American Fiction 1914 to 1945

Titles in the CRITICAL COSMOS series include

AMERICAN FICTION

American Fiction through 1914
American Fiction, 1914–1945
American Fiction, 1946–1965
American Fiction, 1966 to the Present
American Jewish Literature
American Women Novelists and Short
  Story Writers
Black American Fiction

AMERICAN POETRY, DRAMA,
  AND PROSE

American Drama to 1945
American Drama 1945 to the Present
American Poetry through 1914
American Poetry, 1915–1945
American Poetry, 1946–1965
American Poetry, 1966 to the Present
American Prose and Criticism to 1945
American Prose and Criticism, 1945 to
  the Present
American Women Poets
Black American Poetry

BRITISH LITERATURE THROUGH 1880

British Drama: 18th and 19th Centuries
Eighteenth-Century Fiction and Prose
Eighteenth-Century Poetry
Elizabethan and Jacobean Drama
Elizabethan Poetry
Elizabethan Prose and Fiction
English Romantic Fiction and Prose
English Romantic Poetry
Medieval Literature
Seventeenth-Century Poetry
Seventeenth-Century Prose
Victorian Fiction
Victorian Poetry
Victorian Prose

FRENCH LITERATURE

French Drama through 1915
French Fiction through 1915
French Poetry through 1915
French Prose and Criticism through 1789
French Prose and Criticism, 1790 to the
  Present
Modern French Drama
Modern French Fiction
Modern French Poetry
Modern French Prose and Criticism

GERMAN LITERATURE

German Drama through 1915
German Fiction through 1915
German Poetry through 1915
German Prose and Criticism through 1915
Modern German Drama
Modern German Fiction
Modern German Poetry
Modern German Prose and Criticism

MODERN BRITISH AND
  COMMONWEALTH LITERATURE

Anglo-Irish Literature
British Prose, 1880–1914
British World War I Literature
Canadian Fiction
Canadian Poetry and Prose
Commonwealth Poetry and Fiction
Contemporary British Drama, 1946 to the
  Present
Contemporary British Fiction, 1946 to the
  Present
Contemporary British Poetry
Contemporary British Prose
Edwardian and Georgian Fiction,
  1880–1914
Edwardian and Georgian Poetry,
  1880–1914
Modern British Drama, 1900–1945
Modernist Fiction, 1920–1945
Modern Poetry and Prose, 1920–1945

OTHER EUROPEAN AND LATIN
  AMERICAN LITERATURE

African Anglophonic Literature
Dadaism and Surrealism
Italian Drama
Italian Fiction
Italian Poetry
Jewish Literature: The Bible through 1945
Modern Jewish Literature
Modern Latin American Fiction
Modern Scandinavian Literature
Modern Spanish Fiction
Modern Spanish and Latin American
  Poetry
Russian Drama
Russian Fiction
Russian Poetry
Scandinavian Literature through 1915
Spanish Fiction through 1927
Spanish Poetry through 1927

THE CRITICAL COSMOS SERIES

American Fiction 1914 to 1945

Edited and with an introduction
by *HAROLD BLOOM*
Sterling Professor of the Humanities
Yale University

CHELSEA HOUSE PUBLISHERS
New York ◇ *New Haven* ◇ *Philadelphia*

© 1987 by Chelsea House Publishers, a division of Chelsea
House Educational Communications, Inc.

3 5 7 9 8 6 4 2

Printed and bound in the United States of America

∞The paper used in this publication meets the minimum
requirements of the American National Standard for
Permanence of Paper for Printed Library Materials,
Z39.48-1984.

Library of Congress Cataloging-in-Publication Data
     American fiction 1914–1945.
(The Critical cosmos series)
     Bibliography: p.
     Includes index.
     1. American fiction—20th century—History and
criticism. I. Bloom, Harold.   II. Series.
PS379.A53   1986   813'52'09   86–8214
ISBN 0–87754–962–1 (alk. paper)

Contents

Editor's Note   ix

Introduction   1
Harold Bloom

Convention in the Fiction of Edith Wharton   25
Mary Suzanne Schriber

Dreiser's Trilogy and the Dilemma
of Determinism   37
John J. Conder

Modernism: The Case of Willa Cather   61
Phyllis Rose

Toward the Outside: The Quest for Discontinuity
in Gertrude Stein's *The Making of Americans*   77
Clive Bush

Sherwood Anderson: American Mythopoeist   101
Benjamin T. Spencer

Sinclair Lewis and the Implied America   115
James Lea

Negatives of Hope: A Reading of Katherine Anne
Porter   127
Joseph Wiesenfarth

Personal Narrators Playing God and Man:
Henry Miller's Henry Miller   137
Alan Warren Friedman

"Dressing the Unknowable in the Garments
of the Known": The Style of Djuna Barnes's
Nightwood   147
Carolyn Allen

Untroubled Voice: Call and Response in Jean
Toomer's *Cane*   163
Barbara E. Bowen

Dos Passos's *U.S.A.*: Chronicle
and Performance   179
Charles Marz

F. Scott Fitzgerald: The Myth of Gatsby   195
    Bruce Michelson

The Aesthetic of Forbearance: Fitzgerald's *Tender Is the Night*   209
    Maria DiBattista

Fitzgerald: The Tissue of Style   223
    Donald Monk

Faulkner on Time and History   239
    Cleanth Brooks

Literary Self-Criticism: Faulkner in Fiction on Fiction   261
    James G. Watson

The Spectral Road: Metaphors of Transference in Faulkner's *As I Lay Dying*   269
    Patrick O'Donnell

Hemingway: Valor against the Void   285
    Ihab Hassan

Ernest Hemingway: The Meaning of Style   301
    John Graham

Human Time in Hemingway's Fiction   315
    Wesley A. Kort

Why You Can't Go Home Again: Thomas Wolfe and "The Escapes of Time and Memory"   331
    Morris Beja

Steinbeck, the People, and the Party   347
    Sylvia Jenkins Cook

Metaphor, Metonymy, and Voice in Zora Neale Hurston's *Their Eyes Were Watching God*   361
    Barbara Johnson

A Surfeit of Commodities: The Novels of Nathanael West   375
    Jonathan Raban

I Thought I Knew These People: Richard Wright and the Afro-American Literary Tradition   389
    Robert B. Stepto

The Vision of Eudora Welty   405
    Ruth M. Vande Kieft

Biographical Notes   425
Contributors   433
Bibliography   437
Acknowledgments   449
Index   453

Editor's Note

This book brings together what I consider to be a representative selection of the best critical essays available upon the work of the twenty most eminent American fiction writers whose principal volumes were published during the period from the outset of the First World War through the conclusion of the Second. I am grateful to Victoria Forman for her assistance in research.

The editor's introduction provides an overview of the five writers he considers to be the strongest among these twenty: Cather, Fitzgerald, Faulkner, Hemingway, and West. Because of their particular excellence and influence, Fitzgerald, Faulkner, and Hemingway are each given three essays, with only one provided for each of the other authors.

Edith Wharton, who of all American novelists after her master, Henry James, best knew the dialectic of convention—that its function is to liberate us from chaos, while its actual tendency is to stifle—is studied here by Mary Suzanne Schriber as a subtle portrayer of the stifling of women by social convention. A very different dialectic is examined by John J. Conder in his analysis of the manifestations of Dreiser's fierce determinism throughout his ruggedly naturalistic trilogy. Though Conder does not deal explicitly with Dreiser's two strongest novels, *An American Tragedy* and *Sister Carrie*, his account of Dreiser's crude but impressive metaphysical materialism seems to me equally relevant for all of Dreiser's major representations of "reality in America."

Phyllis Rose surveys Willa Cather as a writer who confronted literary Modernism through the "anonymity" of her lucid and unmannered style, thus achieving mythic reverberations as intense as those of Joyce and T. S. Eliot in their stylistic dissociations. Gertrude Stein, a grand dissociative Modernist, is mapped as a quester for discontinuity in relation to literary tradition, in a reading of her *The Making of Americans* by Clive Bush. Another American mythopoeic fiction writer of the plain style, Sherwood Anderson, is seen by Benjamin T. Spencer as being linked to Stein as a stylist of what she called "clear and passionate sentences." James Lea, investigating the vision of America in Sinclair Lewis, suggests that Lewis had a mastery of implication, so that he was at once an astute social critic and a favorite of the audience he roundly damned.

In a reading of Katherine Anne Porter, Joseph Wiesenfarth credits her with an astringent art that represents spiritual blindness as being prevalent, and yet gives us, by negation, images of a certain hope. A writer as different from Porter as can be, Henry Miller, is described by Alan Warren Friedman as a kind of involuntary dualist, playing God and man together even as he depicts himself as the personal narrator, one "Henry Miller." Another writer vastly diverse from Miller, Djuna Barnes, receives an adroit stylistic analysis from Carolyn Allen.

The black writer Jean Toomer, whose *Cane* has now achieved a belated reputation, is presented by Barbara E. Bowen as that rarity, an untroubled visionary of black intensities, who could work in the mode of Walt Whitman yet who consciously did so in the acute realization that his *Cane* was a "swan song" at the end of an age. Another writer who seems now to conclude an era rather than prophesy a future, John Dos Passos, is studied by Charles Marz as an economist of the self, chronicling performances while performing a chronicle.

Three essays upon Scott Fitzgerald begin a sequence on the three major fiction writers of the age: Fitzgerald, Faulkner, Hemingway. Bruce Michelson explores the myth of Gatsby, Maria DiBattista the stoic aesthetic of *Tender Is the Night*, and Donald Monk the general style of Fitzgerald, all of them finding in him a quality at once indomitably ancient and indomitably new. Faulkner, without doubt the greatest American novelist of his age, is analyzed by Cleanth Brooks as a conceptual rhetorician of time and history, while James G. Watson traces the "literary self-criticism" practiced in the fiction and Patrick O'Donnell provides an exegesis of a crucial metaphoric pattern in *As I Lay Dying*, which seems to me Faulkner's masterpiece and the most original American fiction of our period. Hemingway's heroic personal stance, superb knack for creating meaning through style, and humanization of time are studied respectively by Ihab Hassan, the paracritic, by John Graham, and by Wesley A. Kort.

Thomas Wolfe, astonishingly overpraised by Faulkner as the great American novelist of Faulkner's day, is seen by Morris Beja as an Orpheus always looking back, never writing the major novel he might have written. Another novelist of talent who could not develop, John Steinbeck, is judged by Sylvia Jenkins Cook to have experiential strength but little response to intellectual stimuli of any substantive kind.

Essays on four more successfully articulated writers conclude this book. Barbara Johnson analyzes the rhetoric of Zora Neale Hurston's poignant *Their Eyes Were Watching God*, while Jonathan Raban gives an overview of Nathanael West, whose *Miss Lonelyhearts* almost rivals Faulkner's *As I Lay Dying* in its originality and pungency. The pioneering black novelist Richard

Wright receives a deeply sympathetic and richly informed consideration from Robert B. Stepto, who assigns Wright his definitive place in Afro-American literary tradition. Finally, the marvelous vision of Eudora Welty, a great artist still alive among us, is adumbrated by Ruth M. Vande Kieft, fittingly completing our survey of thirty extraordinary years of American fiction.

Introduction

Willa Cather, though now somewhat neglected, has few rivals among the American novelists of this century. Critics and readers frequently regard her as belonging to an earlier time, though she died in 1947. Her best novels were published in the years 1918–31, so that truly she was a novelist of the 1920s, an older contemporary and peer of Hemingway and of Scott Fitzgerald. Unlike them, she did not excel at the short story, though there are some memorable exceptions scattered through her four volumes of tales. Her strength is her novels and particularly, in my judgment, *My Ántonia* (1918), *A Lost Lady* (1923), and *The Professor's House* (1925); fictions worthy of a disciple of Flaubert and Henry James. Equally beautiful and achieved, but rather less central, are the subsequent historical novels, the very popular *Death Comes for the Archbishop* (1927) and *Shadows on the Rock* (1931). Her second novel, *O Pioneers!* (1913), is only just short of the eminence of this grand sequence. Six permanent novels is a remarkable number for a modern American writer; I can think only of Faulkner as Cather's match in this respect, since he wrote six truly enduring novels, all published during his great decade, 1929–39.

Cather's remoteness from the fictive universe of Fitzgerald, Hemingway, and Faulkner is palpable, though all of them shared her nostalgia for an older America. She appears, at first, to have no aesthetic affinities with her younger contemporaries. We associate her instead with Sarah Orne Jewett, about whom she wrote a loving essay, or even with Edith Wharton, whom she scarcely resembles. Cather's mode of engaging with the psychic realities of post-World War I America is more oblique than Fitzgerald's or Hemingway's, but it is just as apposite a representation of the era's malaise. The short novel, *A Lost Lady* (1923), is not out of its aesthetic context when we read it in the company of *The Waste Land*, *The Comedian as the Letter C*,

The Sun Also Rises, The Great Gatsby, and *An American Tragedy*. Subtler and gentler than any of these, *A Lost Lady* elegizes just as profoundly a lost radiance or harmony, a defeat of a peculiarly American dream of innocence, grace, hope.

Henry James, Cather's guide both as critic and novelist, died in England early in 1916. The year before, replying to H. G. Wells, after being satirized by him, James wrote a famous credo: "Art *makes* life, makes interest, makes importance." This is Cather's faith also. One hears the voice of James when, in her essay "On the Art of Fiction," she writes: "Any first-rate novel or story must have in it the strength of a dozen fairly good stories that have been sacrificed to it." Those sacrifices of possibility upon the altar of form were the ritual acts of Cather's quite Paterian religion of art, too easily misread as a growing religiosity by many critics commenting upon *Death Comes for the Archbishop*. Herself a belated Aesthete, Cather emulated a familiar pattern of being attracted by the aura and not the substance of Roman Catholicism. New Mexico, and not Rome, is her place of the spirit, a spirit of the archaic and not of the supernatural.

Cather's social attitudes were altogether archaic. She shared a kind of Populist anti-Semitism with many American writers of her own generation and the next: Sherwood Anderson, Theodore Dreiser, Ezra Pound, Thomas Wolfe, even Hemingway and Fitzgerald. Her own version of anti-Semitism is curiously marked by her related aversion to heterosexuality. She had lost her first companion, Isabelle McClung, to a Jewish violinist, Jan Hambourg, and the Jewish figures in her fiction clearly represent the aggressivity of male sexuality. *The Professor's House* is marred by the gratuitous identification of the commercial exploitation of Cather's beloved West with Marcellus, the Professor's Jewish son-in-law. Doubtless, Cather's most unfortunate piece of writing was her notorious essay in 1914, "Potash and Perlmutter," in which she lamented, mock-heroically, that New York City was becoming too Jewish. Perhaps she was learning the lesson of the master again, since she is repeating, in a lighter tone, the complaint of Henry James in *The American Scene* (1907). She repeated her own distaste for "Jewish critics," tainted as they were by Freud, in the essay on Sarah Orne Jewett written quite late in her career, provoking Lionel Trilling to the just accusation that she had become a mere defender of gentility, mystically concerned with pots and pans.

This dark side of Cather, though hardly a value in itself, would not much matter except that it seeped into her fiction as a systemic resentment of her own era. Nietzsche, analyzing resentment, might be writing of Cather. Freud, analyzing the relation between paranoia and homosexuality, might be writing of her also. I am wary of being reductive in such observations, and someone perpetually mugged by Feminist critics as "the Patriarchal critic" is too battered to desire any further polemic. Cather, in my judgment, is aesthetically strongest and most persuasive in her loving depiction of her heroines and of Ántonia and the lost lady, Mrs. Forrester, in particular. She resembles Thomas Hardy in absolutely nothing, except in the remarkable ability to seduce the reader into joining the novelist at falling in love with the heroine. I am haunted by memories of having fallen in love with Marty South in *The Woodlanders*, and with Ántonia and Mrs. Forrester when I was a boy of fifteen. Rereading *My Ántonia* and *A Lost Lady*, now at fifty-four, I find that the love renews itself. I doubt that I am falling again into what my late and honored teacher, William K. Wimsatt, named as the Affective Fallacy, since love for a woman made up out of words is necessarily a cognitive affair.

Cather's strength at representation gives us Jim Burden and Niel Herbert as her clear surrogates, unrealized perhaps as figures of sexual life, but forcefully conveyed as figures of capable imagination, capable above all of apprehending and transmitting the extraordinary actuality and visionary intensity of Ántonia and Mrs. Forrester. Like her masters, James and Pater, Cather had made her supposed deficiency into her strength, fulfilling the overt program of Emersonian self-reliance. But nothing is got for nothing, Emerson also indicated, and Cather, again like James and Pater, suffered the reverse side of the law of Compensation. The flaws, aesthetic and human, are there, even in *My Ántonia*, *A Lost Lady*, and *The Professor's House*, but they scarcely diminish the beauty and dignity of three profound studies of American nostalgias.

Cather is hardly the only vital American novelist to have misread creatively the spirit of his or her own work. Her essential imaginative knowledge was of loss, which she interpreted temporally, though her loss was aboriginal, in the Romantic mode of Wordsworth, Emerson and all their varied descendants. The glory that had passed away belonged not to the pioneers but to her own transparent eyeball, her own original relation to the universe. Rhetorically, she manifests this knowledge, which frequently is at odds with her overt thematicism. Here is Jim Burden's first shared moment with Ántonia, when they both were little children:

> We sat down and made a nest in the long red grass. Yulka curled up like a baby rabbit and played with a grasshopper. Ántonia pointed up to the sky and questioned me with her glance. I gave her the word, but she was not satisfied and pointed to my eyes. I told her, and she repeated the word, making it sound like "ice." She pointed up to the sky, then to my eyes, then back to the sky, with movements so quick and impulsive that she distracted me, and I had no idea what she wanted. She got up on her knees and wrung her hands. She pointed to her own eyes and shook her head, then to mine and to the sky, nodding violently.
> "Oh," I exclaimed, "blue; blue sky."
> She clapped her hands and murmured, "Blue sky, blue eyes," as if it amused her. While we snuggled down there out of the wind, she learned a score of words. She was quick, and very eager. We were so deep in the grass that we could see nothing but the blue sky over us and the gold tree in front of us. It was wonderfully

pleasant. After Ántonia had said the new words over and over, she wanted to give me a little chased silver ring she wore on her middle finger. When she coaxed and insisted, I repulsed her quite sternly. I didn't want her ring, and I felt there was something reckless and extravagant about her wishing to give it away to a boy she had never seen before. No wonder Krajiek got the better of these people, if this was how they behaved.

One imagines that Turgenev would have admired this, and it would not be out of place inserted in his *A Sportman's Sketchbook*. Its naturalistic simplicity is deceptive. Wallace Stevens, in a letter of 1940, observed of Cather: "you may think she is more or less formless. Nevertheless, we have nothing better than she is. She takes so much pains to conceal her sophistication that it is easy to miss her quality." The quality here is partly manifested by an exuberance of trope and a precision of diction, both in the service of a fresh American myth of origin. Nesting and curling up in an embowered world of baby rabbits and grasshoppers, the children are at home in a universe of "blue sky, blue eyes." Heaven and earth come together, where vision confronts only the gold of trees. Ántonia, offering the fullness of a symbolic union to him, is rebuffed partly by the boy's shyness, and partly by Cather's own proleptic fear that the reckless generosity of the pioneer is doomed to exploitation. Yet the passage's deepest intimation is that Jim, though falling in love with Ántonia, is constrained by an inner recalcitrance, which the reader is free to interpret in several ways, none of which need exclude the others.

This is Cather in the springtide of her imagination. In her vision's early fall, we find ourselves regarding her lost lady, Mrs. Forrester, and we are comforted, as the boy Niel Herbert is, "in the quick recognition of her eyes, in the living quality of her voice itself." The book's splendor is that, like Mrs. Forrester's laughter, "it often told you a great deal that was both too direct and too elusive for words." As John Hollander shrewdly notes, Mrs. Forrester does not become a lost lady in any social or moral sense, but imaginatively she is transformed into Niel's "long-lost lady." Lost or refound, she is "his" always, even as Ántonia always remains Jim Burden's "my Ántonia." In her ability to suggest a love that is permanent, life-enhancing, and in no way possessive, Cather touches the farthest limit of her own strength as a novelist. If one could choose a single passage from all her work, it would be the Paterian epiphany or privileged moment in which Mrs. Forrester's image returned to Niel as "a bright, impersonal memory." Pater ought to have lived to have read this marvelous instance of the art he had celebrated and helped to stimulate in Cather:

> Her eyes, when they laughed for a moment into one's own, seemed to provide a wild delight that he had not found in life. "I know where it is," they seemed to say, "I could show you!" He would like to call up the shade of the young Mrs. Forrester, as the witch of Endor called up Samuel's, and challenge it, demand

the secret of that ardour; ask her whether she had really found some ever-blooming, ever-burning, ever-piercing joy, or whether it was all fine play-acting. Probably she had found no more than another; but she had always the power of suggesting things much lovelier than herself, as the perfume of a single flower may call up the whole sweetness of spring.

It is the perfection of Cather's difficult art, when that art was most balanced and paced, and Mrs. Forrester here is the emblem of that perfection. Cather's fiction, at its frequent best, also suggests things much lovelier than itself. The reader, demanding the secret of Cather's ardour, learns not to challenge what may be remarkably fine play-acting, since Cather's feigning sometimes does persuade him that really she had found some perpetual joy.

II

It is difficult to imagine John Keats writing the fictions of Joseph Conrad, since there is nothing in common between the Great Odes and *The Secret Sharer* or *Heart of Darkness*. But such an imagining is not useless, since in some sense that was Scott Fitzgerald's accomplishment. *The Great Gatsby* does combine the lyrical sensibility of Keats and the fictive mode of Conrad, and makes of so odd a blending a uniquely American story, certainly a candidate for *the* American story of its time (1925). *Gatsby* has more in common with T. S. Eliot's "The Hollow Men," also published in 1925, than it does with such contemporary novels as the *Arrowsmith* of Sinclair Lewis or the *Manhattan Transfer* of John Dos Passos. Eliot's admiration for *The Great Gatsby* is understandable; the book, like the visionary lyric of Hart Crane, struggles against Eliot's conclusions while being compelled to appropriate Eliot's language and procedures. Fitzgerald, the American Keats, and Crane, even more the American Shelley, both sought to affirm a High Romanticism in the accents of a belated counter-tradition. The Keatsian belief in the holiness of the heart's affections is central to Fitzgerald, and *Tender Is the Night* owes more than its title to the naturalistic humanism of the Great Odes.

Fitzgerald's canonical status is founded more upon *Gatsby* and his best short stories, such as "Babylon Revisited," than it is upon the seriously flawed *Tender Is the Night*, let alone upon the unfinished *The Last Tycoon*. Oddly praised as "the best Hollywood novel" despite its manifest inferiority to Nathanael West's *The Day of the Locust, The Last Tycoon* is more an embryo than it is a torso. Edmund Wilson's affectionate overestimation of this fragment has been influential, but will fade away each time the book is actually read. *Tender Is the Night* demonstrates that Fitzgerald, unlike Conrad and Lawrence, cannot sustain too long a narrative. The book, though coming relatively late in his career, is Fitzgerald's *Endymion*, while *Gatsby* is, as it were, his *Fall of Hyperion*. Keats desired to write epic, but was more attuned to romance and to lyric. Fitzgerald desired to write novels on the scale of Thackeray and of Conrad, but his genius was more fitted to *Gatsby* as his mode of romance, and to "Babylon Revisited" as his version of the ode or of the reflective lyric.

The aesthetic of Scott Fitzgerald is quite specifically a personal revision of Keats's hope for Negative Capability, which Fitzgerald called "a romantic readiness" and attributed to his Gatsby. It is certainly part of the achievement of Fitzgerald's best novel that its hero possesses an authentic aesthetic dignity. By an effective troping of form, Fitzgerald made this a book in which nothing is aesthetically wasted, even as the narrative shows us everyone being humanly wasted. Edith Wharton rather nastily praised Fitzgerald for having created the "perfect Jew" in the gambler Meyer Wolfsheim. Had she peered closer, she might have seen the irony of her patrician prejudice reversed in the ancient Jewish wisdom that even Wolfsheim is made to express:

> "Let us learn to show our friendship for a man when he is alive and not after he is dead," he suggested. "After that, my own rule is to let everything alone."

Whether Nick Carraway is capable of apprehending this as wisdom is disputable but Fitzgerald evidently could, since Wolfsheim is not wholly devoid of the dignity of grief. Lionel Trilling commended *The Great Gatsby* for retaining its freshness. After sixty years, it has more than retained its moral balance and affective rightness. Those qualities seem augmented through the perspective of lapsed time. What has been augmented also is the Eliotic phantasmagoria of the *Waste Land* imagery that is so effectively vivid throughout Fitzgerald's vision. Carraway begins by speaking of "what preyed on Gatsby, what foul dust floated in the wake of his dreams." These are also "the spasms of bleak dust," above which you perceive the blue and gigantic eyes of Doctor T. J. Eckleburg, which brood on over the dumping ground of the gray land. "My heart is a handful of dust," the monologist of Tennyson's *Maud* had proclaimed in a great phrase stolen by Eliot for his *Waste Land*. Fitzgerald's dust is closer to Tennyson's heart than to Eliot's fear:

> to where Myrtle Wilson, her life violently extinguished, knelt in the road and mingled her thick dark blood with the dust.
> Michaelis and this man reached her first, but when they had torn open her shirtwaist, still damp with perspiration, they saw that her left breast was swinging loose like a flap, and there was no need to listen for the heart beneath.

Fitzgerald's violence has that curious suddenness we associate with the same narrative quality in E. M. Forster. Something repressed in the phantasmagoria of the ordinary returns, all too often, reminding us that Fitzgerald shares also in Conrad's sense of reality and its treacheries, particularly as developed in *Nostromo*, a novel that we know Fitzgerald rightly admired. *Heart of Darkness*, which Fitzgerald also admired, is linked to "The

Hollow Men" by that poem's epigraph, and many critics have seen Carraway as Fitzgerald's version of Marlow, somewhat sentimentalized but still an authentic secret sharer in Gatsby's fate. Like the Eliot of "The Hollow Men," Fitzgerald found in Conrad a seer of the contemporary abyss of:

> Shape without form, shade without color,
> Paralysed force, gesture without motion;

or, in the language of *Heart of Darkness:* "A vision of grayness without form."

Writing to his daughter about the "Ode on a Grecian Urn," Fitzgerald extravagantly observed: "For awhile after you quit Keats all other poetry seems to be only whistling or humming." Fitzgerald's deepest affinity to Keats is in the basic stance of his work, at once rhetorical, psychological, and even cosmological. In both Keats and Fitzgerald, the perpetual encounter is between the mortal poet or man-of-imagination (Gatsby, Diver) and an immortal or perpetually youthful goddess-woman. Fitzgerald's women—Daisy, Nicole, Rosemary—are not so much American dreams as they are Keatsian Lamias or perpetually virgin moon-maidens. "Virginity renews itself like the moon" is a Keatsian apothegm of Yeats's and the quester in Fitzgerald would have concurred. The murdered Gatsby is truly Daisy's victim; rather more grimly, Diver is emptied out by his relationship with Nicole, and to some degree, by his repetition of that pattern with Rosemary.

This has been read as misogyny in Fitzgerald but, as in Keats, it tends largely to be the reverse. Confronting his immortal women, the Keatsian quester seeks what at last Keats himself obtains from the harshly reluctant Muse, Moneta, in *The Fall of Hyperion:* recognition that he is *the* poet in and for his own time. "I sure should see/Other men here; but I am here alone." Fitzgerald was greatly ambitious, but his audacity did not extend quite that far. Yet his surrogates—Gatsby and Diver—are no more deceived than Keats's poets are deceived. Daisy, Nicole, and Rosemary do not matter as personalities, not to us as readers and not much more to Gatsby or Diver. Gatsby, the more sublime quester, is allowed his famous touch of genius when he dismisses Daisy's love for her husband, the brutal Tom Buchanan: "In any case, it was just personal." Diver, less magnificently, also knows better, but is just as doom-eager as Gatsby. The inadequacies of the actual women do not matter, because the drive is not for satisfaction or for happiness. It is Freud's uncanny death-drive, which replaces the drive for self-preservation, and exists in a dialectical balance with the libido. Gatsby somehow chooses to die in his own fashion, while Diver chooses the death-in-life of erotic and professional defeat.

Tender Is the Night survives the weakness of its characterizations and the clumsiness of its narrative structure precisely because of Diver's own fated sense that there are no accidents. His character is his fate, and his relationship with Nicole is not so much a failed counter-transference as it is another pathetic version of the sublime Romantic vision of sexual entropy set forth overtly in Blake's "The Mental Traveller" and implicitly in James's *The Sacred Fount:* "And she grows young as he grows old." For the Blakean "young" we can substitute "whole," yet for the "old" we cannot quite substitute "weak" but something closer to Fitzgerald's "interior laughter," the quality in Diver that drives him down and out until he ends up practicing medicine in progressively smaller towns in the Finger Lakes Section of the Western Reserve of New York State. The pathos of that dying fall is anything but Keatsian, and may have been Fitzgerald's trope for his own self-destructiveness.

A curious self-appropriation, or perhaps indeliberate self-repetition, links the close of *Tender Is the Night* to the close of "Babylon Revisited," which seems to me Fitzgerald's most impressive single short story. On the day before he leaves the Riviera for America, after his rejection by Nicole, Diver spends all his time with his children: "He was not young any more with a lot of nice thoughts and dreams to have about himself, so he wanted to remember them well." The penultimate sentence of "Babylon Revisited" is "He wasn't young anymore, with a lot of nice thoughts and dreams to have about himself."

Whichever came first, the repetition is central to Fitzgerald. "Nice thoughts and dreams" are the essence, and Fitzgerald's regressive vision, like Gatsby's and Diver's and Charlie Wales's, is a Keatsian and Stevensian study of the nostalgias. Keats, staring at the face of the unveiled Moneta, prophesies the Stevens of *The Auroras of Autumn,* with his unabashed, Freudian celebration of the imago: "The mother's face, the purpose of the poem, fills the room." Charlie Wales, in "Babylon Revisited," longing for his daughter, remembers his dead wife as any man remembers his mother: "He was absolutely sure Helen wouldn't have wanted him to be so alone." As the last sentence of what may be Fitzgerald's most memorable story, it reverberates with a peculiar plangency in American Romantic tradition.

III

No critic need invent William Faulkner's obsessions with what Nietzsche might have called the genealogy of the imagination. Recent critics of Faulkner, including David Minter, John T. Irwin, David M. Wyatt, and Richard H. King, have emphasized the novelist's profound need to believe himself to have been his own father, in order to escape not only the Freudian family romance and literary anxieties of influence, but also the cultural dilemmas of what King terms "the Southern family romance." From *The Sound and the Fury* through the debacle of *A Fable,* Faulkner centers upon the sorrows of fathers and sons, to the disadvantage of mothers and daughters. No feminist critic ever will be happy with Faulkner. His brooding conviction that female sexuality is closely allied with death seems essential to all of his strongest fictions. It may even be that Faulkner's rhetorical economy, his wounded need to get his cosmos into a single sentence, is related to his fear that origin and end might prove to be one. Nietzsche prophetically

had warned that origin and end were separate entities, and for the sake of
life had to be kept apart, but Faulkner (strangely like Freud) seems to have
known that the only Western trope participating neither in origin nor end
is the image of the father.

By universal consent of critics and common readers, Faulkner now is
recognized as the strongest American novelist of this century, clearly sur-
passing Hemingway and Fitzgerald, and standing as an equal in the sequence that includes Hawthorne, Melville, Mark Twain, and Henry James.
Some critics might add Dreiser to this group; Faulkner himself curiously
would have insisted upon Thomas Wolfe, a generous though dubious judgment. The American precursor for Faulkner was Sherwood Anderson, but
perhaps only as an impetus; the true American forerunner is the poetry of
T. S. Eliot, as Judith L. Sensibar demonstrates. But the truer precursor for
Faulkner's fiction is Conrad, inescapable for the American novelists of
Faulkner's generation, including Hemingway and Fitzgerald. Comparison
to Conrad is dangerous for any novelist, and clearly Faulkner did not
achieve a Nostromo. But his work of the decade 1929–39 does include four
permanent books: *The Sound and the Fury*, *As I Lay Dying*, *Light in August*
and *Absalom, Absalom!* If one adds *Sanctuary* and *The Wild Palms*, and *The
Hamlet* and *Go Down, Moses* in the early forties, then the combined effect
is extraordinary.

From Malcolm Cowley on, critics have explained this effect as the
consequence of the force of mythmaking, at once personal and local.
Cleanth Brooks, the rugged final champion of the New Criticism, essentially
reads Faulkner as he does Eliot's *The Waste Land*, finding the hidden God
of the normative Christian tradition to be the basis for Faulkner's attitude
towards nature. Since Brooks calls Faulkner's stance Wordsworthian, and
finds Wordsworthian nature a Christian vision also, the judgment involved
necessarily has its problematical elements. Walter Pater, a critic in a very
different tradition, portrayed a very different Wordsworth in terms that
seem to me not inapplicable to Faulkner:

> Religious sentiment, consecrating the affections and natural re-
> grets of the human heart, above all, that pitiful awe and care for
> the perishing human clay, of which relic-worship is but the cor-
> ruption, has always had much to do with localities, with the
> thoughts which attach themselves to actual scenes and places.
> Now what is true of it everywhere, is truest of it in those secluded
> valleys where one generation after another maintains the same
> abiding place; and it was on this side, that Wordsworth appre-
> hended religion most strongly. Consisting, as it did so much, in
> the recognition of local sanctities, in the habit of connecting the
> stones and trees of a particular spot of earth with the great events
> of life, till the low walls, the green mounds, the half-obliterated
> epitaphs seemed full of voices, and a sort of natural oracles, the
> very religion of those people of the dales, appeared but as another

link between them and the earth, and was literally a religion of nature.

A kind of stoic natural religion pervades this description, something close to the implicit faith of old Isaac McCaslin in *Go Down, Moses*. It seems unhelpful to speak of "residual Christianity" in Faulkner, as Cleanth Brooks does. Hemingway and Fitzgerald, in their nostalgias, perhaps were closer to a Christian ethos than Faulkner was in his great phase. Against current critical judgment, I prefer *As I Lay Dying* and *Light in August* to *The Sound and the Fury* and *Absalom, Absalom!*, partly because the first two are more primordial in their vision, closer to the stoic intensities of their author's kind of natural piety. There is an *otherness* in Lena Grove and the Bundrens that would have moved Wordsworth, that is, the Wordsworth of "The Tale of Margaret," "Michael," and "The Old Cumberland Beggar." A curious movement that is also a stasis becomes Faulkner's pervasive trope for Lena. Though he invokes the imagery of Keats's urn, Faulkner seems to have had the harvest-girl of Keats's "To Autumn" more in mind, or even the stately figures of the "Ode to Indolence." We remember Lena Grove as stately, calm, a person yet a process, a serene and patient consciousness, full of wonder, too much a unitary being to need even her author's variety of stoic courage.

The uncanniness of this representation is exceeded by the Bundrens, whose plangency testifies to Faulkner's finest rhetorical achievement. *As I Lay Dying* may be the most original novel ever written by an American. Obviously it is not free of the deepest influence Faulkner knew as a novelist. The language is never Conradian, and yet the sense of the reality principle is. But there is nothing in Conrad like Darl Bundren, not even in *The Secret Agent*. *As I Lay Dying* is Faulkner's strongest protest against the facticity of literary convention, against the force of the familial past, which tropes itself in fiction as the repetitive form of narrative imitating prior narrative. The book is a sustained nightmare insofar as it is Darl's book, which is to say, Faulkner's book, or the book of his daemon.

Canonization is a process of enshrining creative misinterpretations, and no one need lament this. Still, one element that ensues from this process all too frequently is the not very creative misinterpretation in which the idiosyncratic is distorted into the normative. Churchwardenly critics who assimilate the Faulkner of the Thirties to spiritual, social, and moral orthodoxy can and do assert Faulkner himself as their preceptor. But this is the Faulkner of the Fifties, Nobel laureate, State Department envoy, and author of *A Fable*, a book of a badness simply astonishing for Faulkner. The best of the normative critics, Cleanth Brooks, reads even *As I Lay Dying* as a quest for community, an exaltation of the family, an affirmation of Christian values. The Bundrens manifestly constitute one of the most terrifying visions of the family romance in the history of literature. But their extremism is not eccentric in the 1929–39 world of Faulkner's fiction. That world is founded upon a horror of families, a limbo of outcasts, an evasion of all values other than stoic endurance. It is a world in which what is silent in the other Bundrens speaks in Darl, what is veiled in the Compsons is uncovered in Quentin. So tangled are these returns of the repressed with what continues to be estranged that phrases like "the violation of the natural" and "the denial of the human" become quite meaningless when applied to Faulkner's greater fictions. In that world, the natural is itself a violation and the human already a denial. Is the weird quest of the Bundrens a violation of the natural, or is it what Blake would have called a terrible triumph for the selfish virtues of the natural heart? Darl judges it to be the latter, but Darl luminously denies the sufficiency of the human, at the cost of what seems schizophrenia.

Marxist criticism of imaginative literature, if it had not regressed abominably in our country, so that now it is a travesty of the dialectical suppleness of Adorno and Benjamin, would find a proper subject in the difficult relationship between the 1929 business panic and *As I Lay Dying*. Perhaps the self-destruction of our delusive political economy helped free Faulkner from whatever inhibitions, communal and personal, had kept him earlier from a saga like that of the Bundrens. Only an authentic seer can give permanent form to a prophecy like *As I Lay Dying*, which puts severely into question every received notion we have of the natural and the human. Darl asserts he has no mother, while taunting his enemy brother, Jewel, with the insistence that Jewel's mother was a horse. Their little brother, Vardaman, says: "My mother is a fish." The mother, dead and undead, is uncannier even than these children, when she confesses the truth of her existence, her rejecting vision of her children:

> I could just remember how my father used to say that the reason for living was to get ready to stay dead a long time. And when I would have to look at them day after day, each with his and her single and selfish thought, and blood strange to each other blood and strange to mine, and think that this seemed to be the only way I could get ready to stay dead, I would hate my father for having ever planted me. I would look forward to the times when they faulted, so I could whip them. When the switch fell I could feel it upon my flesh; when it welted and ridged it was my blood that ran, and I would think with each blow of the switch: Now you are aware of me! Now I am something in your secret and selfish life, who have marked your blood with my own for ever and ever.

This veritable apocalypse of any sense of otherness is no mere "denial of community." Nor are the Bundrens any "mimesis of essential nature." They are a super-mimesis, an over-representation mocking nature while shadowing it. What matters in major Faulkner is that the people have gone back, not to nature but to some abyss before the Creation-Fall. Eliot insisted that Joyce's imagination was eminently orthodox. This can be doubted, but in Faulkner's case there is little sense in baptizing his imagination. One sees why he preferred reading the Old Testament to the New, remarking that the former was stories and the latter, ideas. The remark is inadequate except insofar as it opposes Hebraic to Hellenistic representation of character. There is little that is Homeric about the Bundrens, or Sophoclean about the Compsons. Faulkner's irony is neither classical nor romantic, neither Greek nor German. It does not say one thing while meaning another, nor trade in contrasts between expectation and fulfillment. Instead, it juxtaposes incommensurable realities: of self and other, of parent and child, of past and future. When Gide maintained that Faulkner's people lacked souls, he simply failed to observe that Faulkner's ironies were Biblical. To which an amendment must be added. In Faulkner, only the ironies are Biblical. What Faulkner's people lack is the blessing; they cannot contend for a time without boundaries. Yahweh will make no covenant with them. Their agon therefore is neither the Greek one for the foremost place nor the Hebrew one for the blessing, which honors the father and the mother. Their agon is the hopeless one of waiting for their doom to lift.

Faulkner writes tragic farce rather than tragedy, more in the mode of Webster, Ford and Tourneur than that of Shakespeare. In time, his genius or daemon may seem essentially comic, despite his dark houses and death drives. His grand family is Dickens run mad rather than Conrad run wild: the hideous saga of the Snopes, from the excessively capable Flem Snopes to the admirably named Wallstreet Panic Snopes. Flem, as David Minter observes, is refreshingly free of all influence-anxieties. He belongs in Washington D. C., and by now has reached there, and helps to staff the White House. Alas, he by now helps to staff the universities also, and soon will staff the entire nation, as his spiritual children, the Yuppies, reach middle age. Ivy League Snopes, Reagan Revolution Snopes, Jack Kemp Snopes: the possibilities are limitless. His ruined families, burdened by tradition, are Faulkner's tribute to his region. His Snopes clan is his gift to his nation.

IV

Hemingway freely proclaimed his relationship to *Huckleberry Finn*, and there is some basis for the assertion, except that there is little in common between the rhetorical stances of Twain and of Hemingway. Kipling's *Kim*, in style and mode, is far closer to *Huckleberry Finn* than anything Hemingway wrote. The true accent of Hemingway's admirable style is to be found in an even greater and more surprising precursor:

> This grass is very dark to be from the white heads of old
>   mothers,
> Darker than the colorless beards of old men,
> Dark to come from under the faint red roofs of mouths.

Or again:

> I clutch the rails of the fence, my gore drips, thinn'd with
>   the ooze of my skin,

I fall on the weeds and stones,
The riders spur their unwilling horses, haul close,
Taunt my dizzy ears and beat me violently over the head
    with whip-stocks.
Agonies are one of my changes of garments,
I do not ask the wounded person how he feels, I myself
    become the wounded person,
My hurts turn livid upon me as I lean on a cane and
    observe.

Hemingway is scarcely unique in not acknowledging the paternity of Walt Whitman; T. S. Eliot and Wallace Stevens are far closer to Whitman than William Carlos Williams and Hart Crane were, but literary influence is a paradoxical and antithetical process, about which we continue to know all too little. The profound affinities between Hemingway, Eliot and Stevens are not accidental, but are family resemblances due to the repressed but crucial relation each had to Whitman's work. Hemingway characteristically boasted (in a letter to Sara Murphy, February 27, 1926) that he had knocked Stevens down quite handily: " . . . for statistics sake Mr. Stevens is 6 feet 2 weighs 225 lbs. and that when he hits the ground it is highly spectaculous." Since this match between the two writers took place in Key West on February 19, 1926, I am moved, as a loyal Stevensian, for statistics' sake to point out that the victorious Hemingway was born in 1899, and the defeated Stevens in 1879, so that the novelist was then going on twenty-seven, and the poet verging on forty-seven. The two men doubtless despised one another, but in the letter celebrating his victory, Hemingway calls Stevens "a damned fine poet" and Stevens always affirmed that Hemingway was essentially a poet, a judgment concurred in by Robert Penn Warren when he wrote that Hemingway "is essentially a lyric rather than a dramatic writer." Warren compared Hemingway to Wordsworth, which is feasible, but the resemblance to Whitman is far closer. Wordsworth would not have written: "I am the man, I suffer'd, I was there," but Hemingway almost persuades us he would have achieved that line had not Whitman set it down first.

It is now more than twenty years since Hemingway's suicide, and some aspects of his permanent canonical status seem beyond doubt. Only a few modern American novels seem certain to endure: *The Sun Also Rises, The Great Gatsby, Miss Lonelyhearts, The Crying of Lot 49* and at least several by Faulkner, including *As I Lay Dying, Sanctuary, Light in August, The Sound and the Fury, Absalom, Absalom!* Two dozen stories by Hemingway could be added to the group, indeed perhaps all of *The First Forty-Nine Stories.* Faulkner is an eminence apart, but critics agree that Hemingway and Fitzgerald are his nearest rivals, largely on the strength of their shorter fiction. What seems unique is that Hemingway is the only American writer of prose fiction in this century who, as a stylist, rivals the principal poets: Stevens, Eliot, Frost, Hart Crane, aspects of Pound, W. C. Williams, Robert Penn

Warren, and Elizabeth Bishop. This is hardly to say that Hemingway, at his best, fails at narrative or the representation of character. Rather, his peculiar excellence is closer to Whitman than to Twain, closer to Stevens than to Faulkner, and even closer to Eliot than to Fitzgerald, who was his friend and rival. He is an elegiac poet who mourns the self, who celebrates the self (rather less effectively), and who suffers divisions in the self. In the broadest tradition of American literature, he stems ultimately from the Emersonian reliance on the god within, which is the line of Whitman, Thoreau, and Dickinson. He arrives late and dark in this tradition, and is one of its negative theologians, as it were, but as in Stevens, the negations, the cancellings, are never final. Even the most ferocious of his stories, say, "God Rest You Merry Gentlemen" or "A Natural History of the Dead," can be said to celebrate what we might call the Real Absence. Doc Fischer, in "God Rest You Merry Gentlemen," is a precursor of Nathanael West's Shrike in *Miss Lonelyhearts*, and his savage, implicit religiosity prophesies not only Shrike's Satanic stance but the entire demonic world of Pynchon's explicitly paranoid or Luddite visions. Perhaps there was a nostalgia for a Catholic order always abiding in Hemingway's consciousness, but the cosmos of his fiction, early and late, is American Gnostic, as it was in Melville, who first developed so strongly the negative side of the Emersonian religion of self-reliance.

Hemingway notoriously and splendidly was given to overtly agonistic images whenever he described his relationship to canonical writers, including Melville, a habit of description in which he has been followed by his true ephebe, Norman Mailer. In a grand letter (September 6–7, 1949) to his publisher, Charles Scribner, he charmingly confessed: "Am a man without any ambition, except to be champion of the world, I wouldn't fight Dr. Tolstoi in a 20 round bout because I know he would knock my ears off." This modesty passed quickly, to be followed by: "If I can live to 60 I can beat him. (MAYBE)" Since the rest of the letter counts Turgenev, de Maupassant, Henry James, even Cervantes, as well as Melville and Dostoevsky, among the defeated, we can join Hemingway, himself, in admiring his extraordinary self-confidence. How justified was it, in terms of his ambitions?

It could be argued persuasively that Hemingway is the best short-story writer in the English Language, from Joyce's *Dubliners* until the present. The aesthetic dignity of the short story need not be questioned, and yet we seem to ask more of a canonical writer. Hemingway wrote *The Sun Also Rises* and not *Ulysses*, which is only to say that his true genius was for very short stories, and hardly at all for extended narrative. Had he been primarily a poet, his lyrical gifts would have sufficed: we do not hold it against Yeats that his poems, not his plays, are his principal glory. Alas, neither Turgenev nor Henry James, neither Melville nor Mark Twain provide true agonists for Hemingway. Instead, de Maupassant is the apter rival. Of Hemingway's intensity of style in the briefer compass there is no question, but even *The*

Sun Also Rises reads now as a series of epiphanies, of brilliant and memorable vignettes.

Much that has been harshly criticized in Hemingway, particularly in *For Whom the Bell Tolls,* results from his difficulty in adjusting his gifts to the demands of the novel. Robert Penn Warren suggests that Hemingway is successful when his "system of ironies and understatements is coherent." When incoherent, then Hemingway's rhetoric fails as persuasion, which is to say, we read *To Have and Have Not* or *For Whom the Bell Tolls* and we are all too aware that the system of tropes is primarily what we are offered. Warren believes this not to be true of *A Farewell to Arms,* yet even the celebrated close of the novel seems now a worn understatement:

> But after I had got them out and shut the door and turned off the light it wasn't any good. It was like saying good-by to a statue. After a while I went out and left the hospital and walked back to the hotel in the rain.

Contrast this to the close of "Old Man at the Bridge," a story only two and a half pages long:

> There was nothing to do about him. It was Easter Sunday and the Fascists were advancing toward the Ebro. It was a gray overcast day with a low ceiling so their planes were not up. That and the fact that cats know how to look after themselves was all the good luck that old man would ever have.

The understatement continues to persuade here because the stoicism remains coherent, and is admirably fitted by the rhetoric. A very short story concludes itself by permanently troping the mood of a particular moment in history. Vignette is Hemingway's natural mode, or call it hard-edged vignette: a literary sketch that somehow seems to be the beginning or end of something longer, yet truly is complete in itself. Hemingway's style encloses what ought to be unenclosed, so that the genre remains subtle yet trades its charm for punch. But a novel of three hundred and forty pages *(A Farewell to Arms)* which I have just finished reading again (after twenty years away from it) cannot sustain itself upon the rhetoric of vignette. After many understatements, too many, the reader begins to believe that he is reading a Hemingway imitator, like the accomplished John O'Hara, rather than the master himself. Hemingway's notorious fault is the monotony of repetition, which becomes a dulling litany in a somewhat less accomplished imitator like Nelson Algren, and sometimes seems self-parody when we must confront it in Hemingway.

Nothing is got for nothing, and a great style generates defenses in us, particularly when it sets the style of an age, as the Byronic Hemingway did. As with Byron, the color and variety of the artist's life becomes something of a veil between the work and our aesthetic apprehension of it. Hemingway's career included four marriages (and three divorces); service as an ambulance driver for the Italians in World War I (with an honorable wound); activity as a war correspondent in the Greek-Turkish War (1922), the Spanish Civil War (1937–39), the Chinese-Japanese War (1941), and the War against Hitler in Europe (1942–45). Add big-game hunting and fishing, safaris, expatriation in France and Cuba, bullfighting, the Nobel prize, and ultimate suicide in Idaho, and you have an absurdly implausible life, apparently lived in imitation of Hemingway's own fiction. The final effect of the work and the life together is not less than mythological, as it was with Byron, and with Whitman, and with Oscar Wilde. Hemingway now is myth, and so is permanent as an image of American heroism, or perhaps more ruefully the American illusion of heroism. The best of Hemingway's work, the stories and *The Sun Also Rises*, are also a permanent part of the American mythology. Faulkner, Stevens, Frost, perhaps Eliot and Hart Crane were stronger writers than Hemingway, but he alone in this American century has achieved the enduring status of myth.

V

Nathanael West, who died in 1940 at the age of thirty-seven in an automobile accident, wrote one remorseless masterpiece, *Miss Lonelyhearts* (1933). Despite some astonishing sequences, *The Day of the Locust* (1939) is an overpraised work, a waste of West's genius. Of the two lesser fictions, *The Dream Life of Balso Snell* (1931) is squalid and dreadful, with occasional passages of a rancid power, while *A Cool Million* (1934), though an outrageous parody of American picaresque, is a permanent work of American satire, and seems to me underpraised. To call West uneven is therefore a litotes; he is a wild medley of magnificent writing and inadequate writing, except in *Miss Lonelyhearts*, which excels *The Sun Also Rises*, *The Great Gatsby*, and even *Sanctuary* as the perfected instance of a negative vision in modern American fiction. The greatest Faulkner, of *The Sound and the Fury*, *As I Lay Dying*, *Absalom, Absalom!* and *Light in August*, is the only American writer of prose fiction in this century who can be said to have surpassed *Miss Lonelyhearts*. West's spirit lives again in *The Crying of Lot 49* and in some sequences in *Gravity's Rainbow*, but the negative sublimity of *Miss Lonelyhearts* proves to be beyond Pynchon's reach, or perhaps his ambition.

West, born Nathan Weinstein, is a significant episode in the long and tormented history of Jewish Gnosticism. The late Gershom Scholem's superb essay "Redemption through Sin," in his *The Messianic Idea in Judaism*, is the best commentary I know upon *Miss Lonelyhearts*. I once attempted to convey this to Scholem, who shrugged West off, quite properly from Scholem's viewpoint, when I remarked to him that West was manifestly a Jewish anti-Semite, and admitted that there were no allusions to Jewish esotericism or Kabbalah in his works. Nevertheless, for the stance of literary criticism, Jewish Gnosticism, as defined by Scholem, is the most illuminating context in which to study West's novels. It is a melancholy paradox that West, who did not wish to be Jewish in any way at all, remains the most indisputable Jewish writer yet to appear in America, a judgment at once aesthetic and moral. Nothing by Bellow, Malamud, Philip Roth, Mailer, Ozick can compare to *Miss Lonelyhearts* as an achievement. West's Jewish heir, if he has one, may be Harold Brodkey, whose recent *Women and Angels,* excerpted from his immense novel-in-progress, can be regarded as another powerful instance of Jewish Gnosis, free of West's hatred of his own Jewishness.

Stanley Edgar Hyman, in his pamphlet on West (1962), concluded that "His strength lay in his vulgarity and bad taste, his pessimism, his nastiness." Hyman remains West's most useful critic, but I would amend this by observing that these qualities in West's writing emanate from a negative theology, spiritually authentic, and given aesthetic dignity by the force of West's eloquent negations. West, like his grandest creation, Shrike, is a rhetorician of the abyss, in the tradition of Sabbatian nihilism that Scholem has expounded so masterfully. One thinks of ideas such as "the violation of the Torah has become its fulfillment, just as a grain of wheat must rot in the earth" or Jacob Frank's "We are all now under the obligation to enter the abyss." The messianic intensity of the Sabbatians and Frankists results in a desperately hysterical and savage tonality which prophesies West's authentically religious book, *Miss Lonelyhearts,* a work profoundly Jewish but only in its negations, particularly the negation of the normative Judaic assumption of total sense in everything, life and text alike. *Miss Lonelyhearts* takes place in the world of Freud, where the fundamental assumption is that everything already has happened, and nothing can be made new, because total sense has been achieved.

Negatively Jewish, the book is also negatively American. Miss Lonelyhearts is a failed Walt Whitman (hence the naming of the cripple as Peter Doyle, Whitman's pathetic friend) and a fallen American Adam to Shrike's very American Satan. Despite the opinions of later critics, I continue to find Hyman's argument persuasive, and agree with him that the book's psychosexuality is marked by a repressed homosexual relation between Shrike and Miss Lonelyhearts. Hyman's Freudian observation that all the suffering in the book is essentially female seems valid, reminding us that Freud's "feminine masochism" is mostly encountered among men, according to Freud himself. Shrike, the butcherbird impaling his victim, Miss Lonelyhearts, upon the thorns of Christ, is himself as much an instance of "feminine masochism" as his victim. If Miss Lonelyhearts is close to pathological frenzy, Shrike is also consumed by religious hysteria, by a terrible nostalgia for God.

The book's bitter stylistic negation results in a spectacular verbal economy, in which literally every sentence is made to count, in more than one sense of "count." Freud's "negation" involves a cognitive return of the repressed, here through West's self-projection as Shrike, spit out but not disavowed. The same Freudian process depends upon an affective continuance of repression, here by West's self-introjection as Miss Lonelyhearts, at once West's inability to believe and his disavowed failure to love. Poor

Miss Lonelyhearts, who receives no other name throughout the book, has been destroyed by Shrike's power of Satanic rhetoric before the book even opens. But then Shrike has destroyed himself first, for no one could withstand the sustained horror of Shrike's impaling rhetoric, which truly can be called West's horror:

> "I am a great saint," Shrike cried, "I can walk on my own water. Haven't you ever heard of Shrike's Passion in the Luncheonette, or the Agony in the Soda Fountain? Then I compared the wounds in Christ's body to the mouths of a miraculous purse in which we deposit the small change of our sins. It is indeed an excellent conceit. But now let us consider the holes in our own bodies and into what these congenital wounds open. Under the skin of man is a wondrous jungle where veins like lush tropical growths hang along over-ripe organs and weed-like entrails writhe in squirming tangles of red and yellow. In this jungle, flitting from rock-gray lungs to golden intestines, from liver to lights and back to liver again, lives a bird called the soul. The Catholic hunts this bird with bread and wine, the Hebrew with a golden ruler, the Protestant on leaden feet with leaden words, the Buddhist with gestures, the Negro with blood. I spit on them all. Phooh! And I call upon you to spit. Phooh! Do you stuff birds? No, my dears, taxidermy is not religion. No! A thousand times no. Better, I say unto you, better a live bird in the jungle of the body than two stuffed birds on the library table."

I have always associated this great passage with what is central to West: the messianic longing for redemption, through sin if necessary. West's humor is almost always apocalyptic, in a mode quite original with him, though so influential since his death that we have difficulty seeing how strong the originality was. Originality, even in comic writing, becomes a difficulty. How are we to read the most outrageous of the letters sent to Miss Lonelyhearts, the one written by the sixteen-year-old girl born without a nose?

> *I sit and look at myself all day and cry. I have a big hole in the middle of my face that scares people even myself so I cant blame the boys for not wanting to take me out. My mother loves me, but she crys terrible when she looks at me.*
>
> *What did I do to deserve such a terrible bad fate? Even if I did do some bad things I didnt do any before I was a year old and I was born this way. I asked Papa and he says he doesnt know, but that maybe I did something in the other world before I was born or that maybe I was being punished for his sins. I dont believe that because he is a very nice man. Ought I commit suicide?*
>
> *Sincerely yours,*
> *Desperate*

Defensive laughter is a complex reaction to grotesque suffering. In his 1928 essay on "Humor," Freud concluded that the above-the-I, the super-ego, speaks kindly words of comfort to the intimidated ego, and this speaking is humor, which Freud calls "the triumph of narcissism, the ego's victorious assertion of its own invulnerability." Clearly, Freud's "humor" does not include the Westian mode. Reading Desperate's "What did I do to deserve such a terrible bad fate?" our ego knows that is it defeated all the time, or at least is vulnerable to undeserved horror. West's humor has *no* liberating element whatsoever, but is the humor of a vertigo ill-balanced on the edge of what ancient Gnosticism called the *kenoma*, the cosmological emptiness.

Shrike, West's superb Satanic tempter, achieves his apotheosis at the novel's midpoint, the eighth of its fifteen tableaux, accurately titled "Miss Lonelyhearts in the Dismal Swamp." As Miss Lonelyhearts, sick with despair, lies in bed, the drunken Shrike bursts in, shouting his greatest rhetorical setpiece, certainly the finest tirade in modern American fiction. Cataloging the methods that Miss Lonelyhearts might employ to escape out of the Dismal Swamp, Shrike begins with a grand parody of the later D. H. Lawrence, in which the vitalism of *The Plumed Serpent* and *The Man Who Died* is carried into a gorgeous absurdity, a heavy sexuality that masks Shrike's Satanic fears of impotence:

> "You are fed up with the city and its teeming millions. The ways and means of men, as getting and lending and spending, you lay waste your inner world, are too much with you. The bus takes too long, while the subway is always crowded. So what do you do? So you buy a farm and walk behind your horse's moist behind, no collar or tie, plowing your broad swift acres. As you turn up the rich black soil, the wind carries the smell of pine and dung across the fields and the rhythm of an old, old work enters your soul. To this rhythm, you sow and weep and chivy your kine, not kin or kind, between the pregnant rows of corn and taters. Your step becomes the heavy sexual step of a dance-drunk Indian and you tread the seed down into the female earth. You plant, not dragon's teeth, but beans and greens."

Confronting only silence, Shrike proceeds to parody Melville of *Typee* and *Omoo,* or Somerset Maugham's version of Gauguin in *The Moon and Sixpence:*

> "You live in a thatch hut with the daughter of a king, a slim young maiden in whose eyes is an ancient wisdom. Her breasts are golden speckled pears, her belly a melon, and her odor is like nothing so much as a jungle fern. In the evening, on the blue lagoon, under the silvery moon, to your love you croon in the soft sylabelew and vocabelew of her langorour tongorour. Your body is golden brown like hers, and tourists have need of the indignant finger of the

missionary to point you out. They envy you your breech clout and carefree laugh and little brown bride and fingers instead of forks. But you don't return their envy, and when a beautiful society girl comes to your hut in the night, seeking to learn the secret of your happiness, you send her back to her yacht that hangs on the horizen like a nervous racehorse. And so you dream away the days, fishing, hunting, dancing, kissing, and picking flowers to twine in your hair."

As Shrike says, this is a played-out mode, but his savage gusto in rendering it betrays his hatred of the religion of art, of the vision that sought a salvation in imaginative literature. What Shrike goes on to chant is an even more effective parody of the literary stances West rejected. Though Shrike calls it "Hedonism," the curious amalgam here of Hemingway and Ronald Firbank, with touches of Fitzgerald and the earlier Aldous Huxley, might better be named as an aesthetic stoicism:

"You dedicate your life to the pursuit of pleasure. No overindulgence, mind you, but knowing that your body is a pleasure machine, you treat it carefully in order to get the most out of it. Golf as well as booze, Philadelphia Jack O'Brien and his chestweights was well as Spanish dancers. Nor do you neglect the pleasures of the mind. You fornicate under pictures by Matisse and Picasso, you drink from Renaissance glassware, and often you spend an evening beside the fireplace with Proust and an apple. Alas, after much good fun, the day comes when you realize that soon you must die. You keep a stiff upper lip and decide to give a last party. You invite all your old mistresses, trainers, artists and boon companions. The guests are dressed in black, the waiters are coons, the table is a coffin carved for you by Eric Gill. You serve caviar and blackberries and licorice candy and coffee without cream. After the dancing girls have finished, you get to your feet and call for silence in order to explain your philosophy of life. 'Life,' you say, 'is a club where they won't stand for squawks, where they deal you only one hand and you must sit in. So even if the cards are cold and marked by the hand of fate, play up, play up like a gentleman and a sport. Get tanked, grab what's on the buffet, use the girls upstairs, but remember, when you throw box cars, take the curtain like a dead game sport, don't squawk.' "

Even this is only preparatory to Shrike's bitterest phase in his tirade, an extraordinary send-up of High Aestheticism prayer, of Pater, George Moore, Wilde, and the earlier W. B. Yeats:

"Art! Be an artist or a writer. When you are cold, warm yourself before the flaming tints of Titian, when you are hungry, nourish yourself with great spiritual foods by listening to the noble periods of Bach, the harmonies of Brahms and the thunder of Beethoven.

Do you think there is anything in the fact that their names all begin with a B? But don't take a chance, smoke a 3 B pipe, and remember these immortal lines: *When to the suddenness of melody the echo parting falls the failing day.* What a rhythm! Tell them to keep their society whores and pressed duck with oranges. For you *l'art vivant*, the living art, as you call it. Tell them that you know that your shoes are broken and that there are pimples on your face, yes, and that you have buck teeth and a club foot, but that you don't care, for to-morrow they are playing Beethoven's last quartets in Carnegie Hall and at home you have Shakespeare's plays in one volume."

That last sentence, truly and deliciously Satanic, in one of West's greatest triumphs, but he surpasses it in the ultimate Shrikean rhapsody, after Shrike's candid avowal: "God alone is our escape." With marvelous appropriateness, West makes this at once the ultimate Miss Lonelyhearts letter, and also Shrike's most Satanic self-identification, in the form of a letter to Christ dictated for Miss Lonelyhearts by Shrike, who speaks absolutely for both of them:

Dear Miss Lonelyhearts of Miss Lonelyhearts—
I am twenty-six years old and in the newspaper game. Life for me is a desert empty of comfort. I cannot find pleasure in food, drink, or women— nor do the arts give me joy any longer. The Leopard of Discontent walks the streets of my city; the Lion of Discouragement crouches outside the walls of my citadel. All is desolation and a vexation of spirit. I feel like hell. How can I believe, how can I have faith in this day and age? Is it true that the greatest scientists believe again in you?
I read your column and like it very much. There you once wrote: 'When the salt has lost its savour, who shall savour it again?' Is the answer: 'None but the Saviour?'
Thanking you very much for a quick reply, I remain yours truly,
A Regular Subscriber

"I feel like hell," the Miltonic "Myself am Hell," is Shrike's credo, and West's.

What is the relation of Shrike to West's rejected Jewishness? The question may seem illegitimate to many admirers of West, but acquires considerable force in the context of the novel's sophisticated yet unhistorical Gnosticism. The way of nihilism means, according to Scholem, "to free oneself of all laws, conventions, and religions, to adopt every conceivable attitude and to reject it, and to follow one's leader step for step into the abyss." Scholem is paraphrasing the demonic Jacob Frank, an eighteenth-century Jewish Shrike who brought the Sabbatian messianic movement to its final degradation. Frank would have recognized something of his own negations and nihilistic fervor in the closing passages that form a patter in West's four novels:

His body screamed and shouted as it marched and uncoiled; then, with one heaving shout of triumph, it fell back quiet.

The army that a moment before had been thundering in his body retreated slowly—victorious, relieved.

(The Dream Life of Balso Snell)

While they were struggling, Betty came in through the street door. She called to them to stop and started up the stairs. The cripple saw her cutting off his escape and tried to get rid of the package. He pulled his hand out. The gun inside the package exploded and Miss Lonelyhearts fell, dragging the cripple with him. They both rolled part of the way down the stairs.

(Miss Lonelyhearts)

"Alas, Lemuel Pitkin himself did not have this chance, but instead was dismantled by the enemy. His teeth were pulled out. His eye was gouged from his head. His thumb was removed. His scalp was torn away. His leg was cut off. And, finally, he was shot through the heart."

"But he did not live or die in vain. Through his martyrdom the National Revolutionary Party triumphed, and by that triumph this country was delivered from sophistication, Marxism and International Capitalism. Through the National Revolution its people were purged of alien diseases and America became again American."

"Hail the martyrdom in the Bijou Theater!" roar Shagpoke's youthful hearers when he is finished.

"Hail, Lemuel Pitkin!"

"All hail, the American Boy!"

(A Cool Million)

He was carried through the exit to the back street and lifted into a police car. The siren began to scream and at first he thought he was making the noise himself. He felt his lips with his hands. They were clamped tight. He knew then it was the siren. For some reason this made him laugh and he began to imitate the siren as loud as he could.

(The Day of the Locust)

All four passages mutilate the human image, the image of God that normative Jewish tradition associates with our origins. "Our forefathers were always talking, only what good did it do them and what did they accomplish? But we are under the burden of silence," Jacob Frank said. What Frank's and West's forefathers always talked about was the ultimate forefather, Adam, who would have enjoyed the era of the Messiah, had he not sinned. West retains of tradition only the emptiness of the fallen image, the scattered spark of creation. The screaming and falling body, torn apart and maddened into a siren-like laughter, belongs at once to the

American Surrealist poet, Balso Snell; the American Horst Wessel, poor Lemuel Pitkin; to Miss Lonelyhearts, the Whitmanian American Christ; and to Tod Hackett, painter of the American apocalypse. All are nihilistic versions of the mutilated image of God, or of what the Jewish Gnostic visionary, Nathan of Gaza, called the "thought-less" or nihilizing light.

West was a prophet of American violence, which he saw as augmenting progressively throughout our history. His satirical genius, for all its authentic and desperate range, has been defeated by American reality. Shagpoke Whipple, the Calvin Coolidge-like ex-President who becomes the American Hitler in *A Cool Million*, talks in terms that West intended as extravagant, but that now can be read, all but daily, in our newspapers. Here is Shagpoke at his best, urging us to hear what the dead Lemuel Pitkin has to tell us:

> "Of what is it that he speaks? Of the right of every American boy to go into the world and there receive fair play and a chance to make his fortune by industry and probity without being laughed at or conspired against by sophisticated aliens."

I turn to today's *New York Times* (March 29, 1985) and find there the text of a speech given by our President:

> But may I just pause here for a second and tell you about a couple of fellows who came to see me the other day, young men. In 1981, just four years ago, they started a business with only a thousand dollars between them and everyone told them they were crazy. Last year their business did a million and a half dollars and they expect to do two and a half million this year. And part of it was because they had the wit to use their names productively. Their business is using their names, the Cain and Abell electric business.

Reality may have triumphed over poor West, but only because he, doubtless as a ghost, inspired or wrote these Presidential remarks. The *Times* reports, sounding as dead-pan as Shrike, on the same page (B4), that the young entrepreneurs brought a present to Mr. Reagan. " 'We gave him a company jacket with Cain and Abell, Inc. on it,' Mr. Cain said." Perhaps West's ghost now writes not only Shagpokian speeches, but the very text of reality in our America.

Convention in the Fiction of Edith Wharton

Mary Suzanne Schriber

Edith Wharton's "hieroglyphic world" of Old New York society with its "elaborate system of mystification" stands implicitly on a pervasive, powerful cultural construct: the nineteenth-century concept of "woman." The idea of woman, the complement of the male, as innocent, dependent, intuitive, spiritual, and nurturing by the design of God, justified and enforced the social conventions and norms governing women's lives. Given a woman's nature, marriage was the arena in which her God-given traits could best be expressed. Manners, such as allowing men to open carriage doors and conduct the extra-domestic business of life, were taken to be the signs of conformity to that nature. Social conventions were the public manifestations of a woman's private but shared essence, the visible translations of the culture's assumptions about a woman's nature and her consequent role and manner in the Divine economy.

Wharton's fictional treatment of convention, with its implicit connection to the culture's idea of woman, captures three particular aspects of its workings with which Wharton has not been credited. First, Wharton's fiction demonstrates the consequences for individual women and for society of the limitation of women's activities to a single fully approved arena, marriage. The investment by heroines of an enormous portion of themselves in marriage or its pursuit grants to that institution an inordinate power either to make or break their lives. Second, convention in Wharton's fiction tends to lessen human attentiveness, insidiously shrinking, replacing, or even obliterating direct perceptions of the world. Intercepting vision and encouraging the perceiver to attach indiscriminately to behavior the significance ordinarily assigned to it, tradition subjects Wharton's female characters to two injustices: their behavior is often misconstrued, or it is

From *Studies in American Fiction* 11, no. 2 (Autumn 1983). © 1983 by Northeastern University Press.

rendered invisible and therefore unappreciated if it in any way outstrips ordinary expectations of woman. Finally, the expectations that govern women's lives and articulate society's notion of a woman's nature are subject to manipulation by both sexes for either life-denying or life-enhancing purposes. When convention is used to close rather than to open life's possibilities in Wharton's fiction, heroines are usually its prey.

Beginning to record the profound and far-reaching reverberations of the culture's predilection to assign marriage to woman as the single approved source of her identity and the sole outlet for her energies, Wharton established the tie between marriage and identity in an early short story. She then creates heroines variously situated who respond in one of three ways to the culture's expectation that they will marry and be fulfilled. Some heroines refuse the culture's directive, others seize it with a vengeance, and still others fulfill it literally to a fault. Whatever their response to the institution of marriage, heroines inevitably must come to terms with their culture's bias in its favor.

The relationship between marriage and identity for a woman appears in Wharton's second published work of fiction, "The Fullness of Life" (1893). The heroine of this allegorical tale chooses to spend eternity with an irritating husband rather than a "soul mate" for reasons that express her conformity to the culture's idea of a woman: she must " 'look after him, he is so helpless' ", as a wife, she is charged with her husband's happiness. Further, the heroine, drawing attention to the difficulties of caring for her husband, fulfills the characteristic pattern of nineteenth-century women who, isolated from the hurly-burly of the masculine world and looking to create some sense of their own value and indispensability, "sought domestic importance as compensation for societal neglect" and increased their sense of worth by emphasizing the difficulties of their duties. The self and the self-esteem of the heroine of "The Fullness of Life" require a traditional marriage.

The pervasiveness and power of cultural assumptions about woman and marriage and identity are perhaps most tellingly revealed in the lives of Wharton heroines who are not married. Logically, it would seem, unmarried women should not suffer from an institution in which they do not participate. Ironically, that institution and the conventions designed to sustain it govern the lives even of the unmarried, as is the case with Lily Bart of *The House of Mirth* (1905). Whereas the heroine of "The Fullness of Life" decides that she is better off in her wifely place at her husband's side, Lily Bart finds herself with no place in which to conduct her life and validate her existence because she is single. She cannot bring herself to marry any of her available suitors, and thus she feels "rootless and ephemeral . . . without anything to which the poor little tentacles of self could cling before the awful flood submerged them." As Lily says to one of her suitors, " 'I am a very useless person . . . What can one do when one finds that one only fits one hole? One must get back to it or be thrown out into the rubbish heap—.' " The one hole into which Lily would fit is marriage. While perceived as marriageable, Lily is granted some social acceptance. Once it becomes clear that she will not marry, that acceptance is withdrawn. Lily Bart's descent from a tenuous foothold among the aristocracy to a lonely death is marked by her movement from house to house, houses being a woman's appointed place of duty and fulfillment, until finally Lily lands in a dingy boarding house in which she is quite literally a nobody. A woman without a house of her own, Lily is therefore a woman without duties to express and define her potential and give point to her life. Without these, Lily loses first her self-esteem and eventually her will to live. The culture provides no place for Lily Bart, no approved arena outside of marriage in which a woman of her class can satisfactorily conduct her life. As ministers told women in the nineteenth century: "Stay within your proper confines and you will be worshipped; . . . step outside and you will cease to exist."

Such a single-minded view of woman's place is shown in Wharton's fiction to diminish society as well as the lives of individuals like Lily Bart. In *The Custom of the Country* (1912), men and the body social suffer the onslaught of Undine Spragg, a heroine who is driven by the assumption that woman fulfilled is woman married. Not at all the nice young lady who seeks to be cared for by a kind man, in keeping with the concept of woman's nature and consequent role, Undine is an extremely capable and unscrupulously ambitious woman who fully understands woman's place and seeks to fill it with a vengeance. Undine sees that because woman's status is conferred by marriage, it is only intelligent to work the territory of marriage as a salesman works his until the profits are satisfactory. With the potential spirit and energy of the free enterprise system, Undine marries four times, contracting each new marriage in the belief that finally society will make good on its promise: marry and be satisfied. Pursuing the American dream as it is packaged for women, and heeding the call of her "pioneer blood" like her father before her, Undine invests in marriages like her father in his business in order to make something of herself. Undine's only available frontier is marriage. As Elizabeth Ammons points out, during Undine's rare periods as a single woman she is unrecognized, even ostracized, and therefore "she *must* marry again [after each failed marriage] in order to have identity itself, much less power." Although Wharton criticism, in order to explain Undine's genesis, has seized upon the words of a character in the novel who identifies Undine as " 'the monstrously perfect result of the system' " that worships money and power and devalues community and integrity, surely Wharton's novel develops a quite different major theme: only one place, marriage, defines a woman and gives her whatever access she may have to money and power.

In Pauline Manford of *Twilight Sleep* (1927), Wharton develops the consequences of convention understood literally and assimilated uncritically. Less insightful than either Undine Spragg or Lily Bart, who see the gap between the idea of woman and the facts of women's lives, Pauline Manford undertakes her womanly role so earnestly and religiously that she loses the very ends it was designed to secure. She pursues her cultural and domestic duties "as eagerly as her husband, in the early days of his career, used to study the documents of a new case." However, Pauline's eagerness, unlike her husband's is not admirable. The objects of Pauline's efforts and talents are inherently incommensurate with the energy brought to them. Yet these objects and activities are woman's only source of identity, woman's only outlet for her energies, and Pauline Manford is above all an energetic woman. She is said to thrill "like a war-horse to a trumpet" when a practical demand is made on her, and her daughter envisions her mother as a "pioneer wife" who would have nursed her children fearlessly in the wilderness. Unfortunately, there is no more wilderness, no more frontier, no safety valve and no duty worthy of the abundant drive of a Pauline Manford. Therefore she crams her calendar with teas, gurus, hairdressers, pop lectures, and redecorating. As a pioneer might measure success by the territory covered, or as a professional man might measure his by the demand for his expertise, so Pauline busies up her life, lecturing to woman's groups both about abortion and motherhood in order to create for herself some semblance of purpose and usefulness.

While *Twilight Sleep* satirizes Pauline Manford, the novel's satiric effect is tempered by the situation in which Pauline is placed and by the motives ascribed to her, showing on the one hand the stupidity of a woman like Pauline but on the other hand the culture's complicity in her fate. Pauline's frenzied activities are designed not merely to gratify herself but to please her husband, a motive her culture would surely approve. Yet the more Pauline does to win her husband's praise and to fulfill her purpose within her culturally assigned sphere, the more inconsequential her activities become, rendering her progressively more boring to her husband. He then seizes upon Pauline's excesses to justify his flirtation with a much younger (and even more frivolous) woman. Wharton is the first American writer to see that the quantity of a woman's energy and the thoroughness of her pursuit of her womanly work can, as in the case of Pauline, ironically guarantee her failure in her only approved sphere of achievement.

Convention impinges on the heroines of Wharton's fiction in a further and even more insidious way. It tends to limit, distort, or obscure the ways in which they are perceived, whether married or not. Characters allow the traditional idea of woman to mediate their perception of individual women; they substitute an abstraction for flesh and blood. Whereas theoretically any human attribute can be underestimated or minimized by imposing conventional limits on it, Wharton's fiction concentrates on her culture's diminished expectations of two of woman's possibilities, intellect and complexity of character. By obscuring or denying these aspects of women, characters are able to shield themselves from truth and to rationalize their deeds, both of which are invariably destructive of human life in Wharton's fiction.

The narrator of Wharton's first and probably autobiographical novella, *The Touchstone* (1900), states directly the limitations of intellect that are associated with women. The hero of the tale is capable of identifying one woman's intellect as exceptional but incapable of rejoicing in it. Glennard cannot love an extraordinary novelist, Margaret Aubyn, because he has

> an ambitious man's impatience of distinguished women. . . . It was not that she bored him; she did what was infinitely worse— she made him feel his inferiority. . . . If a man is at times indirectly flattered by the moral superiority of woman, her mental ascendancy is extenuated by no such oblique tribute to his powers. The attitude of looking up is a strain on the muscles; and it was becoming more and more Glennard's opinion that brains, in a woman, should be merely the obverse of beauty.

Despite the fact that Margaret Aubyn underplays her superiority, Glennard fixes his attention on the expected incompatibility of woman and intellect. Recognizing that Margaret's intelligence outstrips the categories prepared for it by the concept of woman, Glennard becomes angry and enlists the idea of woman against Margaret, making her wrong to be intelligent in order to make himself right in his lesser gifts.

Predictably, Glennard takes a conventional wife, Alexa. Ironically, he does not revel in her conventional qualities. In *The Touchstone*, no woman can be "right" in the eyes of a man like Glennard who uses *a priori* ideas of woman to protect his ego. Glennard eventually discredits Alexa's intelligence on the grounds that her words are the mere "conventional utterance of a 'nice' woman." Reducing Alexa's grasp of the issue at hand to his own expectations of woman, Glennard unwittingly indicts himself on two counts: he fails to recognize the extent of his wife's intelligence, and he shows himself unable to rest easy with any quantity of intellect in a woman. Margaret Aubyn was unacceptable to him because she was more intelligent than a woman should be, and now Alexa fails to win his approval because she is only as intelligent as a woman should be. In matters of intellect, a woman is wrong to be a woman in *The Touchstone*.

Perhaps the most classic and tragic enactment in Wharton's fiction of convention as a distorting lens occurs in *The House of Mirth*. Lawrence Selden uses social norms to protect himself from the implications of his own motives and ideas. For all of Selden's rhetoric about the Republic of the Spirit, that land in which one supposedly breathes free of the usual proprieties, and for all of his actual observation of Lily Bart, Selden finally substitutes tradition for vision in dealing with her. Because Lily behaves improperly at times, visiting Selden's apartment unchaperoned and violating norms of female conduct, Selden is unable to sustain a consistent, accurate reading of her character. He cannot dismiss the simple significance ordinarily ascribed to behavior like Lily's in order to grasp firmly the authentic, complex person whose integrity he has reason to believe in. It is for this reason that Selden cannot bring himself to marry Lily Bart. While his hesitations and indecisiveness are usually charged to his tepidness of character, the novel shows that the imperceptiveness which convention encourages finally accounts for Selden's failure. Reading Lily's behavior as an indication of questionable character, Selden cannot risk proposing marriage to her. The crucial point at which Selden definitely turns away from Lily is the moment in which Selden escapes from difficult, individual judgment into easy notions about proper women. The sight of Lily emerging late at night from the rakish Gus Trenor's house causes Selden to break his resolve to propose marriage to her. In a scene just prior to this, Selden is made party to information which casts Lily's behavior in an entirely proper light. He is told that Lily planned to visit Judy Trenor that night, and he is also told that unexpectedly, Judy had remained out of town. Yet Selden fails to recall this fact on Lily's behalf. His commitment to the normative idea of woman overwhelms his insight into Lily and his knowledge of her motives. At Lily's deathbed, a similar scene occurs. Although chastened and sorrowful, Selden immediately suspects the worst when he spots an envelope on Lily's dresser addressed to Gus Trenor. A man like Selden who sees life in customary terms cannot entirely believe in or accurately perceive a woman who in any way expands on that framework.

In the case of Lily Bart, convention obscures good qualities and serves to undermine the future of a strong heroine. In the case of Undine Spragg of *The Custom of the Country*, expectations of woman serve to disguise Undine's reprehensible side. Despite Undine's evident strength and energy, her suitor, Ralph Marvell, sees her as a poor, defenseless woman, a damsel in distress, and sees himself as a knight to the rescue: "He seemed to see her as a lovely rock-bound Andromeda . . . and himself whirling down on his winged horse . . . to cut her bonds, snatch her up, and whirl her back into the blue. . . ." Ralph's perception of Undine, like his reading of her on their honeymoon as a soft and unyielding new bride when she is actually seething with boredom and plotting her escape from it, is tragically inaccurate. The traditional idea of woman assists in the destruction of a decent man by contributing to misperceptions so severe that he commits suicide when they are finally corrected.

Convention as a distorting force is of central importance in *The Age of Innocence* (1921). This novel has often been read as Wharton's nostalgic tribute to the New York society of her youth and to the norms that regulated the conduct of her parents and grandparents. The discrepancy in the novel between Newland Archer's views of women and their actual deeds, however, proves *The Age of Innocence* to be Wharton's most far-reaching judgment on the deficiencies of Old New York and her most resounding indictment of fashion used as a mediator, even an interceptor, of reality.

Newland Archer's vision of Ellen Olenska and May Welland is the product of inherited ideas of woman. Reflecting on Ellen's rich history, Archer pictures her in the frame of dark lady whose past includes "marriage to an immensely rich nobleman of legendary fame" met at the Tuileries and possessing "princely establishments" throughout Europe. Reflecting on Ellen's present life, he notes her high spirits and high color, her mysteriousness, and her status as an outcast from New York society. In his eyes she is surely a heroine of romance, "an exposed and pitiful figure, to be saved at all costs from further wounding herself in her mad plunge against fate." Cynthia Woolf credits Archer with an imagination that allows him his vision of Ellen. More accurately, in envisioning Ellen as a damsel in distress as Ralph Marvell had envisioned Undine Spragg, Archer provides himself with the opportunity to play a chivalric role and to think well of himself. Moreover, his response to Ellen is one of many indications of his conformity. It is clear that Archer relies on the stock idea of the dark lady in his thoughts of Ellen, for he is certainly not relying on observation. Ellen, in fact, rather calmly and confidently goes about her life throughout the novel and is only occasionally concerned with society's view of her. It is true that Ellen differs from the women of Old New York: she imprudently changes addresses, acts assertively with Archer, and decorates her quarters exotically. It is equally true that Archer imposes comfortable stereotypes on the raw material Ellen provides, enabling him to conceive of himself as a literary hero rather than a traditional male.

Archer's assessment of May Welland grows out of the same view of woman in which he framed Ellen. It is simply the other side of the same coin, the fair heroine *versus* the dark. Archer makes May seem to be less than the novel shows her to be in order to justify his attraction to Ellen. Ellen, after all, seems so much more vital and exciting once he imputes an excessive conventionality to May, and May seems so much more dull and uninteresting once Ellen flies free from social norms that a man can hardly be blamed for preferring the one to the other. To Archer, May seems guileless. He assumes that because May "had been trained not to possess" versatility and freedom of judgment, it must be that she does not possess them. While critical of his society's efforts to ensure the innocence of young women, Archer assumes that society has succeeded in the case of May and foresees "his task to presently take the bandage from this young woman's eyes, and bid her look forth on the world." So thoroughgoing are Archer's preconceptions of May that when she urges him to agree to an earlier marriage than planned, a clue that her eyes may be less bandaged than he thinks, Archer thinks that "she simply echoed what was said for her." A young woman like May, Archer presumes, would of course not express her own thoughts and perceptions.

Unhampered by Archer's role, the narrator and the action of *The Age of Innocence* have meanwhile shown May in a light different from the one Archer turns on her, a light that exposes and judges Archer's attachment to traditional ideas of woman. Archer is guilty of gross imperceptiveness stemming from the substitution of assumptions for attentive observation. The narrator claims that there was "a certain triteness in these [Archer's] reflections [on May's character]." Worse, his reflections are simply wrong. May was all along aware of Archer's penchant for Ellen, as Archer discovers only years later. Contrary to Archer's impression, May in some matters is calculating rather than spontaneous and innocent. At the time of Ellen Olenska's imminent departure for Europe, when May knew that Archer was tempted to board Ellen's ship, May intimately announces her pregnancy to cousin Ellen—a pregnancy not yet confirmed. While this timely announcement conforms to convention (for women are permitted to trick one another in the interests of marriage and the family), it exceeds the usual expectations of the fair sex because it is based on a precise calculation of the character of May's rival. A less scrupulous woman than Ellen might take what she wanted despite a pregnancy. May, however, more insightful than Newland, understands that Ellen is in many ways a respecter of the code of Old New York; Ellen will not allow Archer to join her under the circumstances. May Welland is, to be sure, a fine, fair, fresh, and traditional woman. The problem is that Archer sees only this aspect of her, the only one of which he can conceive, the only one for which he has an *a priori* category which explains and neutralizes her.

The Age of Innocence, in keeping Archer faithful to May, does not nostalgically lament the passing of a bygone era. Rather, it simply draws to a logical and plausible end the implications of the character the novelist has created. Newland Archer is a protagonist whose only contentment, despite his fantasies, is found in the world of Old New York. Archer's dreams of running off with Ellen are themselves misconstructions of his own character just as surely as his perceptions of Ellen and May are inaccurate. As Marilyn Lyde points out, in Wharton's fiction responsible departures from the paths of convention are reserved for exceptionally perceptive and strong characters who are prepared to suffer social ostracism for morality's sake. Although Newland Archer would like to think of himself among these happy few, he is neither perceptive nor courageous. He is one of the "middling people" spoken of in Wharton's "Autres Temps" who would be knocked senseless by the air of freedom. This is precisely Wharton's point in *The Age of Innocence*, a point deftly made by her handling of tradition as a distorting lens through which Archer perceives the women in his life. *The Age of Innocence* is not Wharton's validation of a conservative life *per se* but a demonstration of the way in which a man in Old New York society goes about making a choice. He arrives at important decisions by unwittingly relying on tradition rather than perception, a procedure that Wharton shows to be defective because of the quantity of life it misconstrues. Far from being an encomium to the old, *The Age of Innocence* is a complaint against an insidious tendency to substitute tradition for the direct apprehension of life.

As the example of May Welland indicates, certain of Wharton's heroines fight back in order to wrest from life some degree of spiritual and material satisfaction. These heroines become themselves a counter-statement to traditional definitions of woman's nature. Recognizing the distance between their actual abilities and the roles into which they are to fit themselves, they cleverly behave in ways beyond usual expectations of woman. Recognizing that *a priori* ideas of woman blind many people to individual women, heroines often exploit convention to render yet more effective their manipulation of it. They put on standard behavior to disguise their real ends, which are sometimes admirable and sometimes not. Heroines play at female roles for a variety of reasons: in an effort to win husbands; to secure selfish and materialistic ends; to preserve, in time-honored fashion, the family; or to evade responsibility.

Lily Bart of *The House of Mirth* is a Wharton heroine who clearly sees that convention confers on women a ritual power that can be and often is used to secure husbands, houses, and money. Further, Lily is perfectly able to exploit traditional roles if she chooses. Knowing full well what men like to find in a woman, Lily behaves in ways that are laughable in light of her actual self but prudent when she goes in pursuit of a husband. Infinitely more intelligent and vital than the eligible but dull Percy Gryce, Lily questions him obsequiously and listens to him patiently on the subject of his Americana collection. Desperate for money and aware of the appeal of female helplessness and dependency to the male ego, Lily cleverly calls upon her vast ignorance of finances in approaching Gus Trenor for a loan and for protection from the harsh world no lovely woman should be forced to confront. Lily repeatedly displays her beauty, which is real, and plays at helplessness and ignorance, which are feigned, in order to maneuver herself into a position to marry. Unfortunately for Lily, however, her soul repeatedly intervenes, preventing her from making full use of a woman's power. Lily is worth infinitely more than society or Selden knows, and she is therefore unable to sacrifice her own integrity on the altar of marriage at any price, including everlasting boredom. This is the mark of her refinement and of the culture's corruption. Lily refuses the prescriptions and the prerogatives that the concept of woman allows. Paradoxically, Lily's recognition that she has no identity and purpose outside of marriage is also her discovery of her true identity: a woman who transcends the culture's concept of a woman, a woman whose self-esteem prevents her from stooping to conquer.

Undine Spragg of *The Custom of the Country*, on the other hand, has no soul to intervene between her desires and the manipulation of tradition. Making Lily Bart seem positively amateurish by comparison, Undine turns cultural expectations into her playthings. Finding herself dissatisfied with Ralph Marvell despite her aggressive pursuit of him to the altar, the worldly-wise Undine seeks another man's sympathy with the affecting lament: " 'What does a young girl know of life?' " Whereas Lily Bart occasionally bends social norms to her purposes, Undine Spragg uses them to cover outright lies. Wishing to impress and then to marry Peter Van Degen, Undine designs a *mise-en-scene* that emphasizes her "recovered freshness and bloom," in consequence of which she "had never been more sure of her power to keep her friend in the desired state of adoring submission." Limit woman's sphere, Wharton's novel seems to say, and women who are intelligent and clever and unscrupulous will wrest from their very imprisonment an occasion for the exercise of power, an occasion created by innocent characters who take stock behavior at face value or by more experienced characters who are rendered myopic by their limited expectations.

May Welland of *The Age of Innocence* is perhaps Wharton's most subtle embodiment of a woman's use of convention for the time-honored end of family unity. May's manipulation of her assumed prerogatives is so quiet that even critics, never mind the characters in the novel, have seldom perceived May's deviousness. May seizes her womanly rights to achieve a most proper end, keeping her husband. Her means, however, are unconventional and therefore invisible to Archer. Aware of his attraction to Ellen, May strategically eschews the obvious role of outraged wife. Instead, she in public proceeds quietly and unobtrusively (as a lady should) to eliminate her rival while avoiding even a private confrontation with Archer on the subject of Ellen, a confrontation which would permanently undermine their relationship and thus render her conquest of Archer partial and her victory over Ellen pyrrhic.

There is a final manipulation of cultural preconceptions of woman in Wharton's fiction which demonstrates the subtlety of Wharton's insight and lays to rest any lingering notions of Wharton as in any simple way an advocate of convention. Whereas society would understand normative behavior as a public expression of a woman's sense of responsibility, Wharton's "Joy in the House" (1933) shows that the opposite can be true. Convention can be used as a refuge from genuine responsibility. The story's heroine, Christine Ansley, enlists traditional norms of female behavior to justify her abandonment of a man who honestly needs her and to whom she has incurred responsibility by her own choices and deeds. She had embarked, with her husband's approval, on a "trial marriage" with an artist. Finding him too intense and demanding, Christine returns to her husband and son. She represents her return as responsible and decent while the story shows it to be an escape into security and complacency. "Joy in the House" renders Christine's return to her husband in terms that refer to tradition and the camouflage and approval it can provide. Christine crawls back home into roles, rejoicing not in the people who greet her but in the forms of address they use: "my daughter," "my wife," and especially "Mrs. Devons Ansley." So pleased is Christine with these designations that she attributes her joy at coming home to the fact that despite all, these people still allow her "to be sacredly and inalienably, 'my wife,' 'my mother'. " Christine even delights in resuming "her household duties, talking over the marketing with the cook, discussing a new furniture polish." She does not yearn for a full life within marriage but for the assigned and approved duties of a wife, shopping and cleaning, in order to escape the human responsibility at issue in the story. Convention built on the concept of a woman's nature may tie woman's identity and purpose to marriage, as in "The Fullness of Life," or it may offer a woman an avenue away from identity and purpose, as it ironically does in the case of Christine Ansley.

The fictional lives of Edith Wharton's characters, constricted in manifold and insidious ways by the codes of behavior dictated by the idea of woman, underscore the need to be attentive to social norms not for reasons of propriety but for purposes of self-defense. Although Wharton's personal history proves her ability to imagine a life beyond traditional manners and mores, she clearly does not reject altogether the uses of convention. It sometimes provides the best available guide to conduct, compensating for limitations of insight and character in those like Newland Archer who are restrained by tradition from actions unsuited to their temperament and their long-term happiness. Nonetheless, the predominant impression Wharton's fiction conveys is that convention, while useful and even necessary, restricts human possibilities. Further, it often dims perceptions of individuals and limits appreciation of their complexity. Wharton's far-reaching, complex critique of the operations of social tradition, particularly in the lives of women, suggests that unless individuals are alert to its power and influence, it will substitute itself first for a direct apprehension of life and then for life itself.

Dreiser's Trilogy
and the Dilemma of Determinism

John J. Conder

In "The Dilemma of Determinism," William James argues for a theory of indeterminism by arguing for the existence, not of man's free will, but of chance. He could well take the position that "the stronghold of the deterministic sentiment is the antipathy to the idea of chance," for to believe that something is "not controlled, secured, or necessitated by other things in advance of its own actual presence" is to deny the fundamental premise of determinism: "For everything that ever happens there are conditions such that, given them, nothing else could happen." If chance exists in the physical universe, then, it seems plausible to believe that man's freedom is a reality as well. Hence it is fitting that Dreiser, the only major American naturalist writer personally and explicitly committed to philosophic determinism, should have pondered the subject of chance during a lifetime that shows strong concern for understanding the ramifications of determinism.

In a section of his *Notes on Life* entitled "The Factor Called Chance," he writes that this concept may be "in most cases only another name for our ignorance of causes." He does grant it some status—it is not possible to know which spider's web will trap which fly—but he never abandons the rigid laws of cause and effect that in fact undermine the concept: "If it were possible . . . to know the exact operations of the entire universe in advance, [then chance would not exist]. But since such prevision is seemingly not granted to any life form, there intervenes the factor called chance."

Although "chance" events do occur in Dreiser's novels—the Chicago fire that initially undoes Frank Cowperwood, for example—their existence is not meant to challenge the concept of determinism. If Dreiser does not bother to explain the causes of the fire, he has good reason for the omission: he wishes to explain the forces which govern human character, not those

From *Naturalism in American Fiction: The Classic Phase.* © 1984 by The University Press of Kentucky.

issuing in the fire. But the very fact that elsewhere he should explore the subject of chance (and many others) in the context of determinism testifies to the firmness of his commitment to determinism and thus sets him apart from a writer like Norris. As a personally committed determinist, furthermore, Dreiser spent much of his career impressing his deeply held doctrine into the service of denying traditional religious and social beliefs, since these assume man possesses freedom of the will. Such denial did not blind him to another fundamental problem raised by his vision, the problem of how man can live with dignity and find order and meaning in a universe that proscribes his freedom. In his last years, he turned to a hazy mysticism, a personal development reflected in Berenice Fleming's study of Brahmanism in *The Stoic*, her own attraction anticipated by Solon Barnes's rejection of materialism and discovery of the spirit of love and purpose in nature and the universe in *The Bulwark*. In his quest for meaning, it would seem as though he abandoned his determinism, but this is not the case. There is a logical connection between these two apparently antithetical poles of his thought, the mechanistic and the "mystical," and the latter, rather than rejecting the former, embraces it.

This connection can be seen in the "trilogy of desire," if one is willing to set aside the usual view of *The Stoic*. The fact that the novel is incomplete has been elevated into a cardinal principle supporting established wisdom: that the work has no inner integrity and cannot be taken seriously as a thematic conclusion to the trilogy. Such wisdom has not gone unchallenged. John J. McAleer has analyzed the trilogy to show that even *The Stoic* has an inner coherence and strong relations to *The Financier* and *The Titan*. I will also leave established wisdom behind to show my own sense of the coherence of the trilogy.

Essentially one long novel, the trilogy possesses the unity of character, plot, and theme necessary to display the harmonious unfolding of Dreiser's thought. But the trilogy is of special value because it shows that the connections between the poles of his thought that gradually unfold depend upon his lifelong exploration of the implications of determinism. In the trilogy, Dreiser pursues those implications to the point where Berenice's conversion seems logical, even if abrupt because the action in this unfinished novel, though fully outlined, still needed further dramatic development. The trilogy, in other words, possesses an inner dynamic dependent on the unfolding of the intellectual premises of the first novel in the second, with the resolution of the philosophic problem raised by the second emerging in the third.

The goal of this chapter is to see how the first novel establishes a deterministic vision; how the second explores the implications of determinism to the point where it arrives at what William James called "the dilemma of determinism"; and how the third resolves that dilemma. Although each section of the ensuing discussion tries to stress the uniqueness of a single novel, the fact that the three novels are essentially one requires a good deal of jumping back and forth for purposes of clarity. The trilogy is a philosophical series of novels, and the meaning of a concept appearing in the second novel may well rest upon a premise established in the first; or the meaning of a subordinate line of thought in the second may require reference to the third in order to establish its full significance. This is the way of a philosophical work, and the critic must adapt to it.

THE FINANCIER

The Financier is an embodiment of "Dreiser's Law," the term used by Dreiser's biographer, W. A. Swanberg, to explain Dreiser's early view of society. According to the first tenet of that law, *"beliefs held by the multitude, the bourgeois and their leaders, are likely to be wrong per se."* The reverse is also true: *"Beliefs held by unconventionalists which fly in the face of orthodoxy are in all probability right."* This law explains Dreiser's attitude toward the two groups of characters in *The Financier*. Needless to say, no distinction is here made between narrator and author. A reader of Dreiser's essays and novels can see that no distinction exists.

Frank Cowperwood and Aileen Butler are the unconventionalists. They scorn the prevailing sexual mores embodied in conventional attitudes toward marriage and the Christian religious system sanctifying the social norm. "Aileen had no spiritual dread whatever. Cowperwood was without spiritual or religious feeling." In numerous ways Dreiser makes it clear that he is on "their" side, not that of their critics, who judge the central characters morally and legally for their transgressions against the laws of God and man. Dreiser's description of "the conventional mind" as "at best a petty piece of machinery . . . oyster-like in its functioning," perceiving "nothing of the subtlety of life," reacting to interferences with "the placid flow of events" with a "grinding" that is "not unlike sand in a machine," is one of several indications of his allegiance. Not only does he show contempt for this kind of mind, but also he exonerates Frank's and Aileen's behavior in terms that make moral condemnation of them irrelevant. Her "innate sensuousness" and that "something chemic and hence dynamic" which in him was "clamoring for expression" are mastering compulsions. As Dreiser states the matter in *The Titan*, Frank Cowperwood "could not control his own temperament any more than Aileen could control hers."

Of course, no one has freedom in the trilogy, so even the moralists in its pages must be exonerated for their actions. Yet, given the pain they cause, or are forced to cause, one must wonder why Dreiser so clearly admires his principals. Why not shed tears over those to whom they are forced to cause pain? Two closely related answers to this question exist, one pertaining to the author's view of Cowperwood, the other to his views of society.

Cowperwood is strikingly like the "creative power" to which Dreiser alludes in his penultimate conclusion to the novel. This power, which expresses itself through nature, is central to Dreiser's determinism. For him, determinism meant that "the physical aspect of the world . . . is not

more than a mechanism through which something . . . expresses itself,"
that all things that exist and all events that occur "are mere manifestations
of energy on the part of something that uses man as man uses a machine."
Like the creative power, Frank Cowperwood is a manipulator of men. His
motto, "I satisfy myself," is a logical extension of this role, for the power
pursues its own purposes (if any) for its own inscrutable ends. Of course
Cowperwood himself is a pawn of that power, which is inaccessible to
man, just as all other individuals, indeed all of nature, are its pawns.
Nonetheless Cowperwood in his role as master manipulator is as close to
a representation of that power as it is possible for a human to be. Since
one cannot help standing in awe and admiration, if not reverence, before
such a power, it is easy enough to transfer such feelings to its human
likeness, the superman.

There is a second reason for Dreiser's admiration, and it can be found
in a section of his *Notes on Life* called "The Theory that Life is a Game."
There he asserts that the creative power has ordained that all things in
nature must engage in contest, man included; for man has been endowed
with vanity and pride as attributes necessary to play the game for victory.
Chance and death give the game its intensity, as "each creature must contest
with something else." With such a view of life, one's sympathies do not
necessarily go to the moral man, whose morality is either a projection of
a temperament not quite fitted to play the game successfully, or a pretext
for defeating a player with no moral pretensions. Men try to bet on a winner
at the Derby. Do they sympathize with the horse that takes last place?

This view, a source of Dreiser's admiration for Cowperwood and
Aileen, accounts for the two sets of characters in *The Financier*. By explaining
their behavior according to "temperament," to "chemistry," and to "instinct," Dreiser allies Frank and Aileen to the world of nature, whereas
other figures, due to their "lack of force," are clearly a part of the social
world, presumably accountable to its laws because there "the chemistry
and physics of life" are not large. This division between "natural" and
"social" characters is enhanced by the distinction between Aileen's chemical
responses, based on physical law, which are the source of her decision to
marry Cowperwood, and the canon law of the Catholic Church to which
her Catholic father subscribes, and which is the source of his opposition
to that marriage. And Dreiser's explanation of Cowperwood's financial
dealings further emphasizes the distinction, for he sees Cowperwood as a
victim of "that subtle chemistry of things that transcends all written law
and makes for the spirit and, beyond that, the inutility of all law." Men of
nature, odd as it may seem, are the true men of spirit. Others are men of
the law, with its pale spirit. They are social men.

This distinction is further enforced by the famous framework of the
book. The first chapter shows Cowperwood's sense of kinship with the
predatory lobster in the fishmarket, which becomes a school for him as he
learns the answer to the question, " 'How is life organized?' " If lobsters

lived on squid, and men on lobsters, then the answer to his question, "And what lived on men?" is self-evident: "other men." This connection between human and animal predators is confirmed in the first coda to the novel, "Concerning Mycteroperca Bonaci," which implicitly associates Cowperwood with the black grouper fish. Its markings changing so that it can "strike unseen," this fish is clearly like Frank Cowperwood in his financial dealings with others and very much like the Cowperwood who, in his adulterous relationship with Aileen, displays the same "power of simulation" it possesses: "For purposes of social success, in order not to offend, to smooth one's path, make things easy, avoid useless criticism, and the like, it was necessary to create an outward seeming—ostensibly conform. Beyond that it was not necessary to do anything."

Not only is Frank Cowperwood a product of nature, but he is absolved of all responsibility for his behavior because of the parallel between him and the black grouper fish and its relation to the creative spirit. In this conclusion to the novel, Dreiser raises several unanswered questions about that relationship, but they are rhetorical ones only. For assuredly that spirit *does* will "that which is either tricky or deceptive"; it does *not* "build this mortal life is such fashion that only honesty and virtue shall prevail." Responsibility for Cowperwood's actions lies with the spirit, not with himself.

At this point in reasoning the distinction between "natural" and "social" men breaks down, for the reader knows that "there was no more escaping the greatness that was inherent in him [Cowperwood] than there was for so many others the littleness that was in them." Their allegiance to conventional social codes reflects that "littleness," which is the mirror of a temperament produced in nature and is in itself one expression of the creative power. As a "natural conservator of public morals," even Cowperwood's first wife, Lilian, is such an expression. Where all are victims of temperament, all belong to the world of nature, and hence all are pawns of, expressions of, the creative power.

Dreiser thus creates an amoral naturalistic axis for action rather than an ethical one in *The Financier*. A creative power wills a contest and creates the conditions for its enactment: the varying temperaments who engage in it. To emphasize the true impulses guiding men, he shows that even morality and legality are facades barely concealing the will to contest and to victory. The point is illustrated by the episode that the chance event of the Chicago fire initiates. Ultimately, the fire exposes Cowperwood's financial chicanery and places him at the mercy of Butler, Mollenhauer, Simpson, and those surrogates of the law who temporarily imprison him. All of these people essentially view Cowperwood's transgressions as "well within his human, if not his strictly legal rights," but they use the law to subdue him in order to achieve a variety of personal victories and goals. Hence the truth of Maxwell Geismar's comment that for them, "ethics is a club, not a code, to finish him [Cowperwood] off." And hence another truth: these men are much like the animal life to which Cowperwood is compared. They are impelled by the same impulses animating the lobster, the black grouper fish, and Cowperwood himself.

The action in *The Financier* thus logically leads to its penultimate conclusion, "Concerning Mycteroperca Bonaci." The novel answers the introductory question, "How is life organized?" The answer is provided by the structure of the action and by Dreiser's commentary, and it is brought out boldly by this first conclusion, which stands in relation to the novel much as the concluding triad of chapters in Henry Adams's *Education* stands in relation to the narrative preceding. That answer is delivered in Darwinian terms. Existence is a struggle, only the fittest survive, and the capacity to create illusions is part of man's equipment for survival. Like the black grouper, some men are fitted to be "an implement of illusion . . . a living lie, a creature whose business it is to appear what it is not, to simulate that with which it has nothing in common, to get its living by great subtlety, the power of its enemies to forfend against which is little." And the greatest illusion of all is morality, for even moral men use it to engage in contest. Save for the very weakest, thus, predator and prey are not rigid classifications but roles that men play interchangeably, when circumstance and chance allow. As Dreiser reminds the reader, man's "feet are in the trap of circumstance; his eyes are on an illusion." The trap is fashioned of temperament and "chance"; the illusion is morality.

If man was not made to know God, to love him, and to serve him, as the religionists would have it; or if man's highest expression of self, even in a godless world, is not to be found in ethical or moral behavior, then the second question that logically follows the first (How is life organized?) is this: What is the end of life? The question implies two others, one related to personal goals and the other to the larger end of existence itself. In answer to the first implied question—What is an individual's personal end or goal in life—the determinist can only declare that it is whatever the creative power dictates for the individual. Dreiser said as much when he raised the question of what man should think of the creative power. "The mechanistic answer to that would be: we are to think what it chemically and physically constructs us to think, no more and no less." If one's views of that power are dictated by it, one's goals will surely be.

Individuals cannot thus transcend their mundane selves to shape their lives according to principles derived from an absolute outside of man, but they can know something about nature, the visible expression of the creative power. Thus, though their private goals may be fated, they can answer the other implied question—What is the end of physical existence?—in larger terms, though not in the largest sense of all, the metaphysical one that would allow them to share divine knowledge. Dreiser makes this distinction clear in the following classic expression of his naturalistic vision:

> Knowledge can only be awareness of the laws of nature or life and
> of nature's skill in applying the same to the creation of forms

functioning within and according to its laws (The acquiring of knowledge is the beginning of wisdom). *Why* its laws came into being, man does not know. . . . *How* its laws came into being, he does not know but surmises, or has surmised, that they are *from everlasting to everlasting*. But that is a surmise. He does not know.

From nature, if not from God, man can answer the question of the end of existence. And the man who believes that life is a game can only conclude that its end is victory, or, rather, the pleasure that victory brings. "For if this life game is not for pleasure," Dreiser writes in *Notes on Life*, "I fail to detect what else it is for." And Frank Cowperwood is the very embodiment of the pleasure principle animating man; his motto, "I satisfy myself," a pure reflection of it. Cowperwood's larger-than-life appearance, of course, makes him seem an exception to human nature, and in some ways he is. Yet, at the same time, his portrayal merely brings out very starkly the impulse in all figures, though its operation may be concealed by a legal code through which some take their pleasure (Butler to revenge himself on Cowperwood, Mollenhauer to fleece him) or by a religious code through which Lilian achieves her temperamental need for stability.

The pursuit of pleasure as life's goal is a theme subdued in *The Financier*, subordinated to answering the question, "How is life organized?" But it is there in Aileen's disregard of her Catholicism brought on by her passionate response to Cowperwood, and in Cowperwood's pursuit of ever-expanding horizons of pleasure: "Wealth, in the beginning, had seemed the only goal, to which had been added the beauty of women. And now art, for art's sake—the first faint radiance of a rosy dawn—had begun to shine in upon him." In *The Titan* this theme becomes dominant, but the point of view that life pursues pleasure receives thematic enrichment from Dreiser's view of illusion.

As a word, "illusion" appears in the penultimate coda to *The Financier*, and it is central to the meaning of its final one, "The Magic Crystal," with its grim forecast for Aileen's and Cowperwood's future: "Sorrow, sorrow, sorrow." Aileen's brilliant society will shine "in a mirage," her love elude as "a will-o'-the-wisp." Her desires or illusions will not be fulfilled. As for Cowperwood, he will become "a soul that was as bereft of illusion as a windless moon." He will see his desires as illusions because their fulfillment brings no pleasure. In *The Titan*, Aileen's prophecy is amply fulfilled, Cowperwood's less so there, though fully so in *The Stoic*. Nonetheless, the final coda of *The Financier* sets the terms for the central tension of *The Titan*: the pursuit of pleasure as opposed to the knowledge that the pursuit is futile, illusory, either because the goal is unattainable or, if attained, is unfulfilling.

THE TITAN

Life is a game, its end is pleasure, and *The Titan* portrays the highest type of victor and victory in this game. The participants' temperaments dictate their pleasures; circumstance determines their fulfillment. Since the trilogy is preeminently the story of Frank Cowperwood, he is the "circumstance" that looms large in the lives of Lilian, Aileen, and Berenice, the other major players in this game. And he, along with these first two women, is introduced in *The Financier* in a way that suggests a scale in the richness and diversity of temperaments allotted humanity and the corresponding pleasures that humans pursue. Dreiser seems to follow what Keats called a pleasure thermometer in his delineation of temperament and pleasure: the richer the temperament, the greater the pleasure. His figures are tropic, seeking pleasure as certain flowers seek the light of the sun, only the hardiest and most luxuriant capable of enduring it for long periods of time. Frank is one of the latter. His interaction with the lesser figures provides both the complexity and the progress of the trilogy as he moves away from lesser figures and their associated pleasures to Berenice and her pleasures. In the process he causes pain, but in *The Titan* he also achieves an awareness of the goal of life consonant with Dreiser's own vision.

The growth of Frank Cowperwood in the trilogy is measured by his successive attractions to the women in his life. Each woman possesses a temperament fated to pursue certain pleasures, and in her turn each offers a new and larger pleasure to Cowperwood. The women, save for Berenice after her conversion, are incapable of further growth beyond the stage they have attained when first introduced. Frank's movement from one to the other is a measure of his own growth, his development from lower to higher pleasures. Hence he is the only dynamic figure in the trilogy.

Through the first novel and most of the second, Cowperwood's temperament develops and grows as instinctively and unconsciously as the banyan tree to which he is later compared. The first stage of the growth is through Lilian, whose "beauty measured up to his present sense of the artistic." As "a natural conservator of the public morals, "Lilian reflects her commitment to public mores in her worry that she is five years older than Cowperwood at the time they marry and in her shame of "the passion that at times swept and dominated her" after their marriage. She finds her pleasure in social institutions, home, and family, and her compensation for pain in religion. *The Titan*'s early pages portray her after Cowperwood has left her for Aileen, and she is still the conventional Lilian handling her problems in a conventional way: "There must be a God. The Bible said so. . . . God would punish her [Aileen], no doubt. He must. So she went to church on Sundays and tried to believe, come what might, that all was for the best."

Although he never comprehended the "palaver about the sanctity of the home" prior to his marriage, Cowperwood "liked . . . the idea of self-duplication," and his early years are comfortable enough to make him conclude, "There was a good deal to this home idea, after all. That was the way life was organized, and properly so—its cornerstone was the home." But that is the way life is organized for Lilian Semple Cowperwood, not for Frank Cowperwood himself. The height of her development is the beginning of his, and its next stage is marked by his involvement with Aileen Butler.

Aileen is "innate sensuousness," "the best that nature can do when she attempts to produce physical perfection," an "*objet d'art*." Unlike Lilian, who is ashamed of her passionate impulses, Aileen possesses the "solicitous attitude . . . more often the outstanding characteristic of the mistress": "It appears to be related to that last work in art, that largeness of spirit which is the first characteristic of the great picture, the great building, the great sculpture, the great decoration—namely, a giving, freely and without stint, of itself, of beauty."

The initial reasons for Cowperwood's attraction to Aileen are, therefore, clear enough. In taking up with her he ascends the pleasure thermometer by discovering an "innate sensuousness" uninhibited by social strictures. In addition, she offers him enduring love, although his is only temporary. In *The Titan* she learns that "the sweet illusion which had bound Cowperwood to her for a time had gone and would never come again." Despite her every effort to control her emotions, she is fated by temperament to continue loving him and hence to suffer from his affairs with other women. She thus becomes an object lesson that "an enduring state of pleasure for anything is not contemplated by Nature as an essential portion of the career of man," as Dreiser puts the matter elsewhere. The meaning of Aileen's situation is simple enough to understand. The crucial question raised by *The Titan* is why Cowperwood can find no enduring pleasure in Aileen.

The answer can only be that, if the goal of life is pleasure, Aileen does not offer the highest kind of pleasure attainable by man; and the temperament of a superman demands no less. "Joy must be innate in energy itself," Dreiser writes in *Notes on Life*, and Frank Cowperwood is distinguished by his capacity for joy, in its highest human terms translated into an appreciation of beauty. In this regard, Aileen is as deficient as Lilian before her. Lilian thought that "Frank was a little peculiar" for liking art, and Aileen "knew nothing of literature except certain authors who to the truly cultured might seem banal. As for art, it was merely a jingle of names gathered from Cowperwood's private comments." And this deficiency of Aileen's is symptomatic of a larger inadequacy that drives the beauty-loving Cowperwood from her. Cowperwood wishes to live his life as though it were a work of art, but Aileen's social ineptitude makes this impossible. A woman who arranges her husband's art works in her home so as to draw the remark " 'Your house reminds me of an art exhibit to-day' " is a woman whose social ambitions are destined to fail, as Cowperwood well knows: "Life had taught him how fortuitous must be the circumstances which could enable a woman of Aileen's handicaps and defects to enter that cold upper world."

Because Aileen does not fully satisfy Cowperwood's aesthetic sense, his love for her dies. The development of this theme of Cowperwood as artist is what distinguishes *The Titan* from *The Financier*. It appears in the early work, of course, but it appears as a theme subordinate to the central interest, an answering of the question, "How is life organized?" His sexual responses in the first novel take on aesthetic values —Lilian's body reminds him of "a figure on an antique vase or out of a Greek chorus," and of course Aileen is an *objet d'art*. Too, his role as financier is equated with the role of the artist: "All the knowledge that pertained to that great art was as natural to him as the emotions and subtleties of life are to a poet." Finance satisfies his love of beauty: "Instead of dwelling on the works of nature . . . he found a happy mean . . . whereby he could . . . rejoice in the beauty of life without interfering with his perpetual material and financial calculations." And of course after developing an interest in wealth and "the beauty of women," he turns to "art, for art's sake": "To the beauty of womanhood he was beginning to see how necessary it was to add the beauty of life—the beauty of material background—how, in fact, the only background for great beauty was great art." It is this subordinate theme that becomes major in *The Titan* as the artist, Cowperwood, moves from an instinctive love of beauty to a self-conscious awareness that its apprehension is man's highest pleasure. In a world divorced from God, beauty substitutes for divine truth. It becomes the only truth man can know with joy.

After a brief introduction providing a necessary transition between two novels, Dreiser immediately introduces the motif of art and artist in *The Titan*. As Cowperwood nears Chicago by train, he sees "as artistic subtlety which touched him." In his eyes, "this raw, dirty town seemed naturally to compose itself into stirring pictures." Dreiser asks for a laureate to sing the praises of "this Florence of the West." His love for Aileen quickly waning, Cowperwood is attracted most to artists, women like Rita Sohlberg and, later, Berenice. "Of all individuals he respected, indeed revered, the sincere artist." In fact, the reader learns what is only suggested in *The Financier*, that "the spirit of art . . . occupied the center of Cowperwood's iron personality." He cannot share art with Aileen, but he can with Berenice, for it is their "one god in common" so that "his mind was fixed on things beautiful as on a shrine." Toward the end of the novel, he suddenly becomes aware of the true end of existence: "At last he saw clearly, as within a chalice-like nimbus, that the ultimate end of fame, power, vigor was beauty, and that beauty was a compound of the taste, the emotion, the innate culture, passion, and dreams of a woman like Berenice Fleming. That was it: that *was* IT. And beyond nothing save crumbling age, darkness, silence."

Dreiser's naturalistic vision of Cowperwood, indeed, depends upon the theme that he is an artist and that the artist creates beauty as his highest pleasure. A passage from each of the first two novels can explain why. In *The Financier*, the reader is told that Cowperwood "admired nature, but somehow, without knowing why, he fancied one could best grasp it through the personality of some interpreter, just as we gain our ideas of law and politics through individuals." Why he prefers an artistic interpretation to the raw material can be inferred from his description in *The Titan*. There he is not simply a connoisseur of art but a practicing artist, one who is "relentless . . . in hewing life to his theory—hammering substance to the form of his thought."

Frank Cowperwood prefers the art work to the raw material that it interprets because in it, the artist puts "nature under foot" and "conforms things to his thoughts," to borrow some phrases from Emerson's *Nature* (1836). The result is congenial to Cowperwood's temperament because he does the same, though on a larger scale. As financier-artist his medium is not the canvas but society itself, and therefore he goes beyond the artist in the scope of his creativity, a fact that is perfectly natural for a superman. As superman he cannot be content to master a portion of his environment, but the whole. And, of course, as superman, his environment is human society, much as the lobster's, the squid's, and the black grouper's environment is the ocean. To master his environment he must become a financier, for only financial relationships give body and form to the whole of it. Hence he becomes one of that band of men who "grow until, like colossi, they bestride the world, or, like banyan-trees, they drop roots from every branch and are themselves a forest—a forest of intricate commercial life, of which a thousand material aspects are the evidence." Hence too the significance of the business aspect of the novel, Cowperwood's attempt to gain fifty-year franchises for his street railway lines. Newspaper criticism of him is in the spirit of the governor's view that the issue is "the ideals of one man and the ideals of men." The superman tries to hammer the substance of the whole, human society itself, to the form of his thought, and this emphasis in the novel successfully unites the themes of artist and financier whose unity some critics have called a failure.

The theme of the financier as artist explains a passage in *The Stoic* describing Cowperwood's response to the beauties of nature on a pleasure trip in Scandinavia. He sees it as beautiful, and he admires the control exhibited by a skipper directing his whaling yacht through the waters, but he nonetheless finds that "the thing that impressed him most about this entire northern scene was the fact that it represented such a sharp and socially insignificant phase of a world that really had no need for any such temperament as his." His artistic nature must have society for its material, for giving form to this medium is the greatest possible challenge to his aesthetic power. Nature can be left to lesser artists. And in another way he is superior to the conventional artist. He can maximize his pleasure in a way unavailable to other artists because he can live within the art work of his creation. Keats may wish to be drawn into the urn, but he can only do so imaginatively. Not so Cowperwood—by virtue of his humanity he can live within his medium. To do so with greatest pleasure, however, he must live there harmoniously. He must be in the foreground of his picture, with society his backdrop, and only the proper woman can regulate his affairs so that together they live within the general harmony of the social picture.

In appearance "the true society woman, the high-born lady, the realization of that ideal" represented by the grandes dames whom Aileen could not equal, Berenice is also a connoisseur of art and, as dancer, sculptor, and painter, its practitioner. Hence she becomes his "pole-star," for Cowperwood recognizes her potential and his need. That potential is made explicit in *The Stoic*. In the second chapter, the reader learns that Berenice "desired not so much to express herself in a given form of art as to live so that her life as well as her personality should be in itself an art form." And Cowperwood knows her value in equally explicit terms, for he believes she can use "her independence and force . . . to achieve temperamental and social perfection" for them in London.

The pursuit of this highest kind of pleasure, the beauty of life lived as art, makes Cowperwood a superman. Conventional artists may mimic his artistic skills, but they lack the force to try to hammer the substance of an entire society to their thought. Yet even the superman has his limitations, for Cowperwood loses his battle for the franchises in *The Titan*. Problems of the sort raised by his loss led Dreiser to explore another implication of determinism, introduced explicitly in the case of Aileen.

For Dreiser, Aileen poses the problem of what compensations for the pains of human existence are available within a deterministic system. In *The Titan*, he asks of her plight: "What shall life say to the loving when their love is no longer of any value, when all that has been placed on the altar of affection has been found to be a vain sacrifice? Philosophy? Give that to dolls to play with. Religion? Seek first the metaphysical-minded." For a person like Aileen, there clearly can be no compensations. She sees through an illusion, her belief that Cowperwood's love for her will endure, yet she is fated by temperament to suffer without compensation because of her enduring love for him. Frank Cowperwood also suffers —he fails in his effort to get his franchises—but he is luckier than Aileen, for his temperament permits him to find compensation in illusions of beauty; in art and in beautiful women.

Ultimately even Cowperwood's compensations fail to satisfy him, however, as *The Stoic* makes clear. To see why and thereby to understand the link between the emphasis on aesthetic experience in *The Titan* and the shift to the differing emphasis on ethical action in *The Stoic*, one must examine Dreiser's private meditations on the subject of compensation.

Central to these meditations is the concept of illusion. Dreiser uses it in three basic ways. First, it is a belief at variance with the structure of reality. Religious belief is one example; Aileen's belief in enduring love, another. He also uses it in reference to art, an illusion because a human creation, a fiction. As such, art is an illusion of an illusion, for Dreiser uses the word ontologically as well. Nature itself—man included—is an illusion because it is only the temporary garb of its wearer, a permanent and enduring energy called the creative power which expresses itself in the world of flux. And this concept, illusion, is intrinsic to the inherent grimness of Dreiser's views, just as it becomes the source of his ultimate salvation.

In his view, life is a matter of luck, one's sum total of pleasures and pains dictated by temperament and chance. Because man is trapped in that "material seeming . . . which . . . is itself an illusion," even the most miserable of men cannot take legitimate comfort from the ultimate compensation for pain when all else fails, a belief in God's goodness. This is so because for most of his career Dreiser insisted that, although the creative power manifests itself in the vale of illusion, its intentions (if any) remain forever unknowable. He saw this situation as one part of life's tragedy.

Not only is man separated from his ultimate source, but his situation is worsened in another way. Even in a godless world, ethical action has been traditionally viewed as the highest good. God may not reward men for the pursuit of ethical goals, but the knowledge that one has contributed to the betterment of others' lives helps to compensate for life's pains. But Dreiser's determinism denies that men can act freely in ethical fashion. His fated selves do only what they can, not what they ought. Describing man's double plight in this way in "The Essential Tragedy of Life," Dreiser exclaims, as well he might, "Herein lies the pathos."

In fact, the inability to find compensation in God never disturbed Dreiser till the end of his life, but man's status as a will-less machine caused him pain. In his *Notes on Life*, Dreiser writes of Einstein: "He will begin by asserting that Free Will is a myth, and in the very same breath assert that man should abolish war. But without Free Will—how?" His essential humanity desired an ethical view of life calling for purposive action for the betterment of the human condition, but his determinism denied his finding compensation for life's pains in ethical action; for such action could only be "ethical" if it were willed, and hence morally superior to other kinds of actions and their attendant compensations. In a world where no action is willed, none can be given ethical priority.

Robert Elias discovered this fact when he interviewed Dreiser. Working with Elias's notes, Swanberg wrote: "Elias found him likeable but illogical. If man was a will-less machine, what was the point in Dreiser's sociological activities and his insistence on the freedom of the individual?" But Dreiser's own determinism dissolves the contradiction: "About determinism and human helplessness, he said of course he was helpless personally and the efforts he made for social equity were not of his own volition but things that he had to do because the forces that moved him required him to."

Trapped in a deterministic world, the man who recognizes that he cannot purposefully alter the world one whit or find any compensations beyond those fated him might well become a pessimist. But despite strong streaks of pessimism. Dreiser's nature was essentially optimistic. His determinism denied man the ability to act purposefully, just as it denied him the knowledge of transcendent meaning and purpose. But his naturalism declared that laws of nature were accessible for all to see and verify, and so Dreiser finds philosophic compensation in the unalterable operations of what he sees as the primary law governing the system of illusions called nature, the equation inevitable. He gives it expression in the conclusion to

The Titan, and his sentiments imply not just an acceptance but an affirmation of Cowperwood's disappointing failure to get his franchises, an affirmation growing from an acceptance of a larger need, the need to sustain a universal balance:

> At the ultimate remove, God or the life force, if anything, is an equation, and at its nearest expression for man—the contract social—it is that also. Its method of expression appears to be that of generating the individual, in all his glittering variety and scope, and through him progressing to the mass with its problems. In the end a balance is invariably struck wherein the mass subdues the individual or the individual the mass—for the time being.

A law that operates to balance opposites is a logical adjunct to Dreiser's view of life as a game. If the essence of life is contest, then life necessarily possesses two basic features. First, it must have opposites. In the game of life, there can be no winner without a loser, and hence no joy without pain. Lilian must suffer for Aileen's good, Aileen for Cowperwood's, and Cowperwood for society's. Its second feature is that life must always remain in an unstable equilibrium. No victory can ever be so complete that the contest is permanently ended; for if the game were over, existence itself could not be. Instead, man would enter the stable equilibrium of what Dreiser refers to in *The Titan* as "Nirvana! Nirvana! The ultimate, still, equation." Life as contest resists Nirvana and demands instability. As he describes it in his conclusion, "For, behold, the sea is ever dancing or raging."

The equation inevitable, therefore, is the principle within the game that guarantees its continuation by prohibiting any victory so complete as to end all contest. It is the law that describes the actual operations of all elements in nature, and even illusions, in the sense of mistaken beliefs, function accordingly. Moral views may falsely assume in man a freedom he does not possess, but their application to Cowperwood in the newspapers and the courts restores the balance between the individual and the mass. Dreiser makes this point clear, too, in his conclusion: "In the meantime there have sprung up social words and phrases expressing a need of balance—of equation. These are right, justice, truth, morality, an honest mind, a pure heart—all words meaning: a balance must be struck. The strong must not be too strong; the weak not too weak. But without variation how could the balance be maintained?"

Without joy *and* pain, joy could not be; ultimately, existence could not be. The law is so central to his thought that in his *Notes on Life* he invests it with religious authority: "So, if there is no god, no surveying and controlling intelligence, there is yet this universal balancing and proportioning of positive against negative, or what may seem good to one against what may seem evil to it and vice versa."

One can now see that Dreiser finds compensation for the pains of human existence in the larger natural process itself. Life for life's sake! he in effect exclaims, and affirms for both pain and joy. In his essay of the same name ["The Equation Inevitable"], he makes it crystal clear that the equation inevitable is his compensation, and he uses language that shows his kinship to Cowperwood:

> In truth, somewhere in the scheme of things is implanted a love of beauty and order as well as their contraries, which can only find expression via equation, and this it is, chemical, inherent awareness of it no doubt, which eases the ache of existence for us all (God, man, devil). For if life loves change, movement, differ-ence, contest, it also plainly loves their contraries, for these exist, and we could not know the one without the other.

Such sentiments, of course, place Dreiser in league with the artist, Frank Cowperwood. Dreiser affirms the importance of oppositions in life for the sake of life itself; and Cowperwood's valuing the harmony of op-posites in art thus translates Dreiser's philosophic view into aesthetic terms, for Cowperwood's zest for art is one expression of his zest for life. In addition, his zest for love and finance, for life as lived as opposed to life as interpreted as art, carries Dreiser's philosophic vision into the story on the level of concrete action. Without experiencing and causing pain, Cow-perwood cannot have the highest kind of pleasure. He thus is a clear illustration of Dreiser's own philosophic commitment, and Dreiser seems to have him in mind when he writes in "The Equation Inevitable":

> Art, the love of life for itself, is nothing more than a synthesis of many equations whereby many lovely harmonies and their op-posites are expressed or implied. Hunger, balanced against satia-tion, creates more beauty. Life builds and wills far beyond the ken of man or his companion animals, and all that he can know is the chemic thrill of life, its joys, the necessity of equation and so-called fair play, or rhythm and balance. For, behold, life is ever dancing and does not will to be still.

Dreiser's thought in his essays and his *Notes on Life* thus shows that he was forced to confront what William James called the dilemma of de-terminism, a dilemma, according to James, "whose left horn is pessimism and whose right horn is subjectivism." Dreiser yearned for an ethical view of life in his role as social crusader, but his determinism forced him to the verge of pessimism on this score, for individuals were trapped by their fated selves and could only do what they could, not what they ought. If men could not through freely willed conduct make a world with abundant evils a better place to live, then Dreiser had to find a way to make such a world reasonably habitable, if he was to avoid pessimism.

His response to the problem closely follows the pattern James observes in "The Dilemma of Determinism," a fact that testifies to the philosophical rigor of Dreiser's mind. If men do *seeming* evil (moral judgment is irrelevant to Dreiser's hard determinism), they also do *seeming* good; and the existence of the good is dependent on that of the evil. "For, behold, the sea is ever dancing or raging." But the determinist is still left with what James calls "the judgment of regret." If good cannot exist without evil, why regret the existence of the evil? Dreiser's judgment of regret is not pronounced in *The Titan*, but he clearly does regret Aileen's suffering, if not Lilian's, and he seems to include even her in his compassion in the novel's conclusion when he intones the consequences of Cowperwood's behavior: "The lives of two women wrecked, a score of victims despoiled." In a determined world, the judgment of regret is itself necessitated, but it is also philosophically erroneous. Since evil is the necessary condition for good, one ought not to regret the evil.

In handling his judgment of regret, Dreiser adopts that very subjectivism which James declares is the only alternative to pessimism for the determinist intent on making his world reasonably habitable. The regret may be philosophically wrong, for the seeming evil was unavoidable and has a positive role to play—Cowperwood is "caught at last by the drug of a personality he could not gainsay"—yet the regret itself emphasizes to its holder how precious is that which has been destroyed. Without the regret, one could never know the qualitative value of love.

In the conclusion to the novel, Dreiser does not speak in direct terms about the value the existence of evil has for heightening consciousness, nor does he mention Aileen by name, yet surely the novel's closing words contain this view and pertain to Aileen, among others: "In a mulch of darkness is [*sic*] bedded the roots of endless sorrows—and of endless joys. Canst thou fix thine eye on the morning? Be glad. And if in the ultimate it blind thee, be glad also! Thou hast lived." There are several meanings in this passage which, taken together, reveal Dreiser's subjectivism. The mulch of darkness sprouts both joys and sorrows, and Aileen experiences both, for she has metaphorically seen the light and been blinded by it. The proper response of the determinist celebrating the equation inevitable is to rejoice, for the blindness has its utility. As Dreiser notes in "The Necessity for Contrast" (*Notes on Life*), "Life . . . must have both ignorance and wisdom, good and evil, morality and immorality . . . for it to function at all as the thing we call life." Without the blindness, light could not be. And blindness has a further utility, for it serves the purpose of knowledge. In the same section of his *Notes*, he writes, "We are only aware of heat because of the possibility of contrasting it with cold, light because of darkness, and so on." Finally, without contrast, value cannot be, for one can only value one moment over another through contrast: "The things that count to any man . . . are the contrasts of this moment . . . his past moment and his next one." Rejoice in the blindness, in other words, for it makes one appreciate the light. The passages' utilitarian levels of meaning thus compound the subjectivism of the last, the value of blindness. For if the darkness is indispensable to the existence of the light, one must value it as well as its opposite.

But even in the trilogy, finally, the subjectivist solution to the dilemma of determinism did not satisfy. James complained that it ultimately led to aestheticism and decadence. In *The Stoic*, Dreiser felt that it led to a restlessness born of an utter loss of meaning in life. He had certainly touched on the problem in his *Notes on Life*, in that part called "The Problem of Progress and Purpose." Commenting that "you, and almost every other person in life, will agree that life without a purpose is meaningless," he concludes: "But see how this works out. Your non self-evoked, non self-created purpose or desire, a thing not originated by you but forced upon you by life, proves very often (not always) a delusion, sometimes a trap, which does for you completely."

In *The Stoic*, Frank Cowperwood illustrates the kind of trap that ensnares man when his purpose in life is preordained rather than freely chosen. That very purpose which is supposed to give life meaning becomes, under this condition, the factor denying it meaning. Judging by what appears in *The Stoic* and is absent from the earlier novels in the trilogy—a concern with endowing life with meaning proceeding from ethical conduct in a deterministic world—one can fairly say that Dreiser's other self, the social crusader, at last demanded a union with the determinist that would not sacrifice the crusader's own autonomy.

THE STOIC

The lives of Dreiser's characters can have no meaning because their selves are fated. Because this statement seems at variance with the obvious relish for life displayed by Cowperwood in the first two novels of the trilogy, some further explanation is needed. If one thinks of life as having meaning in some cosmic sense, then it is clear that from Dreiser's point of view, his characters do not possess such meaning, because it can be derived only from knowing and following divine mandates, to which they have no access. For most of his career Dreiser declared that man cannot even know whether or not the creative power is intelligent or purposive, much less know of its possible design; so characters who think life has cosmic meaning are deluded.

Frank Cowperwood is not one of them. He recognizes the cosmic meaninglessness of his life, fleetingly in *The Financier*, more forcefully in *The Titan*. In the first novel, he gazes at the stars after his imprisonment, thinking "of the earth floating like a little ball in immeasurable reaches of ether," which made "his own life [appear] very trivial." This theme is resumed in *The Titan*. As Cowperwood watches Berenice stroke a fledgling sparrow, the thought comes to him "with great force, how comparatively unimportant in the great drift of life were his own affairs when about him was operative all this splendid will to existence." And in *The Stoic*, this sense of his triviality is translated into the problem of life's meaning, Cowperwood's central problem in that volume. After Cowperwood learns of his imminent death and sails for America, Dreiser tells the reader that "once on the boat, Cowperwood felt alone, spiritually alone, at last admitting to himself that neither he nor any man knew anything about life or its Creator."

This is a sad conclusion to Cowperwood's career, for it is reasonable to assume that he was now aching for some cosmic justification for his existence. Earlier in the novel, at Canterbury Cathedral with Berenice, he envies what he thinks of as her youthful ability "to be so thrilled, to be so deeply moved by color, form, the mystery and meaninglessness of human activity!" Presumably he has lost just enough of his relish for life to require some larger justification for his existence, and this view is borne out by Berenice's concluding thought about Cowperwood, "that his worship and constant search for beauty in every form, and especially in the form of a woman, was nothing more than a search for the Divine design behind all forms."

But there is a second sense in which life can have meaning, what Paul Edwards calls the terrestrial sense. From this angle of vision, the principal thoughts and actions that constitute a person's life become meaningful if they are united into a purposeful pattern and inspire the individual with that satisfaction commonly associated with purposeful action. As Edwards makes clear, a life need not have cosmic meaning in order to have terrestrial meaning; but as he also makes clear, no life can be viewed as possessing legitimate meaning of either kind without freedom.

Cowperwood may be a superman, but he shares the common lot of Dreiser's characters insofar as his life cannot be considered meaningful in even a terrestrial sense. He has a goal, and he pursues it with vigor; but both the goal and the means for its pursuit (means that dictate the nature of the goal) are functions of his fated self. Dreiser's earlier quoted comment on "non self-evoked, non self-created purpose" confirms this fact; and, indeed, he calls all goals and purposes illusions precisely for this reason. They exist simply to assure the continuity of the game that is the life process.

If the lives of Dreiser's characters must be seen as meaningless when observed from without, this fact need not cause them personal distress so long as they are unaware of their enslavement. Or, even if aware, they might like Dreiser take refuge in beauty, affirm that life is, or can be, worthwhile, if not meaningful. In *The Stoic*, Cowperwood becomes aware of his own position and follows the latter route. But Dreiser no longer felt the subjectivist solution to the dilemma of determinism satisfying, for how else explain the novel's conclusion, Berenice's repudiation of a life of pleasure and beauty in order to work for the betterment of the lot of the poor? Dreiser finally demanded meaning from life, meaning to be found in ethical action, and he prepares for this view in his portrayal of Cowperwood.

That the problem of meaning becomes urgent for Cowperwood in *The Stoic* has already been noted, but not the way in which the problem is thrust on him. The specific terms that the problem takes are of special interest. In his life with Berenice, Cowperwood has achieved as much of the beauty of life as circumstance permits (Aileen refuses him a divorce), yet he must continue to pursue his business life as a financier. He is caught in a vicious circle, experiencing the pleasure of the achieved goal of a financier, beauty, while forced to play a game whose end has already been achieved. This conception of Cowperwood dominates the novel throughout, right through the moment when, knowing he is going to die, he reflects on his entire past life.

Early in the novel, he shows that he is dimly aware of his predicament and dissatisfied with it. Before they leave Chicago for London, where he will resume his financial operations, Cowperwood tells Berenice: " 'What I would prefer to do . . . now that I have you, would be to loaf and travel with you, for a time, anyhow. I've worked hard enough. You mean more than money to me, infinitely more. It's odd, but I feel all at once as though I've worked too hard all my life.' " Berenice's reply: " 'You've been like some big engine or machine that's tearing full speed somewhere, but doesn't know exactly where.' "

Her comment is significant because it reveals the true position of the fated self in a determined world, and Cowperwood becomes more clearly aware of this when he expresses amazement to DeSota Sippens, another successful businessman, that "we can get so excited over it"—that is, the pursuit of financial affairs—when "neither of us can do much more than eat a little, drink a little, play about a little while longer." Sippens replies as though he were Dreiser himself: " 'I look on it all as some sort of a game that I'm here to play. . . . And I guess that's the answer: to be doing something all the time. There's a game on, and whether we like it or not, we have to play our parts.' "

Frank Cowperwood still experiences pleasure, but even the experience of it is fated, and this knowledge blunts the pleasure and emphasizes the problem. He wonders again about his financial dealings: "But now, here he was. And what was it all about? What was he to get out of it, other than the pleasure with Berenice, which, had she willed it otherwise, he might have found in a more peaceful way." If one's fate is a happy one, one can value life for its own sake, call life worthwhile, but one cannot quite escape the anguish that is the common lot when one learns the meaninglessness of existence. Cowperwood's reflections after he learns of his impending death bear out the truth of this observation. He reviews his life—"the men, in the main so helpful, the women so entertaining." He thinks of "this lovely hour with Berenice, here by the Thames, and this pleasant lawn that spread before them." And he feels "the fleeting beauty of life and its haunting poignancy." The very thought of death "had a tendency to emphasize the value of all he had been and enjoyed." Yet such comfort is small; for "he could only consider the poetic value of this hour, and its fleetingness, which involved sorrow and nothing but sorrow."

The Stoic thus fulfills the concluding prophecy of *The Financier*: "Sorrow, sorrow, sorrow." Death, the ultimate pole of a polarity without which existence cannot be, enhances the poetic value of the hour; but if the beauty is there and felt, so is the meaninglessness. Subjectivism is not enough.

It would be bad manners to pursue what has already been acknowledged, the weak literary quality of the later part of an action that Dreiser was fleshing out even on the day before his death. This is a matter which was beyond his control. But the framework *is* there, and one can explain its logic.

The problem of the fated self is central to this framework, as it is to the trilogy at large. Man must have freedom if he is to achieve significant meaning of any kind in life, but he can obtain freedom only by escaping the fated self. Short of renouncing his determinism (and Dreiser never did), no such escape seemed possible. But a way out of his dilemma opened in Dreiser's last years as his view of the creative power changed. Earlier he thought its character unknowable, for all man could know is its expression in nature; but late in life he saw greater implications in such knowledge. Adopting an Aristotelian approach to nature, he played a variation on the Thomist theme for proof of the existence of an intelligent God: "I see motion; I infer a mover." Dreiser in effect said, I see artistry, so there must be an artist intelligent enough to create the design. Elias notes that the intelligence of the artist did not immediately suggest that the power was good, but even on this point Dreiser relented. His own sense of unity with nature became sufficient evidence "that the unity of the creative force must be good and that there was involved with it a kind of love."

Elias records the shift to account for the aged Dreiser's exalted view of man: "As *a part of* nature he and his will were tinctured by the aesthetic color and swept up in the universal grandeur of the vast and amazing scheme before the idea of which one could only stand in reverent gratefulness for being alive." But in *The Stoic*, a further implication to Dreiser's changed view of the creative power appears. Even as *a part of* nature, man can escape from his fated self, and Dreiser could now see this other implication in man's unity with nature. As a part of nature man must possess some part of the power that manifests itself in every single aspect of nature. And that part which he possesses must be consistent with those attributes distinguishing him from other creatures in the animal world; for each of the multiple aspects of creative power expresses itself by creating unique things and unique species in nature. In the animal world, man is distinguished by his higher intelligence and by his awareness of concepts like choice and freedom, though his fated self cannot freely exercise that intelligence to make free choices in a vale of illusion. Therefore that part of the power which he possesses must have something to do with the core of his uniqueness, his intelligence and his very awareness of the freedom resident in power itself—must indeed be part of its intelligence and freedom. And that part constitutes a second self whose status is other than the fated one's—that very self, in short, which Emerson celebrates in *Self-Reliance*.

Indeed, such thinking logically proceeds from Dreiser's earlier thoughts on the self. Individuality, he had declared, was a myth. One man could never know another, much less himself, because he cannot know "the forces which are making and operating or driving us and which same we do not even know ourselves." These forces are reducible to mechanical stimuli in the natural world to which the mechanism called man reacts. A true self, Dreiser thus suggested, could only be an autonomous one. When he reached the point where he could distinguish between the self fated by forces created by the creative power and the self that participates in that power's freedom, the question became, How activate that second self?

He must have thought of the possibilities inherent in Cowperwood's sense of his own triviality in *The Financier* and *The Titan*, for in *The Stoic* he links Cowperwood's sense of personal triviality to the problem of meaning and freedom, and through Berenice he makes a recognition of one's personal triviality a precondition for escaping the fated self. Only by recognizing that self's triviality can one see that its existence is a myth, an illusion, and by so much is one liberated from it and the illusions that it pursues.

But there is a second condition to be fulfilled before true selfhood can be attained. One must recognize that one is a part of nature and learn those other implications of this recognition already spelled out, that men possess part of the power of the creative spirit. In *The Titan* Berenice already possesses the feeling of unity with nature that Cowperwood never achieves. As she strokes a fledgling sparrow whose mother stands by, watching, Cowperwood notes that the "splendid will to existence" in nature that inspires his own sense of triviality is not only "sensed by her," but that she feels a part of it. "It was not so much bird-love as the artistry of life and of herself that was moving her." When he asks how she knows the bird's mother feels no fear for its offspring, she replies, " 'Do you think the senses of the world are only five?' ", showing by her response that she has an extra sense linking her to the natural world. She stands in contrast to the Cowperwood of *The Stoic,* who feels out of place in nature on a boating trip to Scandinavia; and she therefore is the likely candidate for attaining true selfhood in the conclusion to the trilogy.

She does so through Brahmanism. Although Dreiser came to respect all religious forms as possible avenues to reaching the creative spirit, not all would do for the trilogy. In a work exploring the ramifications of determinism, Brahmanism was the logical choice, because it permitted him at the same time to retain his determinism (he never abandoned the doctrine) and to transcend it in a world view much like the one he had held all along. For both views, the earthly realm, the realm of nature, is a realm of illusion and enslavement. If Dreiser's sense of enslavement does not come from selves fated to be reborn in an eternal cycle of reincarnation, it does come from selves fated to follow the illusions of nature so long as they remain alive.

Hindus do find freedom from the vale of illusion, however, and they do so through the discovery that they have personal access to the realm of Brahman; through the discovery, that is, that the core of the self is in fact Brahman. Dreiser could draw on this view in *The Stoic* because, as discussed earlier, his view of the creative spirit had changed. He was now in a position to respond to the demand for meaning that had gradually emerged in the determined world of the trilogy. By permitting Berenice both escape from the illusion called individuality and access to the insight and freedom of a self that is part of Brahman, Dreiser provides the freedom without which meaning cannot exist while retaining the vale of illusion that is the world of determinism in which most people live.

In his portrayal of Berenice after Cowperwood's death, Dreiser keeps his focus sharply on the problem of the fated self, to show that it is the central problem of his trilogy and of his mechanistic philosophy. Before Berenice picks up her copy of the *Bhagavad-Gita*, she is troubled by a critical article that "tended to single her out as an opportunist" in her relations with Cowperwood, a view violating her self-image. "For as she saw herself . . . she was wholly concerned with the beauty of life." The passage recalls Dreiser's view that one individual can never really know another, for individuality is a myth. But if her public image is not her true self, neither can her self-image be. She does not utter such a thought directly; but the passage from the *Bhagavad-Gita* that she reads immediately after the offensive newspaper article speaks for her adequately enough. It begins: "Part of myself is the God within every creature."

When Berenice wishes to escape the scenes of her life with Cowperwood, she has a strong practical reason to do so—bad publicity; but Dreiser fashions the terms of that need so as to anticipate the solution to the central problem of the trilogy. After she decides to go to India, she reveals one of the factors in her decision. She recalls that Dr. James, Cowperwood's physician, advised some of his patients to visit a Hindu Swami to relieve their physical and mental distress: "For, as he had noted, there was something about the limited thought of the self that was lost in the larger thought of the not self that brought about forgetfulness of self in the nervous person, and so health."

The dichotomy between self and "not self" thus sets the terms for Berenice's release from the bondage of her fated self. In India she learns the two conditions essential for escape. The first is a lesson in nonattachment, a concept stressed several times by her guru. Such a lesson is equivalent to a lesson in the triviality of the self fated to pursue nature's illusions, and hence a lesson in its own illusory nature. Thereafter she learns the falseness of the "idea of separateness," for her guru asks, "Is not the whole universe yourself?"

This discovery is of great importance. Her acknowledgment of her oneness with the universe is equivalent to an acknowledgment that she is part of nature and yet, paradoxically, free from the illusion of nature and the self that is a part of it. For Brahman is in all of nature, and so her sense of unity with it allows her to discover the truth of that line from the *Bhagavad-Gita*, "Part of myself is the God within every creature." Hence she is in a position to renounce that self which "worshipped beauty in all its forms" and so was beauty's slave. Thereafter she achieves her true identity with its "pure knowledge" and "perfect freedom" promised her by an earlier reading of the *Bhagavad-Gita*. She can thus return to the determined world of fated selves as a free soul.

In this way Berenice becomes the true stoic in this novel, though Cowperwood's centrality in the trilogy would suggest otherwise. Yet Cowperwood is only superficially a stoic, for he fits the commonplace meaning of that word, one who is indifferent to life's pains and joys. Cowperwood's lot has been mainly one of joys but, in the end, though he still experiences pleasure, he must remain philosophically indifferent even to his joys, because they provide his life merely with poetic value, not with meaning. His restlessness indicates that he endures pleasure much as others endure pain, while Berenice becomes the stoic in a more precise sense of that word. In her subsequent life working for the poor, she becomes stoical in the ethical sense that she "does not shrink from doing what is disagreeable," nor does she "long to do what is agreeable," so long as she can translate her divine illumination into concrete ethical action.

Berenice's need to translate divine wisdom into ethical action shows an Emersonian view of religion. In his poem "The Problem," Emerson states his respect for the churchman but stoutly maintains: "Yet not for all his faith can see/Would I that cowled churchman be." There is more than one way to contact God, just as there is more than one way of utilizing the freedom and truth that such contact brings. If one religious form does bring divine illumination, furthermore, what remains important is the illumination, not an unswerving loyalty to the form that provided it. Emerson wore out Unitarianism to go his own way, and there is every evidence that Berenice uses Brahmanism to achieve freedom without feeling any necessity to remain bound to the essential concern of the Brahman, the experience of divine illumination and emancipation from self. Her reflections on India reveal her puzzlement that "a country could have evolved such a noble and profoundly religious philosophy of life and yet, at the same time, have evoked and maintained such a low, cruel, and oppressive social system," and thereby show how American a Brahman she is. That puzzlement also shows that through her Dreiser uses Brahmanism to reconcile what he for so long thought was irreconcilable: his humanitarianism and his determinism. If Berenice had to achieve cosmic meaning in order to gain the terrestrial meaning in life that impels her to work for the poor in New York City, it is clear which level of meaning she finds primary. For her, as for Dreiser, the cosmic is but the condition to gain that freedom without which life could not have a level of meaning that becomes indispensable: the terrestrial.

In viewing Dreiser's development into an American Brahman, one can best recall the truth of William James's comment on the dilemma of determinism. "Remark how inevitably the question of determinism and indeterminism slides us into the question of optimism and pessimism, or , as our fathers called it, 'the question of evil.' The theological form of all these disputes is the simplest and the deepest, the form from which there is the least escape." At the last, "the question of evil" became too much even for the committed determinist. If Dreiser did not seek refuge in the faith of his fathers, the Catholicism of his youth, in his own way he returned to "the simplest and the deepest . . . form from which there is the least escape." But he could never have made his way even this far without finding freedom in a second self. Still, had he not found it, his lot would not have been quite so bad: he would have had aesthetic vision as compensation. Dos Passos could not find even this much comfort when he pointed to the vacuum within society's self.

Modernism: The Case
of Willa Cather

Phyllis Rose

In the 1950s David Daiches cannily predicted that literary historians would
have difficulty placing Willa Cather. He did not foresee that Cather's work
would be underrated because it was hard to place, but such may have been
the case. It could be said that Cather has been ignored because she was a
woman, but that would not explain why her rediscovery has taken ten
years longer than Virginia Woolf's. Generally perceived as a traditionalist,
Cather has been patronized. Many people read her for pleasure, but for
the past twenty years few have taught her works or written about them.
The novels seem curiously self-evident. They are defiantly smooth and
elegant, lacking the rough edges that so often provide convenient starting
points for literary analysis. To a critical tradition that has valued complexity,
ambiguity, even obscurity, the hard-won simplicities of Cather's art seem
merely simple. Her lucidity can be read as shallowness; her massive, abstract forms can be—and have been— viewed as naïvely traditional, the
appropriate vehicle for an art essentially nostalgic and elegaic.

Although I am deeply distrustful of the way in which, for twentieth-
century writers, the term "modernist" is not merely an honorific but the
precondition of attention from literary critics and scholars, I will nonetheless
try to show ways in which Willa Cather's work is allied to modernism. I
do this by way of redressing a balance. Her public stance was so bellig-
erently reactionary (perhaps in order to mask the radically unacceptable
nature of her private life) that she herself encouraged the flattening of her
work into a glorification of the past, a lament for the shabbiness of the
present, which has persisted for decades. The writer who titled a collection
of essays *Not Under Forty* would have been the last person to feel con-
gratulated at being called a modernist. But it is time to risk her wrath. In

From *Modernism Reconsidered*. © 1983 by the President and Fellows of Harvard College.
Harvard University Press, 1983.

part because of her defensive self-presentation, in part because her fiction so perfectly embodies certain aesthetic ideals of modernism—monumentality, functionalism, anonymity—we have overlooked its innovative nature. To see its modernist elements is to readjust and enrich our response to her work—and also to widen our notions of modernism. If Cather is a modernist, she is a tempered, transitional modernist closer to Hardy than to Pound. Nonetheless, her work is moved in important ways by a modernist urge to simplify and to suggest the eternal through the particular. Because we have paid more attention to other aspects of literary modernism—the overtly experimental, the representation of subjectivity, the literary analogues of cubist collage—we react to Cather's novels as though we have stumbled across some giant work of nature, a boulder, something so massive that is seems inhuman, uncrafted. But I would suggest that what we have stumbled upon in fact is something like the literary equivalent of an Arp, a Brancusi, a Moore.

I would point first of all to her scale. I do not mean, of course, the size of her books, for they are conspicuously slender, little masterpieces of economy; I mean the size of the subjects to which her imagination responds. In her strongest work, the land is as much a presence as the human characters, and the landscapes that move her imagination are large and unbroken ones, the plains and fields of the American Midwest, the canyonlands and deserts of the Southwest. Reading *O Pioneers!*, *My Ántonia*, or *Death Comes for the Archbishop*, we experience the exhilarating potential of clear blank spaces. Few novels I can think of are less cluttered than these; they offer the breathing space of all outdoors, and one feels that Cather may be describing herself when she says of Alexandra Bergson, the Swedish immigrant farmer who is her first great female protagonist, that she was uncertain in her indoor tastes and expressed herself best in her fields, that properly speaking her house was the out-of-doors.

The vast Nebraska prairie, which Cather saw for the first time when she was ten, transplanted from the hill-enclosed perspectives of Virginia, determined—or answered to—her sense of scale. Whether it happened when she was ten, or, as seems more likely to me, when as a grown woman, a harried and successful magazine editor in New York, she turned her inner eye back to the landscape of her childhood, the landscape of her dreams, the impact of the prairie on her sense of self was probably such as her narrative stand-in, Jim Burden, describes in *My Ántonia*:

> There seemed to be nothing to see; no fences, creeks, or trees, no hills or fields. If there was a road, I could not make it out in the faint starlight. There was nothing but land: not a country at all, but the material out of which countries are made . . . I had the feeling that the world was left behind, that we had got over the edge of it, and were outside men's jurisdiction. I had never before looked up at the sky when there was not a familiar mountain ridge against it. But this was the complete dome of heaven, all there

was of it . . . I don't think I was homesick. If we never arrived anywhere, it did not matter. Between that earth and that sky I felt erased, blotted out.

To feel "erased, blotted out" is not, from Cather's perspective, such a bad thing. The scale of the landscape erases trivialities of personality, and in one of the most beautiful passages in American literature Cather presents Jim at his happiest, most fully alive, when he has become a mere creature on the earth, sitting in his grandmother's garden, resting his back against a sun-warmed pumpkin, his individuality transcended. "I kept as still as I could. Nothing happened. I did not expect anything to happen. I was something that lay under the sun and felt it, like the pumpkins, and I did not want to be anything more. I was entirely happy. Perhaps we feel like that when we die and become part of something entire, whether it is sun and air, or goodness and knowledge. At any rate, that is happiness; to be dissolved into something complete and great."

Against the background of the plains, only the biggest stories stand out, only stories based on the largest, strongest, most elemental emotions. "There are only two or three human stories," Cather wrote in *O Pioneers!*, "and they go on repeating themselves as fiercely as if they had never happened before; like the larks in this country, that have been singing the same five notes over for thousands of years." If you approach *O Pioneers!* as a naturalistic account of the conquest of new land, four-fifths of the book is anticlimactic, even irrelevant, and you must wonder why the story of the adulterous love of Emil Bergson and Marie Shabata and their murder by her jealous husband is taking up so much space in a book about pioneers. In fact, the love of Emil and Marie, growing as inevitably as Frank's murderous jealousy, is the focus of the story, along with the autumnal attachment of Alexandra Bergson and Carl Lindstrum, Alexandra's ambition, and her fatigue. The rhythms of the seasons are matched by the natural growth of human emotions. Typically, Cather uses a metaphor of seed-corn to compare Emil's guilty passion for Marie with the happy love of his friend, Amédée: "From two ears that had grown up side by side, the grains of one shot joyfully into the light, projecting themselves into the future, and the grains from the other lay still in the earth and rotted; and nobody knew why." As in ballads, motivation is played down; motives in such oft-enacted human stories are assumed to speak for themselves. Amédée dies in the prime of life of a ruptured appendix; Emil dies from the gunshot blast of a man who is so enraged he hardly knows what he is doing and who is presented as acting with no conscious volition. In a curious way, both deaths seem equally natural in this novel which presents the life of man and the life of earth as concurrent, equivalent.

In the American Southwest, which Cather visited for the first time in 1912, she found not only another monumental landscape but the temporal equivalent for the vast spaces of the Midwest. For these were not, like the plains, uninhabited spaces whose history was just beginning. Here and there, tucked in the great half-dome caverns on the cliff-sides of canyons, were the remains of an ancient, civilized people. The cliff-dwelling Indians had lived, cultivated the land, and, in their weavings and pottery, produced art, long before Europeans had landed on American soil. The effect of Anasazi art and architecture on Cather's aesthetic was profound, but for the moment I want to concentrate merely on the imaginative impact of a long-inhabited, long-abandoned monumental landscape. It lengthened the past. If you included the Indians, American history, which had seemed so small and cramped a thing, suddenly became vast. When Thea Kronborg in *The Song of the Lark* and Tom Outland of *The Professor's House* encounter the canyonlands, the effect on their senses of themselves is like the effect of the prairie on Jim Burden: it obliterates the trivial and raises them, spiritually, to its own scale, uniting them to something larger than themselves.

Cather's imagination craved and fed on large scale, both in time and space, and her books repeatedly struggle to break outside the confines of town or city life and make their way, quite against the grain of the narrative, back to the wilderness. *The Song of the Lark* gets to Panther Canyon by way of the unlikely premise that Thea Kronborg, studying music in Chicago, needs the experience of exactly that locale to change her from a good artist into a great one. The relationship between Tom Outland's story of the discovery of the cliff-dweller ruins on the Blue Mesa (a version of the true story of the discovery of Mesa Verde by Richard Wetherill) bears an even more tenuous plot connection to the rest of *The Professor's House*, which concerns a transitional crisis in the life of a midwestern university professor. Thematic justification for the interpolated story may of course be found, but I find it more interesting to note how it does *not* fit into the rest of the novel. In the sudden, eccentric switch to the southwestern locale, we witness a Catherian compulsion. Explaining it, however, as an experiment in form (a tactic that would have been more persuasive had she not done something so similar in *The Song of the Lark*), Cather said she wanted to reproduce the effect of a square window opening onto a distant prospect set into a Dutch genre painting of a warmly furnished interior. She said she wanted the reader first to stifle amidst the trappings of American bourgeois domesticity, then to feel the clean air blowing in from the mesa. This suggests that the contrast between inside and outside worlds is essential to the power of both. But the effect of the massive dislocation within *The Professor's House* is less like the effect of Dutch genre painting, which carefully subordinates one scale to the other, than it is like the effect of surrealism, with its willful changes of scale and its reminders, within a canvas, of the artificiality of the canvas—Magritte's painting of a view out the window blocked by a painting of a view out the window, or Charles Sheeler's ironic *The Artist Looks at Nature* which depicts Sheeler out-of-doors, painting a kitchen interior. It is Cather herself who stifles in the housebound, small-town scenes, craves open air, and inserts the outdoors into the indoors as willfully as Sheeler's self-portrait does the reverse, justifying the change however she can. (The novel's epigraph, a quotation from itself, also seems a justification of the form: "A turquoise set in silver, wasn't it? . . . Yes, a turquoise set in dull silver.") The first part of the novel seems to me strained—overly didactic, underlining all points, the dialogue forced—but when we move to the mesa, the writing achieves that effortless symbolic quality which is Cather's distinctive note and best achievement, in which everything seems radiant and significant, but in a way no one could precisely explain.

The pattern in *The Song of the Lark* and *The Professor's House* is repeated in her work as a whole. She alternates between two modes—a more conventional realism, which is evoked when she sets herself the task of describing people in groups, living in houses, and a more abstract and lyrical mode, evoked by people against a landscape. Writing about indoor people—Thea Kronborg, Bartley Alexander, Godfrey St. Peter—she writes in small strokes, with more circumstantial detail, with more accounts of what people think and say. Her first novel, *Alexander's Bridge*, was in this mode and has always reminded readers of the work of Henry James and Edith Wharton. Later, Cather preferred to think of *O Pioneers!* as her first novel, because it was the one in which she discovered the lyrical mode that she considered her authentic style. It is the mode in which her best books— *My Ántonia*, and *Death Comes for the Archbishop* as well as *O Pioneers!*—are written. Deeply associated with it, perhaps necessary to generate it, is the quality I have been calling scale.

I have already touched on the way in which scale determines an approach to character, but I would like to go into it more fully. The illusion of grandeur in her protagonists is another feature of Cather's most exhilarating work, and this illusion, I suggest, depends on simplification.

We are first introduced to Alexandra Bergson, for example, through the eyes of a traveling salesman who is never named, whose role is never developed, whose sole function is to provide a perspective on the heroine. And what does he think of her? That she is "a fine human creature" who makes him wish he was more of a man. That is, she makes an impact without individuation. Although Alexandra has a good deal of character— she is placid, firm, in some ways a visionary (about the future of the Divide), yet wholly unimaginative about other people's emotions—Cather's presentation of her consists of broad strokes. Alexandra is not clever in the manner of city-bred and well-educated people, such as the characters Cather had written about in *Alexander's Bridge*, and that absence of cleverness allowed—perhaps forced—Cather to treat character in a new way in *O Pioneers!* Alexandra cannot be an interesting "center of consciousness" in a Jamesian sense, because her consciousness is insufficiently complex. Nor is it the most important part of her. "Her personal life, her own realization of herself, was almost a subconscious existence; like an underground river that came to the surface only here and there, at intervals months apart, and then sank again to flow under her fields." Her conscious mind is a "white book, with clear writing about weather and beasts and growing things. Not many people would have cared to read it." So we do not explore her consciousness. We see her resolutely from the outside, and this, along with Cather's persistent contrast of her in terms of size to those around her (" 'What a hopeless position you are in, Alexandra!'[Carl] exclaimed feverishly. 'It is your fate to be always surrounded by little men.' "), creates the illusion of grandeur which is a distinguishing trait of Cather's heroines, although they may be as different in background and personality as Ántonia Shimerda and Marian Forrester.

For Jamesian centers of consciousness, Cather substitutes objects of admiration. Her favorite narrator is the adoring young person, usually a man, creating out of some woman a creature with mythic resonance: Jim Burden and Ántonia, Niel Herbert and Marian Forrester in *A Lost Lady,*, also Nellie Birdseye and Myra Henshawe in *My Mortal Enemy.* Ántonia provides the best example, for she is not so much characterized as mythicized from the opening—"This girl seemed to mean to us the country, the conditions, the whole adventure of our childhood"—to the conclusion: "She lent herself to immemorial attitudes which we recognize by instinct as universal and true . . . She had only to stand in the orchard, to put her hand on a little crab tree and look up at the apples, to make you feel the goodness of planting and tending and harvesting at last . . . She was a rich mine of life, like the founders of early races." Ántonia lingers in the mind more as a goddess of fertility than as an individuated woman; to Jim, certainly, she is archetypal woman, her face "the closest, realest face, under all the shadows of women's faces."

Cather shared the impatience with individuated character that she saw reflected in the way southwestern Indians spoke English or Spanish, dropping the definite articles: not "the mountain" but "mountain"; not "the woman" but "woman." She often presents her characters as conduits for a divine spirit, raised above human powers by some force above or below consciousness, approaching the condition of gods, goddesses, or saints. In her portrait of Archbishop Latour, who could so easily have been made to seem a cathedral-building, executive, and managerial paragon, Cather goes out of her way to deemphasize willed activity. We see him first when he is lost in the desert, able to forget his own thirst through meditation on and identification with Christ's agony on the cross, and from then on, his "story" is largely a record of his finding or losing the spirit of God. Cather repeatedly chooses artists as subjects because she has an archaic sense of the way, in performing or creating, they are possessed by divine inspiration, a sacred breath that blows away consciousness of the petty circumstances of their lives, so that Thea Kronborg, for example, can look harried and fatigued in the afternoon, but that night, performing at the Met, she is the essence of youthful idealism.

Cather's art is peculiarly keen at registering surges of energy and at noting the presence or absence of spirit—in an innocent girl like Lucy Gayheart or in an amoral woman like Marian Forrester, who resembles Lucy only in that she puts her whole heart into everything she does. Indeed, most of Cather's heroines—Lucy, Marian, Ántonia, and Alexandra—have the capacity, sometimes harmful to themselves, to live so intensely that they seem like powers more than people, and one sometimes feels that Cather has set herself the task of portraying pure spirit divorced from circumstance, that background and circumstance are merely accidents, and that in the earth-mother Ántonia as in the bitchy, bitter Myra Henshawe, what is essential is the vital breath. Although she would have been appalled by the terms "blood knowledge" and "head knowledge," Cather resembles Lawrence in her desire to bypass the conscious and intellectual elements in her characters in quest of the instinctual and unconscious. These elements she found most accessible in simple people like the farmers of the Divide, in the devout, like the Old World Catholics of her later books, or, in their ideal imagined form, Indians. (When Mabel Dodge married Tony Luhan, a Taos Indian, and many of her friends asked how she could do it, Willa Cather reportedly said, "How could she not?")

But if Cather and Lawrence were in some sense after the same thing in their characters, they went about it in very different ways, and she attacks him as a mere cataloguer of physical sensations and emotions in her most important critical statement, "The Novel Démeublé." Most of this essay is a rather predictable attack on the novel of physical realism which she calls "over-furnished," overly devoted to description and observation. Balzac serves as her example of misguided labor, as Bennett, Wells, and Galsworthy served in Virginia Woolf's comparable manifestos, "Modern Fiction" and "Mr. Bennett and Mrs. Brown." Balzac, says Cather, wanted to put the city of Paris on paper, with all its houses, upholstery, games of chance and pleasure, even its foods. This was a mistake, she believes. "The things by which he still lives, the types of greed and avarice and ambition and vanity and lost innocence of heart which he created—are as vital today as they were then. But their material surroundings, upon which he expended such labor and pains . . . the eye glides over them." At this point Cather moves away from Woolf, who rejected physical realism in favor of psychological realism, outer for inner, including Lawrence in her camp, and moves instead toward an aesthetic of the archetypal, toward Jung rather than Freud. In a brilliant maneuver, she asserts that it is possible to be a materialistic enumerator about the inner life as well as the outer and offers Lawrence as her example. Cataloguing sensations, he robs the great stories of their intrinsic grandeur. "Can one imagine anything more terrible than the story of *Romeo and Juliet* rewritten in prose by D. H. Lawrence?" The minds of one's characters can be overfurnished, too, and in detailing the crockery and footstools of their interior life we can lose track of the distinctive forms of their humanity.

In her insistence on presenting her characters from the outside, in her refusal to explore their subjectivity, Cather seems to fly most conspicuously in the face of modernism, but that is because we have overidentified modernism in the novel with the techniques of interior monologue and stream of consciousness. Interior monologue and Cather's resolutely external treatment are equally reactions against traditional characterization. If we posit a traditional method of characterization in which the inner expresses itself in the outer—both action and physical surroundings in which character is compassable, knowable, and if we think of this as a middle-distance shot, then interior monologue may be thought of as a close-up, emphasizing uniqueness and individuality to the point of unknowability, and Cather's method of characterization as a kind of long shot, emphasizing the archetypal and eternally human, acknowledging individuality, perhaps, but not exploring it. Joyce tried to incorporate both the close-up and the long shot in his presentation of Leopold Bloom by suggesting that this highly individuated man was an avatar of Odysseus; Virginia Woolf seems to want to present eternal types in *The Waves* and to some extent in *Between the Acts;* and Lawrence likes to show his characters in the grip of cosmic forces, wrenched away from the personal. By abandoning the attempt to represent interior consciousness, by her resolute externality, Cather in her own way participated in the attempt to render the generally human as opposed to the individual. This is what I mean by the urge to abstraction in her handling of character (although "abstraction" is inevitably an imprecise and somewhat irritating word as applied to literature): her downplaying of individuality, her lack of interest in "personality" as opposed to essential force.

Heroic simplification is the essence of Cather's approach to character, and I will offer a visual analogy of this which Cather herself provides. In *My Ántonia*, Jim Burden and the Bohemian girls picnic on the banks of the river, and, as the sun begins to set, they notice a curious and striking phenomenon:

> Just as the lower edge of the red disk rested on the high fields against the horizon, a great black figure suddenly appeared on the face of the sun. We sprang to our feet, straining our eyes toward it. In a moment we realized what it was. On some upland farm, a plough had been left standing in the field. The sun was sinking just behind it. Magnified across the distance by the horizontal light, it stood out against the sun, was exactly contained within the circle of the disk; the handles, the tongue, the share—black against the molten red. There it was, heroic in size, a picture writing against the sun.

When the sun goes down further, the plough sinks back into its own littleness somewhere on the prairie, but it is the moment of heroic magnification that intrigues Willa Cather.

Naïve readers responding to *O Pioneers!* or *My Ántonia* or *Death Comes for the Archbishop* have trouble seeing these works as novels. They appear to be collections of vignettes or sketches, and the connection between the parts is not always evident. This response is useful, reminding us how unconventional Cather's approach to form really is. Except in *The Song of the Lark*, her most traditional novel, Cather pays no more attention to plot than Woolf does in *To the Lighthouse* and looks for unity to mood. "It is hard now to realize how revolutionary in form *My Ántonia* was at that time in America," wrote Edith Lewis, Cather's companion. "It seemed to many people to have no form."

In the first part of *My Ántonia*, for example, one comes suddenly upon a story so powerful that it threatens to throw the novel off track: the story of Pavel and Peter, who, back in Russia, had been carrying a bride and groom home from their wedding in a sled over snow by moonlight, when the entire party was set upon by wolves. To lighten their load and make it to safety, Pavel and Peter throw the bride out of the sled to be devoured by the wolves. At first this violent, horrific story seems separate from the novel as a whole, but with time one's mind weaves it into the fabric. It serves as a prologue to the grim winter in which Mr. Shimerda, unable to endure longer the hostility of nature, shoots himself. And in the sacrifice of the bride so that Pavel and Peter may reach the safety of town, the story states, with the starkness of folktale, the theme of sexuality sacrificed to advancement which is the heart of the book. But the real power of the story, it seems to me, comes from our awareness that Pavel and Peter are ordinary men whose lives had once been suddenly shifted into the realm of elemental forces, then dropped back down again into the ordinary, men metaphorically struck by lightning who go back the next day—or the next month—to milking cows. Their detachment from their horrendous experience is what is so moving, precisely their failure to incorporate it into the texture of their lives. The narrative exemplifies the way in which Cather's fiction moves between the quotidian and the elemental, not forcing the former to render up its potential for transcendence, nor demanding that the latter be everywhere manifest, but acknowledging the abrupt transformations of the ordinary into the ghastly or elemental or transcendent.

Other writers, hardly modernists, have used inset stories—Cervantes and Dickens, for example. But in Cather the folktale material is not framed by the rest of the narrative; it penetrates it, bringing what might be read merely as naturalistic narrative into the realm of the mythic, so that, later in the novel, we are aesthetically prepared, though still surprised and shocked, when a tramp wanders in from the prairie, climbs onto a threshing machine, waves his hand gaily, and jumps head first into the blades. Why should a tramp be immune to despair? Heroic emotions are not just for heroes. Cather routinely works with mythic incident (Jim's killing of the giant rattlesnake, a dragon-slaying episode that proves his manhood, although the rattlesnake is definitely a rattlesnake at the same time as it is, psychically, a dragon), with folk material, and with dreams. Naturalism coexists with symbolism. Lena Lingard may be an upwardly mobile, sexy, independent dressmaker in Lincoln, Nebraska, when Jim is a student there, but she is at the same time what she appears to him in a dream: a woman in a wheat field with a scythe, both a symbol of harvest and a figure threatening death, the pleasant death of his will and ambition by surrender to her compelling sensuality. Lena, the Danish laundry girls, and the three Bohemian Marys are to Jim—and Cather—joyous evocative figures out of

Virgilian rural life ("If there were no girls like them in the world, there would be no poetry"), and Jim, the student, is simultaneously Virgil ("For I shall be the first if I live to bring the Muse into my country").

With such an emphasis on the timeless, with the way in which human beings embody recurrent impulses and attitudes, with Swedish immigrant girls in Nebraska as avatars of Virgilian rustics, no wonder *My Ántonia* defies the traditional temporal organization of plot. Dorothy Van Ghent has noted how, out of homely American detail, Cather composes in *My Ántonia* "certain frieze-like entablatures that have the character of ancient ritual and sculpture." "The suffering of change, the sense of irreparable loss in time, is one polarity of the work; the other polarity is the timelessness of those images associated with Ántonia, with the grave of the suicide at the crossroads, with the mute fortitude of the hired men and the pastoral poetry of the hired girls, and most of all with the earth itself." In appreciating Cather's instinct for the timeless, Van Ghent begins to see the implications if formal terms of that instinct, the "frieze-like entablatures," the sculptural and abstract forms throughout Cather's work. "The boldest and most beautiful of Willa Cather's fictions are characterized by a sense of the past not as an irrecoverable quality of events, wasted in history, but as persistent human truths—salvaged, redeemed—by virtue of memory and art."

Most critics have noticed only the nostalgia, the "sense of irreparable loss in time" in Cather's work, a thematic emphasis that leads them to misperceive her art as traditional. This is like confounding Georgia O'Keeffe's skulls, crosses, and flowers with Landseer's dogs. Leon Edel, for example, demanding a representational three-dimensionality foreign to Cather's art, can only be dissatisfied with *The Professor's House* for offering, as he says repeatedly in his "psychoanalytic" reading of that novel, no explanation for the professor's depression. Forced to invent a narrative wholly outside the text, Edel offers an explanation, essentially that Cather herself was regressive, infantile, and so depressed when she was deprived of Isabelle McClung's maternal attention by her marriage to Jan Hambourg that she wrote her depression into Godfrey St. Peter without enough distinction between herself and her character to provide him with motivation. But Cather has her own notion of personal development, which is very well articulated in *The Professor's House:* she imagines childhood as a stage of pure being, divorced from accomplishment; in the middle years, from adolescence on, fueled by sexual energy, one asserts one's identity both through one's work and family life; old age is a return to a stage of pure being, a sadder or a richer childhood. The professor is at the end of the second stage of his life, his identity played out, his daughters grown and his work accomplished; his depression marks his transition to the third stage. In *Death Comes for the Archbishop* Cather would present her protagonist as having successfully performed the transition that was so difficult and painful for Professor St. Peter. The Archbishop "was soon to have done with calendared time, and it had already ceased to count for him. He sat in the middle of his own consciousness; none of his former states of mind were lost or outgrown. They were all within reach of his hand, and all comprehensible." Van Ghent, with her interest in primitive religion and myth, can understand what Cather is trying to do in her representation of old age. Edel, with his interest in Freudian analysis of a crude sort, insisting on the individual etiology of every "symptom," cannot even begin to understand. For him, *Death Comes for the Archbishop*, one of Cather's masterpieces, is an exercise in nostalgia, signaling Cather's final retreat into the past. That, indeed, is the way most critics of the forties and fifties—all dominated by a moralistic response to Cather, all disposed to condemn her for retreating into the past, all viewing her as a traditionalist—saw that book.

In fact, from a formal point of view, *Death Comes for the Archbishop*, that extraordinary compilation of vivid scenes and great stories which ignores chronological time, is the most daring and innovative of Cather's works. It perfectly embodies the anti-illusionist aesthetic which many of her early books strove for. I will quote Cather's own excellent description of what she was trying to accomplish and, I believe, did accomplish:

> I had all my life wanted to do something in the style of legend, which is absolutely the reverse of dramatic treatment. Since I first saw the Puvis de Chavannes frescoes of the life of St. Genevieve in my student days, I have wished that I could try something a little like that in prose; something without accent, with none of the artificial elements of composition. In the Golden Legend the martyrdoms of the saints are no more dwelt upon than are the trivial incidents of their lives; it is as though all human experiences, measured against one supreme spiritual experience, were of about the same importance. The essence of such writing is not to hold the note, not to use an incident for all there is in it—but to touch and pass on. I felt that such writing would be a discipline in these days when the "situation" is made to count for so much in writing, when the general tendency is to force things up. In this kind of writing the mood is the thing—all the little figures and stories are mere improvisations that come out of it.

Cather had begun her writing career imitating the "dramatic treatment" of Henry James. But what she had always been moving toward was what she calls here "legend." The distinctive note of modernism appears in her aspiration to do "something without accent," in her impatience with "artificial elements of composition," with traditional climaxes and resolutions ("not a single button sewn on as the Bond Street tailors would have it," said Virginia Woolf). Musically speaking, this lifelong lover of opera repudiates the operatic ("holding the note") as a model for fiction and turns instead—rather astonishingly—to jazz, with its emphasis on mood-generating "improvisations."

The attempt to write "something in the style of legend" involved the pursuit of another aesthetic quality: anonymity. This was hard for Cather to achieve. She had been a high school teacher; more important, she had suffered in her youth from the disapproval of her community, who regarded her nonconformity with distaste. She could never quite stop telling them off for it, and the theme of opposition between philistine materialism and artistic dedication too often evokes a marring didacticism in her work. The way she overcame the urge to preach was by complete submission to her material, which she said she learned from the example of Sarah Orne Jewett. And when she suppressed herself, she did it more completely than any writer I can think of.

The clarity and simplicity—the sheer absence of eccentricity—of Cather's prose style contributes to the effect of anonymity. She adheres to the traditional structure of the English sentence—subject, verb, object—as the surest way of suppressing individuality. Rarely does one find any complicated syntax. There are passages in Cather's writing that stop the heart with their beauty, but they are never purple passages in the usual sense. They tend, as in this passage, to depict moments of quiet, and they are signaled, if at all, by a toning down of the prose rather than a keying up:

> In stopping to take a breath, I happened to glance up at the canyon wall. I wish I could tell you what I saw there, just *as* I saw it, on that first morning, through a veil of lightly falling snow. Far up above me, a thousand feet or so, set in a great cavern in the face of the cliff, I saw a little city of stone, asleep. It was as still as sculpture —and something like that. It all hung together, seemed to have a kind of composition: pale little houses of stone nestling close to one another, perched on top of each other, with flat roofs, narrow windows, straight walls, and in the middle of the group, a round tower . . . It was red in colour, even on that grey day. In sunlight is was the colour of winter oak-leaves. A fringe of cedars grew along the edge of the cavern, like a garden. They were the only living things. Such silence and stillness and repose—immortal repose. That village sat looking down into the canyon with the calmness of eternity.

Although the moment Cather describes here is characteristic—the small and particular raised to the monumental, the once-busy seen in eternal repose—the force of this passage resides as much in its style, in the calm, methodical notation of colors and shapes, the note of awe suggested with no overtones of hysteria, as in its content. It insists on the sculptural qualities of its subject, as Cather tends to in her descriptions of prairie and sky as well. The prose is by no means flowery, but neither is it as stark as it might be, as Hemingway's is, for example. There is a softness about it which comes from Cather's willingness to offer neutral elaboration. "In the sunlight it was the colour of winter oak-leaves"—this is a nice detail but not hypercharged, as it might appear in Hemingway, where the excessively stripped-down quality of the prose makes everything seem almost too significant. Cather's range is more comfortable, and the effect is to reduce, symbolically, the glare. Georgia O'Keeffe comes to mind again, as opposed to Dali or Magritte.

O'Keeffe, Sheeler, and other visual artists allied, however loosely, with Precisionism in America offer a good example of aesthetic urges similar to Cather's, generated from analogous but different sources and worked out quite independently. The aim of the Precisionists was simplification of form, and this joined an impulse toward monumentalizing ordinary objects—Sheeler's "Totems in Steel," for example, a rendering of steel girders on a building project, or his eerie stairwells or imperious ladder-back chairs, or O'Keeffe's resonant adobe houses. Cather particularly recalls O'Keeffe in her response to the Southwest, in her homage to the scale of the American landscape, in her ability to monumentalize the ordinary, and in her gift for generating a sense of mystery out of simplified forms. Cather's sources of inspiration invite comparison with Sheeler's. Sheeler's formalism fed on a deeply native tradition which was not in itself modernist: he was a student of Shaker furniture and Shaker barns. Similarly, Cather took strength from what she saw as a native example of functionalism, the stories of Sarah Orne Jewett. In describing Jewett's work, Cather distinguished between two kinds of beauty: the beauty of the Chinese junk, which comes from ornamentation and embellishment, and the beauty of the racing yacht, in which every line is subsumed to purpose. The beauty of Jewett's prose, to Cather, was the sleek, functional, pared-down beauty of the yacht, and although it is possible to imagine a stripping down and functionalism that goes well beyond Cather's—Hemingway, again—that is certainly the beauty she aspired to herself.

Every great writer is an innovator, forging his or her own style in the face of the seductive force of the conventional. We must mean more than that when we use the term "modernist." Critics of the sixties tended to identify modernism in the novel with subjectivity, but newer accounts of modernism tend to emphasize art's awareness of its own artificial status. The modernists themselves, however, did not unanimously recognize that what they were producing was semiotically precocious fiction; nor were all of them effective theorists of their own positions. Joyce talked about the artist refined out of existence. Eliot talked about art as an escape from personality. Flaubert aspired to write a novel about nothing. Woolf talked about capturing the luminous halo of life. In this company, Cather, with her talk of the "novel démeublé," seems the least critically sophisticated, yet it is certainly in this company that she belongs. In modernist critical writings, including Cather's, certain themes recur: an urge to shake loose of clutter, a refusal to accept the mimetic function of art as previously defined, a feeling that a certain "spirit" was escaping the older forms, an urge toward anonymity. The vessel is emphasized rather than the content; art is imagined as a fragile container for the ineffable substance of life. Thea

Kronborg speaks for Cather: "What was any art but an attempt to make a sheath, a mould in which to imprison for a moment the shining, elusive element which is life itself,—life hurrying past us and running away, too strong to stop, too sweet to lose? The Indian women had held it in their jars." The modernists were aware of art as created artifact, not as a mirror reflecting reality or a camera eye absorbing and imprinting it. Nothing could be further from the modernist temper than Dreiser's boast about *Sister Carrie* that it was not intended as a piece of literary craftsmanship but as a picture of conditions. The modernists often, like Cather, looked to Flaubert as their Ur-aesthetician, with his emphasis on style, surface, disciplined craft; but the wittiest theorist of modernism was Oscar Wilde, whose assertion that life imitates art may be seen as the key to the modernist spirit.

If we describe the modernists as self-conscious artificers who rejected mimesis as their chief business, we risk overemphasizing the intellectual, game-playing, Nabokovian element in modernism. Not all experiment took place for the sake of experiment, but out of a conviction that the old forms did not capture something important in life, a "spirit," a force, a religious or spiritual dimension existing somewhere below or above consciousness but beyond the purviews of traditional fiction. Hence modernism's impatience with describing the here-and-now and its persistent urge to see the here-and-now in the light of, united to, all of human history: Eliot in *The Waste Land*, Pound in the *Cantos*, Joyce in *Ulysses*, and, I would suggest, Cather, in her continuing effort to tie contemporary life to a past that stretched back, in America, to the cliff dwellers and to see all human life in relation to the enduring earth.

An interest in the past and particularly in primitive cultures characterized the early twentieth century and was not just a piece of isolated nostalgia or conservatism on the part of Willa Cather. Gauguin had been impressed by Aztec sculpture at the Paris Exposition as early as 1889. Vlaminck began collecting African sculpture around 1903 and was followed in his enthusiasm for primitive art by Derain, Matisse, Modigliani, Brancusi, Moore, and Picasso, who, in 1907, incorporated renderings of African sculptures into *Les Desmoiselles d'Avignon*. Picasso had visited Altamira in 1902 to see the neolithic cave paintings. Lawrence left the Old World for the New in search of civilizations more ancient than the former could offer. The same impulse drove Cather to Walnut Canyon, Arizona, and later to Mesa Verde, where she found in the buildings and pottery of the Anasazi an objective correlative for aesthetic impulses she had felt in herself. Form in these cliff-dwellings followed function; the buildings blended with the landscape; towns were set inside natural caverns with the cliffs themselves providing protection from the elements. The pottery was elegantly functional, embellished only with abstract designs. No more in these designs than in Indian pictographs, no more than in the cave paintings of Altamira or in certain Greek vase painting, was there an attempt to imitate three-dimensionality on a flat surface. It is no surprise that a woman so moved by this art should also have responded strongly to the frescoes of Puvis de Chavannes, whose flat, almost friezelike figures emphasize the picture plane and refuse to create the illusion of receding space. Although Puvis de Chavannes was not himself a modernist figure, he influenced Seurat, Gauguin, Matisse, and Picasso. Most modern painting has stemmed from a refusal like his to create the illusion of three-dimensional space, often encouraged by the example of primitive, non-Western, or pre-Renaissance art. Cather's antinaturalistic *Death Comes for the Archbishop,* a series of stories so arranged as to blur the distinction between the past and the present, the miraculous and the mundane, is, I would argue, a true even if somewhat surprising example in literature of the modernist aesthetic in art, and much of her early work should be seen as moving in that direction.

Visual analogues for Cather's modernism are many. The determining factor, as in so much modernist painting which exploded out of the confines of easel-sized canvases, is scale. One thinks of the wall-sized works of Picasso and Matisse, such as *Guernica* and *The Dance of Life;* one thinks of the giant canvases of Jackson Pollock and the vast areas, made to seem even vaster by their minimalist treatment, of works by Rothko, Frankenthaler, Barnett Newman; one thinks of the murals of Orozsco and Thomas Hart Benton. To work on that scale involves simplification. The reduction to essential forms, which began in the visual arts with Cézanne, finds a literary analogue in Cather's insistence on there being only a few human stories which are told over and over. Her refusal to follow the twists and turns of her characters' individual thoughts, her insistence on seeing them as "human creatures," subject to an endlessly recurring cycle of emotions, recalls Cézanne's insistence that the cone, the circle, and the square are at the basis of everything we see. If her novels seem consequently simple, their simplicity has the same aim as Klee's figures, Matisse's late abstract cutouts, or Picasso's consciously childlike drawings. It is a simplicity that aims to capture the elemental and enduring and that requires the greatest art to produce.

However fragmented their initial impact, both *The Waste Land* in its relation to *The Golden Bough* and *Ulysses* in its relation to the *Odyssey* attempt to transcend the complexity of modern life by annexing the structural simplicities of myth. Embracing multiplicity but animated by an urge to abstraction, they attempt to search through the historical and accidental to the fundamental. The appropriate stance for the artist in the face of such mythic and archetypal material is anonymity. The appropriate style is no style. Joyce in *Ulysses* sought to approximate "no style" by parodying all styles. Gertrude Stein and Hemingway sought to produce an anonymous surface by means of prose styles of the utmost plainness, stripped of all ornament and connotation. But the lucid prose of Willa Cather makes even Hemingway's sentences look mannered. And as for Gertrude Stein, it is one of the many ironies of modernism that the pursuit of simplicity and anonymity produced works of such futile complexity and obtrusive personality. Like many other modernist artists, Cather sought to bypass consciousness and the circumstantial details with which it concerns itself and to produce an art that appealed to the most elemental layers of our minds. Her enduring popularity with readers shows that she succeeded, and critics ought now to take account of her success.

Toward the Outside:
The Quest for Discontinuity
in Gertrude Stein's
The Making of Americans

Clive Bush

"It is only sentimentalists and unexperiencing thinkers whose eyes turn in," wrote Gertrude Stein in her notebooks, and she continued, "Those having wealth of experience turn out or are quiet in meditation and repose." Such a statement, with its suggestions of the connections between vision, experience, emotion, and moral life, constitutes a fundamental guide to Gertrude Stein's first great masterpiece, *The Making of Americans; Being a History of a Family's Progress*. But for Gertrude Stein, in the period of writing this work, 1902–11, it was an insight not easily achieved, and it will be the argument of this paper that its truth formed the basis for an inner moral dialogue, asserted with varying degrees of confidence, in the work itself. This perceptual movement of the eyes, variously supported in philosophy, psychology, and reading of literature, helped to provide Gertrude Stein with the means for writing an enormous satirical fiction, which, in keeping with its conviction of radical ambiguity, depended upon a technique of paradox and irony for its realization. It is, however, no ordinary satire, for object and process of observation are themselves self-consciously analyzed in the narrative, suggesting that the very modes of satire, irony, and ambiguity—the literary modes of English eighteenth-century Tories, late nineteenth-century bourgeois on the run, and teachers in contemporary English departments—constitute a self-defeating circularity both in the process of art and in experience.

The content of the fictional field of *The Making of Americans* is therefore a complex one. On one level it is a very American examination of inherited values. Like her aging contemporary, Henry Adams, and her young contemporary, James Joyce, Gertrude Stein felt bound both to examine the

From *Twentieth Century Literature* 24, no. 1 (Spring 1978). © 1978 by Hofstra University Press. Originally entitled "Toward the Outside: The Quest for Discontinuity in Gertrude Stein's *The Making of Americans; Being a History of a Family's Progress*."

historical legacies of American life and to give an account of the struggles
of the artist to free himself from the immediate realities of his childhood
and adolescence. The result is a kind of romantic satire. The inner narrative
of *The Making of Americans* is autobiographical. More precisely there is an
autobiographical voice at work inwardly mediating the objects of its perception. The objects of that perception are American family life as the climax
of Western civilization originating, in nineteenth-century conviction at
least, in classical times; the consequent struggles between the claims of art
and life, home and freedom, and, since the immediate historical context of
the writing was Europe in the ten years before World War I, between the
European future and an American past with the subsequent impact of this
paradox on the American dream itself.

The inner movement of the eyes engaged home, America, the claims
of personal life, the repetitive neuroses of family living, "society," and the
dignification of "necessity" as moral truth. The outer movement of the eyes
meant rejection of home, the objectification of personal existence, Europe,
the attempt to break loose from family psychology, to free time from the
contentless nature of "society," and to assert that freedom begins once the
boundaries of necessity have been passed or overcome. The technique of
The Making of Americans is carefully designed to investigate both the principles and the content of the process between the interior and exterior
visions. The result, as Leon Katz long ago implied, is an epistemological
investigation of a cultural situation.

The fastest way into this process is first to consider the title of the work
abstractly and then to locate it historically. In the full title every word
signposts the terms of the composition. Let us take the two phrases separately. In the first, "making" has a curiously mechanistic quality reinforced
by its dogmatic definite article. The continuous present participle indicates
not a present, but a past, action in process. "Americans" discloses nationalist content. The whole phrase, governed by the gerundive, concretizes
movement but in so doing cuts off its own future. Beyond "Americans"
there is nothing in spite of the fact that the naming is a process, not an
absolute category. As though dissatisfied with such a completion Gertrude
Stein *adds*, in the second appositional phrase, an analogical process. The
epistemology of style is here empiricist-derived; additive truth and a definition of secret relational meanings in a process of equivalence. But in an
attempt to make the process open-ended, "being" is analogically related
to "making." In fact, the analogy has an atmosphere of insistence, of repetition, and of attempting to move forward between the stasis of history
and progress. Through "being," history becomes the complement of "making." Becoming is a function of being. That is to say, "being" absorbs history
in the "becoming" of family progress. What we are given is not an ingenious
logical statement, but an ironic reflection on a psychology of analogy. The
initial distinction between being and becoming goes back to Aristotle. As
Norman O. Brown once pointed out, *kinesis* is an imperfect form of *energia*.
Becoming is the condition of making history, being the state of freedom

from it. Gertrude Stein's title expresses ironically the frustration of becoming presented analogically as being. Frozen movement replaces the true Aristotelian notion of activity. What we have is a restless stasis of highly charged frustrated becoming. History *as* nationalist "making" reduces activity to a pragmatically successful authorization of the truth of present process; a logical absurdity. The title ironically implies that history preceding truth is the same as history following truth. Total history, in either case, to use Foucault's distinction, obliterates general history. But the indefinite articles of the analogical phrase suggest particularity in history, and work against the totalizing process. "A family's progress" suggests both continuity and change, but the ends are once again blocked off. A family belongs to the realm of necessity, progress to the public world of history and change. Progress suggests ironically a teleology of destiny but analogically relates to an action preserved by memory operating in the past. The isolation of moments of necessity set as "being-in-becoming" elicits a wavelike motion of progress, like a train of prairie schooners straggling across the desert toward the sunset.

The totalizing impulse has always been an object of literary satire. In writing *Melanctha* (written in 1905–06, not published until 1909), for example, Gertrude Stein claimed she was creating a methodology out of Matisse and Swift. We will return to painting, but the major difference between herself and the Tory satirists was the fact that she investigated the psychology of the satiric process as well as using it. Briefly, satire depends on a notion of certainty in order to attack certainty. It attacks real idealism with secret idealism. For eighteenth-century satire depended upon an empiricist view of common sense. *A priori* thinking is repressed as a dogma and described in oblique form as a world of fantasy, dream, madness, and absurdity, celebrated *in* the satire as aesthetic *frisson*. The dislocations between common sense and fantasy are experienced as wit. In psychological terms the effect is melancholy or loving-to-hate. In political terms contradiction is interiorized as neurosis and objectified as paradox and secret inexpressible transcendence. In such a scheme the follies and vices of mankind are located not in history, but in "psychology." The authorial voice exteriorizes itself as wiser-than-thou Stoic to make an "objective"description of "characteristic" behavior. Common sense reveals itself as a totalizing method which attacks totalizing content. A hidden idealism is transferred to a literary perception as process revealing the empiricist world of "human nature." Mechanism is the rationale of the satiric method as well as the object of its attack.

By substituting "making" for "acting" (the true human interaction in the *polis*) in her title, Gertrude Stein revealed a contradictory impulse. On the one hand she attempted to found a procedure which would reveal "truth" and at the same time deny that such a procedure was possible at all. The false unities of "making" are revealed by inward-turning eyes; outward-turning eyes reveal discontinuity. The object of Gertrude Stein's satire, as the quotation at the head of this essay indicates, was the "truth" of American nationhood: *E pluribus unum.* "Making" in the historical process is a notion as old as political theory itself. "Making" connotes continuity, rule, and in classical political theory after Aristotle, the division of action into "beginning" and "achieving." Whereas action in the Aristotelian sense of *bios politikos* was fundamentally entrenched in the *polis*, in Plato it is replaced by "making" in the *societas*. "Making" comes about, in Hannah Arendt's words—and her superb discussion is being followed here—by Plato transferring to the *polis* the "currently recognized maxims for a well-ordered household." Here the two phrases of the title come together. History disappears in the family. The master-slave relations of necessity invade the public realm. The propaganda for its success is "making"; that is to say, technique, fabrication, pretense of objective certainty, the relegation of true action to "means" to obtain "higher" ends. Action becomes instrumental. "Success" validates that action, irrespective of content. For "making" in American speech has connotations of "making it," implying success in business and also in sexuality. Family necessity also reduces response to experience, and as articulated in the preferred terms of sensationist psychology, to Stoicism or Epicureanism. Action is reduced to behavior, the political becomes social. For reasons of training, Gertrude Stein sought to investigate the behavior of the family as a totalization of historical process. In behavior the true activity of the *bios politikos* is submerged in a statistics of analysis and prediction. By applying a totalizing method to a totalizing object Gertrude Stein revealed an America where the dream of eighteenth-century historical progress had turned into twentieth-century totalitarian nightmare.

The terms in which Gertrude Stein naturally thought were philosophical and psychological ones, when the terms still needed each other for definition at the beginning of the twentieth century. Much has been written of her relation to William James, but it is not clearly enough grasped that she attempted to reverse virtually every one of his principles. For James, using the paradoxical Darwinian epistemology of invisible principle (natural selection—involving the paradox of automatic will) and observable fact (spontaneous variation—involving the paradox of temporal break with tradition inside "norm"-related change), attempted to create a psychology of empiricist process which kept the paradoxes but set them in motion.

There is not space to explain Gertrude Stein's point-for-point rejection of James, but one aspect of his work is crucial. It is the attempt to predicate reality on the linguistic form of the sentence. Indeed the famous definition of the "stream of thought/consciousness" depends upon it. Gertrude Stein stretched the traditional use of the sentence to its limit, seriously damaging its credibility as a purveyor of reality in the Jamesian sense. For James it celebrated mere variety with a fixed order of process; for Gertrude Stein it became a method of satirizing reality predicated on analogies of biological evolution. James brandishes it as a mirror of representational reality so that the neurotics and unhealthy-minded may gird up their loins like men. Gertrude Stein, almost whimsically, tosses it back and forth over an epistemological abyss. For James it is the secret and imperishable guide to reality itself; for Gertrude Stein it renders a satire which turns savagely on its own truth. For James its "reality" forces him to admit the exceptional and the discontinuous as "fringe" or "penumbra"; for Gertrude Stein it may produce, or indeed depend upon, any one of its parts being radically discontinuous from any other part, thus undercutting common sense itself. For, in brief, the sentence expressed the reality of Western grammar since the Greeks with its truths of linear time, category, and philosophical dualism, For James, therefore, its inner truth could make sense of nonsense, but for Gertrude Stein it judged reality in the making of it. Gertrude Stein is the first of many writers in the twentieth century to have made an assault on the sentence as the structure of immutable truth. For "to sentence" means to commit to "doing time," and doing time is the experience of the substitution of imprisoned "making" for free activity. In *The Making of Americans* "doing time" is, as we shall see, the narrative experience of the authorial voice and the narrative content of its perception—a double inwardness of "socialized" vision.

For William James the metaphysics of the sentence also underwrote his adulation of habit in the ethical domain. Repetition in the areas of existence are made into moral regulations through analogy in order to enforce necessity. To use Freudian terms, for James habit was the superego (the internalization of social contradiction as conscience); for Gertrude Stein it was undoubtedly "id." By banishing repetition to the level of biological life, Gertrude Stein sought to make a place for herself in which, at the level of culture, analogies for moral life made out of biological process might be epistemologically exposed. James buried the possibility of that exposure by claiming consciousness as a fact of the biologically given. Gertrude Stein's definition of repetition would have encapsuled Nietzsche's remarks that "[t]he real continuous process takes place *below* our consciousness: the series and sequence of feelings, thoughts, and so on, are symptoms of this underlying process." For James habit or behavioral repetition was in the Duke of Wellington's words, which he quotes in *The Principles of Psychology*, "ten times nature." In the growth of the behavioral sciences, the life process as either open or secret ethical analogy for consciousness has, in Hannah Arendt's trenchant irony, "let loose an unnatural growth, so to speak, of the natural."

We can also bring to the Duke of Wellington's words Hannah Arendt's insight that such an unnatural domination of nature is only possible following the invasion of the public realm by the necessities of family life: "With . . . the rise of the 'household' (*oika*) or of economic activities to the public realm, housekeeping and all matters pertaining to the private sphere of the family have become a "collective" concern. In the modern world, the two realms indeed flow constantly into each other like waves in the never-resting stream of the life process itself." That wavelike motion was something clearly understood by Gertrude Stein as she fashioned her sentences. For the drift toward "society" affected the privacy needed for artistic creativity as much as it attenuated the public significance of true activity. If in the romantic period the artist was driven to the rock like Prometheus, or to Hell like Faust, or to the farthest reaches of the Pacific like Captain Ahab, there was still a dialectical significance in his alienation. By the end of the nineteenth century that significance had been eroded and intimacy had replaced privacy as directly as the *polis* had been replaced by the *societas*. The secret narrative of *The Making of Americans*, breaking the surface at various points, is the experience of the narrative voice responding to its loss of public audibility which made the task of distinguishing creative solitude from "social loneliness" the more difficult and the more urgent. *The Making of Americans* shows us the authorial voice breaking with "society" by creating a magnificent epitaph for it. For Gertrude Stein it meant a long apprenticeship, reaching a threshold of release from the tyranny of the sentence with all its implications of reality. The completeness of the break is described in her essay "The Gradual Making of *The Making of Americans*" and realized halfway through *A Long Gay Book*, written after *The Making of Americans*.

We have, of course, described the process too clearly. Gay, *déracinée*, living among bohemians *and* artists, herself exempted from "necessity," Gertrude Stein also had to escape from that pseudo-alternative of American bourgeois life: bohemianism. The *life-style* (a term as dogmatically aesthetic and significant of *behavior* as "way of life") included an interest in psychoanalysis, managing art, collecting, or, as Gertrude Stein herself said in a particularly vicious mood in "The Notebooks," teaching ballet to little girls. We should, therefore, expect from the novel a variety of tones, and indeed contradictory attitudes toward the fate of American history turning into social behavior. The movement goes between inner and outer perception, between nostalgia and hatred, ironic approval and obsessive criticism, chilly analysis and praise of courage face to face with invisible neurosis, between pride and despair. Indeed the tone of the authorial voice matches these varieties as it changes the terms of its address from "gentle reader" of Swiftian memory to "stranger" of twentieth-century nihilistic angst.

Various disciplines merge in the novel. From her training at Harvard and Johns Hopkins she brought the experimental legacy of a classificatory habit of mind, a distrust of teleologies, and a disposition toward evolutionary psychology as a model for human behavior. In Europe she immersed herself in literature and painting. The curious thing to emerge from her prodigious excursions into literature is a double leaning toward eighteenth-century novels, many written by women, and toward histories of military leaders. There is a sexual differentiation of direction toward the private and public realms. It seems as if she needed to ascertain the poles of traditional "feminine" and "male" behavior: the one expressing its conflicts in the early bourgeois novel whose class, economic, and social conflicts mythicized themselves in the Gothic romance; the other betraying *her* fascination with violent male power games which lasted throughout her life. Thus we may at least speculate that in the paralleling of the search for a husband with the search for glory she was looking for the historical origins of psychological types, a favorite nineteenth-century activity.

In satire she found a way of handling the inheritance, for satire turned on the terms of domestic comedy and public tragedy by characterizing human activity as behavior, and by mocking the linear continuities of idealism and destiny. We can see Gertrude Stein thinking about the alternatives in a passage which caught her attention from Lyly's *Euphues,* a tale very much bearing the marks of a sophisticated nonlinear oral tradition and predating the "realism" of the later novel. She copied it down, as Katz points out, inaccurately: "In faith Euphues thou has told me a long tale, the beginning I have forgotten the middle I understand not and the end hangeth not together." Here in a nutshell are the satiric weapons with which to defeat the Aristotelian certainties: "forgetting," absence of "knowing," and "discontinuity." Those certainties were most immediately present to her in Jamesian philosophy and psychology which received the Aristotelian epistemology into its system through British empiricism especially as enunciated in the writings of Locke. Many commentators have noted the childlike voice of the authorial perspective. We must remember that it was Locke and in literary terms Wordsworth (with Goethe, James's favorite poet) who created in the image of the educating child a biophilosophical foundation for an epistemology of experience. Wordsworth's invention of the autobiographical epic where the growth of the child is both object of and perception of experience and in which mature identity is predicated on memory's view of the past as moral code is the key work of nineteenth-century sensibility. Predisposed as an American toward autobiography, how could Gertrude Stein come to terms with such an inheritance of satire and romantic autobiography? Rejecting experience and yet attempting to frame it through category, determined that the child should not be the father of the man, that biological aging and repetitive action based on memory should not be made into simple analogies for human consciousness, Gertrude Stein attempted in *The Making of Americans* to turn the autobiographical child-perception into an "objectively" satirical "naïve" vision, and her own obviously unhappy childhood into an exteriorized plot of family, that is, social, behavior. The implications of the logic of the attempt, which we have not space to explore here, showed that the historically contradictory poles of public satire and private romantic autobiography were but poles of a single self-enclosed system.

The epistemological weapons besides satire with which to break with the Aristotelian tradition in literature and psychology were to be found in her encounter with cubism and Weiningerian psychology. Cubism in those last ten years of bourgeois optimism was an assault on the traditional notions of hierarchy inherent in representational painting and on the specially privileged position of man in nature by a technique of representing the body as planes in space. It made process into an object by isolating spaces with rectilinear boundaries to create patterns which brought traditional three-dimensional depth up to the surface. Cubism helped Gertrude Stein to solve her own epistemological problems. For it is a visual enactment of space as statistical time. The hidden process is made visible. Representation with its invisible power of infinity is replaced by probable reality based on statistical series. Cubism is also an exemplifier of the process which Foucault describes in his *The Birth of the Clinic*, from, in his language, the garden of species (primarily an eighteenth-century static, categorizing, medical mode) to the "internal surface" of a medicine of spaces. In medicine in the early nineteenth century the body becomes an object, the space of disease becomes its cause, the logical sign becomes an index of generalization, the macabre is replaced by the morbid, and death becomes the privilege of the individual suffering his "average" (a statistical term) life. Surely cubism was at once a summary of and satire upon the epistemology of what Foucault calls the "empirical gaze." It both exposed and re-created the hidden assumptions behind the confident realities of pathological psychology. There is not space to develop the argument more rigorously, but the relevance to *The Making of Americans* of this kind of analysis is important, not only because Gertrude Stein took a conscious decision to reject medicine and behavioral psychology, and was consequently bound to find terms for the rejection, but because she was in many ways still struggling to escape from the bases of their styles of thinking and from that revolution in consciousness which marked the coming of age of bourgeois power where the introduction of death as the teleology of disease enabled the structure of "space" and "individual" to emerge.

If we can rid our minds of the clichéd character of the phrase, it is precisely Matthew Arnold's "strange disease" of modern life which is the subject of Gertrude Stein's investigation. Nowhere was life more modern than in America, nowhere were the realities of bourgeois life more entrenched, and nowhere were the principles of the cubist and the psychomedical "space of time" more developed. As Gertrude Stein explained at the end of "The Gradual Making of *The Making of Americans*":

> Then at the same time is the question of time. The assembling of a thing to make a whole thing and each one of these whole things is one of a series, but beside this there is the important thing and the very American thing that everybody knows who is an American just how many seconds minutes or hours it is going to take to do a whole thing. It is singularly a sense for combination within a conception of the existence of a given *space of time* that makes the American thing the American thing, and the sense of this space of time must be within the whole thing as well as in the completed whole thing.

Just as cubism isolated perspective moments in wavelike motion over the picture space, so Gertrude Stein's sentences specifically attacked the depth realism which James had attributed to the sentence form itself. The danger is of course that process becomes its own object alienating the force of the improbable in statistical uncertainty. Marx's critique of Hegel is relevant here, for, as he argued, absolute process may bury true externality in natural alienation: "Thus, his intuition of nature is only the act of confirming his abstraction from the intuition of nature—is only the conscious repetition by him of the process of creating his abstraction." True externality, argued Marx, is not, as in Hegel, a mistake or defect, but a *"self-externalizing world of sense* open to the light, open to the man endowed with senses." The recovery of the senses that are common to all, rather than the common sense of the empiricists, was, I believe, one of Gertrude Stein's aims. In some ways it was unfortunate that she found a method for determining the principles of her investigation into the nature of the novel, the epistemology of psychological perception, and the dissolving of world history in American society, in Otto Weininger's *Sex and Character*.

It had better be said at once that Weininger's book is a vicious libel on mankind, obsessive in its hatred of women and intellectually fraudulent in its attribution of empirically observed behavior to human nature. But as a record of one man's perception of the psychopathology of a world turning from imperialism to totalitarianism it is a crucial document. For Gertrude Stein its method of dualistic sexual characterology with its concept of sexual affinities (a phrase refashioned by Weininger from that other great novel about the "scientific" relation of sexual struggle to the design of space—in this case English gardens—Goethe's *Elective Affinities*) was one which she took over for herself in the book. It helped to reinforce the habit of thinking in character "types" inherited from the well-known early motor-automism experiments. The philosophy of Weininger's book theorizes about empiricist process between poles of maleness and femaleness to characterize behavior. For example, really "male" men are, unlike women, genuinely capable of heroic experience because they are more consistent, capable of memory, of perception of essences, of comparative thought, and therefore of analysis. Weininger psychologizes the psychology of Carlylean heroism and takes abstraction a stage further. It is not merely that the history of the world is the history of great men, but that genius is perhaps most to be found in men who write biography. Psychology becomes theoretical biography. I suggest Gertrude Stein took this very seriously indeed. *The Making of Americans is* theoretical biography.

Weininger's accompanying attack on the family is most interesting as a cry of rage against the invasion of "society" into every area of truly public life. The attack is focused on women as managers of the domain of necessity. But objectively to attribute their slavelike character to their incapacity for the public realm buries logic in the repressed guilt of the slave owner. Weininger mistakes in short the symptoms of repression for human nature. Behavioral analysis as dualistic characterology discovers without much effort the truth of the empiricist gaze: repressive reality made over into natural process.

It is true that, as Katz observes, Gertrude Stein gradually moves out of the crude dualisms of Weiningerian characterology. But nonetheless Gertrude Stein approaches the American family with an only outwardly objective gaze. Like Weininger the memory of personal experience forms the basis for satire in spite of the fact that satire is the humor, in Weininger's words, of the Jews and is hence to be equated with sentimental erotics, passivity, lying, and intellectual second-rateness, supposedly also characteristic of women. We may suppose that Gertrude Stein needed to free herself from Weininger's condemnation while admitting that at the impoverished level of pseudo-objective observation he was mainly correct. The American family did obliterate potential richness of life in boredom; its sexual boundaries forced repetitive neurosis until they seemed like a death design of nature itself. Its unforgiving alternations of marriage and divorce *was* the reality underlying its obsessive moralism and aesthetic romance consciousness, concealing its need for competitive possession in pragmatism. These are the subjects of *The Making of Americans*, and Gertrude Stein examines the Weiningerian certainties in a kind of half-satire and the result is half-victory. Marianne Moore was precisely wrong when she said that *The Making of Americans* was a "kind of living genealogy"; it was a *dying* one. Its family realities forced the eyes inward to consume the self in consciousness of its own process. Her famous remark that "when Leo said that all classification was teleological I knew I was not a pragmatist" must be seen in the light of what followed it: "I do not believe that, I believe in reality as Cézanne or Caliban believe in it. I believe in repetition." This shows in part that she rejected the buried idealistic stasis of pragmatism in order to render a creative movement of space-time more freely in relation to the pleasurable and dangerous "repetitions" of the earthbound id.

The process of *The Making of Americans* is the rejection of inheritance, an externalized autobiography. Gay, Jewish, trained as an experimental psychologist and a pragmatist, she wanted to recover the freedoms of creative consciousness, to be an artist not a teacher, nor only a collector, to reject, perhaps, the kind of life led by her brother Leo with his internalizing interest in Freudian theory which prevented him from outering his vision. The process reached the cleansing threshold of satire and of necessary adolescent rebellion. At that level it is a truly American book. Beyond the level of "social satire" in all the meanings we have attributed to these words, it could not go. But just as those eyes of Picasso's *Desmoiselles d'Avignon* haunt us with innocent, empty, mocking tragedy held as if in the gaze of a child and brought to us in a brilliant redeployment of space by a Spanish artist living the violences of his culture (a culture Gertrude Stein was to parallel strongly with her own culture, as did Hemingway after her), so do Gertrude Stein's characters haunt us in their childlike incapacity to move beyond the cheap behaviorism of natural tragedy. We must now turn to the text itself to examine the realization of these extraordinary and original combinations of issues in the field of her creative attention.

It is fitting that Gertrude Stein opens *The Making of Americans* with a slight modification of a moral tale originally to be found in the *Nichomachean Ethics* of Aristotle.

Once an angry man dragged his father along the ground through his own orchard. "Stop!" cried the groaning old man at last, "Stop! I did not drag my father beyond this tree."

It is hard living down the tempers we are born with. We all begin well, for in our youth there is nothing we are more intolerant of than our own sins writ large in others and we fight them fiercely in ourselves; but we grow old and we see that these our sins are of all sins the really harmless ones to own, nay that they give a charm to any character, and so our struggle with them dies away. . . .

These certain men and women, our grandfathers and grand-mothers, with their children born and unborn with them, some whose children were gone ahead to prepare a home to give them; all countries were full of women who brought with them many children; but only certain men and women and the children they had in them, to make many generations for them, will fill up this history for us of a family and its progress.

The Old becomes the New World in parable form; a very nineteenth-century desire to celebrate nationality in a folk tale embodying "wisdom." The denouement is a commonsense one as befits its Aristotelian source. But its fable element depends upon marrying the repetitious quality of psychological behavior to social repetition in order to make an ethical judgment. The incident is to stand ironically in the book as a dramatic representation of necessity. By changing Aristotle's "out of the house" to "through the orchard" Gertrude Stein grafts Judaic legend onto Greek. More precisely Judeo-Christian "fall" is married to Greek cycle in order to produce an interiorized model of family behavior. The revolution is, absolutely, revolution. The psychology of necessity exposes the static and categorical Freudian insight that "the unconscious aim of the quest for novelty is repetition." This insight is linked with the psychology of "beginning again," which throughout the novel is to characterize the American experience. In this system memory has the quality of defense and palliative, making the eternal truth of behavior bearable. In the realm of necessity there is no way out of the circularity. Repetition counters repetition in order to safeguard repetition. In the moralizing passage which follows, the word "tempers" connects both anger (a quality which, in the *Ethics*, was superior to desire because it contained an element of thinking) and habit of mind. Its connotations reach deep into the Western mind with their various meanings of hardening, softening, tuning, mixing, and reminds us of a now obsolete psychology which predicated behavior on the bodily fluids. Turned into a question of psychological behavior, history becomes a secret repetitive myth of the endless struggle of parent against child. The orchard tree denotes the boundary of forbidden knowledge which, once violated, makes taboo out of guilt. But here the gentle moral tone works against the pattern of determinism, for it tells us also of misplaced struggle.

In *Song of Myself* Whitman defied the European class, economic, and historical boundaries by limiting the meaning of endless genealogies to natural repetition: "born here from parents the same, and their parents the same. . . ." The same confidence is not apparent at the end of the century. Here there is a sense of crushing repetition. The repetition is not acknowledged in order to be free of it but in order to show its power. The biblical echoes of "gone ahead to prepare a home" turn biology into destiny. The child becomes father of the man. But there is irony also in the fact that the children prepare the home, and in the ambiguities of "certain," the depiction of women at the hub of necessity, not to mention a logical paradox in the fact that progress can hardly be "filled up." Filling up refers to space; progress is a movement in time. The space-time reveals a "cubist" vision of patterning space by symbolizing isolated moments whose meaning is their statistical shape.

A series of portraits of the Hersland family (one of the two major families to be described in the book, the other being the Dehnings) ensues in fairly realistic manner. The viewpoint shifts between that of the child and the investigator. The child's vision of the family home, ten acres of American freedom, contrasts with a point of view outside the family, "ten acres, with a rose hedge to fence their joys in." Sexuality is symbolized as romantic boundary and reminds us of Blake's priests "binding with briars, my joys & desires." So bounded real desire dies and Mrs. Hersland turns from her husband to women friends, suppressing gay feelings and leaning toward those who can confirm her status. But the ten acres of American freedom come under continuing ironic pressure as we learn, like a child becoming conscious of its surroundings, the endemic poverty that surrounds it, woeful tales of illegitimacies, crime, and other types of noncentrist behavior. Ambiguous questions arise. Is the house a precarious stay against disaster? a libel on social deprivation? an area of suppressing outward-reaching desire? a prison or a refuge? a children's paradise or a children's hell?

As the portrait of the father, David Hersland, emerges, the terms of the "doing" of necessity (beginning, eating, making a fortune) are revealed as an authoritarian propaganda which patterns a "paternalist" relation with children. David Hersland's most positive acts in relation to his children seem to be buying them a series of governesses paralleling his wife's involvement with the servants. Paternal involvement in "education" does not condescend to the level of content but as with his wife's relation to the servants (she prefers Anglo-Saxons and keeps a useless little blonde for a while) is an expression of social status. The mildly conspicuous consumption is a reflex of the rumors of business life outside the boundary, and out of its reifications of human life come the characterological dualisms of "attacking" and "resisting" *being*, reflecting the debt to Weininger and forming a basis for the analysis of "types."

Being is not an area of truth but of necessity; or more accurately the behavioral response to necessity. The point of view at this stage is that of a woman or child responding to the vague business disasters, rumors of dishonesty, and failure which filter through from the fringe of social consciousness, empty of content, merely giving an atmosphere of inevitability and impotence. The struggle objectively reflects an attempt to exteriorize the vision of the child toward the real world. Parental tyranny plays against the forces calling the child from the family into the public areas. The epistemological question here, as in the rest of the book, is the relation of "knowing" to "being." The American fortune seeker holds a primary relation to "being," the area of necessity. He experiences the endless frustrations of muted sexuality in family life, the endless tasks of work in capitalist conditions. The restlessness that Tocqueville noted as a characteristic of American life is internalized in the father as the neurosis of "beginning again." The accompanying "knowing" incorporates a psychology of heroic individualism with its doctrine of tragic end. Attenuated in *fin de siècle* bourgeois behavior the end is not Byronic death in battle, nor physical Napoleonic exile, but a large fortune which slips away to be replaced by an internalized meditation on death. David Hersland retains, mercifully for himself, ironically for us, only the habit of strength:

> He was strong then in beginning, he was strong in fighting, he was always changing, he was very strong in fighting. In his business living this came out in him, it came out in him in all his living, it came out in him in his ways of eating, in his ways of doctoring, in his ways of educating his children. In his business living no one went with him to an ending, always they would somewhere leave him and go on to their own finishing. To the end of his business living he had in him a big beginning, this never broke down into weakness inside him, this never broke down into impatient feeling, he was full then in his later living with impatient feeling and then later with weakness inside him but always in him too was a big beginning and this was in him to his ending.

So David Hersland sustains the dream to the end, but it appears to be a dream without enlightenment. In the combined characteristic of "strength" and "beginningness" Gertrude Stein etches a fine satire of the American paternalist businessman. Everything is compulsive and *inside*. The sentences reveal an atmosphere of involuntary angst. The irony reveals that "always changing" (itself a paradox) is sandwiched between two statements of fighting. "Fighting" belongs to the "biological" level here moving ironically to the level of "willed behavior." "Strong in beginning" suggests faddishness, novelty neurosis, a frustration of the more positive desire to make things new. These qualities "coming out" show a pseudo-exteriorization, for the compulsions deny interaction with the world. Even birth is a repetitious mechanical process. "Coming out" is a static equation of inside-outside movement; the present continuous tense contradicts the exteriorizing movement in eternal moment. By mechanical juxtaposition, business living is ironically equated with living itself. To become the task

is a lesson in estrangement as Marx knew well: "The machine accommodates itself to the *weakness* of the human being in order to make the *weak*
human being into a machine." It is fighting that underpins the equation,
and also the reductiveness of the struggle. In the social evolutionary scale
the "professions" are "higher" than business activity, but here "doctoring"
and "educating," the very means by which care should be taken of body
and mind, are undifferentiated by juxtaposition with "eating." The *buying*
of everything obliterates the distinction between nature and nurture. To
this day in America, with all too few exceptions, medicine and education
are forcibly related to the area of necessity by economic means. In Hersland's consciousness there is no completion, only endless growth. At the
real ending there is no one with him, for the "varieties" split off in Darwinian manner to continue the same struggle. The business cycles, never
complete, invoke the psychology of the endless task. Taken off the fix,
David Hersland is stuck with the "habit." To be full of "important feeling"
just this side of weakness gives an impression of emotional constipation.
The manner and habit of beginning usurp the *act* of beginning which in
any real activity only happens once. The illusion lasts until death. Human
life needs continuous reinvestment. The business-life equation means that
that reinvestment always takes the same character.

In the Martha Hersland section of the book we see a young woman's
"progress" from childhood, to adolescence, to college, to marriage, and
finally to divorce. The style moves, reversing the procedure of the earlier
section, from abstraction to narrative clarity. The buried innocence of realism is used for the purpose of satire. Martha's college is a suitably bureaucratic, intellectually mediocre, provincial, and incipiently totalitarian
community (totalitarian signifying that combination of liberal propaganda,
actual hierarchy, and bureaucratic terror of criticism which characterizes
most institutions of education) to provide a setting for the claims of marriage
(the area of necessity) in conflict with education (minimal enactment of the
public domain).

The section begins with an epistemological investigation of the nature
of "repetition," defining it initially and in a rare moment of optimism as
the pleasurable repetition inherent in the play of the child:

> Loving repeating is always in children. Loving repeating is in a
> way earth feeling. Some children have loving repeating for little
> things and story-telling, some have it as a more bottom being.
> Slowly this comes out of them in all their children being, in their
> eating, playing, crying, and laughing. Loving repeating is then in
> a way earth feeling. This is very strong in some. This is very strong
> in many, in children and in old age being. This is very strong in
> many in all ways of humorous being, this is very strong in some
> from their beginning to their ending.

The child's play is a true "buttering." The epistemology of "process sensation" reveals that there is almost an unconscious reflectiveness (loving

repeating *in*) in spontaneous activity whereby imaginative impulse (loving repeating) reveals itself in the activity irrespective of "will." Having cleared idealist purpose and empiricist objectivity from the description of "loving repeating," Gertrude Stein matches the outer narrative of her story in the inner revelation of authorial voice:

> Always then from the beginning there was in me always increasing as a conscious feeling loving repeating being, learning to know repeating in every one, hearing the whole being of any one always repeating in that one every minute of their living. There was then always in me as a bottom nature to me an earthy, resisting slow understanding, loving repeating being. As I was saying this has nothing to do with ordinary learning, in a way with ordinary living. This will be clearer later in this description.

What we witness is a struggle between words as *description* (involving objectivity and secret authorial voice) and as *action* (the admission that we act in nature acting upon ourselves). The rhythmic utterance, itself an "outering," puts together its content and its enactment of that content. Long before Charles Olson's essay "Human Universe" Gertrude Stein understood that movement leading to real knowledge lay at the level of the skin, truly at the surface of the senses in multiple rhythmic interaction. This is the difference between true knowledge or learning and the false knowledge of common sense or idealism. In Olson's words:

> There is only one thing you can do about kinetic, re-enact it. Which is why the man said, he who possesses rhythm possesses the universe. And why art is the only twin life has—its only valid metaphysic. Art does not seek to describe but to enact. And if man is once more to possess intent in his life, and to take up the responsibility implicit in his life, he has to comprehend his own process as intact, from *outside*, by way of his skin, *in*, and by his own powers of conversation, *out* again.

The movement toward a full realization of this position is counteracted by a "descriptive" impulse relying on the vicarious rhythms of Jamesian sentence essentialism whose apparent objectivity disguises a subjective plot to reinforce "reality." The now secret, now open inner discourse of Gertrude Stein's narrative mediates and assesses the respective claims. The problem was how to preserve for adult consciousness the rhythmic play of the child without the Wordsworthian conditions of memory, nostalgia, and the internalization of sense data as moral taboo with its accompanying masochistic melancholy. Gertrude Stein's style of "conscious feeling" fully exposes the conditions and epistemology of bourgeois knowing and half-reveals an alternative form of knowing.

In attempting to make "conscious feeling," or a psychology of the emotions, the ground base of knowledge, the true exteriority of the child's play becomes lost in the objective memorizing eye of the investigator. Gertrude Stein attempts to palliate that loss by making the authorial voice confess its unhappiness. The epistemological difficulty is that the "emotions" are imaginative, existential ways of attempting to control action between people, not objective springs of action as in the famous James-Lange theory that we are, for example, unhappy *because* we cry. To *double* the emotional base (the melancholy perception of melancholy) is not to concretize the perception but doubly to negate our freedom of response. "Conscious feeling" does not tell us whether our emotions are conscious attempts to magically control the world or merely awareness of feeling. At best, however, the authorial confessions of emotion which increase from now on break the illusion of realism. It is at least a preparation of a condition in which to gain the freedom to describe what true knowledge may be.

The knowledge toward which the authorial voice describes itself as moving involves that rhythmic play between inside and outside. "Conscious feeling" stands on the threshold of learning and is confirmed in the hearing or seeing of the senses. Mere awareness, however, reflects the contentless series of biological moments of which the whole life span is the shape. Interpreting their significance is the problem. Are the moments characteristic of the whole or do they find their completed action in the whole? The first relies on an epistemology of representation which Gertrude Stein hoped to avoid; the second demands an ultimately death-oriented vision. The first refuses to be surprised; the second admits discontinuity but in a homogenous process. The confession of "difficulty" and sadness by the authorial voice doubles the confusion because in it the idealistic ego declares its capacity for uncertainty and the empiricist ego declares itself a man among men. Gertrude Stein does not in fact break out of the empiricist framework. Her demand for "clarity," however much attention is diverted toward the process of that demand, is still a part of the psychology of the empirical gaze. Indeed at moments of difficulty Gertrude Stein diverts into a self-mocking satire of the investigator and his object in their circle of mutual damnation.

The struggle is between the intensity of the empirical gaze and the utterance or outering of the artist. In the empirical gaze the perceiver is damned in a Faustian movement as revelation pulls at the senses without satisfying them. Only in the utterance is the curse lifted. Loneliness, and here Gertrude Stein takes up the great romantic tradition, is the price of unspeakable visions. In the romantic tradition the process of knowledge becomes the object of the artist. Abstractly at this point Gertrude Stein summarizes in one of the many "portraits" in the work the legends of Faust, the Ancient Mariner, and Prometheus as a process of creative intimacy:

> As I was saying I had heard descriptions of this one, they were ordinary descriptions, they were not very interesting, they had not very much meaning. Then I saw this one, then I looked intensely at this one, then this one was a whole one to me. Then

the whole being of this one was inside me, it was then as possession of me. I could not get it out from inside me, it gave new meanings to many things, it made a meaning to me of damnation. I had then to tell it to this one, that was the only way to loosen myself from this one who was a whole one in me. I had then to tell this one of the meaning in damnation that this one being a whole one inside me had made clear to me. Always then later this one was a whole one to me, it was then a gentler possession of me inside me than when this one first was a whole one inside me, a damned one to me. It was still true to me later inside me the whole of this one but it did not then possess me. This is then one way of learning a whole one, by seeing them completely by one long looking at them. This is now a little more description of this one and being possessed by this one as a whole one inside me. To begin again then.

What the authorial voice attempts in this extraordinary passage is an epistemology of the empirical gaze. In the first instance the completeness of its appropriation by the object (objectivity) neutralizes in dialectical movement the freedom of the observer. Pure gaze and pure object move toward madness. Here Gertrude Stein explores the complexities lying at the heart of her attempt to mitigate objectification of process by confession of procedure. Demonic possession lies at the heart of knowledge—that much is revealed—but there is also a sense of transcendence of possession in the pure process of time as intimate feeling. The consequences of knowledge are neither social nor political but "intimate." The outering is but a half-outering. But the heart of the matter has been exposed obliquely, that the suffering and birth pangs of new meaning lie in a hidden reflexive consciousness between the looking and the "getting it out."

I think Gertrude Stein's instinct was to talk about freedom, not about truth. Unfortunately she had inherited philosophically the vicariously stabilizing bourgeois dialectic of "belief" and "truth" which reduced the importance of activity from both ends. We can sum up this section by saying that three interacting areas are examined as continuous process in the novel: human relations, the object of her discourse; a highly self-conscious authorial voice explaining the perception of that process in spite of the fact that it claims objectivity; and a series of attempts to appropriate reader reaction in confession. The first approaches an existential examination of human power relations which the categorizing dualistic characterology pulls back into satire; the second approaches Cartesian *cogito* against the presuppositions of the method by exposing the paradoxes of objectified self-consciousness; the third betrays the nervousness of the authorial voice in the desire for intimacy and authenticity which reflects the actual loss of a public (a political loss) not least exemplified in the very object of her examination, the socializing of history.

Gertrude Stein's attempt to take a "biological approach to the study of man," as W. F. R. Hardie has said of Aristotle's *Ethics*, and to render inner experience objectively has some strange effects. In some "portraits" her character dualisms are based upon bodily substance in process, a technique which takes us back to Elizabethan times and to the first attempts to describe the anatomy of melancholy. Explaining two of her most crucial categories, "resisting being" and "attacking being," she says in a passage (where one recent critic incidentally can see nothing but "coyness"):

> It is like a substance and in some it is as I was saying solid and sensitive all through it to stimulation, in some almost wooden, in some muddy and engulfing, in some thin almost like gruel, in some solid in some parts and in other parts all liquid, in some with holes like air-holes in it, in some a thin layer of it, in some hardened and cracked all through it, in some double layers of it with no connections between the layers of it. . . .
>
> I am thinking of attacking being not as an earthy kind of substance but as a pulpy not dust not dirt but a more mixed up substance, it can be slimy, gelatinous, gluey, white opaquy kind of thing and it can be white and vibrant, and clear and heated and this is all not very clear to me and I will now tell more about it.

By trying to make substance "fluid" Gertrude Stein still, however, does not attempt to go deeper than physical analogy for a description of behavior. Certainly the clue to this behaviorist vision is in Aristotle: "for outbursts of anger and sexual appetites and some other such passions, it is evident, actually alter our bodily condition, and in some men even produce fits of madness. It is plain, then, that incontinent people must be said to be in a similar condition to men asleep, mad, or drunk." But for Gertrude Stein it is the inhibited passions which cause men to stagger drunkenly in unconscious neurosis. Like a cubist portrait the characters become objects in different states of phase. Perhaps for the precise nature of the "substance" Gertrude Stein is remembering her medical lectures on the function of albuminoids, fats, and carbohydrates, or perhaps even more specifically a passage from Bergson's *Creative Evolution*, where he talks of the albuminoids, which, unlike carbohydrates and fats, are distributed evenly throughout the body with undifferentiated function and hold therefore a kind of fundamental function in physical organization. The clarity and unclarity of the albuminoids directly affect the nervous system and hence behavior. Bergsonian vitalism insisted that the body *is* the nervous system as a continuous interactive complex. The ironic emphasis throughout the book on "ways of eating" as key to bourgeois behavior (and one is irresistibly reminded of Buñuel's *Discreet Charm of the Bourgeoisie*) certainly helps to underwrite this interpretation. In the most positive sense Gertrude Stein occupies a tradition which stretches from Whitman to Michael McClure in its conviction that liberation lies in instinctual pleasure free from the demands of moral pragmatism. The education of the artist must include what we call in our own time the dialectics of liberation. The strongest elements of Gertrude Stein's satire are directed against those who are compulsively indifferent to the real, sensuous world and who in their fear of life and deification of necessity destroy themselves inwardly by outwardly repressing others.

Foucault reminds us, however, that the change from the idea of the body being affected by substances to the idea of it being affected by bodily fluids is inherent in the change from medieval to Elizabethan culture. The origins of romantic mechanism, as powerful in its way as romantic anti-mechanism, lie in the post-Elizabethan world where the movement of qualities are *"immediately* transmitted from body to soul, from humor to ideas, from organs to conduct." The quality may take the opposite nature to itself (hard-soft; like Gertrude Stein's substances here in states of phase), and it can alter according to external circumstance. Foucault gives Lorry's explanation of "melancholia." There are two sorts, one predicated on solids, the other on liquids. Linked with these images of quality is also a theory of the body as penetrable and impenetrable where melancholia becomes located not in physical cause, but within a "certain ethic of desire." We are, indeed, "on the threshold of the nineteenth century, where the irritability of the fibers will enjoy physiological and pathological fortunes." Gertrude Stein's catalogue of psychological types, moving between quality and substance, not merely doubles the theoretical strategy (category and interaction) but presents it as a dialectical process to exhibit the pathology of bourgeois behavior in its own preferred terms of perception.

In her narrative *exempla* of these discussions we see the child's innocent eye progressively turned inward and blinded in its encounter with the authoritarian inheritance of social living. The inward-turning eyes of the young American couple Redfern and Martha Hersland cause them to repeat in their lively "moral" discussions and at a half-conscious level what Gertrude Stein calls in the case of Redfern's own parents "the constant spectacle of an armed neutrality." The question of spectacle is important. Brown reminds us that the superego is based on "incorporation through the eye" of the supervisory parent and the neurosis stemming from the vision of the primal scene. The process begun in childhood takes its irresistible course, increasing unconscious taboos until the self becomes catatonically withdrawn in Kafkaesque anonymity. Here is Martha confronted with marital breakup: "In a dazed blind way she tried all ways of breaking through the walls that confined her. She threw herself against them with impatient energy and again she tried to destroy them piece by piece. She was always thrown back bruised and dazed and never quite certain whence came the blow, how it was dealt or why."

It is in the third section of the novel that the interior voice of the narrative most exposes itself. The confession turns to method itself: "To be using a new word in my writing is to me a very difficult thing." One of the qualities of Gertrude Stein's prose is that it attempts to imitate the sensuous quality of its referents and to make representations without logic or linear argument. Here the new word represents the new perception, or the breakthrough, of a kind of Darwinian spontaneous variation. The emphasis is, however, a very American one, for it makes the new *word* a concrete locus of truth. "In writing a word must be for me really an existing thing, it has a place for me as living, this is the way I feel about me writing." The authorial voice attempts to make the word an act and a place simultaneously. But evolutionary sentences and spontaneous words depict loss of faith in public speech, for they equate the written word with action. They also deny the heuristic principle that the whole can be observed in the parts. The new becomes exceptional and *difficult*, for Gertrude Stein swings between what Sartre calls a totalizing investigation and a "scholasticism" of the totality. For the word cannot be made flesh except by the principle of transcendence which the whole drift of her argument is designed to obliterate. The "word's place for me" makes what should be a public gesture into an intimate act. Public address becomes an object of knowledge. Privacy and public life are replaced by intimacy and authenticity. The irreducible realism of the new word in the irreducible *a priori* of the sentence symbolizing biological process points to a double subjectivity whose consciousness is "unhappy." Existence becomes the "work" of "inner life." The authorial viewpoint struggles with the same problems as the characters it illuminates in its perceptual gaze. At this dark moment the inner and outer visions equate themselves in entropic silence. The new word, rather than denoting an epistemological leap in the dark, reinforces the weight pulling back the hopeless gesture toward freedom. A black comedy results with characters repeating their contorted roles, dancing to the strings of sense ambiguities, power seeking, and the corrosive propagandas of success and failure; a veritable *Dunciad* of Santayana-style fanaticism, everyone redoubling his efforts having lost sight of his aim. The right rich American family living is a space of nightmare, where no one talks to each other, no one listens, and no one comes directly in contact with experience. The hell of half-response emerges chiefly in Julia who is strung between the competitive forces of father and husband, "having some worn out feeling in not having completed passional loving."

The David Hersland section which ends the book is an examination of what happens to history in America. Private-public interaction turns into individualist awareness of intimacy and authenticity in a vision which death has almost entirely appropriated. Verbal nouns denote David Hersland's "habits" which are variously biological *and* cultural, forming "keys" to his behavior: "David Hersland was interested in dying, in loving, in talking, in listening, in ways of eating, in ways of being going on being in living." Self-reflexive consciousness (the Cartesian *cogito*) is made into a statement of alienation. "Interest" alienates. It denotes relational possibility with its overtones of claiming legal title, of disposition to economic matters, not to mention unearned profit. As a passive verb, it is, in the words of the Oxford dictionary, to cause to have an "objective interest or concern" in the "progress or fate of a matter." Personal interest therefore has the same epistemological assumptions as pragmatism and the empiricist approach to behavior. The making of Americans becomes the unmaking of one American. We do not know whether David is objectively or subjectively interested in dying, learning, and so forth. Certainly the verbal nouns connote movement through time, but they are also isolated as moments leading to patterns of contentless multiplicity, not completed linear truth. Each of these verbal nouns is made the subject of a distinct paragraph as the descriptive process is built up. Perhaps the best analogy, ignoring the obvious one of cubism, is from music of the same period because music takes place in time and in sound which comes closer to the writer's art. Certainly *The Making of Americans* has to be read aloud for full effect.

Speaking of the increasing chromaticism in the music of Liszt and Chopin, and the subsequent weakening of the central role of the tonic, Charles Rosen, in a recent book on Schönberg, points to Wagner as accelerating this process until no key could be assigned to a particular phrase, and indeed, any chord might be "ambiguously" interpreted according to position: "This suspension of clear small-scale harmonic sense is what enabled Wagner to give the impression of long-range action, in which the music proceeds in a series of waves and not in small articulated steps. . . . The polarizing function of modulation has been developed so far and so radically that the resistance of the framework that gives it its meaning—the tonic triad—has been weakened beyond repair." In this pattern "stability" is only a local effect. The shape *in* time is more important than the shape *of* time. One might compare the tonic triad in the effect of its traditional classical certainty with the structure of the sentence and its system of subordinations within its never complete realism. Like Wagner's music the Steinian sentence has this suspension of small-scale sense within larger patterns. The process is, strictly speaking, endless. Here are a series of key transformations about David Hersland by way of conclusion:

> He was interested in this thing sometimes almost completely interested in this thing, he was sometimes almost completely interested in being certain that something would be happening, he was sometimes almost completely interested in being certain that something was going to be happening and then that thing was happening.

> He was almost completely clearly feeling being one being living. He was almost completely clearly feeling being one going on being living. He was not completely needing this thing being one going on being living. He was almost completely needing the thing being one being living.

> Some are ones needing being one succeeding in living. Some are ones not needing being one succeeding in living, David Hersland was such a one, he was one needing being one succeeding in living. He was one not needing being one succeeding in living. If

he had gone on in being living he would not have been one succeeding in living, he would not have been one needing being one
succeeding in living. If he had been one going on in being living
he might have been succeeding in living. He might have been one
succeeding in living if he had been one going on being living and
then he would not have been needing being one succeeding in
living. He was not going on being living after the ending of the
beginning of middle living. He was not being living after the ending of the beginning of middle living.

In the first paragraph the "thing" refers to "something would be happening" of the previous paragraph. The representational content is obliterated
in process. The noun becomes a future conditional happening. To take
interest in action as though it were a concrete thing replaces "activity" and
the capacity to reflect on change by internalizing meditation whose correspondence with the outside world is that of secret design. David Hersland
attempts to "outer" his vision but is trapped in empiricist paradox which
reveals itself as a psychological trappedness, not a system of logic. The
"and" preceding the final phrase, the "added" truth of the Jamesian empiricism, destroys "certainty," for it describes the relation of consciousness
to the new as biological awareness only. It shows David Hersland's wavering hold on his capacity for action and its mysterious relation to the real
action, which must be radically discontinuous with it.

The second paragraph performs a reverse function. In the first paragraph the earnestness of "interest" vicariously seeks certainty everywhere
and is ironically undercut by "sometimes," "almost completely," "interested in being certain," and so forth. Here "clearly feeling" attempts to
give emotion a cognitive role whose feeling of itself is paradoxically empiricist "clarity." But the "almost" has two effects. The first two sentences
suggest that being and process, necessity and biological awareness, are the
same thing. "Almost" suggests that David Hersland never quite understands that the drive for emotional clarity is a neurosis reflecting a world
in which bourgeois fear of emotional life has made consciousness into an
object. But it also suggests subtly, in the gap between "almost feeling" and
"almost needing," that clarity is no more necessary in feeling than necessity
itself directly underpins objective realism. It is a rare note of hope. The
third sentence of the second paragraph negates the equation of "being one
being living" and "being one going on being living." David Hersland almost
distinguishes internalized biological awareness from simply living and almost realizes that the very equation is hardly necessary. There is a sense
of exhaustion as well as of freedom. The fourth sentence in Hegelian manner negates the negation, and the "almost" again has a curious role, for it
prevents repetition as much as it prevents consciousness of change. The
restless psychology of dialectic has nothing but its own motion for content.

To put more radically what one critic has already suggested, there is no possibility of real superseding in Gertrude Stein's character dialectics. But she undoubtedly invoked the Hegelian method for her own purposes, not least we may suspect yet again to subvert James, who had attacked Hegel because he dared to "insult" the "bound-respecters" of space and time and in so doing made "manifest his own deformity." Yet it is precisely the "stable distinctions" that Gertrude Stein's whole method attacks while adopting a strategy of proceeding by them. The interior awareness of biological "space-time" process subverts the physical models for psychological stability. But at the same time it refuses to move from awareness to consciousness. The unblocking of awareness at the level of the skin is only a prior condition of freedom, however much "society" seeks to keep the argument at that level. Satire suggests ironically the success of socialized behavior. In short Gertrude Stein's satire is half-done from inside the same system it attacks. Perhaps all satire is, *pace* the academy, negative, and is symptomatic of relinquishing the public realm while expressing its hatred of the necessity for so doing.

The third paragraph, though more confident in tone, is still radically ambiguous. But at least there is a suggestion that success may be disengaged from necessity, thus refusing the crude socialization of Darwinian struggle. David Hersland moves between asserting and denying its possibility. Merely to suggest that "success" may not belong to the realm of necessity, however, inverts traditional American propaganda for the terms of social visibility. There is a sense of threshold reached, and the ironies are muted as biological death is, for the first time, accepted for what it is; that is, something distinct from bourgeois death consciousness, the hidden secret of the family. For a brief moment David Hersland almost breaks free.

But finally for David Hersland biological process becomes an object of knowledge which supersedes everything else. The patterns of bourgeois melancholy are confidently and lyrically exposed. Vicarious decisions are made about the inevitable. "David Hersland was one deciding about eating something." We might compare Prufrock's "Do I dare to eat a peach?" The process is one of catatonic withdrawal.

The real freedom in the novel is reserved for that inner authorial voice. It has freed itself in the exposure of death as the essence of American family living. *The Making of Americans*, like most great satires, ends with a shrug of the shoulders: "Any family living can be one existing and some can remember something of such thing." The triumph of the outer gaze moving from inner narrative perception is complete and the quest for discontinuity made irrelevant. The artist has obliquely and secretly triumphed. But the triumph is achieved as a halfway revolution of intimacy, authenticity, and mere awareness. It is all inadvertently summed up in a booklist note in one of the back pages of her notebooks. That neglect of the public in listening privately to its own freedoms in the artist's public work, the metaphysics of quest which underwrite bourgeois competitiveness and psychological impotence, the barriers to freedom in the totalitarian socializing of history, and the problems of distinguishing the vicarious outering of gaze in "quest from real exteriority, all seem to find a concentrated expression in a concrete image of four words:

> Melville
> White Whale
> Walls

Sherwood Anderson: American Mythopoeist

Benjamin T. Spencer

It is not surprising that during the past generation Sherwood Anderson's literary reputation should have suffered an eclipse, for the renascent American literature which he envisioned and in part exemplified half a century ago was rooted in the soil and in a sense of wonder and mystery alien both to the realism which preceded it and to the sophisticated naturalism that followed it. To be sure, his work has rarely evoked the degree of condescension found in the dictum of Miss Susan Sontag, who, somewhat ironically upbraiding Anderson for taking himself too seriously, recently dismissed *Winesburg, Ohio* as "bad to the point of being laughable." In view of her addiction to the New Wave of French fiction, with its commitment to sensory surfaces and psychic fragmentation as contrasted with Anderson's concern for inwardness and identity, her verdict is inevitable.

That such a reversal in his literary fortunes would occur Anderson himself surmised over forty years ago. Acknowledging himself to be not a great writer but rather a "crude woodsman" who had been "received into the affection of princes," he prophesied that "the intellectuals are in for their inning" and that he would be "pushed aside." And indeed, though more judiciously than Miss Sontag, estimable critics have concurred in assigning Anderson a lesser rank than did his early contemporaries. Soon after the author's death Lionel Trilling, while confessing a "residue of admiration" for his integrity and his authenticity as the voice of a groping generation, nevertheless adjudged him too innocent of both the European literary heritage and the role of ideas in psychic maturity. More recently Tony Tanner, in an analysis of the naïveté of American writers, found in Anderson a distressing example of such writers' penchant for "uncritical empathy" and for dealing in discrete moments of feeling without that "exegetical intelligence" which has shaped all durable literature.

From *American Literature* 41, no. 1 (March 1969). © 1969 by Duke University Press.

Between these two extremes of detraction grounded on the one hand in an aversion to "meaning" and on the other in an intellectualization of art through formal control and complexity, Anderson has consistently had, as a recent volume assessing his achievement shows, his body of apologists. Faulkner, Van Wyck Brooks, Irving Howe, Malcolm Cowley have been among those who have found a distinctiveness and a distinction in the best of his work, especially when it is related to the literary atmosphere of the first quarter of the century. Indeed, Anderson himself throughout his career could never separate his writing from its national context, and this cisatlantic cultural context impelled him toward the mythic, toward the archetypal and the elemental, rather than toward the urban and sociological. Repeatedly he spoke of his love for America, sometimes as "this damn mixed-up country of ours," sometimes as a land "so violent and huge and gorgeous and rich and willing to be loved." Moreover, he thought of himself as representatively and comprehensively "the American Man," as he wrote Brooks, explaining that by virtue of his varied occupational background he could take into himself "salesmen, businessmen, foxy fellows, laborers, all among whom I have lived." But not only did he feel himself to be "a composite essence of it all"; he also could experience, he declared with Whitman-like assurance, an "actual physical feeling of being completely *en rapport* with every man, woman, and child along a street" and, in turn on some days "people by thousands drift[ed] in and out" of him. Like Whitman, too, he contained multitudes and contradictions; he was, as he said, a compound of the "cold, moral man of the North" and "the warm pagan blood of the South . . . striving to become an artist" and "to put down roots into the American soil and not quite doing it."

In reiterating through the second and third decades of the century his view that the crucial deficiency among American writers was that "Our imaginations are not yet fired by love of our native soil," Anderson had in mind of course more than the affirmation of a simple American pastoralism. The "soil," indeed, included the darker lives of the people who lived on it or near it; or, as he wrote to Dreiser in the mid-1930s, the redemption of such lives must lie so far as the writer is concerned not in any philosophical or ideological projection from his pen but in telling "the simple story of lives" and by the telling, counteracting the loneliness and "terrible dullness" that afflicted the American people. He had in mind, no doubt, such a story as the first which he had drafted for *Winesburg*, as he later related its genesis in "A Part of Earth"—a story called "Hands," in which he conveys the pathetic misunderstanding of the character whom he described as the "town mystery" of Winesburg, Wing Biddlebaum, whose hands reached out to others like "the wings of an imprisoned bird." Later the same motif is repeated in the hero of *Poor White*, whose loneliness and vague ambition impel him to a restless wandering and finally to an awkward and alienated marriage, and in the heroine of *Kit Brandon*, whose intense loneliness Anderson asserts to be characteristic of American life. Indeed Anderson's return to his native "soil" led him to the discovery of what he called "the loneliest people on earth," and his sensitive treatment of these people has led the novelist Herbert Gold to call him one of the purest poets of isolation and loneliness. To Irving Howe he seemed to have expressed the "myth" of American loneliness. Even with this theme, therefore, the mythopoeic Anderson apparently had initially found his imaginative stance. He was not, of course, in the strict etymological sense of the word a "mythopoeist," a maker of myths; but his imagination achieved its finest expression in narratives such as "Death in the Woods" or in parts of *Dark Laughter* where the preternatural or archetypal not only gave it unity and direction but also evoked a connotative style approaching the idiom of poetry. The term is therefore broadly used here as the most adequately comprehensive one to indicate the orientation and mode of Anderson's fiction as contrasted with those of such contemporary naturalists or realists as Dreiser and Lewis.

II

This persistent concern with loneliness both in Anderson's own life and in that of his characters, Lionel Trilling has asserted, is in part traceable to his excessive reliance on intuition and observation and to his unfortunate assumption that his community lay in the "stable and the craftsman's shop" rather than in the "members of the European tradition of thought." That Anderson was only superficially and erratically involved with the literary and philosophical past of Europe is undoubtedly true. As late as 1939 he could declare that he did not know what a "usable past" is, and that his concern was rather to live intensely in the present. In effect Anderson was emphasizing the inductive and the autochthonous as primary in the literary imagination, as Emerson, Thoreau, and Whitman had done before him; or, in anticipation of William Carlos Williams, he was committing himself to the principle that only the local thing is universal. By concentrating on the elemental tensions of provincial life he was assuming, as Mark Twain had done with the Mississippi, that the archetypes of human character and situation would most surely emerge, and that by returning to "nature" or the "soil" American literature would find at once its uniqueness and its authenticity. Hence his dismissal also of recent European art as a model for American artists. How irrelevant is Whistler's pictorial mode, he wrote in the 1920s, to a valid expression of the "rolling sensuous hills . . . voluptuously beautiful" in California; and how silly are those painters who follow Gauguin when the varied life and color of New Orleans is available to them. The "half-sick neurotics, calling themselves artists" as they stumbled about the California hills, apparently resembled the "terrible . . . shuffling lot" of Americans he later observed in Paris. Yet from writers whom he venerated as the great fictional craftsmen of Europe—Turgenev, Balzac, Cervantes—he induced what seemed to him to be the fundamental principle for a durable American literature: indigenous integrity. These authors were "deeply buried . . . in the soil out of which they had come," he asserted in *A Story Teller's Story*; they had known their own people intimately and had spoken "out of them" with "infinite delicacy and understanding." With this indigenous commitment, Anderson believed, he and other American writers could belong to "an America alive . . . no longer a despised cultural foster child of Europe."

Though Anderson found only a limited relevance for the cisatlantic writer in the literary modes and cultural traditions of Europe, he was by no means indifferent to the American past. His involvement lay deeper than the love which he professed to Gertrude Stein for "this damn mixed-up country of ours"; it approached, indeed, a mythic assent to what he viewed as a liberating cultural destiny often reiterated from the early days of the Republic—a belief in what his younger contemporaries Pound and Fitzgerald praised as the old largeness and generosity which they felt had marked the ante-bellum national character. The substance and inclination of Anderson's nationality may be inferred from the names of the five Americans whom he concluded, in an evening's discussion with his wife, to be the greatest his country had produced: Jefferson, Lincoln, Emerson, Whitman, and Henry Adams. For Lincoln and Whitman, as well as for Twain and Dreiser, he confessed a special affinity because they, with origins like his own, had had to take time to put roots down in a thin cultural soil and, ingenuous and confused, to confront a "complex and intricate world." The somewhat unexpected inclusion of Henry Adams may be accounted for by the common anxiety that both authors felt not only about the shattering effects of the machine on the older American values but also about the redemptive agency of some new mythic force which would bring unity out of multiplicity in American life. A more sustained influence, however, Anderson felt in Whitman, whose attempt to supplant a narrow and repressive Puritanism with large democratic vistas of brotherhood and loving perceptions he believed had been betrayed by later generations of American authors. Like Whitman he tried to project the democratic beyond concept into myth—into man's link with primordial forces of earth and into an eventual return to what the older poet in "Passage to India" had called "reason's early paradise."

Though early in his literary career Anderson was puzzled that Twain had not generally been placed with Whitman "among the two or three really great American artists," he was especially drawn to the Missouri author as a salient example of the American writer's plight and failure. In Twain he perceived a literary pioneer whom the "cultural fellows," as he termed them, had tried in vain to get hold of. Yet ironically, despite Twain's brave achievement and his bold disregard of literary precedent, Anderson sadly observed, he had never been able to attain full literary stature because the America which nurtured him was a "land of children, broken off from the culture of the world." As a part of this, Twain seemed to Anderson to have been caught up in the country's dominant shrillness and cheapness, with his literary talent thereby perverted and dwarfed. But an additional factor in Twain's failure seemed to Anderson to be his voluntary removal during the latter half of his literary life to the East, where he became subservient to what the latter termed the "feminine force" of the "tired, thin New England atmosphere." It is not surprising, therefore, that in *Dark Laughter* Anderson, through his hero Bruce Dudley, should charge Twain with deserting the imaginatively rich Mississippi River milieu and reverting to childhood or trivial themes which could be summed up as "T'witchetty, T'weedlety, T'wadelty, T'wum!" By ignoring the "big continental poetry" of rivers before it was choked off by the invasions of commerce, Twain in Anderson's eyes was in part responsible for the fact that the great River had become a "lost river," now "lonely and empty," and perhaps symbolic of the "lost youth of Middle America." Indeed *Dark Laughter* may be viewed as Anderson's mythopoeic projection of the repressed Dionysiac forces which the early Twain at times adumbrated and then gradually abandoned for genteel values and concerns. At the heart of the book is Anderson's elegy for a literary ancestor who should have expressed the mythic force of the heartland but who lost his touch with elemental things.

For Anderson, therefore, America evoked both intense devotion and recurrent despair—perhaps an inevitable dualism in one whose deepest cultural convictions were grounded in an ante-bellum version of the American dream as articulated by his five greatest Americans. Jeffersonian as he essentially was, he inclined to trace the confusion and vulgarity of his age to the displacement of the agrarian base of American society. This older America he could envision in *Windy McPherson's Son* as a kind of pastoral paradise, a land of milk and honey wherein the shocks of abundant corn were "orderly armies" which the American pioneer had conscripted from the barren frontier, as it were, "to defend his home against the grim attacking armies of want." It was this agrarian faith, he wrote in *Mid-American Chants*, that had lured the immigrant races westward and had developed a deep affinity with the earth spirit, with the fields as "sacred places" in whose fertility the impulses to human aggression had vanished. And as small organic centers in this agrarian richness, he felt, there had developed the Midwestern villages, which, in turn, had nurtured a vital individualism whereby both men and women lived with courage and hope and with a pride in craftsmanship and independence such as that joyously possessed by Sponge Martin in *Dark Laughter*. Hence Anderson's characterization of Bidwell, Ohio, the setting of much of *Poor White*: it was a pleasant and prosperous town whose people were like a "great family," and, like those in other Midwestern towns in the 1880s, were undergoing a "time of waiting" as they tried to understand themselves and turned inward to ponder the utopianism of Bellamy and the atheism of Ingersoll.

The snake which had crept into this agrarian Eden and its village culture was, in Anderson's reiterated view, a new reliance on the external benefits supposedly conferred by technological progress rather than on the inner resources conferred by Nature and the Soul on the Emersonian and Thoreauvian and Whitmanian self. On this contest of the humane self and the nonhuman machine most of Anderson's major works revolve—especially

Windy McPherson's Son, Winesburg, Poor White, Dark Laughter, and *Beyond Desire*. During his youth, Anderson told a college audience in 1939, the increasing obsession with getting ahead had resulted in a pervasive confusion through the identification of happiness with possessions. Inevitably the towns had become tainted with a competitiveness and greed which left them, as he phrased it in *Windy McPherson's Son*, "great, crawling slimy thing[s] lying in wait amid the cornfields." Young Sam McPherson's success in Chicago, like Anderson's, brought its disenchantment with such "blind grappling for gain"; having "realised the American dream" in its perverted form at the end of the century, Sam felt impelled toward the larger quest of seeking truth—toward the risks of that "sweet Christian philosophy of failure [which] has been unknown among us." Because of a ruthless greed whetted by the new industrialism, Anderson suggests in the novel, "Deep in our American souls the wolves still howl." The consequent dehumanization of the old communities could be seen in both city and village. Reflecting on the brutal crowds in New York, Sam is no doubt expressing Anderson's attitude when he concludes that "American men and women have not learned to be clean and noble and natural, like their forests and their wide, clean plains." And in villages like Winesburg, as Anderson declared in his *Memoirs*, the blind faith in machines had not brought beauty but had left a residue of fragmented grotesques—villagers who, as he explains in introducing the stories of *Winesburg*, in the disintegration of the agrarian community had been driven to seize upon some narrow or partial truth and, in a desperate attempt to sustain their lives, to make it an obsessive and destructive absolute. In a disconsolate mood of acceptance Anderson conceded in his *Memoirs* that "it may just be that America had promised men too much, that it had always promised men too much." In effect he was conceding the subversion of a major myth—one fused by his own experience from the old dream of the garden, Jeffersonian agrarianism, Transcendentalism, the repudiation of Puritanism, and the pastoral abundance of the West. His vision of a land where the earth and brotherhood would allow the satisfaction of the basic human desires had yielded to the reality of masses of "perverse children," lost and lonely.

III

Anderson's mythic focus, however, lay below the national or politico-economic level. America and the West were at last but symbolic media or indices for him, as they had been for the Transcendentalists—transient entities to be valued only to the degree that they proved instrumental in releasing the deific forces of primal satisfactions of man's being. This assumption Anderson made clear in his early days as a writer by insisting in the *Little Review* that the so-called "new note" in American literature was in reality "as old as the world," involving as it did the "reinjection of truth and honesty into the craft" of writing and also the "right to speak out of the body and the soul of youth, rather than through the bodies and souls of master craftsmen who are gone. [¶] In all the world there is no such thing as an old sunrise, an old wind upon the cheeks. . . ." Similarly, as he later recalled in his *Memoirs,* he and other members of the Chicago group during the First World War were, above all, trying "to free life . . . from certain bonds" and "to bring something back," including the "flesh" which the genteel realism of the preceding generation had excluded. In short, they wished to divert American literature from what they conceived to be its secondary focus on the socio-political and redirect it to the primary and recurring experiences —to what Anderson in his later years was willing to call "the great tradition" which, he said, goes on and on and is kept straight only with difficulty. "All the morality of the artist," he concluded, "is involved in it."

Convinced as he was that the greatest obstacle to the return to the "oldness" and the "great tradition" lay in the fidelity to fact espoused by the realistic school, Anderson insisted that American writers look primarily within themselves, for "there is this common thing we all have . . . so essentially alike, deep down the same dreams, aspirations, hungers." In effect Anderson was urging a mythopoetic approach to the same native scenes that Howells and Twain had often depicted. Like Conrad, he believed that "the artist descends within himself" and "appeals to that part of our being which is not dependent on wisdom" by speaking to "our capacity for delight and wonder, to the sense of mystery surrounding our lives; to our sense of pity, and beauty, and pain. . . . " In the Midwestern lives about him Anderson found the "dreams, aspirations, hungers" which could evoke the "sense of mystery . . . of pity, and beauty, and pain," and the transatlantic understanding and approval which his stories had elicited confirmed his belief that the American writer could best strike the universal note through such an emphasis. That the "subjective impulse" and the imagined world should take precedence for the author over fact he continued to affirm throughout his life, proclaiming consistently the satisfactions that he had found as a "slave to the people of . . . [his] imaginary world."

As the clearest repository of archetypal emotions and situations Anderson, like Hawthorne and Twain before him, used the small town or village for his settings. In the commonplace Midwest world, he wrote in 1918 in "A New Testament," there is a "sense of infinite things." As an illustration of this "sense" he proffered his story "In a Strange Town," in which the persona observes an ordinary couple—a woman and a man accompanying her to place her husband's coffined body on the train. The people are of no importance, he explained in a comment on the story, but they are involved with Death, which *is* "important, majestic." The very strangeness of the town, he also explained, served to afford a kind of aesthetic distance in which the irrelevant and superficial disappeared and the elemental constants of mortality emerged. To be sure, Anderson at times and for the most part in nonfictional works, did view the town, both Midwestern and Southern, in a sociological perspective. But even here he frequently sounded mythic overtones, as he did in his perceptive remark in *Home Town* (1940) that the small community had always been the "back-bone of the living thing we call America" because it lies halfway between the cities (which breed ideas) and the soil (which breeds strength).

On this soil as an autochthonous matrix Anderson consistently relied for the vital norms of his stories as well as of the villages themselves, enclosed as they generally were with their cornfields. It was the soil which in his belief gave the "power" to life and literature (to use Emerson's dual terminology from "Experience") as the towns and cities gave the "form." The towns and villages, therefore of *Winesburg* or *Dark Laughter* and *Poor White*, rich as they may be in human archetypes, are never autonomous, but always have their traffic with the surrounding fields and woods. Acknowledging the "bucolic" in his nature, Anderson spoke of himself as a "Western novelist" and of his region as the "corn-growing, industrial Middle West." It is "my land," he wrote in 1918 to Van Wyck Brooks. "Good or bad, it's all I'll ever have." But only incidentally was he concerned with its industrial aspects; for what he wished to do, he said, was to "write beautifully, create beautifully . . . in this thing in which I am born"— indeed, to "pour a dream over it." His perspective was thus visionary; his imagination was committed to distant vistas, not merely democratic but essentially mythic. Stirred during the years of the Chicago renaissance by something new and fresh in the air, as he said in the *Little Review*, he was convinced that "the great basin of the Mississippi . . . is one day to be the seat of the culture of the universe." The current industrialism of the region he interpreted in a quasi-mythic figure as a cold and damp winter beneath whose lifeless surface something was "trying to break through." Envisioning that vernal rebirth in the West when "newer, braver gods" would reign and a new and joyous race would develop, he composed his *Mid-American Chants*—essentially a volume of free-verse hymns extolling an American paradise where nature and man were one. In the very term "chants" Anderson suggested both the style and purpose of his poems. Eschewing both the elegiac disenchantment with the region to be found in Master's *Spoon River Anthology* and the virile bravado of Sandburg's contemporaneous *Cornhuskers*, these visionary poems in their diction and movement and tone are Anderson's most explicit venture into the mythopoeic strain.

In the *Chants* Anderson essentially invoked the earth spirit, as he wrote in "Mid-American Prayer," with its Indian memories and rites to supplant the Puritanism dominant in the region and to remind the Midwestern people of the "lurking sounds, sights, smells of old things." The theme of the repressive sterility of New England was, indeed, and oft-reiterated one in Anderson's most prolific years, for he had come to feel that the major mission of the Midwestern writer, as he explained in his *Memoirs*, was on behalf of a new race to put "the flesh back in our literature" and thereby to counteract the "feminine force" of the older section. The New England notion of America was not blood deep, he asserted in a Lawrentian vein in *A Story Teller's Story*; and since blood will tell, the increasingly thinner blood of the Northeastern man must yield to that type more richly blended from the "dreaming nations" which had settled the Midwest. In place of an "old-maid civilization" derived from a cold, stony New England, Anderson saw emerging from the "rich warm land" and polyglot racial strains a kind of Dionysiac brotherhood in which the humane spirit of Lincoln would be the heroic and brooding presence. Thus, as he wrote in *Dark Laughter*, the "whole middle American empire" would be restored as a land of rivers and prairies and forests "to live in, make love in, dance in."

Despite Anderson's invocation of rivers and forests and the "old savages" therein "striving toward gods," the dominant symbol in *Mid-American Chants* was the pastoral cornfield—a symbol indigenous to the country as a whole, though especially so to the Upper Mississippi Valley. Confessing himself to be a "kind of cornfed mystic," Anderson was always moved by the sight of a cornfield, and later in his life at Marion, Virginia, he remarked that such fields were distinctively American. Not surprisingly, the cabin where he chose to do his first writing in Virginia was, as he wrote Stieglitz, a "deserted one in a big cornfield on top of a mountain. Cowbells in the distance, the soft whisper of the corn." Nearly a decade earlier, in *Windy McPherson's Son* he had protested the popular conception of corn as being merely the feed for horses and steers; instead the shocks of corn stood for him as majestic symbols of a land in which man had been freed from hunger. Yet two years later, in *Mid-American Chants* the cornfields moved from a mere symbol of well-being into the sacramental: they became a "sacred vessel" filled with a sweet oil which had reawakened man to a sense of the beautiful, old things. Moreover, the long aisles of corn in their orderly planting not only signified man's conquest of the forest; they seemed even to run to the throne of the gods. "Deep in the cornfields the gods come to life," he wrote in "War,"/ "Gods that have waited, gods that we knew not." In the cornfields, indeed, Anderson found a new impulse to prayer through what he felt to be their mythic reincarnation of the earth spirit; in them he found an elemental vitality to counteract the sterile religious tradition of New England. Back of the "grim city," Chicago, he saw "new beauties in the standing corn" and, in "Song to New Song," dreamt of "singers yet to come" when the city had fallen dead upon its coal heap. Or again, in "Song for Lonely Roads," he reasserted his faith that "The gods wait in the corn,/ The soul of song is in the land." During these years, indeed, as he wrote in one of his letters, he felt that "a man cannot be a pessimist who lives near a brook or a cornfield"; and in another he confessed to the "notion" that none of his writing "should be published that could not be read aloud in the presence of a cornfield."

IV

By the 1930s, and especially with the stringencies of the economic depression, Anderson's corn gods had proved illusory. In his earlier romantic commitment to the divinely organic he had construed the machine as a seductive threat to a Mid-American reunion with the earth. In those days he could still believe in the triumph of the egg—to use the title of one of his volumes which contains the story "The Egg," a humorous treatment of the effort of the persona's father to subdue a simple egg by standing it on end or forcing it into a bottle. His humiliating defeat, one may suppose, may be taken to reflect Anderson's earlier view of the futility of human attempts to contain or subdue the primal, organic forces of nature. From a similarly organic perspective the inventor-hero of *Poor White* (1920), appearing at evening and pantomiming with his flailing arms and mechanical strides the motions of his cabbage-planting machine, becomes for the farmers a frightening specter whose grotesque movements are a graphic index to consequences which Anderson felt must follow the replacement of the organic by the mechanical. As imposed behavior and technological demands had succeeded freedom and personal pride in craftsmanship, he commented in *Poor White*, men and women had become like mice; and in *Dark Laughter* he spoke of the "tired and nervous" cities, with their "murmur of voices coming out of a pit." Over a decade later in his Southern novel *Kit Brandon* only a few of the mountain girls seemed to him to have retained a self-respect and proud individualism akin to that of "the day of America's greater richness." Of this older richness another symbol was the horse, which as a boy in the livery stable he had found to be the most beautiful thing about him and superior to many of the men with whom he had to deal. In the industrial era, he wrote in *A Story Teller's Story*, since machines had supplanted horses, his own nightmare as a writer was that of being caught as a prisoner under the "great iron bell"—that is, we may interpret, under the great humanly wrought inanimate doom. Perhaps his vivid story "The Man Who Became a Woman," in which a young boy whose devotion to the horse Pick-it-boy has cleansed his lustful thoughts and dreams and who, mistaken for a girl at night in the stable loft by the drunken horse-swipes, flees naked to the neighboring slaughterhouse yard and undergoes a kind of traumatic burial in the skeleton of a horse—perhaps this story reflects something of the psychic effect on Anderson of the destruction of his mythopoeic America. At any rate, even by the time of the publication of *Horses and Men* (1923), in which he celebrated both the vibrant fascination of the horse and the innocence of youth, he confessed to Stieglitz that he had learned at last that horses and men are different and that in the confrontation of human dilemmas the equine would no longer "suffice."

Though by the mid-1920s Anderson felt obliged to abandon many of the mythic assumptions of his Midwestern years, he could not renounce entirely the demands of his mythopoeic imagination. During the last fifteen years of his life, therefore, he sought new centers and media for a viable myth which would bring unity and beauty to his life. This he found in the mill towns of the new industrial South and in the girls who worked therein. Formerly the South had been for Anderson New Orleans and the southern Mississippi, where the dark, ironic laughter of the Negroes had seemed to express for him an elemental spontaneity and a vital sense of life—a "touch with things" such as stones, trees, houses, fields, and tools, as Bruce Dudley enviously concedes in *Dark Laughter*—which made the members of a subject race humanly superior to the sterile life about them. In the later Southern novels the Negroes have all but disappeared, and though the mill girls, who as a vital center supplant them, are too much at the mercy of their factory world to embody any mythic assurance, they do point to a redemptive feminine principle which Anderson, like Henry Adams, found in his later years the surest counteragent to the disintegrating power of the machine. It was the American woman, he concluded in the 1930s, who alone could reintroduce the "mystery" which a technological age had dispelled and without which "we are lost men." Since American women at their best had not yet been "enervated spiritually" by the machine or accepted from it a "vicarious feeling of power," perhaps women, he argued in his book entitled by that phrase, might rescue the American man "crushed and puzzled" as he was in a mechanical maze.

Yet, just as Anderson's phrase "perhaps women" suggests an acknowledged tentativeness in his later mythic formulations, so his treatment of the machine in his late works often discloses a new ambiguity. As his recourse to woman for salvation reflects Adams's adoration of the Virgin, so his discovery of the poetry as well as the power of the machine follows the example of another of his five "greatest Americans," Whitman, who abandoned the pastoral milieu of "the splendid silent sun" to discover the poetry of ferries and locomotives and crowded streets. Yet Anderson, with his earlier sustained distrust of the machine, could not free himself from an ambivalence in his later years; he felt both awe and impotence, he confessed, in the presence of the vast order and power and beauty of machinery, and his tribute to Lindbergh as an emergent culture hero, the new type of machine man, as well as his sympathetic portrayal of the speed-obsessed Kit Brandon, the heroine of a late novel, betrays an uneasiness not present, say, in his characterizations of Sponge Martin and the Negroes in *Dark Laughter*. Yet watching the superb technology of the whirling machines, his hero Red Oliver, in *Beyond Desire*, no doubt reflected much of Anderson's later attitude by confessing that he felt "exultant" and that here was "American genius" at work—America at "its finest." Two years earlier, in 1930, Anderson had declared that he would no longer be "one of the . . . protestors against the machine age" but henceforth would "go to machinery" as if it were mountains or forest or rivers. Hence his poem to the beneficence of the automobile and his attempts to catch the excitement of the cotton mills in his "Machine Song" or "Loom Dance." Yet he also felt impelled to express the more sinister admixture of fear and awe experienced in the presence of the textile machines, whose hypnotic speed and incessant shuttle rhythms could induce in Molly Seabright, a mill girl in *Beyond Desire*, an indifference and confusion which led to a loss of identification with the human world about her. Modern American industry, he concluded ambivalently in *Perhaps Women* (1932), was indeed a "dance," a "flow of refined power," to which men lifted up their eyes in worshipful adoration. Surely in such statements the failure of Anderson to approach the machine as if it were mountains and rivers is manifest. The earlier mythopoeic imagination has become bifurcated into myth and poetry; the validity of the myth is not felt, and the poetry is an act of will rather than of imagination. In this bifurcation and desiccation one may no doubt find much of the explanation for Anderson's decline in his later years.

V

To his inclination and commitment to a mythopoeic approach to American experience both Anderson's literary achievements and his shortcomings may ultimately be traced. From the time of the First World War until his death at the beginning of the Second, he consistently aligned his writing with a focal purpose summarily stated in *A Story Teller's Story:* "It is my aim to be true to the essence of things." In probing for the "essence" he ran the romantic risk of neglecting the existential substance of American experience, and hence one may feel, as Lionel Trilling has asserted, a deficiency of the sensory and concrete in his work. If one adds to this mythic concern for patterns and forces behind the phenomenal world Anderson's addiction to the psychic and intuitive as the arbiters of reality, one approaches what to Anderson seemed the "poetic" factor in the mythopoeic imagination. Hence neither the region nor the nation was a substantial entity for him; neither ideologies nor sociological formulas were significant norms for his fictional perspective. The "new note" in American literature, as he said, was really a return to the old sensations and desires; and hence his women have few social concerns or ambitions, nor are they regional types: Aline Grey and Clara Butterworth and Kit Brandon play their roles rather as versions of the White Goddess reasserting primal humanity, as did Adams's Virgin.

Anderson's style, like his larger fictional perspective, is an organic product of his mythopoeic approach. Rooted in the naive, in wonder, in the mystic and the intuitive, his expression shapes itself subjectively from emotions or associations, as Tanner has shown, at the expense of tight syntax, controlled structure, and purified or precise diction. And yet Anderson's vagaries are, for the most part, those which he inherited (and somewhat intensified) through a major native tradition initiated by the Transcendentalists and involving in its course Whitman, Twain, Stein, and Salinger. If from Anderson's pen this style becomes one in which each sentence affords only a fragmentary glimpse, as Tanner contends, perhaps the limitation is in part explained by Anderson's conclusion that in an immense land where all men are strangers to one another, the writer can "only snatch at fragments" and be true to his "own inner impulses." That a cisatlantic orientation may be necessary to the full comprehension of Anderson's style, with its indigenous tone and idiom, is suggested by Gertrude Stein's contention that "Anderson had a genius for using the sentence to convey a direct emotion, this was in the great american [*sic*] tradition, and that really except Sherwood there was no one in America who could write a clear and passionate sentence." Early in his career Anderson in "An Apology for Crudity" asserted that if American writing were to have force and authenticity, it would have to forgo objectivity for the "subjective impulse," and that an honest crudity would have to precede the "gift of beauty and subtlety in prose." However consciously stylized and contrived his own apparent artlessness may be, his "subjective impulse" extended outward like Whitman's in an effort to catch "the essence of things," and his reputation will be most secure among those who can accept the mythopoeic assumptions which nurtured and shaped his imagination.

Sinclair Lewis
and the Implied America

James Lea

That Sinclair Lewis recorded the social history of a major sector of the American population in the first third of the twentieth century is a generally accepted literary axiom. An ear for the rhythms of Midwestern speech and a descriptive power which E. M. Forster likened to that of photography combined with intelligent curiosity to produce in him one of the country's most astute social critics. Especially during the decade of the twenties, the mirror which his novels held up to the material crassness and spiritual befuddlement of middle-class Americans established Lewis as a forceful cultural commentator, a best-selling novelist and the darling even of those whom he damned.

But Sinclair Lewis wrote—or, we should say created—another sort of American history as well. In the work of most social satirists, criticism of the contemporary world derives in large part form the writer's assumption that there was, or is, or could be a better world. Lewis assumed that there *had been* a better world, or at least a better America, and that his twentieth century had betrayed the potential for freedom and productive happiness implicit in the people, life, and very land itself of eighteenth- and nineteenth-century America. Sheldon Grebstein has observed that "the theme of Lewis's serious books, beginning with *Main Street*, is disillusionment." But disillusionment is more than a theme; it is the tonal foundation of Lewis's major works. Lewis's picture of a banal present is underpinned by his concept of a more meaningful past, a concept which is manifested both in implication by contrast and in detailed representation throughout his principal novels. The center-stage actions of Lewis's novels—the struggling of Carol Kennicott, the blustering of George Babbitt, the soul-searching of Neil Kingsblood—are always played against a back-drop depicting the

From *Clio* 3, no. 1 (October 1973). © 1973 by Robert H. Canary and Henry Kozicki.

America that has been, and that by extension could be, but is being perverted.

To aid the process of delineating the character of the American past which is continuously implied by Lewis, I have chosen to examine seven novels which present an interesting historical chronology through the periods in which they are set. *The God-Seeker*, although not published until 1949, is Lewis's only work that follows Sir Walter Scott's classic definition of the historical novel. Its action is laid between 1830 and 1856. *Main Street* (1920) covers the years 1907 to 1920, *Babbitt* (1922) the years 1920 to 1922. *Arrowsmith* (1925) is set between 1897 and 1923, and *Elmer Gantry* (1927) between 1902 and 1926. *Dodsworth* (1929), called by some Lewis's last great novel, covers the years 1903 to 1928. *Kingsblood Royal* (1947), lying far beyond the limits of Lewis's "golden decade" with respect to quality as well as to publication date, treats the period 1944 to 1946. While Lewis calls upon his vision of the American past in other novels, these seven offer particularly illuminating examples of the methods by which he describes what may be called his Implied America.

When Sinclair Lewis was a boy, in the late years of the nineteenth century, Sauk Centre, Minnesota, was only two generations removed from the crude huts and the cavalry stockade of the early plains pioneers. It is quite probable that when he boarded the train for New Haven and the lifetime that lay beyond, he took with him at least a germinating sense of the land which earlier eyes had seen and earlier feet had walked. This imaginative perspective, reinforced by the sort of research which stood behind every Lewis novel, appears in the setting and characters of *The God-Seeker*. In this, the last Lewis novel published during the author's lifetime, Aaron Gadd traces in microcosm the trail of the Yankee missionaries and merchants who settled the northern plains in the mid-1800s. Physically, Aaron moves from his boyhood home in Clunford, Massachusetts (where his American lineage is firmly established in the person of his grandfather, a Revolutionary War veteran) to a missionary post among the Sioux and Chippewa, and from there to the growing frontier camp which becomes St. Paul, where he sets up shop as a housing contractor. In the course of his progress, Aaron is identified—either directly or by association—with most of the forces which shaped the character of the American frontier as Lewis sees it represented in pioneer Minnesota. Perhaps more idealistic than many of the early migrants, Aaron departs Massachusetts "to go west! To bring order and civilization to the aborigines!" Traveling by train, river boat, canoe, and horseback to his job at the Mission, he encounters the fur-traders, voyageurs, gamblers, soldiers, preachers and barons of commerce who are writing the history of the territory. His frontier mentors are Caesar Lanark, one of the traders who "pioneered the way for a lot of scoundrels who want to butcher the Indians at once, instead of gently pasturing them and milking them over the years." Squire Harge, the missionary whose mission is to impose his own Christianity upon a people with a centuries-old cultural identity of their own, and the St. Paul carpenter

Seth Buckbee, whose social posture in the free, new land is supported by his belief that "the Irish and the Scandanavians were as shiftless as the Injuns." Among them and the proud but desperate Indians, and on the face of the Minnesota wilderness, Aaron finds his place alongside other frontiersmen, "men with stars in their heads and solid boots on their feet, men with a sense of elevated piety and of slick politics and land-options, in their violent and everwestering lives."

If Aaron Gadd's physical travels and his contact with the western up-and-comers seem to reflect the movements of the Yankee pioneers, his spiritual progress represents the development of Lewis's ideal of the nation-builder. Beginning in a youthful innocence shaped by his father's New England Puritanism, Aaron is seized by a religious conviction and a mis-sionary fervor which are perhaps similar to the fever for free land and a free life which drove more than one mid-nineteenth century easterner west-ward. His service at the Mission loosens his resolution and implants in his mind grave doubts about the superiority of his creed and his white race. His escape to St. Paul and his success as a carpenter in a town where building is as much a function of the heart as of the hands mark his initiation into that class of men who neither advertised nor traded but actually pro-duced the flesh and bone of America. Aaron's representative spiritual com-pleteness is not realized, however, until he takes the ultimate democratic step and helps his own employees organize a labor union. So Aaron Gadd—and, Lewis seems to say, all those who helped shape "a just, orderly and enduring commonwealth"—travels the circle from the innocence of exter-nally ordered youth to the dawning human awareness of autonomous manhood.

The God-Seeker must be judged one of Lewis's weaker novels. But in the consideration of his formulation of an American past clearly in contrast with his American present it holds an important place. In this novel Lewis establishes his idea that the crassness and pettiness of the twentieth century are both a perversion of the ideals of a time when "men cast longer shad-ows" and at the same time directly traceable to it. For as Aaron Gadd ascends to success on the Minnesota frontier, Lewis continues to remind us that "the future history of Minnesota, like that of every other state in the Union, would be the inept struggle of mechanics and farmers and shopkeepers to get back a little of what they never intended to give away in the first place." *The God-Seeker* probably should not be read as Lewis's "final statement," but rather as an indication of his late recognition of the need for a preliminary statement. The total impact of the body of Lewis's major work resides not only in its social character, but in its historical character as well; it is in *The God-Seeker* that Lewis gives substance to that age of promise against which his age of disillusionment is measured.

From this level of historical perspective, we read more than irony in the frontispiece note to *Main Street*: "Main Street is the climax of civilization. That this Ford car might stand in front of the Bon Ton Store, Hannibal invaded Rome and Erasmus wrote in Oxford cloisters . . . Our railway station is the final aspiration of architecture." For Lewis seems to consider it very important that we understand that the life and times of Gopher Prairie which he is about to present are of historical value in a double sense: they are a representation both of what we are and of what we have made out of what we could have been. Main Street does not exist as an independent construct, but as a point on the continuum of time, accountable to the past and to the future.

The Implied America makes briefer appearances in *Main Street* than in *The God-Seeker*, but it appears early. The novel opens with a description of Carol Milford (later to be Mrs. Will Kennicott) standing "on a hill by the Mississippi where Chippewas camped two generations ago." It is 1907, and the Chippewas Lewis refers to are the sons and grandsons of the Chippewas whose hunting grounds Aaron Gadd had walked. In those two generations, much has changed; the Indians and the frontiersmen are gone, although their presence remains woven into the fabric of the era: "She saw no Indians now . . . Nor was she thinking of squaws and portages, and the Yankee fur-traders whose shadows were all about her."

Main Street, of course, marked Lewis's turn, as Robert J. Griffin phrases it, from "the celebration of national potentialities to the castigation of national failings." Lewis's five novels which preceded it were buoyant little books of apprenticeship, and, except for *The Job* (1917), they are rarely discussed today. In those early novels, Lewis treated the escape of the young innocent from the village into the outside world, a sort of idealized spiritual autobiography. By 1920, however, his vision seems to have panned down from the fresh leaves fluttering in the blue sky to the roots of life in America and the native soil in which they were sunk.

While Lewis's five apprenticeship novels dealt with the native Midwestern villager confronting the smug big city establishment, *Main Street* relates the confrontation between urban naïveté and small-town smugness. Carol Kennicott was brought up in "Mankato, which is not a prairie town, but in its garden-sheltered streets and aisles of elms is white and green New England reborn." Her childhood is delightfully secure, her education—both at home and at Blodgett College—is entertaining and shallow. She steps out on the trail to Gopher Prairie garbed in Aaron Gadd's Yankee innocence and idealism, a cultural pioneer armed with the Good Book-and-broadaxe of her own Romantic self-assurance.

Though she finds the plains no longer menaced by outraged Indians; though "the days of pioneering, of lassies in sunbonnets, and bears killed with axes in piney clearings, are deader now than Camelot"; still Carol encounters history in Gopher Prairie. There is the sense of the seemingly eternal land, into which she retreats in her most desperate moments. There are the Scandanavian farmers, belying the calender by clawing the earth as their pioneer predecessors had done fifty years before: "a forest clearing: pathetic new furrows straggling among stumps, a clumsy log cabin chinked with mud and roofed with hay."

There are the last frontiersmen, the Champ Perrys, whom Carol sees as merely another possible means to her end, but whom Lewis suggests are the remnants of an age degraded by "the era of aeroplanes and syndicalism." And there are the records of the Minnesota Territorial Pioneers. Carol muses for a moment over the years when Gopher Prairie consisted of four cabins and a stockade, when men and women lived with difficulty and vigor and a certain buoyancy, now lost. For Carol, stranded in an America which is "neither the heroic old nor the sophisticated new," the past is a panacea which she frivolously schemes to reclaim.

For Sinclair Lewis, the past is yesterday's reality. Miles Bjornstam is its only vitally extant embodiment in the novel. His socialism is the modern echo of the dead frontier equalitarianism. In a sense, he is a tragic anachronism, caught, as Mark Schorer would say, between "the individual impulse for freedom and the social impulse to restrict it." Bjornstam no sooner abandons his freedom of foot and spirit for an attempted accommodation with twentieth-century domesticity than he is crushed. When he leaves Gopher Prairie to find a new starting place, his directions are northward to Alberta and backward to the frontier past. Bjornstam's judgment upon the town, Lewis suggests, is the judgment of American history upon the Main Street of the American present.

For all its high towers of commerce and sprawling circumference of modern economic splendor, the city of Zenith, as Lewis depicts it in *Babbitt*, is built over a pit. Located in Lewis's mythical Midwestern state of Winnemac, Zenith was "an ancient settlement in 1897, one hundred and five years old, with two hundred thousand population." By 1920, it is a city on the make, rudely displacing its nineteenth-century buildings with "clean towers . . . thrusting them from the business center," re-surfacing its land— formerly a "wilderness of rank second-growth elms and oaks and maples"—with the "bright roofs and immaculate turf and amazing comfort" of Floral Heights. If in 1856, Aaron Gadd's St. Paul was on its way to becoming "the most mammoth, gorgeous and powerful metropolis on this globe," Zenith is Lewis's unpleasant representation of what the realization of such a goal can produce.

Turning from his examination of the mid-American village to a study of the mid-American city, Lewis finds a social phenomenon inflated to the bursting point with the hot air of its own gusto. Zenith has long since lost touch with its agricultural beginnings; that aspect of its history is no longer even relevant. For generations its citizens have occupied themselves with the manufacturing of products, the buying and selling of property, the lending of money and other vocations which contribute to the collection of masses of people into easily manipulable units. In the process, they have all but eradicated the city's link with the land and their own link with their forebears. For their own purposes, they have no history: in Zenith in 1920, Lewis writes, "an old house is one which was built before 1880."

The result of Zenith's exorcism of its past to make room for a booming present and a "promising" future is reflected in the befuddlement which creeps into the soul of George Babbitt. Outwardly brash and blustering,

Babbitt inwardly represents a population in limbo, at a point in history when, as Walter Lippman has written, "they have lost the civilized traditions their ancestors brought from Europe and are groping to find new ways of life." Cut off from a vital past, they have lost the vitality to pursue their personal dreams: Babbitt is a real estate salesman who has dreamed of being a lawyer; Paul Riesling is a roofing salesman who has dreamed of playing the violin; even Chum Frink, author of versified pap and "Ads That Add," has once dreamed of being a poet.

It seems that Zenith's pioneer past is all the more conspicuous because of its absence in the present. Modernity's hollowness and shallowness go unrelieved, except when Babbitt discovers the restorative effects of a vacation in the Maine woods with Paul Riesling. It is a return to the frontier for Babbitt, a chance to touch "something sort of eternal" that has eluded him in the city. The woods invite Babbitt's dreams of what is strangely like an idealized frontier life: "If he could but take up a backwoods claim with a man like Joe, work hard with his hands, be free and noisy in a flannel shirt, and never come back to this dull decency!" The plague of city life disappears as Babbitt imagines "Moccasins—six-gun—frontier town—gamblers—."

But in the end it is too late for Babbitt. The frontier is too far past. He can't draw from it sufficient courage to face down the forces of materialism that Zenith can marshall at the first sign of individual diversity. At the end of the novel, there is a quiet note of hope as Babbitt encourages his son to "Tell 'em to go to the devil!" But Babbitt disappears again into the crowd of faces—mindless behind their smiles—of Americans who have severed themselves from history.

In April, 1926, Sinclair Lewis was awarded the Pulitzer Prize for his ninth novel, *Arrowsmith*. With considerable malice aforethought, he rejected the award on the grounds that he would not be bought off by an agency of the tasteless American literary establishment. Given the probability that after the Pulitzer debacle of 1920 Lewis would have welcomed any opportunity to snub the Columbia University trustees, it is nonetheless interesting that *Arrowsmith* gave him that opportunity. For Martin Arrowsmith is also a man who will not be bought off by the establishment, and this is only one of the traits which mark him as Lewis's most nearly autobiographical character.

With this novel, Lewis undertook a series of studies of the professional person that developed from Arrowsmith the doctor through Gantry the preacher to Dodsworth the retired manufacturer and others. Each of these different characters moves in a milieu in which the historical past, Lewis's Implied America, plays a significant role. In *Arrowsmith*, the role is dual, incorporating history both as personal lineage and as a standard for the measurement of modern contrasts.

The story of Martin Arrowsmith opens sometime in the early nineteenth century, with a brief vignette in which a fourteen-year-old girl is driving a wagon westward. Despite the pleadings of her fevered father and her responsibility for a horde of younger brothers and sisters, she presses on: "There's a whole lot of new things I aim to be seeing!" The girl turns out to be Martin Arrowsmith's great-grandmother, and thus Lewis establishes an historical referent for Arrowsmith's character, linking him personally to the past.

Because he has a new story to tell, Lewis revolves his artistic gels a few turns and sheds a new light on Winnemac and Zenith. As he describes it, the character of Zenith's contemporary population has not changed noticeably since Babbitt, but Lewis works to re-establish the area's historical groundings. Prior to taking a satiric crack at the University of Winnemac, Lewis explains that the state's tradition goes back to the Revolutionary War. Zenith, as we learned earlier, was founded in 1792—the year Kentucky joined the Union—but outlying counties were not settled until 1860. (Of Elk Mills, Martin's hometown, we learn nothing directly.) Then, having established that Winnemac is to a notable degree rooted in history and that Martin Arrowsmith is very much rooted in it, Lewis seems to drop the matter. His chief interest in this novel is the development of a contemporary pioneer stalking the frontier of science.

Hazard offers an interpretive construct of American history as representing three stages of pioneering: the regional stage, in which man attempts to control nature; the industrial stage, in which man attempts to control the labors of his fellow men; and the spiritual stage, in which man attempts to control himself. She suggests that *Arrowsmith* contains elements of all three stages, that Martin's ancestors were the regional pioneers, that his contemporaries are the industrial pioneers and that he becomes a spiritual pioneer in the manner of the Transcendentalists when, at the end of the novel, he resigns wealth and celebrity in New York and goes off to the Vermont woods to pursue pure science. Hazard's speculation should be extended somewhat, for from his first practice in the plains village of Wheatsylvania, Martin is seeking first of all to serve his fellow man. There is, therefore, a strain of the spiritual pioneer running in him throughout.

But Lewis is treating modern science in much the same way he treated the physical wilderness in *The God-Seeker* and the cultural wilderness in *Main Street*—that is, as an untracked space in which man could leave prints as deep and as permanent as he could make them. Martin Arrowsmith remains the regional pioneer in this open domain, much as Miles Bjornstam remains one in the broad lands beyond the short horizons of Gopher Prairie. Both of them occasionally pass through the clutches of their industrial contemporaries, sometimes with tragic consequences. But in the end each succeeds because each is free. For Martin this freedom is the fruit of the dogged determination inherited from his pioneer great-grandmother. Arrowsmith is characterized as Lewis may have characterized himself: a solitary and beleaguered spiritual survivor of the frontier past.

Although *Elmer Gantry* is set between the years 1902 and 1926, the voice of the narrator obviously speaks from the late years of that span. In the chapters dealing with Elmer's days as a student at Terwillinger College and as a rising young cleric, the voice is almost reflective in tone: "His Mother was able to give Elmer the three hundred dollars a year which, with his summer earnings in harvest field and lumber-yard, was enough to support him—in Terwillinger, in 1902." Speaking not in the past tense but in a sort of past-imperfect, Lewis writes of Gritzmacher Springs, the home of Terwillinger College: "The springs have dried up and the Gritz-machers have gone to Los Angeles, to sell bungalows and delicatessen." On the day of Elmer's ordination ceremony, "It was 1905; there was as yet no Ford nearer than Fort Scott." The author's sense of historical distance becomes clearer when he writes: "In the virginal days of 1905 section gangs went out to work on the railway line not by gasoline power but on a hand-car, a platform with two horizontal bars worked up and down like pump-handles." This impression of a distance in time and place between the narrative voice and the action of the novel is one which Lewis manages to achieve in several pieces of his fiction. One effect of this device is to raise the reader above the plane of the story, to give him a share in the author's omniscience, to allow him to view plot and characters in the temporal context in which the author has placed them. Rather than weaving historical dates and events into the narrative, Lewis alludes to their presence outside the narrative. By this means, the action of the novel is historically anchored, and, at the same time, the reader is aware that the action is distinct from, but contiguous to, other events of its time.

The clarification of this distinction is particularly important to the reading of *Elmer Gantry*, for in this novel Lewis has created his least sympathetic character. Elmer is a universal type, rather than a character representative of some national epidemic of the heart. He is the operator immemorial, egocentric and ruthless. He is Squire Harge with no core of sincere religious zeal; he is Juanita Haydock with no limit to his perfidy; he is Babbit with no suspicion of his fallibility. Elmer Gantry's prototype is the ahistorical Ananias.

But Elmer does not move independently of history. There are around him the identifiable characters of the twenties: Billy Sunday, Amiee Semple McPherson, and others. And there is the suggestion that historical perspective itself can be manipulated, as when Katie Jonas, of Utica, New York, acquires enough money to be able to put on the aristocratic home, lineage, and name of Sister Sharon Falconer.

So while *Elmer Gantry* is set before Lewis's ubiquitous backdrop of history, the relationship between the present and the past is somewhat different in this novel from that in those novels we have previously examined. Lewis is describing here not so much a society brought to its present state by its betrayal of its own past, as a phenomenon—Elmer—emerging in a society that is as historically ready for him as its early nineteenth-century counterpart was ready for the revivalists of that time.

Maxwell Geismar has offered the idea that the plots of Lewis's early apprenticeship novels turn on the confrontation between the aristocratic Easterner (or his tradition) and the Western democratic hero, and that the novel's complications arise from this conflict of cultural values. By comparison, *Dodsworth* turns largely upon the confrontation between a johnny-come-lately American and an historically imposing Europe. By the time *Dodsworth* was published in 1929, Sinclair Lewis's fame and increasing fortune had allowed him to make several trips to Europe and to get glimpses both of Europeans at home and of Americans away from home. The sense of contrast which such glimpses aroused in him, and the notion that between the American and his European heritage was a gulf even wider than the one which separated the American from his own national past, were manifested in Lewis's thirteenth novel.

Dodsworth is another admirable frontiersman who has outlived his time. The Champ Perrys of *Main Street* were of this sort, lost in an age when their courage and determination no longer had the focus provided by torturing elements and belligerent Indians. In the industrial twentieth century, Dodsworth has pioneered new designs and techniques in the building of automobiles. He has outfought the industrial reactionaries and the financial bamboozlers, and he has lasted long enough to see the Revelation, the product of his own work and bearing the stamp of his own imagination, become a world-famous motorcar. By 1925, he has become the victim of advancing civilization; his outpost on the leading edge of the industrial frontier has been overrun from behind by a more efficient—albeit less refined—technology. Dodsworth at age fifty is an analogical national soul who has experienced the rigors of regional and industrial pioneering and now—like America in the 1920s—stands at the threshold of a new spiritual frontier and a new self-perception.

Dodsworth's European experience is Lewis's idealization of a post-pioneer America learning to live comfortably and unobtrusively with itself. From a posture of boom-time smugness rooted in the mood of *Main Street*— "Three guests had come in these new-fangled automobiles, for it was now 1903, the climax of civilization"—Sam evolves through self-doubt to an ultimate new sense of his place in the commonality of human experience. Europe is a testing ground on which his personal character—and, by implication, America's national character—is tried. His first considered reaction to Europe is historically framed. Though he is enchanted by the atmosphere of England and disgusted by the superficiality of the Continental salons, he—like Irving's Geoffrey Crayon a century earlier—is unequivocally impressed by the air of solid permanence which he senses in old Europe. He finds Paris "stately, aloof, gray with history, eternally quiet at heart for all its superficial clamor." This captain of American industry responds to Europe with the shrinking awe of a small child: "Gee . . . this town has been here a long time, I guess. . . . This town knows a lot. . . . I wish I did!" He reflects on the lost bliss of his egocentric American ignorance. "Life was a lot simpler then. We knew we were It. We knew that Europe was unbathed and broke, and that America was the world's only bulwark against Bolshevism and famine."

Dodsworth becomes first defensive, then contemplative in response to Europeanism's challenge to Americanism. In defense, he calls not upon America's "steel-and-glass skyscrapers and miraculous cement-and-glass factories and tiled kitchens and wireless antennae and popular magazines," but upon the tradition of his national past: "the tradition of pioneers pushing to the westward, across the Alleghenies, through the forests of Kentucky and Tennessee, on to the bleeding plains of Kansas, on to Oregon and California, a religious procession, sleeping always in danger, never resting, and opening a new home for a hundred million people."

After the disintegration of his marriage, and under the subtle tutelage of Edith Cortwright, Sam achieves a stability of perspective which suggests a new Lewis vision of the place of America in the history of the world. Sam is no longer unsure of himself as "the rich American . . . uncouth and untraditional" in comparison to the European cultural heritage. Fully aware of his failings, he learns to revel in being "a most American American." After despair and self-denunciation, Sam can gloat "I am real!"

Dodsworth, in the chronology of Lewis's Implied America, marks a shift in setting and characterization from the Midwest of the Kennicotts and the Babbitts and an expansion in the scope of Lewis's historical perspective. No longer does a ponderous American history loom behind a frantic modern Zenith, reducing its loftiest self-serving ambitions to sheerest banality. In this novel, Lewis's vision of the entire American character, past and present, is re-adjusted through a thoughtful comparison with European civilization. Dodsworth himself is "not a Babbitt, not a Rotarian, not an Elk, not a deacon." He is as sound and sympathetic an American character as Lewis created before 1930. When, at the conclusion of the novel, Sam establishes something of a hold on happiness, he becomes complete as Lewis's post-pioneer American, still endowed with his natural awkwardness, perhaps, but possessed of a new historical and societal equilibrium.

Kingsblood Royal was a highly topical novel when it was published in 1947, since it deals with racial tension in the small Midwestern city of Grand Republic. It also provides a chronologically and thematically satisfactory culmination to this study of Lewis's use of an implied American past. In the central plot device in the novel—Neil Kingsblood's discovery of his own past and that discovery's effect upon him and those around him—Lewis seems to have found a feasible working model of his own sense of history and the individual's relationship to it.

In 1944, Neil Kingsblood has "always wanted to be a frontiersman, an Astor Company trader of 1820 on the Minnesota border," but his life is a world and a couple of World Wars away from the frontier. It is his father's unlikely theory that the family line may carry the blood of Henry VIII which puts Neil on the trail of the genealogy of his mother's ancestors. He is excited enough to press his research when he learns that this great-great-great-grandfather was one Xavier Pic, "a voyageur for the Hudson's Bay Company," a man belonging "not to evening and mist and gossiping cowbells but to alert mornings on the glittering rapids of unknown rivers." Neil's investigation gives form to the desire of a more mature post-war

America to ally itself with a national past which, two decades before, it had been happy to ignore.

The startling discovery that Xavier Pic was a full-blooded Negro—thereby making Neil a Negro by legal definition—opens the door to another exercise in spiritual pioneering, and also lays the foundation for Lewis's explication of his own hypothesis on the relationship of the past to the present. As Neil determines to testify to his racial status, regardless of the cost, the confluence of forces which time brings to bear upon the equilibrium of any given moment becomes apparent. The mixture of blood lines in Neil's ancestry is like the mixture of social, political and economic forces which, along with the whims of countless individuals, accounts for the character of an age. The inevitable conclusion to the story, with Neil waging a valiant but futile fight for his rights as a human being, rounds out not only Lewis's condemnation of racism in America, but also his implication that a nation must be willing to recognize and act upon the obligations imposed by its own past.

The chronological domain of these seven Sinclair Lewis novels spans more than a century of American history. During that century, America changed more radically in structure and character than any other nation had ever changed in an equal amount of time. The Upper Midwest passed from a state of wilderness to a state of prosperous modernity, and Lewis took it as one of his artistic tasks to chronicle that passage. As an observer of American life, he planted himself squarely in the twentieth century, but his vision ranged backward to the beginning and forward to the unknown but hopeful future. In *The God-Seeker*, he attempted to capture the flavor of optimism and expectancy and the nearly equal potentialities for glory and for ruin which pervaded the nineteenth-century frontier. He warned his readers to look carefully upon those pioneers, for what they did and saw and said would count for something in the development of the quality of the years which followed theirs. *Main Street, Babbitt, Arrowsmith, Elmer Gantry,* and *Dodsworth*, written amidst the fury of the decade in which they were set, described the harvest which the twentieth century was reaping from its own reckless tending of the national garden. *Kingsblood Royal* suggested the degree of courage which is necessary for a people to ride successfully the crest of their own history.

It would be presumptuous, even silly, to suggest that the body of Sinclair Lewis's novels constitutes a grand epic of the American Midwest. But the evidence of his attention not only to documentary accuracy but also to historical perspective in the recording of his era's manners and meanness clearly implies that Lewis was generally and artistically conscious of the prominent role which history plays in the affairs of his most memorable characters.

Negatives of Hope: A Reading
of Katherine Anne Porter

Joseph Wiesenfarth

Through the telescope of time Katherine Anne Porter looks like an early prophet of ecology: "We may indeed reach the moon someday," she wrote in 1950, "and I dare predict that will happen before we have devised a decent system of city garbage disposal." Before muggings and bombings made headlines daily, before assassinations in the 1960s and skyjackings in the 1970s became commonplace, before anarchy became a way of death in everyday life, Miss Porter wrote, "The savages and thugs and hoodlums have really broken loose all over the world, we have mob rule and no mistake, so much for our liberal and humane notions!" But one does not read Porter for prophecy. She is a truth-teller. She speaks of what was and what is; what will be follows as day does night. What she wants most to do and what she does best is to penetrate the present darkness with a compassionately merciless eye. Therefore she praises Thomas Hardy, who said, "My motto is, first correctly diagnose the complaint—in this case human ills—and ascertain the cause: then set about finding a remedy if one exists."

It is neither strange nor curious, then, that one or another of Katherine Anne Porter's stories should reveal some unhealthy symptoms, or that taken together they should compose an anatomy of man in the modern world. Moreover, Miss Porter's view of modern life makes this pathological concern inevitable: "All the conscious and recollected years of my life have been lived to this day," she said on June 21, 1940, "under the heavy threat of world catastrophe, and most of the energies of my mind and spirit have been spent in the effort to grasp the meaning of those threats, to trace them to their sources and to understand the logic of this majestic and terrible failure of the life of man in the Western world." Taken collectively, as a record of her attempt to understand, Katherine Anne Porter's stories project

From *Renascence* 25, no. 2 (Winter 1973). © 1973 by the Catholic Renascence Society.

a disordered world in which conflict is generated in lives where self-knowledge and love have failed to find their place. If individual men and women
fail, how can those collocations of men and women we call nations succeed?
With a classically hard-headed sense of human frailty, Porter insists that
many cannot succeed where two or three have failed. To diagnose the
"cause of human ills," then, she goes straight to the individual to test his
self-knowledge and his love.

"I have not much interest in anyone's personal history after the tenth
year," Porter writes, "not even my own. Whatever one was going to be
was all prepared for before that." Her story "The Downward Path to Wisdom" is a gloss on this remark. It tells how a child of kindergarten age,
Stephen, becomes "badly mixed up in his mind." It opens one morning
with Stephen eating peanuts in his parents' bedroom.

> "Bright-looking specimen, isn't he?" asked Papa, stretching his
> long legs and reaching for his bathrobe. "I suppose you'll say it's
> my fault he's dumb as an ox."
> "He's my little baby, my only baby," said Mama richly, hugging
> him, "and he's a dear lamb." His neck and shoulders were quite
> boneless in her firm embrace. He stopped chewing long enough
> to receive a kiss on his crumby chin. "He's sweet as clover," said
> Mama. The baby went on chewing.
> "Look at him staring like an owl," said Papa.
> Mama said, "He's an angel and I'll never get used to having
> him."
> "We'd be better off if we never *had* had him," said Papa.

To the father the retarded child is a bird or a beast, an owl or an ox; to the
mother he is more politely inhuman: he is a lamb, he is clover, he is an
angel. In the narrator's words, Stephen with his parents is "like a bear cub
in a warm litter." To his parents the child is never a person and consequently to the observer his parents are less than human.

The husband's remark that no child at all would be better than Stephen
brings about an argument with his wife which so terrifies Stephen that he
throws up his breakfast and is taken by his nurse Marjory to his grandmother's. With Grandma and her crochety maid Old Janet, Stephen is
alternately indulged and scolded. To straighten him out his Uncle David
teaches him to say "please" and "thank you," to blow up balloons and to
box. As a child in a world of grownup confusion, Stephen can understand
neither his elders nor himself. Kindergarten is Stephen's only happiness:
"The people around him were his size; he didn't have always to be stretching his neck up to faces bent over him, and he could sit on the chair without
having to climb. All the children had names, like Frances and Evelyn and
Agatha and Edward and Martin, and his own name was Stephen. He was
not Mama's 'Baby,' nor Papa's 'Old Man'; he was not Uncle David's 'Fellow'
or Grandma's 'Darling,' or even Old Janet's 'Bad Boy.' He was Stephen."
To maintain this sense of self and foster goodfellowship, Stephen takes on

one occasion some of Uncle David's balloons, and on another he takes lemon and sugar to make lemonade for his classmate Frances. Old Janet accuses him of stealing, and Uncle David calls him a thief, finding him a true son of his brother-in-law. Stephen must now leave Grandma's. The balloons become a pretext for a bitter argument between Uncle David and his sister, but Grandma, having had enough, dismisses her son and daughter: " 'I'm sick of you both. Now let me alone and stop this noise. Go away,' said Grandma in a wavering voice. She took out her handkerchief and wiped first one eye and then the other and said, 'All this hate, hate—what for? . . . So this is the way it turns out. Well, let me alone.' " A moment later Stephen supports Grandma with his own epiphany of hate: "Stephen began suddenly to sing to himself, a quiet, inside song so Mama would not hear. He sang his new secret; it was a comfortable, sleepy song: 'I hate Papa, I hate Mama, I hate Grandma, I hate Uncle David, I hate Old Janet, I hate Marjory, I hate Papa, I hate Mama . . . ' " This story, told from a child's point of view, is anything but childish. It is an account of civilized disorder is a respectable middle-class family. The child, like everyone else in the story, can gain no self-understanding within the context of the family. Moreover, Stephen's world of needs is as foreign to his elders as theirs of codes is to him, and they use the child's unwitting mistakes to fight maliciously with each other. This is precisely how the major crises of the story are brought about: the pretexts for arguments between adults are peanuts, lemonade, and balloons. The child who is presumed retarded is the natural symbol of the truly retarded grownups. Given enough people like those who surround Stephen and martyr him, hating themselves without knowing it, the world would be entitled to its measure of terrible confusion and awful failure. Certainly this is Porter's logic in "The Downward Path to Wisdom."

At the opposite end of the age-scale, Stephen's counterpart is Granny Weatherall, who, in her eightieth year and at the moment of her death, realizes that she has built her life for sixty years on a failure to love. Having been jilted at age twenty, she married another man, reared a family after his death and in face of hardship, and entered into an agreement with God about her salvation. At the moment of her dying she drops her rosary beads and grabs the hand of her son because she realizes that beads will not do, she must have something alive. But the order of Granny's whole life has been like the beads in her hand and has substituted for the love she did not have and even denied needing. The truth forces itself on Granny, however, who affirming the submerged mode of her existence blows out the light of her life. What she has missed, Stephen now misses. Youth and age are one in the need to know themselves and to love another, and neither code nor order can substitute for such needs.

If Stephen's story is that of a child in search of himself—of his attempt to find his "I" as Stephen rather than as "Baby" or "Fellow" or "Bad Boy"—the short novel "Noon Wine" is the story of a man without any personal identity or desire for self-knowledge. It is the story of a man making every attempt to live an orderly life without ever learning that order must emanate from within.

When the strange and quiet Olaf Helton appears one day on his run-down farm, Mr. Royal Earle Thompson takes him on as a hired man. Through the industry of Helton over a period of nine years the farm is put on a paying basis and the lives of Thompson, his wife and two sons are set in a semblance of order. With Helton on the farm, Thompson is able to achieve that measure of social prestige that alone has attracted him. One day, however, his idyll comes to an end with the arrival of Homer T. Hatch, a bounty hunter, who reports that Helton is an escaped lunatic. In a foray, during which Helton's life seems endangered by Hatch, Thompson's lawyer has the weak-eyed Mrs. Thompson lie for her husband by saying that she witnessed the whole incident. This causes Ellie to suspect her husband of murder, and Thompson himself, with qualms about his courtroom conduct, attempts to convince each of his neighbors of his innocence by having his wife repeat her lie to each of them singly. But all is to no avail. Neither Thompson's wife nor his sons nor any of his neighbors sees him as anything but a murderer. Thus this man who lived on the good opinion of others really died the moment he killed Hatch. His suicide merely certifies the death of the *persona* which he had substituted for the self he never knew.

In this story Mr. Thompson only knows the importance of appearance. "All his carefully limited fields of activity were related somehow to Mr. Thompson's feeling for the appearance of things, his own appearance in the sight of God and man. 'It don't *look* right,' was his final reason for not doing anything he did not wish to do." The collapse of the appearance of "looking right" is his death. The complete inadequacy of Thompson is pictured in the run-down condition of the farm at the beginning of the novel and the disintegration of his family life at the end. Into this disordered existence comes Mr. Helton, whom the Thompsons think queer because he is not like them; that is, he is a person in his own right. But it is Helton, the benign lunatic, who sets the farm in order and even effects a temporary familial harmony by way of his own orderly life. And at the end of each day he reaffirms the new order by his ritual playing of the same song on one of his harmonicas. The story confronts one, then, with the extraordinary irony of an insane man creating order among sane people and reminding the sane people of this order through the symbolic order of his music. The irony is compounded when Hatch, a servant of society, arrives and announces: "Fact is, I'm for law and order, I don't like to see law-breakers and loonatics at large." Here a servant of the society from which Mr. Thompson exacts life-giving respect comes in the name of law and order to destroy order and to return the Thompsons' life to worse than pre-Heltonian chaos.

"Noon Wine," then, is the dramatization of the life of a man without any form of self-reliance based on self-knowledge and, consequently, without any ability to set up a meaningful mode of existence to sustain himself and his family. The source of his failure within the limits of the story is in the lie he lives—in the *persona* which cannot cope with the reality of evil in the person of Hatch, who contests Thompson's mediocrity for the possession of a good in the person of Helton.

Other stories of Katherine Anne Porter explore both of the dimensions that "Noon Wine" dramatizes: first, law and order as a substitute for personal and real order; second, life as impoverished by a failure of truth and love. "Magic" and "Theft," respectively, capture these themes in their essence. "Magic" is a story in which a human being is valuable only as a commodity. It tells simply of a madam who through magic secures the return of a dismissed prostitute when her clientele becomes disorderly because of the absence of the popular Ninette. The girl's return reestablishes social tranquility. Even the police are pleased. Here in a story Kafka-like in its savagery the profoundest human disorders are masked by the order of a brothel. Love becomes lust and freedom becomes servitude in a situation where disorder wears the costume of order. The point that Porter makes is that a society which proceeds without a recognition of the dignity of the human person and of his responsibility to a meaningful love has as its analogue the whirligig order of a brothel.

The savagery of "Magic" is balanced by the pathos of "Theft." Here a woman of perhaps early middle-age has her gold purse stolen by her janitress. All the woman has allowed herself to miss—especially the love of the man who gave her the purse—comes vividly to mind. The woman finds that anyone who steals her purse steals trash, because, basing her life on a vague general faith, she has been the thief of her own happiness. The purse calls from her memory the unpleasant ghosts of missed opportunities and innumerable losses, and her life converges in a pathetic epiphany that leaves her, in the last sentence, staring into a cup of cold coffee that she has substituted for the wine of life.

The failure of Ninette in "Magic" and the woman in "Theft" is the disordering failure of human love. The one is forced to accept the imposed order of love as lust, the other must see in her gold purse the poverty of her existence. Life without love in these two stories is revealed mainly as endurance, and endurance itself is an inadequate answer for human life.

This inadequacy of endurance divorced from love is realized in stories like "He" and "A Day's Work," in which the demands for social recognition and religious devotion are used by Mrs. Whipple and Mrs. Halloran as substitutes for self-knowledge and love of another. The one seeks to fulfill herself by having her neighbors recognize the extent to which she has sacrificed herself to care for her idiot son, and the other attempts to enforce Christian virtue on her husband by way of Catholic observance without liking him at all. "He" ends with Mrs. Whipple learning that her child, though simple, has feelings which are deep and that her loudly professed love for him has hidden a secret death-wish which her neighbors clearly understand: "His head rolled on her shoulder: she had loved Him as much as she possibly could, there were Adna and Emly who had to be thought of too, there was nothing she could do to make up to Him for His life. Oh, what a mortal pity He was ever born. Them came in sight of the hospital, with the neighbor driving very fast, not daring to look behind him." "A Day's Work" ends with Lacey Halloran beating her helpless husband with a knotted wet towel because, among other things, he drinks and filches change from her hoard and habitually walks through their flat in sock feet. One thinks of Porter's remark on Hardy's Angel Clare in Lucy Halloran's case: "His failure to understand the real nature of Christianity makes a monster of him at the great crisis of his life."

Ship of Fools, twenty years in the writing, is Katherine Anne Porter's most thorough exploration of her perennial theme of the restless and frustrating search of human being for the order of human love. The reader is invited to watch two different couples make two different kinds of love in the presence of an English bulldog. He is invited to contrast the lust of Arne Hansen and that of William Denny, the one open-handed, liberal, and satisfied by the love he buys, the other close-fisted, brooding, and eminently thwarted. He is invited to compare the gentle kiss of Dr. Schumann and the sleeping Condesa with the brutal kiss of the young officer and Mrs. Treadwell. He is invited to contrast the violence of Pepe and Amparo's usual vigorous love-making with the new and searching love of Johnny and Concha. In short, the reader is invited to the spectacle of the world making love.

Lovemaking is the most important of the many daily activities of man aboard the *Vera*, the ship of fools. People eat and drink, dress and undress, talk and read, as well as love and hate. The reader is spectator to a life of order that seems as meaningless as the daily promenade around the ship's deck. In short, the reader is spectator to life's order in its ultimate disorder. Through a pattern of fixed and repeated actions, Porter examines the eternal in man through his daily activities.

The captain of the *Vera* is a megalomaniac named Thiele who is concerned about the good order of his ship alone. He is so blind and rigid that he can take a knife away from a woodcarver and at the same time ignore the Zarzuela dance troop, which turns the last night of the ship's voyage into a *Walpurgisnacht* during which the patterns of established order disintegrate and the mad pursuit of lovers ends variously in sexual satisfaction or brutal frustration. At this point in the novel everything collapses according to plan because each person seems more intent than usual on acting the way he always acts. Thus the captain dissociates himself from the passengers and goes to the bridge where clicking heels and saluting officers allow him to pretend the ship is in order. Meanwhile the Zarzuelas have so taken over the ship that disorder and debauchery are rampant: the drunken Denny is drunker than ever, the frustrating actions of David and Jenny are more frustrating than ever, the frigidity of Mrs. Treadwell culminates in the savage beating of Denny, who is more savagely in pursuit of Pastora than ever before. In this manner the established patterns of action end in the disorder that they continuously hinted at throughout the novel. One night out of Bremerhaven is the focal point toward which all lives converge to produce a symmetrical picture of disorder in which lust is the closest a person can come to love.

Standing outside this pattern and measuring it are Dr. Schumann and La Condesa. The man, though sentimental, actually good and noble; the woman, though a criminal, actually saintly. The doctor gives her what he considers a guilty kiss and the Condesa accepts it as the most innocent love of her life. But she sends no answer to his note which offers her the continuing solicitude of his affection, and her silence proves to be this noisy novel's most magnificent gesture. Both end their affair before the *Walpurgisnacht* and both establish their generosity as the anti-model to the selfishness that stands as cause to effect in the disorderly and loveless lives of so many on the *Vera*.

In the *Ship of Fools* Katherine Anne Porter writes her constant theme: "It is hardly possible to exaggerate the lovelessness in which most people live, men or women: wanting love, unable to give it, or inspire it, unable to keep it if they get it, not knowing how to treat it, lacking the humility, or the very love itself that could teach them how to love: it is the painfullest thing in human life." The reason that Porter names her ship of fools *Vera* is to indicate that she believes that only by seeing the truth about themselves will people have a chance to change. Truth for her is a prelude to love.

These stories we have looked at repeat some truths that must be recognized. Sexual frustration is part of them all. Stephen and He are unwanted children. Ellen Weatherall's children substitute for those she might have had by George who jilted her. The woman in "Theft" has substituted a "baseless and general faith" in humanity for her love for Eddie. Ninette's sex is a commodity that men miss. Mrs. Thompson refuses to sleep with her husband, and his sons threaten his life. Thwarted sexual desire turns to aggression in "The Downward Path to Wisdom." The last six whacks Mrs. Halloran gives her husband with the wet knotted towel are "for your daughter and your part in her." Mrs. Treadwell beats Denny bloody with her spiked-heel shoe in *Ship of Fools*, where varieties of frustration and aggression are set in kaleidoscopic patterns.

The usual escape from the sexual self is the embracing of some external form of order. The family ideal and moral rectitude are celebrated in "A Downward Path" and "The Jilting of Granny Weatherall." Social recognition in "He" and "Noon Wine." Law and order in "Magic" and "Noon Wine." Humanity in "Theft." Religion in "Granny Weatherall" and "A Day's Work." And all of these are upheld by Captain Thiele in *Ship of Fools*, where the captain himself is projected as the image of a modern God who wants the floating planet shipshape even if the crew itself is a hopeless wreck. As long as there is some external order to distinguish virtuous from vicious, Porter suggests, those who do but slenderly know themselves and those who do but slenderly love others can always fill themselves up with self-righteousness.

The moral pettiness of such external orders are always demonstrated by the way they are supported. Stephen is condemned by peanuts, lemonade, and balloons. Mr. Halloran by sock feet. An empty purse is all that is left of a woman's love. Homer T. Hatch supports law and order for a bounty. Granny Weatherall is worried at her death by love letters she did not destroy and altar wine she has failed to deliver. The witchcraft that secures the return of Ninette is worked with tufts of her hair, powder from her puff, clippings from her finger- and toe-nails, and blood from her sheets all mixed together in Ninette's chamber pot with the spit of the witch and the madam. The knife that Captain Thiele takes from the woodcarver forces the peasant to suicide. Children, lunatics, prostitutes, drunkards, and art- ists are the victims of the trivia that righteousness uses against them.

Katherine Anne Porter's stories everywhere dramatize what she else- where says in her essays. "All human life since recorded time has been a terrible struggle from confusion to confusion to more confusion." Human nature is a "snake-pit." And "human relationships are the tragic necessity of human life . . . every ego is half the time greedily seeking them, and half the time pulling away from them." Personal existence is possible only if a way to order is found. Art is one way: "Chaos *is*—we are in it. My business is to give a little shape and meaning to my share of it." Love is another way: an "unalterable belief in the first importance of individual relationships between human beings founded on the reality of love—not in the mass, not between nations, nonsense!—but between one person and another." Despair comes from tottering under one's "share of human per- versity of thought and feeling." The "destiny of Man [then] is to learn the nature of love and to seek spiritual rebirth."

Given the fragility of human existence as Porter has written of it, how does one learn the nature of love and seek spiritual rebirth? One has to reverse the processes seen in the stories discussed. Passion, sexual or other- wise, must be admitted and consciously dealt with. Order must be created realistically from within rather than imposed from without. Self-righteous- ness must be avoided. And things must take a place secondary to human relationships. In "The Cracked Looking-Glass" Rosaleen tries to order her life by dreams because her marriage to Dennis, twenty-five years her senior, is painful to her. Yet all her dreams prove lies. There are she and Dennis and no one else. The cracked looking-glass is a mirror of their marriage, not a distortion of her beauty. Dennis, not "The Lover King," must be the object of her love. She must admit these things and accept them and she finally does when their truth is forced upon her mind. She then breaks the pattern of her life, refuses to believe in dreams and in romantic love, and takes Dennis to herself: "She sat up and felt his sleeves carefully. 'I want you to wrap up warm this bitter weather, Dennis,' she told him. 'With two pairs of socks and the chest protector, for if anything happened to you, whatever would become of me in this world?' " Rosaleen has done what Porter in "St. Augustine and the Bullfight" describes as converting an adventure into an experience. "Adventure is something you seek for plea- sure, or even for profit, like a gold rush or invading a country; for the illusion of being more alive than ordinarily, the thing you will to occur; but experience is what really happens to you in the long run; the truth that finally overtakes you." Rosaleen seeks adventure in New York at the movies and in Boston with Hugh Sullivan and even near home with Guy Richards, but Rosaleen discovers her real life must be with Dennis. She draws on her adventures to find her experience, and faithful to him she breaks the pattern of illusion that has put the crack in the looking-glass that symbolized their marriage.

For Katherine Anne Porter the truth, no matter how unpleasant, is the beginning of possibility. She celebrates the Mexican writer Lizardi whose appearance in the streets caused crowds to gather and cheer that "he told them the naked truth." She admires Circe and St. Augustine because Circe showed clearly that most men want to be pigs and Augustine was not afraid to show men acting piggishly: the story of a sensitive young man who scrupulously avoids the gladitorial contests only finally to go to the Coliseum and enjoy the blood-bath being a case in point. She says harsh things about human nature and she narrows the limits of human possibility.

> The refusal to acknowledge the evils in ourselves which therefore are implicit in any human situation is as extreme and unworkable a proposition as the doctrine of total depravity; but somewhere between them, or maybe beyond them, there does exist a possibility for reconciliation between our desires for impossible satisfactions and the simple unalterable fact that we also desire to be unhappy and that we create our own sufferings; and out of these sufferings we salvage the fragments of happiness.

The knowledge of self and of the human situation leads inevitably to another Porter imperative: "Love must be learned, and learned again and again; there is no end to it." Acedia, spiritual sloth, in the activity of knowing and loving is the cause of man's moral collapse and of his creation of codes and systems that destroy the human spirit. Whatever heroes and heroines there are therefore in Porter's stories are heroes and heroines of the spirit. And perhaps she herself is her own greatest heroine because she has never stopped searching for the spirit of man amid the confusion of his life and the rubble of his civilization. "I shall try to tell the truth, but the result will be fiction," she told a Paris audience in 1934. "I shall not be at all surprised at this result: It is what I mean to do; it is, to my way of thinking, the way fiction is made."

This astringent and subtle art of truth which Porter practices so relentlessly is a certain sign of hope in human life. One who does not want another to see does not for half a century hold up a mirror to his nature. Katherine Anne Porter's stories show man how and why he is spiritually blind and how and why he hates and they show with as much intensity, if more rarely, how and why he can be reborn and love again. Her stories are the shape of existence, fiction that is truth, art that is life. They are stories that live by faith in the man whose illness they diagnose. As such, they will endure. And with the last word, Katherine Anne Porter tells us why:

> In the face of . . . [the] shape and weight of present misfortune, the voice of the individual artist may seem perhaps of no more consequence than the whirring of a cricket in the grass; but the arts do live continuously, and they live literally by faith; their names and their shapes and their uses and their meanings survive unchanged in all that matters through times of interruption, diminishment, neglect; they outlive governments and creeds and societies, even the very civilization that produced them. They cannot be destroyed altogether because they represent the substance of faith and the only reality. They are what we find again when the ruins are cleared away.

Personal Narrators
Playing God and Man:
Henry Miller's Henry Miller

Alan Warren Friedman

Autobiographical self-projections, whether avowedly fictional or not, assume various tones and forms. The speaking voice relates to the implicit author along a spectrum of possibilities ranging from identity to antithesis. In instances of identity, the work claims literal reality as its basis, like Augustine's and Rousseau's confessions, Cellini's and Franklin's autobiographies. Where narrator and implied author are clearly distinct, the work proclaims itself as fiction—*Fanny Hill, Moll Flanders, Great Expectations*—although many affinities still exist between the two personae despite the fairly common difference in gender. Structurally and tonally most interesting are fictions which, like Proust's *Remembrance*, fuse literal and imaginative realities into an inseparable unity by confounding our attempt either to equate implied author and narrator or else to distinguish them completely from each other. Proust's fictive world, for example, subsumes people and places he has experienced directly in a way that at times suggests a *roman à clef*, and its presiding genius bears and shares his name. In his preface to *A Moveable Feast*, Hemingway says, "If the reader prefers, this book may be regarded as fiction. But there is always the chance that such a book of fiction may throw some light on what has been written as fact." Similarly, Norman Mailer subtitles *Armies of the Night*, his firsthand account of antiwar protests in Washington, "History as a Novel/ The Novel as History," and like Henry Adams in the autobiographical *Education*, refers to himself always in the third person. With such writers, we enter the realm of memoir/ confession/autobiography as nonfictional novel, a mode that forces us to define our own uncertain relationship to outspoken yet protean narrators who appear as both artisans and artifacts.

The range of possible relationships between narrator and evolving self,

From *Multivalence: The Moral Quality of Form in the Modern Novel*. © 1978 by Louisiana State University.

like those between implied author and narrator, is also extensive. The narrator may be totally self-approving of his younger self from the first, like Cellini or Franklin or Frank Harris in *My Life and Loves*, condemnatory of a younger self that is, however, educable and therefore perhaps salvageable (St. Augustine, Dante in *The Divine Comedy*, Pip in *Great Expectations*, Henry Adams in his *Education*), or relatively neutral, portraying himself as, in one mood, Hamlet does his father: "He was a man, take him for all in all." Thus Rousseau proclaims: "This is my work, these were my thoughts, and thus was I. I have freely told both the good and the bad, have hid nothing wicked, added nothing good. . . . I have exposed myself as I was, contemptible and vile some times; at others, good, generous, and sublime." In the same spirit, Mark Twain had his autobiography suppressed until after his death so that he need hold nothing back.

The plot structure of such narratives is developmental, the dramatized process usually defined as maturation or education, as an awakening or reawakening, as a movement from darkness to light; and the purpose of the work is to serve as exemplum. The reader is usually expected to feel superior—as the narrator himself does except when he identifies completely with his younger self from the first—to the ignorant, misguided, or lost protagonist he encounters at the start, to participate vicariously in the journey from innocence to experience (often via revelation or conversion), and finally to feel impelled to take a similar journey or to be left among the uninitiated. As in Whitman's "Crossing Brooklyn Ferry," we look back on a figure portrayed as inferior to us (if only because past), observe the process of his moving up to and even beyond us, and then often find that *we* are being looked back on. Whitman's persona speaks, first, of being on the ferryboat with "the hundreds and hundreds that cross returning home," and he addresses "the others that are to follow me," those "that shall cross from shore to shore years hence." But then the present, and we, are caught and passed:

> It avails not, time nor place—distance avails not,
> I am with you, you men and women of a generation, or ever so
> many generations hence,
> Just as you feel when you look on the river and sky, so I felt,
> . . . .
> These and all else were to me the same as they are to you.

The poem invites us to participate if we would in the pert's double journey, not only the spatial one *on* the ferry, but also the temporal one that transcends the physical and enables us to look back upon an event that is simultaneously present and past. *We* experience such literature, as we do certain heightened moments of our own lives, as both participant and observer, as in effect both spontaneous artist and removed analyst.

Henry Miller's Henry Miller has affinities with all the self-portrayers mentioned above. As in true autobiography, but also as in Dante and Proust, Miller confers his own name on the protagonist/narrator who appears in most of what he writes. Relatively late in his career, Miller says: "There was just one book I always wanted to write. . . . Even had I lost the notes, it would not have mattered: everything that ever happened to me had been burned into my brain. The writing of this one and only work has been going on for many, many years—the greater part of it in my head. . . . How the final edifice will shape itself I still do not know." The single work that is the Miller canon is both autobiography and fiction, both an accurate representation of the life whose outlines and details it dramatizes and an imaginative structuring by a detached implied author playing god (in his constructing) and playing equally human games of rhetorical strategy (in denying that he is playing god). An author named Henry Miller both shapes and identifies with a narrator of the same name; the narrator turns the same trick on the character who similarly bears his name. Fiction and nonfiction, reliable and unreliable narration, identification and irony—the categories and terms break down for a writer who both proclaims and denies distance between implied author and narrator and between narrator and protagonist. No wonder Miller's writings have eluded our classificatory instincts: their basic thrust is a full-scale attack on such instincts. We thought we knew about protagonist/narrators: their lives were wrong from the start (like Augustine and Dante), and they would teach us the lessons they have learned; or they were always in the right (Cellini, Franklin, Frank Harris), and, like Shelley's Ozymandias, they would have us look on their works and despair; or they proclaimed a fidelity to truth (Rousseau, Twain, Malcolm X), and let the chips fall where they might. Miller, of course, embraces all three approaches— denouncing his early life in America, asserting his consistently valid vision, and yet proclaiming his utter fidelity to truth—and so leaves us with a chaos of categories comparable to that he finds in his world: "There was never any time when I was living *one* life, the life of a husband, a lover, a friend. Wherever I was, whatever I was engaged in, I was leading multiple lives. Thus whatever it is that I choose to regard as *my* story is lost, drowned, indissolubly fused with the lives, the drama, the stories of others." Not only does such an artist refuse to do our job for us, he denies the terms and validity of our attempting to do so. Like Miller, and Whitman before him, we must ourselves play democratic bard in order to reinvent and repeople a world whose verities such writers seem constantly to deny. We must turn, with Whitman, and look back on ourselves looking back at him, and create, with Miller, the single organic work which we would do well to call "song of myselves."

Following Whitman—who speaks of being vast and containing multitudes—Miller carves out a complex relationship to the protagonist speaking for him, for they both blithely emit contrarieties without pause or concern. Miller's narrator maintains that everything is true "about this universe of ours," even the most outrageous and deliberate lies; that art can reveal the truth of life, yet that no one can tell the truth; that art is at odds with life, "only a make-shift, a substitute for the real thing," but that it can lead you to life; that the artistic process has greater importance than "what one has to tell," yet through art one can transcend, even destroy, art in order to reenter life. Miller proclaims that only the natural, the spontaneous (like him), has value: "What is not in the open street is false, derived, that is to say, *literature*. I was born in the street and raised in the street. . . . To be born in the street means to wander all your life, to be free." As a logical extension of this view, Miller denounces all efforts to distinguish his life from his writings, to view them as other than coextensive and inspired by a single source. The central paradox lies, perhaps, in what Miller presumes and asserts here: that his writing accurately and directly reflects his life, that while he has lived willfully, self-assertively, the writing results from the opposite, a passivity, a Keatsian "negative capability," and thus is not literature (which is bad) but byproduct; not Wordsworthian "experience recollected in tranquility," but a direct and immediate access to unreflected experience.

Miller maintains that no thought or consideration determines his writing, that everything flows as from "a writing machine. The last screw has been added. The thing flows. Between me and the machine there is no estrangement. I am the machine." And he never revises, never alters what he writes, for "I detest the eraser"; he has, he says "made a silent compact with myself not to change a line of what I write. I am not interested in perfecting my thoughts, nor my actions. Beside the perfection of Turgenev I put the perfection of Dostoevski. . . . Here, then, in one and the same medium, we have two kinds of perfection. But in Van Gogh's letters there is a perfection beyond either of these. It is the triumph of the individual over art."

Miller's books do seem to reflect a dislike for erasers, for they are commonly redundant, associational, anarchic—like several dozen random versions of cut-and-paste jobs done on one vast, flowing diary. The themes, the settings, the imagery are few, but the variations on them are infinite, or seemingly so. The artist endlessly shapes identical blocks—those not "gone, scattered, wasted in talk, action, reminiscence, dream,"—under the same inspiration, and the products vary only through accidents of time and sometimes place. Only the haphazardness of human nature and conditions, it seems, prevents the results from being mechanically identical.

Yet as with Thomas Wolfe, a writer with whom Miller has much in common, artifice and art coexist in the published books; for all their length and verbiage, Miller's works result as much from pruning as accretion. "My books," he says, "are purely autobiographical," implying that they are coextensive and of a piece with his life. But like a good modern craftsman he then speaks of technique: "In telling the story of my life I have frequently discarded the chronological sequence in favor of the circular or spiral form of progression." Sometimes, in fact, his books will fail to appear because they are never satisfactorily realized. Benjamin DeMott refers, for example, to one work that Miller wrestled with for decades as "a catastrophically complicated, luckily abandoned book about D. H. Lawrence." Miller himself speaks of elaborately reworking *The World of Sex* for a second edition:

"As I reread the book I began making certain corrections; it became a game which I could not resist playing to the end. Every page of the original version I went over in pen and ink, hatching and criss-crossing until it looked like a Chinese puzzle. In the new edition a few photographic copies of these corrected pages have been inserted; the reader may judge for himself what a task I gave myself."

In a classic exchange, Edmund Wilson congratulates Miller for his brilliantly imaginative creation of character, setting, and theme in *Tropic of Cancer*—and an outraged Miller responds that he doesn't write fiction.

> Wilson praised Miller for his skillful ironic portrait of a particular kind of "vaporing" poseur, for making his hero really live, "and not merely in his vaporings or his poses. He gives us the genuine American bum come to lead the beautiful life in Paris; and he lays him away forever in his dope of Pernod and dreams." To all of this praise for irony, Miller replied, "The theme is myself, and the narrator, or the hero, as your critic [Wilson] puts it, is also myself. . . . If he means the narrator, then it is me. . . . I don't use 'heroes,' incidentally, nor do I write novels. I am the hero, and the book is myself."
>
> (Wayne C. Booth, *The Rhetoric of Fiction*. Chicago and London: University of Chicago Press, 1961)

Both Wayne Booth and Philip Stevick cite this interchange as illustrating the contemporary critic's dilemma when considering the crucial question of distance between author and character, and they sympathize with Wilson for making a natural error. Stevick comments that "the immediate impasse in this exchange between novelist and critic is point of view. But dependent upon that central matter of technique is every other value in the novel. Presumably, if Edmund Wilson were to accept Henry Miller's own statement of intention, he would be obliged to find *Tropic of Cancer* not a detached and perceptive work at all but a banal and silly one. A whole history of the novel . . . could be written around just such problems in the perception of point of view." Aside from the sticky question of the effect avowed authorial intention can have on the validity of a work, the important consideration that Booth and Stevick fail to pursue is that, despite the protestations of Miller and his protagonist, Wilson is basically right. For the first-draft manuscript of *Tropic of Cancer* was three times the length of the published version, and three times Miller rewrote the book. About his Chronology, a supposedly factual account designed to settle many such difficulties, Miller has said, "There are times when I myself no longer know whether I said and did the things I report or whether I dreamed them up. Anyway, I always dream true. If I lie a bit now and then it is mainly in the interest of truth."

The same attitude prevails throughout what Miller calls his "autobiographical romances." After vividly detailing an extensive series of sexual conquests, the protagonist of *Tropic of Capricorn* comments: "It was going on this way all the time, even though every word I say is a lie." As Kingsley Widmer, in the best book to date on Miller, has noted, "it is unavoidable in discussing Miller's work to call the central figure Henry Miller, as does Henry Miller, though this is not a claim that the experiences are literal fact. . . . In all probability Miller's writings about Miller are not true, in several senses." In another sense, of course, all of it *is* true, even the outrageous lies, because intensely experienced and proclaimed by both author and character.

For Miller, and artist despite himself, both form and substance follow function. The manic release of automatic writing flows from the depression engendered by endless rewriting; similarly, a nonstop exuberance for life emerges from personal despair. For the half-hidden central plot of all of Miller's writing concerns the failure of passion consequent to youthful love gone awry. The Miller we see, although obviously obsessed with the *idea* of sex, is largely indifferent to it in reality. Taking a woman to bed— although he does so at every opportunity—seems always to be someone else's idea: the various women who accost him in the streets or the cafes, the blushing Hindu afraid to venture upstairs in a brothel alone, the friend who offers him the loan of his own latest bedmate. Miller's reaction to the latter is typical: "I didn't know whether I wanted to or not," he says, but of course he does. It is free, it is convenient, and it saves him the cost of a night's lodging.

Earlier in *Cancer*, he speaks of watching his friend Van Norden "tackle" one of the inevitable nameless prostitutes:

> It seems to me that I'm looking at a machine whose cogs have slipped. . . . I am sitting on a chair behind him, watching their movements with a cool, scientific detachment. . . . It's like watching one of those crazy machines which throw the newspaper out. . . . The machine seems more sensible, crazy as it is, and more fascinating to watch, than the human beings and the events which produced it. My interest in Van Norden and the girl is nil. . . . As long as that spark of passion is missing there is no human significance in the performance. The machine is better to watch."

Miller's own lack of passion, the antithesis and source of his manic exuberance, ties in with his pivotal theme of "the misery and inspiration connected with the Dark Lady of passion. She is partly the *femme fatale* of the romantic, an inverted traditional muse of the artist, the Eve-Lilith of primordial knowledge, a witch-goddess of sexuality and power, and, according to Miller's insistence, his second wife. Under the names of Mona and Mara, she haunts most of Miller's work; and she appears, at least briefly, in almost every book he has written."

Certainly her appearances are brief and intermittent, for her story is as fragmented as everything else in Miller's discontinuous narrative. Nonetheless, Miller's treatment of her constantly emphasizes her emotional centrality to his life and to his work. For one thing, the Mona/Mara passages are remarkably free of both censorable language and excremental references. Descriptions of Mona and of scenes with her, unlike those of the other women in the *Tropics*, never become flights of nihilistic, semiabstract imagery indulged in for their own sake. Of the significance of Mona, the "Her" to whom *Capricorn* is dedicated, Miller writes: "Everything I endured was in the nature of a preparation for that moment when, putting on my hat one evening, I walked out of the office, out of my hitherto private life, and sought the woman who was to liberate me from a living death."

In *Cancer* she appears initially as a figure of almost virginal purity, a kind of antiwhore who embodies love rather than sex. Miller has been eagerly awaiting her return to Paris when "suddenly," he writes, "I see a pale, heavy face and burning eyes—and the little velvet suit that I always adore because under the soft velvet there were always her warm breasts, the marble legs, cool, firm, muscular. She rises up out of a sea of faces and embraces me, embraces me passionately. . . . I hear not a word because she is beautiful and I love her and now I am happy and willing to die." Then in bed their intense passion finds expression, as do Miller's tenderness and love—and a new emotion, fear.

> She lies down on the bed with her clothes on. Once, twice, three times, four times . . . I'm afraid she'll go mad . . . in bed, under the blankets, how good to feel her body again! But for how long? Will it last this time? Already I have a presentiment that it won't. . . . Finally she drops off and I pull my arm from under her. My eyes close. Her body is there beside me . . . it will be there till morning surely. . . . My eyes are closed. We breathe warmly into each other's mouth. Close together, America three thousand miles away. I never want to see it again. To have her here in bed with me, breathing on me, her hair in my mouth—I count that something of a miracle. Nothing can happen now till morning.

But in the morning everything happens. They wake to find each other crawling with bedbugs; Mona, wanting a bath, food, and adequate clothing, loses her temper at Miller's having forgotten to provide for money; and, although Miller does not detail the rest of the sequence of events, by the next page Mona disappears from the narrative—not to be even mentioned again for some 120 pages. Again he longs for her, wondering how different life might be with "a young, restless creature by [his] side"; but his image of her has altered drastically, and, bitterly, he sees her as alien to his European world. If she ever should return, he wryly speculates,

> She'll probably tell me right away that it's unsanitary. That's the first thing that strikes an American woman about Europe—that it's unsanitary. Impossible for them to conceive of a paradise without modern plumbing. . . . She'll say I've become a degenerate. I know her line from beginning to end. She'll want to look for a studio with a garden attached—and a bathtub to be sure. She wants to be poor in a romantic way. I know her. But I'm prepared for her this time.

Exactly what is good about being poor in an unromantic way Miller never explains, but certainly he is correct about being prepared for her—for he manages, at least for the moment, to blot from his mind everything that belongs to the past, especially those few years when they were together and life was, if not edenic, at least vital and intense. Now when he thinks of her—and he is unable to keep himself from doing so entirely—it is "not as of a person in a definite aura of time and space, but separately, detached, as though she had blown up into a great cloudlike form that blotted out the past." Regardless, he adds, "I couldn't allow myself to think about her very long; if I had I would have jumped off the bridge. It's strange. I had become so reconciled to this life without her, and yet if I thought about her only for a minute it was enough to pierce the bone and marrow of my contentment and shove me back again into the agonizing gutter of my wretched past." And yet, no matter what the reason, a man who willfully destroys his past, as Miller begins to realize, commits spiritual suicide: "It seems as if my own proper existence had come to an end somewhere, just where exactly I can't make out. I'm not an American any more, nor a New Yorker, and even less a European, or a Parisian. I haven't any allegiance, any responsibilities, any hatreds, any worries any prejudices, any passion. I'm neither for nor against. I'm a neutral." But this statement serves first as manifesto and only subsequently as actual fact, for after the climactic moment when he recognizes the irrevocable loss of Mona, he gives way to a despairing loneliness so profound and so terrible that all else seems irrelevant. Yet in his hopelessness he comes full cycle, rediscovering his affinity with all the sordid and cancerous aspects of Paris, a city that "attracts the tortured, the hallucinated, the great maniacs of love," a Paris that "is like a whore. From a distance she seems ravishing, you can't wait until you have her in your arms. And five minutes later you feel empty, disgusted with yourself. You feel tricked." Ultimately there are only the streets for refuge—the streets which, in the childhood reminiscence of *Black Spring*, define his freedom in America—for the streets take every man's torments, every man's raging despair that is so precious because it confirms his significance as an individual capable of suffering, and the streets make of it something neither for nor against, but simple neutral. Miller, as we see him at the end of *Cancer* and then again at the end of *Capricorn*, is a diminished figure wondering "in a vague way what had ever happened to [his] wife." "A vague way"—the phrase is revealing—for it suggests, and this is borne out in the later writings, that the failure of the relationship may well have resulted from Miller's intrinsic inadequacies. As Widmer has put it: "While his version of the Dark Lady myth aims to show Miller as the victim of love, he really presents himself as the victim of his own lovelessness."

But Miller anticipates us in this as he does in everything else we might care to say about his writing. Early in *Capricorn* he says, "Things were wrong usually only when one cared too much. That impressed itself on me very early in life. . . . This caring too much—I remember that it only developed with me about the time I first fell in love. And even then I didn't care enough. If I had really cared I wouldn't be here now writing about it. . . . It was a bad experience because it taught me how to live a lie." As much as such things ever can, this recapitulation explains Miller's self-projection in all he has written and been, for his assertion of himself as a writer who never revises is of a piece with his assertion that he cares for no one, for nothing.

Thus, the manic self-dramatization is a way of both confronting and avoiding, a way of defining oneself that denies momentary disasters of every kind and wills a reality that endures for poets and children. For a certain kind of writer, usually sophisticated Americans insecure in their sophistication, a public persona represents, in Ben Jonson's phrase about his son, "his best piece of poetry." Franklin's pious spouter of platitudes, Frost's kindly old country grandfather, Hemingway's super-macho Papa, Mailer's endlessly belligerent good bad boy—all represent imaginative constructs in a grand style. Miller, too, offers a self-dramatization above all, himself as a twentieth-century fulfillment of Whitman's call for spontaneous democratic bard, a poet by instinct rather than training now returned to the land where such willful creation of self seems most possible and necessary. "The United States themselves are essentially the greatest poem," Whitman writes. "Of all nations the United States with veins full of poetical stuff most need poets and will doubtless have the greatest and use them the greatest." But, as Anaïs Nin pointed out in *Cancer's* original preface, Miller is no more an untutored, spontaneous genius than Whitman, and seeming naïveté is willed and purposeful: "Here the symbols [of art] are laid bare, presented almost as naïvely and unblushingly by this over-civilized individual as by the well-rooted savage. It is no false primitivism which gives rise to this savage lyricism. It is not a retrogressive tendency, but a swing forward into unbeaten areas." What then, we might ask, is Miller up to?

Tropic of Cancer, Miller's first writing success after several unpublished novels, may be read as a scatological *Down and Out in Paris and London*, for both books concern the quest for food and shelter (among other things) during the days and nights of the Parisian Depression— only Orwell seeks even the most menial and degrading work in order to survive at any cost. Miller, on the other hand, becomes a parasite in order, as he maintains, to survive on his own terms (that is, without working) but also, despite his protestations, in order to make literature of the experience. At the beginning of *Cancer*, Miller offers us a miniature portrait of the artist and his art.

> It is now the fall of my second year in Paris. I was sent here for a reason I have not yet been able to fathom.
>
> I have no money, no resources, no hopes. I am the happiest man alive. A year ago, six months ago, I thought that I was an artist. I no longer think about it, I *am*. Everything that was literature has fallen from me. There are no more books to be written, thank God.

> This then? This is not a book. This is libel, slander, defamation
> of character. This is not a book, in the ordinary sense of the word.
> No, this is a prolonged insult, a gob of spit in the face of Art, a
> kick in the pants to God, Man, Destiny, Time, Love, Beauty . . .
> what you will. I am going to sing for you, a little off key perhaps,
> but I will sing.

Art, then, becomes both art and non-art, for it is not only formless and
eclectic, negative and destructive, but is serves for the artist both as an end
in itself and also as a means to life. Elsewhere, Miller writes that "art is
only a stepping-stone to reality. It is the vestibule in which we undergo
the rites of initiation. Man's task is to make of himself a work of art. The
creations which man makes manifest have no validity in themselves; they
serve to awaken." They can, in fact, serve as means for passing beyond
the immediate, beyond fiction and reality, beyond even truth and its antithesis: "For years I have been trying to tell this story and always the
question of truth has weighed upon me like a nightmare. Time and again
I have related to others the circumstances of our life, and I have always
told the truth. But the truth can also be a lie. The truth is not enough.
Truth is only the core of a totality which is inexhaustible." Further, "The
sum of all knowledge is greater confusion. . . . Truth comes with surrender.
And it's wordless." "I believe," he adds, "that one has to pass beyond the
sphere and influence of art. . . . All art, I firmly believe, will one day
disappear. But the artist will remain, and life itself will become not 'an art,'
but *art*. . . . Once art is really accepted it will cease to be. It is only a
substitute, a symbol-language, for something which can be seized directly."
Thus, the artist must cease "immolating himself in his work," must cease
creating out of a martyrdom "of sweat and agony. . . . We do not think of
sweat and tears in connection with the universe; we think of joy and light,
and above all of play." Despite the evidence of his own experience, the
artist assumes this art to be a spontaneous outpouring, an automatic byproduct of unrecollected and untranquilized emotion—because, at least in
Miller's case, it serves the purposes of art and life, of narrators playing god
and man. The paradox, the contradictoriness, becomes the point, the message as well as the medium for the persona projecting himself as *both* the
literal and created embodiment of his author's psyche. Identification between the two is of course inexact, but the very dichotomy—in a form that
seeks to deny that there is any—has much to teach us not only concerning
protagonist narration but also about distancing techniques in fiction and
elsewhere. Despite appearance and expectation, blatant self-assertion in
the service of complex revelation about fiction, art, reality, life— or in Miller's terms, "God, Man, Destiny, Time, Love, Beauty . . . what you will"—
may be not the most accessible or trustworthy mode of communication,
but something approaching its opposite.

"Dressing the Unknowable in the Garments of the Known": The Style of Djuna Barnes's *Nightwood*

Carolyn Allen

Investigations of style in fiction by women most often begin with the opinions of Virginia Woolf. Her comment that Dorothy Richardson had invented "a psychological sentence of the feminine gender" has led recent critics interested in women's fiction to posit a "woman's style," presumably a way of writing with features common to most women writers and distinct from most male writers. But Woolf goes on to say that Richardson's is a woman's sentence "only in the sense that it is used to describe a woman's mind by a writer who is neither proud nor afraid of anything that she may discover in the psychology of her sex." Woolf's interest is in description of the female mind rather than in formal characteristics of the sentence itself. Critics following Woolf tend to jump from her yearning for sentences in which syntax would accurately capture the psychology of a woman's mind to a conviction that such sentences, and other sex-specific features of style, exist in women's literature. It is a leap, I believe, that has been made too hastily and without sufficient information; thus, my description of style in Djuna Barnes's *Nightwood* is intended not to argue for a theory of woman's style, but to give critics interested in such theories additional basic material with which to work.

Before coming to *Nightwood*, however, I would like to outline one problem raised by reading recent formulations of woman's style. In the criticism there is a lack of discussion about what the word "style" in the phrase "woman's style" includes. No such lack exists in less specifically directed discussion of literary style, but as feminist critics look for commonalities among women writers and begin to trace a heretofore missing women's literary history, they have, at least temporarily, set aside definitional questions. Though defining what one means to include by the term

From *Women's Language and Style* (Studies in Contemporary Language, no. 1). © 1978 by E. L. Epstein. L & S Books, 1978.

"woman's style" will not immediately bring to a halt arguments about whether or not there is such a thing, it will at least allow the arguers to be more in control of the terms of their dispute. Some critics use "style" broadly to include forms of thought and repeated choices or treatments of subjects. Others have in mind a narrower sense, one limited to forms of writing determined by conscious or unconscious linguistic choices. Too often critics intend one sense, readers understand another, and the substantive argument gets lost in the middle. It is not my purpose here to debate the merits of these two views, but rather to point out that the term has been taken both ways by critics of women's fiction and to suggest that for distinguishing a tradition for female writers one seems to hold more promise than the other.

In Josephine Donovan's essay "Feminist Style Criticism" and in Annette Kolodny's critique of it in "Some Notes on Defining a 'Feminist Literary Criticism', " "woman's style" is used to mean both habits of mind revealed in subject choice and attitude of the writer toward that subject, and ways of writing about the subject, though more emphasis is given to the former. Donovan speaks of the repeated tendency of women novelists to have as their primary interest the "inner, under-the-surface life of the heroines." In discussing passages from Richardson and Woolf as examples of writing well-suited to rendering the inner life, she speaks of the effects of punctuation in Richardson, and less specifically, of the rhythm of Woolf's sentences. Both discussions are brief and do not take up specific syntactic and lexical choices. So although Donovan asserts the notion of sex-specific uses of language, she does not provide much support for it. Her discussion of feminine style follows Mary Ellmann in noting the tone of authority present in male writers but appropriately absent in female writers trying to capture the inner life. Ellmann, however, (as Donovan acknowledges) does not believe it possible to determine a "woman's sentence"; she stresses that in Richardson's novels, the feminine tone Woolf admires is a function of subject choice. While Ellmann delineates differences in forms of thought between male and female writers, she does not argue for sexual differences as the determining factor in linguistic choice. Donovan seems to hold that a woman's style means both forms of thought and forms of writing, but she does not discuss the latter in much detail.

While applauding Donovan's intentions, Kolodny rightly criticizes her for accepting the notion of a woman's style on the basis of too few examples and insufficient explanation of her generalizations. Kolodny goes on to discuss "demonstrable repetition of particular thematic concerns and image patterns" that she has discovered in contemporary women writers. She also asserts that there are similar repetitions in "stylistic devices" and "often-repeated sentence constructions," features that I take to be crucial in determining whether there is a uniquely woman's style—style in the narrower sense of linguistic choice rather than in the broader sense of epistemology, subject choice, and attitudes. Kolodny does not, however, elaborate what these devices and constructions are.

Feminist linguists Julia Stanley and Susan Robbins in their essay "Toward a Feminist Aesthetic" (delivered at the Conference on Language and Style, Graduate Center, CUNY), do discuss specific sentence constructions in describing what they call the "conjunctive style" of woman writers. Wisely, however, they limit themselves "to a few observable linguistic trends in women's emergent writing, specifically that of self-identified feminists." They are then able to draw not only on the writings themselves, but also on statements of authors who have spoken of creating a woman's style suitable for their overtly feminist material.

Like Ellmann, I am not convinced that syntactic and lexical choices are made on a sex-specific basis without regard to such variables as literary period, class, race, or perceived place in a societal hierarchy. Nor do I believe any literary critic has wholeheartedly made such an argument. Stanley and Robbins define their notion of "style" more linguistically than do Ellmann, Donovan, and Kolodny, but for the most part they limit their examples to a few well-chosen contemporaries. Donovan's and Kolodny's definitions of "woman's style" include more than linguistic choice and, by taking "style" to include habits of mind and predilection for certain literary subjects, they extend the discussion beyond the narrower goal of finding a specifically sex-determined syntax. All these theorists raise interesting possibilities in their formulations of woman's style, but future readers will want to keep in mind their definitional differences when coming to their own conclusions about the existence of a woman's style.

Donovan and Kolodny call for further close analysis of women writers as a base for asking additional questions about woman's style, however it is defined. My essay on *Nightwood*, Djuna Barnes's best-known novel, is a contribution to that effort, a description of a particular woman's linguistic and structural choices and the ways in which they are appropriate, even necessary for her subjects.

In *Nightwood*, what readers hail as stylistic innovation begins not so much with Barnes's desire to experiment as with her recognition that current modes of discourse were inappropriate for her subject. In *Nightwood*, she eschews the language of rationality, often nominal in emphasis, dichotomous in argument, and factual in description, because it cannot adequately portray her subjects, the power of the night, of irrationality and the unconscious; and the nature of love, particularly love between women. To evoke them, Barnes uses instead an indirect, associative style that depends on reader intuition rather than on logic. The style of *Nightwood* tries to avoid naming directly, and so concentrates on not-naming, on using syntactic and semantic structures that signal indirection. Direct description would, for example, place in too distinct a relief a woman like Robin Vote, the novel's central force, who is best conceived as a presence rather than as a character. In passages describing her there is a syntactic preference for the passive voice suitable to her title, "la sonambule," and frequently for negation in keeping with her "presence-in-absence." In addition, love between women, in which self-knowledge comes from loving one who is different from yet resembles the self, requires a language tending toward synonymy rather than antonymy. Appropriately then, the principal mark of Barnes's style is the analogy, the terms of which are basically alike though superficially different. The talk of the two main speakers, Matthew and Nora, is heavily metaphoric as if single words or direct description were inadequate to convey the nature of their subjects, the discoveries and despairs of love. The syntax is complicated, heavily embedded and often appositional, another suggestion that single phrases alone cannot name what is occurring. Throughout individual passages and among widely separated sections, words and phrases are repeated, sometimes with a shift in meaning, and the reader must associate these words with earlier occurrences of them in order to see how Barnes depends on lexical sets rather than on narrative or characterization to convey her ideas.

Ironically and purposefully, the novel's highly metaphoric and oblique style makes a crucial point: words do not work. For Matthew and Nora, talk, even elaborately constructed talk, does not convince or sustain or serve in experiences of extremity. Although conversations about the night world are the substantive center of the novel, speakers have either collapsed into chaos or fallen silent before its conclusion.

Traditional plot development is of scant interest to Barnes, and in *Nightwood* it operates as pretext rather than context. The novel's two interwoven stories have at their centers Robin Vote, "a wild thing caught in a woman's skin," who leaves her husband Felix and comes in time to live with her lover, Nora Flood. But Robin, enclosed in the solipsistic world of the sleepwalker, cannot return Nora's love any more than she could Felix's, and she finally breaks with Nora to take up a relationship with another woman, Jenny Petherbridge. In agony, Nora turns for solace and wisdom to Matthew O'Connor, who serves as her advisor and confessor/priest. His long monologues on the world of the night occupy much of the novel but ultimately fail to cure Nora of her obsessional love for Robin. By the novel's end Matthew has collapsed physically, spiritually, and rhetorically, Nora and Felix are left without Robin, and Robin herself has returned to the "deep-shocked realm" from which she had fitfully emerged.

At the macrostylistic level, the scant importance of the few plot-advancing events and the strong concern for emotive states is clear in the novel's structure. Except for the brief last chapter, the action is completed at the end of chapter four (of eight). Yet oddly we also feel that the "action" does not begin until chapter five. Chapters one through four introduce the main characters, each of the titles a phrase associated with a character: Felix, "Bow Down," Robin, "La Sonambule," Jenny, "The Squatter," and Nora, "Night Watch." Matthew is the lone exception. His descriptive chapter, "Watchman, What of the Night," is reserved for the second half of the novel befitting his stature as a commentator on events as well as his confessor role. He interprets the foregoing events, which he has witnessed, for Nora and Felix. Each of the first four chapters opens with a description of its central character—with two instructive variations. The opening of

"Bow Down" dwells at some length on Felix's parents since he is dominated by his sense of an insufficient history. The opening of "La Sonambule" begins not with Robin but with Matthew. Robin's first appearance is delayed until the middle of the chapter in keeping with Barnes's general strategy of presenting Robin indirectly, out of established narrative patterns. At the end of chapter four we learn that Robin and Jenny leave Paris and go to America. Chapter five begins the significant action of the novel, talk—talk generated by Robin's leaving first Felix, then Nora, and departing with Jenny. In chapter five Matthew discourses to Nora about Robin's associations with the night, and in six, to Felix about the fate of Guido, his son by Robin. The seventh chapter begins with Matthew trying to cure Nora of her obsessional memories of Robin and ends by Nora's silencing Matthew with her own verbalized understanding of Robin's sleep-state. The final chapter breaks the pattern by its focus on action without talk. In its four pages Barnes countermands the emphasis on Matthew's verbal persuasion by bringing Nora and Robin silently together, only to have them divided by their dissimilarity.

Within this framework, departures of narrated time from chronological time reflect Barnes's interest in the psychological and indicate how structure emphasizes content. The narrated time first departs from the chronological when we are taken into the past to hear the history of Felix's parents. This departure stresses the obsession with history that determines his life's direction. The second disjuncture coincides with the coming together of Robin and Nora; their brief union both distorts ongoing time and slows it down when Nora's confusion becomes the subject of Matthew's long monologues. In addition, the only actions which are repeated in the telling, those on the night when Nora loses Robin to Jenny and those of Robin's increased night wanderings, testify to Nora's desire to keep Robin as her lover.

Periodically Barnes mentions dates: "This was in nineteen hundred and twenty seven," "In nineteen hundred and twenty Felix was in Paris," not to develop the plot, but to remind us that our deep involvement with the characters' psyches prevents our noting the passage of time. In addition, the dates call attention to a traditional novelistic linearity and orderliness that Barnes rejects in capturing through analogic commentary the unorderly chaos of emotional life.

Two other features of *Nightwood*'s structure need comment. The first is Barnes's preference for interior settings. Even the outdoor places are "interior." Note, for example, the enclosed sense of the *place* where Matthew lives: "This relatively small square through which tram lines ran in several directions, bounded on the one side by the church and on the other by the court was the doctor's 'city.' What he could not find here to answer to his needs could be found in the narrow streets that ran into it." The constriction here is matched by the rococo room of Felix's parents, Jenny's cluttered house, Nora and Robin's memento-crowded apartment, Matthew's filthy chamber, and the crowded carriage in which Jenny, Robin, Matthew, and others drive through the streets of Paris. The novel's metaphoric interiorality suggests the extent to which the characters' private dilemmas pressure them emotionally, as if their bodies, like the rooms they live in and the sentences that describe them, cannot contain their intensity.

Enclosure as a condition of emotional pressure exemplifies the metaphoric method by which Barnes writes indirectly rather than directly about her subjects. Both narrative presentation of characters and ideas of the characters themselves testify to Matthew's (and Barnes's) belief that it is not possible to "dress the unknowable in the garments of the known." That is, abstractions like love, memory, irrational passion, and emotional pressure are discussable only in terms of something concrete, like cluttered rooms. The psyche remains in part mysterious and the reader, like the characters, can only intuit what might be occurring in the unconscious.

At the same time, her presentation of the unconscious is always self-conscious on the part of the characters, and one of the most singular features of *Nightwood* is the way Barnes makes interior feeling a topic of exterior conversation. The metaphoric language in which Matthew and Nora discuss abstract mental constructions calls on techniques often associated with interior monologue. One critic mentions Barnes's "frequent employment of the interior monologue" even though the novel's monologues are actually exterior and conscious. Some passages seem interior because states of mind are the principle subject of conversation and because the talk about them is removed from what we ordinarily associate with everyday conversation; people do not usually talk like Matthew, though interior monologues in novels may employ his degree of metaphor. Furthermore, the style of *Nightwood* as a whole is so idiosyncratic that it often seems as if Barnes were writing an essay instead of a novel. All the characters talk in the indirect style used in the narrative descriptions. Though in one sense Barnes keeps her reader at an impersonal distance by her indirection, in another she creates a personal voice which the characters all share. It is difficult to avoid thinking of a single metaphor-maker behind Matthew's and Nora's voices and narrative passages. As a result, the largely undifferentiated and highly self-conscious language may be thought of as Barnes's own "interior monologue" though formally there is nothing interior about it. Like Joyce and Faulkner, she is interested in what goes on in the mind, but instead of mimetic "streams" of consciousness or unconsciousness she relies on indirection in narrative observation, characterization, and figurative language.

By indirect narrative observation I mean that Barnes often presents scenes and characters so that the reader seems to be at one remove, as if watching the action through a camera in the process of capturing the scene. To introduce her characters she frequently uses a verb of observation in the passive voice with a hidden agent followed by one or more participles: "Here he had been seen ordering details for funerals . . . buying holy pictures . . . displaying vestaments and flowering candles." Or later on the same page: "He would be observed staring up at the high towers . . . running a thick worn finger around his throat, where, in spite of its custom his hair surprised him, lifting along his back and creeping up over his collar." Other examples at random:

> All these could be seen sitting about her oak table before the huge fire, Nora listening, her hand on her hound, the firelight throwing her shadow and his high against the wall.

> Then walking in the Prater he had been seen carrying in a conspicuously clenched fist the exquisite handkerchief of yellow and black linen.

> Baron Felix . . . had been seen in many countries standing before that country's palace gate, holding his gloved hands before him . . . contemplating relics and parts.

This construction suggests the presence of a narrative eye through which the reader sees the characters at a distance, much as if a camera were filming a scene from an anonymous but personal viewpoint. By placing this "eye" between reader and character and by focusing it on continuous action, Barnes avoids the immediacy a direct, finite verb of action would suggest and achieves a sense of distance and impartiality that keeps the reader from identifying very closely with the figure observed.

This narrative observation is related to another kind of indirection in the novel—the use of tableaux. Because the characters are introduced by this distanced narrative observer, the tableaux which follow their introductions carry the same sense of distance, as if that camera stops on a particular frame. Robin especially is caught in these stopped moments. We see her holding her son above her head as if to smash him on the floor, embracing Jenny beneath her garden's statue, or momentarily transfixed as a circus lioness bows down before her. At one point Barnes is explicit about this visual freeze-frame. She describes a meeting between Jenny and Robin. They are seated at a table, Jenny leaning forward, Robin leaning back: "They presented the two halves of a movement . . . that can divulge neither caution nor daring, for the fundamental condition for completion was in neither of them, they were like Greek runners, with lifted feet but without the relief of the final command that would bring the foot down— eternally angry, eternally separated, in a cataleptic gesture of abandon." Here the action is stilled because completion is impossible; Jenny is too shallow to love; Robin, too self-absorbed. But the "frozen gesture" is more than a metaphor for their incomplete relationship. It is a mode of Barnes's perception through which she does not describe action so much as prevent it by favoring stasis over activity, retelling over direct description. Her interest is not in events but in states of mind and the final inability of language to express those states.

The tableaux are one of several techniques Barnes uses to keep Robin before the reader as a present power rather than as a shaped character. Just as the tableaux allow us to see Robin from a distance, so Barnes's descriptive language, by focusing attention on her exotic surroundings and thus forcing the reader to associate Robin with it, evokes rather than presents her directly, as in the passage when we first see her:

> On a bed, surrounded by a confusion of potted plants, exotic palms and cut flowers, faintly over-sung by the notes of unseen birds, which seemed to have been forgotten—left without the usual silencing cover, which, like clouds on funeral urns, are cast over their cages at night by good housewives—half flung off the support of the cushions from which, in a moment of threatened consciousness she had turned her head, lay the young woman, heavy and dishevelled. Her legs, in white flannel trousers, were spread as in a dance, the thick-lacquered pumps looking too lively for the arrested step. Her hands, long and beautiful, lay on either side of her face.

The long first sentence delays naming Robin as its grammatical subject until near its end. Before coming to her the reader must process clauses and phrases that refer not to her but to her surroundings. It begins with two past participles which refer to Robin, although the reader does not recognize the referent immediately because of the inverted sentence order. Quickly, however, the direction shifts away from Robin in two relative clauses whose deep-structure subjects are not Robin, but first "birds," then "cover," then "cushions." Each succeeding relative clause asks the reader to suspend asking who is on the bed and focuses attention instead on what is in the room. Thus the largest percentage of words in the passage does not describe Robin; it calls attention to her surroundings and at the same time maintains suspense about the woman by delaying her grammatical "entrance." The passive voice of "are cast" in the metaphor and "were spread" in the second sentence together with the reduced passive past participles and the intransitive, low-activity main verb, "lay," repeated once, become syntax-as-metaphor to emphasize the physically passive posture of the woman on the bed.

Barnes's evocation of Robin is sensuous as well as indirect and passive. We see the exotic palms and hear the birds before we come to the woman who is to become the center of attention. The diction obviously heightens the sense of Robin as primal, but along with the plants, palms, and flowers are a group of words that suggest something missing: "*unseen* birds, which seem to have been *forgotten*—left *without* the usual *silencing* cover." Similarly the consciousness is "threatened," the step "arrested." Throughout there is a sense of negative presence or of partial presence signalled by the "not" feature of the words in the collocation appropriate to Robin who is perceived primarily by her absence. She is "an amputation that Nora [can] not renounce."

Robin is further evoked by negation in the following passage where the repetition of "un-," "no," and "never" reinforces her unmistakable "notness." Note how the normal syntax of the opening sentence is reordered to shift the negative "unaware" to a position of end-focus:

Yes now, when they were alone and happy, apart from the world in their appreciation of the world, there entered with Robin a company *unaware*. Sometimes it rang clear in the songs she sang, sometimes Italian, sometimes French or German, songs of the people debased and haunting, songs that Nora had *never* heard before, or that she had *never* heard in company with Robin. When the cadence changed, when it was repeated on a lower key, she knew that Robin was singing of a life that she herself had *no part* in; snatches of harmony as tell-tale as the possessions of a traveller from a foreign land; songs like a practiced whore who turns away from *no one* but the one who loves her. Sometimes Nora would sing them after Robin, with the trepidation of a foreigner repeating words in an *unknown* tongue, *uncertain* of what they may mean. Sometimes *unable* to endure the melody that told so much and so little, she would interrupt Robin with a question. Yet more distressing would be the moment when, after a pause, the song would be taken up again from an inner room where Robin, *unseen*, gave back an echo of her *unknown* life more nearly tuned to its origin. Often the song would stop altogether, until *unthinking*, just as she was leaving the house, Robin would break out again in anticipation, changing the sound from a reminiscence to an expectation.

These negatives are supported by words with negative force, including "debased," "turns away," "whore," "foreign," "foreigner," "stop," "distressing," "trepidation." The use of the "would" instead of the simple past tense also evokes rather than describes directly because it conveys a repeated condition rather than a definite complete action.

Perhaps no single mark of Barnes's style contributes so powerfully to the language of evocation as the use of metaphor. Though the metaphor is especially elaborate in connection with Robin and with the descriptions of the night, it is a mark of the novel's style throughout. It contributes to the evocative quality of *Nightwood* by relying on analogy to suggest the implications of the novel's situation. Metaphor, and I am using the term broadly to include various tropes, conceits, and analogies, ranges from the relatively straightforward, ("as if Robin and she . . . were a pair of opera glasses turned to the wrong end, diminishing in their painful love") to the obscure ("Such a woman is the infected carrier of the past: before her the structure of our head and jaws ache—we feel that we could eat her, she who is eaten death returning, for only then do we put our face close to the blood on the lips of our forefathers"). This description of Robin depends on the context of the novel as a whole. Unlike the comparison with the opera glasses, it can be understood only as part of a larger set of associations identifying Robin with the forces of early evolution. The language of *Nightwood* requires the reader to make associations among suggestions that are scattered throughout the novel. Thus the description of Robin as an "infected carrier" of a past that extends backward to the moment of the "beast turning human" becomes meaningful as one of a number of references to the "way back," to beasts both actual and mythical and to the pre-verbal realm from which she comes. These evolutionary references are related in turn to another set, again referring to prehistory, but instead of to beasts, to "the fossil of Robin, intaglio of her identity," "the hieroglyphics of sleep and pain," figures of design, and references to tracing.

Furthermore, the sets themselves are not merely repeated patterns of images; they are groups of associations which have a collective meaning within each group and from set to set. Thus to understand Robin, the reader must respond to the language of evocation associatively rather than analytically. Barnes makes individual tropes part of a series whose items may shift metaphoric shape without losing their relatedness to the whole lexical or semantic set, and whose meaning is not fully graspable without the reader's power of intuition. As a result, logical reconstruction must be suspended in favor of allowing the collective sets to *suggest* rather than *present* meaning.

The reader's problem is complicated by Barnes's insistence not only that associations between spatially separated metaphors be made and allowed to reshape each other, but also that syntactically linked pairs of opposites and near-opposites be tolerated. That is, by connecting words that are semantically opposed, she refuses to acknowledge their dichotomous tensions:

> Amid loud and frantic cries of *affirmation and despair* Robin was delivered.

(Note, too, how the passive voice separates Robin from the birth, a process she has refused to participate in actively and soon renounces by leaving husband and son.)

> The equilibrium of her nature, *savage and refined*, gave her bridled skull a look of compassion.

> Her gaze was anchored in *anticipation and regret*.

> Her head moved perceptively with the broken arc of two instincts, *recoil and advance*.

> Two spirits were working in her, *love and anonymity*. Yet they were so "haunted" of each other that separation was impossible.

In a small way the language of the last example speaks to the predicament of the entire novel. Opposites are so bound up in each other that duality is impossible. This stylistic joining prefaces Nora's most important personal discovery—that in loving Robin she loves herself, for they are of the same kind, mirror images of one another. What appears initially as different is finally the same: "She is myself."

Nora's discovery of the self-recognition and self-knowledge possible in loving a woman finally cannot be contained by the novel's most forceful and brilliant rhetoric. The two long monologues of Matthew O'Connor are marked by the same stylistic features that characterize the narration and the speech of the other characters. But in his speeches those features, extended analogy, associative semantic sets, and oppositional pairings, are expanded so that the ultimate failure of Matthew's talk is particularly dramatic.

From his first appearance Matthew embodies language and discourse. We first see him speaking to an audience of eleven at a party, a group gathered "by the simple device of pronouncing at the top of his voice . . . some of the more boggish and biting of the shorter Saxon verbs." The comic note here often reappears in connection with Matthew; in fact his own droll stories and comic put-downs create a distance between himself and his listeners that finally destroys rather than protects him. Later in the evening of that party the "insistent hum" of his words puts his companion to sleep and we get some sense of the final ineffectiveness of talk. He knows he substitutes talk for living: "I've given my destiny away by garrulity . . . for no matter what I may be doing, in my heart is the wish for children and knitting," but still he fills the air with words.

In his first monologue, "Watchman, What of the Night," he tells Nora "how the day and the night are related by their divisions," again seeking to bring together two contraries. But he cannot do it directly; he must instead compare French nights to American ones and pose numerous rhetorical questions to Nora who grows more and more desperate because she wants specific information about why Robin lives as she dies, not a seemingly endless stream of epigrams ("the brawl of the Beast leaves a path for the Beast"), comic descriptions ("You can imagine how Jenny trembled when she saw herself going toward fifty without . . . anything in her past that would get a flower named for her"), elaborate curses, quotes from Donne, Cibber, Montaigne et al, extended tropes, and self-mythologizing. But finally he comes to Nora's problem. In his own figurative way and in his own time he relates his understanding of Nora's pain and tells the story of the "night of nights." For the length of his monologue Matthew is conscious and purposeful about his indirection. He knows that "even the greatest generality has a little particular," and says he has a narrative "but you will be put to it to find it . . . there is no direct way. The foetus of symmetry nourishes itself on cross purposes." He acknowledges "my mind is so rich that it is always wandering." Matthew's method in the monologue is Barnes's throughout the novel. There is no adequate way to speak directly about the night, whose inhabitants have no conscious control over their actions, or about Robin, who wanders in the dark, or about Nora's love, which sends her in search both of Robin and of unknown parts of herself. Even at this point halfway through the novel, Matthew, and through him Barnes, speaks to the failure of language: "We who are full to the gorge with misery should look well around, doubting everything seen, done, spoken, precisely because we have a word for it and not its alchemy."

Intuition and indirection are the touchstones both of Barnes's style and epistemology in *Nightwood* because its central subject, the power and difficulty of love, does not yield itself to the logical language of direct statement.

The inadequacy of the word suggested in "Watchman, What of the Night" becomes the complete failure of verbal communication in Matthew's second long encounter with Nora, "Go Down Matthew." Its opening question signals a shift in roles from "Watchman." " 'Can't you be quiet now?' " says Matthew to Nora and though he is still the principal talker in most of the chapter, Nora comes to speech before its conclusion while Matthew eventually ceases his talking in despair. The more Matthew tries to convince her to give up hoping for Robin's love, the more Nora understands why she cannot. Focused on discussions of memory as fiction and love between women, and ending in Matthew's lamentation for his own lost life, the chapter brings together the main concerns of the novel and discusses them in the same powerful style of the earlier monologues.

When Nora's voice takes precedence, it resembles Matthew's, but is more personal. In the following exchange, for example, Matthew speaks generally, Nora personally:

> He got up and crossed to the window. "That priceless galaxy of misinformation called the mind, harnessed to that stupendous and threadbare glomerate compulsion called the soil, ambling down the almost obliterated bridle path of Well and Ill, fortuitously planned—is the holy Habeas Corpus, the manner in which the body is brought before the judge—still—in the end Robin will wish you in a nunnery where what she loved is, by surroundings, made safe, because as you are you keep bringing her up as cannons bring up the dead from deep water."
>
> "In the end," Nora said, "they came to me, the girls Robin had driven frantic—to me, for comfort!" She began to laugh. "My God," she said, "the women I've held upon my knees!"
>
> "Women," the doctor said, "were born on the knees; that's why I've never been able to do anything about them; I'm on my own so much of the time."
>
> "Suddenly, I knew what all my life had been, Matthew, what I hoped Robin was—the secure torment. We can hope for nothing greater, except hope. If I asked her, crying, not to go out, she would go just the same, richer in her heart because I had touched it, as she was going down the stairs."
>
> "Lions grow their manes and foxes their teeth on that bread," interpolated the doctor.
>
> "In the beginning, when I tried to stop her from drinking and staying out all night, and from being defiled, she would say, Ah, I feel so pure and gay! as if the ceasing of that abuse was her only happiness and peace of mind; and so I struggled with her as with

the coils of my own most obvious heart, holding her by the hair, striking her against my lap, as a child bounces in a crib to enter excitement, even if it were someone gutted on a dagger. I thought I loved her for her sake, and I found it was for my own."

The rate of first-person pronominals is five times greater in Nora's speech than in Matthew's. In addition, Matthew's less personal voice sounds in his abstract nouns ("misfortune," "mind," "compulsion," "soul," "manner") and stative verbs. Nora recalls specific incidents and uses concrete action verbs and verbals ("struggled," "holding," "striking," "raised," "dropped," "bounces," "gutted"). Matthew's opening speech is notable both for its Latinate word choice and its mixed metaphors. Classic derivatives like "galaxy," "misfortune," "stupendous," "glomerate," "compulsion," "obliterated," "fortuitously," culminate in "holy Habeas Corpus" which in turn is part of the legalistic diction surrounding God as judge. But at the same time this polysyllabic self-important rhetoric is in tension with the "harnessed," "ambling," "bridle path" set which suggests nothing more than a buggy out for a leisurely ride in an overgrown park. Typically, the degree of visuality in the metaphor is low. With the mind as galaxy and the soul as compulsion it is not quite possible to imagine which is the cart and which the horse. The lack of specificity is part of Barnes's sense that language cannot fully capture, especially directly, what she wishes to convey. The combination of the legal and carriage metaphors together with the borrowed allegory in "Well" and "Ill" is comic because of the incongruity of juxtaposition. In the next sentence, indicated here by dashes, Matthew moves rapidly from the comic to the prophetic (signalled by "wish") and yet another analogy for Robin and Nora's relationship. The reference to the cannon bringing up the dead is the kind of indirection so central to Barnes's style—reference to emotional connection by concrete analogy. Nora's voice in the speech concluding this passage also depends on comparisons, "as if it were a game," "as some people strike their hands," but she eschews Matthew's incongruity, inflation and prophecy and speaks of her own experiences rather than relying on abstract exempla.

In the passage which ends their "conversation" and leaves Matthew in "confused and unhappy silence," Nora realizes that in death, where memory is obliterated, she and Robin might come together. This excerpt is a fine example of Barnes's indirection and of her associative style.

"Looking from her to the Madonna behind the candles, I knew that the image, to her, was what I had been to Robin, not a saint at all, but a fixed dismay, the space between the human and the holy head, the arena of the 'indecent' eternal. At that moment I stood in the centre of eroticism and death, death that makes the dead smaller, as a lover we are beginning to forget dwindles and wastes; for love and life are a bulk of which the body and heart can be drained, and I knew in that bed Robin should have put me down. In that bed we would have forgotten our lives in the ex-

tremity of memory, moulted our parts, as figures in the waxworks
are moulted down to their story, so we would have broken down
to our love."

As so often in Barnes, Nora's discovery is made in terms of something else:
she recognizes her relationship to Robin by mentally transforming a young
woman's candle to the Madonna into a sign of Robin's relation to herself.
Her language in the first sentence depends on the metaphoric construction
A is B, but the features of B, though they grow increasingly concrete,
"dismay"—"space"—"arena" violate the reader's expectation that B will
somehow be visual and concrete enough to elucidate A. The violation and
the appositional structure permit Barnes to suggest that the naming power
of language is insufficient to make Nora's love for Robin perceivable to the
reader. The lines of the passage also show a predilection for explaining one
thing in terms of another by analogy. Death makes the dead smaller "as a
lover we are beginning to forget dwindles and wastes," "we would have
forgotten our lives . . . as figures . . . are moulted down to their story."
Additional metaphors include "I stood in the centre," "for love and life are
a bulk," "that bed," and "moulted." Every sentence of the passage is in
some way metaphoric and though not every sentence of the novel is equally
so, the passage is typical rather than atypical. The indirection suggested
by her use of analogy and metaphor is supported by her use of apposition
in which one phrase is followed by an elaborating one, as in the dismay—
space—arena sequence and again in the elaboration of "forgotten our lives"
by "moulted our parts." It is as if a single description were insufficient and
that several attempts are needed to convey the meaning.

The passage also typifies the way in which a full reading of *Nightwood*
depends on associations made by the reader among repeated words or
ideas. The central idea that death brings with it the obliteration of memory
culminates a series of references to memory and forgetting in the chapter,
such as "I can only find her again in my sleep or in her death; in both she
has forgotten me," "Robin can go anywhere, do anything . . . because she
forgets and I nowhere because I remember," "and because you forget Robin
the best, it is to you she turns," "I have been loved . . . by something
strange and it has forgotten me." In context, these remarks are individually
inconsequential; together they form one of the text's principal preoccupa-
tions. But many novelists count on repetition to support the force of an
idea not directly addressed. Barnes stands out because virtually every noun
and several verbs in the passage belong to a repeated series which in turn
signals a thematic concern. In addition to the obvious interest called up by
the collocation of death, emotion, and love, "madonna," "candles," "image," and "saint" recur in relating the danger of passionate worship. "Figure" and "story" recall the emphasis on the stories and storytelling of
Matthew, the fictional life of Felix, and the destructive fabrications of Nora's
memory. "Broken down" belongs to the semantically related set of verbs
including "go down," "going down," "bow down" that Kenneth Burke

calls the "transcendence downward" mode of *Nightwood*. "Moulted" itself is not repeated, but references to birds and birdnests recur several times. These latter differ from items like memory, death, love, in that they are less thematically significant, but their recurrence signals Barnes's associative style by indicating that even metaphoric terms used to call up different ideas are recurrent. Matthew speaks of the lining of his belly as a bird's nest "flocked with the locks cut off love in odd places" and later tells a story meant to keep Nora from being so protective of Robin, about an English girl who made nests so well that the birds forgot how to do it themselves. Another reference connects birds not with over-enthusiastic protection, but with lying: "Do I wail . . . of every lie, how it went down into my belly and built a nest to hatch me to my death there." The change in referent from love to lie is in keeping with the novel's connection between love and fictionalizing.

This passage, with its complex set of associations, completes Nora's coming to speech and immediately precedes Matthew's recognition that talking does not alleviate pain. Nora's obvious turmoil and more personal metaphors force Matthew to leave his impersonal role as comforter of the world's wounded and sum up his own life. What he sees is not that he is "a good man doing wrong, but the wrong man doing nothing much." He continues by recognizing the failure of his talking: "I wouldn't be telling you about it if I weren't talking to myself. I talk too much because I have been made so miserable by what you are keeping hushed." Nora has forced him out from under his stone and he is finally naked, laboring to comfort her. He cannot talk her out of her commitment to Robin; instead, he brings her to speech at the very time he recognizes fully that words are useless. Thus for all his extravagant language he fails twice over: he does not "cure" Nora and he makes her uselessly articulate. His probing of her love for Robin forces him to acknowledge the emptiness of his own life. He has substituted talk for love and that recognition leads to his final collapse: "I've not only lived my life for nothing, but I've told it for nothing—abominable among the filthy people—I know, it's all over, everything's over and nobody knows it but me—drunk as a fiddler's bitch—lasted too long—." He tried to get to his feet, gave it up. "Now," he said, "the end—mark my words—now *nothing but wrath and weeping!*"

In her slow coming to speech, Nora articulates for the first time the source of her passion for Robin and the reason for Matthew's failed efforts to dissuade her. In loving a woman she comes to know and love herself as well: "A man is another person—a woman is yourself, caught as you turn in panic; on her mouth you kiss your own. If she is taken you cry you have been robbed of yourself." To express the "outsideness" of love between women, Barnes reorders the patterns of ordinary discourse, eschews its propensity for naming directly, and creates a sense of doubleness in which states of mind are understood only in terms of metaphors that gather force from a context of related associations. In so doing she forges a style apart from the standard "great tradition," one perfectly suited to the novel's exploration of sexual possession, threat, pain, and love outside and beyond the conventional.

When in the brief final chapter, Nora and Robin converge on a small chapel, even the indirect language of that style is impossible; their meeting is wordless. We do not know when Nora, unpersuaded by Matthew's elaborate speeches, returns to America or how Robin's wanderings bring her "up to Nora's part of the country." We do know that Jenny "strikes herself down," putting accusations against Robin into words, and that Robin brings silence with her into the woods near Nora's home. Instinct, not argument, draws Nora and Robin together but Robin, unable to survive a love that requires her to be fully conscious, moves back into the preverbal world from which others had awakened her only briefly. We last see her on her hands and knees beside Nora's hound, both of them "crying in shorter and shorter spaces, moving head to head." Finally Robin gives up, "lying out, her hands beside her, her face turned and weeping." *Nightwood* has at its silent center a recognition that even the most brilliant rhetoric, the most suggestive metaphor cannot deny the power of haunted love or the magnetism of the night world.

Untroubled Voice: Call and Response in Jean Toomer's *Cane*

Barbara E. Bowen

If there is a single gesture which characterizes Jean Toomer's *Cane*—a book even its most vigorous supporter called a "chaos"—it is the gesture of listening for a voice. *Cane* begins with the word, "Oracular," a call for voice from "deep-rooted cane," and enacts again and again the same scene of calling for voice. The most powerful version of the scene comes in "Esther," where it appears in doubled form: first a kind of silent call, a crowd's hushed anticipation of speech, then a story of calling and responding. The sketch begins with the crowd's gathering to listen to King Barlo:

> A clean-muscled, magnificent, black-skinned Negro, whom she had heard her father mention as King Barlo, suddenly drops to his knees on a spot called the Spittoon. . . . Soon, people notice him, and gather round. His eyes are rapturous upon the heavens. Lips and nostrils quiver. Barlo is in a religious trance. Town folks know it. They are not startled. They are not afraid. They gather round. Some beg boxes from the grocery stores. From old Mc-Gregor's notion shop. A coffin case is pressed into use. Folks line the curb-stones. Business men close shop. And Banker Warply parks his car close by. Silently, all await the prophet's voice.

The first words Barlo speaks are an announcement of an answer to his call; it is the answer that makes him a prophet. "Jesus," he begins, "has been awhisperin strange words deep down, O way down deep, deep in my ears." Twice more he tells the crowd that Jesus has been awhisperin in his ears before he will let them hear what Jesus said. While he is heightening their eagerness for Jesus' words, he is at the same time focusing attention relentlessly on his own voice. It is Barlo's voice that turns Jesus' message into an event, an intimate drama of father and son—"He called me to His

From *Black Literature and Literary Theory*. © 1984 by Methuen, Inc. Originally entitled "Untroubled Voice: Call and Response in *Cane*."

side an said, 'Git down on your knees beside me, son, Ise gwine t whisper in your ears' "—and Barlo's voice that releases us from the tautness of the narrator's prose. Listen to the freeing of rhythm as Barlo begins to speak:

> The crowd is hushed and expectant. Barlo's under jaw relaxes, and his lips begin to move.
> "Jesus has been awhisperin strange words deep down, O way down deep, deep in my ears."

And, finally, it is Barlo's voice that enables the crowd to speak. Silent until he speaks, the crowd finds voice in response to him. An "old sister" interrupts with "Ah, Lord," and later, "Ah, Lord. Amen. Amen," while someone else shouts, "Preach it, preacher, preach it!"

Barlo, too, has found voice after hearing a response to his call. Jesus' message is for him not a chance revelation but an *answer* to his own voice. He inserts himself into the story of Jesus' message and shapes the message as a response to his readiness to hear; only after Barlo says "Thy will be done on earth as it is in heaven" does Jesus speak. And the "strange good words," when at last we hear them, are nothing more, or less, than instructions on how to speak. "Tell 'em," Jesus says to Barlo, "till you feel your throat on fire." Barlo does not need to ask what he is to "tell 'em"; he knows he has been enfranchised to preach. That a voice responds to his call suddenly confirms his own ability to speak.

The real event, then, in the drama Barlo narrates is not his hearing of Jesus' message but his own discovery of voice. Jesus' words are almost forgotten as Barlo's sermon becomes the center of the crowd's attention. By the end of the scene, the shift of voice from Jesus to Barlo is complete; despite Barlo's emphasis on hearing Jesus speak, it is his own voice that is finally compelling. And the sermon he preaches is testimony to what affirmation of voice means. Watch what happens the moment Barlo is authorized to speak: "An He said, 'Tell em till you feel your throat on fire.' I saw a vision. I saw a man arise, an he was big an black an powerful—" Suddenly he is able to imagine a past; for the first time, Barlo sees himself not as an actor in a private drama but as a member of a community. The vision he sees connects him with Africa and provides a symbolic ancestor for the whole Afro-American community. "He was big an black an powerful," Barlo tells us, "—but his head was caught up in the clouds. An while he was agazin at the heavens, heart filled up with the Lord, some little white-ant biddies came an tied his feet to chains." For Barlo, affirmation of voice is affirmation of presence and release from what Geoffrey Hartman calls "the terror of discontinuity." Barlo no longer needs a responding voice to establish continuity with his world; he has created his own continuity by envisioning a shared history.

His language bears lively witness to his faith in continuity, for it enacts the process of affirming continuity with a group. As Barlo tells the story of the captured African—"They led him t the coast, they led him t th sea . . . "—his words begin to shape themselves into a perfect blues stanza:

> "They led him t the coast,
> They led him t th sea,
> They led him across the ocean,
> An they didnt set him free.
> The old coast didnt miss him,
> An the new coast wasnt free,
> He left the old-coast brothers,
> T give birth t you an me.
> O Lord, great God Almighty,
> T give birth to you an me."

The statement–variation–response sequence which is the essence of the blues is a development of the call-and-response pattern of collective work-songs and spirituals. For the blues singer, the importance of the call-and-response pattern is its continual affirmation of collective voice. As antiphonal phrases repeat and respond to each other, the singers are assenting to membership in a group and affirming that their experience is shared. When Barlo slips easily into the blues, he is giving rhetorical expression to the continuity he discovered with assurance of voice.

More important, though, than Barlo's sense of continuity with the past is the promise of a future it implies. The crowd hears his vision of the past as a vision of the future; they turn his story of oppression into a prophecy of regeneration. As Barlo preaches, he is transformed for them into the African he describes: "Barlo rises to his full height. He is immense. To the people he assumes the outlines of his visioned African." Barlo has made the past present for his audience and embodied it in himself. That he can imagine continuity with the past enables them to imagine regeneration in the future, and their belief in regeneration takes the form it always has for Toomer: prophecy of a black messiah. As its narrators long for sexual consummation and search unsuccessfully for a black madonna, *Cane* is registering the struggle for belief in renewal. Barlo is a figure of such magnetism because he enacts the assurance of renewal as he teaches his people to hear a response to their call. Their response, too, comes from deep, deep down when Barlo enjoins them, "Open your ears": "Years afterwards Esther was told that at that very moment a great, heavy, rumbling voice actually was heard. That hosts of angels and of demons paraded up and down the streets all night. That King Barlo rode out of town astride a pitch-black bull that had a glowing gold ring in its nose. . . . This much is certain: an inspired Negress, of wide reputation for being sanctified, drew a portrait of a black madonna on the courthouse wall." This is the same portrait that appears in "Fern," and there the connection with depth and the earth is even stronger. "I felt strange," the northern visitor observes, "as I always do in Georgia, particularly at dusk. I felt that things unseen to men were tangibly immediate. It would not have surprised me had I had a vision. People have them in Georgia more often than you would suppose. A black woman once saw the mother of Christ and drew her in charcoal on the courthouse wall. . . . When one is on the soil of one's ancestors, most anything can come to one." Kabnis, too, standing on the soil of his ancestors, is moved to comment: "Things are so immediate in Georgia." As his characters locate the source of visions and voices in the soil, Toomer is subtly shifting the source of the messiah. While voices come to white prophets from the heavens, they come to black prophets from the earth. And specifically the Georgia earth, where the name of the state comes from the word for "earth." If the white messiah descends from heaven, the black messiah rises from the earth; and the earth takes on its enormous significance in *Cane*, reminding us of fertility, birth, and the womb.

Over and over, Toomer's narrators hear the empowering response to their calls from deep, deep down and figure the response as the birth of a black messiah. In "Box Seat," where the narrator is perhaps closest to Toomer himself, there are two striking moments of confidence in rebirth. First, as Dan Moore waits for Muriel, he resolves to stop merely watching—"I'll never peep"—and begin actively listening:

> I'll listen. I like to listen.
> Dan goes to the wall and places his ear against it. A passing street car and something vibrant from the earth sends a rumble to him. That rumble comes from the earth's deep core. It is the mutter of powerful underground races. Dan has a picture of all the people rushing to put their ears against walls, to listen to it. The next world-savior is coming up that way. Coming up. A continent sinks down. The new-world Christ will need consummate skill to walk upon the waters where huge bubbles burst.

Dan's sense of the earth is a southerner's—and also a poet's—sense; when a streetcar rumbles beneath him he hears not the sounds of northern technology but the stirrings of a fertile earth. Without hesitation he declares the noise to be "the mutter of powerful underground races." By transforming the streetcar rumble into speech, he has given the earth voice; and in the process found his own voice. That he can make the earth speak to him confirms his own authority to speak and gives him the same assurance of renewal that was charcoaled on the courthouse wall. In his essay on apostrophe, Jonathan Culler suggests why response from nature is crucial to the poet's authority to speak. "The vocative of apostrophe," he writes, "is a device which the poetic voice uses to establish with an object a relationship which helps to constitute him. To object is treated as an *I* which implies a certain kind of *you* in its turn. One who successfully invokes nature is one to whom nature might, in its turn, speak. He makes himself poet, visionary." For Dan, as for Barlo's audience, hearing a response so strongly confirms the self that it denies discontinuity and allows a vision of lasting renewal.

Dan's second vision of renewal is again centered in the earth; it is his realization of what it means to stand on the soil of one's ancestors. Sitting in the theater, he catches "the soil-soaked fragrance" of the Negress next to him, and suddenly the whole theater comes to life in a scene of intense eroticism:

> Through the cement floor her strong roots sink down. They spread under the asphalt streets. Dreaming, the streets roll over on their bellies, and suck their glossy health from them. Her strong roots sink down and spread under the river and disappear in blood-lines that waver south. Her roots shoot down. Dan's hands follow them. Roots throb. Dan's heart beats violently. He places his palms upon the earth to cool them. Earth throbs. Dan's heart beats violently. He sees all the people in the house rush to the walls to listen to the rumble. A new-world Christ is coming up.

Hearing a voice from deep in the earth allows Dan a fantasy of the sexual consummation he never achieves in reality. The throbbing of the earth beneath him is for Dan the evidence of a responding voice, and again the voice carries a promise of renewal through a black messiah.

Here, the promise is intensified because Dan feels as well as hears nature's response to him. In one of the transformations of image which animate this section of *Cane*—think of the house in "Rhobert" or the street in "Seventh Street"—the woman's fragrance changes from roots under a city to a network of roots under a river and finally to blood-lines. By turning roots into blood-lines, Toomer suddenly invests blood-lines with new meaning; they become literally lines of blood: like roots, tangible lines of sustenance and connection with the sources of regeneration. Evocative of soil and the sugar-cane plant, roots appear throughout *Cane* and are one of the persistent figurations of the rebirth it constantly seeks. What is important about Toomer's choice of roots as an image of rebirth is that they are a specifically Afro-American symbol, part of the vitality of southern black life that *Cane* celebrates.

Perhaps the most daring instance of Toomer's insistence on an *Afro-American* renewal is his revision of the standard Romantic image of mist or smoke. The first section of *Cane* could almost be a manifesto for a new literary tradition, based on community and belief rather than alienation and doubt. "Karintha" takes one of the most celebrated Anglo-American poems of its day and pointedly rewrites a central image. Here is the famous beginning of T. S. Eliot's "The Love Song of J. Alfred Prufrock":

> Let us go then, you and I,
> When the evening is spread out against the sky
> Like a patient etherised upon a table;
> Let us go, through certain half-deserted streets,
> The muttering retreats
> Of restless nights in one-night cheap hotels
> And sawdust restaurants with oyster-shells:
> Streets that follow like a tedious argument
> Of insidious intent

To lead you to an overwhelming question . . .
Oh, do not ask, 'What is it?'
Let us go and make our visit.
   In the room the women come and go
Talking of Michelangelo.

   The yellow fog that rubs its back upon the window-panes,
The yellow smoke that rubs its muzzle on the window-
      panes,
Licked its tongue into the corners of the evening,
Lingered upon the pools that stand in drains,
Let fall upon its back the soot that falls from chimneys,
Slipped by the terrace, made a sudden leap,
And seeing that it was a soft October night,
Curled once about the house, and fell asleep.

Now Toomer's "Karintha":

At sunset, when there was no wind, and the pine-smoke from
over by the sawmill hugged the earth, and you couldnt see more
than a few feet in front, her sudden darting past you was a bit of
vivid color, like a black bird that flashes in light. . . . A sawmill
was nearby. Its pyramidal sawdust pile smouldered. It is a year
before one completely burns. Meanwhile, the smoke curls up and
hangs in old wraiths about the trees, curls up, and spreads itself
out over the valley. . . . Weeks after Karintha returned home the
smoke was so heavy you tasted it in water. Some one made a
song:

      Smoke is on the hills. Rise up.
      Smoke is on the hills. O rise
      And take my soul to Jesus.

Toomer has learned from Eliot how to personify smoke, and he calls attention to his source with the phrase "spreads itself out" and the repetition
of "curls up"—both echoes from Eliot's opening lines. But if Eliot's fog,
like the winding streets of his city, is an emblem for Prufrock's endless
uncertainties, Toomer's pine-smoke is a physical sign of continuity between
earth and heaven, a straightforward answer to the problem of reaching
Jesus. The final brilliant stroke in the passage from "Karintha" is to turn
Eliot's urbane and intellectual fog into the smoke of a southern spiritual.
The primitive prayer to lift the smoke from the valley is also an expression
of belief in a personal, fatherly Jesus; "Rise up" is as much a statement of
the simple belief that Prufrock could never share as it is an exhortation to
the heavy smoke. The pine-smoke wreathes throughout the first section of
Cane, always as a symbol of the belief in renewal expressed in "Karintha" 's
spiritual. In "Becky," for instance, the trees themselves are given voice,
and the phrase "The pines whispered to Jesus" becomes a kind of refrain,
promising regeneration with Jesus despite Becky's failure to bear the black

messiah. Or in "Georgia Dusk" we hear that "the pine trees are guitars" and "the chorus of the cane / Is caroling a vesper to the stars." Finally, in "Song of the Sun" the pine-smoke is entrusted to carry the last vestige of a disappearing culture.

> Pour O pour that parting soul in song,
> O pour it in the sawdust glow of night,
> Into the velvet pine-smoke air tonight,
> And let the valley carry it along.
> And let the valley carry it along.

Cane's most dazzling moment of regeneration is enabled by another image of connection: the tongue. Like roots and curls of smoke, the tongue can be pictured as a winding line, and it is in this form that it becomes the center of "Her Lips Are Copper Wire," a poem which must be *Cane*'s most stunning single piece:

> whisper of yellow globes
> gleaming on lamp-posts that sway
> like bootleg licker drinkers in the fog
>
> and let your breath be moist against me
> like bright beads on yellow globes
>
> telephone the power-house
> that the main wires are insulate
>
> (her words play softly up and down
> dewy corridors of billboards)
>
> then with your tongue remove the tape
> and press your lips to mine
> till they are incandescent.

This is Toomer's display of real virtuosity. His control of assonance and rhythm—in the third and last lines, for instance—produces a poem that is at once startling and seductive. Toomer has learned from the Metaphysical poets how to transform a technological instrument into an image for emotion or eroticism; his sensuous telephone wires owe much to Donne's "stiff twin compasses." At the same time, the image of copper-wire lips unites the northern and southern sections of the book, combining technology and sexuality. With the union of north and south comes the only true possibility of sexual consummation in the book. The "incandescence" of the poem's last stanza is the regenerating sexual union—and perhaps the promise of a black messiah—that *Cane*'s narrators can never achieve. And the union, of it is possible, will be enabled by voice: lips and tongue. "Then with your tongue remove the tape," the speaker urges, "and press your lips to mine." If in "Esther" and "Box Seat" the discovery of voice produced a vision of renewal, in "Her Lips Are Copper Wire" it provides the renewal itself. The final stanza, then, with its deep eroticism, is a description of finding voice. Like Barlo and Dan, the poet is listening for a response; he asks the woman literally to empower his voice by removing the tape which keeps him silent. Thus the confidence and power of the closing line is as much a display of new-found voice as an expression of sexual fulfillment.

What is at stake for Toomer in hearing a response to his voice is perhaps clearest when we consider the source for his dilemma, the Romantic lyric. The Romantic poets sought oneness with nature, at least in part because they wanted to reverse the dualism and discontinuity imposed on us by the Fall. It is because Adam's naming of the animals in the Garden is our image of perfect continuity—man and nature, word and thing—that it becomes the Romantics' model for an unfallen poetry. The Adamic model informs Romanticism in America even more than in England, and perhaps most explicitly in the work of Walt Whitman. In poems such as "To the Garden the World," "As Adam Early in the Morning," and "There Was a Child Went Forth," Whitman's project is to pose a new Adam, "peering and penetrating" in perfect communion with nature. One version of the new Adam is the child who becomes the world he observes:

> There was a child went forth every day,
> And the first object he look'd upon, that object he became,
> And that object became part of him for the day or a certain part
> of the day,
> Or for many years or stretching cycles of years.

When Whitman made his poet a new Adam in the Garden, he was giving expression to what R. W. B. Lewis calls an "emergent American myth." The myth is crucial for Toomer, because it is against this myth that *Cane* defines itself. The "American Adam," Lewis writes, was

> an individual emancipated from history, happily bereft of ancestry, untouched and undefiled by the usual inheritances of family and race; an individual standing alone, self-reliant and self-propelling, ready to confront whatever awaited him with the aid of his own unique and inherent resources. It was not surprising, in a Bible-reading generation, that the new hero . . . was most easily identified with Adam before the Fall. Adam was the first, the archetypal, man. . . . And he was the type of the creator, the poet par excellence, creating language itself by naming the elements of the scene about him.

If the figure for the American myth is Adam, the figure for the Afro-American myth is Cain. In Genesis, God tells Cain, "And now art thou cursed from the earth, which hath opened her mouth to receive thy brother's blood from thy hand . . . a fugitive and a vagabond shalt thou be in the earth." Cain is the first fugitive, the archetypal wanderer. As self-consciously as Whitman in his Adam poems, Toomer in *Cane* is offering a new cultural myth. While the American poet seeks the authority to speak by trying to recover an unfallen continuity of language and nature, the Afro-American poet seeks authority by trying to recover an unexiled con-

tinuity of speaker and listener. As Toomer's narrators listen for a responding voice and figure their response as pine-smoke, cane-roots, copper-wire
lips and a black messiah, Toomer is posing an emphatically Afro-American
solution to the essential Romantic problem: finding authority to speak in
a discontinuous, dualistic world. For Romantic poets, response from nature
assures the continuity that empowers voice; for Afro-American poets, the
empowering response is from their people. *Cane* is the record of Toomer's
discovery that call and response—the drama of finding authority through
communal voice—has enabled the creation of a distinctively Afro-American
literary form.

That *Cane* records the discovery of a literary form helps to explain
Toomer's notoriously cryptic statement about its structure. Writing to
Waldo Frank in December 1922, Toomer claimed:

> From three angles, *Cane*'s design is a circle. Aesthetically, from
> simple forms to complex ones, and back to simple forms. Region-
> ally, from the South up to the North, and back into the South
> again. Or, from the North down into the South, and then a return
> North. From the point of view of the spiritual entity behind the
> work, the curve really starts with Bona and Paul (awakening),
> plunges into Kabnis, emerges in Karintha, etc., swings upward
> into Theater and Box Seat, and ends (pauses) in Harvest Song.

Toomer is suggesting that *Cane* contains a kind of counterpoint, a dialectic,
between content and form. The literary form that Paul awakens to and
Kabnis loses sight of is the form the book itself employs from the beginning.
It is as if Toomer wants to display the resources of a distinctive Afro-
American form in order to give meaning to his protagonists' discovery of
it. What gives *Cane* its richness and subtlety is the tension between style
and narrative: at the same time that the book is stretching a literary form
to its utmost, its protagonists are questioning and finally realizing their
distance from the same form.

From its opening moments, *Cane* displays a restlessness with conventional forms. "Karintha" defies classification as either prose or poetry; it
alternates from Joycean verbal density to peasant diction, and combines
complex patterns of imagery with unsophisticated spirituals. Toomer seems
to share the impatience with convention, the sense that the Anglo-American
tradition cannot contain what he has to say, that moved Ralph Ellison to
remark: "I became gradually aware that the forms of so many of the works
which impressed me were too restricted to contain the experience which I
knew. . . . [*Invisible Man* attempts] to burst such neatly understated forms
of the novel asunder." For Toomer, the way to burst asunder the forms of
the Anglo-American novel was to turn to the form he discovered in the
black south: the spiritual. If *Cane* is an elegy, it is an elegy for a form; what
moved Toomer to write was the sense that the spiritual would soon be lost
to us. "There was a valley," he recalls in an autobiography,

the valley of "Cane," with smoke-wreaths during the day and mist at night. A family of back-country Negroes had only recently moved into a shack not too far away. They sang. And this was the first time I'd ever heard the folk-songs and spirituals. They were rich and sad and joyous and beautiful. . . . I realized, with deep regret, that the spirituals, meeting ridicule, would be certain to die out. With Negroes also the trend was towards the small town and then towards the city—and industry and commerce and machines. The folk-spirit was walking in to die on the modern desert. That spirit was so beautiful. Its death was so tragic. Just this seemed to sum life for me. And this was the feeling I put into "Cane." "Cane" was a swan-song. It was a song of an end.

Barlo's invocation of the blues, then, with its pattern of call and response, is emblematic of Toomer's impulse in *Cane*. From the moment he finds voice, his project is to shape his message through the forms of call and response. There are moments in *Cane* of straightforward spiritual or work-song—in "Rhobert" or "Cotton Song," for instance—but what distinguishes Toomer's work is that he is as demanding of his form as the Anglo-American novelists are of theirs. Toomer pushes the form of call and response as hard as Joyce pushes the form of the novel. And *Cane*'s most successful moments come when Toomer opens up for us what it means to turn the call-and-response pattern into a literary form.

In "Blood-Burning Moon" Toomer takes one of the basic elements of the pattern and explores how it can generate a new narrative structure. The story forms the culmination of *Cane*'s first section, and the lynching it dramatizes is, in a sense, the event towards which the whole first section has been leading. What Toomer discovers in repetition is a way to wrench the story out of sequential time and give its central event the weight of inevitability. Tom Burwell dies figuratively so many times that his real death seems more a fulfillment of prefigurations than an event which results from the mob's violence. Toomer suggests the source of his narrative structure in the blues stanza that occurs three times in the story:

> Red nigger moon. Sinner!
> Blood-burning moon. Sinner!
> Come out that fact'ry door.

The stanza follows what Sherley Williams identifies as the classic blues pattern of statement, variation, and response, in which both variation and response intensify the meaning of the statement and place its situation "in stark relief as an object for discussion." As the second and third lines repeat and respond to the first line, they force our attention back to it and become meditations on its significance. Ralph Ellison talks in *Shadow and Act* about the impulse in the blues "to keep the painful details and episodes of a brutal experience alive in one's aching consciousness, to finger its jagged grain, to transcend it, not by the consolation of philosophy but by squeezing from it a near-comic, near-tragic lyricism," and it is in the dwelling on the first line of a stanza that we can locate the impulse. For Toomer, the blues structure means that a single event can become isolated and intensified until all other events seem merely to prefigure or repeat it. In "Blood-Burning Moon" the lynching of Tom Burwell acquires a kind of terrifying inevitability as every scene becomes charged with the significance of an omen. Even the mob's chilling plan of "Two deaths for a godam nigger" cannot compare with the horror of a death that happens figuratively over and over before it at last actually takes place.

The lynching is so intensely foreshadowed that it seems to have happened even before the story begins. "Portrait in Georgia," the poem that precedes "Blood-Burning Moon," invokes the Petrarchan device of cataloguing a woman's features, but turns it into a grotesque description of a charred body:

> Hair—braided chestnut,
> coiled like a lyncher's rope,
> Eyes —fagots,
> Lips — old scars, or the first red blisters,
> Breath—the last sweet scent of cane,
> And her slim body, white as ash
> of black flesh after flame

Thus when "Blood-Burning Moon" begins with this incantatory paragraph the meaning of its omens is already clear: "Up from the skeleton stone walls, up from the rotting floor boards and the solid hand-hewn beams of oak of the pre-war cotton factory, dusk came. Up from the dusk the full moon came. Glowing like a fired pine-knot, it illumined the great door and soft showered the Negro shanties aligned along the single street of factory town. The full moon in the great door was an omen. Negro women improvised songs against its spell." Skeleton stone walls, rotting floor boards, a fired pine-knot, a full moon in the great door, and finally the songs the women improvise: all these are foreshadowings of Tom's death. As the story continues, the omens take on more and more meaning and the lynching seems to be enacted in every passage. Thus, when Toomer lavishes attention on a description of the smoke from burning sugarcane, we sense that he is also describing the smoke from Tom's lynching: "Up from the deep dusk of a cleared spot on the edge of the forest a mellow glow arose and spread fan-wise into the low-hanging heavens. And all around the air was heavy with the scent of boiling cane. . . . The scent of cane came from the copper pan and drenched the forest and the hill that sloped to factory town, beneath its fragrance. . . . One tasted it in factory town. And from factory town one could see the soft haze thrown by the glowing stove upon the low-hanging heavens." Or here, as an old woman draws water from a well, Toomer seems to be giving us a description of the fight which is to come: "The old woman lifted the well-lid, took hold the chain, and began drawing up the heavy bucket. As she did so, she sang. Figures shifted, restlesslike, between lamp and window in the front rooms of the shanties. Shadows of the figures fought each other on the gray dust of the road." By the time the lynching occurs it seems outside of sequential causality and part of a larger scheme of prefiguration and repetition. Toomer has used the call-and-response patterns of the blues to defeat conventional time schemes and give a single event a stark, unmistakable significance. The final scene of "Blood-Burning Moon" has the intensity of a blues statement, every word almost unbearably charged with meaning. When the blues stanza appears for the last time, it is finally an explicit call for a response; Louisa is asking Tom to come out that fact'ry door:

> Louisa, upon the step before her home, did not hear [the yell], but her eyes opened slowly. . . . Where were they, these people? She'd sing, and perhaps they'd come out and join her. Perhaps Tom Burwell would come. At any rate, the full moon in the great door was an omen which she must sing to:
>
> > Red nigger moon. Sinner!
> > Blood-burning moon. Sinner!
> > Come out that fact'ry door.

From the beginning, then, the song has been a plea to undo the lynching which becomes inevitable. The strength of "Blood-Burning Moon" is the allusive, self-affirmative quality of its prose, and it is Toomer's development of the call-and-response pattern as a literary form that earns him the right to his style.

The pattern of call and response empowers, too, some of Toomer's most searing social criticism. Toomer finds in the spirituals, another form that originated in the call and response of collective work-groups, a demonstration of the way language can become an alternative source of political power. While the slaves singing in the fields were not in control of conventional sources of power, they were in control of language; they turned the words of their oppressors' own songs against them with what DuBois calls "veiled and half-articulate" messages. "Kabnis," a play about violence which remains literally and figuratively underground, begins with a demonstration of how language can be turned against itself in a fine counterpoint of overt and covert meaning. "Whiteman's land. / Niggers, sing," urges the first spiritual in "Kabnis," and it could almost be a motto for the whole play. That white men own the land, the song suggests, will not change; all blacks can do is sing, but their singing is their resistance and finally their victory.

The version of "Rock-a-by-baby" that Kabnis imagines dramatizes the struggle to gain power through language. Kabnis has just leapt out of bed to kill a chicken in the coop where he sleeps, when his violence is interrupted by this passage of strange lyricism:

> With his fingers about [the chicken's] neck, he thrusts open the outside door and steps out into the serene loveliness of Georgian

autumn moonlight. Some distance off, down in the valley, a band of pine-smoke, silvered gauze, drifts steadily. The half-moon is a white child that sleeps upon the tree-tops of the forest. White winds croon its sleep-song:

> rock-a-by baby . . .
> Black mother sways, holding a white child on her bosom.
> when the bough bends . . .
> Her breath hums through the pine-cones.
> cradle will fall . . .
> Teat moon-children at your breasts,
> down will come baby . . .
> Black mother.

Kabnis whirls the chicken by its neck, and throws the head away. Picks up the hopping body, warm, sticky, and hides it in a clump of bushes. He wipes blood from his hands onto the coarse scant grass.

The act of violence that frames the song provides a guide to its meaning. Kabnis's killing of the chicken acts out the violence against a small helpless creature that lies behind the song. The black nurse croons a white sleep-song, but she gradually wrests the song away from her white masters and gives it her own meaning. What begins as a lullaby ends as a wish to kill the white child she suckles. In the lines of narration between the lines of the song, Toomer gives us the process by which the slaves invested the spirituals with veiled messages: the collective experience underlying the call-and-response pattern allows them to share a meaning inaccessible to whites. The story of the black nurse becomes the subtext which decodes the song and establishes membership in the community. Kabnis's "Rock-a-by baby" dramatizes the creation of a literary form which allows words to subvert themselves and a calm linguistic surface to express violent meanings. The black mother who remains at the end of the song achieves through language a triumph over her oppressors that makes her perhaps the only real black madonna of the book. And Kabnis's victory suddenly shrinks beside hers.

Crucial for the play between surface and hidden meaning is an assumption of a shared perspective among the audience. In his "Rock-a-by baby" Toomer creates the shared situation, the kind of context the spirituals take for granted, in the story of the black nurse. By giving us the sketch of the nurse suckling a white woman's children, he makes us the community for which the song has special meaning. Both the spirituals and the blues have an assurance of communal voice built into their form, and it is on this unique strength that Toomer draws in "Kabnis." The assurance of collective voice gives the speaker in the spirituals or the blues an untroubled authority to speak. Michael Harper puts the source of this authority succinctly when he notes that the blues audience hears "we" when the speaker says "I," communal response for the blues singer, as for Barlo, confers the authority to speak.

But Toomer is not simply singing the blues or preaching the coming of a new messiah; he has learned from the Romantics that hearing a response to one's voice cannot be unproblematic. *Cane* brings to the call-and-response pattern it celebrates all the questioning of voice we find in Whitman; it invests an Afro-American form with the problematic of Romanticism. When Toomer tells us that "the spiritual entity behind the work" awakens in "Bona and Paul," plunges in "Kabnis," emerges in "Karintha," swings upward in "Theater" and "Box Seat" and ends (pauses) in "Harvest Song," he is charting the discovery of the problematics of response. What Paul awakens to is the realization that he cannot elicit from his people the response that would confirm his own voice. Paul's moment of luminous vision is followed by a lack of response so complete as to be almost comic. " 'I came back to tell you,' " he declares passionately to an unconcerned doorman,

> "That something beautiful is going to happen. . . . That dark faces are petals of dusk. That I am going out and gather petals. That I am going out and know her whom I brought here with me to these Gardens which are purple like a bed of roses would be at dusk."
> Paul and the black man shook hands.
> When he reached the spot where they had been standing, Bona was gone.

For Toomer, the meaning of isolation from one's own people is intensified by his own racial isolation. Like Paul, he was of mixed race, and perhaps it is his own separation from a community that makes his narrators' failures to get a response particularly acute.

When Kabnis sets out for the south, then, he is taking Toomer's journey to find a way to participate in the literary form at the heart of *Cane*. *Cane* gives us first the form—as it appears in the spirituals, blues and variation-and-repetition patterns throughout the book—then the writer's sense of separation from the form he celebrates. Toomer's story of failed response begins in the middle of the book, and takes him back through all the narrators whose failure to consummate love is emblematic of their failure to hear a response. Muriel's analysis is finally the right one; frustrated with Dan's harangues, she accuses him of being a "Timid lover, brave talker." By the end or, as Toomer puts it, the pause of the story, the narrators are afraid even to talk. "Harvest Song" is a poem about failure to speak for a community. Before hearing Toomer, let us recall Langston Hughes writing four years later on the same subject:

> I bathed in the Euphrates when the dawns were young.
> I built my hut near the Congo and it lulled me to sleep.
> I looked upon the Nile and raised the pyramids above it.

> I heard the singing of the Mississippi when Abe Lincoln went
> down to New Orleans, and I've seen its muddy bosom turn
> all golden in the sunset.

Now Toomer:

> I am a reaper whose muscles set at sundown. All my oats are
> cradled.
> But I am too chilled, and too fatigued to bind them. And I hunger.
>
> I fear to call. What should they hear me, and offer me their grain,
> oats, or wheat, or corn? I have been in the fields all day. I fear I
> could not taste it. I fear knowledge of my hunger.

Both poets adopt the strategy of embodying a community in a single voice; but while Hughes can range freely over history and geography, absorbing all voices into his as he goes, Toomer feels that he is in trouble from the moment he speaks. Almost immediately he feels he must qualify his definition of himself as a reaper. If he is part of a harvest, it is a failed harvest. In the poem which marks the end of Toomer's own journey, he returns to the work-songs which generated the pattern of call and response, then insists over and over that he cannot respond.

Cane enacts the confrontation of Romanticism and Afro-American culture. The untroubled assumption of voice at the heart of the call-and-response pattern is no longer possible in a world altered by Romanticism. The distinctive Afro-American form cannot survive Romanticism unchanged any more than southern blacks can blend unchanged into northern society. *Cane* in the deepest sense is about a clash of traditions, and what such a clash will mean for Afro-American literature. Perhaps, though, there is a more profound confrontation being enacted in *Cane*, one that is inevitable in any meeting of self-consciousness with nostalgia for untroubled voice. When Toomer wrote that *Cane* was a "swan song," is was this confrontation that he seems to have had in mind. "It was," he says, "a song of an end. And why no one has seen and felt that, why people have expected me to write a second and a third and a fourth book like 'Cane,' is one of the queer misunderstandings of my life." There can be no second or third *Cane* because the call-and-response form which *Cane* explores and celebrates is exactly the form it shows is no longer possible.

Dos Passos's *U.S.A.*: Chronicle and Performance

Charles Marz

John Dos Passos records and resists in *U.S.A.* the extinction of the private voice, the invasion of the private space, by the devastating forces of history. The landscapes of the text, like those of *Three Soldiers* and *Manhattan Transfer*, are strewn with that devastation's debris—the residue of character, the remains of narrative. Dos Passos chronicles in the trilogy the voices and the acts of residual men—the echoes, the fragments that compose America.

U.S.A. expands the themes and techniques of *Three Soldiers* and *Manhattan Transfer*. Structurally it is even more artificial and patterned. The usual criterion of realistic style, that it vanishes before the reality of the subject, does not apply to its pages. As in *Manhattan Transfer* Dos Passos deforms the voices of America, the bankrupt speech of anonymous men. *U.S.A.* is more than what Kenneth Lynn has described as "an anthology of the American idiom— of Texas drawl, Harvard broad 'a,' and immigrant pidgin; of middle-class female twaddle and proletarian male coarseness; of popular songs, advertising slogans, and fragments from the yellow press," more than the ultimate extension of Twain's famous prefatory note to the *Adventures of Huckleberry Finn*. *U.S.A.* is not a recording of America. And it is not a story about America. Traditional novelistic unities of character and action are abandoned; beginnings and endings of persons and events are fortuitous. There is little progress, little growth, little development of character; there is no real concern with representation, illusion, or empathy. The trilogy is not held together by any chain of events or "story line"; it must be apprehended spatially and not sequentially. Sequence yields to a structure characterized by the juxtaposition of disconnected and often incompatible word blocks. *U.S.A.* is a continent and a composition ruled by crisis and collision; it is fragmented, radically incomplete, and as amorphous and incoherent at times as its characters' lives.

From *Modern Fiction Studies* 26, no. 3 (1980). © 1980 by the Purdue Research Foundation. Originally entitled "U.S.A.: Chronicle and Performance."

The trilogy is a medley of juxtaposed and layered voices. Its meanings are generated by the thematic and structural tensions among its compositional blocks, by the complex and various juxtapositions of Camera Eyes, Newsreels, Narratives, and Biographies. Public and private lives and events constantly intersect; public and private voices collide. Dos Passos records the sound of the collisions, the noise of the public sphere and the silence of the private space during the first thirty crisis-ridden years of this century in America. But as he chronicles he resists the murderous forces of history, the triumph of the world. Neither the composition nor the country disintegrates. The performing voice of the novelist-historian, and his accomplice, the reader, survive the tale told as history and fiction of a world too much with us.

The conflict between the destructive chaos of public voices and the private voice that seeks survival in the world is manifested in the collisions of the Newsreel and the Camera Eye sections of *U.S.A.* The Camera Eye is the last preserve of the sensitive and embattled individual. It is the last remnant of the individual voice —the end product of Martin Howe, John Andrews, and Jimmy Herf— or perhaps the waste product. For the Camera Eye is a residual voice; it is what remains of the intense subjectivity of the early works.

The Camera Eye is not the autobiographical voice of John Dos Passos. It is not simply a method of smuggling chunks of personal "stream-of-memory" into an impersonal novel. It is not an autobiographical novel within a novel. It may be true that much of the material in the Camera Eye passages concurs with Ludington's, Cowley's, and Bernardin's accounts of Dos Passos's "hotel childhood," his love of Malory and Gibbon, his association with the Harvard Aesthetes, the Norton-Harjes Ambulance Service, and the Sacco and Vanzetti case. But the fact that the Camera Eye sections of *U.S.A.* might compose a partially autobiographical history of Dos Passos from the turn of the century to the early thirties is irrelevant to their use and meaning in the trilogy. Matching the life and text of the author is a critical game we need not play. *U.S.A.* is not a *roman à clef*.

The Camera Eye selections in *U.S.A.* contain both historical and fictional materials. They are representations and not samples of a private voice, and their meaning is not autobiographical. It is the manner more than the matter of the telling that is significant. The conversational expression, the direct address of the reader, the unfamiliar allusions, and the paratactic constructions create a sincere and private presence. It gives the appearance of real or natural speech and seems autobiographical, at times even confessional. It remains, however, essentially fictive discourse—the private voice of a fictive self speaking anonymously from the interior of the text. It is a portrait of a Self more than a self-portrait. And the speaker, as in the first Camera Eye, remains the embattled individual, often the stranger, the exile, "The Man Without A Country," the unknown soldier— always the sensitive observer isolated and buried by the world.

The Camera Eye of *The 42nd Parallel* is the protected "I" of youth. It is the most insulated voice, the most interior level of perception in the trilogy. In it the world is reduced to entirely personal (if not necessarily autobiographical) history; the camera eye is turned on the most private circumstances, the most intimate perceptions and sensory experiences of the autonomous and inviolate individual. In it the significant space of that individual is preserved; it is preserved, however, in isolation from the world and the text. It is the solitary space of the aesthete and solipsist; it is a cultivated voice under a bellglass, a powerless voice in retreat from the NOISE THAT GREETS THE NEW CENTURY. And it is the guilt-ridden voice of the spectator. The preservation of that private space, that highly rhetorical and complicitous voice, becomes in the trilogy an increasingly difficult, an increasingly irresponsible task. The World presses on the Camera Eye, and the bellglass is shattered by the central event of the trilogy—The Great War—the public NOISE that kills.

The voice of the Camera Eye in *Nineteen Nineteen* is familiar to the reader of *One Man's Initiation—1917* and *Three Soldiers*. It is the spectatorial voice of the ambulance driver, the voice of the gentleman-volunteer, and it exists at the margin of the War and the text. The voice of the gentleman-volunteer remains detached; it observes, describes, but does not protest the devastation; it is a passive voice, drained of moral content. The war becomes a modern museum of the grotesque, and the voice of the Camera Eye the voice of the spectator, the tourist. That aesthetic detachment becomes more difficult to maintain in a world rapidly filling with horrible exhibits. Retreat is no longer possible. The War and The City have become interchangeable landscapes, both debris-laden, both ruled by the slogans and lies of the public voice. Death is ubiquitous; the unknown soldier becomes the unknown citizen; both travel as strangers in strange lands, unrecognizable, faceless. Identities merge, blur and fade away like old photographs. The residual voice becomes difficult to locate and identify:

> the poem I recited in a foreign language was not mine in fact it was somebody else who was speaking it's not me in uniform in the snapshot it's a lamentable error mistaken identity the service record was lost the gentleman occupying the swivelchair wearing the red carnation is somebody else than

> *(U.S.A. The Big Money)*

The disembodied voice of the Camera Eye represents the slow dissolution of a coherent, private individual. That dissolution is consistent with Philip Fisher's notion of the changing territory of the self:

> Memories, secrets, feelings, and interior chatter of the mind—the whole realm of what we call "privacy" . . . this residue was in the age of individualism what was meant by the self and was located inside the body . . . Now, it is one of the most interesting facts about the representation of modern characters . . . that this territory of the self within the body has vanished or declined in interest or investment.

The Camera Eye chronicles the disappearance, the gradual bankruptcy of the self. It also resists that disappearance. The private voice of the Camera Eye resists subordination—both syntactically and politically. It is expansive and unpredictable; it rebels against order and form, history and society. Violence (linguistic and political) is done to syntax and organization. The world is deformed; it becomes asyntactical. The beginnings and endings that constitute normal historical and narrative order—the "conspiracy" of history we call "plot"—are resisted. And so finally are the echoes and clichés, the headlines and slogans, the word-debris that buries the individual, the nose that silences him. The private voice of the Camera Eye retreats from and resists the world; it is a voice haunted by possible complicity, by the deformations of word-slinging and slogan-mongering; it enlists the reader (also complicitous in his aesthetic detachment) in the struggle to find an authentic private voice — a voice that will successfully combat the public noise.

The pressure of contemporary events increases in *The Big Money*. It culminates in the trial and execution of Sacco and Vanzetti—symbolically the last of America's embattled individuals. They are the victims of an oppressive culture, and they have been betrayed by the word-slingers, destroyed by the public voices. It is up to the speaker of the Camera Eye to renounce the lies that kill. But our efforts are to no avail; the voice in the last Camera Eye of *U.S.A.* has become collective; we are ultimately all complicitous. Sacco and Vanzetti die; the world triumphs; we stand looking into now familiar coffins:

> our work is over the scribbled phrases the nights typing releases the smell of the printshop the sharp reek of newsprinted leaflets the rush for Western Union stringing words into wires the search for stinging words to make you feel who are your oppressors America
>
> America our nation has been beaten by strangers who have turned our language inside out who have taken the clean words our fathers spoke and made them slimy and foul . . .
>
> we line the curbs in the drizzling rain we crowd the wet sidewalks elbow to elbow silent pale looking with scared eyes at the coffins
>
> we stand defeated America
>
> *(The Big Money)*

The last Camera Eye of *U.S.A.* is an expression of defeat and an expression of shame. It is the voice of the spectator, the tourist, the gentleman-volunteer; it is the private voice of Martin Howe, John Andrews, and Jimmy Herf, and it has nothing to say to the prisoners of *U.S.A.*, nothing to express but the certainty of their destruction: "the men in jail shrug their shoulders smile thinly our eyes look in their eyes through the bars what can I say? . . . what can we say to the jailed? *(The Big Money)*." The voice that survives is guilt-ridden; it is a residual and powerless voice; it is the voice of the reader.

The public world with us has become the private world . . . The single individual, whether he so wishes or not, has become part of a world which contains also Austria and Czechoslovakia and China and Spain . . . What happens in his morning paper happens in his blood all day, and Madrid, Nanking, Prague are names as close to him as the names by which he counts his dearest losses.— Archibald MacLeish

The Newsreels of *U.S.A.* operate at several levels of meaning. Most obviously and, perhaps, least significantly, they mark time chronologically. The panoramic, historical aspect of *U.S.A.* is now a critical given. The Newsreels locate the historical background for the action of the trilogy; they provide its setting; they generate atmosphere; they indicate the passage of him in the world and in the text. It seems also given that the Newsreels may be linked to themes and actions in adjacent narrative, Camera Eye, and biographical passages; they date, comment on, and link the various persons and events in the trilogy. However, even if we could identify the historical source or referent for each of the Newsreel fragments, even if we could "plot" (as "conspiratorial" critics engaged in the "burial" of the text) the chronological progression of the trilogy from Newsreel I to Newsreel LXVIII, we would be no closer to explaining the power of *U.S.A.*, no closer to articulating the significance of the Newsreels. The trilogy must be understood dynamically. Its power and meanings come ultimately from vertical, atemporal, simultaneous events, and not from horizontal, biographical, successive actions. They are not generated by the historical exactness but by the random collisions of voices. The voices in the Newsreels collide with one another and with the rest of the text. These collisions generate grotesque ironies. It is not uncommon in a Newsreel to find juxtaposed celebrations and horrors of America, the dream and the nightmare. Dos Passos resists as he records the noise of history. Random collisions set off random explosions; the novelist is historian and saboteur.

The Newsreels chronicle the voices of the public sphere; they are the most banal, most impersonal, most mechanical registration of persons and events in the trilogy; they are the "nightmare of history," uncolored and uncontrolled by the private voice of the Camera Eye. Violence is objectively reported. The lies of the public voice reveal themselves in absurd and ironic incongruities. Death is reduced to statistical tabulation and the exalted rhetoric of the Great War; it is reported in the same manner and in the same space as a surge in the market. Devastations of vastly different magnitudes—though typographically and structurally equivalent— collide:

For there's many a man been murdered in Luzon and Mindanao
GAIETY GIRLS MOBBED IN NEW JERSEY

(*The 42nd Parallel*)

ARMY WIFE SLASHED BY ADMIRER
THREE HUNDRED THOUSAND RUSSIAN NOBLES
SLAIN BY BOLSHEVIKI

(*1919*)

Our sense of scale is annihilated; experience in the public sphere is reduced to the formula, cliché, echo of the headline; war and politics to the front page, love to the society page, and death to the obituary column. In a world in which private voices give way to the public noise, all private experience soon becomes public knowledge. The army wife slashed by her admirer and the death of three hundred thousand Russian nobles become equivalent public events. The most private destinies become public, and all men become—if only for a moment— celebrities.

As the noise of the world increases, the Newsreel demands economies of presentation, the brief notation of persons and events; it becomes an automated, dehumanized, faceless form of communication. There is neither the time nor the space in the public sphere for the continuous enactment of coherent, private lives. Narrative and voice contract, atrophy, and disappear. And all that remains in the Newsreels is the residue of voice, the debris of character, action, and experience. *U.S.A.*, like *Manhattan Transfer* before it, is a novel of physical and spiritual erosion. Dos Passos continues to catalogue the wreckage, the fragmentary form, the broken objects that invade and bury persons and landscapes. The Newsreels are composed of unintelligible and multiple verbal fragments in agitated motion. They surface, collide, and disappear much like the garbage in the Ferryslip section of *Manhattan Transfer*. Significance is drained from any single event by typographical uniformity, by the mechanical equivalence of the presentation:

> PARIS SHOCKED AT LAST
> TEDDY WIELDS BIG STICK
>
> . . . .
>
> MOB LYNCHES AFTER PRAYER
> (*The 42nd Parallel*)

Each headline is a verbal snapshot, a mechanical recapitulation of some part of the world. Each snapshot is a short-lived event, incompletely defined at any particular moment, and limited by space-time constraints to verbal accidents or collisions. Persons and events are "shot" and the Newsreels preserve their remains: "SNAP CAMERA: ENDS LIFE" (*The 42nd Parallel*). Susan Sontag has noted that photography makes forgetting the world, escaping history's debris, increasingly difficult. The reader of the Newsreels, like the photographer, must passively receive and suffer the world and its debris. The world prints the image. Transitory meanings are occasionally available in the accidental configurations and collisions of fragments. But the wreckage and the noise increase, and it is not enough simply to chronicle the devastation. The collisions of public voices generate that devastation, the noise of history that creates Dos Passos's dilemma—perhaps the central dilemma of his time —how both to chronicle and resist a disintegrating world.

In the Camera Eye passage of *U.S.A.*, there is a refusal to abdicate personal control; the embattled individual stands at the center of the world, almost to the exclusion of it; there is an intense —though never transcendent or religious —residual individualism. In the Newsreels, however, the person exists nearer the periphery of the world. And the subject, the ever-present "I" and "you" of the Camera Eye, recedes. The public voices of the Newsreels are speakerless. They are voices over which men have no control. Individuals are not subordinated—they simply cease to exist. There are no coherent or continuous interior lives in the Newsreels. The space alloted to persons contracts. And the Newsreels become collages of torn spaces, broken and layered samplers of persons and events. The subjects of actions are often collective or absent. Occasional subjects may be public figures or anonymous individuals or groups. The Newsreels are spoken by anonymous public voices, spoken by the conspiratorial "they" of Camera Eyes 49 and 50. The world of the Newsreels is a lawless, violent world out of control, a world of personalities or celebrities and not characters, personalities whose lives are only as complete as the information available in the headlines. The speakerless world of the Newsreels is a constantly eroding world, a world without human responsibility or moral content. The dispassionate, technological voices of the Newsreels speak constant destruction and violence; they register the nightmare that is history. And in that nightmare the human scale is reduced; things become the locus and power of values. The individual is "heaped" by the world, slowly buried by its objects and its debris. Philip Fisher has noted that "for a man inside the city his self is not inside his body but around him, outside his body." And for a man in the U.S.A. that Dos Passos chronicles, his voice is not inside his body, but around him, outside his body in the verbal objects that engulf him—in the public space.

The Newsreels are ultimately verbal objects—word and world debris. They are the residue of the natural world, divested of their original functions and contexts, wrenched from private and public occasions. In the trilogy they become ahistorical, non-contextual verbal acts, always possible but never actual verbal utterances. They are in many ways like "found poetry" in that their presentation invites a certain critical ingenuity; they are "the representation of a natural utterance in an implicit dramatic context, designed to invite and gratify the drawing of interpretive inferences"; they exist at the margins of discourse.

The borders between natural and fictive discourse, history and fiction, shift and dissolve in *U.S.A.* History is introjected and eroded in the text. And the Newsreels are the location of the debris. They are cemeteries and museums (both burial grounds of objects) of verbal artifacts. They preserve the afterlife of verbal objects — echoes and clichés. In them the world is dematerialized; scale is destroyed as persons and events are uniformly fragmented in space and in time. Those verbal fragments of the world are catalogued and displayed. The voice fragments exhibited become increasingly remote as one moves away from familiar historical persons and events. What may once have been most public, most accessible —most immediately verifiable news—becomes most strange. We are without access to reported historical circumstances. Contexts are ignored and unexplained; the most intriguing observations remain hermeneutically sealed. The reader is estranged from the text by the insufficiency and the incompleteness of information. An intimate relation with the text is denied. We must scan the text—as we must scan the world—as strangers, in search of recognizable characters and actions. And as the text and the world erode we must deal with their debris—with the bits and pieces of lives and events—with the fragments of experience.

The meanings of the Newsreels are not located finally in the world of historical actions and consequences. Tracing the former lives of these artifacts is irrelevant. For they do not simply date the action of the trilogy; they do not simply provide atmosphere. They invade the text; they collide with the Camera Eye; scraps of reality, records of things, vestiges of the past set adrift, the wreckage of public voices buries the individual and silences him. Man is gradually replaced by his artifacts, by world and word debris, by the slowly and inevitably triumphant noise of history.

As the world becomes increasingly public, as private lives and voices atrophy, and as man is buried and silenced by the relics of history, the nature of the novel—traditionally a genre of and for private spaces— changes. Rather than insisting on the quality and interest of private lives (in the manner of Joyce, Proust, or Woolf), Dos Passos records in the Camera Eye the contractions of the private space, the dissolution of the private voice, and in the Newsreels the concurrent triumph of the world. In the narrative and biographical passages of *U.S.A.* the residual voice of the Camera Eye and the speakerless voice of the Newsreel give way to a voice of the "middle-distance," the performing voice of the chronicler-novelist. The performer and his complicitous audience, the reader, remove themselves from and resist the world by deforming it. Irony becomes the rhetorical strategy most useful in that deformation. It records as it deforms the public voice; it locates the disparity between word and thing; it demands the mutual participation and understanding of writer and reader; and it provides their necessary expiation. It is, after all, fundamental to an understanding of *The Great War* and *The Big Money*. As Paul Fussell has recently noted, "there seems to be one dominating form of modern understanding; that it is essentially ironic; and that it originates largely in the application of mind and memory to the events of the Great War." Through ironic subversion, the world of public voices, of clichés and headlines, is mined by the writer as saboteur. The explosions that result from that subversion generate the energy of the text.

Survival becomes difficult in the noisy, debris-laden world of the Newsreel, a world constantly recorded, imaged, and fragmented. Persons are "shot," then their remains, their remnant images and voices, litter the landscape. Obliteration in the form of private or public apocalypse is imminent at every moment for the individual. Thus the cultural imagination seeks, creates, and clings to pseudo-heroes who survive that danger, personalities who derive their stature precisely through their ability to survive, if not to dominate, in the world. They remain visible if only as image. They remain audible if only as echo. They are the gods of a new pantheon; they are America's celebrities and newsmakers.

In the biographical passages of *U.S.A.* Dos Passos records the lives and voices of the public space. He chronicles the destruction of America's last heroes — embattled individuals who attempt to hollow out the expanding and consuming public space and preserve an authentic, private voice. And he chronicles and deforms the lives and voices of the survivors, the pseudo-heroes, the word-slingers who contribute to and sustain the public noise—the noise that kills.

Eugene Debs, Bill Haywood, John Reed, Randolph Bourne, Bob LaFollette, Thorstein Veblen, Joe Hill, and Wesley Everest—like Sacco and Vanzetti—are embattled individuals ultimately destroyed by the public noise. Debs is a threat to the power of the public voice; he resists the lies that kill. Big Bill Haywood campaigned for Debs for President in 1908; he spoke for cowboys and lumberjacks, harvesthands and miners, and participated in major strikes in Lawrence, Patterson, And Minnesota. He, like Debs, resists the public voice and is ultimately "buried" in Leavenworth. Debs, Haywood, Hill, and Everest are all men who refuse to submit to the conventional wisdom of public platitudes and clichés. Each of them is ultimately destroyed for his resistance; each is reduced to debris, "the mangled wreckage" of America: "As Wesley Everest lay stunned in the bottom of the car, a Centralia businessman cut his penis and testicles off with a razor. . . . They jammed the mangled wreckage into a packing box and buried it"(*1919*). Debs, Haywood, Everest, LaFollette, Veblen, Reed, and Bourne knew that the truth about America was grim. They identify the disparities between the way things are and the way they are reported by the public voice, by Mr. Creel's bureau in Washington. They identify the real meanings of Wilson's empty phrases, the Lies of the public voice.

Dos Passos identifies the lies and points to the liars. Carnegie, Hearst, Morgan, and Wilson represent the survivors, the conspiratorial "they" of the Camera Eye. "They" are responsible for the destruction of the embattled individual, for the dissolution of the private voice, for the execution of Sacco and Vanzetti, for the defeat of Debs and Haywood and Hill and Everest and LaFollette and Veblen and Reed and Bourne. "They" are the "strangers who have turned our language inside out," the liars "who have bought the laws and fenced off the meadows and cut down the woods for pulp and turned our pleasant cities into slums and sweated the wealth out of our people and when they want to they hire the executioner to throw the switch"(*The Big Money*).

William Randolph Hearst controls the presses, the distribution of print and images. That "print" and those "images" invade the trilogy in the headlines of the Newsreels; it is the word-debris that litters the novel. Hearst, however, survives in splendor. The newspaper headline, after all, serves not to communicate information as much as to sell newspapers. It is an efficient if inauthentic mode of communication. With the Taylor Plan and Henry Ford's assembly line individual lives and voices give way to the demands of efficiency and public consumption. Men are reduced to cogs in the industrial machine. They are dehumanized; they become the voiceless debris of a beaten nation, used by the word-slingers and then discarded. They are the remains of the City and the War; they are the mechanical echoes, the hollow men, the citizens of *U.S.A.*

Survival demands submission to the public voice. Valentino spends his life in the public eye. Even the celebrity's death remains an entirely public affair. Dos Passos chronicles the funeral as if it has no existence other than that given it by the public voice of the *New York Times:* "The funeral train arrived in Hollywood on page 23 of the *N. Y. Times.*" And survival demands submission to public values, to dehumanizing efficiency, to profit, even at the expense of life. It is that dedication to the dollar that Dos Passos detests in Carnegie and Morgan.

One survivor in the trilogy receives a more devastating treatment than any other. That man is the embodiment in Dos Passos's eyes of the Great War, the Big Money, the inauthentic public voice. "Meester Veelson" "lived in a universe of words," and his every action betrayed the meaning of those words. He takes the "clean words our Fathers spoke and makes them slimy and foul." Dos Passos suggests the Great War was fought for something other than "to make the world safe for democracy." The meaning, the power, the energy of the Biographies is generated by controlled, subversive collisions. In his biography of Wilson, Dos Passos locates the disparities between what Wilson said and what he did. Public expressions of "neutrality in thought and deed" and "too proud to fight" prove meaningless lies betrayed by actions. Wilsonian rhetoric is exploded by the writer as performer and saboteur. *U.S.A.* may be a chronicle of destruction, but it is also a subversive performance.

The lives and voices of the public space, of the Newsreels and Biographies, penetrate the trilogy. They invade and determine the world and the text in which the narrative characters act and speak. Historical and fictional lives collide. "Big Bill," for example, immediately precedes "Mac," a narrative section in which Big Bill Haywood speaks at a union meeting that Mac (Fenian MacCreary) attends in Goldfield, Nevada. The world and the text interpenetrate; history and fiction blur. Fictional lives, the habitual voices of average Americans, echo the recognizable historical gestures and voices of the public space. In the narrative passages of *U.S.A.*, Dos Passos chronicles the echoing voices and actions of hollow men. Characters are voiceless and nearly invisible; they are like Reginald Marsh's illustrations as described by William Steadman, "silhouettes of people . . . whose features illustrate only too well the irreparable damage of time." They have no depth; their outlines are often broken; and there is no difference between the space of their interior and exterior lives.

The damage of the public space is inescapable; headlines—the word-debris that kills—stains the lives of the fictional characters: "A rancid smell of printer's ink came from it; the ink was still sticky and came off on her gloves. "DECLARATION OF WAR" *(1919)*. Lives are stained and shaped by the daily papers. The propaganda of Mr. Creel's bureau in Washington becomes the material of characters' actions, thoughts, and values.

The embodiment of the inauthentic voice, the voice that purveys the lies of the Great War and the Big Money, the voice of salesmanship without moral content, the voice that is merely an echo, is the Public Relations Counsel J. Ward Moorehouse. He is a confidence man who betrays the meaning of words if it will make a profit; he reduces language to advertising clichés and lies in order to manipulate and deceive his audience, in order to mold the public mind. Moorehouse is the public voice, the publicity agent for America, Woodrow Wilson's advance man. He "does propaganda for the Morgans and the Rockefellers"; he is, as Jerry Burnham tells Eveline Hutchins, "nothing but a goddam megaphone . . . a damn publicity agent." He has no interior life; his soul is hollow; his every activity is an echo. Moorehouse is incapable of feeling, incapable of expressing private sentiments—sentiments that originate with him and not his clients. He is an American Success, much like Jay Gatsby or Citizen Kane as described by Robert Carringer:

> The chief misfortunes of the [three] men seem to stem not so much from an inability to keep public and private apart as from there being practically nothing private to separate. The defect seems to be ultimately traceable to their American personae. An all-consuming persona inevitably also consumes its wearer; the mask eventually becomes inseparable from the face.

Moorehouse's private self is sacrificed in pursuit of public images. Like Gatsby and Kane, he is incapable of interpersonal relationships, incapable of love. Moorehouse worries about divorce in much the same way that Charles Foster Kane worries about Susan leaving him—in terms of the harm it will do his public—not his private—life; divorce is simply bad business.

U.S.A. is ultimately an "economic novel of the self." That is not to say that it is simply a commentary or record of the American economy. It is a chronicle of inflated and officious sentiments (public voices), of counterfeit verbal transactions (echoes), of the loss of personal value (private space) in pursuit of the Big Money. *U.S.A.* is the record of the bankruptcy of the self. As one character remarks, "we hocked our manhood for a brass check about the time of the First World War." The Great War is an investment of human capital; losses are strictly financial, investments in the Big Money. In a society stripped of satisfactions other than financial the stock broker's office becomes a holy place. In that society interpersonal as well as religious relationships are reduced to economics, to sexual transactions. Marriages are seen as potentially profitable relationships. J. Ward Moorehouse suggests to Richard Savage that the consummation of their business relationship with Doc Bingham will be marrying him off to one of the Bingham girls. Sex is a commodity, marriage a negotiable contract, and divorce the dissolution of an unsuccessful business venture. Private lives must give way to the public space. Savage will not marry Daughter when he gets her pregnant because it stands in the way of his career with Moorehouse. Ben Compton and Helen Mauer will not have children because all of their strength must be devoted to the movement. And so Helen Mauer has an abortion. *U.S.A.* is replete with the debris of loveless relationships. Mary French, like Helen Mauer, has an abortion. Margo Dowling, raped by her stepfather, marries a Cuban homosexual and has a deformed child. Children are the residue of the private space, the reduplication of history's debris.

There are no love relationships in *U.S.A.* Women are bought, sold, and raped. Frenetic love (and business) affairs are abortive. Successful public men pursue public values during business hours. Their women serve as night deposit boxes—the pun captures the vulgarity, the sordid truth of the devalued, impersonal transactions.

The characters of *U.S.A.* drift through the narrative out of control, occasionally colliding and littering the landscape with their debris. They are not alienated; they are exhausted, invisible, and silent. Persons are subsumed by the public space, silenced by the public noise, the voices of the war and the exchange. They are purged of emotions, volitionless, and obedient. And they exist in a world without moral content or complication. Survival in that world demands the relinquishment of will, action and voice.

Dos Passos chronicles in the narratives of *U.S.A.* a society of stenographers, interior decorators, and advertising men, the counterfeit voices of a bankrupt society. In that society lives are conducted in relation to public values. Voices are conditioned by the invasion of the private space by the Newsreels and Biographies. Mac echoes Joe Hill and Wesley Everest, and Big Bill Haywood. Ben Compton and Mary French and Don Stevens are echoes of Eugene Debs. Margo Dowling is an echo of Isadora Duncan and Rudolph Valentino. And Charley Anderson is an echo of Henry Ford. Other characters are echoes of echoes, imitations of themselves. As Moorehouse is an echo of Wilson and Morgan so Janey Williams, his stenographer, and Richard Savage, his aide, are echoes of Moorehouse. Williams literally records his voice; Savage then repeats it.

Characters dissolve in the narrative passages of *U.S.A.*; they become transparent images of one another, echoing verbal structures. Private lives and voices disappear and history usurps the space of character. In narrative that becomes essentially iterative, lives become structurally identical and selves are erased. Futures remain uncertain in a world and text in which apocalypse is imminent at every moment, in a world and text in which men do not act out their own lives. Characters experience the world as oppressive; it is no longer the tangled predicament James experienced dramatically; men are no longer actors in the drama of life. Some 120 characters are introduced, interrupted, terminated, or forgotten in the narrative passages of *U.S.A.* None, however, is memorable. Characters in *U.S.A.* are not individually significant. Action and voice remain public. There are not the epiphanies or illuminations of Joyce, Woolf, or Lawrence. There are not the interesting interior lives of Proust or Dostoevsky. And there are not the dramatic portraits of human beings found in Dickens or James, for Dos Passos chronicles a world in which the psychological space disintegrates. The first person is indirect, occasional, and residual; characters are not flat; they are hollow.

The absence of interior life explains the physical intensity of Dos Passos —the strong sense of disintegrating animate and inanimate "things." As interior space disintegrates, so too does the space of representation. Characters in *U.S.A.* exist within a space as two-dimensional as the photographic landscapes of *Manhattan Transfer*. Characters are presented cinematically, as expanded Newsreel notations:

> All is as in a scene from the silent movies; the picture is flat, not always too clear; the movements of the characters are jerky as the movements of the machine which controls them . . . On the screen two-dimensional Macs and Bens flicker and fade, reel after reel, to the dreary denouement of their lives . . . Restless, synoptic, the telescoping action of the narrative sweeps back and forth across the country recording the triumph of the money-machine and the debasement of human life.

Characters survive in *U.S.A.* by adaptation to the "money- machine." They escape dissolution by constant reduplication of themselves, by the monotonous reaffirmation of public identities and voices. They simply repeat one another's actions and words. That repetition is grotesquely mechanical, the inhuman repetition of meaningless acts. And the narratives of the trilogy are ultimately chronicles of the bankrupt, the dehumanized, the habitual voice; they are cinematic chronicles of mechanical lives, of Taylor's American Plan.

The residual lives of the Narratives, the Biographies, the Newsreels, and the Camera Eyes meet and join in the young man at the beginning of each novel, in "Vag" and in "The Body of an American." In those passages history and fiction become indistinguishable. In the world and in the text, character is reduced to anonymity, to the vagrant and the unknown soldier. The road and the war become the dumping grounds for society's debris. The tramp and the soldier are rootless and mobile, in perpetual states of "vagabondage." They occasionally collide, but relationships on the bum and on the battlefield are always transitory. The content of their lives is determined by anonymous public voices. Advertising, radio, film, and Wall Street invade the consciousness of Vag: "ads promised speed, own your home, shine bigger than your neighbor, the radio-crooner whispered girls, ghosts of platinum girls coaxed from the screen, millions in winnings were chalked up on the boards in offices." And the brain of the unknown soldier has been charged with "savings print headlines":

> Now is the time for all good men knocks but once at a young man's door, It's a great life if Ish gebibbel, The first five years 'll

be the Safety First, Suppose a Hun tried to rape your country right or wrong, Catch 'em young What he don't know won't treat 'em rough, Tell 'em nothin,' He got what was coming to him he got his, This is a white man's country, Kick the Bucket, Gone West.

Character in Dos Passos is bombarded by the public noise, by the buzz of history. The continuous roar of the City (Vag) and the War (Body of an American) is inescapable. The anonymous citizen is overwhelmed by the remains of voices:

The young man walks by himself, fast but not fast enough, far but not far enough (faces slide out of sight, talk trails into tattered scraps . . . the cars are caught tight, linked tight by the tendrils of phrased words, the turn of a joke, the singsong of a story, the gruff fall of a sentence, linking tendrils of speech twine through the city blocks, spread over pavements, grow out along broad parked avenues.

The world of *U.S.A.* is littered with the tattered scraps of voices. Its debris-laden landscapes reek of the devastation of The City and The War. The stench that lingers in the nostrils of Vag is the stench of the battlefield.

The point to which all things descend in the world and in the text of *U.S.A.* is "thememorialamphitheaterofthenational cemeteryatarlingtonvirginia." The cemetery is the location of the remains of things, and the national cemetery is the location of the remains of a nation. The anonymous debris of that nation, "The Body of An American," is buried at the center of the world and the text. It is the residue of a culture, of the nightmare of history, "history the billiondollar speed up":

WhereastheCongressoftheunitedstatesbyaconcurrentresolution
adoptedonthe4thdayofmarchlastauthorizedtheSecretaryofwarto
causetobebroughttotheunitedstatesthebodyofanAmericanwho
wasamemberoftheamericanexpeditionaryforceineuropewholost
hislifeduringtheworldwarandwhoseidentityhasnotbeenestablished
forburialinthememorialamphitheaterofthenationalcemetery
atarlingtonvirginia

(1919)

In "The Body of an American," Dos Passos explodes the solemn and official rhetoric of the public voice. He sabotages the empty ceremonial gestures that disguise and disfigure reality for the public's sake.

Dos Passos (and the reader) survive the devastation of the public noise. They do not retreat into anxiety-producing and complicitous aestheticism; they instead engage and resist the world; they participate in its ironic deformation. Dos Passos wires the ironies; the reader pushes the plunger.

The reduction of the human scale to the anonymity of the vagrant and the unknown soldier reminds us of our common humanity and warns us of our common fate. Dos Passos chronicles the disintegration of hollow men, but he does not unqualifiedly condemn them. For he, his characters, and his readers are linked in their susceptibility to reduction and anonymity. All are embedded in the echoing public space —in the space of the text and the world. We, as readers, are in the same relation to the characters as they are to one another. We collide and know nothing of them but what we see and hear. We search for permanent, developing relationships, coherent and continuous lives, meaningful characters who mirror what we imagine to be our own human significance. We search, in short, for reassurance.

We are, however, like Vag, estranged from the world and the text. The continuity of our response to discontinuous lives is deliberately and continuously disrupted. As strangers we wander anonymously through the text (and the world). Our reduction to "The Body of An American," the waste product of *U.S.A.*, is the negative function of our estrangement. There is, however, a positive function of that estrangement, that tenuous connection to the world and the text. Dos Passos recognizes the subversive energy that often exists in society's outcasts. The stranger might escape "habit, piety, and precedent," the mechanical automatism that cultural patterns provide. The vagrant is both given off by and in search of a world. The young man of the text is bum and picaro, a culture's debris and its last best hope. The young man is driven by the world of echoes; he is driven, and he is in search of authentic voices: "he must catch the last subway, the streetcar, the bus, run up the gangplanks of all the steamboats, register at all the hotels, live in all the boardinghouses, sleep in all the beds." That young man and the reader travel *U.S.A.*, a catalogue of American debris, an exhaustive inventory of American people and places, in search of authenticity. Each stands in the midst of the great public noise, in the midst of a world too much with us.

Dos Passos refuses to relinquish his voice to the public space. He resists the invasions of history that determine and reduce lives, the public nightmares, the Newsreels. He resists voices that have become public, that demand conformity, that rest in cliché. He refuses to be silenced by the public voice, yet he does not retreat into solipsism. Silence and exile are not viable alternatives. There is only cunning. *U.S.A.* is a chronicle of word-debris, of language betrayals, of treasonous voices. It is also, however, a subversive performance. Its meanings lie neither in documentation (Newsreels), nor in conviction (Camera Eyes). They lie somewhere in between, in that frontier between history and fiction, in the ironic, performing voice of the author in concert with the reader, in their cunning resistance to the public voice, in our controlled deformation of the text and the world.

F. Scott Fitzgerald:
The Myth of Gatsby

Bruce Michelson

Among a set of characters marvelously palpable and vital—I would know Tom Buchanan if I met him on the street and would avoid him—Gatsby is somewhat vague. The reader's eyes can never quite focus upon him, his outlines are dim. Now everything about Gatsby is more or less a mystery, i.e. more or less vague, and this may be somewhat of an artistic intention, but I think it is mistaken. Couldn't he be physically described as distinctly as the others, and couldn't you add one or two characteristics like the use of that phrase "old sport,"—not verbal, but physical ones perhaps.
 —Letter of 20 November 1924, in *Dear Scott/Dear Max*, ed. John Kuehl and Jackson R. Bryer (New York: Scribner's, 1971).

Writing to Scott Fitzgerald in the spring of 1924, Maxwell Perkins was right, of course. The remarkable fact is that he was right still, even after Fitzgerald took this letter to heart, went back to the details of the Fuller-Magee case, pressed Zelda to "draw pictures until her fingers ache"—all in a struggle to make Jay Gatsby less of a wraith. A few weeks later, Fitzgerald wrote to Perkins that he, Fitzgerald, knew Gatsby now "better than I know my own child"; but Nick Carraway's mysterious neighbor, this Gatsby in whom so many readers have found a character of mythic proportions and resonance, Gatsby whose story comes so quickly to mind as a fable for our nation and our time, remains a ghost, not a man with a knowable face and soul. Perhaps this is as it should be, given three decades of general and accepted talk about *The Great Gatsby* as some sort of myth for the modern age. At least one kind of true myth, the kind about an everyman who, for the rest of us, strives with the gods, must have a faceless hero. The Bellerophons, Arachnes, Niobes, and Phaetons who try those glorious foolish gestures that we all want someone to try for all mortals' sake, can be known to us only by their desire, if they would represent us all. But sheer facelessness certainly is not enough; and with Gatsby, a handsome young felon with arrested ideas about love and a wrong young woman to practice them on—we need to ask how this somewhat tawdry story is made the substance of modern myth. Further, if Fitzgerald, in conceiving the book, was not imagining Gatsby as someone clear, unique, and real, who or what *was* Fitzgerald thinking of, and how has this novel convinced so many readers that an important, permanent tale is in it? All of this only restates an old question, the source of *The Great Gatsby's* mythic powers; however, it is

From *Modern Fiction Studies* 26, no. 4 (Winter 1980–81). © 1980 by the Purdue Research Foundation. Originally entitled "The Myth of Gatsby."

one which we can make some headway with if we can come at it a little differently. In doing so, the first task is to clarify what mythic heritage Fitzgerald was schooled in and drawing upon, in the wake of *The Waste Land* and *Ulysses*'s triumph, when, consciously or not, Fitzgerald turned mythmaker himself; and to which ancient hero in particular Gatsby owes his greatest debt. The second and far more important matter is to look at the novel *as* a myth with a definite heritage, and to see better those immemorial needs—of the teller and the listener alike—which the new tale fulfills in the manner of the old.

The Great Gatsby is a classic in great part because Fitzgerald had a classic imagination, classically trained. For all his fame as a bad student, for all his failed examinations, misspellings, malapropisms, and botched grammar, there is no question that he knew his Greco-Roman literature and mythology. The Newman School dedicated itself to preparing its Roman Catholic boys to succeed at the Protestant Yales and Princetons. Princeton required three years of Latin simply for admission; and we know that Fitzgerald, in Princeton's literature curriculum, was taking advanced Latin (however badly) even into his junior year. Late in his life, when he prided himself on little else, Fitzgerald was still vain about his knowledge of literature, and all through his career he could use that background gracefully when it pleased him to do so. His use of Greco-Roman lore was not just a matter of dropping a Narcissus here and a Trimalchio there; his classical background often plays a much more important part in his storytelling. Sometimes it shows up for a joke, as in the opening paragraphs of the 1920 story "May Day":

> There had been a war fought and won and the great city of the conquering people was crossed with triumphal arches and vivid with thrown flowers of white, red, and rose. All through the long spring days the returning soldiers marched up the chief highway behind the strump of drums and the joyous, resonant wind of the brasses, while merchants and clerks left their bickerings and figurings and, crowding to the windows, turned their white-bunched faces gravely upon the passing batallions.
>
> Never had there been such splendor in the great city, for the victorious war had brought plenty in its train, and the merchants had flocked thither from the South and West with their households to taste of all the luscious feasts and witness the lavish entertainments prepared—and to buy for their women furs against the next winter and bags of golden mesh and varicolored slippers of silk and silver and rose satin and cloth of gold.
>
> So gaily and noisily were the peace and prosperity impending hymned by the scribes and poets of the conquering people that more and more spenders had gathered from the provinces to drink the wine of excitement.

And so on through another paragraph thick with Athenian and Roman festivity. The story finally gets down to modern Americans wandering around a delirious New York, looking for whiskey, love, casual sex, or a good street brawl to celebrate the end of the World War.

But the classical modes inspire more than parody. From the late note-books, for example, come echoes of a different kind— different, and more unmistakably his:

> Wait for what? Wait while he swam off into a firmament of his own, so far off that she could only see his feathers gleaming in the distance, only hear distinctly [sic] the clamor of war or feel the vacuum that he created when sometimes he fell through space. He came back eventually with spoils, but for her there was always another larger waiting—for the end of youth, the blurring of her uniqueness: her two menacing deaths beside which mortal death was no more than sleep.

They are all here, all of Fitzgerald's most familiar dreams and woes. The wish for some glorious transcendence, the fear of that mortality which dooms hope, youth, intensity, and all the dimly-seen magnificence in life: these are surely the themes which pervade the major writings. And no classical allusion could encompass them better than this, the image of the skyborne mortal ascending towards the heavens on feathered wings, flying madly far and high, shaking the world with his earthward plunge. The flying, heroic, and doomed mortal comes, of course, straight out of myth; he is Icarus on his wax wings, Bellerophon on Pegasus, Phaeton in the sun's golden car. These stories are all one: a bold young man sacrifices everything for a few moments of impossible glory, pays with his life for an instant of supreme privilege, for living out the wildest fantasy of youth. The young doomed heroes, too, are all one: they are all faceless, known to us only in the mad, fine dreams they share with everyone. To Ovid, and to the galaxy of ancient myths brought to life in *The Metamorphoses*, Fitzgerald's mind turned when he thought of his own most desperate self, and of those sky-gazing desperate men he created, at least in part, in his own image.

As it happens, *The Great Gatsby*'s image patterns and even the workings of its plot show more than a general family resemblance to classical tales of flying men. The legend of Phaeton is the one which echoes in this novel most persistently and strongly—so strongly that there is cause for wondering whether Phaeton isn't as deliberately called up here as Odysseus is in Leopold Bloom's wanderings around Dublin. We shall see that this is a riddle worth puzzling over: in writing what he called his "new and delicate and intricately textured" something, a book which he himself thought of (in his happier moments) as "something really NEW in form, idea, structure—the mode for the age that Joyce and Stien [sic] are searching for, that Conrad didn't find," and which he accused all reviewers of misunderstanding, was Fitzgerald trying to be more Joycean than he ever admitted? But on this matter, puzzling is as far as we can go. There is no proving that Fitzgerald consciously turned to Ovid in designing *The Great Gatsby*. He apparently never said a word about doing so; and we can be sure that if Phaeton was on Fitzgerald's mind, other tales were haunting him too. One of his working titles for the novel, *Trimalchio in West Egg*, certainly makes the case for *The Satyricon*, but there are also shadows of *The Waste Land*, and recently some interesting parallels have been turned up between passages in *Gatsby* and lines in *The Golden Bough*. The point, then, of looking at the Phaeton tale in *The Great Gatsby* is not to make an argument for one literary debt and one alone, or to arrive at one pat explanation of how the novel works and what Fitzgerald meant by it. If *Gatsby* borrows something from Phaeton, it might very well be an unconscious borrowing. But one way or the other we are left with the fact that parallels between the stories turn up in uncanny profusion, that the implications of those parallels need to be followed out, and that the closeness of the new myth to the old one helps us understand better how Gatsby's story *is* a myth, how the rise and fall of a deluded and childlike gangster turns into a vital classic of *our* time.

To summarize the Phaeton story as Ovid tells it: a true son of a god, young Phaeton lives in a land of mortals far to the west of Apollo's palace. Nobody takes the young man seriously when he speaks of his noble birth, and so when he has grown up strong and reckless, Phaeton journeys to the east edge of the world, the blazing home of the divine horseman, the golden palace which Ovid describes with such flourish. From one of the many "trots" to *The Metamorphoses* available in 1916: "The palace of the Sun stood high on lofty columns, bright with glittering gold and bronze that shone like fire. Gleaming ivory crowned the gables above; the double folding-doors were radiant with burnished silver. And the workmanship was more beautiful than the material. For upon the doors Mulciber had carved in relief the waters that enfold the central earth, the circle of the lands and the sky that overhangs the lands. The sea holds the dark-hued gods: tuneful Triton, changeful Proteus, and Aegaeon."

And so on through many more radiant furnishings. When Phaeton arrives on high, his remorseful father hastily swears by the Styx to give the boy anything he desires; and Phaeton claims the sun and the golden chariot for one day. Apollo warns the boy of the power of the wild winged steeds, the perils of the course through the sky, the dangers of his cargo, the twistings, turnings, and grotesqueness of the path that seems so easy and perfect from below. But Phaeton is unshakable. Dawn on the fatal day throws open "her purple gates, and her courts glowing with rosy light," and Phaeton mounts to the god's place in the golden car. The young usurper manages things for a while, but soon the great horses are out of control, racing, swerving from the path, and setting the world ablaze: "The earth bursts into flame, the highest parts first, and splits into deep cracks, and its moisture is all dried up. The meadows are burned to white ashes; the trees are consumed, green leaves and all, and the ripe grain furnishes fuel for its own destruction. But these are small losses which I am lamenting.

Great cities perish with their walls, and the vast conflagration reduces whole nations to ashes."

The earth cries to heaven for mercy; with Apollo's consent, Zeus hurls his thunderbolt; and Phaeton, afire, streaks down through the air like a falling star. His body falls into the Eridanus, the river no living man has ever seen; and his sisters, grieving at his tomb, are subsequently transformed into poplars, forever dropping their amber tears into the water. Ovid's epitaph for Phaeton:

> Hic situs est Phaeton currus auriga paterni
> Quem si non tenuit magnis tamen excidit ausis.

Here lies Phaeton, who drove his father's golden car. He failed greatly, but still more greatly did he dare. Ovid begs the question: did Phaeton turn out all right in the end? Was he a true son of the god, or just a "poor son of a bitch"? As one of Ovid's flashiest tales, Phaeton's fall offers perfect raw material for making a modern hero. Here is a true mortal with his sublime and preposterous dreams, one who would risk everything for a simple "golden moment"—and as soon as he has what he wants, his world burns (literally, in this case) to ashes before his eyes. The story lives precisely because it has at its heart the paradox which haunts all the great myths of mortals who strive with gods: it appeals to our most fabulous dreams even as it cautions us to leave those dreams alone.

The golden car, the disastrous careening ride through the ash-strewn world—the general likenesses of Gatsby's story to Phaeton's fall will be immediately clear to anyone thinking of *The Great Gatsby* with Ovid in mind. But all the plot borrowings in the world could not make a modern Phaeton of Gatsby, could not make his story a living myth, were it not for Nick, a storyteller with a genuine capacity for wonder. The raw bones of a myth might be waiting for him in West Egg, just as the older tale waited centuries for Ovid; but Nick, like Ovid before him, proves the true mythmaker. Nick finds the details and the language to perform the magic, to suspend us, as he himself is suspended, somewhere between wonder and scorn for the hero of his tale, to enchant us with the very spirit that the story builds its tragedy around. The myth of Gatsby is a myth made as much of small moments and well-chosen words as it is of grand gestures, and with these small shadings we must especially concern ourselves.

To do this, we need to begin at the beginning of *The Great Gatsby*, with the first dramatic situation in the book, Nick's social call on the Buchanans. All through the novel Nick is of course Gatsby's witness; but at times Nick is also Gatsby's surrogate, and he begins the book by paying the visit Gatsby ought to be paying himself, to the house of sun-girl. Nick goes visiting in the evening. He travels across to East Egg, on the other side of the water, and finds a house ablaze with light. Fire and brightness catch Nick's eye much more than does the architecture itself: "The lawn started at the beach and ran toward the front door for a quarter of a mile, jumping over sundials and brick walks and burning gardens—finally when it reached the house drifting up the side in bright vines as though from the momentum of its run. The front was broken by a line of French windows, glowing now with reflected gold and wide open to the warm, windy afternoon."

Daisy, the days-eye, shares the house with West Egg's master of horses, posed in his riding habit above the glowing world as Nick drives up. Tom is a polo-player, *the* polo-player, according to Gatsby, and by Tom's own boast "the first man who ever made a stable out of a garage." The horseman and Nick survey the domain (Tom's eyes "flaring" as he himself looks over it), and then Nick is led into the glowing house, where he finds a girl in white with a face "sad and lovely with bright things in it, bright eyes and a bright passionate mouth." And here too is a tanned companion with sun-strained eyes, Miss Baker, veteran of three hot-sounding cities, Asheville, Hot Springs, and Palm Beach. In a few minutes Nick, Tom, and the two white-garbed women move to dinner out on a rosy-hued porch, where Daisy makes her first completed gesture in the novel. Snuffing out the lesser lights at the table, she lets everyone know what a days-eye does with her time:

> "Why *candles*?" objected Daisy, frowning. She snapped them out with her fingers. "In two weeks it'll be the longest day of the year." She looked at us all radiantly. "Do you always watch for the longest day of the year and then miss it? I always watch for the longest day in the year and then miss it."

Sad fate, always to miss the best of all chances to be radiant. Milton Stern and others have already gone to great trouble demonstrating Tom's connections with fire and light, and Daisy's general, recurring likeness to the sun; Stern takes the resemblance as a restatement of the metaphoric link between sunshine and the Good Life—but Fitzgerald may have had more specific connections to suggest. Nick talks about sunlight more than any other narrator in our major fiction, and radiant Daisy and horsey, powerful, philandering Tom are ever his sunlight people, carrying the fire and light and heat with them everywhere they go. When this polo-playing Apollo takes a ride to the high, white penthouse where he has installed his mortal "girl," Myrtle—like Daisy, Myrtle too is a name with a pun in it—the place fills with "cheerful sun," making it an inspiring sight for the other mere mortals down in the streets below. Or so Nick imagines the effect in a moment of dizzy enchantment, as he too finds himself on high: "high over the city our line of yellow windows must have contributed their share of human secrecy to the casual watcher in the darkening streets, and I was him too, looking up and wondering."

Of course, Daisy can do the same sort of trick when she is in the mood. The rain falls from a gloomy sky on the afternoon of her coming to tea at Nick's house and finding Gatsby again; the storm lightens to a mist when she arrives, falls again on their awkward, unheard reconciliation (Nick waits out the conversation outside in the downpour, under a tree). But sun comes out strong when Daisy, now in a much brighter mood, has made up her mind to come to the house of her admirer. Once they are all inside Gatsby's mansion the rain comes on again, stopping only for a moment when the sun-girl needs some small-scale fireworks:

> "Come here *quick!*" cried Daisy at the window.
>
> The rain was still falling, but the darkness had parted in the west, and there was a pink and golden billow of foamy clouds above the sea.
>
> "Look at that," she whispered, and then after a moment: "I'd like to just get one of those pink clouds and put you in it and push you around."

In her own way, Daisy is quite a hand at pushing clouds and people around, dazzling people, burning them up. Of course, she is more a travesty on radiance than the real thing, just as Tom is a parody of an Apollo— but the arrangement is not quite that simple. The effect these people have on us is not cheap irony, not another dreary recognition of how far the sublime world has fallen. Thanks to Nick, Tom and Daisy come off as travesties which respect the myth and in a strange way revive it: Tom is a new Apollo in much the same way that Molly Bloom, munching her potted meat in bed with Blazes Boylan, is a New Penelope. That is, Nick shows us enough of the real thing in Tom, enough genuine presence in him, and enough mysterious brightness in Daisy to place both of them somewhere between parody and incarnation. Like Molly, Daisy and Tom seem, through Nick's eyes, a little grander than human, even as they are so much less than good. We see the aura around these people because Nick sees it and makes us see it too; we believe in it precisely because Nick does—in spite of himself and his persistent wish to suggest his detached contempt. As an excitement betrayed rather than acknowledged, it is all the more powerful. That excitement shows itself not simply in the diction and the detail Nick heaps up, all the blazing, radiating, and flashing; it shows itself, too, in the mute, stumbling, reverential stupidity Nick is driven to in this world of the mock-divine. In fact, Nick's enormous skill with language, turning up in every line of his narrative, only underscores the speechless enchantment he feels in the Buchanan Palace. Led into Daisy's presence, Nick comes silent, murmuring an apology as he enters awestruck with the command of the room; he is just as reverent and tongue-tied for just the same reasons on being introduced to Jordan Baker: "Miss Baker's lips fluttered, and she nodded at me almost imperceptibly, and then quickly tipped her head back again—the object she was balancing had obviously tottered a little and given her something of a fright. Again a sort of apology arose to my lips. Almost any exhibition of complete self-sufficiency draws a stunned tribute from me."

A joke flashes upon Nick when Daisy asks if she is missed back in Chicago —but like everything else he has tried to say among and about his hosts, the joke pays tribute even as it pokes fun: " 'The whole town is desolate. All the cars have the left rear wheel painted black as a mourning wreath, and there's a persistent wail all night along the north shore.' "

"How gorgeous!" cries Daisy, taking (as we would expect) the homage along with the jest. It is no surprise that this extravagance should come to Nick's lips so readily. These people do have a touch of Olympian grandeur, arrogant, foolish, and untrustworthy though they are—and to be sure, arrogance, foolishness, and treachery are no strangers to Olympus either. The Buchanan world, down to the very claret they serve at dinner, is "corky but rather impressive" at the same time; everything in it astonishes, charms, and cloys all at once. The scene in East Egg is, in sum, a remarkable feat of balancing. Already we find ourselves suspended in that vertiginous limbo between wonder and derision, that odd, mixed mood which grows stronger as Gatsby's story gets underway. Nick's translating consciousness has made the necessary mock-divinities, but, in doing so, he has given them an edge of the true Olympian; and already the moral vertigo of a living myth has established itself in the novel.

Out of his exile in the western hinterlands, into the home of the sunshine—where he believes he rightly belongs— comes the usurper. Once a James, he calls himself Jay now, a name more befitting one who aspires to flight in the high heavens. Nick calls him a "true son of God—a phrase which, if it means anything, means just that," fresh from the dark fields of the republic, and ready. He has riches now, "Valor Extraordinary" and medals to prove it, an east-facing palace which catches the light, a golden heliotropic car that moves, as a dazzled Nick tells us, "with fenders spread like wings, scattering light through half Astoria," a car with a "labyrinth of windshields that mirrored a dozen suns." Of course Gatsby, better than any other character in American literature, knows how to dress the part of the special mortal who strives with the gods. When he lays claim to the sunshine in Nick's cottage, he comes in that array of white suit, silver shirt, and gold tie which Marius Bewley, among many others, has found "dogmatically Olympic." Everything he surrounds himself with is dogmatically Olympic too, and heliotropic, meant to flash and bloom in sunlight; nothing about him, not even his vast house, looks good in gray weather. The most sun-oriented thing, perhaps the most memorable item in Gatsby's possession, is the car, and not simply because it has the key role in its owner's downfall. In one sense it is a peculiar choice for Gatsby. One might suppose that a drive into town to see the notorious Wolfsheim, or around the countryside later on with another man's wife, would require something less ostentatious, more closed-up. In one way—but not of course in the mythic one—Gatsby would be much better off in his Rolls Royce than in this golden, open, flamboyant thing with its canvas tops and picnic boxes and hat boxes—this supreme touring car—or to use the motoring jargon of the twenties, this phaeton to end all phaetons.

Sun-seeking Gatsby has been after the sunshine in his life for five years, and his path has been a twisting and turning one. Just after his return from the Great War, he made a dejected pilgrimage to the place where light had shone. In true Ovidian fashion, Nick loses himself utterly in his fantasies of Gatsby's passage out of Louisville, whose sacred streets the days-eye had once walked, but walks no more. The ride out of town is a passage into exile from the life-giving fire: "The track curved and now it was going away from the sun, which, as it sank lower, seemed to spread itself in benediction over the vanishing city where she had drawn her breath. He stretched out his hand desperately as if to snatch only a wisp of air, to save a fragment of the spot that she had made lovely for him. But it was all going by too fast now for his blurred eyes and he knew that he had lost that part of it, the freshest and the best, forever."

This denial of the light is too much to bear; and so when Jay Gatsby comes east he comes as a kind of mirror, establishing himself just across the water from the sun-girl. He settles in West Egg, the new-rich community that catches and reflects and diffracts the sunlight, rather than radiates it as East Egg does. Nick observes that when the East Eggers do come west, they come "carefully on guard against its spectroscopic gaiety." And Milton Stern is certainly right in associating Gatsby with the moon—which, of course, shines by reflection—but we should note, too, that Gatsby by night is the spectroscope, the prismatic transformer of the white sunlight he catches into the thousand colored lights of his enormous parties, the lights of which "grow brighter as the earth lurches away from the sun." Gatsby lives for the light he catches; to the sun-light's place across the water (marked at night only by a green light), he makes an appeal of a thousand colors. But the sun will not come to him—until, that is, he plays his trick to get her, just as Phaeton cannot possess the sun without tricking his father into giving it up. The trick to bring the sun-girl into his mortal hands is set, with Nick's and Jordan's help. Now, suddenly, the lights at Gatsby's house are no longer spectroscopic glints; the white fire boils from inside the mansion itself, not from across the water. Nick sees the transformation in the early morning on his way back from the city.

> When I came home to West Egg that night I was afraid for a moment that my house was on fire. Two o'clock and the whole corner of the peninsula was blazing with light, which fell unreal on the shrubbery and made thin elongating glints upon the roadside wires. Turning a corner, I saw that it was Gatsby's house, lit from tower to cellar.
>
> At first I thought it was another party, a wild rout that had resolved itself into "hide-and-go-seek" or "sardines-in-the-box" with all the house thrown open to the game. But there wasn't a sound. Only wind in the trees, which blew the wires and made the lights go off and on again as if the house had winked into the darkness. As my taxi groaned away I saw Gatsby walking toward me across his lawn.
>
> "Your place looks like the World's Fair," I said.

Gatsby tells Nick that he has been "glancing into some of the rooms," an excuse which Nick finds preposterous enough to recall only after he goes home. There is no explaining these fireworks in the small hours, except perhaps as a kind of midnight welcome of the sun's coming sunshine, a suggestion that the golden fire has indeed found its way into the sunworshippers' charge—to fill his life with radiance, and soon after to set his world ablaze.

The sun-girl comes; the rain clears; and white-suited Gatsby finds himself with the thing he has most wanted. To rule the days-eye is to rule over time itself—or so thinks Gatsby, with his faith that people can make the present out of the past. The drizzly afternoon is full of skips and halts and eddies in time. The weather is a blur. There is rain, and then sun, then rain again and sun again, and rain once more. There is a defunct clock on Nick's mantle to catch in the hands and wonder at; there is even Klipspringer (the very name suggests erratic paces, haywire timepieces), the guest left over from some party or other, to spring out of nowhere and sing songs about making love "In the meantime, inbetween time." The son of God has caught the sun; but the son of God is only a mortal, and already the smooth order of days and time is beginning to come apart under his command.

To Gatsby's brief life in-between-time Nick gives only a few paragraphs, a few peripheral moments. Tom, on horseback, comes by the house and deals out a snub which only emphasizes his own powerlessness, now that somebody else has domain over his sunny charge; Gatsby throws one more great party, at which Tom must go round as "the polo player," and Daisy, late in the evening, worries about an eclipse—the one catastrophe sun-girls must fret over: "What would happen now in the dim, incalculable hours? Perhaps some unbelievable guest would arrive, a person infinitely rare and to be marvelled at, some authentically radiant young girl who with one fresh glance at Gatsby, one moment of magical encounter, would blot out those five years of unwavering devotion."

But no truer radiance shows up. Gatsby fires his servants, ends his parties, and fills the house with Wolfsheim's henchmen—and then suddenly it is the hottest day of the year, a day when the seats of the railroad cars "hovered on the edge of combustion," a day when the sun-god, whose very body (in Nick's daydream) grows "far too hot to touch this afternoon," he who, on an earlier afternoon, has proclaimed himself Apollonian patron of "—oh, science and art, and all that," declaims now on the solar apocalypse: "I read somewhere that the sun's getting hotter every year," said Tom genially. "It seems that pretty soon the earth's going to fall into the sun—or wait a minute—it's just the opposite—the sun's getting colder every year."

Whichever. But Tom knows whereof he speaks in foretelling a fiery end "pretty soon." Before the climactic excursion to the roasting city, there is time only for Tom to grasp the truth, and one front-porch Arcadian reverie about winged sails crossing the sound, bound for "the scalloped ocean and the abounding blessed isles"—to which one of their party will be fated to pass in a day's time.

At this point, of course, *The Great Gatsby*'s plot takes its most elaborate turn.

> "Shall we all go in my car?" suggested Gatsby. He felt the hot, green leather of the seat. "I ought to have left it in the shade."
>
> "Is it a standard shift?" demanded Tom.
>
> "Yes."
>
> "Well, you take my coupé and let me drive your car to town."
>
> The suggestion was distasteful to Gatsby.
>
> "I don't think there's much gas," he objected.
>
> "Plenty of gas," said Tom boisterously. He looked at the gauge. "And if it runs out I can stop at a drug-store. You can buy anything at a drug-store nowadays."
>
> A pause followed this apparently pointless remark. Daisy looked at Tom frowning, and an indefinable expression, at once definitely unfamiliar and vaguely recognizable, as if I had only heard it described in words, passed over Gatsby's face.
>
> "Come on, Daisy," said Tom, pressing her with his hand toward Gatsby's car. "I'll take you in this circus wagon."
>
> He opened the door, but she moved out from the circle of his arm.
>
> "You take Nick and Jordan. We'll follow you in the coupé."

All of this, capped off by Tom's declaration to George Wilson that the yellow car is Tom's, eventually causes Myrtle to run out into the Phaeton's path, causes Wilson to blame and assassinate Gatsby, and Tom to involve himself as the last betrayer. No one finds fault with the roundaboutness and implausibility of this car-swapping, and no one, really, has a right to. The object is not tidiness, but holocaust, and Fitzgerald achieves here one of the most powerful, memorable holocausts in a literature that abounds with it. Assuming that Fitzgerald had several options open for killing off Gatsby and showing Tom and Daisy for what they are, and assuming that we, who have an endless choice of lurid disasters in the modern novel, feel a rare and special intensity in this one, what is it that makes the nightmare in *Gatsby* so right and all the elaborate preparations for it perfectly justified?

The careening, bloody ride back from town strikes deep because it perfectly symbolizes Gatsby's disaster—the disaster that has *already* befallen him—and because the symbolic episode is drawn directly from the climax of the Phaeton legend. Consider the hero's plight: even his golden car now belongs to the sun-god, Tom having publicly laid claim to it, just as he has publicly laid claim to Daisy again, and made it stick. Gatsby is every inch the failed and powerless usurper: his no longer are the reins, nor the sun, nor the golden car; he tears along now at the mercy of fate and of his own overreaching ambitions, spreading not light now but death through a world of ashes, watching the car spread the destruction which will soon bring down on himself the retributive stroke. The killing of Myrtle is Daisy's fault, but it epitomizes Gatsby's failure. He has had the sun and could not keep her; he has lost his grip on his own life; he rides helplessly through a once-bright world now gone up in smoke, and ashes, doomed himself by that which he has most desired.

Phaeton falls like a glowing star into the secret waters of the Eridanus; the tears of his transformed sisters fall on the water as amber. Gatsby goes home and dons his "pink rag of a suit," the "bright spot of color against the white steps" of his empty and hopeless house. He spends one black evening with Nick, groping around in the darkness for cigarettes—and the next morning he is found drifting in the swimming pool he has not entered all summer. The gardener has warned him that "Leaves'll start falling pretty soon," and they start falling sooner than he or anyone else would expect, falling that very day upon another ambitious young hero floating dead in the water: "With little ripples that were hardly the shadows of waves, the laden mattress moved irregularly down the pool. A small gust of wind that scarcely corrugated the surface was enough to disturb its accidental course with its accidental burden. The touch of a cluster of leaves revolved it slowly, tracing, like the leg of transit, a thin red circle in the water."

Again, what can we make of all this? That a classic myth has been deliberately and ingeniously revived? Or is it rather that *The Great Gatsby*'s imagery, descriptive diction, and essential plot structure parallel the Phaeton legend with amazing persistence? There is no settling that matter to everyone's taste; and finally it is not important that we do so. The vital question about *The Great Gatsby* remains the question of what it is *about* and what exactly is Nick's stake in telling the story. I have said that the tale, an inarticulate bootlegger's fixation on a worthless woman, is in itself almost nothing. It becomes everything, or rather it becomes truly mythic and haunting in its reverberations, precisely because Nick experiences it as a myth, and tells it as a myth of the classic kind. The Phaeton story, and for that matter all of the great western mythology, seeks to explain how the world is, and what the teller's and the listeners' place is in it—that much is self-evident. The gods are always around somewhere, attending to the godly business which we had better avoid; we mortals have our own lower place, and our own ungorgeous lives to attend to. And these tales of the mortal dreamer who seeks Olympian power and delight are important because they help us to come to terms with our own wild dreams. The Phaetons and the Gatsbys live those dreams for us, allow us to enjoy the great adventure and still escape alive. Their legends are not cautionary lessons, but vicarious thrills as well; they celebrate the persistence and power of the dream even as they warn against trying to live it out. The great myth does not choose between tempting and teaching. It does both. It is the achievement of such a duality, more than anything else, that marks *The Great Gatsby* as a modern myth. Nick both tells and responds to the story as myth, losing himself imaginatively in the fulfillment and the inevitable disaster of the Gatsby in himself, the garish, gorgeous, foolish believer and doer that part of this cautious, removed, ascetic Nick Carraway yearns to be.

Nick is a superb mythmaker, in other words, because he is Jay Gatsby as well as Nick and because he loses neither identity when becoming the other. Everyone notices that Nick, in many ways, acts as Gatsby's double, riding around New York with him and being mistaken for a "business gonnegtion," taking up Daisy's friend Jordan—the other girl of the matched set—arranging the reunion of the lovers, answering Gatsby's telephone, arranging the funeral, running the house and protecting it after the murder. But more important to the story is Gatsby's role as *Nick*'s surrogate, creating for Nick moments of overwhelming imaginative transcendence, making Nick feel, even after Gatsby's death, those mysterious possibilities, those dreams which still lure, however "foul dust" might gather in their wake. Nick is part-Gatsby to the very end; Gatsby's death is not, for Nick, the dashing of all that Gatsby suggested to him alive. Always poised at the edge of things, on the edge of Gatsby's blue lawn, the edge of Wall Street's glorious, tawdry business, the edge of friendship, the edge of love, Nick is in the end still in that condition, treading a border between "unaffected scorn" for Gatsby's ruthless hubris, and celebration for Gatsby's great dare. Too often the final page of the novel is discussed as a straight dirge for The American Dream, a proclamation that all the dreaming and striving go for nothing. We need to read more carefully than this, for the ending of a true myth is more complex than the moral on a fable. When this composed and controlled Nick goes down to sprawl on Gatsby's empty beach, the gesture itself suggesting a kind of surrender, he gives himself once more to the very dream he has been trying, tries even now, to shuffle off. It is for Nick that the houses now grow "inessential" and pass away; for Nick that the old island reveals itself, flowering still as it flowered (he imagines) long ago —and it is Nick, finally, who finds himself "compelled" by his own reverie "into an aesthetic contemplation he neither understood nor desired, face to face for the last time in history with his capacity for wonder." Even here, Nick dreams up more surrogates, nameless old Dutch sailors to dream his dreams for him, feel what he himself feels but wishes to keep at a safe distance. But as has happened through his history of Gatsby, Nick's own wonder, his own history, emerges through these others. Gatsby is dead; his dream (at least this time) is defeated; but neither has lost a grip on Nick's imagination, or on ours. Nick is free to go home to Minnesota, but he has found no safe distance from which imaginatively to experience Gatsby's adventure. At the end of the novel the "American Dream" is alive because Nick's imagination is still under its spell. If Gatsby has lived that dream to an inevitable, disastrous conclusion, he has done so in a fashion as much classic as American, and Nick has been classic in telling of it, not simply in allusion and metaphor but in condition of mind. Phaeton may be here in Gatsby by contrivance, or he may not; but *Gatsby* is certainly more akin to Ovid than it is to the Fuller-Magee case or Ben

Franklin's *Autobiography* or *Hopalong Cassidy* or the Alger stories or any other rise or rise-and-fall tales that Fitzgerald ever knew of. The story is ancient in more than one way, and that is precisely why it stays with us, not only powerful, but invincibly new.

The Aesthetic of Forbearance: Fitzgerald's *Tender Is the Night*

Maria DiBattista

"Forbearance, good word." This curt entry in F. Scott Fitzgerald's notebooks is the tempered reflection of the private man. The public Fitzgerald was more rash. The man who, on meeting his idol James Joyce, offered to jump out of the window to demonstrate his adulation, lacked, unquestionably, the instinct to forbear. Forbearance conventionally prescribes a standard of behavior, a "good" word in that it designates a social virtue, a deliberate restraining of self-assertive impulses. Yet such acts of restraint, social or moral, were probably uncongenial to a writer of Fitzgerald's temperament, a romantic novelist attracted to personality defined as "an unbroken series of successful gestures," the uninterrupted, sweeping gestures of the self.

That Fitzgerald's praise of forbearance surfaces in the literary musings of his notebooks suggests, rather, that forbearance is a good word primarily in Fitzgerald's private vocabulary of art, a word connoting a determined fictional strategy within a determining moral stance. Forbearance as an aesthetic attitude emphasizes the active sense of the word—a withholding, a deferral until the proper moment for expression declares itself. Forbearance, aesthetically conceived, implies a suppression of narrative information and as such represents a guiding principle in the construction of plot. A forbearing fiction demands a canny narrative treatment of history, of character, and of appropriate generic and mythic material to insure that the ironic mystery of its fable is protected against sentimental, moralistic readings.

In a letter of "uncalled for" advice to John Peale Bishop, Fitzgerald counsels the aspiring novelist on the primacy of mystery over morality in the novelistic treatment of causality and human destiny:

From *Novel: A Forum on Fiction* 11, no. 1 (Fall 1977). © 1977 by Novel Corp.

Life is not so smooth that it can't go over suddenly into melodrama. That's the other face of much worry about inevitability. Everything's too beautifully caused—one can guess ahead. Even the movies condemn a story as "too straight." My own best solution to date is the to-and-fro, keep-facts-back mystery stuff, but it's difficult.

The "to-and-fro, keep-facts-back" fictional ploy is what Fitzgerald means by forbearance. As an aesthetic demeanor cultivated by the artist, forbearance is the stuff of mystery, not morality. Only in melodrama do mystery and morality meet without embarrassment, but the result, Fitzgerald intimates, is debased art. His implied objection to melodrama, as a form of art or life, is that its projected ending is "too straight" in a double sense—too rigid in its moral attitudes and too predictable in its vindication of those attitudes. The good plot is devious; it conspires against conventional expectations and their attendant moral complacencies. Only good form insures good values, and the good plot forbears reproducing life's lapses into melodrama.

Fitzgerald's social conscience, based as it is on his aesthetic, makes the same *generic* objection to America's national demeanor. Writing in the thirties, Fitzgerald observed: "Fifty years ago we Americans substituted melodrama for tragedy." His critique of America is directed against the corrupt fictions endemic to the continent whose popular imagination produced the cowboy, the bootlegger, and the ruthless entrepreneur—all avatars of the unforbearing spirit—as distinctly native "types." In *The Great Gatsby*, for instance, Fitzgerald's cautionary tale about the dangers lurking in "bad" form, Fitzgerald successfully exploited the ironies of America's fatal substitution of melodrama for tragedy. The ending of *The Great Gatsby*, the too beautifully caused murder of the romantic idealist by the mindless revenger, marks the triumph of the popular over the literary imagination. The vigilante—whose generic home is melodrama—defeats the finest "type" of the American novel—the American naïf, whose tragic destiny had been explored by Hawthorne and Melville, partially modified in the dark comedies of Twain, and finally illuminated in the work of Henry James. *The Great Gatsby*'s purposefully melodramatic denouement, adapted, Fitzgerald hinted, after the "arbitrary blood-letting of Flaubert, Stendhal, and the Elizabethans" represents the triumph of "vulgar" reality over the sophisticated myths of the New World.

In *The Great Gatsby*, the exigencies of theme necessitated Fitzgerald's flirtation with the arbitrary blood-letting of melodrama. Gatsby's story, like Madame Bovary's or Julien Sorel's, simultaneously comprises a cultural history of *accomplished* betrayal to cultural ideals, a nation's select and self-serving fictions. Historically, America's lack of forbearance expressed itself in the populist melodrama of the westward movement, whose unchecked expansionism was legitimized by the myth of manifest destiny. In Fitzgerald's ironic critique, the historical betrayal lies not in the originating, but in the finalized vision of a destiny already made manifest. Gatsby's famous slip, relocating San Francisco in the Midwest, betrays the historical as well as geographical ignorance of the American Adam. San Francisco marks the temporal and spatial limit of the expansionist adventure in the New World. But, indoctrinated in the popular faith in an inexhaustible frontier, Gatsby naïvely believes that the American romance is a continuing, not a completed, history.

Plot, then, as the temporal dimension in narrative, functions as a commentary and corrective for America's naïve historical understanding. It provides an alternate, secular model of destiny to the Edenic myth of providential history. Thus, the plot of *The Great Gatsby* is constructed around a series of accidents that dramatize how the unpredictable contingencies of ongoing historical time subvert Gatsby's personal myth of a stable, and therefore renewable, past. Gatsby is the American hero of untutored imagination who believes that the course of history is decided by the sheer effort of human will. In *Tender Is the Night,* a novel Fitzgerald compared to Thackeray's *Vanity Fair,* that is, a novel "without a hero," the American imagination is educated into an attitude of forbearance. Gatsby's naïveté yields to Dick Diver's sophisticated knowledge that he is the instrument, not the shaper, of historical forces.

In a rare moment of perception, Nicole Diver observes that her husband behaves "as though an incalculable story was telling itself inside of him, about which she could only guess at in the moments it broke through the surface." In *The Great Gatsby*, too, Fitzgerald ironically qualified Gatsby's original "mystery" by belatedly invoking the "story" told in Ben Franklin's *Autobiography*, especially those sections involving schedules for the programmatic shaping of the self. Diver's incalculability, like Gatsby's "mystery," is finally, if not an open, at least a simple literary secret. In the novel's opening sequence, we are introduced to, among others, one McKisco, who, his garrulous wife explains, is finishing his first novel:

> "It's on the idea of Ulysses," continued Mrs. McKisco. "Only instead of taking twenty-four hours my husband takes a hundred years. He takes a decayed old French aristocrat and puts him in contrast with the mechanical age—"
>
> "Oh, for God's sake, Violet, don't go telling everybody the idea," protested McKisco.

Questionable as the informing idea of McKisco's novel may be, his novelistic instincts are sound when he interrupts his wife at the point when the full plot of the novel is about to be disclosed. McKisco's forbearance is Fitzgerald's. The basic idea shaping the apparently incalculable story of Dick Diver's life is a novelistic treatment of an epic theme—the odyssey of acculturation and adjustment undertaken in the Vanity Fair of the mechanical age.

Joyce's Ulyssean Bloom is the immediate progenitor of Fitzgerald's Odyssean hero, and Homer's Odysseus is surely an impressive forebear.

Yet Fitzgerald's treatment of the idea of Ulysses differs markedly from theirs. Joyce's and Homer's heroes remain fundamentally paradigmatic figures whose idiosyncratic characters may qualify, but never oppose their substantive epic being. Diver, however, is presented as a novelistic "character" unprotected by the epic machinery that governs the irresistible destiny of Homer's Odysseus or the epic scaffolding that supports and upholds Joyce's Bloom even in his most bathetic moments as a besieged Dubliner. Schooled in an intransigent American tradition that prefers folk heroes to mythic prototypes, Fitzgerald underplays Diver as an incarnation of the mythic hero in a continuing literary tradition. Instead Diver's biography is Fitzgerald's vehicle for testing the process by which historical figures, like Benjamin Franklin or Andrew Jackson, come to embody the literary idea of a life story: how, that is, the randomness and openness of historical life assumes the inevitability of a closed narrative form. The "real" Ulysses whose story haunts *Tender Is the Night* is Ulysses S. Grant, the genius of warfare in a mechanical age.

After summarizing the central data of Diver's life, the narrator concludes: "The foregoing has the ring of a biography, without the satisfaction of knowing that the hero, like Grant, lolling in his general store in Galena, is ready to be called to an intricate destiny." The life of Ulysses S. Grant serves as a potentially imitable model of heroic life because it conforms to the American version of the myth of destiny—the success story. The satisfaction implicit in such stories derives from a knowledge of the end accessible to the reader, but denied to the historical or literary character. Fitzgerald emphasizes the satisfaction in "guessing ahead" by initially focusing on his heroic model, as did Homer and Joyce, *in medias res*. The apparently purposeless middle, Grant lolling in his general store, reveals its historical purpose in a future already known and documented: Grant's triumphant return to the center of American life at a decisive historical moment. In the "straight" Odyssean epic narrative, the return is *nostos* or homecoming. *Nostos* not only reinstates the heroic warrior to his rightful position as national leader; *nostos* also reinstates the idea of an epic destiny. *Nostos* is the triumph of forbearance, the satisfaction awaiting the cunning hero who, like Grant lolling in Galena, knows how to bide his time.

But the American warrior of modern warfare knows no such straight triumph. That Grant, the hero of the Civil War, becomes the scandal-ridden president of Reconstruction is also part of the reader's knowledge of Grant's intricate destiny, perhaps the decisive part. Such knowledge irreversibly complicates the conscious parallel between the life of Ulysses S. Grant and the history of Dick Diver, descendent of Mad Anthony Wayne, another warrior ill-suited for the work of peace. Grant's biography not only serves as a generic model of the heroic life seen in distinctly American terms; it also provides an object lesson in the realities of historical life, realities that may intersect but never completely vindicate the myth of transcendent destiny.

The intricacies of destiny in the modern world thus undermine the satisfactions of a straight biographical or mythic narrative that concludes with the unqualified triumph of the hero. One source of thwarted satisfaction is the historical irony associated with Grant's emergence into heroic life and subsequent disgrace as a national folk-hero, namely, the qualified return. Fitzgerald translates this disappointment into the delusory satisfactions of false homecoming. False homecoming is the keynote of the first important scene in *Tender Is the Night*, the reunion of expatriates the Divers host. Rosemary Hoyt, the naïf of the party, "as dewy with belief as a child from one of Mrs. Burnett's vicious tracts," is duped by the surface good cheer prevailing at the Villa Diana into "a conviction of homecoming, of a return from the derisive and salacious improvisations of the frontier." The novel associates dewy visions of homecoming with naïve, infantile, and finally dangerous forms of belief. Fitzgerald was always fascinated by the peculiarly American mind that combined the vicious and the child-like, a fascination that accounts for his singular contribution to the profile of the American naïf—the destructive child, a Daisy Buchanan, a "Baby" Warren. But his sophisticated hero, Dick Diver, knows better. He forbears embracing the doctrinaire and degraded idealism that envisions an untroubled transition from war to peace, an immediate restitution of the departed past. His Atlantic crossing to the true homeland, the still untamed American frontier, is to say goodbye to all his fathers, not to re-embrace them.

Diver's homage to his American "Fathers" proves, however, a meager gesture of respect and atonement. For Diver harbors a more subtle form of viciousness peculiar to his times. The vice-ridden "Lost Generation" reneges on its historical obligations, deliberately cutting itself off from its renewing and renewable source in the improvisations, however derisive and salacious, of the frontier. Its wanderings over the face of a ravaged Europe are never redeemed by a final homecoming, because for many wandering has become an end in itself. Homer's and Joyce's Ulysses are involuntary exiles; Fitzgerald's wanderers are expatriates, voluntary exiles. The American in Europe, James's great subject, is reinterpreted as the prime symbol of the modern Ulysses who prefers the comfortable life of exile in the devitalized and decadent Phaeacia of the Old World to the difficult work of repatriation in the New. The post-war generation conceives of homecoming, as does Rosemary, as a return from, not a return to their native ground.

Thus despite the novel's focus on conviviality and hospitality, feasting and drinking—the normative values in epics of acculturation—its heroes abjure their true historical mission: the reclamation of the homeland that, like Ithaca, awaits the return of her native sons from foreign wars. The viciousness of post-war life can be seen in the festivities that occupy much of the novel's narrative time, festivities not held to celebrate the return of conquering heroes, but to mask moral defeats. Diver, the Belasco of the post-war party, looks back "with awe at the carnivals of affection he had given, as a general might gaze upon a massacre he had ordered to satisfy an impersonal blood-lust." The violence inherent in the simile is startling and puzzling, and it is not immediately apparent what the affinity is between the forced gaiety of expatriate life and the barbarism of the battlefield. Yet the persistent use of military tropes to describe carnivalized life argues that the connection is not casual, but definitive. In a more sober lenten mood, Diver reflects on "the waste and extravagance" involved in his carnivals of affection. Diver's entertainments and the massacres of a general are extravagances in a double sense: a "waste" of material and human resources and, as the etymology of extravagance implies, a misguided expense of energy. Extravagance comes from the Latinate root for "wandering" (Fr. "vagari"), denoting a digression beyond proper limits. Carnival time and wartime are both times of excess, times in which the stricture to forbear, with its promise of containment, is more needed than ever. A massacre to satisfy an impersonal blood-lust strategically oversteps the military objectives of battle. Similarly, a carnival to satisfy a need for affection transgresses beyond the bounds of civilized sociability.

The relaxation of moral and social norms accounts for the carnival mood of *Tender Is the Night*. Carnival is the holiday of release that winks at promiscuous and indecorous behavior. Fitzgerald is not alone in equating the decadence of post-war society with the unforbearing spirit of carnival. In *The Sun Also Rises*, Hemingway employs a carnival setting—the Pamplona festival—as his climactic and definitive image of the chaotic and undirected life of the Lost Generation. Dos Passos concludes his great trilogy, *U.S.A.*, with an orgiastic party to dramatize the moral and political bankruptcy of America in the twenties. Carnival in its radical sense—*carne vale*—denotes a farewell to the flesh. But the extended holiday taken by post-war society argues a more pervasive *ubi sunt:* a goodbye to a belief in the privileged destiny of an "elect" or incorruptible self. In all three works, carnival culminates with the destruction of a once intact personality: *U.S.A.* concludes with a suicide, *The Sun Also Rises* with the seduction and contamination of the "pure" Romero by the decadent Lady Brett, and *Tender Is the Night* is punctuated throughout with Nicole's schizophrenic breakdowns, retreats into a private madness that complement and comment on the public surface of carefree life.

The carnivalistic attitude toward the world characteristic of post-war American fiction can be illuminated in part by Mikhail Bakhtin's brilliant analysis of "carnivalized" attitudes toward reality. Bakhtin's study of carnival is exhaustive and cannot be reproduced here. However, his general theory of the meaning of carnival is helpful in understanding *Tender Is the Night* and its contemporary fictions that stress carnivalized modes of life. Bakhtin argues that the basic ritual performance in carnival—the crowning and uncrowning of the carnival king—forms "the very core of the carnivalistic attitude to the world—the pathos of vicissitudes and changes, of death and renewal" : "Carnival celebrates change itself, the very process of replaceability (*'smeniaemost'*), rather than that which is replaced. Carnival is, so to speak, functional, not substantive. It absolutizes nothing; it proclaims the jolly relativity of everything." Fitzgerald's transposition of carnival attitudes into his modern Odyssean narrative contributes to the intricacy of his conception of novelistic destiny. Diver's carnivalized life is inimical to his heroic potential. Carnival celebrates replaceability as the principle of communal destiny. The heroic observes the absolutizing of a unique destiny. The result of combining two antithetical views of human destiny is the paralyzed, schizoid hero. Carnival becomes dysfunctional for Diver, since as a displaced heroic leader in the novel, he can be eliminated, but never adequately replaced. He can expect neither carnival renewal nor heroic fulfillment. He is suspended *in medias res*, between the functional carnival king and the substantive epic hero.

Yet the carnivalized texture of *Tender Is the Night* does more than vitiate the epic potential of its theme: return and readaptation to peace. It also determines the time order of the novel. It has become a truism of Fitzgerald criticism that his fiction is rooted in nostalgia, a theory most succinctly put by Wright Morris. "Nostalgia," claims Morris, "is simply all there is." Perhaps this is true of *The Great Gatsby*, where the narrative impulse is to return to an originating past. But *Tender Is the Night* entertains no such project. In carnival time, the past intersects the future in the immanent present. Carnival simultaneously releases the imagination from its bondage to the past and absolves the novelist from, in Fitzgerald's words, "too much worry about inevitability." At the heart of carnival pleasure is the pleasure of the moment. Rosemary's happiness among the festive Divers, for example, is the happiness of the moment: "Later she remembered all the hours of the afternoon as happy—one of those uneventful times that seem at the moment only a link between past and future pleasure but turn out to have been the pleasure itself." The essence of pleasure is the uneventful, undirected middle, the "long years of sheer being" that characterize Nicole's life with Dick and that "had had an enlivening effect on the parts of her nature that early illness had killed." Fitzgerald's subject in *Tender Is the Night* is the interval of convalescence, not the dramatics of cure. Even McKisco's Ulysses takes one hundred rather than ten years or one day to complete his odyssey of reacculturation. Fitzgerald consistently defers the moment of narrative resolution. The "end" is resisted because it completes the process of becoming at the expense of timeless being. Fitzgerald's Ulysses is the wanderer portrayed by Homer on Calypso's isle, the Ulysses who lingers.

Nowhere is Fitzgerald's historical sense more apparent than in his treatment of the life of exile as a distinctly economic phenomenon. Dick Diver's lingering on foreign soil is a sign of his class as well as his mythic or psychological status. His withdrawal from professional life, initially justified by the exigencies of his wife's illness, serves to promote and perfect "the exact furthermost evolution of a class" : "The Divers' day was spaced like the day of the older civilizations to yield the utmost from the materials at hand, and to give to all transitions their full value." The historical stability of the older, inherently aristocratic civilizations is grounded in a paradox: the aristocracy has survived because it has refused to be pressured by time.

The poor or the petit-bourgeois, entrapped, like the hard-working Kaethe Gregorovius, in "the eternity of toil and decay" succumb to the material pressures of existence. They have neither the time nor the money to exploit the pleasures—and values—of transitions. What constitutes these values is suggested in Thorstein Veblen's *The Theory of the Leisure Class*.

Veblen contends that the cultivation of leisure functions both as a certificate of status and as a protest against "the vulgarisation of life." Veblen is careful to establish that leisure "does not connote indolence and quiescence." What is does connote, Veblen maintains, is the non-productive consumption of time. Veblen argues: "But leisure in the narrower sense, as distinct from exploit and from any ostensible productive employment of effort on objects of no intrinsic use, does not commonly leave a material product. The criteria of a past performance of leisure therefore commonly take the form of 'immaterial' goods." Leisure is essentially a *performance* accompanied by some token of accomplishment. Veblen cites scholarly and artistic endeavors and the range of "social facts" that includes manners and breeding as immaterial products of such leisured performances.

In Fitzgerald's analysis, however, leisure has become an end in itself. The immaterial good produced in Diver's leisure time is unconnected to either cultural or social reality—repose. At one point he boasts that "no American had any repose, except himself." The ambiguous usage of "had" indicates that repose is regarded both as a personal attribute and as a possession. In no sense is repose the prelude or the aftermath of productive employment. Rather, it is the concrete form vitality assumes in the psychic and social life of the leisured class.

The economy of psychic life, like the economy of material life, is subject to the law of diminishing returns. Prolonged repose, dramatized in the Divers' relaxed regime, converts productive into entropic energy. Entropy, the mechanistic diminution of vitality, becomes the deciding rhythm of life. The novel anticipates Diver's psychic dissolution in Warren Devereux's deathbed escape:

> "It was instinct," Dick said finally. "He was really dying, but he tried to get a resumption of rhythm—he's not the first person that ever walked off his deathbed—like an old clock—you know, you shake it and somehow from sheer habit its gets going again."

Habit alone provides the impulse for ongoing social and biological movement in the diseased and devitalized who instinctually, never willfully, resist their inevitable end: total repose. Thus Dick Diver's resumption of psychiatric practice after Nicole's recurrent breakdowns is the desperate move of a man who knows he is "really" dying. As such, it represents, as do so many events in the novel, a belated effort to resume the rhythm of vitality, a qualified "return" to a chosen destiny.

Even when Diver returns to his practice, he is surrounded by appealing specters of impending psychological and biological collapse: the "Iron Maiden" who yearns for a final defeat; a Portuguese general "who slid almost imperceptibly toward paresis." The novel's clinical terminology becomes substantive when repose—the innate attribute of the hero—is associated with paresis, a medical term denoting both mental and physical paralysis. The Greek root of paresis—"parienai"—means "to let go," indicating that the origin of the dysfunction is in the organism's desire for total relaxation. If carnival dramatizes a social rebellion against the stricture to forbear, paresis incarnates the internalized revolt of the unforbearing spirit. Dick commits himself to caring for the emotionally paralyzed when his carnival life of entertaining the morally atrophied is over. Both activities betray his sympathy with those who let go rather than withhold vital energies. Dick himself becomes an increasingly enervated hero, what Fitzgerald elsewhere terms an "homme epuisé."

In a letter to Mrs. Edwin Jarret, who was staging an adaptation of the novel, Fitzgerald refined his notion of Dick Diver as "homme epuisé": "he is after all a sort of superman; an approximation of the hero seen in overcivilized terms—taste is no substitute for vitality but in the book it has to do duty for it. It is one of the points on which he must never show weakness. Just as Siegfried could never show physical fear." Fitzgerald's assertion that taste may do duty for vitality is not borne out by the novel itself. In the novel's opening pages, Violet McKisco identifies Dick, the so-called superman of taste, as "the assistant hero" in the conspiracy of tasteful emigrés against the McKiscos' own arriviste community. Given his initial reduction in heroic stature, the over-civilized hero cannot prevent the total hegemony of the vulgar society that triumphs at the novel's close. It can be said of his final social eclipse what Dick feared was said of his father "with smug finality in the gilded age: very much the gentleman, but not much get-up-and-go about him."

For Diver's taste, which historically grounds him in the material refinements of the gilded age, is really a diluted version of the Odyssean hero's capacity for acculturation. Homer's Odysseus and Joyce's Bloom, for example, pass through a plurality of cultures, yet neither loses sight of his homeward destination. Diver, on the other hand, refuses to get up and go. He prefers the "diffused magic" of transitional space—the Riviera, the modern equivalent to the land of the Lotus-eaters. Rosemary, "half in the grip of fashion" for the indolence traditionally associated with shorelines, at least recognizes that her lingering transitional presence in "the lull between the gaiety of last winter and next winter while up North the true world thundered by" evinces "an unhealthy taste for the moribund." As arbiters of taste, fashions, like transitions, are vehicles of change; to absolutize one's taste for either is a sign of morbidity, not gentility.

The novel's extended symbol for the fatal enchantments of the landscapes of repose is Nicole's Riviera garden. The enclosed garden is pervaded by a tender damp, its path "atrophied and faintly rotten." The richness of the garden is the richness of internal decay. Its landscaping recalls the "verdurous glooms" of Keats's "Ode to a Nightingale" to which Fitzgerald acknowledged his debt both in the title and epigraph of the novel:

> Already with thee! tender is the night . . .
> . . . But here there is no light,
> Save what from heaven is with the breezes blown
> Through verdurous glooms and winding mossy ways.

Fitzgerald's ellipses deliberately omit Keats's vision of the object of desire—the Queen-Moon who renders the night so tender:

> And haply the Queen-Moon is on her throne
> Cluster'd around by all her starry Fays;

"Haply" is the key word for Fitzgerald. Keats's Queen-Moon, obviously commemorated in the Villa Diana, remains an inaccessible form of romantic desire. The chaste moon, like the haunting song of the nightingale that reverberates throughout the opening sequence of *Tender Is the Night*, represents the goal of romantic desire: the bliss of union that cancels temporality and its inevitable alienation of lover and beloved. In Keats's ode, all misery proceeds from finite existence, "Where youth grows pale and spectre-thin and dies." Fitzgerald's romanticism, however, sees in desire itself the source of much human suffering. All pathology proceeds from the desire that invests the real with the radiance of the ideal, that confuses real time with ideal time. Romantic psychology explains why Dick is divided between two competing female figures, one personifying an idealized past, the other an idealized future.

Because women become objects of desire for Diver through their association with ideal and not "real" times in his life, the novel rightfully discards the chronological exposition conventionally observed by novels wedded to the canons of realism. The complexities of erotic desire are irreducible to such a straight treatment. Fitzgerald maximizes the psychological tensions implicit in his narrative by exploiting the "to-and-fro" mystery of Diver's wavering desire. Of course, much has been made of Fitzgerald's later rearrangement of the novel into a strict chronological narrative, perhaps in reply to early critics who objected that the "Rosemary's Angle" section that opens the original version constituted a "false start." Malcolm Cowley has since canonized the theory that the "straight" exposition of the revised manuscript represents Fitzgerald's definitive version. Cowley, overlooking the theme of the extended middle so central to the novel's temporal and psychological order, works on the assumption that Nicole represents Dick's "real" past. But Nicole is never associated, psychologically or narratively, with Dick's past. She originates the call to an "intricate destiny"; with her, Dick's moment begins rather than ends. It is Rosemary, whose name is emblematic of remembrance, who recalls Dick's idealized past. The novel's original opening is structurally consonant with the novel's determined subject. Not only does it place the hero *in medias res*, thereby preparing for the ironies of his unfulfilled destiny, but it defines the transitional, crisis-ridden middle, Dick torn between Rosemary (his lost youth) and Nicole (his undetermined future).

Rosemary incarnates one bequest of America's past that Fitzgerald deplored and admired at the same time: the "exigent idealism" inculcated by generations of frontier mothers ignorant of necessitarian arguments. That Rosemary, "embodying all the immaturity of the race" is equipped with "an opportunistic memory" becomes evident when she and Dick visit Thiepval. The scene of "the last love-battle" in the nineteenth century's *haut bourgeois* romance becomes in her eyes the stage of "a thrilling dream." She never comprehends Dick's mature, if elegiac, vision that Thiepval was the theater where a decisive confrontation spelled the end of the dreams upheld by "the whole-souled sentimental equipment" of "middle class love."

Even the more immediate and personal Oedipal past, painfully documented in Nicole's case history, is subject to sentimental revision by the indomitable idealizing imagination. Elsie Speers, whose last name betrays the determined idealism disguised by her innocuous manner, surrounds her daughter Rosemary with the unreal air of a nursery. It is she who nourishes and approves of the idealization of the Oedipal child into "Daddy's Girl," the role that makes Rosemary famous. "Daddy's Girl" shows the inherent viciousness of the sentimentality extending from Mrs. Burnett's vicious tracts to Elsie Speer's protective ardor. Its last shot is of Rosemary and her "father" united "in a father complex so apparent that Dick winced for all psychologists at the vicious sentimentality."

Fitzgerald's most brilliant and original use of nascent Freudianism and its insights into individual and cultural pathology was to see in the Oedipal project a vivid metaphor for the "vicious" idealism endemic to the New World that discounted or ignored the claims of past history in determining individual or national destinies. As Faulkner well knew, incest was the logical outcome of America's "exigent idealism" that encouraged withdrawal and self-insulation as guarantees for the Emersonian ideal of self-reliance (Elsie Speer's great virtue) and self-determination. Incest involves a hoarding of emotional as well as sexual energies, a hoarding justified by the mind's need to preserve its original *intactness* by confining its energies to the originating structure of biological and social life—the family. But as Dick Diver knows, both personally and professionally, the price of intactness is incompleteness.

In a novel filled with introverts, Dick Diver represents a moral alternative: extroversion. "Lucky Dick" must be, as the narrator says, "less intact, even faintly destroyed": "If life won't do it for him it's not a substitute to get a disease, or a broken heart, or an inferiority complex, though it'd be nice to build out some broken side till it was better than the original structure." Dick's marriage to Nicole is one effort to break down the intact self and its incestuous self-idealizations. His "work" with Nicole is to build out of the broken side of her psyche a compound, if less intact, identity—Dicole. Concomitantly, it is an attempt to wed "moral" love to the self-sufficiency demanded by the exigent idealist. Their marriage thus occasions a last great American love-battle pitting "her unscrupulousness against his moralities."

Rosemary, then, represents the love battles already lost, Nicole the battles yet to be decided. Her schizophrenia is congenital to the American psyche in which the embattled mythologies of the Puritan ideologue and the materialist entrepreneur (the self-made man) contend for power. Fitzgerald hints at the inevitable outcome when Nicole resolves to be sane crook to Dick's mad Puritan. In Nicole's final decision, the guarded secret of the future is contained. As Rosemary herself intuits, Nicole is "the incalculable force" behind Dick's incalculable story. She is the female fate, a Pallas Athene manqué: "I am motionless against the sky and the boat is made to carry my form onward into the blue obscurity of the future, I am Pallas Athene carved reverently on the front of a galley."

Yet as the novel moves into the obscurity of the future, it reveals an unstable and mythically debased destiny. For Nicole is no Pallas Athene, the commanding figure of domestic and civic art, the champion of the Odyssean hero, although she does preside over the final section of the novel, which Fitzgerald, remembering the Odyssean motif in his narrative, entitled "The Way Home." Nicole proves a rather sorry Penelope, "Hands never idle — distaff flying," as Dick sarcastically observes. In an ironic reversal worthy of Joyce, Nicole-Penelope chooses the barbarian usurper over the hero of taste, the mercenary soldier over the committed warrior of love. Manifest destiny is always a westward movement, but in electing Tommy Barban as her future husband, Nicole allies herself with the decadent Mongul East:

> She liked his bringing her there to the eastward vision. . . . Symbolically she lay across his saddlebrow as surely as if he had wolfed her away from Damascus and they had come out upon the Mongolian plain. Moment by moment all that Dick had taught her fell away and she was nearer to what she had been in the beginning, prototype of that obscure yielding up of swords that was going on in the world about her.

Nicole's eastward vision, the vision of decadence, prompts her to exchange her past, the decade spent wandering with her Ulysses in foreign lands, for the anarchy of her lover. To suggest, as many critics have done, that her exchange constitutes a necessary and therapeutic transference from the over-civilized, dying hero (Diver) to the vital, primordial Barban would be another instance of "vicious sentimentality" in the American reading of reality. Nicole's break with Dick is not a sign of recovery, but of a relapse into an original passivity, a submission to the insane "yielding of swords that was going on in the world about her." Her surrender to Tommy Barban excites fantasies of wolfish men, barbarian hordes engaged in the wholesale rape of captive women. Nicole remains at the end of the novel what she was in the beginning, the passive sexual victim of men with appetites for disorder. Tommy Barban becomes in fantasy what Warren Devereux was in reality—a partner in decadent love.

Thus, in her end as in her beginning, Nicole illustrates "very simple principles containing in herself her own doom," principles of ceaseless change endemic to the carnival spirit. As Dick notes, Nicole "was a carnival to watch—at times primly coy, posing, grimacing and gesturing." Dick recognizes, too, the pathos of that carnivalized spirit: "sometimes the shadow fell and the dignity of old suffering flowed down into her finger tips." The pathos of carnival culminates in Nicole's final breakdown on the ferris wheel. The novel's most explicit image of carnivalized life, the ferris wheel symbolizes the process of endless revolution unredeemed by the carnivalistic faith in revolution as a form of renewal. Dick capitulates to Nicole's insane rhythm of purposeless change "not without desperation feeling the ethics of his profession dissolving into a lifeless mass."

Dick, the psychiatrist and *soi disant* hero of taste, if finally overcome by "the versatility of madness . . . akin to the resourcefulness of water seeping through, over and around a dike." Again, the image invoked is extravagant, equating the versatility of madness with the transgression against limits prescribed by a forbearing power. Dick's progressive alcoholism, as symptom of his submission to the resourceful madness of carnival that "makes the downright world amorphous," recalls the same desire for death and dissolution as the entirely liquid Mr. North." Alcoholism in the novel functions as both symptom and metaphor for the death wish of schizophrenia in its acute and downhill phase. Dick's increasing "liquidity" precipitates the split of the compound identity—Dicole—into the moribund will of Diver, who seeks his extinction in boundlessness, and the resurgent, anarchic will of Nicole, who accommodates the amorphous as an inner principle. What began as a private love affair becomes a historical fable. In the "broken universe of the war's ending," only those like Nicole and her lover Barban, who flourish in the chaotic, survive. Those like Diver, who raise their voice to oppose the anarchy of the age, are silenced: "Again he had offended someone—couldn't he hold his tongue a little longer? How long? To death then." Holding his tongue is the final gesture of the hero of taste who forbears to the death.

Fitzgerald admittedly modelled his ending after Conrad's example, concluding his narrative with a "dying fall," an ending in which the illuminating figure is eclipsed and absorbed by an enveloping darkness. The dying fall recommends itself to a fiction exploring the ironies of an unfulfilled destiny. "Dying" is a gerund, expressive of life in the process, not in the completed state of dissolution and final repose. The dying fall is the ultimate strategy in the aesthetic of forbearance, a postponement of the desired end. It protects the aura of mystery Fitzgerald sought to preserve in his fiction. The hero does not die; he simply fades away. Dick Diver is Fitzgerald's ironic comment on the literature of the disappearing hero produced by the post-war imagination. Diver cannot even be *located* in the novel's final sentence, so complete is the absorption of the heroic figure in the non-heroic ground: "Perhaps, so she [Nicole] liked to think, his career was biding its time, again like Grant's in Galena; his latest note was postmarked from Hornell, New York, which is some distance from Geneva and a very small town; in any case he is almost certainly in that section of the country, in one town or another." Galena, like Thiepval, represents hallowed historical ground, the fateful place where national destinies are decided. The final ironic allusion to Grant in Galena underscores the untraversable distance between one American Ulysses and another, between Grant's temporary exile and Dick's permanent exile spent in ignominious times and anonymous places.

But there is a final irony in this eclipse of the hero in the guise of a qualified return. Forbearance, biding one's time, becomes allied with inconclusiveness and indecisiveness. The danger in forbearance is in failing to see that one's moment has passed, like Gatsby, or in waiting too long, like Diver. Fitzgerald knew the agony of the forbearing spirit. In "Sleeping and Waking" he writes:

> The horror has come now like a storm—what if this night prefigured the night after death—what if all thereafter was an eternal quivering on the edge of an abyss, with everything base and vicious in oneself urging one forward and the baseness and viciousness of the world just ahead. No choice, no road, no hope—only the endless repetition of the sordid and the semi-tragic. Or to stand forever, perhaps, on the threshold of life unable to pass it and to return to it.

Fitzgerald's angst is rooted in a generic predicament. The tragic refuses to yield itself to him. He cannot imaginatively bridge the gap between the self, grounded in the baseness and viciousness of its history, and its appointed "tender" night of foreordained destiny. This is the negative side of forbearance as a standard of behavior and of art—a refusal to give in to the urge forward, an inability to cross the threshold of new life. Fitzgerald, like Diver, remains the genius of the shore, a sentinel stationed, forbearingly, at the edge of an abyss. For implicit in the aesthetic of forbearance is an overvaluation of thresholds, an undervaluation of ends. Fitzgerald, as he says of Diver, is a "spoiled priest" of the imagination, a term borrowed from his idol, James Joyce. And like the agony of Stephen Dedalus, Joyce's spoiled priest, Fitzgerald's torment may be that of a disappointed Aristotelian who can never confirm that "the motion is ended." Endless repetition of the sordid and the semi-tragic or the melodrama of unrealized life— these are the nightmares from which the forbearing spirit tries to awake.

Fitzgerald: The Tissue of Style

Donald Monk

> The last light
> fades and drifts across the land—
> the low, long land,
> the sunny land of spires;
> the ghosts of evening
> tune again their lyres
> and wander singing in a plaintive band
> down the long corridor of trees;
> pale fires echo the night
> from tower top to tower:
> oh, sleep that dreams,
> and dream that never tires,
> press from the petals of the lotos flower
> something of this to keep,
> the essence of an hour.
>
> *(This Side of Paradise)*

Printed as poetry this representative passage from Fitzgerald's first novel differs from the post-1915 debasement of Imagism (what Ezra Pound called "Amygism") in only two significant aspects: it has a higher incidence of rhyme and is, if possible, even more devoid of content. Its voice defines the novel's protagonist, Amory Blaine, much more memorably than do his character and actions. Derived from the vaguely erotic style Pater developed in *Marius the Epicurean* (1885) and popularized by Wilde's *The Picture of Dorian Gray* (1891), this verbal swoon, made over into a Princeton accent, places Fitzgerald in the Romantic Decadence. Its derivative quality should not, however, blind us to the work it entailed for Fitzgerald, accumulating

---

From *Journal of American Studies* 17, no. 1 (April 1983). © 1983 by Cambridge University Press.

these inter-echoes during the re-writings of the novel. Whatever else the development of such a style indicates, it shows us a man painstakingly aware of the weight stylistic effects, in their own right, can bear.

Fitzgerald's obsession with style implies a counterforce to impermanence: "material, however closely observed, is as elusive as the moment in which it has its existence unless it is purified by an incorruptible style and by the catharsis of a passionate emotion." Given the unsummonability of deep emotion at will, Fitzgerald at a low ebb felt that this stylistic emphasis condemned him to a treadmill of technical variations: "we authors must repeat ourselves. . . . We have two or three great and moving experiences in our lives. . . . Then we learn our trade, well or less well, and we tell our two or three stories—each time in a new disguise—maybe ten times, maybe a hundred, as long as people will listen." Such doubts about the invention of new material are alarming. But the commitment to "great and moving experiences" and not the disguises which trick them out is persuasive. Fitzgerald takes his stand with the great body of Romantic belief which insisted on the primacy of emotional intensity and on the "organic" literary form true to it. His lasting conviction was that such transmission of emotion involved short-circuiting or bypassing logic. Coming close to the terminology of T. S. Eliot's "auditory imagination," Fitzgerald says, "Almost everything I write in novels goes, for better or worse, into the subconscious of the reader." Writers naturally play to their strengths. But this disdain for such aspects of narrative as originality and variety makes it no surprise to us, though it was to him, that his days as a best-selling chronicler of the Jazz Age were numbered.

Fitzgerald's most evident vulnerability, his weakness at plotting, is almost as proverbial as his bad spelling. Henry Dan Piper, a sympathetic but not unamused observer of the phenomenon, comments on "the minor role that plot played in Fitzgerald's art," a crippling weakness when it came to making a living in Hollywood. Fitzgerald's aversion to and awkwardness with sequential methods means that "practically all his poorer stories suffer from the burden of too much plot." His successes do not occur when he happens upon superior plots but when this issue of plot is bypassed. In the best of his short stories narrative plays a minimal role. "The Diamond as Big as the Ritz" is a marvellously titled Jazz Age allegory, but the private anti-aircraft guns defending the diamond make Hawthorne look a master of realism. The religious disclosures in "Absolution" add up to bog-Irish religiosity whilst compression of personality, place, and atmosphere in "Babylon Revisited" and "Financing Finnegan" are anecdotal in the extreme. These, his best work in the short story genre, are memorable not for narrative but for stylistic evocation of mood and atmosphere. It comes back to the pre-eminence of emotional intensity: "If you have anything to say, anything you feel nobody has ever said before, you have got to feel it so desperately that you will find some way to say it that nobody has ever found before, so that the thing you have got to say and the way of saying it blend as one matter—as indissolubly as if they were conceived together."

Again organic form; again absolute insistence on intense emotion; again, bewilderingly, a total vagueness as to means. But the sought distinctiveness cannot but be stylistic, a Keatsian "fine excess." Fitzgerald not only felt a temperamental affinity with Keats but also measured himself against his productions: "those eight poems [Keats's greatest] are a scale of workmanship for anybody who wants to know truly about words, their most utter value for evocation, persuasion or charm." "To know truly about words," especially in respect to "charm," sums up the best effects of the two writers. But the implicit independence on stylistic effects is also responsible for the quasi-hallucinatory sense of words becoming their own substance, their own *raison d'être*, which one can feel when in a mood unsympathetic to the pair of them.

Meanwhile we are still left with the question, What produces this "evocation"? Joseph Conrad was the model ("influence" seems too weak a word). Fitzgerald insisted, "Conrad has been, after all, the healthy influence on the technique of the novel." Time and again in his correspondence he cites the importance of the Conradian intention in the Preface to *The Nigger of the Narcissus*—"before all—to make you *see*." (Agreement on this crucial imperative underpinned his relationship with Hemingway.) Particularly Conradian is Fitzgerald's definition of fiction: "the purpose of a work of fiction is to appeal to the lingering after-effects in the reader's mind as differing from, say, the purpose of oratory or philosophy which respectively leave people in a fighting or a thoughtful mood." "Lingering after-effects" is a clearer formulation of "what goes into the subconscious of the reader." But it is still a curiously vague profile. Fidelity to the original emotion, transmission through an organic form, bypassing the conscious mind to produce "lingering after-effects" make a likelier formula for poetry than prose.

Plot, dialogue and character—all we usually see as the province of fiction—are scarcely mentioned in Fitzgerald's letters or elsewhere. Such occasional comments as we find can be of a brutal factuality. Advising his friend John Peale Bishop on the tricks of the trade, he begins, "Try and find more 'bright' characters; if the women are plain make them millionairesses or nymphomaniacs, if they're scrubwomen, give them hot sex attraction and charm." Behind the humorous despair at the appetites of the reading public we see how moral, aesthetic, and realistic considerations fly out of the window. Composition of characters becomes as plastic as the range of vocabulary: "my theory [is] utterly opposite to Ernest's, about fiction, i.e. that it takes half a dozen people to make a synthesis strong enough to create a fiction character." Equally clearly this plasticity could lead to recurrent problems. The notorious lack of definition in Gatsby's portrayal ("I never at any one time saw him clear myself") exists because "he started as one man I knew and then changed into myself." When a transformation of this kind is only half-completed, as in the case of Dick Diver, the great dangers in working from primary personal emotion become insurmountable. Having spent his life as a professional writer, Fitzgerald always regretted the limits this laid on his own experience, portioned out between his five novels. The directly autobiographical is not so much the problem as a blurring of outline as the self inconclusively projects itself— evident enough in the protagonists—Blaine, Patch, Gatsby, Diver, Stahr.

One major problem is that of style unavoidably blurring into the problem of *life*-style. Style could be said to be as close as Fitzgerald came to a philosophy. His protagonists are measured not by the success of their attempts to do well or nobly or conscientiously, but to do *stylishly*. Midwestern unease with the style of New York in the Twenties accounts for the ironic dimensions of *The Great Gatsby*. The life in the prose is then a surer index of artistic control than plot, character or action.

Fitzgerald is here a little more forthcoming about the production of "lingering after-effects": "in *Gatsby* I selected the stuff to fit a given mood of 'hauntedness' or whatever you might call it, rejecting in advance in Gatsby, for instance all of the ordinary material for Long Island, big crooks, adultery theme and always starting from the *small* focal point that impressed me." "Hauntedness," like a "lingering after-effect," is plainly what reaches to the "subconscious of the reader." Here, as perhaps elsewhere, it means a rejection of "ordinary material." Instead we have the personal, intensifying level of "the *small* focal point that impressed me." What we have seen in the breakdown of style in *This Side of Paradise* as the amplification of the highest possible degree of verbal echo has been worked up into scenic echo, the multiplication of "*small* focal point[s]."

Henry James, of course, had spoken for this method but his disciple Conrad was the one who simultaneously "made you see" yet redoubled the visual effects into a sense of "hauntedness." In *The Secret Agent*, for example, Conrad's refusal to discriminate between criminal and police motivation is as shameless in its own way as Fitzgerald's advocacy of "scrub-women . . . with hot sex attraction." The anarchist Verloc and the Assistant Commissioner are more interesting in the similarity of their domestic problems than in being on this or that side of the law. Likewise the sexual vagaries in *The Great Gatsby* are never judged, except by juxtapositions at least as aesthetic as they are moral. Symmetry claims its own priority, a symmetry almost at first undetected, which is the basis of the method and its effect. The multiple echoes thus generated form a sound which lingers with us, a sound we did not at first realize we were hearing. Individual characters and actions become as pliable as the individual words. Accumulation and accentuation of meaning in this way were the chief literary invention of the earlier part of the century. An Eliot poem, a Conrad novel, even an Orwell essay each operate on this principle. The New Criticism, following this lead, disregarding plot and character and action, saw image-patterns as the basic stuff of literature. Meaning, as paraphrasable meaning disappeared, became inseparable from its constituent images. Novels like *The Secret Agent*, with its carefully contrived oppositions—of light/dark, criminal/respectable, sanctioned/unsanctioned, overt/covert—made up the intellectual climate within which Fitzgerald created his major work.

II

The Great Gatsby, designed as a multiple complex of its local meanings, continues this tradition. The obviously aligned image-patterns in the book—those of water, sport, couples, riches, class, family and self-image— are not independent and disparate entities. They overlap, interrelate, fuel and adjust each other's meanings. To track any one of the major aligned patterns is to reach the core of the novel, but at the cost of slighting the master design which so organized the patterns for mutual reinforcement. Echoes and correspondences, operating laterally as well as sequentially, are the muscle tissue of the novel.

To show the method at work I have chosen the pattern of *sport*, not the most obtrusive, but more pervasive than one would think and with an interesting ironic undertone. Jordan Baker is fashioned entirely in the image of a sportswoman. When we first see her at the Buchanans' she refuses a drink because she is "absolutely in training." Her body—small-breasted, erect, shoulders thrown back, heavily suntanned—proclaims her athleticism and defines what it is that comes to attract Nick Carraway sexually, "a clean, hard, limited person . . . leaned back jauntily." Later, when their romance begins to peter out this undertone of boyishness takes on a less pleasant aspect: "Usually her voice came over the wire as something fresh and cool, as if a divot from a green golf-links had come sailing in at the office window, but this morning it seemed harsh and dry." Nick, at first flattered to go places with a golf champion, doesn't see the full implications of this attractiveness: "I noticed that she wore her evening-dress, all her dresses, like sports clothes—there was a jauntiness about her movements as if she had first learned to walk upon golf courses on crisp, clean mornings." This dry, almost antiseptic healthiness, with its attendant self-confident image, comes in the end to seem a kind of mask, a charade performed for a gullible public. When Nick last sees her "she was dressed to play golf, and I remember thinking she looked like a good illustration, her chin raised a little jauntily, her hair the color of an autumn leaf, her face the same brown tint as the fingerless glove on her knee." Significantly, Jordan always appears for Nick as if posing for a portrait. For the truth is that Jordan's famed "jauntiness" is a matter of self-image, and beneath the air of athleticism there is something close to a void. Like most of the characters in *The Great Gatsby* she lives out an image of herself, not a reality. Unsurprisingly, what reality does surface is radically at odds with the wholesomeness of the package.

From the very first Nick is troubled by the familiarity of her looks, and only gradually does he locate this unease:

"Jordan's going to play in the tournament tomorrow," explained Daisy, "over at Westchester."

"Oh—you're *Jordan* Baker."

I knew now why her face was familiar—its pleasing contemptuous expression had looked at me from many rotogravure pictures

of the sporting life at Ashville and Hot Springs and Palm Beach.
I had heard some story of her too, a critical, unpleasant story, but
what it was I had forgotten long ago.

Jordan's contemptuous expression speaks for the life of leisure and privilege
which captivates Nick for a while. Then

> suddenly I remembered the story about her that had eluded me
> that night at Daisy's. At her first big golf tournament there was a
> row that nearly reached the newspapers—a suggestion that she
> had moved her ball from a bad lie in the semi-final round. The
> thing approached the proportions of a scandal—then died away.
> A caddy retracted his statement, and the only other witness ad-
> mitted that he might have been mistaken. The incident and the
> name had remained together in my mind.

The realities of sport, as Fitzgerald's friend Ring Lardner made a point of
illustrating, did not correspond to the attractiveness of the image put before
the public. Jordan, like the Buchanans, is one of the "careless people" who
use wealth and status to screen out inconvenient aspects of reality. Her
cheating in a golf tournament resonates with Tom Buchanan's cheating
with Myrtle and over the murder of Gatsby. People in their position can
arrange cover-ups so that what appears in the newspapers brushes over
the scandal of their lives. Apart from Jordan's brief, abortive romance with
Nick this information about her sporting career is as much as we find out
about her and it leads directly to Nick's dismissive summing-up—"She was
incurably dishonest." Most interestingly, the way in which Nick only gradually recalls her involvement in the golf scandal precisely mirrors the way
in which Gatsby emerges from the rumours about him (that he had killed
a man, that he was the Kaiser's nephew) and is revealed in his self-made,
self-deluding simplicity. But Gatsby's image is true to his own conception
of himself, whereas Jordan's is true only to that of high-life fashion
magazines.

   With that economy of means that is the most striking characteristic of
the novel, Fitzgerald links Gatsby with Nick and Jordan via this same rose-
spectacled vision of sporting morality. Asking the favour of an introduction
to Daisy, Gatsby assures Nick of his proposed adultery, "Oh, it's nothing
underhand . . . Miss Baker's a great sportswoman, you know, and she'd
never do anything that wasn't all right." In Jay Gatsby too there is an
element of masquerade in the sporting outfits he wears: photographed in
a blazer "with a cricket bat in his hand" or with his early mentor Dan Cody,
both "in yachting costume." Typical of the man the images are a truth, but
only a part of the truth, interim self-images pieced together along the way
to his becoming what he believes will recapture Daisy. One of the few times
we see him clear is when Fitzgerald is at some pains to show how boyish
this image is: "He was balancing himself on the dashboard of his car with
that resourcefulness of movement that is so peculiarly American—that

comes, I suppose, with the absence of lifting work in youth and, even more, with the formless grace of our nervous, sporadic games." But if there is an infantile and escapist aspect to these games there is a darker side also—just as the pool Gatsby never uses all summer ends by bearing his bathing-suited corpse. For money is needed to sustain these glossy images of yachting and cricketing gear, and Gatsby, without the Buchanans' inherited wealth, will do anything to acquire it. It is Meyer Wolfsheim, of course, who is responsible for Gatsby's meteoric rise, a gambler who fixed the World Series in 1919, prompting Nick's response, "It never occurred to me that one man could start to play with the faith of fifty million people— with the single-mindedness of a burglar blowing a safe." Sport and criminality are explicitly linked here, almost blinding us to the larger irony of so much of a nation's "faith" being so childishly invested.

Gatsby's grandeur is of an equivalent kind, desperately trying to put the squalor of his youth into a dream, the pathos of which is exactly caught in his "SCHEDULE" for September 12, 1906, where his work-day is bracketed by "Dumbbell exercise and wall-scaling 6.15–6.30 a.m." and "Baseball and sports 4.30–5.00 p.m." A parallel ironic dichotomy can be seen in his rival, Tom Buchanan, who "brought down a string of polo ponies from Lake Forest. It was hard to realise that a man in my generation was wealthy enough to do that." But a ruthless physicality accompanies Tom's life-style. He had been "one of the most powerful ends that ever played football at New Haven" and his power is expressed in "a body capable of enormous leverage—a cruel body." These ironic sporting innuendoes are never allowed to drop from our attention, hearing Gatsby's perpetual use of "old sport" and of "the polo player" for Tom Buchanan. "There's sport for you," says Tom, looking wistfully out at a yacht, wishing himself out there as, parodically, Gatsby once looked at Dan Cody's yacht and went to find his fortune on it.

We see that sport and money and self-image are very closely aligned. This further emphasizes the economy of the novel: full explication of the image-patterns would much exceed the length of the novel. The resonances we have seen build up within one sequential pattern, of sport, multiply alongside the other patterns. *The Great Gatsby*'s plot of masked adulteries and social climbing, even including the revealed past of a Midwestern boy, intent on success with a girl a class above him, does not make a long telegram. However, the narrative technique of the semi-involved narrator is itself used to made a redoubling. Nick is in some sense a *doppelgänger* of Gatsby, another Midwesterner on the wrong coast of the bay, ineffectually involved with Gatsby's girl's best friend, out in New York to make money but not doing too well at it. In terms of character too his main pride (that honesty is his "cardinal virtue") is ironically set beside other elements in the story—his attraction to the dishonest Jordan and his being an intermediary in the extra-marital liaison of his cousin.

The perfection of the method, then, involved only a perfunctory need for character, plot and action. Resemblance is so much the technique of the novel it could also be called virtually its material, Tom Buchanan possessing Daisy by a status, power and wealth Gatsby vainly tries to displace, whilst Nick and Jordan pallidly re-enact Gatsby's grand affair, vicariously re-living it. These tenuous strands, radiating from the ironic centre of the novel—the powerful glamor of money and its distortion of emotional life—are fragile in themselves, but interlocked produce the tensile strength of a spider's web. No occasion is lost to reinforce the theme of the illusions produced by wealth. The street pedlar who sells a "police dog" to Tom and Myrtle is "a gray old man who bore an absurd resemblance to John D. Rockefeller." Judged by material success, the fact that he has the millionaire's expressionless, cadaverous face is indeed absurd. But the very pettiness of how he makes his living casts its own ironic light on Rockefeller penny-pinching his way to a fortune by ways as unsavoury as Gatsby's. And what is implied about Carraway's vaunted honesty when he remarks on his own resemblance to the great-uncle who founded the family fortune?

> we have a tradition that we're descended from the Dukes of Buc-
> cleugh, but the actual founder of my line was my grandfather's
> brother, who came here in fifty-one, sent a substitute to the Civil
> War, and started the wholesale hardware business that my father
> carries on today.

So early in the novel we find in capsule form the definitive theme relating the source and prestige of money. The great-uncle avoided danger, built a business, used money to buy a safe cloak of respectability. Gatsby, war-hero, "son of God," bootlegger, tragically comes to the same game too late, his amoral pursuit of success much more patently visible than the Carraway's past. Yet the very crudity and maladroitness of his ambition put him in the old unsophisticated American tradition, so that he finds his tragic dimension through a simplicity the New York of the Twenties was turning its back on. The method by which Fitzgerald reveals this is infinitely suggestive, a texture of "lingering after-effects."

III

The success of *The Great Gatsby* rests in large measure on the multiple amplifications of the barest of anecdotes. Sadly, *Tender Is the Night* did not offer such economies. Fitzgerald's difficulties in resolving the plot are legend. Again seeking a "big" theme, he began with the "Melarky version," dealing with matricide. Thereafter, the thematic interest began to shift towards demoralization and sexual incompatibility, taking shape as Nicole Diver's parasitic absorption of her husband's energies. The sexual hostility Fitzgerald wished to analyse, "the American Woman's . . . clean-sweeping irrational temper that had broken the moral back of a race and made a nursery out of a continent," remained constant but the evidence cried out for simplification, not ramification. What male weakness contributed to the matriarchy? Was it especially an American problem? Where, if at all, did money enter the equation? Jay Gatsby's fatal confusion of success and sexuality, so accurately dissected, now becomes Fitzgerald's own. The ambivalence of his feelings collapses the moral centre of the novel. Nicole is presented as a potential killer, but Dick Diver's anger and hatred are directed towards himself. Reinforced by the complex sexual disorientation of expatriate life, fine local detail though this gives, the malaise spreads beyond diagnosis. Even the most evident weakness of technique, the evasively restricted narrator of "Rosemary's Angle," comes from the same source, an unlocalized and bathetic fascination with Hollywood's "Daddy's Girl." The strands snarl and tangle without the carefully gauged ironic parallels of *The Great Gatsby*.

Under the stress of these centrifugal forces the easy stylistic grace takes on an implausible note. The ironic control, so remarkable in *The Great Gatsby*, falters: Rosemary's love, we read, "had reached a point where now she was beginning to be unhappy, to be desperate. She didn't know what to do—she wanted to talk to her mother." These sentimental abstractions—"love," "unhappy," "desperate"—find no significant distance from the romantic fiction from which they derive. The bathos of "she wanted to talk to her mother" is scarcely under control at all. Failure to distinguish between erotic and familial love sucks Fitzgerald into the incestuous morass he should be analysing. It is difficult not to feel that the author finds the success and charm of his monstrous regiment of women attractive in much the same way as Diver does, and instead of analysing the phenomenon is similarly deflected into brooding on the corrosion of will-power.

Everywhere this uncertain definition of the point of view oozes into and undermines the style. The earlier novel's brilliant axiom, "personality is an unbroken series of successful gestures," mixed with a recall of the magic in Daisy's voice, disintegrates into slack self-parody as Rosemary Hoyt listens to Dick: "his voice promised to unroll an endless succession of magnificent possibilities." The jaded exoticism of the Riviera life-style can indeed summon touches of Fitzgerald's old ironically glamorous phrasing, e.g. "the hotel with its bright tan prayer rug of a beach." This is exactly right for the modern narcissistic worship of the sun. But where in *The Great Gatsby* the reverberations of the phrase would have been held within the ironic redoubling, here the filaments spread in too many directions. Echoed elsewhere, a confusion of style and life-style diffuses the effect. Nicole's self-regard, a narcissistic religiosity, as she prepares for her seduction by Tommy Barban, "reverently crossing herself with Chanel Sixteen," comes as an echo from a different world than the phrase for the battles of attrition on the Somme, "leaving the dead like a million bloody rugs." The hedonism of the rich on Europe's beaches may have been a revulsion against the Great War, but it cannot be located as the same force of self-sacrificial loyalty that endured the war. Fitzgerald's real battleground was in fact the sexual one, but this can destroy an intended historical dimension when Dick's maudlin lament that "All my beautiful safe lovely world blew itself up here with a great burst of high explosive love" mixes a shallow Freudianism with the idea that European decadence comes from not carrying civil arms for two centuries. Metaphorical lushness of the same kind, displacing any real analysis of society, emerges when Dick sums up his own fate: "he had been swallowed up like a gigolo, and somehow permitted his arsenal to be locked up in the Warren safety-deposit vaults." "Gigolos" and "safety-deposit vaults" may define the perimeters of the Warren world, but Dick's *macho* view of his talents as an "arsenal" is at odds with his psychoanalytic background and marked lack of manliness. *Tender Is the Night* is awash with images similarly briefly breaking surface, unfocused by the control of the earlier novel.

Unintentional nuances also blur the focus in the incest—vampire theme. Even as evidence of the depths of Dick Diver's self-pity there is a diseased note in seeing Nicole's dependence on him as "her dry suckling at his lean chest." Likewise his resentment of his children for "what he had to give to the ever-climbing, breast-searching young." The trans-sexuality of the images, mammary and not testicular, shows that conveying the theme of deterioration through images and not analysis is almost certain to rot the images in the absence of a clearly determined point of view. And since that is denied by Dick Diver's very condition there is no solution to the problem. The earlier style of "lingering after-effects," derived from Conrad, was perfectly adapted for characters who lie to themselves and have it exposed in a crisis—Lord Jim, Verloc, Razumov and Gatsby himself. The fatal difficulty in *Tender Is the Night* is that the moment of crisis never arrives, its plot being predicated on a continual postponement of the moment of truth. That we can accept the random, diseased images thus left to speak for themselves as the thought-processes of a gifted psychiatrist is impossible. Psychiatry treats in the analysis of metaphors; it can hardly be composed of them. Dick Diver's incessant speculation in this mode undercuts any credibility in the great future he believes he has squandered on the Warrens. We may concede the bloodsucking tendencies of the spoiled rich, but Dick Diver remains a hemophiliac.

With so many diverse objectives in *Tender Is the Night*, the novel may never have been manageable for Fitzgerald. The evocative redoubling of phrase and incident, "the small focal point" of *The Great Gatsby*, was not suited to a larger novel. There are indications, however, that Fitzgerald was experimenting towards a more expansive, free-flowing, less localized effect:

> For her sake trains began their run at Chicago, and traversed the round belly of the continent to California; chicle factories fumed and link belts grew link by link in factories; men mixed toothpaste in vats and drew mouthwash out of copper hogsheads; girls canned tomatoes quickly in August or worked rudely at the Five-and-Tens on Christmas Eve; half-breed Indians toiled on Brazilian coffee plantations and dreamers were muscled out of patent rights in new tractors—these were some of the people who gave a tithe

to Nicole, and, as the whole system swayed and thundered onward it lent a feverish blush to such processes of hers as wholesale
buying, like the flush of a fireman's face holding his post before
a spreading blaze.

Impressive though this is, it is not a style for a case history. Even as a
setpiece, the metaphoric generalities begin to weaken towards the end,
signalled by the perfunctory transition "these were some of the people."
Why should the accurate railway-system metaphor be abandoned for the
localization of the fireman at his post? What would be the large-scale consequences of having this "flush" and "fever" spelled out in terms of Nicole's
life? Even the initially persuasive "tithe" with its exact nuance of feudal
rights, percentage and the religion of money could have begun to look very
odd if fully integrated into the meanings of the novel. Had more pervasive
use been made of this effect, the novel might well have rippled throughout
with individual touches of colour, like a *pointilliste* painting, but only at the
cost of harder outlines. The wide-cast net of psychological exhaustion
would have become even more diffuse, the style even less sure of its own
perspectives.

Nevertheless, *Tender Is the Night* still functions best out of the vitality
of its metaphors:

Mountain-climbing cars are built on a slant similar to the angle of
a hat brim of a man who doesn't want to be recognised. As water
gushed from the chamber under the car, Dick was impressed with
the ingenuity of the whole idea—a complementary car was now
taking on mountain water at the top and would pull the lightened
car up by gravity, as soon as the brakes were released. It must
have been a great inspiration.

An image of this kind is unexceptionable. On a walking tour the mountain
car is a likely enough object to encounter. Dick Diver's preoccupation with
it is also natural. He is an ingenious man who seeks to rise to the top,
stylishly, without the appearance of effort. The pulled-down hat brim is
another telling touch, for already Dick is furtively speculating how far the
patient—doctor relationship with Nicole can be stretched. But it is the inner
dynamics of the passage that is most impressive. In its mechanical expression of balance and symbiosis, transference of mass and energy, it ironically
reverses his own dreams of any easy climb and instead prefigures how his
strength will be poured into Nicole. More than anything Henry James found
in *The Sacred Fount*, or even William Blake in "The Mental Traveller," ex-
plorations of identical themes, the image is sharp, persuasive and able to
speak for itself. Dick Diver examines the principle of the mountain car,
pleased by it, even as overtones of his own predicament shade the prose.
There is not the usual blurring of image and personality. The mysteries
that connect Nicole and Dick are seen *through* a medium, not *as* a medium.
For once the image is given focus. Conceivably all might have been well

with *Tender Is the Night* had Fitzgerald again constructed by images, not sociological analysis. The pity of it was that the book could not rely on images that find their intensity from psychological abysses Fitzgerald was in no position to stand back from and evaluate. He had guessed at the source of the evil but, in a sense like Diver, believed it could be charmed away. So *Tender Is the Night* compromises on a blur of style and life-style, a smooth-surfaced charm supposedly the antidote to, yet at the same time the symptom of the disease.

IV

The constructional lapses in *Tender Is the Night* brought home to Fitzgerald that he would need new methods to express his overriding theme—what it is that drains energy from such dreams as Gatsby's and Diver's and his own, and how to live in the shadow of its loss. Something more than charm and evocativeness was required. The clarities, stylistic as well as autobiographical, of the confessional essays in *The Crack-Up* had become imperative on many counts.

In *Tender Is the Night* there are signs that Fitzgerald had already begun to formulate his theory of "emotional bankruptcy." When Dick gives the time as 1.30 p.m., and adds in an ominous overtone, "It's not a bad time . . . It's not one of the worst times of the day," the indications are there. Tightened by the stringencies of *The Crack-Up* style, this would lead variously to "every act of life from the morning tooth-brush to the friend at dinner had become an effort" and "in a real dark night of the soul it is always three o'clock in the morning, day after day." Equally sharply phrased is the central proposition of his self-analysis: "I began to realise that for two years my life had been a drawing on resources I did not possess, that I had been mortgaging myself physically and spiritually up to the hilt." The re-awakened alertness of the style is unmistakable—economical, pungent, colloquial, turning away from "lingering after-effects." Sergio Perosa correctly observes, "His language here is simple and flowing, discursive and easy; by reducing the expressive means to the level of conversation he achieves unexpected results. Expressing in everyday words his inner crisis, Fitzgerald detached himself, as it were, from his person, and he stood by to contemplate and record." The self seen as Other (like Rimbaud's "*Je* est un autre") brought Fitzgerald out of the cloudy self-projections of *Tender Is the Night*. Seeing himself clear, as he never saw Dick Diver, also involved the renewing and the refreshing of the style.

The theory of "emotional bankruptcy" is not an edifice of gigantic erudition. It is the quintessential drinker's theory: the hangover as unpaid interest on the night before's excesses, up to and including the insolvency of alcoholism. But it sufficiently covered his own case, and that of the collapse of Boom into Depression. In *The Crack-Up*, for the first time, Fitzgerald's natural genius for metaphor operates within a known historical dimension. The Jazz Age which had infatuated him is revealed as "borrowed time anyhow—the whole upper tenth of a nation living with the insouciance of grand ducs and the casualness of chorus girls." His analysis of the Thirties is etched with the same directness: "money and power were falling into the hands of people in comparison with whom the leader of a village Soviet would be a gold-mine of judgement and culture." A Marxist dimension has begun to temper the awe with which his Carraways and Divers once viewed the wealth and arrogance of the Buchanans and Warrens. We feel that Fitzgerald has earned the right to juxtapose his colloquialisms ("gold-mine," "borrowed time") with the historical overturn of the century ("village Soviet," "grand ducs") creating again, with an acerbic nostalgia, an ironic glamor. The shoddiness of what post-1918 America made of its Dream is felt personally and historically alongside the sterner realities of the USSR. It is true to say that Fitzgerald does judge "a general crisis of which his own personal crisis was merely a reflection," much as Robert Lowell was to do in *Life Studies*.

This new toughness of mind and manner is omnipresent in *The Last Tycoon*, tragically incomplete at the time of his death. Fitzgerald's new hero, the movie mogul Stahr has, like Fitzgerald in *The Crack-Up*, an accurate vision of himself. Stahr, like the remodelled Fitzgerald, is a dreamer aware of the insubstantiality of his dreams even as he makes them happen. In Stahr he had found an artist-figure with a societal dimension. There is a concomitant emphasis on sequential plot. Stahr's progress is from scene to scene, cinematic; though we shall never know how, or if, Fitzgerald would have handled the time-shift problems of an emotionally involved narrator. But the ironic perspective that attaches to Stahr—"he cherished the parvenu's passionate loyalty to an imaginary past"—is sound and workable, based as it is on the author's own self-irony.

The newly found historical perspective carries over also. It seems that in the studio system we were to have seen the American class system in microcosm. *The Last Tycoon* promises to flesh out a world of observed political realities: the emergent Communism of the film technicians, the Mafia-like connection of Brady with the gangsters he hires against Stahr, Stahr's own merciless pragmatism. Even in its incomplete state we view a world in which people act and live and, most importantly, *work* as nowhere else in Fitzgerald. The humour of Wylie White giving his background—"I was born near here—the son of impoverished southern paupers. The family mansion is now used as an outhouse. We had four servants—my father, my mother and my two sisters"—is not merely local. It catches the cynical accent of an intelligent man working in a system he can only tolerate for the money, something of the professional self-disgust Fitzgerald felt when he had to dramatize Margaret Mitchell's *Gone with the Wind*, not permitted to alter a word in it, as though it were Holy Writ.

Hollywood did have a kind of sacred idiocy about the dreams it manufactured. The Knights of Columbus visit a set: "they had seen the host carried in procession, but this was the dream made flesh." Stahr, above all in his ability to control teams of script-writers set one against the other and to convince his colleagues to make a quality film at a loss, is both credible and unmysteriously superhuman. If Stahr is a workaholic who revels in the exercise of power, Fitzgerald is at pains to differentiate him from the self-made materialists of the Gilded Age "who have merely gypped another person's empire away from them like the four great railroad kings of the coast." Fitzgerald captures the ethos of American capitalism, as he had in *The Crack-Up*, in the easy use of "kings" and "empires." But in the use of the colloquial "gypped," undercutting this self-deluding grandeur, we see the influence of Hemingway: "About *adjectives:* all fine prose is based on the verbs carrying the sentences. They make sentences move." The style of this final novel is noticeably fined down in order to convey the realities of a world of action.

Psychological depths are similarly under control. Stahr, in common with all Fitzgerald's heroes, never loves a woman: his dead wife Minna and her near-double, Kathleen, are "girls." But this adulation of youth and inability to face up to ageing is now accompanied by an awareness of their romantic inadequacy: "In love with Minna and death together—with the world in which she looked so alone that he wanted to go with her there." Maybe the prose is still tinged with purple, but the sparse, elegiac, ironic note of *The Crack-Up* fits with Hollywood's world of evasion and nascent disaster. When Schwarz commits suicide because he is now excluded from the respect of Stahr and his peers, his death-wish is equally firmly identified: "At both ends of life man needed nourishment: a breast—a shrine. Something to lay himself beside when no one wanted him further, and shoot a bullet into his head." Simple opposition of the emotive ("a breast—a shrine") alongside the harsh reality ("shoot a bullet into his head") bypasses the treacherous sentiments they would have occasioned in *Tender Is the Night*, cutting into a tone of mingled illusion and catastrophe which constitutes Fitzgerald's Hollywood. He had worked for his intimacy with this "mining town in lotus land."

The Last Tycoon clearly functions like the cinema in its rapid intercutting from scene to scene. The airplane flight broken by the visit to Andrew Jackson's home, Stahr's life at the studios contrasted with the isolation of his uncompleted beach-house, the papers scattered from Stahr's briefcase in the fatal plane crash, and the superb stroke of the flood which washes the Hollywood sets away, improbably bearing him the image of his dead wife on the head of Siva—these are remarkable not only for their immediate, local force but also their montage-like suggestion of Hollywood bizarreness. Juxtaposition of such large-scale scenes was matched by close verbal control of ambiguities. What Fitzgerald had long known as his own special *forte* for romantic irony—the Dantesque "I like to balance a beautiful word with a barbed one"—is becoming an overall principle. His sense of the Depression's "brave gloom" as "California was filling up with weary desperadoes" ensured his stylistic tightening exactly matched this intensely glowing, but corrupt, celluloid world. Even what stands out as his major problem, a narrative line largely dependent on the callow Cecilia, might in the end have been malleable to the same forces.

For Fitzgerald was still learning, and it is in the analysis of the characteristic craft that an abiding interest lies, not in the spuriously romantic myth of alcoholism, nor the perfunctory Jazz Age exercises. The popularizers' focus on cocktails and bobbed hair and bead dresses deflects attention from his real achievement. In Edmund Wilson's balanced view, in his poem on the death of his friend, what Fitzgerald made is

> Not the great Ritz-sized diamond you desired
> But jewels in a handful, lying loose . . .
> Some tinsel zircons, common turquoise; but
> Two emeralds, green and lucid, one half-cut,
> One cut consummately.

For Fitzgerald's failures are such only by the highest standards, and more can be learned even from his local flaws than more facile successes. Even the gloss and glamor of much of the surface is directed as commentary on a period and a world infatuated with the superficial.

Faulkner on Time and History

Cleanth Brooks

Much has been written about Faulkner's sense of place —and properly so. His very creation of Yoknapatawpha County underscores the importance he attached to place. A writer had to write about what he knew, and if his "own little postage stamp of native soil" was what he truly knew, he must write about that. The area did not need to be large or famous; even in its obscurity and ordinary character it could serve his purposes as a writer, for, as Faulkner insisted in his various interviews, in all lands and throughout all epochs men are essentially the same. You could find even in Yoknapatawpha County a sufficiently full representation of the human predicament, examples of man's virtue and of his baseness. So much, for my present purposes, for Faulkner's abiding concern with place.

Something more needs to be said, however, about Faulkner's concept of time. Though various writers have had perceptive remarks to make on this subject, much of what has been written seems to me misleading or confused. Moreover, what Faulkner, on one occasion or another, is quoted as having said about time needs to be put into its proper context. In particular, his acknowledgement of his debt to Henri Bergson stands in need of clarification.

In an interview with Loïc Bouvard, Faulkner apparently did say: "There isn't any time. In fact I agree pretty much with Bergson's theory of the fluidity of time. There is only the present moment, in which I include both the past and the future, and that is eternity. In my opinion time can be shaped quite a bit by the artist; after all, man is never time's slave." As stated, however, this is a rhetorical, not to say poetic, utterance. That it is poetic in character does not, of course, mean that it is necessarily false, but the assertion as given may need to be translated and expanded. In any

From *William Faulkner: Toward Yoknapatawpha and Beyond.* © 1978 by Yale University. Yale University Press, 1978.

case, the passage quoted comprehends at least three propositions, which in this compact statement are not so much related to each other as simply pressed together.

Before beginning our examination, it might be best to compare with the statement to Bouvard another that Faulkner made some ten years later. (This later one, by the way, occurs in the very paragraph in which Faulkner spoke of his "little postage stamp of native soil.") Speaking of the characters who are made to inhabit his mythical county, Faulkner says "[the fact] that I have moved [them] around in time successfully . . . proves to me my own theory that time is a fluid condition which has no existence except in the momentary avatars of individual people. There is no such thing as *was*—only *is*." In both statements what is stressed is the fluidity of time, though only in the first does Faulkner link his theory of time with Bergson's. What Bergson meant was that time as experienced by human beings is continuous—a flowing stream, carrying in it memories of past experience and foreshadowings of prospective actions. What Faulkner seems to have meant by time's fluidity was that it has "no existence" except as it is experienced in the consciousness of individual human beings. In writing, "There is no such thing as *was*—only *is*," Faulkner jumps ahead to another point: we experience the pastness of the past and experience an impending future only in a *present* moment of consciousness. So what is past (Faulkner's "was") exists only in a *present state* of human consciousness. So also with Faulkner's "shall be": it too exists only in a moment of present consciousness. (Compare the earlier statement: "There isn't any time.")

A passage in *The Wild Palms* puts Faulkner's conception of time more clearly than he was able to state it in the interviews from which we have quoted. Faulkner has Harry Wilbourne speak "of the current of time that runs through remembering, that exists only in relation to what little of reality . . . we know, else there is no such thing as time." I take it that "what little of reality we know" means in this context the present moment—what we have immediately in our consciousness. Apart from some human being's consciousness of a felt continuity, time is a mere abstraction and so does not really exist.

The matter of continuity is of the greatest importance. As Wilbourne puts it, time is felt as a "current" that "runs through remembering. . . ." It flows out of the past through the present and toward the future. This is how Faulkner stresses Bergson's concept of time as *fluid*. A little later in the same passage Wilbourne will go on to say that before we were born, time did not exist for us. When we become aware of ourselves and of reality, "time begins" and is immediately sensed as "retroactive"; time can only be conceived of as a current flowing *from* somewhere *to* somewhere. Such is my interpretation of Wilbourne's cryptic "Then *I am*, and time begins, retroactive, is was and will be." Wilbourne goes on to say: "Then *I was* and so I am not and so time never existed"; that is, when I am dead and no longer possess consciousness, then time does not exist for me and indeed, so far as I am concerned, might as well never have existed.

The best specific evidence for Bergson's influence on Faulkner, I am convinced, is to be found in this passage. Yet it should be noted that the idea of the "presentness" in the human consciousness of the past and of the future long antedates Bergson. For instance, it was put forcefully by St. Augustine in his *Confessions*, Book XI, Section 23:

> For if times past and to come be, I would know where they be. Which yet if I cannot, yet I know that, wherever they be, they are not there as future, they are not yet there; if there also they be past, they are not longer there. Wheresoever there is whatsoever is, *it is only as present*.
>
>   [Trans. by Edvard Bouverie Pusey; my italics.]

In citing St. Augustine, I do not mean to imply that this was Faulkner's source. He may well have got the notion from a number of sources, including Henri Bergson. In his 1952 interview with Bouvard, he pointedly includes Bergson among the French writers to whom he was indebted. He had been "influenced by Flaubert, and by Balzac. . . . And by Bergson obviously"; and he adds: "I feel very close to Proust."

To sum up, I interpret Faulkner to be saying that time does not exist apart from the consciousness of some human being. Apart from that stream of living consciousness, time is merely an abstraction. Thus, *as actually experienced*, time has little to do with the time that is measured off by the ticking of a chronometer. Such a conception of time, however, did not impel Faulkner to destroy his own watch as Quentin Compson did (in *The Sound and the Fury*). Though clock time, as an abstraction, might be deemed to be in some sense unreal, Faulkner, like Bergson himself, conceded that clock-and-calendar time had its uses and that no human life of the slightest complexity could get along without constant reference to it.

When, in his 1952 interview with Bouvard, Faulkner declared that "man is never time's slave," he was simply affirming that time as man experienced it could never be adequately or accurately measured except by the human heart. For Romeo and Juliet on their wedding night, time is incredibly swift; on the next morning the sun rises all too soon. But for the lover awaiting the appointed hour to see his mistress, time seems hardly to move at all. In general, the way in which men see the world is altered both by memories of past experience and by their expectations of the future. Such a view of time is immemorially old.

Why make these points here at such length? Because I think that what Faulkner got from Bergson was essentially a confirmation, from a respected philosopher, of something that he already knew. I doubt that Faulkner read Bergson very deeply or thoroughly. I believe that the influence of Bergson on Faulkner has been generally overestimated and that its importance has been occasionally pushed to absurd lengths. In several of the articles and dissertations that argue for a strong Bergsonian influence on Faulkner, the authors manage to write as if they had forgotten that Bergson's own system was a dualism in which the philosopher found room and *need* for objectively measured time as well as for time as *duration*. Far from dismissing the spatial-temporal world as irrelevant or unreal, Bergson needed this inorganic world to set over against the organic world that was dynamic and "alive." As Thomas Hanna has put it, "[Bergson's] contention that the inner movement of duration is the very stuff of reality becomes not only a key for an understanding of the nature of time and of memory, but, inevitably, becomes the interpretive basis for understanding the evolving character of mankind as well as of organic life in general. All of organic life is linked together in time by an enduring reality which relentlessly preserves the past, as this living past gnaws its way further into the present." (Compare Harry Wilbourne's reference to "the current of time that runs through remembering. . . . ") The inner movement of duration has, to be sure, a plus value. It is more truly "real," but for Bergson, the inorganic world also had its own reality as the necessary foil to that "human reality" in which Bergson is primarily interested.

Faulkner's statements to the effect that time exists only in the present of some human consciousness may well account for the fact that a number of characters in his fiction assert that the past is not truly past. See for example what Gavin Stevens says in *Intruder in the Dust* and Mr. Compson's remark in *The Sound and the Fury* to the effect that "was [is] the saddest word of all[;] there is nothing else in the world[;] its not despair until time[;] its not even time until it was." Even this riddling passage begins to make some sense in view of Faulkner's special concept of time.

Because Bergson obviously attached special importance to the inner, organic, and dynamic force which, in the evolutionary process, for instance, was "gnaw[ing] its way" further into the static, inorganic world, many readers of Faulkner apparently regard as Bergsonian such remarks by Faulkner as his pronouncement that "Life is motion and motion is concerned with what makes man move—which are ambition, power, pleasure." Perhaps they are right, though I think that Faulkner did not need to be told by Bergson or anyone else that life involves motion.

Life has always been associated with motion. But for neither Faulkner nor Bergson was it enough to simply be in motion. I grant that Faulkner does not condone mere passivity in the face of adversity. He understands and may pity, but cannot approve those who retreat into the past. In a moment of bitter insight, Gail Hightower admits to himself that he has never in his whole life really lived. Moreover, though Faulkner was obviously fascinated by the Southern past, he was realistic about it too — about its faults, limitations, and sins. He often also warned about the necessity for change and man's need to adapt to new conditions. Yet merely to survive, merely to stay alive, was not at all what he meant by "endurance." Flem Snopes, for example, was able to cope with the situation in which he found himself. He did not remain passive; he did not retreat into the past. But it never occurred to Faulkner to say of Flem that he "endured," even though in a very real sense Flem not only endured but—in the language of *A Fable*—"prevailed" over other men. For Faulkner, mere financial success was a shoddy achievement.

Those who write about Faulkner, therefore, ought to be more careful about citing some of the oversimple observations that he occasionally made, particularly in interviews. For Faulkner believed that there were some things that a man must not do even as the price of his survival. There were some causes for which a man ought to be willing to give up his life.

If it was indeed Bergson who taught Faulkner to be aware of the limitations of pure ratiocination, to trust the heart, to believe in man's potentialities for growth and improvement, and to see that time as humanly experienced was an unbroken stream flowing out of the depths of his past and moving with a forward surge into a yet unexperienced future—then his debt to Bergson was indeed large. For these are the basic assumptions on which Faulkner erected his literary work. But he might easily have learned these things elsewhere, and he could have learned nothing from Bergson that made calendar time something with which man did not need to concern himself because it was "unreal." The evidence that Faulkner's characters have to contend with clock time and the intractabilities of static "things" is to be found in the fiction itself.

For instance, though Joe Christmas distrusted laws, commandments, and conventions of all kinds, and seems to have arrived at his decisions through intuitions—intuitions so spontaneous that it may be difficult for the reader to grasp their meaning—in the end, even Joe Christmas comes back to calendar time. Wandering in the woods, sought for days by the sheriff's posse, he suddenly finds that he simply has to know what the day of the week is. When a black man on a wagon tells him the day—"It's Friday. O Lawd God, it's Friday"—Joe starts immediately for his destination. His subsequent actions are those of a man who is maintaining a tight schedule in order to keep an important engagement. He needs to be present at a particular place and at a particular time.

To take another example, Harry Wilbourne spends weeks with Charlotte in a kind of Eden-like retreat. They have removed themselves from the world. But one day Harry suddenly finds that he simply has to know the calendar date, and at once begins to construct a calendar. Wilbourne has a quarrel with the modern world, and he tries to keep its inhuman stultifications out of his intensely experienced life with Charlotte. He even speculates on the possibility that time can be "abrogated" altogether. He cites his first sexual orgasm as proof that such abrogation is possible: "for that one second or two seconds that you were present in space but not in time" (*The Wild Palms*). We have here a reference to a time that is not time, maybe a glimpse of eternity itself. Nevertheless, Wilbourne feels the necessity for mentioning clock time also: "one second or two seconds." Both kinds of time occur in Faulkner's world, and, on reflection, could it be otherwise?

To come at the problem from another direction: in spite of Faulkner's acceptance of Bergson's conception of time as fluid and continuous (time as "duration"), it is hard to think of a novelist who exceeds Faulkner in his careful attention to the details of clock time and calendar time. I am thinking here particularly of the chronology of his novels. Each conforms not only to a generally consistent time scheme; the details of the time scheme are often very precise. Indeed, it is a revelation to go through a Faulkner novel, giving special attention to its chronology, and so discover how many unobtrusive but specific time-clues Faulkner has planted. Though such clues often do not call attention to themselves, yet when noted and put together, the chronology that they plot is much too consistent to be unpurposed. Even if Faulkner did not mean for every reader to be aware of these buried chronologies, we may be sure that he was himself in command of the sequence of events.

It must be conceded that he occasionally makes mistakes. Usually these are obvious contradictions of the overall pattern. Thus, on page 322 of *Light in August* Faulkner says that Joe Christmas was captured on a Friday—a date that doesn't fit with other events in the scheme—but nine pages later the date is set right (to Saturday). Again, in *Absalom, Absalom!* we are told that Judith and Bon saw each other for "a total period of seventeen days," but a few lines down on the same page the number is said to be twelve. In the Texas MS the text reads "seventeen" in both instances. Obviously, when Faulkner decided to revise the number downward to twelve, he corrected the second instance but overlooked correcting the first.

How careful Faulkner could be in organizing a consistent scheme is revealed in his first published novel. Other striking instances occur in *Sanctuary*, in *The Wild Palms*, in *Absalom, Absalom!*, and even in "Miss Zilphia Gant" the chronology is carefully ordered. In *Light in August* it is perhaps possible to assign the precise calendar date of Joe Christmas's murder of Joanna Burden. Faulkner's characters clearly lived their lives and underwent their passions in Bergson's *temps durée*, but this fact does not absolve them from living through a time that could be ticked off by the clock and measured by the calendar.

It has also been argued that Bergson's theories of time had a powerful influence on Faulkner's conception of art. Susan Resneck Parr puts the matter thus: "Life after all is dynamic, [Faulkner] believed, while art, by its very nature, is static. Life is an ever ongoing process. It is motion, change, becoming. Art, in contrast, has as its aim stillness, permanence, completeness." How then, she asks, could art "communicate the motion of life and the reality of a moment. . . . " Miss Parr goes on to quote the following passage from Faulkner's interview with Jean Stein: "The aim of every artist is to arrest motion, which is life, by artificial means and hold it fixed so that 100 years later when a stranger looks at it, it moves again since it is life."

Faulkner's statement is a sound way of putting the artist's age-old problem: how to salvage from the onrushing stream of time a story or episode or simply a moment of insight or revelation, and preserve it in a form impervious to time so that hundreds of years later it will exist not merely as a static entity, but, under the reader's gaze, will begin to flow once more with the movement of life. Bergson had shown that reality is not fixed but mobile, continuous, and ongoing, whereas words are basically static, and, as names given to objects, manage to freeze out of the flux of reality little objective "things," which, in their definite outline and immobility, falsify the flow of reality that they propose to imitate.

Miss Parr argues that Faulkner's acquaintance with Bergson stimulated him to develop certain narrative and descriptive techniques. I do not find her argument convincing. If the problem as described by Bergson does arise from the very nature of reality and the very nature of words, the one fluid and dynamic, the other fixed and static, then such has been a problem for the literary artist from the first beginnings of language, and it existed for Homer and Sophocles, Dante and Shakespeare, as well as for Faulkner. Moreover, unless we want to argue that Homer and Sophocles, Dante and Shakespeare labored in vain, the problem of using the medium of words to convey a sense of life is not insoluble. It has been solved, more or less satisfactorily, over and over again. One of Faulkner's favorite poets, by writing what was to become perhaps Faulkner's favorite poem, the "Ode on a Grecian Urn," solved it very much to Faulkner's own special satisfaction.

So much for a common-sense view of what Faulkner did not need to learn from Bergson. If, however, we insist on applying very literally and narrowly to literary art what Bergson has to say on this subject of how the intuition grasps the nature of reality as distinguished from the way in which the intelligence is compelled to deal with it, we would have to argue that any genuine solution of the problem had to wait upon the invention of the movie camera. I have in mind the following passage from Bergson's *The Creative Mind*.

> To think intuitively is to think in duration. Intelligence starts ordinarily from the immobile, and reconstructs movement as best it can with immobilities in juxtaposition. Intuition starts from movement, posits it, or rather perceives it as reality itself, and sees in immobility only an abstract moment, a snapshot taken by our mind, of a mobility. Intelligence ordinarily concerns itself with things, meaning by that, with the static, and makes of change an accident which is supposedly superadded. For intuition the essential is change: as for the thing, as intelligence understands it, it is a cutting which has been made out of the becoming and set up by our minds as a substitute for the whole.

How is the literary artist to get from little "cuttings" or slices of reality to the movement of real life? From individual static photographs to something resembling the flow of time? If we take Bergson literally, he is saying that the problem cannot be solved by the artist whose medium is words. Since nouns are names and clot the dynamic flow of reality into little static pseudo-entities ("things"), a poem or a story necessarily denies the true nature of reality. If we insist upon a narrow interpretation of Bergson, the only arts that do not falsify reality would be such arts as music, the dance, and preeminently the art of the moving picture. In that art, the static "cuttings" from reality become a sequence of frozen moments (as seen by the camera's eye), but these are projected upon a screen so rapidly that the observer "sees" not static "things" but virtual movement.

This "cinematic" solution of the problem is, of course, not the only or even necessarily the best solution. Granted that some moving pictures do attain a very high level of art, it must be conceded that cinematic art has its own limitations. What is in fact produced in cinematic art is often mediocre if not meretricious. At all events, the cinema has certainly not pushed the other arts into an inferior category. I have cited this essentially mechanical solution of the problem of how to present the vital movement through what are essentially static items as a warning against a literalistic interpretation of Bergson. In his discussion of intuition and the artist, he surely meant something more profound. If cinematic art is truly to catch and convey the movement of dynamic life, the camera itself has to be employed by a sensitive and imaginative artist. After all, the camera is simply one more tool.

One of the best articles in which the case for Bergson's influence on Faulkner is argued is that by Darrel Abel. He points out that the "resource of the intuitive artist [for] conveying his intuitions to practical men, who must have reality represented to them in 'states' and 'things,' is symbolism," and he quotes Bergson's own assertion to that effect in *The Creative Mind:* Intuition "will have to use ideas as a conveyance. It will prefer, however, to have recourse to the more concrete ideas" and, of these, "those which still retain an outer fringe of images. Comparisons and metaphors will here suggest what cannot be expressed." Though "No image will replace the intuition of duration, . . . many different images . . . will be able, through the convergence of their action, to direct the consciousness to the precise point where there is a certain intuition to seize on."

Quite so. But with this concession that the literary artist can solve his problem by recourse to images, metaphors, and symbols, we have no proclamation of a revolutionary technique —rather, a confirmation of the age-old and thoroughly traditional means employed by the literary artist. I am not scolding Bergson for failing to produce a new technique. My purpose is rather to moderate the inflated claims of Bergsonian influence on Faulkner's technique. In this matter of narrative techniques, I believe that Faulkner learned more from Conrad and Joyce or, more largely, from Shakespeare and Keats and Eliot than he could ever have learned from Bergson.

Darrel Abel's discussion of *Light in August* is, by the way, one of the best of the earlier accounts of this fascinating novel. Abel offers excellent insights and provides a sound emphasis on what themes in this novel are truly central and important. But his insights have little to do with his argument that Faulkner has been influenced by Bergson. Actually, what Abel says would seem to imply the influence of Nietzsche rather than Bergson. For example, Abel comments on Hightower's rather detached view of the life that swirls around him as follows: "In the Dionysian dance of life there comes a serene moment of Apollonian vision." By contrast, Lena Grove "knows no reality beyond her subjective moment. She represents ordinary naive mankind, inviolably innocent because it cannot enter the realm of ideas." True enough; but how does this state of affairs square with Bergson's claim that it is only by intuition that we can grasp the dynamic reality of life? Since Lena is subjective and nonintellectual, it would appear that it is she who lives in "duration" and by intuition. She swims in the very current of life and life seems to flow through her. By contrast, it is Hightower who has withdrawn from life as a "becoming," a process, and who is the creature of ratiocination and intelligence.

In Nietzsche's scheme (as described in *The Birth of Tragedy*), such a contrast makes sense: the artist is able to give Apollonian "form" to the Dionysiac dance. He has to be able to detach himself from the dance and so "see" it. The person who is wholly caught up in the dance cannot see what he is doing; he is blind to its pattern. In a famous poem Yeats asked: "How can we know the dancer from the dance?" But in the somewhat altered context presented here, the question is, how can the ecstatic dancer distinguish herself—"know" herself—from the dance. I am not here trying to convict Abel of a contradiction. Rather, I wonder whether the contradiction is not Bergson's own. If so, it would not be the first or the last time. Bergson is noted for his contradictions.

The most extreme claims for Bergson's influence on Faulkner almost inevitably come to a head in discussions of *Absalom, Absalom!* Several commentators have pointed to this great novel as the special showcase for exhibiting Faulkner's way of handling the problems of truth. We are told, for example, that Quentin and Shreve begin to use what Bergson calls a "dynamic method of perceiving and responding to reality . . . as opposed to a static method." Though "dynamic" and "static" are rather slippery terms, let us grant, for the sake of the argument, that Quentin and Shreve do employ a dynamic method. Nevertheless, they first assemble all the evidence (the static facts) that they can. They use deductive methods when these apply. They make use of the law of contradiction. They eliminate some hypotheses as unlikely and others as frankly unreasonable. They do not start out by making a set of uneducated guesses. They sort a lot of evidence before they resort to intuition.

Intuition may discover truth, but some intuitions come closer to the truth than others do. (Some intuitions amount to arrant nonsense.) In any case, intuition has to have a context. There must be a problem—not merely an empty space into which to fire off random guesses; and the context itself usually sets limits to the intuitional operation. A given context may eliminate certain possibilities and call attention to others.

One commentator on *Absalom, Absalom!*, eager to make the case for

Faulkner's use of a Bergsonian method, lays great stress on the discrepancies to be found in *Absalom, Absalom!* We are urged not to try to explain them away, for these "discrepancies" have been deliberately set down by Faulkner. Furthermore, by printing at the back of the book a genealogy and chronology that differ in some details from the text, Faulkner has meant to add to the reader's uncertainty as to what is true and what is not. In short, Faulkner deliberately confuses his reader since a main theme of his novel is the "elusiveness of truth."

Several of the characters in *Absalom, Absalom!* do indeed expatiate on the difficulties of understanding history and the impossibility of ever discovering the truth about what happened to the Sutpens and why. But if the difficulties are to be made absolute or nearly so, then the quest for truth becomes pointless. To make even murkier the murkiness that envelops the Sutpen story seems a curious way of recommending Bergson's intuition as a means of discovering truth.

To sum up, though Bergson may have confirmed some of Faulkner's notions about time and about the ways in which human beings can know reality, and though Bergson may have stimulated Faulkner to experiment with the verbal presentation of motion and action, I find little in Faulkner's narrative treatment that can be certainly attributed to Bergson's influence. Many of Faulkner's techniques turn out to be simply skillful and imaginative adaptations of traditional narrative methods, but if one were to specify particular influences it would not be Bergson's so much as Conrad's, the early Eliot's, and Joyce's. Whatever Faulkner's indebtedness, his handling of time reached perhaps its most brilliant achievement in *Absalom, Absalom!*

Faulkner's concern with time is closely related to his concern with history; and it is just here, I believe, that one could most plausibly make a claim for Bergsonian influence, though the proponents of that influence seem to have overlooked this opportunity. I refer both to the sense in which the past "exists" only in the present and to a related matter: the past as a living force in the present, a force that moulds our sense of the present. These concepts have everything to do with the importance that Faulkner assigns to history. Whether or not he derived these ideas from Bergson, they do constitute his profound belief. Faulkner's own personal experience, of course, had much to do with his sense of history. Most of us who grew up, as he did, in the South of the early decades of this century had talked to Confederate veterans, who were in some instances our own grandfathers. We felt a sense of identity as "Southerners." We believed that we really constituted a kind of subnation within the United States, and were very much aware of the consequences of the South's defeat in the war. Such a defeat did make a difference in one's present life. Our loss of the war had political and economic consequences that had affected and continued to affect us.

There was of course nothing unusual about such a situation. The victors in a war quickly forget it; it is the losers who do not. In the British Isles, the Scots, the Welsh, and to a much greater extent the Irish appear to be peoples caught up in a similar cultural situation. Yet the South had not been locked into its old agrarian culture merely by custom and tradition: discriminatory freight-rate differentials, unfavorable tariff laws, and lack of capital made it very difficult to shift to an urban-industrial culture — even for those Southerners who wanted to make the shift. There was more than its own inertia that kept the South in the role of the producer of raw materials which would be shipped abroad or into the northeastern quadrant of this country for processing and consumption. In short, the South's was a colonial economy, and the region found it almost as difficult to shake off its colonial yoke as the emerging countries (as we call them today) find it difficult to shake off theirs.

Faulkner's fiction clearly reflects this general cultural situation: there was poverty, extreme at one end of the social scale and not much better than genteel at the other. The habits and customs of an older America persisted. The South's was essentially an agricultural society, a society of small towns and farms, a hunting society where everybody had a gun and supplied the table from time to time with squirrels, rabbits, partridges, and, very occasionally, with venison.

It was family centered, both in its upper and in its lower classes. A real folk culture persisted, both in the white population and in the black. Like nearly all folk societies, there was a live tradition of story-telling, folk songs, and oratory of both the pulpit and the political varieties. For those who want to insist on time as felt *duration*, time in the South had slowed down as compared with the rest of the country. Naturally, there was a strong sense of history—local, family, and regional—but history not so much book-learned as passed down from father to son or from mother to daughter, or simply absorbed through a process of cultural osmosis. (Quentin felt that he had always known the basic outlines of Thomas Sutpen's story. Just when or from whom he had learned this or that circumstance, he would not always have found it easy to say.)

All of this has a bearing on Faulkner's sense of history. For him, the Civil War seemed a living memory in which he had not directly participated but which was *his* nevertheless. Let us grant that Faulkner sometimes gets the date of a battle wrong or is confused about this or that happening; yet there is no contradiction. He was so certain of what he knew that it apparently did not occur to him to get out a book and look up the episode. History is here passing over into myth, but I do not mean that history is thereby falsified; rather, history has become a part of lived experience, as immediate as other aspects of lived experience, and not an abstract pattern that never engages one's day-to-day life. When history as myth is reshaped by a mind of genius, it may even improve upon formal history. Certainly, in Faulkner's conception, history was more than a chronicle of events, more even than a collection of verified facts and statistics. It was a meaningful story.

Faulkner allowed some of his characters —Isaac McCaslin in "The Bear" is a notable instance—to see history as providential, something more than a sequence of causes and their effects—as a story with a purpose, even as a story that bore a high promise. Clearly he rejected the notion that history was meaningless. On the other hand, he also rejected any notion of mankind's inevitable and automatic progress. His view of history was too complex to allow him to accept either of a pair of alternatives so simple as these.

Yet before undertaking to describe Faulkner's philosophy of history—though how he would have winced at this phrase—it will be necessary to clear the ground a bit by disposing of two or three persistent misapprehensions. A sense of history does not imply an irrational reverence for the past or an antiquarian's disparagement of the present world, or some nostalgic yearning for vanished glories. To clarify my position in this matter, and to clarify what I take to be Faulkner's, will require at least a brief consideration of *change,* the *past,* the *nature of history,* and the *nature of myth.*

It has been insisted on by some critics that Faulkner regarded what is unchanging as worse than merely passive—as simply dead and inert, since he believed that change was the very principle of life and vitality. Now there is an element of truth in such observations—namely, that change is part of the process of growth in all living organisms and that change is a symptom that the organism is alive. But it is a careless, not to say a specious, logic which arrives at the conclusion that change is necessarily good. History deals out change in all shapes and sizes, all the way from the change in hairstyles to the fall of the Roman Empire. What Faulkner constantly reprehended was something very different: the failure to *cope* with change.

In his novels Faulkner has presented a number of characters who are unwilling to accept change or are unable to cope with the changes that have occurred. One thinks immediately of a Quentin Compson or a Gail Hightower. As we have noted earlier, Faulkner believed that to isolate the past from the present was to falsify the very nature of time. It was a fallacy in which some of Faulkner's characters were trapped, but never Faulkner himself. The authentic human being lives in the past and future as well as in the present. Indeed, the present as such is an abstraction—an arbitrary knife-edge, over which time future constantly moves into its condition of time past. How long is the "present"? A year, a week, a day, a half-hour, a split second? Faulkner was, as we have seen, quite as clearheaded on this matter as was St. Augustine. The past does continue to live in the present, not only in the sense that it is alive in our memories, but also because we ourselves, and our very capacity to remember, have been shaped by the past. Gavin Stevens does not always express Faulkner's own opinions and beliefs, but when he says, as he does more than once, that "There's no such thing as past, . . . " he voices Faulkner's own conviction. A Quentin or a Hightower, who lives only in the past, is not fully alive. But then neither is a man like Jason Compson, who repudiates the past and lives only in future expectations.

The Sound and the Fury presents a third mode of incomplete human life, that of the third brother, Benjy. Since Benjy, the idiot, cannot distinguish between past and present and has no real prevision of the future, he lives virtually at the animal level—is barely human. Considerations of this kind lead us to a definition of history as the specifically human realm. Creatures at the animal level truly have no history. Possessing almost no memory and no sense of the future, birds and beasts live in what is to all intents and purposes a timeless present. Their basic drives and responses to their environment are largely instinctual. They are so deeply immersed in nature, they so completely lack man's self-consciousness, that they are barred out of the realm of purposes and responsibilities, which constitute the realm of history.

Though we think of history as the record of the past, human history (and there is really no other kind) tells of the deeds and misdeeds of a creature whose conscious life comprehends a continuous effort that links up his own past with the present and extends it into the future. The birds and beasts, on the other hand, live in what is a virtual present—in what amounts to a timeless dimension. Every creature, of course, will die, but it is only man who *knows* he will die—and thus conducts his whole life from babyhood onwards under the sentence of death. This is both his burden and his glory.

Since man participates in both nature and history, it is important that he should keep these realms distinct and not confuse one with the other. One such confusion involves regarding history as simply a natural process in which an empire grows like a great tree, flourishes, falls into the sere and yellow leaf, and finally crashes to the ground. When history is so regarded, there may be danger of losing the human dimension altogether. Men who really believe that the tendencies of history are simply blind natural forces may be inclined to throw up their hands and say, "What's the use of our actions?" For such a mentality, history has been eaten up by nature. On the other hand, nature may be eaten up by history. If we come to believe that man can manipulate nature to suit his own purposes, nature becomes assimilated to history—that is, we come to consider history to be simply the story of man's unlimited Promethean will as he remakes the physical universe to suit his own purposes. Such pride indeed goeth before a fall. If history teaches anything, it surely teaches that.

Most of us use the word *history* to mean the record, oral or written, of what has happened in the life of a people or a civilization. Yet, since history is possible only to a self-conscious creature like man, a creature who can remember and who can try to interpret the meaning of his past, the quality and complexity of recorded history will obviously differ some-what from culture to culture, with the extent of its knowledge of the past and the nature of its world view. It will be difficult to find a truly objective history containing no element of emotional and subjective bias.

The history of certain primitive tribes is more accurately described as being mythic rather than truly historical. If their experience as a tribe has been little more than the cyclic round of "birth, copulation, and death," with no epochal events, no crises, no turning points—if their history seems to be going nowhere in particular—it will not be so very different from the "history" of unselfconscious birds and beasts; that is, it will be no history at all. It may amount to not much more than a cosmic myth, telling how the universe began and the story of a heroic eponymous ancestor whose descendants are the members of the present tribe.

Yet, though civilized man sometimes looks with a patronizing scorn on the mythic histories of primitive peoples, it is difficult to eliminate from any history the element of myth. Popular history is usually heavily tinctured with myth. We wage our wars and define our political objectives largely in terms of myths. Our professional historians are thus set a difficult task: to try to eliminate at least the more fanciful myths and to ground history, as nearly as possible, on fact; and yet to provide an interpretation of history—not just a dry chronicle of facts—something that will possess the dynamics of myth even though based on actual happenings.

With this observation one can return to the matter of Faulkner's attitude toward the Southern past and to the charge, still often made, that his fiction veered dangerously toward a celebration of what enlightened people now know was merely a myth—the account of a fabulous Old South that never really existed. Actually, Faulkner's picture of the antebellum South is no gilded dream. It is a solid world, of the earth earthy. Faulkner finds the Southerners of that time both good and bad, with the usual mixture of vices and virtues. He is essentially realistic in his account of slavery. If his novels of that older time show us some slaveholders who were fundamentally decent and honorable men, they show others who were callous and inhuman.

Moreover, in his novels he gives a great deal of attention to the whites who owned few or no slaves. Faulkner depicts a yeomanry that possesses a proper self-esteem along with the sturdier virtues. The poorer whites, including those who had been beaten down and damaged by a life of brutal toil, are usually treated with comprehending sympathy, as are the blacks, whose humanity and basic dignity have, in Faulkner's account, survived their condition of servitude.

Considering the zest with which so many of Faulkner's characters tell stories about the Civil War, it is impossible to believe that Faulkner himself did not take pride in the fight that his homeland had put up against such heavy odds. The Civil War was a bloody war and one that had grave consequences for his people and his own family. Moreover, the issues involved were too complicated to be accommodated under the rubric "a crusade to free the slaves." In *Go Down, Moses* Isaac McCaslin observes that the Southerners "had fought for four years and lost to preserve [slavery] . . . not because they were opposed to freedom as freedom but for the old reasons for which man (not the generals and the politicians but man) has always fought and died in wars: to preserve a status quo or to establish a better future one to endure for his children. . . . " The war was really a clash between two cultures possessed of differing manners, customs, and world views.

The antebellum South, in spite of the curse of slavery and its penchant for frontier violence, had provided a scope for courage, honor, and heroism. Faulkner even went so far as to write after the conclusion of World War II, in a letter to Lambert Davis, that there were times when he believed "there [had] been little in this country since [1860-70] good enough to make good literature, that since then we have gradually become a nation of bragging sentimental not too courageous liars. We seem to be losing all confidence not only in our national character but in man's integrity too. The fact that we blow so hard so much about both of them is to me the symptom." The circumstances of these comments are worth reporting. Davis had sent Faulkner a copy of Robert Penn Warren's *All the King's Men*. Faulkner had read the novel and had been much taken with the Cass Mastern episode, the principal events of which occur from about 1854–55 to 1864. In comparison with what man had had to face and had heroically faced up to nearly a century ago, the men of the mid-twentieth century did not come off well. Yet Faulkner's outburst represented more than the momentary impact on him of this fine long story. What Faulkner says here has close affinities with the speeches that he put into Ike McCaslin's mouth in *Go Down, Moses* and into Gavin Stevens's mouth in *Intruder in the Dust*.

The history of this Southern subnation was, as Faulkner depicts it, tragic in Aristotle's sense of the term. One remembers how in the *Poetics* Aristotle observed that you cannot make a tragic hero out of a base and contemptible man. The tragic hero must be literally "worth the killing." Though he has a tragic flaw, he must possess real virtues; otherwise the evocation of pity and terror that Aristotle regarded as the hallmark of genuine tragedy could not occur. For Faulkner, the tragic flaw of the South was its harboring of chattel slavery, yet the slaveholders, and in general the soldiers of the Confederacy, the majority of whom were not slaveholders at all, were essentially brave and worthy men. That was why, for Faulkner, the collapse of the Old South was authentically tragic.

There is, however, another way of approaching this matter of Faulkner's relation to the myth of the Old South. Most critics of that myth make the assumption that they themselves stand on firm historical ground. They are bringing solid truth to bear on a flimsy fairy tale. But the situation may in fact be rather different. It is entirely possible that we have here not a myth confronted by history, but one myth confronting another. For if there is a myth of the Southern past, we must recognize that there is a myth of the American future—its more respectable name is the American Dream—and with reference to the charge that the Southern myth erred in describing its past as golden, one might point out that the American myth has consistently insisted that its future was made of the same precious metal. But a golden future, never quite here, always about to be, may turn out to be quite as much a falsification. If it is dangerous to glamorize the past because one's future is dark or uncertain, the reverse process may falsify quite as much: to gild the future because the past is drab and unsatisfactory.

We are not condemned to either alternative, though the American myth has applied a constant pressure toward this either/or choice. Thus, in his day Emerson divided the American intellectuals into those who belonged to the Party of Memory and those who belonged to the Party of Hope. In doing so, he offered a false option, for there is not the slightest reason why a writer like Faulkner, who remembers, should thereby forfeit his right to be hopeful—unless, of course, one assumes that one is forced to choose between losing his memory and losing his hope. In a world of such mad choices as that, a man might as well lose his mind too and be done with it.

Faulkner may be said to have participated in both myths, that of the Old South and that of America. As an American, he felt the attraction of the American Dream, particularly as it is expressed in the opening sentences of the Declaration of Independence—the promise of freedom, equality, and the right of the individual to pursue his own notion of the good life. But Faulkner was no Emersonian; nor was he a Whitmanian, rejoicing in the promiscuous bonhomie of urban crowds. Faulkner was more realistic— some would say more pessimistic—about the general cantankerousness of human nature and the difficulties of directing the course of history, even of *predicting* its outcome. To be sure, he never quite despaired of man, but neither was he buoyantly optimistic about man's future. In 1955, some several years after his Nobel Prize speech, he observed in a letter to a friend: " . . . human beings are terrible. One must believe well in man to endure him, wait out his folly and savagery and inhumanity." Faulkner did "believe well in man," but his was no naive belief. It was a hard-won faith.

If Faulkner was willing to criticize the myth that he had inherited from his family and his local community and his region, he was also willing to criticize the myth of America, to make a realistic estimate of how far we were still from a realization of the American Dream. In 1955, he published an article entitled "On Privacy." He was always sensitive, perhaps hypersensitive, to what he regarded as invasions of his private life. What he had published was open to discussion and criticism, but his personal life was not the business of the public. He resented bitterly the fact that a magazine like *Life* should consider that everything he had ever said or done was in the public domain. But though it was a personal incident that provoked his essay, Faulkner tried to rise above the merely personal occasion. He made it plain that the issue raised was general and had reference to basic principles. It is significant that he gave his essay the subtitle: "The American Dream: What Happened to It?" He even wrote to a friend at this time that he wanted to write five or six essays on this matter of the degeneration of the American Dream. The essays might make up a small book on the subject.

The five or six additional essays were never written. But from the one that he did publish and from the novels and short stories of his later career, one can make out what his developed thesis would have amounted to. The American Revolution had been fought to free the individual citizen from all sorts of tyrannies. One's right to keep his personal life free from gossipmongers and meddlers and censors was an essential part of his freedom.

Consequently, when a soul-less corporation could invade a citizen's privacy by flaunting a banner emblazoned "Freedom of the Press" or "The Public's Right to Know," the real issues had been perverted and the individual citizen's freedom subverted. Greed for money to be made by truckling to the curiosity of a mass audience had undone what the Declaration of Independence had proclaimed and the Constitution had been intended to confirm.

The growth of the money power represented a degeneration from the republican ideal of the Founding Fathers. The transformation of a free citizenry into a mindless mob amounted to an even worse corruption, the kind of corruption that Thomas Jefferson had foreseen as a possibility and had warned against. Harry Wilbourne (in *The Wild Palms*) may well be speaking for Faulkner when he argues that present-day America's special vices are "fanaticism, smugness, meddling, fear, and worst of all, respectability."

I do not know that Faulkner ever consulted Alexis de Tocqueville's *Democracy in America*, but had he read Tocqueville's second volume he would have found an account of the very process by which a government set up to protect the individual's rights might end up by subverting them. Though the Founding Fathers of the United States had indeed conceived the individual to be the sole bearer of rights and responsibilities, and though democratic political institutions were devised to protect the individual's rights and privileges, Tocqueville points out that the whole tendency in a democracy is toward the standardization of culture and toward a homogenization of the mass of the citizenry. It is the needs of the average citizen that it seeks to satisfy, not those of the special person here and there whose needs are highly individual. The greatest good of the greatest number, indeed. How much could a Faulkner's rather odd desire for privacy count against the desires of the several million readers of *Life* who wanted to read all about him?

This is the sort of situation that Tocqueville foresaw; and though he thought well of democracy and hoped for the best, he was apprehensive that a democratic state might come to institute a quiet despotism, though ostensibly for the benefit of the people themselves. As Tocqueville puts it: "I have always thought that servitude of the regular, quiet, and gentle kind which I have . . . described might be combined more easily than is commonly believed with some of the outward forms of freedom, and that it might even establish itself under the wing of the sovereignty of the people."

Had Faulkner gone on to write his five or six essays on what had happened to the American Dream, would he have touched upon such matters as the dissolving of community, the breakdown of the older values, and the increasing isolation and insecurity of the individual? I think it very likely, for if one examines his fiction, he will find implied a coherent ethical and moral position that is traditional and conservative. It is not mindlessly opposed to all change, nor is it unduly pessimistic about man's future, but it has little patience with utopian ideas and none with leveling tendencies.

Since I have characterized Faulkner's world view as "conservative," I should at least intimate what I mean by that term. I can do no better, I believe, than to quote two paragraphs from Robert Nisbet's *Quest for Community* (which should be read entire by those interested in Faulkner's general intellectual position). Nisbet writes:

> The family, religious association, and local community—these, the conservatives insisted, cannot be regarded as the external products of man's thought and behavior; they are essentially prior to the individual and are the indispensable supports of belief and conduct. Release man from the contexts of community and you get not freedom and rights but intolerable aloneness and subjection to demonic fears and passions. Society, Burke wrote in a celebrated line, is a partnership of the dead, the living, and the unborn. Mutilate the roots of society and tradition, and the result must inevitably be the isolation of a generation from its heritage, the isolation of individuals from their fellow men, and the creation of the sprawling, faceless masses.
>
> The conservatism of our own age of thought is new only in context and intensity. Through the writings of such intermediate figures as Comte, Tocqueville, Taine, Maine, Arnold, and Ruskin, the root ideas and values of early nineteenth-century conservatism have found their way straight to our own generation and have become the materials of a fresh and infinitely diversified veneration for community.

Since he was essentially a conservative, history meant a great deal to Faulkner. He was fully aware of what the mutilation of the roots of society and tradition could mean. In portraying the life of Joe Christmas, he had actually provided a brilliant study of what a complete release from the context of community entailed, including the "isolation of individuals from their fellow men."

Faulkner believed that history might serve as a guide to mankind because he believed that fundamental human nature did not change through the ages. Man did not, even in a different epoch, become an essentially different creature. The man of the present could recognize his own lineaments in the characters described in the *Iliad* or in the Old Testament.

Though Faulkner's novels are drenched in history, they are not "historical novels" in the sense in which Hollywood costume-dramas are. Faulkner's concern is not antiquarian. His primary intention is not the exploitation of those historical differences in order to provide colorful dress and language for the old, worn, stock characters of romance. The element of escape is never his emphasis. The past is made to reveal a connection with the present.

Faulkner's insistence on making the past impinge meaningfully on the present— on his own present, at least—shows itself in the very time scheme of his novels. The action of *Absalom, Absalom!* begins in 1833 but it does not end until 1910. *The Unvanquished* reaches back to the 1850s, but the man who narrates it does not make what is the crucial decision of his life until 1876, and, as we learn from *Flags in the Dust*, he does not die until 1919. The first episode of *Go Down, Moses* occurs in 1859, but the last episode is to be dated 1941. One might add that even *Light in August* makes use of the same basic pattern. It contains two short but very brilliant flashbacks that deal with the grandfathers of Joanna Burden and Gail Hightower, but the impact of these men on their grandchildren does not reveal its full consequence until 1932.

In sum, the past is never for Faulkner a realm of irresponsible fantasy. For his characters, the past may seem to be a doom, a judgment, a portent, a responsibility, even a providential hope. But it is never simply irrelevant— something that is finished and done with.

Faulkner, of course, was not alone in his concern for the past. The literary artists of our day have been especially concerned with it. One thinks, for instance, of Yeats, Pound, Tate, Eliot, to name only a few. Yet— and here is a sort of paradox—perhaps not for centuries has history counted for so little in the culture as a whole. The man in the street simply doesn't concern himself with it. His eyes are bedazzled by the future. Robert Penn Warren has put the matter bluntly and with somber emphasis: ours, he says, is "a world in which the contempt for the past becomes more and more marked."

The triumphs of modern technology have indeed been staggering. As a virtuoso technological exhibition, our series of moon landings, for example, is almost incredible. But less spectacular technological accomplishments had already altered the total culture. Henry Ford's humble Model T eventually put the whole nation on wheels and, by doing so, drastically altered our daily lives —where we lived, the kind of work we did, and even the makeup of the family unit. Whether or not Ford ever really said that history is bunk, his Tin Lizzie helped persuade the average citizen that history *is* bunk, and in the process also changed the average citizen's conception of nature.

The two phenomena are obviously related: Eliot's or Tate's or Yeats's interest in history is not at all like the pleasant nostalgia with which Sir Walter Scott, a century and a half ago, viewed the past in his historical novels. Nor does it reveal the spirit of detachment which forty years ago allowed millions of readers of *Gone With the Wind* to enjoy the exciting adventures of Scarlett O'Hara. Such excitement could remain a harmless diversion just because the world of Scarlett O'Hara had indeed gone with the wind.

Writers like Yeats, Eliot, and Faulkner find the past frighteningly immediate, inextricably tied up with the present, and full of portent for the future. They cannot dismiss the past as truly past. The temptation of the man in the street to dismiss mankind's earlier experience as obsolete is precisely the circumstance that portends danger. Our technology does not in itself foredoom us. What is frightening is the confidence of the man in the street that the past has been safely buried, that history holds no wisdom for him, and that he is a new, emancipated creature, a rather modest but quite authentic model of Friedrich Nietzsche's Superman.

It is just here that we encounter once more the American Dream. That Dream has always had its ingredient of millennialism, for from the very beginning the American has felt that in setting sail for the New World he had rid himself of the past, and in setting foot on the shores of a virgin continent he had dismissed his old life and had become the New Adam. The New World meant another chance for man. It meant the end of the old despotic tyrannies that hampered man from realizing his proper freedom.

Faulkner, like most of the rest of us, had felt the attraction of the American Dream. He took its promises seriously. I judge that he never repudiated the ideals for human life that shimmered through it, but he fairly soon must have come to realize that it was unattainable or at least all but unattainable. One of his most idealistic characters, Isaac McCaslin, is made to talk to the issues directly in *Go Down, Moses*. Isaac tells his elder kinsman that he believes that Columbus's discovery of America was providential; that God did mean to give man a new chance. Out "of the old world's worthless evening," God had "discovered to [man] a new world," one in which "a nation of people could be founded in humility and pity and sufferance and pride of one to another." But then Isaac goes on to say that this new American land was "already accursed . . . already tainted even before any white man owned it." Yet the white men also were tainted. It was as if the sails of their ships were filled with "the old world's tainted wind."

In short, the white men from the Old World were not somehow miraculously purged of their sins through their action in crossing the Atlantic. They had within them plenty of the Old Adam, the Adam who had been expelled from Eden long ago, and so could be expected to bring into the new American Eden a prosperity for evil. (I am aware that I have been quoting one of Faulkner's characters, not the author himself. Nevertheless, I see no reason to believe that Isaac McCaslin in this passage is not expressing Faulkner's own view. Such a view is implicit in the whole canon of his works.) Isaac, to be sure, is far from hopeless. He even insists that God almost miraculously brought on the Civil War because he loved the South and meant to save it from the curse of slavery; and so saw to it that the Southerners were defeated because apparently "they [could] learn nothing save through suffering, remember nothing save when underlined in blood."

Isaac, and maybe Faulkner himself, could hope that the South might eventually find "a happy issue out of all its afflictions," even out of a shattering defeat. Since history was not meaningless, even suffering could be redemptive. All this amounts to a kind of religious faith; but we confront here something different from the American Dream, different at least from the later modes of the American Dream. For Isaac is here taking a realistic view of man's capacity for evil. He is also taking history seriously. Instead of dismissing history as irrelevant, he is trying to make sense of it.

The millennialist believes that man is perfectible, that he can learn the laws that govern society, and so eventually determine the course of history. A millennialist tendency is to be seen in the very beginnings of the American experience. The Puritans of New England, constituting the militant left wing of Protestantism meant to return to God's plan as set forth in Scripture and so establish the New Jerusalem, the divine society as ordained by God, on the soil of the New World. They were, of course, sufficiently orthodox not to presume that man was perfectible, or that all the human miseries, including sickness, old age, and death, could be done away with. They still held firmly to the doctrine of original sin. They had no illusions that they could restore man to his immortal state, living once more in the happy garden of an unfallen nature. Yet as the doctrine of original sin faded, and as man's powers to control nature grew more and more powerful, the millennial ideal gradually became secularized. The Puritan determination to build the perfect society, far from weakening, was simply redirected from the eternal to the temporal, from the City of Heaven to an earthly city of the here-and-now.

St. Augustine, in his famous discussion of the city of God and the city of man, certainly expected the Christian to use the heavenly city as the model for his earthly enterprise, but he made it plain that it could not be built through man's efforts, but only by God's grace, and in God's own good time. In fact, whenever it was achieved, time would be at an end and the citizens of this New Jerusalem would be living in the light of eternity. The secularization of this view of history took centuries. Yet men did finally come to believe that it was possible, provided that one had a privileged insight into history and a proper social and industrial technology, to control and direct the historical process so as to achieve the perfect society on this earth.

American millennialism has never been as violent as the various revolutionary movements of Europe have been—Marxism, for example—but it has remained from the seventeenth century onward a driving and shaping force in our history. One can find it in the essays of Emerson, in the poetry of Walt Whitman, and almost nakedly in Julia Ward Howe's "The Battle Hymn of the Republic." It is still a powerful force right down to the present day, though it is now so familiar to most of us that we never refer to it by a term so formidable as millennialism, but speak of it rather fondly as simply the American Dream.

The issue of millennialism is, however, one that sets Faulkner off from a great many other American writers. He does not, of course, stand alone; yet his more old-fashioned notion of history has disquieted and confused many a twentieth-century literary critic, and it sets him off sharply from such writers as Hart Crane or, to mention one whose talents he greatly admired, Thomas Wolfe. Faulkner is far less visionary than Wolfe, less optimistic, less intoxicated with the greatness of America. By contrast,

Faulkner's view is more "Southern," and though one should not claim him for Christian orthodoxy, much closer to St. Augustine's view of history.

In calling Faulkner's view more "Southern," I am thinking of what C. Vann Woodward has to say in the course of *The Burden of Southern History* and particularly of such observations as the following: "An age-long experience with human bondage and its evils and later with emancipation and its shortcomings did not dispose the South very favorably toward such popular American ideas as the doctrine of human perfectibility, the belief that every evil has a cure, and the notion that every human problem has a solution."

Faulkner did not scorn the American Dream. Rather, he mourned the fact that it had not been fulfilled. He grieved at having to conclude in 1955 that "the American air, which was once the living breath of liberty [has] now become one vast down-crowding pressure to abolish [freedom], by destroying man's individuality. . . . " Faulkner, however, was skeptical about the full realization of *any* utopian dream, even the noblest. That is to say, he was evidently seriously concerned that his country might be undone by her sometimes overweening faith in the future, by her belief that progress was inevitable, by her confidence that man's happiness would result from sociological know-how and the right set of plans, by her reliance on her technological might, by her incautious trust in her own virtues and good intentions, and, most dangerous of all, by her unprecedented record of military victories. (Faulkner died before Americans went into Vietnam.) Americans could easily get the impression that they, unlike the other nations of the earth, were immune to defeat, loss, and evil. Such innocence might in the end prove disastrous.

Literary Self-Criticism:
Faulkner in Fiction on Fiction

James G. Watson

The self-critical impulse in modernist writing is a useful context in which to examine William Faulkner's fiction, much of which, like Eliot's and Joyce's, is reflexive in this way. The Faulkner canon, no less than Eliot's, is full of new starts and Faulkner's own different kinds of failure, and we can see him trying to learn to use his own words from text to text and within individual fictions. Faulkner might insist on his lifelong commitment to overall fictional design, as he did in 1955, but the example of his own work is of irregular heights and drops. *Pylon*, for example, is sandwiched between the great Yoknapatawpha novels of the 1930s, yet that wordy, derivative book somehow freed his imagination of the detritus of New Orleans and made it possible for him to finish *Absalom, Absalom!* So much is this seemingly wayward progress the case with Faulkner's fiction that Hugh Kenner has complained, "ideally we should have his entire work before us at once, including—also, alas, ideally—the books he would have written in a second lifetime; which is only to say that his work was impossible to finish, and even, in detail, impossible to accomplish. God himself has not yet stopped.

That his work was impossible to accomplish to his own satisfaction, at least, is testified by his famous judgment that his most splendid book was his "most splendid failure." Retrospective authorial judgments aside, *The Sound and the Fury* does corroborate in itself its own failings and records the struggle that Faulkner undertook to overcome them. Probably none of the four attempts to tell the Compson story is satisfactory as a discrete narrative, and none represents a complete action, not even Quentin's. Nor probably were they so intended. The kind of failure that Faulkner meant is better suggested by his recurrence in the text to particular problems of form. The difficulty of self-expression in the novel is an illustration of what

From *The Southern Quarterly* 20, no. 1 (Fall 1981). © 1981 by The Southern Quarterly.

I mean. Ben's futile "trying to say" to the Burgess girl is motivated by a heightened memory of Caddy and punished with castration. Quentin's inevitable disappointments derive from the disjunction between his inexpressible ideal of himself and a reality that will not let him be a hero of tragedy. As the boys fishing outside Cambridge say, "he talks like they do in minstrel shows." Even his suicide fails his splendid intention and he knows that it will even as he commits the act. Quentin's longing for a palpable emblem of his ideal of womanhood is analogous to Faulkner's own artistic need to realize his grand imaginings in concrete fictional forms. Mr. Compson phrases the dilemma to Quentin in terms that apply to art as well as suicide when he says, "you are contemplating an apotheosis in which a temporary state of mind will become symmetrical above the flesh and aware both of itself and of the flesh it will not quite discard you will not even be dead." In just this way *The Sound and the Fury* is an apotheosis of Faulkner's splendid vision of it, a form "symmetrical above the flesh" that is self-aware of its own strategies of composition. As great an achievement as the novel is, the realized form is not ideal, could never have been, and so the strategies of its making are questioned and requestioned. Ben's inability to speak, Quentin's several failures of self-expression, and Jason's neurotic insistence on "what I say" depict a pervasive frustration with language in the novel that is comparable to the several sexual incapacities and frustrations of the brothers. The conjunction of linguistic and sexual impotence in this self-aware book challenges its own realized form—the word-as-deed as Faulkner elsewhere phrases it—in the same way that Jason implicitly does when he turns the artistic cliché Great American Novel to a description of his castrated brother, Ben, whom he calls "the Great American Gelding." Nonetheless, it is one achievement of *The Sound and the Fury* that it in fact affirms its vitality by such repetitions and modifications as these. Recurring in each section to the problem of self-expression, Faulkner made each section a commentary on the limitations and achievements of expression in each other section—including the final one, told from the authorial point of view, and even the "Appendix: Compson" that he added fifteen years later. Like his title, with its overt appeal to Shakespearean symmetries, Faulkner's historical "Appendix" and his retrospective judgments of his book are stages in a progressive structure of self-criticisms that comment on the achieved splendors and the failures of *The Sound and the Fury*.

Such a progression might also include Faulkner's apprentice work, where the false starts and tentative solutions to artistic problems are sometimes as significant measures of his development as his masterworks. We may imagine that through the 1920s Faulkner was working from a steadily enlarging pool of material, some of it theoretical but much of it then still quite personal, and much of it rooted in his fiercely maintained ideals of art. In New Orleans and in Europe in 1925, he also was working more or less seriously in several mediums—writing poetry, prose sketches, and extended fictions, drawing and even painting. As might be expected, this

work is largely characterized by art-conscious commentaries and self-portraits. In his "Foreword" to *Sherwood Anderson and Other Famous Creoles* in
1926, he declared himself a brother to all of the painters in the French
Quarter, and the prose sketch "Out of Nazareth" contains judgments of
the Andrew Jackson bronze in Jackson Square, Cézanne's appreciation of
light, and the emotional precisions of Housman's verse. The title "Out of
Nazareth" and his statement that "words are my meat and bread and drink"
suggest that he was already committed to the sacrament of art. At the least
he was its priest, and in his published sketches and novels and his unpublished work from this period there is enough art-smitten gesturing and
posing that it is difficult sometimes to know which positions are in fact
Faulkner's own. His critical comments sometimes affirm an identity, sometimes repudiate. Often the best that can be said is that they too represent
positions or problems that he was working out for himself when he wrote
them: How might the literary man dip his brush in light as Cézanne had?
How might he embody his personal and artistic ideals in his art like
Housman?

One book where Faulkner approaches these problems through a persona identifiably his own is the hand-lettered-and-illustrated *Mayday* that
he gave to Helen Baird as a courtship gift in late January, 1926. Modelled
on popular mock-romances such as Cabell's *Jurgen, Mayday* is an allegory
of the author's disappointed love in which a young knight named Sir Galwyn of Arthgyl is given a vision of a perfect woman with "a face all young
and red and white, and with long shining hair like a column of fair sunny
water." In company with the spectres Hunger and Pain, Galwyn rides in
search of his vision and encounters on the way three princesses, each of
whom falls short of his ideal by her eagerness to seduce him. At the end
of the quest he is instructed by the good Saint Francis that his vision exists
only as "Little sister Death." To find her, and by finding her relieve his
frustration with an imperfect world, Galwyn drowns himself in the stream
of oblivion. Allegorically, Galwyn is Faulkner, the ideal woman more beautiful than Yseult and her lustful sisterhood is Helen Baird, and Galwyn's
suicide symbolizes the threatened end to unrequited love. In the drowning,
as in some other details, Sir Galwyn looks forward to Quentin Compson
and *Mayday* to *The Sound and the Fury*. Unlike other early work where there
are verbal echoes and foreshadowings, however, the line of development
from *Mayday* to *The Sound and the Fury* links that novel to a book that is
overtly self-critical. In addition to its autobiographical and apprentice interest, *Mayday* is in several important respects an apparently intentional
self-portrait of the artist and his art. The sullied idealist driven by a lover's
vision portrays more openly than *The Sound and the Fury* Faulkner's own
struggle to give significant form to the figures of his imagination, and there
is in Sir Galwyn's suicide the same narcissistic impulse that drove Faulkner
to write. As the Semitic man says in *Mosquitoes*, published a year after
Mayday, "you don't commit suicide when you are disappointed in love.
You write a book."

Nonetheless, if art was to be Faulkner's antidote to life, the evidence of *Mayday* and *Mosquitoes* suggests that it was not yet an effective one. In the dedication to *Mayday* Faulkner called it "a fumbling in darkness," and a "fumbling" the little book decidedly is: a fumbling for detachment with a very personal love-experience, a fumbling with his idea of himself and his art, and a fumbling with an allegorical form that would not quite fit his need. In *Mosquitoes*, which is likewise dedicated to Helen Baird and draws on some of the same personal materials, Faulkner attributed those same uncertainties to his mentor, Sherwood Anderson. The Anderson character, Dawson Fairchild, is called "a man of undoubted talent, despite his fumbling bewilderment in the presence of sophisticated emotions"; according to the Semitic man, "His writing seems fumbling, not because life is unclear to him, but because of his innate humorless belief that, though it bewilder him at times, life at bottom is sound and admirable and fine." Faulkner's parody of Anderson suggests that he felt himself above such fumbling idealism, but the issue in 1926 and 1927 was still unresolved. Years later, in a tribute to Anderson, Faulkner recalled that his style "had the appearance of fumbling but actually it wasn't: it was seeking, hunting." *Mayday* testifies to the same questing impulse in the younger Faulkner.

A related characteristic of his art-consciousness at this period is his searching and experimenting with different artistic mediums as well as literary styles. In the case of *Mayday*, the allegorical images in the text are complemented by the pictorial dimension of the book. Like his 1920 college play, *Marionettes*, *Mayday* is decorated with Beardsley-like black-and-white drawings. It also has three watercolor paintings, one of only two of Faulkner's extant books to be so made. The watercolors are in the body of the book and illustrate the story. In the first, Sir Galwyn is shown kneeling at prayer to receive his vision; in the second, he flies with Princess Aelia in her dolphin-drawn chariot. The third watercolor is unique in that the event it depicts does not actually take place in the text. Positioned near the end of the book opposite the page where Galwyn must choose between a new life and death, the painting is conventionally romantic: a night scene in which Galwyn stands with his arm about the waist of his beloved beneath an approving new moon. For Galwyn the scene in the painting represents the ideal life he has envisioned and an alternative to suicide; for Faulkner the hoped for outcome of his courtship of Helen. That Faulkner knew *Mayday* would never actually bring about that romantic conclusion is illustrated by the black-and-white drawings that decorate the endpapers of the book. The first illustrates his purpose in making *Mayday*: it shows a bearded satyr piping for a naked woman who faces away toward the images conjured by his music. These include the spectres from the allegory, Hunger and Pain, and in the upper left corner a second satyr pursuing two female figures who dance away ahead of him. The satyr, or faun, is a figure that Faulkner often took for himself, and it is clearly appropriate to a romance celebrating May Day and the rites of spring as *Mayday* does. If we take the woman in the foreground of the drawing to be Helen Baird and the music to represent Faulkner's book, then the goatish piper must be the artist himself, piping the self-reflexive music of sexual pursuit. The faun symbolizes the complex, even divided relationship between the man and the artist. Like the story in which he portrays himself as a knight, the drawing that illustrates the story is a multiple self-portrait in which Faulkner the illustrator depicts Faulkner the piper depicting Faulkner the man pursuing Helen through the several mediums of his art. The repetition of the satyr as both piper and pursuer is more than a sly hint of the idealist's actual lust: it combines artistic and sexual vitality in a single figure that stands as the one alternative to the sex-death conjunction set forth in the text, where the quest fails and Sir Galwyn drowns himself. That image is the subject of the final drawing: although the musical motif is maintained in the second black-and-white illustration at the end of the quest and the book, the satyr is absent, replaced by the ghost of Sir Galwyn brooding above his own grave.

For all of its interest as an unusual artifact, this multi-faceted little book is still no masterpiece. Yet its fumbling for expression in different mediums and with materials and attitudes toward art that were to be carried forward into the major fiction makes of it a significant document in the development of Faulkner's art and record of his earliest understanding and adaptation of modernist practices. It was even strangely prophetic, for a year later, on May Day 1927, Helen Baird announced her engagement to another man. *Mayday* predicts such an outcome and more. Sir Galwyn's solution to disappointed love was to recur in Quentin's suicide; Faulkner's, perhaps, found expression still later in Harry Wilbourne's decision in *The Wild Palms* to live with his grief. Harry's ideal woman, Charlotte Rittenmeyer, is also modelled on Helen Baird, but in that novel it is Charlotte who dies while Harry, in a self-parody of Faulkner's earlier personae, decides, *"between grief and nothing I will take grief."*

Self-parody is a form of self-portraiture: like autobiography it is inherently self-analytic, but parody repudiates instead of affirming the value of one's previous identity. Taking *Mayday* as a point of reference, Faulkner's use of parody as self-criticism is evident in his recurrence during the 1930s to the pictorial self-portraits in that book: the faun in the first pen-and-ink drawing and the knight and his lady in the final watercolor. The faun he borrowed initially from Swinburne and the French Symbolist poets, and it appears repeatedly in his work from his first published poem, "L'Après-Midi d'un Faune" in 1919, through *The Marble Faun* in 1924, to occasional poems and prose sketches later in the 1920s. Working on his autobiographical novel "Elmer" in Paris in 1925, he grew a beard and illustrated his letters home with pen-and-ink drawings of himself so faunlike that he might have used them a year earlier to illustrate *The Marble Faun* or six months later for the decorations in *Mayday*. Andre Bleikasten has called the figure of the marble faun an enigmatic symbol reflecting "the young poet's own impasse: both thirsting for the experience of reality and tempted by the timeless vision of art, and too self-involved to achieve a working relationship with either." The drawings in the Paris letters and in *Mayday* accord with the sense of a divided self evoked in the long poem. After the publication of his first masterpieces, however, Faulkner's self-awareness drove him to purgations and renunciations of his youthful intensities. The faun was a literary figure dating from his own age of uncertainty, and typically, self-critically, he expunged it by literary means. In 1934 when the story "Black Music" appeared in *Doctor Martino and Other Stories,* Faulkner's personal involvement with the faun symbol was distanced by comedy. The tale of Wilfred Midgleston's transformation into a "farn" and his boozy service to a virile and vengeful Pan is as much a portrait of the artist in its way as is *The Marble Faun* or *Mayday,* but the artist it portrays is no longer frustrated by his exclusion from life. Like Faulkner, perhaps, Midgleston is described as "a small, snuffy nondescript man," and like Faulkner the artist in 1934, he too has "done and been something outside the lot and plan for mortal human man to do and be." Both have been fauns, but Faulkner no more than Midgleston was a "sad bound prisoner" of paralyzing self-consciousness when he wrote "Black Music"; instead, he could comically confirm the artistic vitality of the faun symbol at the same time he repudiated its frustrations.

An occasional piece written in 1937 for his French translator, Maurice Coindreau, completed the process of purgation. In "Afternoon of a Cow," Faulkner turned the French Symbolists' early influence on him back upon itself in a way that the Frenchman Coindreau would surely have appreciated. The title parodies his own title, borrowed from Mallarmé, "L'Après-Midi d'un Faune," and the sketch itself mocks his early poetic posturing. Instead of the faun who speaks in the poem, the narrator of "Afternoon of a Cow" is Faulkner's self-declared ghost writer, the priggish, fastidious "Ernest be Toogood"; instead of an idealized nymphet, the object of their quest is a cow, "the lone female among three men . . . helpless victim of her own physical body," and instead of haughtily rejecting Mr. Faulkner's advances, this terrified Io defecates on him. The story represents Faulkner's fictional encounter with situations from his own previous fictions and poems. His response is a comment on his repudiation of the faun persona and of what he by then saw as the pretensions of the European conventions that informed it. These last he projected onto Toogood, according to whom Mr. Faulkner's response "was couched in that pure ancient classic Saxon which the best of our literature sanctions and authorizes and which, due to the exigencies of Mr. Faulkner's style and subject matter, I often employ but which I myself never use although Mr. Faulkner even in his private life is quite addicted to it and which, when he employs it, indicates what might be called a state of most robust, even though not at all calm, wellbeing." The passage offers an example of a divided self in which a previous aspect of the writer's persona ironically affirms his present solution to the problems of language and voice that troubled and divided him then.

A variation on this comic resolution that relates to *Mayday* through

Faulkner's paintings occurs in the long story he crafted from his Paris novel and called "A Portrait of Elmer." In some respects that story is as much autobiography as the satyr in *Mayday* is a self-portrait: it carries forward unchanged from the earlier, unfinished work events from Faulkner's own European trip, his artistic ambitions then, and his idealized love for Helen Baird. Elmer's Myrtle Monson is "arrogant with youth and wealth . . . like a star: unattainable for all her curved pink richness." Myrtle is touring Europe as Helen had in 1925, and like Faulkner Elmer tries to win her by painting a picture. At this point in his narrative the story of Elmer Hodge ravelled out, and Faulkner turned from the fragment to *Mosquitoes*. When he returned to the "Elmer" material in the 1930s, he wrote into it a personal, parodic self-judgment of *Mayday* and his Helen Baird period. "A Portrait of Elmer" brings the painter to Paris where he buys watercolors, drives to a "blue hill" in the Forest of Meudon, and paints "a picture of three trees and an inferior piece of an inferior river." In 1926, within a month of his return from Paris, Faulkner had painted nearly the same picture for Helen's book. The third watercolor in *Mayday* shows Sir Galwyn's imaginary meeting with his ideal woman: it is a night scene, set in an enchanted forest, with a blue hill, three trees, and a piece of a river. Elmer's fictional picture parodies the picture in Faulkner's fiction. About to be reunited with Myrtle Monson, Elmer is beset not with a sexual nor even an artistic frenzy but with diarrhea, and he uses the painting neither for courtship nor Fame but as toilet tissue. Like a drowning man with his life passing before him, Elmer "seems to see his life supine before the secret implacable eyeless life of his own entrails like an immolation" as he onomatopoetically repeats the name of his beloved—"Myrtle. Myrtle. *Myrtle.*" For the purposes of the story, this comic ending is an end in itself: it is an appropriate irony that the Fame-struck artist who first painted on newspaper as a child must use his first painting as toilet tissue in lieu of newspaper as a child might. In the fuller context of the story's antecedents and connectives, however, the scene performs an act of criticism on *Mayday* that repudiates Faulkner's early self-characterization as the brother to all painters in the way that "Afternoon of a Cow" does the faun symbol. Faulkner also painted from childhood, and in *Mayday* he put himself into his watercolor paintings as a knight. Paradoxically, Elmer puts himself into his watercolor when he marks it with his excrement. The resulting canvas is likewise a self-portrait, one produced in his own ironic image by his own hand and the only pictorial "portrait of Elmer" in the story of that title. This is parody that draws not only on Faulkner's life but on his own autobiographical fictions and paintings. Recasting the story from the autobiographical novel he had begun with such enthusiasm in 1925, he could hardly have avoided rethinking his personal and artistic attitudes as he rethought the story itself. By ending "A Portrait of Elmer" as he did, he purged himself of the self-involved persona he had assumed to write the previous, unfinished version entitled simply "Elmer." The excrement on Elmer's "portrait" represents Faulkner's retrospective judgment of the artist-as-man. It is also a measure of the distance he had come by mid-1930 from his own practices during the earlier period when he worshipped Cézanne, who "dipped his brush in light."

Like their own self-critical conclusions, "Afternoon of a Cow" and "A Portrait of Elmer" themselves conclude a series of poems, illustrations, and fictions done over more than a decade in which Faulkner assessed and reassessed the methods and materials of his art. His self-consciousness is classically modernist in tendency. In his 1923 review of *Ulysses*, T. S. Eliot argued that rather than turning away from living experience to the mummified forms and modes of the literary "museum," "one can be classical in tendency by doing the best one can with the material at hand." And in that material, he said, "I include the emotions and feelings of the writer himself, which, for that writer, are simply the materials which he must accept—not virtues to be enlarged or vices diminished." For Faulkner, doing the best one can involved almost constant artistic attention to his own interwoven virtues and vices, which were after all the materials of his emotional life and the sources of his ideals and uncertainties. Less intellectually detached than Eliot claimed to be, his inwardness is no less a mark of his own modernist sensibility. It is the stuff of *Mayday*, and it is a primary component in the pool of material that gathered for him through the mid-1920s in Oxford and Toronto, New Orleans and Paris. Later the turn inward was followed by a complementary turn homeward, in *Flags in the Dust* and then *The Sound and the Fury*, to his own "little postage stamp of native soil," the actual environment from which he was to cast his apocryphal "cosmos." That the fictional cosmos should at times openly affirm or correct the virtues or failings that Faulkner found in the actual South is a function of its foundations in his ancestry and experience as a Southerner. It is equally an extension of the self-analytic tendency that evolved in the apprentice work preceding the Yoknapatawpha books. Faulkner's criticism of his fiction in his fiction measures more accurately than any retrospective statements of his the developing self-assurance and reconciliation to his art and life that were necessary to his creation of the cosmos he called "a kind of keystone in the Universe." Because it is himself that the Southerner is writing about," he wrote in 1933, "not about his environment . . . the [Southern] writer unconsciously writes into every line and phrase his violent despairs and rages and frustrations or his violent prophesies of still more violent hopes. That cold intellect that can write with calm and complete detachment and gusto of its contemporary scene is not among us." Such dark complexities of the self, where sexual and artistic vitality are conjoined and death is the alternative to both, comprised the materials at his hand from his first maturity. To the fictional implications of that interior landscape he was as scrupulously, as critically, attentive as to the geography of north Mississippi itself.

The Spectral Road: Metaphors of Transference in Faulkner's *As I Lay Dying*

Patrick O'Donnell

William Faulkner's intense concern with both the social and ontological implications of language is nowhere more evident than in *As I Lay Dying*. Perhaps, too, it is in this work that Faulkner is most aware of both the connection between language and metaphysics, and the difficulty involved in using language to observe its own operation as the vehicle for expression of being, word, or act. In one sense, the novel creates a "hermeneutic circle," wherein the attempt to interpret its world is circumscribed by the means for understanding it—i.e., language. In just this way, the significance of the Bundrens' journey is only revealed within the confines of the journey itself as it moves haltingly toward Addie's burial. The irony of this situation informs everything about the novel, from its narrative structure, to its use of "voice," to what I am most concerned with here, its metaphoricity—by which I mean its exhibition of metaphor on the surface as, traditionally, a rhetorical device and, more deeply, as an epistemological conveyance of the novel's concern with the "meaning of meaning."

As I Lay Dying is clearly one of Faulkner's most heavily metaphorical fictions. For one critic of Faulkner's artistic evolution, the binding power of metaphors in the novel, which creates coherence between disparate elements of the world, "can establish in consciousness a relationship of virtual presence between subject and environment . . . expressed perfectly in language." That is, the novel's metaphors form a network of correspondences and cross-references that gives the novel the texture of a systematic world, a world wherein journeys—like metaphorical language—lead toward certain ultimacies of desire, purpose, and expression. However, at the same time, the fractured metaphorical links of the novel compel one to question the validity and strength of this "virtual presence"— created by the binding power of the metaphors.

From *Papers on Language and Literature* 20, no. 1 (Winter 1984). © 1984 by the Board of Trustees of Southern Illinois University.

In the novel, Faulkner relies on the ambivalence of metaphor; the progression toward ultimacy and meaning, projected in the Bundrens' journey, moves forward by contraries. The fading, circuitous roads of the novel can be seen as metaphors for the act of metaphor in which meaning is borne or transferred from one point to another; they suggest that the unfolding significance of the journey turns upon itself and falls into question, making the outcome of the journey ironic. Similarly, the novel's many vessels and containers can stand for the idea of metaphor as a significant shape embodying meaning. However, the shapes, frames, and containers of *As I Lay Dying* seem to form themselves around a lack, absence, nothingness, as if the transcendent realm of significances that narrates a world of purposeful actions had disappeared. The ironic and complex metaphorical motions of the novel define its subject as a reflection upon the meaning of both funereal and metaphorical journeys. My intention here is to test the metaphorical ambivalences of *As I Lay Dying*. In so doing, I suggest that Faulkner, by means of the metaphors he creates, questions the tenuous connection between fictional language and the apparent "world" to which it refers, or between the unfolding of a comic journey and the journey's end.

Traditionally, metaphor has been viewed as a trope of resemblance. According to Paul Ricoeur, "the dynamic of metaphor [rests] on the perception of resemblance." The use of metaphor creates identity and cohesion, so that "the splitting of meaning" that historically occurs when language evolves from its simple, concrete roots and lends itself to abstraction, returns, through metaphor, to "the original unity" of language and world. Metaphor's ability to connect the concrete and the abstract, to create analogy, even to structure discourse, confers upon it this effective power of "binding" and establishing coherences, identities, and resemblances. At the same time, the use of metaphor involves "the apprehension of an identity within the difference between two terms." The act of metaphor in the oldest sense, as a "transfer" of meaning or quality between one term and another, designates the inherent differences between the terms, so that identity and difference are named at the same time. One can see the operation of "sameness-within-difference" that metaphor facilitates as fundamental to the structure of any discourse, where meaning arises through the work of resemblance, transference, and differentiation.

This view has been altered somewhat by more recent considerations of metaphor, and it is both observed and challenged by Faulkner's use of metaphor in *As I Lay Dying*. The traditional view assumes that metaphor is a stabilizing force in language, that it provides moments of cohesion and concretization in the flow of discourse. But because the relationship between signifier and signified, "vehicle" and "tenor," or image and idea has been so thoroughly questioned by modern rhetorical theory, the totalizing concept of metaphor has come under close scrutiny. In the "post-romantic" consciousness, according to Manfred Frank, we can see "the emancipation of metaphor from the law of analogy" as we discover, increasingly, that what words refer to and signify is more a matter of context and intertext than of their "relationship to some fixed, fundamental" universe of mean-ings. As it "transfers" meaning, the act of metaphor can cause us to be conscious of the essentially arbitrary relations metaphors create, as well as of the fragile structures defined by the contexts they build. Metaphors, like the texts in which they appear, present the possibility of "an open-ended, non-centered play of metaphorical textual desplacements." In these con-siderations, metaphors are not kernels or knots of meaning; rather, they are signs of the *relationality* of language conceived of as a series of semantic shifts. They reveal the unceasing flux of relations which is language strug-gling and desiring to achieve what it cannot: a perfect cohesion between medium and message such that discourse ceases to question its own ability to mean. Metaphors thus serve a double task. They allow the flow of relations and emerging significances to continue because these assemble identities and differences; however, at the same time, they force the dis-course where they appear to question how meaning is conveyed by met-aphor, particularly in that literary language where the abundant use of metaphors becomes self-conscious.

The metaphors in *As I Lay Dying* are observed by a reader who is also privy to fifty-nine monologues of fifteen speakers. Within the framework of a completed journey, the varied, repeated metaphors which these speak-ers provide may represent some "ultimate fusion," forming a "living net-work of symbols, a full and vibrant image of the world, an epiphany of reality." This fusion can be seen as the result of "a repetition as binding" that will "allow us to grasp the text as a total metaphor." In this view, *As I Lay Dying* can then "mean" itself as a metaphor: the "total metaphor" of the novel carries us from the tangible events of the journey to the unseen, unspeakable burial of the mother who is the source of life and meaning. The novel becomes a metaphor for death, in which all meaning and motion, all the diverse, metaphor-filled, Addie-filled perceptions of fifteen voices focus around an ultimate, significant act—Addie's burial. The novel thus allows the satisfaction of closure, along with the promise that, despite the inherent ironies of the Bundrens' mental and physical meanderings, mean-ingful action in this world recurs as a new Mrs. Bundren appears at the end, and a new journey is undertaken.

However, the novel's metaphorical ambivalences, while they partially affirm these critical views of the novel's coherence, also undermine them, suggesting Faulkner is undertaking to try the power and limits of meta-phorical language. Addie's and Darl's monologues, in particular, reveal the complexity of these metaphorical trials. The voice of Addie tells us that a word, "love," is "just a shape to fill a lack," a "vessel" or "jar" of "sig-nificant shape profoundly without life like an empty door frame." Though this is the view of only one character, the perception might be extended to all the vessels and shapes of the novels, the rhetorical figures and tropes that promise significance but, in the end, stand empty, void of life and meaning. The journey is completed; Addie is buried; thus, the novel may, at one level, reflect "a triumph of fraternal feeling" as the family joins together in burying Addie. Or it may embody the desire for the merging of "word and act," as the language through which each Bundren articulates his/her understanding of "mother" or "journey" is finalized and directed toward the completed act of burial. But the disruptive, fragmented tropology of *As I Lay Dying* undermines any unproblematic reading of the novel's drive toward closure as a final, significant act that triumphantly concludes this particular episode of the Bundrens' perambulations in the world and leads to a new journey homeward with the new Mrs. Bundren.

Reading the novel exposes one to a barrage of analogies that asks him to undertake a restless search for that never-revealed significance which will "glue" the shifting, dispersed shapes and vessels of metaphor together. What is known in the novel's world is only known because it moves, it slides; motion is life and, as Darl says during the disastrous crossing of the river, where animals and men only occasionally touch bottom, *"it was only by means of that slipping contact that we could tell we were in motion at all."* This traversal literally refers to the act of fording a river, but it also refers, metaphorically, to the act of signification. It is part of a chain of analogies that represent modes of transmission: roads, rivers, coffins, and meaningful gazes. The novel encourages a collective reading of these manifestations of transference, not only as literal vehicles for journeys, but as metaphorical commentaries on linguistic operations. Indeed, all of the novel's metaphors of transference work on these two levels. They define concretely a particular consciousness or mode of perception, specific anxieties about the progress and ends of the journey, memories of Addie, or concretizations of desire. But each metaphor is also a description of its own "metaphoricity," which is its work as a rhetorical, semantic device that conveys meaning, or makes problematic the conveyance of meaning. Darl's image of "slipping contact" suggests that as men ford rivers—by the sliding movement of feet along the river bottom, against the steady, impervious onrush of the current—only so is motion or forward progress known. In essence, motion, certainly the substance of the journey as well as, to some extent, its end, is only made apparent by slippage, counterturn, or movement that calls into question the "reality" of the journey's progress. As "metalinguistic" commentary, the metaphor suggests that the "work" of language is carried forward only through the constant slippage, elision, and erosion of Faulkner's language, or only by the failure of figures in language to stand still for any one thing in particular. For Faulkner, these metaphorical gesticulations define the act of signification, which never arrives at the ultimacy it foreshadows.

One may take the crucial image of the road in the novel as an example of Faulkner's metaphorical technique. The road to Jefferson is a type of vehicle; it is the pathway along which Addie's coffin is transferred from the Bundren farm to the cemetery. From the perspective that the novel's metaphoric network is revelatory of a structured world of significances tending toward some final end, the road would represent a sign of linkage and connection, a metaphor for the act of metaphor as it joins and binds.

While moving along the road, the Bundrens successfully pass through the trials of fire and water as they complete their journey, causing the community, represented by Tull, Samson, and Armstid, to gather around them in mutual effort. The metaphor of the road appears to be an image of coherence as it defines the relation between the inception and *telos* of the journey. Near the end, Darl observes that the road to Jefferson runs parallel to "the massed telephone lines," gives a view of "the clock on the courthouse [that] lifts among the trees," and stops "where the square opens and the monument stands before the courthouse." This road is, again according to Darl, "like a spoke of which Addie Bundren is the rim": it parallels the conduits of communication [the telephone lines], and it gives a prospect of the orderly progression of time that lends to human experience a meaningful historicity (the courthouse clock). It ends in the public square, a gathering place of the community, in sight of a heroic monument and the courthouse itself, that law-giving edifice that confirms the social order. From their backwoods point of origin the Bundrens have somehow managed to progress along a road to this place where information is exchanged and around which the community molds itself. The purpose of their journey thus becomes part of a celebration of the communal desire to signify and organize itself as an entity that has a meaningful shape within historical and temporal horizons. In this sense, the journey becomes "a parable of creation, the motion of travel implying a process in which the separate inert elements of the world combine into living forms." The journey inspires the creation of the small Bundren community taking on a purposive task, and even the inert Anse is spurred to action in his "courtship" of the second Mrs. Bundren. The smaller community is analogous to the community of the world, which exists because it has order, information, and social purpose: it generates significance. The image of the road, here, serves as a metaphorical conveyance that leads to the creation of meaning.

Furthermore, the novel's roads and paths are often envisioned by Darl who, ever concerned about matters of progress and connection, tries to make sense out of the journey. The perceptions of the road which Darl, the predominant speaker of the novel, conveys within his nineteen monologues suggest his concern with connection and completion, and his desire that the journey generate its own significance. But his descriptions of the road are also replete with images of blockage, interruption, erosion, and spectrality, suggesting a more crucial, ironic understanding of order and disorder, progress and repetition in the world he inhabits. His negative perceptions agree with Dewey Dell's vision of the road as "empty with waiting" and Anse's judgment that the road in its "horizontality" is a perversion of the earth. In its creation, the road "switched the land around longways" and conveyed to Anse a series of disasters, from the drafting of Darl into the army to the appearance, at Addie's deathbed, of Peabody, about whose fee Anse is anxious. Darl's conception of the road is essentially in accord with Anse's, who surmises that "the Lord put roads down for traveling. . . . When He aims for something to be always amoving, He makes it longways, like a road or a house or a wagon, but when He aims for it to stay put, He makes it up-and-down ways, like a tree or a man." Anse's perception reveals an anxiety about traveling and the road, a well-founded fear that journeys mean constant movement, labor, and uncertainty, and a concurrent desire that things "stay put." Journeys are necessary, even for the lazy Anse or the anxious Darl, but they create a desire for the satisfaction of the journey's sensible completion—a task undertaken and well done, then a lapse back into stasis.

Darl's desire that the journey's end be meaningful is reflected in his first words, which describe the path he and Jewel traverse as they come in from the fields. The path "runs straight as a plumbline, worn smooth by feet and baked brick-hard by July, between the green rows of laid-by cotton, to the cottonhouse in the center of the field, where it runs and circles the cottonhouse at four soft right angles and goes on across the field again, worn so by feet in fading precision." This circuitous passage is filled with metaphoric resonances that echo throughout the novel: to some degree, it inscribes the geometry of *As I Lay Dying.* The path is "straight as a plumbline," the anterior referent an architect's or builder's tool used to determine the straightness of a vertical measurement. The vision of a road running straight to a structure that is the house of the dead (the future repository of the "laid-by" cotton) anticipates several other similar images. Most notably, it parallels the image of the road as a "line" leading straight to the cemetery with Addie's coffin "tied" to one end of it (Darl speaking here of yet another road) similar to the road along which Darl and Jewel travel to haul a load of timber that, in Darl's perception, "vanishes beneath the wagon as though it were a ribbon and the front axle were a spool." It is as if the road, line, or ribbon is taken up in the act of traversal, as it both connects and differentiates object and intention. This movement signifies a transference taking place, and the road is the conduit of that transference.

Another metaphoric parallel to Darl's image of the cottonhouse path occurs in the scene at Tull's ford when the overturned wagon is held fast in the torrent by a rope which Jewel, still standing on the ford (and thus on the old road passing along the river bed), has managed to seize. Tull observes "the rope cutting into the water, and we could feel the weight of the wagon kind of blump and lunge lazy like . . . Like it was a straight iron bar stuck into the bottom and us holding the end of it. . . . There was a shoat come by, blowed up like a balloon . . . It bumped against the rope like it was a iron bar and bumped off and went on, and us watching that rope slanting down into the water." Like the path Darl describes, the rope that stays the coffin is a plumbline, a straight extension of the road. It is an iron bar that arises from the chaos of the flooded river and signifies the continuance of the journey, since by it Addie is not allowed to slip away into the flood. The "iron bar" of rope allows for the emergence of discrete objects—the momentary appearance of the shoat out of the undifferentiated mass of water—analogous to the operation of language as the differentiating function of an otherwise silent, monolithic existence. The current of the river is seen by Darl as "silent, impermanent and profoundly significant, as though just below the surface something huge and alive waked for a moment of long alertness out of and into light slumber again." In opposition to the road, which connects things, the chaotic, flooded river threatens to obliterate the pathways and bridges between points, to destroy the topographical or linguistic networks of correspondence in the world, as it conceals its own monstrous, nihilatory significance. The rope holds back from this ceaseless onrush of "sleeping significance" the significant object of the coffin; it is part of the road that is the linkage which makes possible the subsequent transference of Addie's casket. The metaphor of transference reflected in the "iron bar" of rope is thus opposed to the apocalyptic log that rushes toward the coffin in the river, uncannily phallic, with its "long gout of foam [that] hangs like the beard of an old man or goat" from its end, which, as an embodiment of the river's destructive force, threatens the success of the journey. Seemingly, the metaphors of rope and road convey to us the sense that, despite disaster, the journey is progressing slowly, straight as a plumbline, through the river instead of over or around it, toward the completed accomplishment that will confer upon the journey its meaning.

A second look at Darl's conception of the path to the cottonhouse reveals that it "turns and circles the cottonhouse at four soft right angles" and that it is "worn smooth . . . in fading precision." Immediately, the metaphoric significance of the road, previously discussed, is deeply questioned. Like this path, the road that runs straight to Jefferson through the flooded river is, paradoxically, roundabout. When Jewel walks through the windows of the cottonhouse to the other side "with the rigid gravity of a cigar store Indian dressed in patched overalls and endued with life from the hips down," and ignores the circular path that Darl takes, his rigid physicality and Darl's impractical decision to follow the path despite its twistings is underscored. For Darl, the road only leads back upon itself. In addition to the circularity in the "four soft right angles" formed by the path to the cottonhouse, Darl sees it also when he views the road alternately as the spoke of a constantly turning wheel of which Addie is the hub, a ribbon winding back onto a spool, most dramatically a "looping string" that, like time and the river, is a "doubling accretion," a phenomenon that embodies the illusion of progress while it endlessly repeats itself. Like the circling vultures with which Vardaman is obsessed, "ceaselessly interrupting the straight line of the Bundrens' progress," the road acts as "an emblem of the book's structure."

To Darl, who is most conscious and conscientious about the journey's progress, the road ultimately leads nowhere in its twisted straightness. Coming into Jefferson, he observes the vultures circling "with an outward semblance of form and purpose, but with no inference of motion, progress or retrograde." From his vantage point sitting backwards on the end of the wagon, Darl notices "the mileboards diminishing, becom[ing] more starkly reaccruent: 3 mi. 2 mi."; going down a hill into town, he sets a riddle: "We descend as the hill commences to rise." The images suggest paradox and repetition. The road does not progress but appears to rise as it falls, the distance to Jefferson diminishes, but Darl notes the backward accruence of mileage designated by the signs leading away from Jefferson. The sense of transference and completion is subverted here in the semantic puzzle of diminishing reaccruence, as it is in the final outcome of the journey. Darl has been too concerned about forward movement. He is obsessed with having to go *somewhere*, designated and specific, despite his insights about the failure of this desire, hence, his despairing act of giving the journey a contrived ending by burning the barn in which Addie's coffin rests. The failure of completion, connection, and signification is represented by his final doomed words " 'Yes, yes, yes, yes, yes, yes, yes, yes,' " while the second Mrs. Bundren appears as merely a substitution for the first, indicating the endlessness of the journey. Darl envisions in his madness the figures of a coin and a view in a French spyglass of "a woman and a pig with two backs and no face." The transference of meaning and the act of signification is nullified by these images of perverted and incestuous repetition without difference, as Darl suffers a form of semantic death. The coin has "a face to each backside and a backside to each face," an image wherein obverse and reverse become functions of continual exchange, losing their distinction as the boundaries and markers of significant shapes. The spyglass portrayal of bestiality depicts an act that can never, unthinkably, lead to any productive conclusion or issue; the shoat in the flood reappears, not caught up now momentarily by the iron bar of signification, but part of a spectacle "with two backs and no face," lost in an unimaginable merging of identities where there can be no transference of sexual or semantic significance. Thus Darl's road ends in this paradoxical, static, and perverse vision of ceaseless flux and repetition.

The complexities of the road metaphors are deepened by Darl's perception that the path to the cottonhouse is "worn so by feet in fading precision." He observes near the outset of the journey "a white signboard with fading lettering: New Hope Church. 3 mi. It wheels up like a motionless hand lifted above the profound desolation of the ocean." Tull says of the washed-out bridge near his farm where the Bundrens will ford the river that it was "shaking and swaying under us, going down into the moiling water like it went clean through to the other side of the earth, and the other end coming up outen the water like it wasn't the same bridge a-tall and that them that would walk outen the water on that side must come from the bottom of the earth." Both are images of fading and breakage— metaphors in which the power of metaphor to convey meaning becomes inoperative. Darl's path is, ironically, a worn-out metaphor. The signs along the road direct one down a path "empty with waiting" (according to Dewey Dell) toward a "profound desolation" (according to Darl) as they fade. Tull's metaphoric bridge between shores and points of reference is dysfunctional; no change in the consciousness of any character results from this immersion. Nothing is transferred or transformed as a result of this "crossing."

Everything remains altogether different and utterly disconnected, even though the bridge itself is "whole."

In a crucial passage, Darl makes this observation of the "old" road that designates the ford in the river:

> He [Cash] looks about quietly, at the position of the trees, leaning this way and that; looking back along the floorless road shaped vaguely high in the air by the position of the lopped and felled trees, as if the road too had been soaked free of the earth and floated upward, to leave in its spectral tracing a monument to a still more profound desolation than this above which we now sit, talking quietly of old security and old trivial things.

Here, the road has become a "spectral tracing," "floorless," "shaped vaguely," "soaked free of earth," as Darl tries to imagine how it appears where the ford might be. Its position is designated by "lopped and felled trees," the dead markers of a ghostly road, no longer a connecting or binding entity, but a sign of that which has been covered over by the river. Like the other fading metaphors, Darl's spectral road is only an indicator of desolation. It does not act as a conveyance of men or meaning, but only traces out the lost significances that cannot be named and about which men can only sit and tell stories of some mythic "security." Because of these lost significances they may only talk in ancient, worn trivialities. The road signifies its own obliteration as it fades and disappears; as such, it can only be demarcated by fading or dead signs and by the endless movement of the Bundrens' wagon upon its surface. In its own labyrinthine fluidity it winds and rewinds, erodes, and provides only the "slipping contact" which Darl, again, says exists between men and earth as the sign of life, motion, and knowledge: "*I felt the current take us and I knew we were on the ford by that reason, since it was only by means of that slipping contact that we were in motion at all.*" Language and metaphysics converge in this complex image, which suggests that the act of analogy, transference, and metaphor—the work of language—is known only by its motion and erosion, which is a kind of failure to mean, to come to a conclusion. In the world of the novel, this entropic notion of metaphor is all that "means," and it seems preferable to the undifferentiated flood of the murderous river or the hell of repetition into which Darl is cast at the end. Put in other terms, Faulkner denies the reader the satisfaction of a cohesive, purposive world at the same time that he celebrates, in an appropriately millennial frame of reference, the ability of existence to speak itself in terms of its arbitrariness, its ceaseless movement *toward* stasis, decomposition, and disconnection. These seem at the root of the differentiating principle that founds his universe. One cannot hope that the road will lead anywhere; one can only see, by its tracing of what it once was (unspeakably whole, rising above the flood) that it still exists as a broken means of transference.

Addie's coffin is transported along this broken road and is seen as an object of mystery and horror to the farmers who observe its passing. The vessel of the coffin contains the concealed Addie, who is the lifeblood of the Bundren family and its motivating force, even in death. The druggist Moseley describes the coffin when it comes into Mottson as "a piece of rotten cheese coming into an ant hill," an image that suggests the grotesque magnetism of the coffin as an entity around which force and power are focused. Conveyed along the road of the novel, the coffin acts as the locus of its plot and purpose. In one sense, it signifies a successful transference, a completion, since it does reach its destination, though it entombs Addie, the source of significance, who is buried only as a result of the scattered, overdetermined desires of her straying family. The coffin would then seem to be the origin of power and revelation. It contains the mystery of death and the enigmas of life, being, and non-being—incarnated in Addie's existence and represented by her monologue on matters of generation, suffering, renewal, and death.

Vardaman bores holes in her coffin with an auger in order to allow whatever living-dying entity he thinks lies within to breathe, and twice opens the windows to the dead Addie's room for the same purpose. His act, which results in the disfigurement of the corpse's face with two holes corresponding to its unseeing eyes, may be viewed as an attempt to reveal the mysteries and auguries the concealed presence in the coffin has to offer. In his imagined reconstruction of the coffin's making, Darl envisions the casket as a completed and perfected composition which holds within its frame a sleeping presence: "It is light, yet they move slowly; empty, yet they carry it carefully; lifeless, yet they move with hushed precautionary words to one another, speaking of it as though, completed, it now slumbered, lightly alive, waiting to come awake." Even before Addie is in the coffin, Darl suggests that it is the receptacle of some living, significant presence. The language of the passage is similar to that in which Darl conceives of the river as a surface covering something alive but unformed, only known as it "wakes" occasionally and ripples the surface. The coffin seems a significant shape fashioned with "the tedious and minute care of a jeweler," containing some form of "awakeness" which later is snatched from the flow of the river by the care of Jewel's hands. The carefully made artifact of the coffin can be seen as "a product of love, of preserving form, and in its craftsmanship a predication of human dignity." It may contain "the word" or significance that form defines, only spoken or conceived because of "the spatial form of every narrative structure," without which words and significances would become "impeccable," transformed into "an overflowing river," or lapse into "the dark voicelessness of the land." Seen in this manner, the coffin becomes another metaphor of metaphors transferred and composed around a meaningful presence.

In one metaphorical movement, Addie seems to reflect Darl's desire that she be a source of concealed significance. Within the coffin, Addie is veiled so that, as Tull says, "the auger holes in her face wouldn't show." As he struggles with his brothers to move the unbalanced coffin from the house to the wagon, to Darl, the veiled Addie seems alive in death: "For an instant it resists, as though volitional, as though within it her pole-thin body clings furiously, even though dead, to a sort of modesty, as she would have tried to conceal a soiled garment that she could not prevent her body soiling." And, as the inertia is broken and the coffin moves freely, "seeing that the garment was about to be torn from her, she rushes suddenly after it in a passionate reversal that flouts its own desire and need." Darl's image of Addie in the coffin is one of secreted knowledge, guilt, and desire, a concealment that reveals the nature of Addie's existence, as if her being-in-the-world was entombed and preserved beneath the surface of the feminine coffin with its "bleeding plank[s]" "bearing on their flanks in smooth undulations the marks of the adze blade." In death, as in life, Addie's presence is concealed, yet the source of revelation. She is the blood and life that generates the Bundren family, the creative principle of the house, land, and world, wherein she is the silent, orderly center, depicted in the image of her nursing of Jewel: "With Jewel . . . the wild blood boiled away and the sound of it ceased. Then there was only the milk, warm and calm, and I laying calm in the slow silence, getting ready to clean my house."

However, in the continual play of metaphorical possibilities which the novel enacts, the image of the coffin as presence signified often is expunged by its portrayal as "just a shape to fill a lack," a shell surrounding nothingness, like Addie's view of the spoken word. For Cash, who does not dwell upon what lies within it, the coffin is an artistic frame that will outline perfectly the "composition" defined by its borders, just as, in Darl's reconstruction of the scene, a window sill frames the dying Addie's face when she looks out to see Cash making the coffin:

> He looks up at the gaunt face framed by the window in the twilight. It is a composite picture of all time since he was a child. He drops the saw and lifts the board for her to see, watching the window in which the face has not moved. He drops a second plank into position and slants the two of them into their final juxtaposition, gesturing toward the ones yet on the ground, shaping with his empty hands in pantomime the finished box. For a while still she looks down at him from the composite picture, neither with censure nor approbation. Then the face disappears.

Addie in the window is a prefiguration of Addie in the coffin, and in this scene of "pantomime" what is notable is the gesturing emphasis put upon the shaping, construction, and composition of the coffin, together with the total absence of sound or word. In her monologue, Addie says that a word, Anse's name, is an overflowing vessel or "a significant shape profoundly without life like an empty door frame." The image corresponds to the scene of Addie framed in the window while Cash imagines her "framed" in the uncompleted coffin, suggesting that the act of framing or shaping infers the limits of art and language, and that what is within is "empty," a lack of presence. Faulkner's irony will not even allow for the perfectibility or preservation of the frame surrounding a lack: the coffin is continually defiled in the novel, when Vardaman drills holes in it, when it is scarred and smeared by the ravages of the river, when it is scorched by the fire. It is ever off-balance because Addie has been laid within backwards since her family will not allow her fanned-out dress to be ruined by correct placement within the clock-shaped coffin. As a metaphor of metaphor, the image of the coffin, like that of the road, suggests that no stable significance dwells within or is revealed, that the "frame" of metaphor is all, and that it is imperfect, ever-changing, subject to the erosion time and transference bring.

In a reversal of his own desire and need, Darl intuits that the coffin is made of boards that "look like long smooth tatters torn from the flat darkness and turned backside out." The image is one of inversion as the inside of the coffin becomes the outside in Darl's mind. Its exterior becomes a mere repetition of its interior, like Darl's coin, all surface, endlessly repeating its own inversion. The coffin reveals itself not to be the tabernacle of some sacred or obscene presence, but only the receptacle of "flat darkness." Indeed, *As I Lay Dying* is filled with figures of inversion and repetition associated with the coffin. Darl depicts Cash making the coffin as an obsessed Vulcan at his forge, hewing out the artifact in a sulphurous atmosphere and subject to torrential rains, "the immediate air in reverberant repetition," so soaked that he looks "as though he had been abruptly turned wrongside out, shirt and all." Peabody notes that the boards of the coffin "look like strips of sulphur," as if it was made out of the annihilating, reverberant atmosphere in which Cash works, while Tull reports the fact that Addie's body is reversed inside. In a double inversion, Darl observes the fire he has started at Gillispie's and the "conical façade" of the barn with its "square orifice of doorway broken only by the square squat shape of the coffin." This portrayal of a frame within a frame is analogous to Addie's image of the empty shape of a doorway. The coffin is set within the "orifice" of the doorway, its square opening like another broken vessel that contains the voiceless absence contained by the coffin. The image echoes Darl's vision of a bucket of water as "a still surface . . . a round orifice in nothingness." Minutes later, Darl sees the doorway disappear in a rain of fire as Jewel attempts to save the coffin: "We watch through the dissolving proscenium of the doorway as Jewel runs crouching to the far end of the coffin and stoops to it. For an instant he looks up and out at us through the rain of burning hay like a portiere of flaming beads." The moment is apocalyptic, and some revelation seems at hand; the language of the passage suggests that Darl, at least, is on the verge of discovering what coffin and mother "mean." The doorway seems like a curtain hiding some mystery, a stage set for revelation; in its burning it is a veil like the one that covers Addie's face. But this metaphorical movement toward disclosure is simultaneously countered by a movement toward dissolution; it is only in the "dissolving proscenium" and in the disappearing, flaming "portiere" that Addie's casket is framed, as if revelation *is* dissolution—

the conveyance of meaning caught up in its own dissolving the instant meaning is produced. The coffin is preserved, but Jewel is forced to bear the marks of this negative revelation. In the metaphoric counter-current that characterizes the tropological discourse of *As I Lay Dying,* like the broken road which is only known by slipping contact or the river which evidences itself through sleeping wakefulness, the coffin reveals its significance within the language of erosion. Appropriately, we are never given an account of Addie's burial; we never see the final concealment or disclosure of that which is signified and has borne significance within the novel. The burial occurs as an ellipsis, the end of transference and motion thus never allowed to take place in the endless metaphoricity which is the novel's deforming force.

These, as well as other metaphors of transference present within *As I Lay Dying*— eyes and vessels, Jewel's horse and Vardaman's fish—reveal the operation of all tropes which, according to Paul de Man, are "always on the move, more like quicksilver than like flowers or butterflies, which one can at least hope to pin down and insert into a neat taxonomy—but they disappear altogether, or least appear to disappear." In the novel, Faulkner's effort is to create an intricate metaphorical labyrinth of rhetorical relations that always point to their own relationality. This shifting, fluid linguistic network expresses both the desire to signify the depths and heights of some transcendent value or meaning and the doubt that it can do so. The tropology of the novel, pervasively self-reflexive as it dwells upon the journey of words and beings to meaningful ends, purports that language denies the possibility of this ultimate significance while ever working *toward* signification. It is like the words that Addie says are "just gaps in other people's lacks, coming down like the cries of the geese out of the wild darkness in the old terrible nights." In her image, language is gap-filled, composed of disconnected voicings and evanescent cries that arise from and fade into the "terrible night" of silence. The desire and labor of language do not end in Faulkner's view: significance is never "achieved" because the end of the desire to signify is stasis, silence, and death, and Faulkner is far too interested in the cacophony of unstilled voices (the matter of *As I Lay Dying*) to let things rest there.

Of the novel's speakers, only Darl and Addie seem aware, on some level, of the metaphysical implications Faulkner's presentation of metaphor elicits. After crossing the river at Tull's ford, Darl watches Jewel and Tull search for Cash's lost tools in the water:

From here they do not appear to violate the surface at all; it is as though it had severed them both at a single blow, the two torsos moving with infinitesimal and ludicrous care upon the surface. . . . As though the clotting which is you had dissolved into the myriad original motion, and seeing and hearing themselves blind and deaf; fury in itself quiet with stagnation. Squatting,

Dewey Dell's wet dress shapes for the dead eyes of three blind
men those mammalian ludicrosities which are the horizons and
valleys of this earth.

In Darl's vision, it seems that motion is stopped, that being is "clotted" as
it dissolves into "the myriad original motion," and that there is a kind of
metaphorical and semantic halt to the flow of language, come to rest in a
static scene of men joined in labor to the original, elemental flow of the
universe. But the polarities and shiftings of the passage create a torrent
that breaks through the placid surface of Darl's image. There is a "clotting"
of presence and being, but it is "dissolved" into a "motion"; seeing is blind,
hearing is deaf, fury is quiet; Tull and Jewel seem to move only upon the
surface, yet they are part of the depths. Life and death merge in the scene:
blindness, deafness, clotting, stagnation, and severance are put alongside
motion, origin, and fury; even the regenerative, ludicrous image of the
pregnant Dewey Dell's breasts, as "horizons and valleys of the earth,"
partake of surface and depth simultaneously. The language of the passage
attempts to pin down a moment of simple presence and fails in its un-
stoppable figurative movement; yet this failing, Faulkner strongly suggests,
is all that language can and must do. As Darl's and Addie's complex digres-
sions on the topic tell us, *As I Lay Dying* is about the attempt of a mutable,
evanescent language to define, through the vehicle of figure, what "being"
is, and what in a tale of life-dying it is that signifies.

What signifies is motion. Or, more precisely, what is "meaningful" in
the world of the novel is noise and movement—any disruption of the placid
surface of silence as a text and a journey are born out of jarring incongruities,
comic reversals, or unfulfilled desires. In a concrete sense, as the scene
toward which the entire novel gestures is not portrayed—Addie's burial—
so Faulkner avoids the "death" of his own novel in favor of its ungrounded,
unending "life" of incomplete journeys and fractured relations. "Being" in
As I Lay Dying is a continual outpouring of words that cannot stop short
of deathly silences, as reflected in Addie's crucial metaphor arising from
the contemplation of Anse's name: "I would think about his name until
after a while I could see the word as a shape, a vessel, and I would watch
him liquefy and overflow." But in the moment of motionlessness, the instant when surface and depth are one, where meaning may be contained
in the shape of a word, the word is forgotten and erased: "and then I would
find I had forgotten the name of the jar." To Addie, simple "being" is the
resolution of the terrible rift between language and its ends, yet an equally
terrible acknowledgment of that resolution's impossibility. Addie thinks of
"how words go straight up in a thin line, quick and harmless, and how
terrible doing goes along the earth," of how words seem "like spiders
dangling by their mouths from a beam, swinging and twisting and never
touching." In her conception, and in her role as the embodiment of death,
silence, and the desire for meaningful ends, language is cut off from being;
language does not lead anywhere, as "doing" does, but is just a series of

dangling, shifting relations separated from some other, more vital realm of quiescent action. She does not seem to understand, as does Darl in his severely limited fashion, that "doing" in the world of the text is also a matter of language, or else incommunicable.

In his meditation on sleep and emptiness, Darl reflects upon the incongruity of the position that says words cannot signify, yet words in motion are signs of "being" desiring to signify itself: "In a strange room you must empty yourself for sleep. And before you are emptied for sleep, what are you. And when you are emptied for sleep, you are not. And when you are filled with sleep, you never were. I don't know what I am. I don't know if I am or not." Darl's words ceaselessly shift between "emptiness" and "filling," "is" and "was," "am" and "am not," so that his being in sleep, in past and present, in a strange room is defined, eradicated, confirmed, and denied by the voice through which he speaks. There is no sense of fusion here between word and being, only the continual movement of sliding differences and arc-like polarities, a state of affairs that Darl cannot ultimately accept. The metaphoric pressures of Faulkner's novel ask us to accept this unaccountable proposition within the context of a world that labors under the fiction of significant ends (Cash completing the coffin; Anse getting his teeth) while ever moving toward the unseen significance it never achieves.

The tragicomedy of *As I Lay Dying* employs these semantic ironies and incongruities because they are what give rise to journeys and novels. These disruptions keep sojourners or readers moving in their search for ends and means, conveyed by the meaningful voices of "being" undergoing, and undoing, its own scrutiny. The novel explains, to some extent, Faulkner's repeated hope "to put everything into one sentence—not only the present but the whole past on which it depends and which keeps overtaking the present, second by second." The expressed desire is twofold: to contain all time and motion within a single semantic vessel, and yet, because it must express everything, to create an infinite sentence, one that continually moves and expands, never able to speak the place of its beginning. That language cannot do what Faulkner asks in his fiction is both beside the point and the point, for it is this tension between the unspeakable finality of word or sentence and its striking out toward significance, its embodiment or conveyance of *that* as an overflowing vessel or a broken road, which defines his understanding of language and being. Only by this ironic indirection does Faulkner allow us to take our passage along the crossings and byways of *As I Lay Dying* to the paradoxical revelations of its concealing figurations.

Hemingway: Valor against the Void

Ihab Hassan

Wherein lies the man's achievement in literature, and how does he participate in the life of the avant-garde? Like the Symbolist poets, Hemingway
wants to purify the language of the tribe; like the Dadaists and Surrealists,
he disdains "literature." He values the rigor of art; he abhors untruth.
Hemingway suspects the power of literature to falsify experience, its readiness to mediate vitality and concreteness. "I used to wish . . . ," he writes,
"that I lived in the old days before all the books had been written and all
the stories told for the first time. In those days it was no disgrace to drink
and fight and be a writer too." Superficially, Hemingway objects to gentility. On a deeper level, he distrusts the accretions of language.

Hemingway's distrust of language has many guises. His vocabulary is
perhaps the smallest of any major novelist. To speak is to lie, Burroughs
avers; this is fanatic. Hemingway is merely taciturn; he advises curtness in
feeling, in action. He emulates the clipped speech of the English upper
classes and of the laconic Westerner. The few words he imports from foreign
languages tend to be simple, even obscene; the essential task is to confront
nada with *cojones*. For Hemingway, true obscenity is something else. It can
be described as "unsoundness in abstract conversation or, indeed, any
other metaphysical tendency in speech." Knowing that the currency of
words has been inflated by fustian or mendacity, that the connotations of
words have been counterfeited, he seeks new values for language in slang,
in fact, in understatement.

Slang is a colorful form of reticence. It is metaphor in the process of
becoming cliché. Alive, it refers to concrete situations; dead, it serves as
impersonal response. Moreover, slang shuns sophistication as it shuns
loquacity. It is not only metaphor or cliché, but also protest. It issues from

From *The Dismemberment of Orpheus*. 2d ed. © 1971, 1982 by Ihab Hassan. The University
of Wisconsin Press, 1982.

the underground of fiction. Fact, on the other hand, speaks on behalf of reality, and challenges the imagination to a keener effort. In his interview with George Plimpton, Hemingway states that the *Racing Form* represents "the true Art of Fiction." This statement, which may suggest the current technique of the "non-fiction novel," actually pleads for constructionism. Hemingway makes his point clear: "From things that have happened and from things as they exist and from all things that you know and those you cannot know, you make something through your invention that is not a representation but a whole new thing truer than anything true and alive, and you make it alive, and if you make it well enough, you give it immortality." On fact, the house of fiction stands; without it, the house collapses in a rubble of sentiment. Understatement, by refusing to exceed the authority of language to interpret fact, helps to keep the edifice spare. Hemingway's understatement stems from a private conviction that good things deserve to remain unexpressed; it ends by serving an artistic purpose. Understatement requires omission, and the art of omission is one that he learns from the great Impressionist painters, Cézanne particularly. Referring to his early years in Paris, Hemingway speaks of his "new theory that you could omit anything if you knew that you omitted and the omitted part would strengthen the story and make people feel something more than they understood." Omission compels participation. Thus the house of fiction, with its empty spaces, is finally inhabited.

But slang, fact, and understatement, as verbal modes, are equivocal. They appear to harden the surface of language; at first, they seem techniques of semantic restraint or even absence. They produce a stillness. Yet their end is to create meaning; they finally function as techniques of semantic presence. Such is the duplicity of silence in Hemingway's fiction. Literature creates itself in self-opposition, and style evolves into a pure anti-style.

The mannerisms of Hemingway's anti-style are only too memorable. Repetitions of word and phrase, suggested by the rhythmic experiments of Gertrude Stein, insinuate their significance precisely because they avoid expansion and customary elaboration. Substantives carry the burden of his statements, and make all analysis superfluous. The conjunctive "and," strung on end, gives equal weight to different parts of a period that moves without syntactic modulation. The little that stands before us stands sharply, brilliantly present; the rest is ruthlessly banished. Often, action replaces speech; thought and feeling remain implicit. As Harry Levin puts it, "the act, no sooner done than said, becomes simultaneous with the word, no sooner said than felt." We are in the huge and abrupt present, given to us without connectives or transitions. If judgments must be made, they can be made ironically, and Hemingway's irony can be cruel and bitter.

These celebrated traits are seldom viewed in the perspective of anti-literature. The clue comes from Sartre who saw in the chopped-up, discontinuous style of Camus's *The Stranger* the form of an absurd vision. The same may be said of Sartre's own *Nausea* as of Hemingway's *In Our Time*.

The simple accretion of invariable units, the succession of discrete events, defy synthesis. We are indeed close to the assumption of nonsense. For nonsense depends on verbal distinctness and precision. "Nonsense . . . ," Elizabeth Sewell says, "will have to concentrate on the divisibility of its material into ones, units from which a universe can be built. This universe, however, must never be more that the sum of its parts, and must never fuse into some all-embracing whole which cannot be broken down again into the original ones." Fastidious and disjunctive, nonsense devises its own structures, abolishing reference, approaching number. Toward these structures, the anti-style of Hemingway often moves without forfeiting its tragic reference. Its rigor, terseness, and repetitions, its intractable concreteness and vast omissions, resist rhetoric, resist even statement, and discourage the mind from habitual closures. The style emerges from silence and tends toward it again by a process of exclusion; in between, it defies insanity.

Style engages human conduct, and conduct engages fate. Hemingway, we know, abhors the cant of ideology; his ethic is elementary. If you "feel good" after an action, you have acted morally. Morality, then, is a subjective response; but it is the response of one who accepts a code of skill and courage, and knows that death exposes the shabbiness of human endeavor. This difficult code offers few comforts and relies on fewer presuppositions. It leaves out much of what history has bequeathed to us of philosophy and religion. The radical skepticism of Hemingway is backed only by what a man truly possesses: his flesh, the home of his morality. As a result of this reductive ethic, the characters of Hemingway are forced to be tough; they avoid all unnecessary responses to the world around them. But they also exact from themselves the extreme response when circumstances warrant it: speechless violence. In the moment of violence, Frederick J. Hoffman shows in *The Mortal No,* men function neither as rational nor as historical creatures; they put themselves beyond humanity.

This is why the ethic of Hemingway's characters is not only reductive but also solitary. What they endure, they can never share with others. Existentially, they remain alone; they find momentary communion only in a dangerous ritual. Always, they disengage themselves from the complexities of human relations, and simplify their social existence to the primary functions of the body. "The only thing that could spoil a day was people," Hemingway writes. "People were always the limiters of happiness except for the very few that were as good as spring itself." In eating and drinking, in love-making, in combat, his heroes silence the shrill demands of civilization, and elude the mind's perversity and the heart's deceit. Their epicureanism is a search for truth, and truth in their day has a withering touch. Truth finds itself by exclusion though in Rabelais's lustier day it offered to devour the world entire.

When we exclude enough, we are left with nothing, *nada*. This, and not physical death, is the destiny of Hemingway's heroes. As a symbol of non-being, of the void, of life's ineluctable emptiness, death chills the spine of the bravest: there is no answer to it but suicide. The old fisherman, Santiago, thinks that "man can be destroyed but not defeated." Yet man can indeed be defeated, as the earlier work of Hemingway repeatedly shows. The defeated are not merely tough; they are embodiments of oblivion. Still, even the defeated may possess dignity. The old man in "A Clean Well-Lighted Place" has failed in his attempt at suicide, but remains a "clean old man." The old waiter who parodies the Lord's Prayer by reciting "Our nada who art in nada, nada be thy name" understands his client; for he too has excluded all but light and cleanliness from his life. Exclusion is a principle of negation, and as Freud has taught us, the very words "No" and "Not" serve the powers of Thanatos in subtle ways. Exclusion finally leads to death-in-life, the fate of Hemingway's unredeemed. Theirs is the stillness we hear beneath the finicky language.

Yet it is perverse to see only the emptiness of Hemingway's world. In its lucid spaces, a vision of archetypal unity reigns. Opposite forces obey a common destiny; enemies discover their deeper identity; the hunter and the hunted merge. The matador plunges his sword, and for an instant in eternity, man and beast are the same. This is the moment of truth, and it serves Hemingway as symbol of the unity which underlies both love and death. His fatalism, his tolerance of bloodshed, his stoical reserve before the malice of creation, betray a sacramental attitude that transcends any personal fate. Though man is doomed to stand and struggle alone, he may carry his initiative, "push his luck," too far; he may transgress by ignoring the tacit harmonies of the universe. The process of nature continues, heedless of human effort, like the Gulf Stream: "the palm fronds of our victories, the worn light bulbs of our discoveries and the empty condoms of our great loves float with no significance against one single, lasting thing—the stream." Suddenly, we understand those innumerable, small ceremonies of magical penance and propitiation the Hemingway's heroes constantly perform: they are secret invocations of Being at its source. His redeemed characters know that the universe is not Naught but One. And they all cast, like one man, a single shadow across death, the unifier of all our tales. Hemingway himself says "all stories, if continued far enough, end in death, and he is no true storyteller who would keep that from you." The story rests in silence.

Silence serves as a metaphor of Hemingway's fiction though his fiction is unsilent. In 1926, Hemingway says to Samuel Putnam that he wants to "strip language clean, to lay it bare down to the bone." A year earlier, he realizes that aim in *In Our Time.*

The collection begins with a scream: "The strange thing was, he said, how they screamed every night at midnight. I do not know why they screamed at that time. We were in the harbor and they were all on the pier and at midnight they started screaming. We used to turn the searchlight on them to quiet them." The scream and the beam, darkness and clarity: therein lies the achievement of Hemingway's style. The same sketch ends with the image of mules, their forelegs broken, dumped in the shallow bay. The author remarks, "It was all a pleasant business. My word yes a most pleasant business." Then comes the story "Indian Camp." Young Nick Adams watches his father perform a caesarian operation on an Indian woman, and sees the body of her husband in the upper bunk, razor still in hand, his throat cut from ear to ear. The story resolves itself in an incantation of repeated sounds in distinct images.

> They were seated in the boat, Nick in the stern, his father rowing. The sun was coming up over the hills. As bass jumped, making a circle in the water, Nick trailed his hand in the water. It felt warm in the sharp chill of the morning.
>   In the early morning on the lake sitting in the stern of the boat with his father rowing, he felt quite sure that he would never die.

The initiation to birth and death, the vitality of nature, the reliance on the father, the deceptions of the self, remain purely implicit in discrete sensations, and in the magic reiteration of certain words, "boat," "father," "morning," "water." This is the Hemingway scene.

The pointillism of the scene can be more obvious. In "Cat in the Rain," for instance, Hemingway writes:

> Italians came from a long way off to look at the war monument. It was made of bronze and glistened in the rain. It was raining. The rain dripped from the palm trees. Water stood in pools on the gravel paths. The sea broke in a long line in the rain and slipped back down the beach to come up and break again in a long line in the rain. The motor cars were gone from the square by the war monument. Across the square in the doorway of the cafe a waiter stood looking out at the empty square.

This is a scene painted by an Impressionist. The eye provides the frame; the mind provides the transitions; the beholder interprets the pattern. Hemingway controls our perceptions by a careful disposition of lacunae. Each event seems to occur independently; each seems coeval with all other events. The effect is abrupt because it is pristine; a great blankness lies behind it.

Brusqueness also conveys the rush of action. "The Battler" begins with a breakman throwing Nick Adams off a moving freight train. Nick walks up to a solitary figure huddled by a camp fire:

> "Hello!" Nick said.
> The man looked up.
> "Where did you get the shiner?" he said.

This is how people meet in a world where violence seldom has antecedents. The slang term is apt; the speaker is a mad prize fighter whose life may be read in his face: "It was like putty in color. Dead looking in the firelight." Ravaged by publicity more than by blows, the battler roams no-man's land, loathing everyone. His sole attendant is a mannerly Negro who hits him with a blackjack whenever he turns dangerous. This emptiness, common to so many characters of Hemingway, affects another battler, Krebs, the veteran in "Soldier's Home." "Krebs acquired the nausea in regard to experience that is the result of untruth," the author succinctly explains. Krebs loves no one, not even his mother; his single passion is to avoid complications. Both battlers are anomic creatures, their lives delimited at one end by violence and at the other by the void.

Even in that perfect idyl, "Big Two-Hearted River," the hero constantly senses the contingencies of the void. Nick feels happy in the ritual simplifications of his fishing trip, and he is alone. "He felt he had left everything behind, the need for thinking, the need to write, other needs. It was all back of him." He makes camp: "Now things were done. There had been this to do. Now it was done. It had been a hard trip. He was very tired. That was done. He had made his camp. He was settled. Nothing could touch him. It was a good place to camp. He was there, in the good place." These rhythms suggest a ceremony of exorcism, as Malcolm Cowley has noted; they are the feelings of a happy man hanging on to happiness by the skin of his teeth. A strange threat chokes the mind, discovering thereby its verbal equivalent of silence. But the specific nature of the threat is deleted from the story; the powers of darkness emerge only in a symbol of the greatest reticence, the swamp. "In the swamp the banks were bare, the big cedars came together overhead, the sun did not come through, except in patches; in the fast deep water, in the half light, the fishing would be tragic. In the swamp fishing was a tragic adventure. Nick did not want it. He did not want to go down the stream any further today."

The cold swamp encircles *In Our Time*. Yet the stories have the ring of a bell heard over the frozen air. Between their pure sound, the vignettes flash across the eye once and are never forgotten. The garden at Mons where the Germans get potted as they climb over the wall; the absolutely perfect barricade jammed across an enemy bridge; the six cabinet ministers shot at half past six; Maera lying still, face in the sand, while the bull's horn gores him repeatedly; and Nick, hit in the spine, propped against a church—all represent the same awful moment. Story and vignette, sound and sight, blend perfectly, enclosed by the same deep stillness. It is the stillness of terrible truth, and it helps to make the collection the best written by an American in our century.

Hemingway sees life as he sees art: a process of laying bare to the bone. Men strip their illusions as they must shed their flesh. The boy who learns of the death, and of the dishonesty, of his father in "My Old Man," concludes: "Seems like when they get started they don't leave a guy nothing." "They" are agents of the withering truth, and their influence prevails in Hemingway's two best novels, *The Sun Also Rises* and *A Farewell to Arms*.

The Sun Also Rises persists as our paradigm of radical loss. The sun rises on characters, like Jake Barnes, who need to sleep with electric lights switched on six months of the year, rises and sets and rises again without dispelling the dark. In this wasteland, the Fisher King is fated. Were his physical wound to heal miraculously, nothing would really change. "Oh Jake . . . we could have had such a damned good time together," Brett says at the end, and Jake, who knows better, replies, "Yes. . . . Isn't it pretty to think so?" Hemingway compresses the terror of his novel into that ironic question. The terror has no reason and no name; it is simply the presence of an absence; and the only recourse of the characters is to discover a rhythm, a style, of endurance. For the best among them, like Romero, there is grace under pressure, which may be the only grace man can ever know.

The novel is predictably circular in structure; we end to begin again. The characters also form themselves in a circle about the hollow center, Lady Brett Ashley, her slouched hat hiding an exquisite despair. The contrast is between Robert Cohn, shabby romantic in a purple land (W. H. Hudson's), and Jake Barnes, maimed stoic and ironist of the night. In this parable of modern love, whores dance with homosexuals, and the impotence of the hero matches the heroine's nymphomania. The quality of Book One is the quality of a nightmare barely kept in abeyance. "It is awfully easy to be hard-boiled about everything in the day time, but at night is another thing," Barnes says in a cold sweat.

In Book Two, fishing and bull-fighting deflect the dread. Brett goes off to San Sebastian with Cohn; Barnes and Bill Gorton go off fishing in the Burguete. The intricacies of love are hushed, the urgencies of worship muted. Barnes tries to pray in a Spanish church: "and as all the time I was kneeling with my forehead on the wood in front of me . . . I was a little ashamed, and regretted that I was such a rotten Catholic, but realized there was nothing I could do about it." The cold high country near Roncevaux, where Roland once gave his life for God and Emperor and the Twelve Peers, beckons; there the trout swim in clear streams. "I shut my eyes," Jake says. "It felt good lying on the ground."

Down on the lower ground, at Pamplona, the society of spiritual cripples waits to receive life from the Feria of San Fermin. The passion they lack they hope to find as *aficionados* (*afición* also means passion) of the ring. By the time the feria is over, Brett has robbed all the men around her of their manhood. Romero stands alone. Can she redeem herself in him? Will she only bring his ruin? Romero has innocence, courage, and grace. His knowledge is from another time, another place. He understands that the bull is his equal, perhaps his other self: "his left shoulder went forward between the horns as the sword went through it, and for just an instant he and the bull were one. . . . Then the figure was broken." He can pay homage to Brett, in the ring, without diminishing himself. But when he offers her the bull's ear, she forgets it in the drawer of a bed-table. There can be no true meeting of Brett and Romero, as there can be none between Brett and Barnes. The feria turns into a bad dream; the characters disperse.

The reducing cycle nears completion in Book Three. Brett decides "not to be a bitch," and releases Romero. "It's a sort of what we have instead of God," she explains to Jake who has hurried to her side in Madrid. In his view, Brett's sacrifice is genuine because she has paid. "You paid some way for everything that was any good. . . . Either you paid by learning about them, or by experience, or by taking chances, or by money," Jake believes. Everyone pays. Some, like old Count Mippipopolous, pay gallantly; others pay badly. But payment is always reduction, divestment; at the end, the skin shrinks tighter on the skeleton. The best lay down their life against death, and no one can offer to pay more. Such is Romero who functions in the novel more as a symbol than as a character. His existence incarnates the crucial insight of *The Sun Also Rises:* only in confrontation with death does life acquire meaning and lose its terror. In this stark paradox, terror is transcended.

The keynote of *A Farewell to Arms* is not terror but doom. The world breaks everyone impartially, and death falls on the earth like a steady rain. Death comes in war, "suddenly and unreasonably"; and it comes in peace to those who would give birth: "Poor, poor dear Cat. And this was the price you paid for sleeping together. . . . This is what people got for loving each other." Nature finds its final unity in decay.

But there is also the unity of love. Within the great circle of decay, two lovers strive to keep intact: "there's only us two and in the world there's all the rest of them. If anything comes between us we're gone and then they have us," Catherine says to Frederic Henry. There are not two, there is only one. For as Catherine goes on to say: "There isn't any me any more. Just what you want." But the circle of decay tightens. There is no place really "to drop the war," as Catherine reminds Frederic; their "separate peace" in Switzerland is only part of a greater biological war. "You'll fight before you'll marry," Nurse Fergus tells the lovers. "You'll die then. Fight or die. That's what people do. They don't marry." Catherine, of course, dies. Love also finds its unity in doom.

In the Italian mountains, "the picturesque front," the war seems to mark an end to history. "Perhaps wars weren't won any more," Henry wonders. "Maybe they went on forever." It is more certain that the war confutes the collective experience of mankind. In a famous passage, Henry says:

> I was always embarrassed by the words sacred, glorious, and sacrifice and the expression in vain. . . . There were many words that you could not stand to hear and finally only the names of places had dignity. Certain numbers were the same way and certain dates and these with the names of places were all you could say and have them mean anything. Abstract words such as glory, honor, courage, or hallow were obscene beside the concrete names of villages, the numbers of roads, the names of rivers, the numbers of regiments and the dates.

Universal violence compels language to be mute; the public and the private fates of characters converge. The novel ends fittingly with an apocalyptic image. Frederic Henry recalls a log crawling with ants that he had thrown into a camp fire. "I remember thinking at the time," he says, "that it was the end of the world and a splendid chance to be a messiah and lift the log off the fire and throw it out where the ants could get off on to the ground." But the messiah only steams the ants with whiskey and they perish.

Yet *A Farewell to Arms* is richer than its macabre insistencies. Rinaldi, Ferguson, the army priest, the barman at Stresa, all move with stringent, with stubborn life. Catherine Barkley, who appears stilted, oddly unreal, finally forces her hidden hysteria upon our consciousness, and in death acquires dignity. Henry remains the Hemingway hero, laconic and inevitable as tragedy. But the novel reminds us that, for Hemingway, country is more ample than people. The novel breathes the seasons; it gives the firm touch of places. We see the pebbles white in the sun, and the blue water moving swiftly in the channels. We shiver when the weather turns cold at night and the rain commences to fall the next day. Still, the narrowness of death ends by pinching our response. Like Frederic Henry, lying wounded in an ambulance, we feel the blood of a dead soldier drip as "from an icicle after the sun has gone." It drips always on the same spot of our skin.

The great phase of Hemingway's art closes with *A Farewell to Arms*. The stories of *Men without Women*, unlike some earlier pieces, cannot be charged with "the kinetographic fallacy" which Carlos Baker defines as "the supposition that we can get the best art by an absolutely true description of what takes place in observed action." But their depth is sometimes attained at a price: Hemingway loses the rigor of omission and exposes his sentimentality. The collection, nevertheless, contains such classic fictions as "The Undefeated." Hemingway still knows that words belong to the public domain; the hidden world requires a subliminal language. This is the language that conveys evil in "The Killers." It is also the language of the death of love in "Hills Like White Elephants":

> "They look like white elephants," she said.
> "I've never seen one," the man drank his beer.
> "No, you wouldn't have."

This dialogue may have been composed by Samuel Beckett. Here it is again, in the incredible opening sentence of "In Another Country": "In the fall the war was always there, but we did not go to it any more." The threat of oblivion presses syntax into ineluctable shape. The narrator of "Now I Lay Me" lies in the dark listening to silk-worms chewing; he dares not close his eyes lest his soul depart. The predicament of Hemingway is much the same: he dare no more ignore than articulate the dark. The tension of the void bestills his art.

Silence is not only a metaphor of Hemingway's work; it is also the source of its formal excellence, its integrity. He begins to lose his virtue, his *areté*, in the thirties and never recovers it completely. Edmund Wilson is probably right in saying that Hemingway succumbs to "deliberate self-drugging" in the period. The opium of the people may be identified as sex, bread, or religion, as Mr. Frazer bitterly reflects in "The Nun, the Gambler, and the Radio." But what is the opium of Mr. Frazer himself who suffers from "the horrors"? In lieu of the gambler's courage or the nun's faith, it is a radio whispering thoughtlessness in the dark.

Winner Take Nothing, which contains that story, contains others that reveal the grotesqueness of American life. The huge whores in "The Light of the World," the religious fanatic who asks to be castrated in "God Rest You, Merry Gentlemen," the absurd tourists in "Homage to Switzerland," the old French couple struggling through Prohibition in "Wine of Wyoming," express the dislocations of spirit when the times are out of joint. Hemingway forces himself to acknowledge the social fact, and admits reluctantly the sense of community. A new poignancy, foreign to his best work, unsettles the stories; a kind of disgust wavers between society and self. When Hemingway returns to his true form in "A Clean Well-Lighted Place" or "A Way You'll Never Be," the style contracts again and sings madly. The latter story portrays Nick Adams in a state of shell shock; he "can't sleep without a light of some sort." "That's all I have now," he explains to a fellow officer. The next moment, Nick rants about locusts, and silently babbles: "And there was Gaby Delys, oddly enough, with feathers on; you called me baby doll a year ago tadada you said that I was rather nice to know tadada with feathers on, with feathers off." This is Hemingway still inward with his terror, a terror he can still overcome, artistically, in the unflawed "The Short, Happy Life of Francis Macomber."

But the embarrassing evidence against him accrues. When *To Have and Have Not* appears in 1937, critics on the Left hail it as proof of Hemingway's conversion to the gospel according to Marx. The social question implied by the main narrative is this: how does a brave man, Harry Morgan, come to be an outlaw? The subplots of the novel are glutinous, and they concern a number of sordid and arbitrary figures from the worlds of politics, finance, entertainment, and literature, whose soft corruption contrasts with the hero's violence. Needless to say, the reader sees only Harry Morgan.

Morgan fits D. H. Lawrence's image of the American, "hard, isolate, stoic, and a killer." His big blonde wife, Marie, can also testify to his ithyphallic character. Morgan relates to no one though he remains an excellent provider for his family. He acts swiftly, and his actions are part of no moral or political scheme. It is a question of survival, and of *cojones.* Mean, pitiless to others as he is toward himself, he stands in nature rather than in civilization. The fact that men are deprived of their dignity by the Depression, or that the Conchs are starved out of the Florida Keys to make room for tourists, or that the veterans are abandoned by the government to perish in a hurricane, hardly seems relevant to his buccaneer's outlook.

Hemingway evades these implications of his character. Throughout the novel, the reader feels that Morgan struggles heroically to escape from an image imposed on him by the ethos of the times. "They don't give you any choice *now* [italics mine]," Morgan says. Hemingway knows very well "they" never did. And Morgan knows it too. When one of the Cuban gangsters lectures him on the necessity of terrorism in the revolution, Morgan silently fumes:

> F—— his revolution. To help the working man he robs a bank and kills a fellow works with him and then kills that poor damned Albert that never did any harm. That's a working man he kills. With a family. . . . The hell with their revolutions.

The inevitable showdown comes. The Cubans are all killed single-handedly; Harry Morgan lies on the cockpit floor in a pool of his own blood. He mutters in delirium the famous lines: "One man alone ain't got. No man alone now. . . . No matter how a man alone ain't got no bloody f——ing chance." Hemingway adds: "He shut his eyes. It had taken him a long time to get it out and it had taken him all his life to learn it." It may also take the reader a lifetime to believe it. Morgan's bloody conversion seems less convincing than contrition wrested from the jaws of death in some obscure Jacobean play. What Morgan lacks at the end is not the strength of "mortal interdebtedness," but simply the use of both his arms. *To Have and Have Not* fails because the essential vision of Hemingway clashes in it with an ideology felt merely as sentiment. The form of the novel reflects the strain as the narrative attempts to expand its focus, change its ground, and alter its point of view egregiously.

The same clash is willfully resolved in the play, *The Fifth Column;* its hero chooses justice rather than love. As a counter-espionage agent, Philip Rawlings is barely credible, and his girl, Dorothy, develops merely as a type. What can she offer but love and sex, and that, as Philip states, is "a commodity you shouldn't pay too high a price for." Philip himself enjoys a dual personality. During the day he is hard, breezy, or efficient, as the Loyalist cause may require. At night he is tender, vulnerable, and suffers from the "horrororous," or "super-horrors." At bottom, he is still the hysterical Hemingway hero, holding on to himself for dear sanity. But the tension in Philip's life is external. He confronts no real choices, and his mistress serves mainly as an idea, a fleshless seduction. As Hemingway himself puts it in the preface, "There is a girl in it [the play] named Dorothy but her name might also have been Nostalgia." Thus melodrama resolves itself in allegory.

For Whom the Bell Tolls can be read more seriously. It is the most traditional of Hemingway's novels, the most novelistic. It seeks to give violence a context, assign to it a public motive. From the title, which argues after John Donne that no man is an island entire of itself, to the ending, which denies Jordan the relief of suicide so long as he possesses enough life to serve others, the book declares itself for human solidarity. In war, men rid themselves of the self. Even the renegade Pablo ends his desertion because his loneliness becomes insupportable. Love itself ceases to be entirely personal; Jordan says to Maria, "I love thee as I love liberty and dignity and the rights of all men to work and not to be hungry." And at the headquarters of the International Brigade in Madrid, Jordan recalls the feeling of light coming through the great windows of Chartres Cathedral.

Yet, once again, the action of the novel complicates, even undercuts, its avowed theme. The Communists who gossip and wrangle at Gaylord's stymie the military efforts of the Republic. The most terrifying scene in the novel shows Pablo at work, forcing the village fascists to run a gauntlet of drunken peasants armed with hooks and flails. And Jordan—who wonders how many true fascists are among all the men he has killed—is left at the end of the novel with Lieutenant Berrendo, a careful and humane officer, in the sights of his machine gun. The bridge is destroyed, but the fascists win the war.

Indeed, the closer we move to the center of the novel, the more familiar becomes the Hemingway pattern. Jordan is no Marxist. "You believe in Life, Liberty, and the Pursuit of Happiness. Don't ever kid yourself with too much dialectics," he admonishes himself. He believes that people ought to be left alone. He wants love to clear the mind of revolutionary and patriotic clichés. "Continence is the foe of heresy," he concludes. He is chary of thought: "Turn off the thinking now," he says; "Don't lie to yourself. . . . Nor make up literature about it. You have been tainted with it for a long time now." In the face of danger, Jordan calls on his grandfather, a guerrilla hero of the American Civil War—the father is a "coward" who shoots himself! Gradually, the personal motive displaces the rest; we are again alone, in the noisome presence of death which Pilar describes so that none can ever forget.

At the very center of the novel, love and death fuse in the timeless present. Maria becomes indistinguishable from Robert. "Can you not feel my heart be your heart?" she asks him, and he replies, "Yes, there is no difference." The life of both is always "Now, *ahora, maintenant, heute.*" The present, created by love and death, devours all memory and circumstance. The present explodes in orgasm: "They were having now and before and always and now and now and now. Oh, now, now, now, the only now, and above all now, and there is no other now but thou now and now is thy prophet . . . one only one, there is no other one but now, one, going now, rising now, leaving now, wheeling now, soaring now, away now, all the way now, all of all the way now; one and one is one, is one, is one, is one, is still one, is still one." In this passage, which expresses purely, absurdly, the unitary vision of Hemingway, style moves toward anti-style, toward silence, toward the point around which the novel turns and turns and turns again. The first and last sentences of the novel circle and meet on the pine-needled floor of the forest on which Robert Jordan loves and dies.

Despite its amplitude of character, of incident, despite its earthy setting and available reference, *For Whom the Bell Tolls* clings to Hemingway's original vision. Jordan has conquered his nightmares and can sleep under the stars. But his word still owes fealty to death. If he moves in that world with a confidence, a naïveté, that Barnes or Henry might envy, it is because

Jordan can act: he can kill. The novel becomes trivial or prolix whenever it becomes explicit; the thoughts of Jordan can be ludicrous. Yet there is no contradiction in the art of this fiction, only redundance, only sentimental superfluity.

Across the River and into the Trees usually sends the critics howling. It is a bitter novel, sadly and bitterly uncontrolled. The obsessions of Hemingway's life now disrupt his art, and his reductive tendencies frankly reveal themselves in a preparation for death. Colonel Cantwell waits for a fatal heart attack as his experience contracts around him. "Everything is much smaller when you are older," he says. He can only care for those mutilated by life: "you only felt true tenderness and love for those who had been there and had received the castigation that everyone receives who goes there long enough." The cutting edge can still be felt. "Every day is a disillusion," Renata says; and Cantwell answers: "No. Every day is a new and fine illusion. But you can cut out everything phony about the illusion as though you would cut it with a straight-edge razor." And so Cantwell mocks and rails against the world with his angry and shriveled heart, and seeks in vain to purge his anger in love. But his true solace is the void. As he lies in bed beside Renata, he tries to think of nothing, "as he had thought of nothing so many times in so many places." Instead of ecstasy, he finally draws "sleep's other brother." Everything Hemingway knows about silence appears in the novel, defaced by self-pity and shoddy rage. The language buckles under pathology.

The last stand of Hemingway, in *The Old Man and the Sea*, takes the form of a parable, a fantasy really, of old age. Santiago is a gaunt old man, deprived, alone. The sail of his skiff is patched with flour sacks and looks like a "flag of permanent defeat." His inner life is limited to stark dreams: "He only dreamed of places now and of the lions on the beach." Eating bores him; a water bottle sustains him. Talking is superfluous at sea and Santiago respects the code, talking rarely to himself. *La mar* stands as the original, fertile silence. Reduction now leads to this: a "strange old man," an image of the Self which does not think but only endures.

Santiago has a single fate, and it is the big fish, his Other Self. He pities the great marlin, he joins it: "His [the marlin's] choice had been to stay in the deep dark water far out beyond all snares and traps and treacheries. My choice was to go there to find him beyond all people. Beyond all people in the world. Now we are joined together and have been since noon. And no one to help either of us." The fish and Santiago's two lacerated hands make three brothers, a trinity of one. Three sunrises witness the unendurable struggle. "Come on and kill me," Santiago breathes at the end. "I do not care who kills who." The fish is finally strapped to the skiff, its dead eye like the eye of a "saint in a procession," and the passion of the fish is shared by the man as the sharks begin to hit its noble body. Santiago returns to his hut alone, shouldering the mast uphill; he sleeps on his face, arms outstretched, palms turned up. There is only the boy, Manolin, to cry over the bleeding hands of Santiago asleep. A woman tourist, looking at the great skeleton on the beach, says: "I didn't know sharks had such beautifully formed tails." Irony within irony: sharks are a spineless specie.

The fable is elemental, the scene stripped. A single, heroic protagonist stands before us. His tragedy seems to be the classic tragedy of transgression. Santiago fears that he has gone out too far and violated his "luck." His sacramental sense prompts him to confess: "I am glad we do not have to try to kill the stars." Clearly, Hemingway assays the simplest, the most universal, statement of the human condition. Where, then, is his error?

Is it not rather a failure of nerve? Hemingway retracts from a limit of experience he had previously attained, from a deeper knowledge of violence and evil. He composes a noble fantasy of old age after tasting from the bitter cup of Lear. The sharks devour the fish and defeat Santiago —the sharks out there in the sea. Their evil seems entirely external. Yet Hemingway knows that sharks also inhabit the mind. If the agents of destruction are merely adventitious, the fate of man is merely absurd. Yet Hemingway knows that violence engages both freedom and necessity, that true terror corresponds to a void within. There is only a hint of this in *The Old Man and the Sea*. Here is how the first shark, a terrifying Mako, appears: "The shark was no accident. He had come up from deep down in the water as the dark cloud of blood had settled and dispersed in the mile deep sea. He had come up so fast and absolutely without caution that he broke the surface of the blue water and was in the sun." Hemingway, however, loses the hint. The language falters, and instead of the ineluctable recognition, we get words such as these:

> It is silly to hope, he thought. Besides, I believe it is a sin. Do not think about sin, he thought. There are enough problems now without sin. Also I have no understanding of it.
>
> I have no understanding of it and I am not sure that I believe in it. Perhaps it was a sin to kill the fish. I suppose it was even though I did it to keep me alive and feed many people. But then everything is a sin. Do not think about sin. It is much too late for that and there are people who are paid to do it. Let them think about it.

And later, when the fish is half-ravaged: " 'Half-fish,' he said. 'Fish that you were. I am sorry that I went too far out. I ruined us both. But we have killed many sharks, you and I, and ruined many others. How many did you ever kill, old fish? You do not have that spear on you for nothing.' " Language becomes a mannerism; silence becomes a parody of itself. The condition of the old Cuban fisherman, splendid as he is, fails to carry the symbolic burden of the human condition. The style still holds back, though it has little to withhold.

The black paradox of Ernest Hemingway remains the same: he can never stray far from the reticence of death, madness, and the void without betraying his vision. Critics have speculated about the "fourth" and "fifth" dimensions that Hemingway believes can be given to prose fiction. They have suggested the dimensions of death, transcendence, and the mystic present. Silence, which bears some relation to these topics, may be conceived as an added dimension to his prose. In that dimension, the exclusive rage and unitary obsession of Hemingway find their best expression.

Yet there is some infirmity, perhaps, in that silence, and it must be acknowledged. It disguises a deliberate restriction of feelings, the tightness of holding tight. Philip Young, we know, relates this attitude to the trauma of Hemingway's wound at Fossalta and to a subsequent neurosis identified by Fenichel as "primitivation." Everything must be simplified. Everything must be simplified and repeated. During his life span, Hemingway doubles up on his tracks across three continents to conquer the fright of being. His compulsion to repeat turns the later work into a parody of the earlier.

We need not speculate on the disease of genius. Whatever ravages Hemingway's life, whatever insanity finds its way to the end, he still manages to create a unique literary style, and manages to create a style of survival that compels envy and emulation the world over. He offers also a parable of the literary imagination nearing the end of its tether, of consciousness struggling against the nihilism that consciousness alone can engender. In his work, literary statement approaches the edge; language implies the abolition of statement. A minimal assertion holds the world of Hemingway together against madness. We are prepared for Kafka. We can see how literature begins to purify itself valiantly in modern acknowledgement of an old void. Naked, Orpheus enters the great, empty spaces of violence.

Ernest Hemingway:
The Meaning of Style

John Graham

Hemingway, in the opening pages of *Death in the Afternoon*, insists that he, his characters, and ultimately, his readers be aware of the active existence of persons, things, and actions. Too often, however, critics seem to accept this as meaning simply the accumulation of concrete details by a sensitive observer. Furthermore, the vitality of Hemingway's novels has been attributed to a number of factors ranging from his plots and characters to his simplicity of theme and control of language. These elements in their many aspects are, of course, contributory but are subordinate to a more constant cause: the active presentation of subject and object (observer and thing observed) and the continuous, intimate, and conscious relationship between subject and object. The characters' conscious reception of present fact (not judgment of or even response to fact) is so pervasive in Hemingway's novels that it appears to be a mode of thought for Hemingway, rather than a conscious artistic device. It is in this constant activity of sensory perception of active objects, and, still more important, in the subjects' awareness of relationship to these objects that the vitality of the writing is found.

The total effect of activity in the novels is gained by a simplicity of plot, a directness of human relations, and a basic impermanence of situation. The major circumstances are keynoted by impermanency: the hero is in a foreign land or, in the case of Santiago of *The Old Man and the Sea*, a foreign element. No matter how familiar the protagonist may be with the place, he is not expected to settle there. The characters "use" countries, hotels, cafes, and houses, but there is never a real act of possession. The reader waits for the next move. The main plot is dominated by violence of war, combat and/or erratic movement from place to place; the characters reflect these highly unstable conditions by their attention on the immediate

From *Ernest Hemingway*. © 1973 by McGraw-Hill, Inc.

present and by their lack of demand on the future. They are active, direct and, one might argue, uncomplicated people with an almost fatalistic acceptance of life. Since they are so uncomplicated in their relations and attitudes, more of a burden falls on the "working out" of the action if the novel is not to die for lack of physical, emotional, or intellectual life.

These elements of circumstance, plot, and character achieve their effects of total vitality cumulatively rather than constantly. On the other hand, it is the continuous and aware relation of active subjects and objects that vivifies the novel at all times. By the nature of Hemingway's plot and characters, and his idea of conflict, the "movement" of this relation takes on added importance since, because of its pervasiveness, it sustains the vitality, giving more flexibility in the presentation of the other elements. Without going into extended detail, the plots of the novels are certainly no more vivid, often less so, than thousands of others. While the subject is often war or physical combat, which by their very nature are intensively active, such subjects, even when coupled with credible participants, do not guarantee life but simply physical exercise. The characters may fade in and out of the action, emotionally alert but divorced from the source of the emotion. Hemingway, with the possible exception of some ruminations of Robert Jordan in *For Whom the Bell Tolls*, does not permit his characters to retreat so far from the facts of their existence that the reader concentrates on the emotion rather than on the motivating force.

A second negative point concerning the importance of this sustaining element of relation with the active concrete is the lack of development of Hemingway's characters. In a surprisingly brief time, Hemingway establishes character; in the first few chapters the reader learns all he is to know about the central actors, and these actors are as knowing about each other as they are ever to be. The action and relations which follow serve only as illustrative incidents which fix more firmly what was openly presented and readily grasped many pages before. There is nothing new to learn; even with the various crises, the characters simply observe. While they seem to understand what they do and what goes on about them, they never seem to assimilate this knowledge and, if they react, they do not change as a result. There would be a real danger of stagnation in the characters if they were not intimately aware of and actively connected with the active material world as well as the incidents in which they take part.

The final negative element that heightens the importance of movement is the lack of complexity in the conflicts presented in the novels. The simplicity, directness, and obviousness of the conflicts give the characters knowledge of the facts of their various situations. There is no challenge to the characters or the reader demanding extended mental activity, subtle or otherwise. The testimony of the participant's senses can be accepted as objective, if limited, fact. While such a simplicity is of value to a forward moving and well controlled narrative, it lessens the possibility of establishing tensions which will keep the novel alive and meaningful as it moves through its rises and falls. Vitality is preserved by the constant and conscious reception of more, though basically unvaried, information concerning the living world in which the characters operate.

The *constant* effect of vitality is gained by the rather obvious quick shifts (particularly within the unit of the paragraph) from one type of expression to another. The writing ranges freely and briefly through narration, description and exposition, monolog and dialog, and first, second and third persons. Shifting points of view add a more organic variation to these essentially artificial devices. But the real force of life is conveyed by the *consciousness* of the relation between characters and an *active* material world. These relations may be physical, emotional or mental, active or static, and actual, potential, hypothetical, or desired. They may be simple, one-directional relations, or become involved exchanges, expanding in both time and place.

This element of "movement" in Hemingway's novels can be observed even in his very brief and seemingly simple descriptions of people. In the description of the Russian, Karkov, there is a limited range of sensory perception, no present physical action on the part of the object, and a rather simple physical, emotional, and mental relation of subject to object:

> He had liked Karkov but not the place. Karkov was the most intelligent man he had ever met. Wearing black riding boots, gray breeches, and a gray tunic, with tiny hands and feet, puffily fragile of face and body, with a spitting way of talking through his bad teeth, he looked comic when Robert Jordan first saw him. But he had more brains and more inner dignity and outer insolence and humor than any man he had ever known.
>
> *(For Whom the Bell Tolls)*

Even in such a seemingly ordinary paragraph there is much conscious relation and active detail. The opening statement of Robert Jordan's reminiscence first connects him with Karkov and indicates generally the atmosphere of the relations; this is emphasized by the concluding phrase *but not the place*, which also forces the question "why?," then "why not?" to become prominent. This question leads to the second which explains the first and implies, by *most intelligent* and *ever*, an act of evaluation and the passage of time. *Had . . . met* is the direct physical and social act which leads to the description of Karkov. The description is brief, rather disorderly, but ranging progressively in detail from clothing to physique to typical action. The inanimate articles are given a type of life by their relation to Karkov, by the participles *wearing* and *riding* and by the reader's action of forming a uniform from the separate pieces of clothing. The mannerism, *a spitting way of talking through his bad teeth*, presents two actions with a relation between each other and a further relation to an audience, specific and general. The concluding detail, *his bad teeth*, is connected intimately with the verb *talking* by the preposition *through* which in itself is an "active" preposition denoting passage from one place to another. The independent clause presents an active judgment, *looked comic*, the temporal clause reveals an implied continuation of physical relation by the adverb *first*. *First* also anticipates the later change of Jordan's conclusion which is revealed in the next sentence, a concluding statement of Robert Jordan's opinion of Karkov. This statement has the implied comparison with other men, then a connection between Jordan and Karkov in *had ever known*, and a shift from *inner* to *outer* man.

Robert Jordan, the subject, has a definite activity here of both the senses and the judgment; his relation to the object, Karkov, is not only logically set forth but is explicitly reiterated. Action for Karkov is restricted and potential, but he is the cause of the activities of Jordan. The interplay of the content and the implications of the perception present the basis for the mental activity of the reader.

Other descriptions are more complex, expanding in time and in place and presenting reciprocal relationships. While Karkov may be considered "potential activity," Santiago is the result of the passage of time and action:

> The old man was thin and gaunt with deep wrinkles in the back of his neck. The brown blotches of the benevolent skin cancer the sun brings from its reflection on the tropic sea were on his cheeks. The blotches ran well down the sides of his face and his hands had the deep-creased scars from handling heavy fish on the cords. But none of these scars were fresh. They were as old as erosions in a fishless desert.
>
> *(The Old Man and the Sea)*

The activity and unity here is one of cause and effect; the continuous action of nature and of past experience on the old man has produced the present figure. Although the old man is "doing" nothing, the involvement of the relationships (indicated by the blotches and scars, the results, which exist in the present) gives a history of past action and forces the reader to shift from one point to another for his perspective and evaluation of the scene and condition.

Both Karkov and Santiago are presented with a sufficient amount of concrete detail for the reader to gain a direct and concrete picture of the characters. The approach to Brett Ashley is, however, quite different. In the entire novel, the only static details we are given about Brett are that her hair is short and her figure slender. She is attractive. There is no attempt at *ut pictura poesis*, no set piece as in Scott or Balzac. Hemingway gives Brett "body" by suggesting to the reader a type: he reveals her in settings, attitudes, and actions that bring out a compulsive, jaded, unconventional animalism, and the reader may choose, from imagination or experience, the physical embodiment for these qualities. A pertinent quotation may be drawn from Jake's observation in a Paris scene: Jake and Bill have come up to a bar; Mike strides forward and greets Jake cheerily; the two talk socially: "Bill had gone into the bar. He was standing talking with Brett, who was sitting on a high stool, her legs crossed. She had no stockings on," *(The Sun Also Rises)*. The point of concentration which has existed for the long evening has been broken; the reader no longer sees the relaxed Bill-Jake combination but an unsettled one of Mike-Jake. The reader's line of observation moves from Jake, one half of the original point of concentration, to Bill, the other half, who is the immediate object of Jake's vision. Bill Gorton has not waited for an introduction to Mike (who certainly makes himself conspicuous) but goes straightway to Brett, Brett who sits reigning insolently on a high bar stool. This shift uses the person we are with, Bill, to draw us closer to Brett, who has just come into range.

The shift demanded is not only a physical one but an emotional one involving change of tone. Jake, surrounded by the alcoholic garrulity of Mike, is in sharp contrast with the intimacy of the conversation at the bar. The present activity of Brett and Bill *talking*, the past activity of shifting up onto the *high* stool and of crossing her legs and the partially incompleted past action of dressing *(no stockings)*, fills the paragraph with an undercurrent of physical activity contributing to the scene's vitality. A still further note of vitality lies in Jake's either intellectual or emotional disapproval of this scene, a scene which expands, reaching through the novel and presenting Brett for what she is: attractive, alcoholic, unconventional, loose and inclined to justify her activities. The reader is given the woman in her particular active relation to particular friends, places, and actions; the character and life are there, although Brett herself is not defined overtly or given a set, static description.

Within the limits of the paragraph, the unit under discussion, vitality might be achieved most easily and effectively in a scene emphasizing the relationships of human beings who were reacting to each other on a number of levels and with varying intensity. While this is true and important for complexity, Hemingway often gains surprisingly active effects with the simple relations of a human subject and an inanimate object to preserve a sense of continuous vitality and to instill an awareness of an immediate and direct contact with the physical world. In an act of seemingly casual observation, Robert Jordan's eyes shift from one point to another as he looks at the snow stretched out before the machine gun: "The sun was bright on the snow and it was melting fast. He could see it hollowing away from the tree trunks and just ahead of the gun, before his eyes, the snow surface was damp and lacily fragile as the heat of the sun melted the top and the warmth of the earth breathed warmly up at the snow that lay upon it" *(For Whom the Bell Tolls)*. Not only is Robert Jordan aware of the existence of the snow, but the snow is in active relation to the sun, the trees, and the earth, changing before the man's gaze. The sun and the earth act on the snow, transforming it; the snow acts in relation to the trees, withdrawing from them; and the snow surface has a static relation (its position) ahead of the gun, before his eyes. The interconnected activity of the inanimate has its own life, independent of the observer yet in relation to him.

While Robert Jordan is rather passively conscious of the active snow object above, he is physically and emotionally very actively conscious of the view and of his relation to it as he lies above the bridge waiting for dawn and the attack.

> Robert Jordan lay behind the trunk of a pine tree on the slope of the hill above the road and the bridge and watched it become daylight. He loved this hour of the day always and now he watched it; feeling it gray within him, as though he were a part of the slow lightening that comes before the rising of the sun; when solid things darken and space lightens and the lights that have shown in the night go yellow and fade as the day comes. The pine trunks below him were hard and clear now, their trunks solid and brown and the road was shiny with a wisp of mist over it. The dew had wet him and the forest floor was soft and he felt the give of the brown, dropped pine needles under his elbows. Below he saw, through the light mist that rose from the stream bed, the steel of the bridge, straight and rigid across the gap, with the wooden sentry boxes at each end. But as he looked the structure of the bridge was still spidery and fine in the mist that hung over the stream.

> *(For Whom the Bell Tolls)*

The activity and relations here are many and varied, but the scene is dominated by Jordan's observation of and identification with the coming light and the hanging mist. In this fluid context, he shifts his gaze from detail to detail and watches as the objects grow clearer. He is acted upon (wet by the dew), reacts (feels) to a movement (the give of the forest floor). The vividness of the activity of light and of the connection of detail with detail in a static physical relation is ultimately dependent on the unity and vitality of Jordan's awareness of his sense perceptions.

To emphasize this intimate connection between subject and object, and their mutual relation to activity, Hemingway is fond of presenting a picture of the countryside as seen by a moving observer. Perhaps "picture" is inexact for it is rather an impression which reveals the movements of the observer on an equal scale with the general nature of the landscapes. The activity of the single observer's continually changing perspectives and objects is transferred to the rather disconnected details and unifies and vivifies them. A simple example of this approach may be drawn from the trip that Jake and Bill take from Paris to Bayonne: "We ate the sandwiches and drank the Chablis and watched the country out of the window. The grain was just beginning to ripen and the fields were full of poppies. The pastureland was green, and there were fine trees, and sometimes big rivers and chateaux off in the trees" *(The Sun Also Rises)*. Here the vitality of the rich growth of the expanding vista is closely connected to the vitality of the aware and pleased observer, and the gain is mutually reinforcing.

An additional virtue of these travel episodes is that the action has a consciously sought goal of a destination which aids in the movement; "the bridge" in *For Whom the Bell Tolls* serves in a similar capacity, generating an almost compulsive drive toward a conclusion. The sense of conscious purpose in the activity of a character can increase the intensity of a scene, putting a particular demand on the person as, for example, during the retreat from Caporetto: Hemingway is not simply "picturing" or establishing an external world in which his characters will operate in some possible future. The character observes and records that external world because he *must* understand it.

> Crossing the field, I did not know but that someone would fire on us from the trees near the farmhouse or from the farmhouse itself. I walked toward it, seeing it very clearly. The balcony of the second floor merged into the barn and there was hay coming out between the columns. The courtyard was of stone blocks and all the trees were dripping with the rain. There was a big empty two-wheeled cart, the shafts tipped high up in the rain. I came to the courtyard, crossed it, and stood under the shelter of the balcony. The door of the house was open and I went in. Bonello and Piani came in after me. It was dark inside. I went back to the kitchen. There were ashes of a fire on the big open hearth. The pots hung over the ashes, but they were empty.
>
> (*A Farewell to Arms*)

Here the goal of the subject is not simply one of perception or destination but of specific and necessary information. As he crosses the field to reach the farmhouse, Frederic describes the place in active terms but the description is, in a sense, accidental to his act of peering for an enemy. This farmhouse has a vital and direct significance to Frederic; it is not presented simply as a concrete detail in a landscape. The "purposeful observation" is the usual method employed for the apparently "incidental" presentation of concrete surroundings. Sometimes the description will have an immediate and specific significance; at others a very general one. This utilitarian aspect of observation is one of the strongest links between the characters and their world.

An interesting aspect of this purposeful relation between the observer and the world is the semi-professional view that the characters often take of their world as if they were evaluating it for an immediate or future specific use. The major characters often reveal a handbook view of an object, a view conditioned by their function as professional observers. Santiago looks at sky, water, and light for indications of future weather and fishing conditions. Frederic and Robert, as soldiers, consider roads, bridges, and terrain in terms of men, movement, and equipment, though Frederic Henry does so with a dull and jaded eye while Robert Jordan is always interested and often pleased; finally, Jake, the newspaper man, views spectacles in the colorful manner that might be expected of a journalist and sojourner. These special variations of purposeful observation are the results of two basic conditions of the Hemingway protagonists that elicit the consciousness of particular or professional knowledge. The hero is often a foreigner; even though he may know the language fluently, he is in some way an outsider, not really in the stream of tradition or daily life. As a result he must learn rather consciously as much as possible about the alien world if he is to deal with it; terrain and customs must be assimilated. Furthermore, while the hero's senses are alerted in his learning process, he, as a "professional," has something to teach the other characters, whether it be bull fighting, warfare, fishing, or eating and drinking. The hero as either student or teacher needs to be aware of the world around him—persons as well as places and things—if he is to survive as a personality and, often, as a physical entity.

The final example of a presentation of the inanimate is an extremely carefully worked out picture of the bull corral in *The Sun Also Rises*. An orderly inter-weaving of concrete detail and of the crowd's restrained activity carries the observing party from the ticket gate to the top of the wall; the simple, direct narration of activity and the orderly expanding description are such that neither could have existence (to say nothing of meaning and vitality) without the order. The eye does not stop at the top of the wall; the area is opened and expands up and out to the horizon, gathering more details and more aspects of life, in particular, people who are in turn focusing their gaze toward the center of the scene. " 'Look up there,' I said. Beyond the river rose the plateau of the town. All along the old walls and ramparts people were standing. The three lines of fortifications make three black lines of people. Above the walls there were heads in the windows of the houses. At the far end of the plateau boys had climbed into the trees" *(The Sun Also Rises)*. Just as the composition of a painting directs the viewer's eye to rest or to follow a certain direction, so this place, the first-person narrator, and Hemingway's description urge the reader to move from one concentric ring to another. It is as if the viewer were a sentient stone sending out ripples in a pool, aware of the expanding circles and the movement of points (i.e., people) on them.

Until this stage the examples considered have been of relationships of persons, places, and things. These relationships have been active, significant, and recognized by the observer. The emphasis has been on the concrete fact rather than on incident. The following examples have been chosen as examples of action but they are more than that alone; the combination of narration and description does not make the distinction of "descriptive unit" or "narrative unit" simple and clearcut. But then this is just one more of the devices for integrating all aspects of the life presented in the novels.

Within the context of the regular plot of the novel, there will be many incidents of subordinate actions contributing toward the whole. To drive the point further, parts of incidents are again subordinate actions contributing to their particular whole. Obviously this can be pushed back to the sentence or phrase or even word, each element being filled with actual or potential movement. The extent to which the writer "packs" his action scenes is, of course, dependent on the precise effect he wishes to achieve, but Hemingway's tendency is toward gaining as much internal action as possible and relating it closely to the characters.

The simplest form of action is the rather automatic performance of commonplace deeds. The flat economy of this narrative or type can achieve a variety of effects, especially when used for contrast, but more significantly the act described is the narrator's attempt to get out of his unrecognizable emotions, to establish contact with the non-self. The drained Jake retreats to San Sebastian after the fiesta: "I unpacked my bags and stacked my books on the table beside the head of my bed, put out my shaving things, hung up some clothes in the big armoire, and made up a bundle for the laundry. Then I took a shower in the bathroom and went down to lunch. Spain had not changed to summertime, so I was early. I set my watch again. I had recovered an hour by coming to San Sebastian" (*The Sun Also Rises*). Jake must "establish" himself in San Sebastian, must be consciously aware of his relation to a world just as he was aware when he and Bill walked through Paris or fished in a stream. It is a part of the self-centeredness of the Hemingway protagonist who must relate all things to himself if either self or things are to have meaning. He must make a world of conscious relation. Slowly the detachment is overcome, slowly a richness of consciousness emerges, and Jake can again enjoy as well as perceive. "I walked around the harbor under the trees to the casino, and then up one of the cool streets to the Cafe Marinas. There was an orchestra playing inside the café and I sat out on the terrace and enjoyed the fresh coolness in the hot day, and had a glass of lemonjuice and shaved ice and then a long whiskey and soda. I sat in front of the Marinas for a long time and read, and watched the people, and listened to the music" (*The Sun Also Rises*). The world and Jake's orderly relation to it have been reasserted. The impersonality is gone, and Jake can contact only the life he wishes and come alive. The actions of the subject, the passage of time, the sights, sounds, tastes, and the transition from the heat of the day to the cool of the evening all fill this paragraph with a leisurely movement of quiet consciousness.

To the relaxed action of this scene an interesting contrast is the animal vigor and pleasure of Rafael, the gypsy, as he walks toward Robert Jordan, who has just killed a cavalry man and is setting up a machine gun in anticipation of discovery and attack: "Just then, while he was watching all of the country that was visible, he saw the gypsy coming through the rocks to the left. He was walking with a loose, high-hipped, sloppy swing, his carbine was slung on his back, his brown face was grinning and he carried two big hares, one in each hand. He carried them by the legs, heads swinging" (*For Whom the Bell Tolls*). Not only is his walk animated but his whole body is working: arms, hands, face. Even the dead rabbits are a part of the action as they swing in the gypsy's grasp.

As satisfying as these presentations may be in their movement, restraint, and solidity, one turns with interest to the presentation of violent actions such as that of the bull's entrance in *The Sun Also Rises*:

> I leaned way over the wall and tried to see into the cage. It was dark. Some one rapped on the cage with an iron bar. Inside something seemed to explode. The bull, striking into the wood from side to side with his horns, made a great noise. Then I saw a dark muzzle and the shadow of horns, and then, with a clattering on the wood on the hollow box, the bull charged and came out into the corral, skidding with his forefeet in the straw as he stopped, his head up, the great hump of muscle on his neck swollen tight, his body muscles quivering as he looked up at the crowd on the stone walls. The two steers backed away against the wall, their heads sunken, their eyes watching the bull.
>
> *(The Sun Also Rises)*

The activity here is literally explosive as the bull bursts from the dark of the cage into the sunlight of the corral. Jake's anticipatory action establishes him as a concerned part of the scene; the heralding noises prepare for the entrance; then the charging, quivering bull dominates the picture. The bull defies the crowd; the steers wait with frightened resignation. Except for the crowd itself, all relationships here are active and intense and anticipate future action.

The simplicity and directness of the lines of actions in the examples already cited give an immediacy of impact and a quick-paced reception of active fact. More complex devices of presentation vary and control this communication. One technique employed is the revelation by grammatical structure of separate but concurrent actions that become mutually involved. United by no logical relation or by cause and effect, the actions draw into closer relation characters or things which reveal or clarify each other. One obvious use of this device may be observed in *For Whom the Bell Tolls*:

> Robert Jordan unrolled the bundle of clothing that made his pillow and pulled on his shirt. It was over his head and he was pulling it down when he heard the next planes coming and he pulled his trousers on over the robe and lay still as three more of the Heinkel bimotor bombers came over. Before they were gone over the shoulder of the mountain, he had buckled on his pistol, rolled the robe and placed it against the rocks, and sat now, close against the rocks, tying his ropesoled shoes, when the approaching droning turned to a greater clattering roar than ever before and nine more Heinkel light bombers came in echelons; hammering the sky apart as they went over.
>
> *(For Whom the Bell Tolls)*

The two actions are channeled grammatically—Robert Jordan's dressing in the independent clauses, the planes' flight in the temporal ones. The independent clauses present a base of commonplace activity and flat rhythm from which operates the harshly poetic flight and the climactic rhythm of the dependent clauses. It is through the earthborn, the personal, the individual of the guerrilla that we approach the diabolic symbol of distant, impersonal mechanization.

Another method of involving forward pace while keeping the action immediately alive is to shift from one object to another with a real or implied shift of subject: "The count was looking at Brett across the table under the gaslight. She was smoking a cigarette and flicking the ashes on the rug. She saw me notice it. 'I say, Jake, I don't want to ruin your rugs. Can't you give a chap an ashtray?' " (*The Sun Also Rises*). Jake, the subject, looked at the count who was watching Brett; the subject momentarily and implicitly shifts from Jake to the count, the object from the count to Brett. Then Brett's action of flicking the ashes occurred; "When she saw me notice it," the subject becomes Brett, the object, Jake, and then is immediately reversed. Brett requested an ashtray in a vaguely guilty manner. The shifting of subject and object, and the limited action of the scene have combined to form a vital whole. The intimate relation of Jake and Brett, her attractiveness to other men and her awareness of that attraction, her carelessness and Jake's control over that carelessness, are all revealed in the conscious observations in these few lines. The significant interplay is alive and active within itself without having any direct role in a specific incident in the usual meaning of the term.

In the preceding scene, the people are conscious of themselves and of each other. A different type of consciousness, more introspective and articulated, is presented by Frederic Henry as he floats down the icy river, clinging to a heavy timber. Not only is he uncomfortably aware of the present and very much involved in it, but his thoughts range back and forth in time and place.

> You do not know how long you are in a river when the current moves swiftly. It seems a long time and it may be very short. The water was cold and in flood and many things passed that had been floated off the banks when the river rose. I was lucky to have a heavy timber to hold on to, and I lay in the icy water with my chin on the wood, holding as easily as I could with both hands. I was afraid of cramps and I hoped we would move toward the shore. We went down the river in a long curve. It was beginning to be light enough so I could see the bushes along the shoreline. There was a brush island ahead and the current moved toward the shore. I wondered if I should take off my boots and clothes and try to swim ashore, but I decided not to. I had never thought of anything but that I would reach the shore some way, and I would be in a bad position if I landed barefoot. I had to get to Mestre some way.

(*A Farewell to Arms*)

The activity of the subject, both mental and physical, is continuous as is the contact with the reader. The lieutenant explains to the reader the sensation in the river and the problem of judgment, considers cause and effect, admits good fortune, fears, accounts, speculates, judges, anticipates, and then doggedly fixes his mind on getting "to Mestre some way." His is an observation and consideration of both the facts and the possibilities of the situation in which he finds himself.

This intense sense of involvement with the present action, as is quietly revealed in the foregoing quotation, is nowhere more brilliantly dramatized than in the opening scene of Chapter XXI from *For Whom the Bell Tolls*, a section too long for inclusion here. In this incident, the vivid description and rushing action fuse into a whole in which the characters act, react, and are acted upon. After opening rather "idyllically" in the quiet peace of the morning, the sound of hoofbeats comes to Robert Jordan, anticipating the entrance of the young cavalryman. The dynamiter is caught up immediately in a three-way relation: he warns Maria, readies himself, and watches for a horseman. The rider appears and the pistol roars; the man is killed and the camp aroused to frantic activity.

The section is vivid, economical, and controlled. To consider just a part of it:

> He reached his hand down toward the scabbard and as he swung low, turning and jerking at the scabbard, Robert Jordan saw the scarlet of the formalized device he wore on the left breast of his khaki blanket cape.
>
> Aiming at the center of his chest, a little lower than the device, Robert Jordan fired.
>
> The pistol roared in the snowy woods.
>
> *(For Whom the Bell Tolls)*

The brilliance of the movement, detail, and sound merge to give a piercing sensory impression. The simplicity of *the pistol roared in the snowy woods* has been prepared for in every respect: the quiet country setting with the snow melting and falling is shattered by the harsh shot ringing from the heavy automatic pistol held in both hands. The idyllic is broken by the ugly; we knew both existed but their juxtaposition gives us the drama. Both of these elements are picked up again as the scene is worked out; the cavalryman is dragged through the snow, the horse tracks are a matter of concern, and Robert Jordan nervously comments on the pistol and lanyard, as he reloads. The entire section is the perfect example of the union of vital parts in a living frame to produce a dramatic and significant reality. All facets previously discussed have been integrated in this passage.

There are three factors which have been examined in this study: one, the object which is under observation; two, the subject, who, in one way or another, does the observing; and three, the nature of the relation between subject and object. Because of the usual integration of these three aspects, it has been unnecessary and impossible to prescind too sharply from any two. The conclusions reached from these discussions are briefly: the activity of the object and subject may be either physical, emotional, or mental. These activities may be presented as actual, potential, hypothetical, desired, past, or implied. The relation of the subject and object is most often one of conscious or effective recognition by one or more of the senses; the subject often seeks to observe the object for a specific, sometimes necessary, purpose. (The reader, acting as external subject, must make subtle adjustments to varying types of expression.) The sense of immediacy in Hemingway's novels is gained not by the reproduction of the object for itself or even in the perception of the object by the subject so much as by the subject's awareness of his act of perception and the activity of the object perceived.

These are pedestrian facts by way of conclusion. The actual use of this view gives a concretely interrelated world to which the characters continually testify as present *now* and accounts for Hemingway's particular achievement in such vivid scenes as the fishing trip in *The Sun Also Rises*. Depending little on the cataloging of static details in the manner of Zola and Norris, Hemingway constructs the connection of character and action which always enlivens and solidifies the characters and humanizes scenes and actions. Before, and below the level of, the formation of the Hemingway "code"—his ideal of actions, courage, endurance, and technical competency—lies the involvement with and awareness of the material and interrelated world and of the characters' recognition of that active world. This constant movement gives the novels their vitality.

Human Time in Hemingway's Fiction

Wesley A. Kort

Three tendencies in Hemingway criticism distract attention from the nature and importance of human time in his fiction: the tendency to subject the texts to the context of his life; the tendency to consider character and tone to be the dominant elements of his narratives; and the tendency to assume that Hemingway's fiction reflects or expresses a philosophical skepticism or an existentialism which situates the person in a contrary relation to his world. These tendencies minimize the importance and distort the nature of human time in his work.

The subjection of the texts to the context occurs so often, of course, because of the undeniable and controversial character of the author. Whether this subjection takes the archeological direction of Philip Young's psychological treatment of the texts or the teleological direction of Carlos Baker's desire to establish the writer as artist, whether it deals with Hemingway's increasing involvement with a hostile world, as in Benson's book, or with Hemingway's interests in establishing a public image of himself, as in Scott Donaldson's study, the narrative texts are used to illustrate a point or make a case about the man. Text is subjected to context. It will be important for this paper to point out that Hemingway's fictions ask the reader to prefer the text to the context, to take the text as primary.

The tendency in Hemingway criticism to make character and tone the dominant elements in his fiction is closely associated with the preference for context; the principal characters of the fiction often resemble Hemingway himself or duplicate moments in his life, and he was himself so associated with a particular style. Indeed, the Hemingway hero and the Hemingway style, the code and the economy, are very likely the two keys to his fiction which any student coming into a course on Hemingway can

---

From *Modern Fiction Studies* 26, no. 4 (Winter 1980-81). © 1980 by the Purdue Research Foundation.

be counted on as having in hand. But it can be argued that time in his fiction may dominate character and style. In his novels characters seem to be carried along by events, to be changed by them as they are not able to change themselves, and tone seems to subject itself to a rendering of what actually occurred. Of course, critics have pointed out that time is an important element in Hemingway's work. Carlos Baker says, for example, that "the symbolic underpainting which gives so remarkable a sense of depth and vitality to what otherwise might seem flat and two-dimensional," this *Dichtung*, can be construed as the relationship between "the temporal and the eternal." By "the eternal" Baker means those constants that underlie the changing surface of life, "seed time and harvest, bread and wine, heat and cold, the rising-up and the going-down of the sun, and the slow turn of the seasons." Furthermore, Baker is aware, especially in his discussion of *The Old Man and the Sea*, of the rhythmic patterns in Hemingway's work, the alternation, especially, of pressure and relaxation, "as in the systolic-diastolic movement of the human heart," and this insight of Baker's has prompted another critic to see a rhythmic pattern as the basic structural design of all of Hemingway's fiction. Sheldon Grebstein adds a further point along these lines, one to which we shall return later, namely, that Hemingway's stories and the episodes of his novels often begin with a movement out of or into a building or room, toward or away from a locale of action, a movement which creates a pattern of action in which characters are "impelled into conflict" and retreat from it. Points of this kind, while helpful in indicating the importance and the nature of time in Hemingway's fiction, do not resist the tendency to take character and tone as always more important in the fiction than narrative.

The tendency of Hemingway criticism to assume or to argue that a generally negative or specifically hostile relation between the individual and his world is central to his fiction and constitutes a kind of philosophical skepticism or existentialism is supported by the other two tendencies, the interest in Hemingway's conflict-ridden life and the subjection of time to character and style. This third tendency can also be found in treatments of the nature and significance of human time in Hemingway's fiction. Earl Rovit, for example, posits a basically contrary relation between the character and the natural and historical time in which the character or narrator exists. Memorable moments of individual time are plucked out of "the meaningless ticking of sequential time," and this "seized time" takes on for the individual "the immortality of *always* time." For Rovit, the so-called Hemingway code is the way in which the author and his characters *impute* "meaning and value" to time, "to the seeming futility of man's headlong rush toward death."

These tendencies reduce the importance or distort the nature of narrative time in Hemingway's fiction. Rather than submit to them, let us ask whether textual time is preferred to the time of the context in Hemingway's work, whether time often becomes the dominant element in his fiction, and whether the "meaning and value" of time inhere within time and are not imputed to it. Let us address these questions, primarily using two texts for answering each of them.

I

The question of the relation of text to context is an important one for modernist literature generally. The tension that characterizes this relation in modernism has within it the rejection of judgment by the text of the context, especially by means of images of the war and the city, and the advocacy by the text of its form as offering or adumbrating a preferred world. In Hemingway's fiction there is both a rejection of the context and a preference for the time of the text. Let us look at *In Our Time* and *A Farewell to Arms* so see if and how this is true.

The first query concerning the relation of text to context arises, for *In Our Time*, from the juxtaposition of the stories and the sketches. This query is not easily answered, since the reason for and the results of the juxtaposition are not completely clear. The two forms cannot easily be divided from one another because there is a good bit of overlap as well as distance in their relation. It is true that the sketches tend to deal with more public, and the stories with more private, events and situations; the sketches also tend to report external events while the stories turn toward more inward matters of personal experience and relationships. Another important distinction is that the sketches tend to be static while the stories have more temporal movement. Knowing as we do how important contraries and contrasts are in Hemingway's fiction—light and dark, life and death, violence and peace, mountains and valleys—we can take this contrast between the static and the moving as important for the work as a whole. Without the sketches the temporal movements of the stories would be less noticeable. If we take these characteristics of the sketches together—their predominant orientation to the public and external, their likeness to reports and to reports of reports, and their static quality—we can take them as a part of the text which not only is separable from the text of the stories but also is closer to the context. They provide, in other words, a kind of vestibule text within the work standing between the texts of the stories and the context. This structure places the text of the stories two steps removed from the context.

As we turn to the stories, the first thing to note is that the characters often come into the story from some other place. We step into the story with them, as though across a threshold. Primarily what has been left behind is the city and the war. The war has clearly been left behind in "Soldier's Home," but something like war has also been left behind as one enters the world of "Big Two-Hearted River." The Nick Adams stories also leave behind the city and deal with a natural world in which Nick and his family are not native and which Nick is always, then, entering.

The second point to make about the stories is that entering is the first stage of a larger, cyclical movement. This movement can be broken down into its parts: entering, confronting, withdrawing, and reflecting. "The Battler," for example, opens at the end of one cycle, at the moment of reflection; Nick reflects on the encounter he has just experienced and draws its lesson: "They would never suck him in that way again." The story then allows a new cycle to begin: Nick enters the camp, confronts the two men and their relationship, and withdraws. The story ends before reflection begins, thereby formally tying the ending to the reflection with which the story began. This pattern of cyclical movement also determines "Indian Camp," "Soldier's Home," and "Big Two-Hearted River." Other stories concentrate on only one moment of the pattern, especially reflection, as in "The Three Day Blow" and "Cross Country Snow."

The third characteristic of these stories, in addition to the fact that some less desirable world is left behind and that the entering is part of a cyclical movement with several stages, is that this temporal movement is productive. It teaches wisdom, a more reliable understanding of the world as it actually is and not, presumably, as it has been distorted or concealed by cities and war. The result is freedom from illusion and miscalculation, although the teaching process is often painful or involves divestment and loss. Furthermore, the young man who appears in these stories has no guide to follow in the figure and actions of his father. Finally, he is handicapped by a habit of underestimating the complexity and difficulties of the world he enters. Occasionally, the movement is not one of divestment but of gaining or reappropriating. In "Big Two-Hearted River" an older Nick Adams returns from some undesirable context to reappropriate the benefits of an actual world with which he has learned to align himself.

The time of these stories involves the reader and character in an initial or repeated entrance into a world apprehended as more valuable than the one left behind. Implicit in the time to which the stories grant access is the affirmation that in every occurrence apart from the context of cities and war and in every human relationship there is an underlying lesson or directive as to how things are and how one should act. The value of the movement is reinforced by the lesson, alignment, or appropriation. The value and meaning are not imputed to the time; rather, they arise from the coming together of a situation and a responsive character. Nor do the value and meaning arise from some a priori rule or code as to how one should act; how one should act or should have acted is taught by the encounter and is a function of alignment and appropriation.

Contrast is also an important aspect of the structure of *A Farewell to Arms*. The two stories, one of war and one of love, stand as a story within a story, with the war story closer to the context. The relation of the two stories to one another, then, is the most immediate and most difficult of the structural questions.

The first thing to note is that enfolding both stories is the natural time of days, seasons, and weather. The opening chapters render the passing of two years primarily through the noting of seasonal changes. The rest of the book presents a year in the life of Frederic Henry, beginning with the spring of 1917. Natural time, by which the other times of the work are enfolded, exerts a determining force on the events of the work, since the war depends on the weather and since the relationship between Frederic and Catherine is strongly affected by the pregnancy and is terminated by the deaths the pregnancy causes. In fact, little is more important for the work than the natural time over which human beings have no control, which changes their lives and relationships, and which is responsible for growth and loss, life and death. Natural time is encompassing, determining, and double-faced. The force and results of natural time complicate the already far from simple relation of the war and love stories to one another.

Although the war and the love stories are to be distinguished, they are related in two important respects. First, Frederic Henry is unprepared for either war or love. A drifter, a student of architecture, and an alien, Frederic, at the outset, is not a person whose intentions in relation to the war are clear; nor is he capable of a responsible, committed relation to another person. His reflections on how he spent his leave make clear his dissatisfaction with this state (chapter 3). But however dissatisfied he may be and however attractive the idea of a different kind of life, such as that represented by Abruzzi, may seem, Frederic Henry is not able to produce needed changes in his behavior. The second way in which the two stories resemble one another is that in both Frederic Henry is changed as he would not have been able to change himself.

The first transformation occurs in Henry through his experiences with war. Both he and Catherine, she in an almost grotesquely romantic way, have underestimated and mistaken the nature of this war. Henry, after a series of shocks—his wound, the chaos of the retreat, the death of his friend, Aymo, and the executions at the bridge—recognizes the nature of war, severs himself from it, and enters the time of the love relationship. The war becomes the context for the second story.

The change which occurs during the love story, while always to be related to the painful experiences of war, is productive. At the outset of his relation to Catherine, Henry reveals himself to be self-centered, able to lie easily, and incapable of commitment. He associates with Catherine because her companionship is preferable to that of prostitutes, of whom he seems to have tired. Within the story Henry grows in his ability to commit himself to Catherine and care for her. Although Catherine is preoccupied with Henry's interests and protects him, creating thereby, a relationship which favors his well-being, the relationship is a process through which a new capacity for commitment and care is created in Henry.

The contrast between the story of Henry's change and the context of the war is sharp. But the question remains as to the relation of these contrasting times to the natural time of seasons and years, of life and death. Crucial to this question is the well-known passage toward the end of the work in which Henry speaks about the "they" who "killed you gratuitously like Aymo. Or gave you syphilis like Rinaldi." To understand this passage we should remember, first, that Henry has protected himself and has been protected by Catherine from a full knowledge of the risks of the pregnancy and the pains and losses that love makes possible; now he has confronted these aspects of life fully and unexpectedly. Furthermore, as Scott Donaldson points out, his indictment of the cosmos projects a burden of responsibility for what has happened which Henry is unwilling to accept himself, even in part. Finally, Henry is in a state of regression brought on by his anger, and he recalls the experiences he had once had with ants on a burning log. What occurs at this moment, then, is Henry's identification of his former self, coldly detached and indifferent to the fate of the ants, with the "they" of the cosmic powers. His anger rends the fabric of the narrative and reinvokes a time that precedes his experiences of war and love.

In the text the worst time is not natural time but the human time of war. Although contained by natural phenomena, such as weather and terrain, the time of war is unnatural and disruptive, a time of disillusionment and loss. Contained within natural time is also the time of love in which creative events occur, particularly the process by which Henry is changed as he could not have changed himself. As the times of war and love are able to reveal the range of possibilities for peace and disruption within human life and relationships, so natural time, by which human life is enfolded, is a complex reality with a wide range of possibilities. Henry does not appreciate, as does the implied author, the primacy and complexity of the human relation to natural time.

There are, it is now possible to say, four times in the work. There is the time of Henry before the war and the love, the time of detachment and drifting. There are the times of war and love, which we have been considering. But finally, there is the natural or cosmic time, large, complex, enfolding, which Henry does not adequately appreciate. Rather than one story within another, we have in this work a series of context-text relations, a stepping stone sequence leading to, but not fully entering, the story of a person's relation to natural time.

The series of context-text relations, which constitutes the structure of the work, makes interpretation difficult. Perhaps the presence in the narrative of an image of the context, especially the war, reduces the discontinuity between text and context and produces an interdependent relationship between them. We do not have such compromise of the contrast in other texts; *The Sun Also Rises*, for example, leaves the context behind, and Jake Barnes enters the story with the war wound. In *Across the River and into the Trees*, Colonel Cantwell comes to Venice as to a place apart from the half century of warfare he has known. True, in *For Whom the Bell Tolls*, the time of war, which forms the context for the love, is rendered, but here a distance is created between the warfare in the mountains or behind the lines and the warfare of the general, more distant, context. Those texts which leave the context behind maximize the potential meaning that lies in the contrast between context and text. The context represents a time of drifting and disillusionment, of destruction and dislocation. The experiences of the texts, though painful, produce a deeper immersion into and appreciation of life. The time of the context is alienating and scattering, a time of disruption, disorientation, and unrootedness. The texts grant access to another time, a time of growth as well as loss, of insight as well as shock, of a new footing in the world.

II

When we turn to the question of the nature and importance of time in the narratives of Hemingway, we should keep in mind what has already come before us, the contrast between text and context and textual time as cyclical and productive. We recall the pattern of entering, encountering, retreating, and reflecting, and we recall the process by which Frederic Henry is changed as he needed to be changed but was unable to change himself. We may now look at the nature and importance of narrative time more directly, with emphasis on *For Whom the Bell Tolls* and *The Old Man and the Sea*.

The time of *For Whom the Bell Tolls* at first seems linear, directed, by Jordan's orders, toward the destruction of the bridge and, by virtue of the risks involved in the project, toward his death. As the story progresses, this arrow-like quality of the time is stressed because risk increases: the fascist preparations indicated by the passing airplanes; Pablo's resistance to the plan; the loss of El Sordo and his men; the snow; and the theft by Pablo of some of the demolition tools. The fatal end is prefigured by conversations and stories about death, especially those involving Pilar: her reading of Jordan's palm, her scent for death, her story of Pablo's execution of the fascists and the demolition of the train. But this movement of events in a direct line toward the end is modified, and the time of the work is altered in a number of ways.

First, the slow pace relieves the pressure on the ending. This pace results from the close attention to details, especially to bodily movements and expressions, the many conversations, some of them extended, and departures from the main story, either through stories told by characters or through inserted stories, such as that which relates the journey of Andrés with Jordan's message.

But more important than the pace for relieving pressure on the end is the cyclical movement of time in the work, a movement which takes the linear time into itself and modifies it. The largest cycle, of course, is marked by the presence of Jordan near the bridge both at the beginning and at the ending of the work. But within that circle are the smaller rounds of the three days and three nights. For these smaller, internal rounds, the cave and not the bridge is the center. During the three days and nights movement is to and from, within and without, the cave.

The most important consequence of the cyclical time for the linear direction toward death is that Jordan's involvement in the cyclical pattern alters his attitude toward dying. As he himself recognizes, he has been changed in the days of contact with these people, especially with Anselmo, Pilar, and Maria. One of the things he learned from them is that in cyclical time the status and meaning of past events can be altered.

The fact that the past can constitute a burden from which a person needs to be redeemed is made clear in the character of Pablo. His present loss of nerve and his unreliability are due to the violence he has caused and witnessed, especially the execution of the fascists by the drunken, angry mob. If he could, Pablo would alter the past and undo it, " 'would bring them back to life,' . . . 'Everyone.' " But Pablo is unable to alter the past or to be free from its burdens and their resulting reduction of his stature.

Other characters, however, believe in or experience an alteration of the past through cyclical or repeated time. Anselmo is not so burdened and diminished by the past as is Pablo because he believes that some kind of ritual can be instituted by which the consequences of past actions, particularly the guilt, can be overcome.

The burden of the past is created for Maria not because of what she had done but because of what has been done to her. Maria believes what Pilar has taught her, that sexual relations with Jordan, because of their love, will erase the strains of the rape she has suffered: " 'She [Pilar] said that nothing is done to oneself that one does not accept and that if I loved some one it would take it all away.' " Although the pain of the scars remains, her repeated acts of love with Jordan affect the status of past events.

It is with Jordan, however, that we have the most important instance of cyclical time affecting the past. His past is a burden to him primarily because of his father's inadequacies. Jordan's behavior compensates for the weakness of his father, the sentimental leave-taking when Robert left home for college, and his father's suicide. Jordan's own dying and his taking leave from Maria overcome the burden of the past and the deficiencies of the father. The repetitious or cyclical character of time relates present to past events, alters the status of the past, and relieves the present of the burden of past events.

In addition, the cyclical time of Jordan's relation to the cave produces a change in his character. At the outset he is a person for whom work is of first importance and is quite separate from personal feelings. But at the end Jordan's work and his love for Maria come together and his life is whole:

> He had never thought that you could know that there was a woman if there was battle; not that any part of you could know it, or respond to it; nor that if there was a woman that she should have breasts small, round, and tight against you through a shirt; not that they, the breasts, could know about the two of them in battle. But it was true and he thought, good. That's good. I would not have believed that.

A unification of his life, an overcoming of the separation between love and work, war and peace, acting and resting, giving and receiving, is not something Jordan does for himself; it occurs to him as a product of the time.

Finally, the time produces a fusion of the lives of Jordan and Maria. The marriage which their ecstasy seals results in a permanent intertwining. When Jordan tells Maria, as they part, that he goes with her, he is not simply trying to make the break less difficult for her; the words express his belief: "Stay with what you believe now. Don't get cynical." The union of their lives, with the unification of Jordan's private world and the alteration of the events of the past, are results of time and not the products of intentions; they are the boons of a kind of temporal grace. And these boons transform the linear movement toward his death in a way that political commitments, duty, or individual resourcefulness could not have done.

In *The Old Man and the Sea*, linear or sequential time plays a less important role than in *For Whom the Bell Tolls*, although the advanced age of Santiago and the fact that he has gone eighty-four days without success in fishing put pressure on the narrative's cyclical, rhythmic, and repetitious time. The time of the narrative is principally the going out and return of Santiago. Within this cycle are others, the days and nights at sea, the rhythms of the waves, and the patterns, both mental and physical, of Santiago's tightening and relaxing, after the marlin has been hooked.

As in *For Whom the Bell Tolls*, the rhythmic or cyclical time has qualities of repetition which relate the present to the past. In this work, however, the past is a resource and not a burden, as it is for characters in the former novel. Santiago, in addition, has adequate models, while Nick Adams and Robert Jordan do not. The importance of models in the work is extended by the relation of the admiring apprentice Manolin to Santiago. Implied in this layering of time is the belief that the past is a resource, that human acts can be guided and enlarged by their relation to an ideal. Santiago wants to "be worthy of the great Di Maggio who does all things perfectly even with the pain of the bone spur in his heel." By virtue of their common vocation, Santiago also feels related to St. Peter. Finally, almost instinctively, Santiago acts in ways that relate him to the trials of Jesus.

In addition to its relation to ideals, however, admirable human action breaks new ground. Working under ideals is not a subservient position, not a simple duplication. Santiago goes out further than other fishermen. This means that there are in each experience unprecedented and individual challenges, the new as well as the repeated.

The third characteristic of admirable human action is that it reveals rapport with nature. While distinct from and, because of intelligence, superior to the marlin, Santiago has a deep admiration for, and adjusts his acts in response to, it. Furthermore, he feels a rapport with other aspects of the world he has entered, the sea, the sky, the birds and the wind, while the attacks of the sharks bring out of Santiago a vicious and desperate rage.

Human actions, in this emerging model, have an intimate rapport with the movements and forces of nature. Yet, Santiago is not absorbed into the natural world as he is not absorbed into the ideal.

Narrative time in *The Old Man and the Sea* is an instance of admirable human action. Admirable human action arises from confidence, something Santiago does not lose in spite of the long draught, and is distinctive; it is encouraged and enlarged by models and ideals; and it is action that is aligned with nature.

III

The importance of models and paradigms for the narrative time of Hemingway's fiction brings us to a topic which receives far less attention in studies of his work than do the aspects of human time which relate it to nature or which have the quality of unprecedented and individuating action. We shall look now at the role of paradigms for the meaning of narrative time in both an early and a later novel in order to suggest that models and paradigms in Hemingway's fiction are not confined to work of a limited period in his career.

The first thing to say about the meaning or paradigmatic aspect of human time in his work, however, is that, as we already have indicated, it should not be divorced from the movement of the time. That movement is productive: it teaches lessons in wisdom, it changes characters as they need to be changed but cannot change themselves, and it creates models of significant human action. Meaningful human time is narrative time, in conflict with the context, rhythmic, and productive.

The paradigmatic aspect of human time is an articulation of the meaning and value inherent in the movement. The paradigm present in *The Sun Also Rises* is most immediately available through the tripartite structure of the work. The three parts order time according to a Dantesque pattern of inferno, purgatorio, and paradiso. This structure articulates the overall meaning of the time rendered by the work, its productive capacity to turn the pain of irrevocable loss into a sense of new individuality and peace. This development is not caused by the character-narrator; it is not the product of individual intention or force of will. It is the result of a process.

In the first part of the book, set in Paris, the narrator presents himself in a state of decline, in a time which, with a few exceptions (primarily the moment at the opening of chapter 5), was frustrating and disorienting. The problem brought into the narrative from the context is, of course, the injury Jake suffered in the war, the exact nature of which, while not directly stated, is indicated by other details in the work and corroborated from extra-textual sources to have been the loss of his penis. What accounts for the decline and pain in this part of the narrative is that Jake has not yet fully faced the consequences of this loss for his life and his relation to other people. He picks up a prostitute, Georgette, only to admit to the difficulty when she makes, as could be expected, a sexual advance. Jake has also not fully faced the consequences of his loss for his relation to Brett; he is angered and frustrated by her associations with other men, especially with Cohn, and he continues desperately to salvage or to negotiate with her some kind of relationship in spite of his loss. In chapter 7, for example, after Brett has sent Count Mippipopolous away and they are in Jake's bedroom, Brett attempts to comfort Jake in his distress and apparently succeeds in granting him some measure of sexual gratification. Jake pleads for a continuation of their relationship. During this first part, Jake must descend to the point of recognizing fully the consequences of his loss for his relation to Brett and to other women as well.

The Dantesque paradigm is suggested at two other moments in this part. First, we have Cohn's remark that he and Jake are mid-way through life, an allusion to the age of Dante at the opening of the *Divine Comedy*. Cohn says to Jake,

> "Don't you ever get the feeling that all your life is going by and you're not taking advantage of it? Do you realize you've lived nearly half the time you have to live already?"
> "Yes, every once in a while."
> "Do you know that in about thirty-five years more we'll be dead?"
> "What the hell, Robert," I said. "What the hell."

The other reference to the *Divine Comedy* is the figure of Mippipopolous, whose arrow wounds and wide experience give him an heroic stature that offers Jake a respite analogous to Dante's moments with Mippipopolous's Greek ancestors in the *Inferno*.

In the second part of the narrative the movement of Jake Barnes up from the point of a full recognition of his situation begins. The movement is helped by the arrival of Bill Gorton. A healthy, natural, even innocent person, Bill plays a role analogous to that of Virgil in relation to Dante; he helps, but only part of the way, toward the needed wholeness and sense of peace. The part begins with Jake, like Dante at the outset of the Purgatorio, in the company of pilgrims, in this case a trainload of them from Dayton, Ohio. Like the Purgatorio, too, this part of the narrative is highly ritualistic and at times liturgical.

The fishing trip sets forth the major consequence of ritual and liturgy, rootedness. Bill lectures Jake on the importance of rootedness, a topic that addresses accurately Jake's uprooted condition because of his physical loss and his spiritual disorientation. The line in the water is a figure for the rootedness of which Bill speaks, the connection with what is natural, hidden, and mysterious. But the inadequacy of Bill's attitudes for Jake's condition is indicated by his comment, " 'We should not question. Our stay on earth is not for long. Let us rejoice and believe and give thanks' " (*The Sun Also Rises*). Admirable as it may be, Bill's childlike attitude toward life is not available to his companion; Jake has lost his first innocence and, if he is to have peace, must find a second one, a new beginning of life.

Church-going plays a minor but repeated role in this part. Jake goes into churches deliberately, and he even tries to perform religious acts: "I'm pretty religious," he later tells Brett. These visits to churches and attempts at acts of piety should be seen as integral to this part of the narrative; they extend and fortify its ritualistic and liturgical quality. Churches and Catholicism offer spiritually what nature offers in its way, something large, inclusive, and mysterious to which the person can be related. But we should not over-emphasize these specifically religious matters; they constitute only one of several ways by which Jake comes into contact with realities, both natural and spiritual, which are larger than himself.

The rounds of celebrations involve Jake in the antics of his friends but they also cause conflict and a break with his friend Montoya. At first Montoya tolerates Jake's friends; later he visits Jake's room to make explicit those values that are tacit in the community of *aficionados*; finally, at the beginning of the third part, Montoya does not appear when Jake and Bill are having lunch. The result of the conflict between the two groups of Jake's friends is that it deprives him of both circles. At the end of part 2 Jake is alone.

Among those moments in the second part which contribute to its ritualistic quality, the bull fighting is, of course, the most important. The bull fighting is the reason for the trip to Pamplona, and the other actions, the natural characteristics of the fishing, the ecclesiastical and Catholic acts, and the celebrating all culminate in this event. In addition, bull fighting, because of its associations with fertility, its tragic and comic aspects, the risks and style of it, and the certainty of death in involves, is the most comprehensive and resonant of the inclusive activities in which Jake participates. It is a worthy object of Jake's interest and an occasion for the dissolving of his personal condition in a larger, even universal whole.

There is conflict, pain, and loss in the second part of the narrative, but Jake is changed during this part into a man able and content to be alone. When the festival is over and even with Brett gone he seems at peace; we read, early in the third part, "It was pleasant to be drinking slowly and to be tasting the wine and to be drinking alone." In order to reach this peace, Jake, through participation in rituals, has had to come to the point of not being dependent upon his friends.

It is fitting for the Dantesque parallel that early in the third part Bill Gorton leaves. Like Virgil for Dante, Bill is too natural a person to accompany Jake to the end. In addition, this part, like the Paradiso for Dante, is the most personal of all. The center of the part lies in Jake's two swims. The first begins with a reminder of his injured state; a couple sits on the raft, the girl with her bathing straps undone. But Jake dives deeply, the second time staying down a long time. During the second swim he floats on the water, rising and falling with the swells: "The water was buoyant and cold. It felt as though you could never sink." That the water is both deep and supportive suggests what kind of benefit Jake receives from swimming. It may be important to note that the ability to be alone and the benefit he receives do not occur for Jake by means of a repression of his painful past. He has been thinking of Brett, since learning from Mike that he had borrowed Brett's last money from her. When she summons him, he goes to help her, moving in his new strength to address her pain and loss.

The paradigm of the work which is most immediately available in its structure and which is parallel to Dante's *Comedy* allows for an articulation of the meaning inherent in the narrative's movement. Specifically it reveals that a person can find a new wholeness and peace on the other side of traumatic loss and pain providing he recognize the full weight of that loss, relate himself to realities that have primacy and magnitude, and allow a new sense of internal peace to be born. Meaning is not imposed on narrative time by the Dantesque pattern; rather, the pattern can be extracted from the work as an articulation of the meaning inherent in the narrative time.

Hemingway's use of Dante, while no less important in *The Sun Also Rises*, is more noticeable in *Across the River and into the Trees*, primarily because Dante is so often mentioned. We find this latter novel to be that work in Hemingway's corpus which is most attentive to the meaning or paradigmatic aspect of human time.

Colonel Cantwell takes more of the context into the text than Jake Barnes takes into *The Sun Also Rises*. Cantwell rehearses his war experiences, and his age coincides with the age of the century, while his vocation corresponds to the century's principal occupation, war.

The time of the text is complicated by the combination of two stories, the duck hunting with which the book begins and which is continued again near the end, and the story of Cantwell's arrival and stay in Venice. The duck hunting takes place on Sunday, the other during the few days preceding, especially the Saturday. The duck hunting provides a frame because the principal action, the relation of Cantwell to the surly boatman, is not resolved until the story is taken up again. A critical question, to which we shall return, concerns the relation of these two stories to one another.

As in *For Whom the Bell Tolls*, linear time, the chronology of a half-century of wars and Cantwell's movement toward his death, is transformed by cyclical or ritualistic time. Cyclical time also eases the tension between the two stories, making the return to duck hunting less abrupt than it otherwise would be. Furthermore, chapters usually begin with a movement over a threshold, the characters going out of or into a building or room. The main exceptions to this pattern are the chapters of Cantwell's confession to Renata. The cyclical character of the movement of time is further supported by Cantwell's return to Venice after many other visits; he knows the city, its history, and many people there very well.

Since this visit to Venice seems understood by Cantwell to be his final return, he resolves matters which have been a burden to him. As in the rituals of *For Whom the Bell Tolls*, the status of the past is altered by ritual; Cantwell repays and relieves himself at the site of his wound at Fossalta.

He must also accept his failings as a military leader during the second war, failings which seem to constitute a burden. He confesses to Renata and then to her portrait in order to relieve himself of the burden of his past.

The process of unburdening and relieving has its counterpart in the increasingly free rounds of activity in which Cantwell and Renata engage. They act without plans about how to spend this weekend together, one they seem to recognize as their last. They are playful, spontaneous, celebrative. And there is a good bit of gift giving and receiving.

To determine the meaning of the cyclical or ritualistic time, we must begin with the contrast between Cantwell and his surroundings. While he admires Venice and knows about its history and art and while he loves the radiantly beautiful and personally gracious Renata, Cantwell is not himself a refined man. He is received into Venice by Renata as someone both bearing the scars of the context and sharing some of its violent characteristics.

The city into which this battered and dying man is received is characterized by its painting, architecture, and literature. Especially important for discussions of painting are images of Madonna; the most important literary figure is Dante, who is mentioned on at least eight occasions. The contrast between Cantwell and Venice is a contrast between a refugee from the world of the context and the world of beauty, antiquity, and art. Within Venice, Renata holds for Cantwell an exalted position as his last and only true love, as an ideal that is epitomized in her portrait.

Contact with Renata and the city changes Cantwell. During the days before Sunday he is still somewhat short-tempered, as Jackson his driver or as the elevator boy whom he reprimands would testify. But during the Sunday of the duck hunting Cantwell tolerates the unpleasantness of the surly boatman and, even more importantly, the breach of hunting etiquette of which the man is guilty. The juxtaposition of these two stories and the suspension of the first until the end make clear the meaning of the time in Venice: the world of beauty and grace has brought out of the bitter and battered man a latent capacity for honesty, generosity, and gentleness.

It is in the redemption of Cantwell that Dante becomes important. For both, there is a movement from one world to another, from the perplexing world of the context to a world of beauty and grace. Venice, the realm of art, truth, and grace, is more durable than the world of the context; it is able to receive Cantwell and, through generosity and confessions, to allow him to change. Secondly, the figure of Renata takes on some of the qualities that Beatrice and the Virgin have for Dante. Associations are made between Renata and the Virgin, the perpetually young woman who receives the broken body of the dying man. Renata is the figure of beauty and grace, the giver of gifts, the fully accepting and renewing woman. Her role is shared by the city and by others who live there, especially the Maestro.

All of these matters, however, are preliminary to what is central to the work, the dying of Colonel Cantwell. In relation to his dying, the *Divine Comedy* seems to have an importance similar to that which it has in *The Sun*

Also Rises. Dying is hellish, purgatorial, and paradisical. It is first of all the threatening, enervating, and final undoing of the person. Cantwell is aware of it as hellish, and he bears on his body and in his memory the marks of its sudden and gradual assaults. But death is also an antagonist with which one can struggle, a struggle in which one has his say, too. Struggle makes dying a human event, ritualizes it, allows it to draw resources out of the self. Finally, death is also a benefit. The use of Stonewall Jackson's words for the title, the need Renata's mother feels to leave Venice periodically for a place where there are trees, and the references to American trees during the reverie of Renata and Cantwell suggest death as a place of desirable rest. Death offers an attractive peace beyond the truthful, beautiful, and gracious world which the Maestro, Venice, and Renata represent.

The meaning or paradigmatic aspect of human time, inherent in the movement, is especially important to *Across the River and into the Trees*. While the movement of the human time in Hemingway's fiction seems easily related to natural rhythms, its meaning is articulated most fully with paradigms of an aesthetic and spiritual nature. Human time is, in his fiction, neither only natural nor only spiritual; as meaningful movement, it is both.

Human time in Hemingway's fiction, then, is opposed to the time of the context. It is not a time dominated by character or style; it is a time which is productive of those changes in character which are urgently needed but cannot be brought about by the characters themselves. Its movement is primarily cyclical, rhythmic, and repetitious, and its meaning is articulated by means of paradigms that are aesthetic and spiritual. The fiction does not force a union between natural*ism* and spiritual*ism* but embodies natural and aesthetic figures to release and expand on the movement and meaning of human time which are inseparable. Hemingway's fiction, then, grants access to a human time which is primary, which is rhythmic, and which is productive of healing, wisdom, and peace.

Why You Can't Go Home Again: Thomas Wolfe and "The Escapes of Time and Memory"

Morris Beja

> *I know there is nothing so commonplace, so dull, that it is not touched with nobility and dignity. And I intend to wreak out my soul on paper and express it all. This is what my life means to me: I am at the mercy of this thing and I will do it or die. I never forget; I have never forgotten.*
> —THOMAS WOLFE, *Letters to His Mother*

Thomas Wolfe never forgot, had never forgotten: that, it turned out, was his trouble. His realization late in his career that "you can't go home again" had for Wolfe complex moral, social, and psychological implications—but for his readers its chief interest is in the *artistic* import that Wolfe gave to it. For as a statement about art it emphatically denies the most sweeping assumption in Wolfe's own work: that you can create valuable art by returning to your personal past—indeed, by permitting your art to be "at the mercy of" that past.

Wolfe had made this assumption ever since he had turned away from his early attempts at writing drama and had begun to write autobiographical novels. From then on, his work showed an overwhelming emphasis on his own recollections, intensified by his possession of so powerful a memory that he seemed capable of total recall. His famous discussion in *The Story of a Novel* of the three elements of time —"actual present time," "past time," and "time immutable"—has, I think, received more notice than it deserves. Systematic reasoning was not one of Wolfe's strengths, and his comments on time are after all neither profound in themselves nor very enlightening in terms of his own work. The one time element that really monopolized his attention was the past, together with one's memories of its individual moments. Although his preoccupation with it was closely related to many of his other important themes—notably the origins and functions of art, the search for a father, and the relationships between the South and the North, Europe and America—it towered above them all in significance.

In his records of the moments of his past, Wolfe was to a degree attempting what James Joyce's Stephen Dedalus meant by his conviction that the task of the artist is "to record . . . epiphanies with extreme care,

From *Modern Fiction Studies* 11, no 3. (Autumn 1965). © 1965 by the Purdue Research Foundation.

seeing that they themselves are the most delicate and evanescent of moments." Wolfe, of course, greatly admired Joyce's work; my point here is that he did so largely because he felt that Joyce was able to do successfully what he himself longed to do: he believed, for example, that in *Ulysses* "the effort to apprehend and to make live again a moment in lost time is so tremendous that . . . Joyce really did succeed, at least in places, in penetrating reality." In *Of Time and the River*, Wolfe refers to this compulsion as "the intolerable desire to fix eternally in the patterns of an indestructible form a single moment of man's living, a single moment of life's beauty, passion, and unutterable eloquence, that passes, flames and goes." In this essay, I shall try to examine the effect this attempt to fix forever moments of the past had on Wolfe's novels, and how it led him to —and illuminates— his eventual realization that, after all, you can't go home again. I pay particular attention to two of the most striking and pervasive forms his effort took: the "recapture" of the past; and the sudden attribution of new and immense significance to moments out of lost time which originally made no distinct impression whatsoever, and which may have seemed, indeed, all but forgotten.

In Marcel Proust's strict sense of the term, "recapturing" the past involves not merely recalling an event but actually living through it again in all its original reality, with all its physical and mental associations. During his privileged moments, consequently, it seems to Proust's Marcel that the past he relives fuses with the present and becomes contemporary with it, while Wolfe writes that once, when George Webber noticed the first signs of spring, the color green so worked upon his memory that "the past became as real as the present, and he lived in the events of twenty years ago with as much intensity and as great a sense of actuality as if they had just occurred. He felt that there was no temporal past or present, no *now* more living than any reality of *then*" (*The Web and the Rock*). Eugene Gant has the same experiences, and they always occur in an epiphany, suddenly: "always when that lost world would come back, it came at once, like a sword thrust through the entrails, in all its panoply of past time, living, whole, and magic as it had always been" (*Of Time and the River*). Not everyone, however, is capable of recapturing the past; it would seem that one must have a virtually abnormal awareness of the sensations of the present in order to feel them again when they have gone, or at least when most people would say they have "gone." One needs the almost neurotic ultrasensibility of a Marcel—a quality already part of Eugene's make-up when he is "not quite six": "his sensory equipment was so complete that at the moment of perception of a single thing, the whole background of color, warmth, odor, sound, taste established itself, so that later, the breath of hot dandelion brought back the grass-warm banks of Spring, a day, a place, the rustling of young leaves, or the page of a book, the thin exotic smell of tangerine, the wintry bite of great apples" (*Look Homeward, Angel*).

Wolfe believed that he himself possessed such a sensibility and that his memory was characterized "in a more than ordinary degree by the intensity of its sense impressions." As an illustration, he describes in *The Story of a Novel* how one day he was sitting in a Paris Café, when suddenly and for no apparent reason he remembered the iron railing on the board-walk at Atlantic City: "I could see it instantly just the way it was. . . . It was all so vivid and concrete that I could feel my hand upon it and know the exact dimensions, its size and weight and shape." Wolfe asserts that this experience —and others like it, all of which also took place, paradox-ically, in Europe —enabled him to discover his America, which he had begun to feel was lost to him. Both his fictional counterparts also undergo the same discovery while in France: the incident that causes Eugene to look homeward occurs toward the end of *Of Time and the River*, when a church-bell in Dijon brings him back to the bell in college at Pulpit Hill, and then even further back to his childhood and "the lost America"; the incident that takes George home again occurs in Boulogne, as he enters a hotel room for the first time yet "feels that he has been here before"—in a sensation of *déjà vu* very similar to what happens at the beginning of Proust's priv-ileged moments —and then revives an evening in the Old Catawba of twenty years before *(The Web and the Rock)*.

In the other kind of moment rescued from lost time stressed by Wolfe, an event produces a revelation, but only long after the event itself has occurred—in what might be called a moment of delayed revelation, or a "retrospective" epiphany. Such moments are so numerous in the novels of Thomas Wolfe that it would be pointless to quote many examples here; they form the bulk of the long catalogues of Eugene's and George's mem-ories that fill so many pages in his books. And *The Story of a Novel* describes how, when Wolfe began to work on the first book of an intended series, he compiled vast lists of almost every conceivable sort, as if he strove in some way to find in the material details and fleeting trivia of the past the sense of value and permanence for which he longed. Some of these lists were put among sections of his manuscripts headed by the words "Where now?":

> Under such a heading as this, there would be brief notations of those thousands of things which all of us have seen for just a flash, a moment in our lives, which seem to be of no consequence what-ever at the moment that we see them, and which live in our minds and hearts forever, which are somehow pregnant with all the joy and sorrow of the human destiny, and which we know, somehow, are therefore more important than many things of more apparent consequence. "Where now?"

Where now?: the question figures not only in Wolfe's manuscripts, but in the catalogues recorded in the published versions of his novels as well. Like his desire and evident ability to recapture lost time, it reflects the general infatuation with the past that Wolfe brought to his art when he first began to write novels.

Art reflects the mind and world of its creator in more ways than one;

while many of the moments of intense emotion in *Look Homeward, Angel* are based, as everyone is aware, on the actual remembrance of things past by its young author, a large number of its apparently purely imaginary incidents also involve the recollection or recapture of lost time, by various characters themselves. Oliver Gant goes through such a moment when, to his dismay, the local madam buys his statue of an angel for a prostitute's grave. The importance to Gant of this angel has been prepared for by the first epiphany in the novel—one which, significantly, dealt with the discovery of artistic longings. Gant, fifteen years old, was walking along a street in Philadelphia when he saw a statue of an angel outside a stone cutter's shop, and it instilled a lifelong desire "to wreak something dark and unspeakable in him into cold stone," to "carve an angel's head," to "seek the great forgotten language, the lost lane-end into heaven." The angel purchased by the madam is not the same one; it has been imported from Italy. But it is as close as Gant has ever come to carving his own angel and to finding the forgotten language. As he and the madam conclude their transaction, their thoughts turn to the years that have gone by since their youth. They look out upon the town square, where everything seems suddenly "frozen in a picture": "And in that second the slow pulse of the fountain was suspended, life was held, like an arrested gesture, in photographic abeyance, and Gant felt himself alone move deathward in a world of seemings as, in 1910, a man might find himself again in a picture taken on the grounds of the Chicago Fair, when he was thirty and his mustache black, and, noting the bustled ladies and the derbied men fixed in the second's pullulation, remember the dead instant, seek beyond the borders for what was there." "Where now?" Wolfe asks, "Where after? Where then?"

At the end of the novel, Gant's son Eugene sees in the same square a vision of his entire past and all his younger selves, in a scene apparently meant to illustrate Wolfe's assertion in his note to the reader that "we are the sum of all the moments of our lives":

> And for a moment all the silver space was printed with the thousand forms of himself and Ben. There, by the corner in from Academy Street, Eugene watched his own approach; there, by the City Hall, he strode with lifted knees; there, by the curb upon the step, he stood, peopling the night with the great lost legion of himself—the thousand forms that came, that passed, that wove and shifted in unending change, and that remained unchanging Him.

> And through the Square, unwoven from lost time, the fierce bright horde of Ben spun in and out its deathless loom. Ben, in a thousand moments, walked the Square: Ben of the lost years, the forgotten days, the unremembered hours. . . .

> And now the Square was thronging with their lost bright shapes,

and all the minutes of lost time collected and stood still. Then, shot from them with projectile speed, the Square shrank down the rails of destiny, and was vanished with all things done, with all forgotten shapes of himself and Ben.

When the images of the past have disappeared, Eugene experiences another "moment of terrible vision," this time of "his foiled quest of himself," of the same hunger that has "darkened his father's eyes to impalpable desire for wrought stone and the head of an angel"; we are thus brought back to the first epiphany in the novel. Ben reveals in an "apexical summation" that what Eugene seeks must be found within himself ("*You* are your world"), and that the object of his quest—"the forgotten language, the lost world"—involves the past as much as the future. But it is forward that Eugene tries to look as he expresses in his final words his confidence that he will someday find what he desires, just as at the end of *The Story of a Novel* Wolfe himself is confident that we may all "find the tongue, the language, and the conscience that as men and artists we have got to have." The last chapter of the novel has generally suggested the visions in Joyce's Nighttown episode in *Ulysses;* but it is Stephen Dedalus's affirmation on the last page of *A Portrait of the Artist*—that, as artificer, he will forge the uncreated conscience of his race —that is called to mind by the last page of *Look Homeward, Angel,* with the young artist's determination to attain what his father has sought but never found in the carved angel: "the forgotten language, the lost world."

In general significance and radiance, this final vision and the others I have cited are exceptions to most of the frozen moments of new enlightenment in the book, which are plentiful and often individually effective, but which too frequently have no real function in relation to the rest of the novel. They reveal a good deal about specific people, but little in regard to comprehensive themes, and they sometimes even seem like merely irrelevant intrusions, included for no other reason than that they personally interest the novelist; the result is that they contribute toward one's impression of the novel as a compilation of fragments. Occasionally, however, as at the end, a moment of revelation will not only give us insight into one of Wolfe's characters, but also serve broader purposes of form by bringing together various themes or threads in the story.

Such structural weaknesses in the use of epiphanies are in one way alleviated in *Of Time and the River,* where a measure of unity is provided by the fact that many of Eugene's visions occur while he is a passenger on a train, as he looks out a window onto an evanescent world which disappears as soon as he has seen it, but the sight of which has a permanent effect upon him; often, for example, glimpses of people whom he will never see again powerfully impress upon Eugene, as his train rushes past them, a sense of the essential isolation in which we all live. Railroad journeys occur throughout the novel, and such visions connect all its sections, early, middle, or late, whether the action takes place in the South or in the North, in America or in Europe. They also help integrate *Of Time and the River* as a whole into the sequence of volumes that tell the life story of the Wolfe hero, for no symbol is more pervasive in Wolfe's work than the train. But in none of the other novels do they play so large a role in providing a degree of internal coherence; in fact, a more appropriate title for the book might well have been *Of Time and the Railroad*, for the image of the river does not even approach in importance that of the train. Wolfe himself, when he tries to describe the "design" of the novel, does not refer to the continuous flow of a river, but is forced instead into the realization that he "can liken these chapters only to a row of lights which one sometimes sees at night from the windows of a speeding train" *(The Story of a Novel)*. As this remark suggests, the limited coherence achieved by the image of the railroad and the visions centering on it is more than offset by the disjointed effect created when countless revelations of all types run through the novel with little or no attempt at relating most of them to each other.

Wolfe's problems in this regard are further compounded by the novel's climax. *Look Homeward, Angel* had at least ended with a powerful and unifying vision; *Of Time and the River* ends with what is probably the chief example in Wolfe of a non-functional and even harmful epiphany, one which seems completely out of place in the novel it is meant to conclude. In the final scene, Eugene is leaving Europe and returning to America; he is in a small boat with a number of other people, waiting to board the ship that is to take them home. All the travelers feel the strange power of the huge liner as it towers over them, but Wolfe gives special attention to the effect of this "magic moment" on a woman named Esther, whom we have never encountered before. We are then shown her own effect on Eugene, as he turns toward her; from the moment he sees her, his spirit is "impaled upon the knife of love." As if that were not bad enough, "at that instant" he also loses the "wild integrity" and the "proud inviolability of youth." Whereupon the novel ends. As the conclusion to an already ill-structured book, this revelation, which should form the forceful climax to the entire novel, succeeds only in leaving the reader hanging in the air. Eugene's loss of his youth can hardly be regarded as a dramatic or convincing corollary of what amounts to an epiphany of love at first sight. Besides, Wolfe's hero instantaneously loses his youth forever very often, and in this case the supposed loss is so unpersuasive as to be embarrassing. One would like to be able to find some alternative thematic function served by this incident: to regard it, say, as a culmination of the search for a mother—which, despite Wolfe's claim that the controlling idea in *Of Time and the River* is "man's search to find a father" *(The Story of a Novel)*, often seems as central in his work as the father theme. But the scene does not really fit this interpretation either, and though eventually Esther does in some degree become a mother figure, that role is of course not evident until the George Webber novels. Indeed, no matter how one looks at it, this scene is so unrelated to the context of the rest of the novel that it can only be regarded as a passage that starts threads that are entirely new. Strictly speaking, moreover, those threads were never taken up and no sequel to the book was ever written, for Wolfe never published another novel about Eugene Gant—though in the end, to be sure, we must ignore Wolfe's switch from Eugene to George Webber.

One of the most frequently cited causes of the structural defects of *Of Time and the River*, and of Wolfe's other novels as well, has been his inability or unwillingness to control the flow of memories he so freely permitted himself to record in his fiction—so freely that the flow became a deluge. Of course, Wolfe was correct in believing that there is much to be said for what he called, in a famous letter to F. Scott Fitzgerald, the "putter-inner" (as opposed to the "leaver-outer") approach to fiction. But this approach also entails great dangers, and too often Wolfe's own work does not overcome his obsession to be a putter-inner of everything. Yet it is an oversimplification to say that Wolfe's "chief fault," in his own words, was merely that he "wrote too much" (*The Story of a Novel*); a lack of critical judgment was also involved. He devoted so much space to autobiographical details which the reader can only regard as at best unessential that his novels frequently give the impression—valid or not—that he failed to understand that not every moment personally important to him need also be artistically significant. To Wolfe, all the myriad experiences he gives his hero are important, even essential; all of them at least potentially involve revelations. And the ones explicitly described as revelations are so numerous as to appear in almost every scene. By itself, each might be fully credible—but not as simply one out of a massive crowd; under such conditions, they take on something of the character of a mere artistic "convention." And Wolfe aggravates his difficulties by treating every one of the illuminations as if it were of cosmic proportions. Instead of subordinating some of them in comparison with others, he uses the same superlative adjectives to describe what would seem to be relatively unimportant moments of insight as he uses in the accounts of those he obviously regards as vital or climactic, such as the ones which end all his novels. We are so frequently told that this or that moment will never be forgotten and produces a revelation completely changing the course of Eugene's life that each such passage loses much of its intended force, and after a while we begin to treat these statements with skepticism—perhaps we even cease to notice some of them.

After the publication of *Of Time and the River*, Wolfe became increasingly conscious of the dangers inherent in his striving for all-inclusiveness. *The Story of a Novel*, having described the manuscripts included under the heading of "Where now?," suddenly rejects both them and the uncontrolled use of memory they seem to imply. In an unexpected and disconcertingly brief passage, Wolfe writes:

> It may be objected, it has been objected already by certain critics, that in such research as I have here attempted to describe there is a quality of intemperate excess, an almost insane hunger to devour the entire body of human experience, to attempt to include more,

experience more, than the measure of one life can hold, or than
the limits of a single work of art can well define. I readily admit
the validity of this criticism. I think I realize as well as any one
the fatal dangers that are consequent to such a ravenous desire,
the damage it may wreak upon one's life and on one's work. . . .

And now I really believe that so far as the artist is concerned, the
unlimited extent of human experience is not so important for him
as the depth and intensity with which he experiences things.

As here presented, Wolfe's new attitude is as yet vague and undefined,
but it does suggest a stronger realization that his work has suffered from
his lack of selectivity. It is of course inconceivable that Thomas Wolfe could
ever really have become a leaver-outer. But though the "Where now?"
method was inevitable and even justifiable for the early stages of his particular career, he now sees that it must be modified so as to take into
consideration the quality of remembered experience as much as, or even
more than, its quantity; not every event that had occurred to him is worthy
of being recorded in art as what I have called a retrospective epiphany.
This new point of view indicates a degree of reaction against the almost
completely free play he had thus far given his memory in the fictional
chronicle of his life; and therefore, as far as it goes, it is a sign of Wolfe's
transition from the attitude we have seen in his youthful letter to his
mother—"I intend to wreak out my soul on paper and express it all. . . .
I never forget; I have never forgotten"—to his eventual conviction that you
can't go home again. I say "as far as it goes" because in itself this passage
is anything but a clear and emphatic statement, and its context contains
further qualifications. Nevertheless, it is one of the first signs of a significant
shift in his thinking.

There are a few less questionable signs in his next published volume,
though again only a few. *The Web and the Rock*, like *You Can't Go Home Again*
(Wolfe, of course, meant them to form a single novel), was never corrected
or even finished by Wolfe himself, and it had to be posthumously edited
by Edward C. Aswell. Much of it, moreover, was written as early as *Of
Time and the River*, and it is therefore doubly difficult to depend on it in
order to trace the development of Wolfe's techniques and ideas. However,
we do know that except for a few passages, notably the ending, the last
half was written before the first, though he did rewrite "small portions of
it" before he died. This situation leads to some awkward discrepancies
between various viewpoints expressed within the novel itself, as well as
with what Wolfe had said elsewhere. Conflicts are especially apparent in
his comments on the role of memory in George Webber's art, and readers
who have read *The Story of a Novel* carefully, but who are unaware of the
peculiarities in the chronology of composition of *The Web and the Rock*, will
be particularly struck by a number of passages in the novel that contradict
the position toward which Wolfe had seemed to be groping. Thus, in the

second (earlier) half of the book, Wolfe occasionally speaks approvingly of George's great reliance upon his powers of recollection, which make the past "as real as the present." "The majestic powers of memory," we are told, "exerted a beneficent and joyful dominion over his life, sharpening and making intensely vivid every experience of each passing day," and enabling him to remember "a thousand fleeting and indefinable things which he had seen for the flick of an eye in some lost and dateless moment of the swarming past." Yet such remarks, though published after Wolfe's death, are not indications of a late reversion to the attitude that had produced the "Where now?" catalogues, but are rather another early product of that attitude. The newly written sections of the book, in contrast, reflect Wolfe's more recent concern about the pernicious effect on his work of his emphasis on memory. When George begins to write his first novel, his memory is said to have grown so "encyclopaedic" and preoccupied with the "minutest details" that it impairs his art and becomes, "instead of a mighty weapon," a "gigantic, fibrous, million-rooted plant of time which spread and flowered like a cancerous growth." Eventually, as George begins to realize that he has been trying "to pour the ocean in a sanitary drinking cup," he does attempt to set down merely "a fractional part of his vision of the earth." However, he is not really prepared to control the crushing power of his past, much less to discard it, and in another year his modest effort has—and Wolfe repeats his previous phrase—"spread and flowered like a cancerous growth": "From his childhood he could remember all that people said or did, but as he tried to set it down his memory opened up enormous vistas and associations, going from depth to limitless depth, until the simplest incident conjured up a buried continent of experience, and he was overwhelmed by a project of discovery and revelation that would have broken the strength and used up the lives of a regiment of men." We have here a description of essentially the same power as the one that had previously been depicted as exerting over George "a beneficent and joyful dominion," only now there is a marked difference in outlook toward its desirability. But though this and similar statements are significant, they are still isolated, infrequent, and counterbalanced by the passages that sharply contradict them.

A more pronounced symptom of Wolfe's doubts about his reliance on his own past in his fiction was his adoption of a new hero, whom he gave a childhood quite different from his own. This attempt to abandon strict autobiography was, perhaps inevitably, abortive; but it did bring him face to face with one of his most important failings—the almost complete absence from his work of objectivity. The novelist who works in the autobiographical form should not only be able to select the significant from the inconsequential; he should also be able to look at himself and his hero with a certain amount of perspective. And if he records his own epiphanies, as Joyce says it is for the man of letters to do, he will be most successful if he can do so with the impersonal self-analysis of a Proust, a Conrad, or of Joyce himself. Wolfe's treatment of many of his, on the other hand, is romanticized and theatrical. It would be absurd to condemn his novels because they are autobiographical. But it would, I am afraid, be correct to accuse them of being *too* autobiographical, in the sense that he seems to have seen his hero first as a reflection of himself, and then as a character in a work of art: he usually—though by no means always—failed to achieve that unique blend of subjective interest and objective insight that Edward Bullough called Psychical Distance.

Extreme subjectivity controls not only Wolfe's own attitude toward his experiences, but also the attitudes of his heroes toward theirs. Far from attaining any true and balanced view of the world around them during their moments of revelation, at such times they frequently have a view that is if anything even more individual and distorted than usual. They can see neither themselves nor others in perspective: they are self-deluded as well as self-absorbed. Their egotism is so excessive, and they are so unable to look at the world except through their own highly distorted glasses, that the credibility of their moments of supposed insight into the lives of other people is greatly affected, and despite the many moments in which Eugene or George feels an overpowering communion with other people, one's general impression is that of a bitter man more capable of abhorrence than of sympathy. For every stranger in the streets of Boston or New York to whom he feels his heart go out, there is someone, barely an acquaintance perhaps, whom he knows and—consequently—hates, fears, and despises. As a result, the sudden insights during which he is said to fathom completely some person or object are frequently unconvincing, for we find ourselves wondering if he is really capable of such insights. Generally, his abnormally self-centered relationships with other people, and his consequent inability to understand or communicate with them except on his own very peculiar terms and according to his own unusual needs, lessen the stature of the Wolfe hero as a human being; specifically, they lessen the seriousness with which we can react to some of his most important epiphanies, for we tend to regard his moments of compassion as more rhetorical than real.

The rhetoric of the epiphanies at the end of *The Web and the Rock*, when George confronts not someone else but his own reflection in a mirror, is an especially interesting example of some of Wolfe's major tendencies, including his inclination to take his hero too seriously, and his technical handling of moments of revelation. George is in a hospital in Munich after having participated in a brawl at the October Fair. His face has been beaten into an awful sight, but as he looks at it in the mirror across from his bed he suddenly grins, and then laughs: "The battered mask laughed with him, and at last his soul was free. He was a man." After that last remark, we too are inclined to grin, and perhaps laugh. As we have seen, this is not the first of the spiritual *bar mitzvahs* Wolfe gives his heroes—nor is it the last, for that matter. But the embarrassingly mawkish today-I-am-a-man quality of this scene is particularly noticeable. Then, for the final epiphany, the reflection even becomes vocal, and he and George have a dialogue — their talk, as might be expected, centering on the past: George lovingly describes to his image his memories of childhood, the "good time." "But," the reflection reveals in the very last words of the novel, "you can't go home again." As a climactic epiphany, this scene is almost as inadequate as the end of *Of Time and the River*, and for essentially the same reasons. It is unprepared for and in its context even seems irrelevant. The revelation it produces seems artificially imposed and is not in the least convincing as the conclusion of all that has preceded it, much of which it in fact appears to contradict. One is therefore not surprised to learn that this scene was probably written much later than most of the last half of *The Web and the Rock*—which dates from the period of *Of Time and the River*, before Wolfe himself had actually come to believe that you can't go home again. Of course, Wolfe did not intend that his manuscript be split in two here, so he can hardly be blamed for the inappropriateness of this scene to its final position, though as the novel stands it is nonetheless inappropriate. It is also ineffectual and unsatisfactory in itself, despite the fact that Wolfe regarded the whole episode of the October Fair as one of the most central in all his work. At one time, he even planned to use *The October Fair* as the title of the novel dealing with the period of his life covered by both *Of Time and the River* and *The Web and the Rock*.

It is not until the end of *You Can't Go Home Again* that, for the first time since *Look Homeward, Angel*, we have an effective climactic epiphany in one of Wolfe's novels. George, having returned to his beloved Germany as a famous author, is now on a train leaving it once more. At Aachen, the last stop before the border, he and the other travelers in his compartment are shocked to see that one of their fellow passengers — a nervous little man, whom George has privately called Fuss-and-Fidget — has been seized by the authorities. The rumor circulates that he is a Jew caught trying to escape with all his money. As the terrified little man tries to persuade the officers to let him go, since there must be some misunderstanding, he is led past his former traveling companions, his eyes glancing at them for just a moment. But he does not betray them by showing in any way that he knows them, and they board the train, leaving him behind on the platform.

> And the little man . . . paused once from his feverish effort to explain. As the car in which he had been riding slid by, he lifted his pasty face and terror-stricken eyes, and for a moment his lips were stilled of their anxious pleading. He looked once, directly and steadfastly, at his former companions, and they at him. And in that gaze there was all the unmeasured weight of man's mortal anguish. George and the others felt somehow naked and ashamed, and somehow guilty. They all felt that they were saying farewell, not to a man, but to humanity; not to some pathetic stranger, some

chance acquaintance of the voyage, but to mankind; not to some nameless cipher out of life, but to the fading image of a brother's face.

The train swept out and gathered speed—and so they lost him.

As so often before, Wolfe has used a scene envisioned from a train window to dramatize a symbolic isolation. But this time the person seen is not a complete stranger; he has had some sort of contact with George and the other passengers. Perhaps that is why this isolated, helpless little man becomes in the end less an image of solitude than of the unity of all mankind. He has achieved a bond—even an identity—with all men, but especially with the people in the train. He is not even aware of it, and it would be little comfort to him if he were. But it is apparently of the greatest importance to those who see him; and, paradoxically, he could never have attained this bond were he not isolated and manifestly doomed.

This episode is one of the best things Wolfe ever did. Its power does not so much rely on the impassioned rhetoric so frequent in his work—though there is still some rhetoric, of the quieter sort—as on its relative calm, the frighteningly low key of its presentation. Even the discussion of the personal significance of the incident for George is treated concisely and with restraint. And the long letter to Foxhall Edwards that then closes the novel discussing some of the broader ramifications of this experience is also handled relatively well; though it follows the climax, it does not really seem anti-climactic. For we soon understand that this event does more than simply reveal to George the true nature of Nazi Germany or even teach him about humanity, though it does both these things; it goes much further and teaches him about himself, enables him to see himself with an objectivity he has never previously known. It thus prepares him for the evaluation of his entire life and career that he undertakes in the letter to Fox. And when we begin to see the full significance of all he has learned, we realize that if this vision of a brother may be compared in effectiveness to Eugene's vision of Ben at the end of *Look Homeward, Angel*, it must be contrasted to it in theme. For instead of involving the recapture of the past, it centers on the future: "He saw now that you can't go home again—not ever. There was no road back. . . . And there came to him a vision of man's true home, beyond the ominous and cloud-engulfed horizon of the here and now, in the green and hopeful and still-virgin meadows of the future." The little man's capture has been for George a catalytic agent producing a violent reaction against much that he has taken for granted in the past— and, even more important, against his great emphasis upon that past itself. You can't go home again. This time the phrase is packed with implications.

George's new discovery comes to him as a sudden shock despite the fact that he has already supposedly learned in a moment of revelation that "you can't go home again"; for the passage at the end of *The Web and the Rock* is a careless addition, as well as a late one. It is completely inconsistent with subsequent passages in *You Can't Go Home Again*, throughout which it is clear that George has yet to discover the truth of this phrase, though he occasionally comes close. Early in the novel, on a train heading toward Libya Hill, he meets Judge Rumford Bland, a figure of evil but also of a kind of dark wisdom. "And do you think," Bland asks him, "you can go home again?" George's hesitant, "almost frightened" affirmative response ("Why—why yes! Why—") makes it clear that he has not yet had the new awareness attributed to him at the end of *The Web and the Rock*, that he still has much to learn, but that he is already beginning to be uncomfortable. He realizes that Bland's question refers not merely to the physical act of returning to the town of Libya Hill, and he is beginning to suspect—and this thought represents no less than a revolution in Wolfe's ideas —that lost time cannot be recaptured. Indeed, this discovery is the one that George finally makes at the end of the novel, when it is stated not simply as an inevitable fact, but also as a moral principle: you *ought* not to recapture the past, you *must* not go home again. The attempt to do so is not merely futile; it is wrong. I do not mean to imply that Wolfe rejects the past itself; that would be absurd and useless. Nor does he repudiate his "home" when he sadly realizes that he cannot go there again. Rather, he rejects the idea that you can or should re-live the past, that it can entirely control your life and art.

Wolfe had once written to Julian Meade of his emphatic conviction that "in no sense of the word" could writing be considered "an escape from reality"; in fact, it is "an attempt to approach and penetrate reality." As an example of what he meant, he cited *Ulysses*, with its "effort to apprehend and to make live again a moment in lost time." But Joyce had been able to exercise strict control over this effort, while Wolfe, as he himself now saw, had made it almost his sole preoccupation. Consequently, he had so distorted its importance that it had become "an escape from reality" after all. The means of escape were the things that make up the mysterious dream world of what used to be. Wolfe described the essence of his new knowledge in a letter written a few months before his fatal illness to Edward C. Aswell, who adapted Wolfe's words for the bridge between the German episode of the little man and George's letter to Fox:

> the whole book might almost be called "You Can't Go Home Again"—which means back home to one's family, back home to one's childhood, back home to the father one has lost, back home to romantic love, to a young man's dreams of glory and of fame, back home to exile, to escape to "Europe" and some foreign land, back home to lyricism, singing just for singing's sake, back home to aestheticism, to one's youthful ideas of the "artist," and the all-sufficiency of "art and beauty and love," back home to the ivory tower, back home to places in the country, the cottage in Bermuda away from all the strife and conflict of the world, back home to the father one is looking for—to someone who can help one, save

one, ease the burden for one, back home to the old forms and
systems of things that once seemed everlasting, but that are changing all the time—back home to the escapes of Time and Memory.
. . . But the conclusion is not sad: this is a hopeful book—the
conclusion is that although you can't go home again, the home of
every one of us is in the future: there is no other way.

The "escapes of Time and Memory" comprehend all the others, and the
radical nature of his departure from them, with all its personal, moral, and
artistic implications, was not lost upon Wolfe—nor upon George, who
admits to Edwards: "No man that I have known was ever more deeply
rooted in the soil of Time and Memory . . . than was I".

To Wolfe, the notion that you can't go home again applies specifically
to *art* in two principal ways: in its essentially moral statement that you can't
use art itself as an escape from reality; and, more important for its complete
reversal of Wolfe's former views, in its essentially aesthetic statement that
you can't create worthwhile art through the particular escapes of Time and
Memory. Wolfe had already come to the realization that a novelist must
be selective in his use of the past; perhaps because he has as yet been
unable to put this realization into practice to his own satisfaction, he now
suspects that one must not use the past at all, and his statements suggest
a belief that the attempt to base one's art upon personal memories is *always*
mistaken, even if carried out with the utmost selection and control: "He
saw now that you can't go home again—not ever." He thus reacts against
his former methods even more forcefully than reason might have dictated,
though in his case such a fierce reaction is perhaps necessary. In the letter
to Fox, George laughs at all the people who have spread rumors that he
would never be able to start another novel. The ironic truth is that he has
found it impossible to finish anything; his trouble, far from being an inability to begin, is an inability to stop recording all he remembers. His
"huge inheritance" had become a "giant web" in which he had entrapped
himself; in admitting this to Fox, George repeats the phrases that had
become so familiar in Wolfe's novels: "forgotten memories exhumed . . .
until I lived them in my dreams," "nothing that had ever been was lost,"
"I lived again through all times and weathers I had known," "the forgotten
moments and unnumbered hours came back." But though this language
has appeared before, and despite George's obvious relish in reverting to
it, there is now an unshrinking recognition that his "torrential recollec-
tiveness" has been a burden, has brought about a distorted attitude toward
life and art, and has produced a "million-fibered integument" which has
bound him to the past and therefore stifled his creativity.

Wolfe's statements are not specific enough for us to be able to tell the
extent to which he consciously intended his new position as a criticism of
all that he himself had so far written, but it is natural that his readers look
at it in terms of the light it sheds upon Wolfe's accomplishments. One's
attitude toward it necessarily involves an evaluation of Wolfe's entire career;

insofar as one regards the view taken at the end of *You Can't Go Home Again* as valid, then so much lower must his estimate be of all of Wolfe's novels, for that view rejects their very basis: the assumption that you can return to the past. But it is not a perfectly simple matter to judge the validity of Wolfe's notion that he had been wrong to try to go home again, for though his memory produced some of the most glaring of his artistic defects, it often contributed much of the value and uniqueness his novels do have. It was at times his strength and at times his weakness.

One critic who believes that Wolfe would have been correct to discard his own past as a subject for fiction is Louis D. Rubin, Jr. Yet at the same time Rubin is convinced that at its strongest Wolfe's memory did produce his most powerful work, and that because Wolfe's recollections of his childhood were his clearest and sharpest, and because the lapse of many years yielded a degree of perspective, *Look Homeward, Angel* is his greatest novel; when he begins to record his adult experiences his books "exhibit a sharp decline in the quality of the recall." Rubin's position boils down to a disagreement with Wolfe's phrase, "you can't go home again." Like the early Wolfe he admires most, Rubin seems to believe that you *can* go home again, though only to a limited extent and, perhaps, to certain periods of one's life; and Wolfe, so to speak, used up all his homecomings in *Look Homeward, Angel* and a few other accounts of his childhood. In other words, Rubin seems to say that you can go home only so many times. Wolfe, on the other hand, goes so far as to say that once you have left it you can *never* go back: "you can't go home again—not ever." Look to the future; there is no other way.

There is much to be said for Rubin's view as he presents it, but I think that in this instance it was Wolfe himself who recognized his problems most acutely. His main difficulty was not that he was too infrequently able to utilize his past, but that he was too exclusively concerned with it. He had allowed his obsession with his memory and its epiphanies to take over and run free, and they had thus impaired even his best work. Rubin feels that it was the poor quality of their memories that ruined the last three novels; but in fact those memories were in quality so intense that they could not be suppressed: the stronger Wolfe's recall, the weaker the art. The superiority of *Look Homeward, Angel* by no means shows that Wolfe was at his best when he gave his memory the most free play; on the contrary, it shows that he was at his best when he exerted the most restraint over it. Of all his novels, *Look Homeward, Angel* is the one that least displays the defects of too much use of personal memories; shorter than his later books, it nevertheless covers the longest period of time, deals fully with the largest number of characters, and is thereby most selective in the choice of incidents that were powerful enough to be included.

Actually, it is doubtful whether Wolfe ever would or could have given up autobiographical fiction; and it is at least questionable whether his future work would have been better if he had. One suspects he would have discovered that, like Orpheus, he had to look back whatever the cost. And if in the end Wolfe had found himself unable to write effectively about anything but the memorable moments out of his own past, regardless of all the dangers they entailed, he surely would have gone back to them with little hesitation—he was never one to be entrapped by a consistency, especially a foolish one. But his growing awareness of the dangers inherent in his use of such moments might have led him at last beyond a mere lip-service recognition of the need to control Time and Memory rather than to continue to let his art be controlled by them. He might have come to treat them as tools, not escapes—to create the great novel he never wrote, but which he had it in him to write.

Steinbeck, the People, and the Party

Sylvia Jenkins Cook

In 1930 Michael Gold, the left wing's literary hit man, provided a vitriolic foretaste of the controversies of the coming decade in his review for the *New Republic* of the works of Thornton Wilder. Gold attacked Wilder for turning his back on the ravages of capitalism in America and for retreating into remote historical settings and decadent religiosity. The *New Republic* was immediately flooded with letters exhibiting such extremities of partisanship on both sides that Edmund Wilson later recognized in the exchange the advent of "the literary class war." In this intellectual milieu—New York in the early 1930s —few young writers could remain unaware of the ardent political debates of the day, the urgent prescriptions for a revolutionary proletarian literature or the immediacy of the social crisis. However, it was at exactly this point in his career that John Steinbeck was farthest removed, geographically, intellectually, and politically from the left-wing ferment in New York. When the literary class war was declared there in 1932, Steinbeck was in California working on *To a God Unknown*, a novel examining the mystical, pagan instincts that inform the relationships of people to the land they tend. Of his two previously published books, one dealt with the adventures of a seventeenth-century Welsh pirate and the other with the propagation of a curse in a utopian western valley. His favorite reading was neither the *New Republic* nor the *New Masses* but Xenophon, Herodotus, Plutarch, and Sir Thomas Malory, and at this time he was beginning to find the greatest stimulus to his intellectual life not in the Marxist dialectic but in the tide pools of the Pacific, where he became something of an expert in marine biology. To borrow some of the terminology with which Michael Gold scourged Wilder, it all seems rather "erudite and esoteric." Yet in 1941, when Michael Gold summarized the literary 1930s at the fourth and

From *Literature at the Barricades: The American Writer in the 1930s.* © 1982 by The University of Alabama Press.

final Congress of American Writers, he chose Wilder and Steinbeck to measure the two poles of achievement in that decade, arguing that "what had happened . . . between Wilder and Steinbeck was a revolution of taste, morals, aspirations and social consciousness. American literature and the audience that read it had reached a certain maturity. A people's culture and hundreds of fine novels, plays and poems impregnated with proletarian spirit had battered down the barricades set up by the bourgeois monopolists of literature."

One might well assume that nothing less than a revolution could have caused the author of *Cup of Gold* and *The Pastures of Heaven* to create a novel of such remarkable timeliness and ideological appropriateness for the 1930s as *The Grapes of Wrath*; yet there is no evidence in Steinbeck's fiction, his letters, or the outward course of his life that he underwent any dramatic conversion away from the remote, heroic, and mystical concerns of his early work to the more topical, naturalistic, and political orientation of *The Grapes of Wrath*. What there is ample evidence for is a gradual and logical evolution of the social metaphors in which Steinbeck embodied his biological interests, which caused him to shift his focus from the marine life of the tide pools to the Communist party and thence to the Joad family. This shift was aided not by literary ideologues in New York but by his empirical observations in California, where he spent almost the entire decade. In this environment Steinbeck had the advantage of detachment from the endless wrangling over revolutionary art and posturing over proletarian causes; however, he was also isolated from the significant reaction that was forming, in a writer, for example, like James Agee, against artistic portrayals of squalor and poverty that seemed to pander to a fashionable taste for exposés of suffering. He was more innocent of both ideology and its exploitation than a writer in Agee's world could ever be. Thus the tumultuous reception of *The Grapes of Wrath* bewildered Steinbeck; he had neither anticipated becoming, as he did, an immediate public institution, nor being characterized, as he was, as a liar, a Communist, and a Jew. He had set out to search for fictional vehicles for rather arcane biological theories and had arrived, in the context of a decade of social upheaval, at the heart of the depression's last literary class war.

The artistic stimulus that Steinbeck found in his biological studies is first articulated in a letter to his friend Carlton Sheffield, dated 21 June 1933. The fact that Steinbeck bothered to date a letter with precision indicates that it had an unusual significance for him, and indeed the text is often incoherently excited. Three years of random scientific observations had suddenly taken a clear philosophical direction so that he now felt the urge to seek what he called "the symbolism of fiction" to act as a vehicle for them. These observations and experiments are derived largely from his study of the coral insect, but in the context of the United States in the depression they all have obvious human and political dimensions. There are three main issues of importance, the first of which he called the group or phalanx idea. This concerns the properties of a group organism and their difference from the properties of the individual units that compose the group. The ideological extension of this interest in the society of the 1930s is the clash of totalitarianism and individualism, communal and selfish behavior. The second concern is with the advantages and disadvantages of nonteleological thinking; in this area Steinbeck's friend and mentor, Ed Ricketts, urged on him the value of constantly seeking to understand and accept what is, rather than a "preoccupation with 'changes and cures' "— that is, the role of the detached scientific questioner rather than the advocate of a cause. This issue manifests itself not only in the technique of Steinbeck's fiction, where he experiments with the idea of having what he calls "no author's moral point of view," of being "merely a recording consciousness," but also in his version of naturalism, wherein the best-laid schemes of mice and men are inevitably destined to defeat. Steinbeck was not optimistic about dreams of a more perfect future, yet in the 1930s, the alternative pattern of American pragmatism, of limited and nonidealistic thinking, seemed increasingly inadequate to deal with the magnitude of the social crisis. The last of John Steinbeck's biological themes is a sense of the unity and interdependency of all life forms and their environment. It appears early in Steinbeck's fiction as an instinctive veneration of the natural world by man; however, when this kind of pantheism is placed in the contemporary context of the decay of agrarian life, the mechanization, industrialization, and despoilage of land, it clearly may provoke political as well as religious responses. None of these biological concerns ever became systematized for Steinbeck into rigid theories; they are constantly reexamined in his fiction in changing circumstances. However, the fact that these circumstances include Communist efforts to organize a strike among fruit-pickers and the exploitation of migrants who are forced off their land lures the reader of Steinbeck to measure him against the orthodoxies of his time, even if his progress there was oblique and unorthodox.

Steinbeck's interest in the phenomenon of group behavior was certainly not new to American fiction, as Mark Twain's description of the mob in *The Adventures of Huckleberry Finn* will testify: "The pitifulest thing out is a mob . . . they don't fight with courage that's born in them, but with courage that's borrowed from their mass." In the 1930s a more positive characterization of group behavior emerged in the many proletarian novels that dealt with the solidarity of the union, where workers could acquire dignity, strength, and power, all inaccessible to the exploited and impotent individual. What distinguishes Steinbeck's interest in group man from either of these examples is his reluctance to attach any moral judgment to the group phenomenon. In his original letter describing his fascination with the possible manifestations of the group, he writes that "Russia is giving us a nice example of human units who are trying with a curious nostalgia to get away from their individuality and re-establish the group unit the race remembers and wishes. I am not drawing conclusions." By the following year he had begun work on what he called " the Communist idea" which was to become *In Dubious Battle*. That Steinbeck's stated intentions for this novel are not wholly congruent with the effect it achieves is a measure of the gap in Steinbeck between the behavioral theories of the amateur biologist and the broader perspective of the artist, a gap that was to increase throughout the 1930s. He denied that the novel was anything other than a harsh scientific investigation of "man's eternal warfare with himself," saying, "I'm not interested in strike as means of raising men's wages, and I'm not interested in ranting about justice and oppression. . . . I wanted to be merely a recording consciousness, judging nothing, simply putting down the thing." Steinbeck felt that he had found in this study of the manipulations of a group of migrant workers by Communist party organizers an ideal crucible for testing the development of his group-man notions; but as soon as the material took form in a specific historical setting, Steinbeck's more complicated sympathies and prejudices altered the novel's supposed impartiality: it is not propaganda, but it clearly illustrates the problems of nonpartisanship.

Group man in *In Dubious Battle* is illustrated by a crowd of striking apple-pickers in the Torgas Valley in California. Individually, they are as far as is imaginable from the conventional image of the deserving poor: they are lazy, careless, cruel, cowardly, envious, and selfish. They refuse to cooperate voluntarily to secure even minimal sanitary arrangements for their camp. The men exploit the women sexually, and the women provoke the men to blood lust. It could never be said of these strikers, as it was of the Okies in *The Grapes of Wrath*, that they bear only the physical but not the spiritual stigmas of poverty and injustice. Yet Steinbeck refuses to indulge in such rationalizations here for the repulsive qualities of his pro- tagonists. When these same men are unified into a group animal by the skill of Mac, the Communist organizer, the new creature is powerful, reck- less of danger, savagely ferocious. It is neither more nor less decent than the individuals who compose it, but it is vitally different in many of its attributes. There is no alternative view in the novel of American working men en masse. The two characters who conduct the intellectual debate of the novel over Communist tactics are in complete agreement with this vision of group man though they differ in their responses to it. Mac, the doctrinaire field organizer, sees the group animal as something to be fed and goaded in the service of Communist political ideals; his images for the group are inevitably contemptuous animal analogies. Doc Burton, the "dreamer, mys- tic, metaphysician" who gives free medical attention to the strikers, but is himself "too God damn far left to be a Communist," sees group man as something to be studied and analyzed in the service of knowledge; he rejects Mac's animal images but substitutes for them images of germs and cells that are certainly no less dehumanizing. The only denial in the novel of the totalitarian implications of this vision of human nature comes from the hypocritical president of the Fruit Growers' Association, who has most to gain by it. Yet the brutal detachment Steinbeck professed and aimed at in *In Dubious Battle* is not absolute; while the group animal and its analysts Mac and Doc Burton clearly engaged his intellectual interests, it was not apparently a sufficient vehicle for his less impersonal artistic sensibility. Thus the novel contains two characters, a father and son, who remain completely outside the theoretical scheme of the novel but who clearly have Steinbeck's sympathy. These are the Andersons, who operate a small, independent farm and a low-profit lunch wagon; they are genial, self-reliant, and efficient men who have their livelihoods destroyed because they side with the aims of the strikers. Since they are so much closer than the fruit-pickers to a benevolent image of the people, they suggest a possible evolution for Steinbeck away from the mechanical and faceless mob —the product of his emotional detachment—to the more heroic and dignified people with roots in history, culture, and region who will form the group animal in *The Grapes of Wrath*.

This is not a simple transition from scientific detachment to emotional involvement on Steinbeck's part—it is also a recognition that the context in which the group phenomenon is studied alters its significance. Thus one Marxist critic of *In Dubious Battle* called it the most lifelike and satisfying proletarian novel of the 1930s. The label is false if used in the conventional sense of the term since the novel does not seek to promote the cause of revolution, but it indicates the partisan nature of Steinbeck's chosen setting—any fiction that dealt with labor activities in the depression and stopped short of opposing it might incur such a label.

Between the publication of *In Dubious Battle* in 1936 and *The Grapes of Wrath* in 1939, Steinbeck wrote a short story, "The Leader of the People," that may serve to emphasize further how the "fictional symbols" in which he embodies the group theory can alter its ideological effect. The story is about an old man who, at one time in his life, had found himself a special kind of cell in a group organism, much as the Communist Mac had in *In Dubious Battle*. He had been the leader of a group of westward-trekking pioneers who had survived a grueling journey across the continent. When they finally reached the Pacific the leader's function had disappeared and to his family he has now become a boring and garrulous figure, endlessly recalling his adventures. The old man is eventually trapped into admitting the authentic nature of the experience: it was a group phenomenon rather than a heroic act. "It wasn't Indians that were important, nor adventures, nor even getting out here. It was a whole bunch of people made into one big, crawling beast. And I was the head. It was westering and westering. . . . I was the leader, but if I hadn't been there, someone else would have been the head. The thing had to have a head." However, his grandson Jody, like the reader of *The Grapes of Wrath*, cannot shake off the heroic associations of westering. In that novel they are revived forcefully, together with all the resolution and hope of the earlier pioneers.

Steinbeck presents the movement of the Okies to California as mysterious and biologically determined, but the context of the people and the evocative associations of their journey recall other, more human standards by which to judge it. The historical context of pioneering is only one of the differences in setting between the filthy, cowardly, and brutish workers of

In Dubious Battle and the noble and enduring Okies of *The Grapes of Wrath*—two groups of people who might otherwise seem so contradictory in their conception as to suggest that Steinbeck radically altered his whole view of human nature between the two books. The Okies, unlike the striking fruit-pickers, are presented as victims of a natural disaster as well as an economic crisis: since the earth has failed them, they must begin anew. Thus there is an impelling logical reason for their migration that makes it both sensible and sympathetic. The Okies are also placed in a cultural tradition that gives dignity and stature to their predicament; they are the descendants of the people who helped clear and settle the continent, who fought in the Revolution and the Civil War. They carry suggestions of the chosen people as they seek for the Promised Land in California. None of these dignifying factors negates the essential biological nature of the mass movement of the group in *The Grapes of Wrath*, but they add an epic and legendary quality to the adventure that suggests that Steinbeck's evolving concern for the migrants has led him to a new and less dispassionate metaphor for his scientific interests.

The group unit itself is given a more varied portrayal in *The Grapes of Wrath*; it is no longer limited to the single feral body of strikers but may be seen in the Joad family moving into unified action to slaughter pigs; it may be a camp of migrants that comes into existence for one night only; it may be a field of cotton-pickers or a chorus of fanatical Jehovites; it may be the massive migratory group, crawling like insects along the highways; or it may be the ultimate macrocosmic group, Manself. These groups, true to their original biological conception, have properties different from those of their individual members: "The bank is something else than men. It happens that every man in a bank hates what the bank does, and yet the bank does it. The bank is something more than men, I tell you. It's the monster." However, with the illustration of such a variety of group formations, Steinbeck also reveals group properties that are clearly differentiated from each other and on which he now appears to make moral and political judgments. The howling, whining, and thumping of the religious enthusiasts does not make an admirable contribution to the life of the people, while the instinctive communal behavior in the roadside camps does; there, "in the evening a strange thing happened: the twenty families became one family, the children were the children of all. The loss of home became one loss, and the golden time in the West was one dream"—this is clearly beneficial to the mutual welfare as laws are established and property shared. The groups continue as in *In Dubious Battle* to respond to emotional goading, but unlike the arbitrary scenes of bloodletting created by the callous and opportunist Communists to stimulate the strikers' lust, in *The Grapes of Wrath* the provocation is completely integral to the situation, and the reader responds to it even before the Okies themselves:

> The people come with nets to fish for potatoes in the river, and
> the guards hold them back; they come in rattling cars to get the

dumped oranges, but the kerosene is sprayed. And they stand still and watch the potatoes float by, listen to the screaming pigs being killed in a ditch and covered with quicklime, watch the mountains of oranges slop down to a putrefying ooze; and in the eyes of the hungry there is a growing wrath. In the souls of the people the grapes of wrath are filling and growing heavy, growing heavy for the vintage.

Anger changes in this novel from a carefully fostered biological urge to a moral obligation; and the mob man is now labeled Manself, willing to "suffer and die for a concept, for this one quality is the foundation of Manself, and this one quality is man, distinctive in the universe."

Had Steinbeck rested *The Grapes of Wrath* on this ideological refinement of group man, it might well have been a more satisfactory proletarian novel; instead he chose to extend the context of the group not just beyond the biological to the political and moral level, but beyond that to the mystical and transcendental: the final apotheosis of group man in *The Grapes of Wrath* is not to socialist unity but to the Oversoul. In *In Dubious Battle*, the subversive Doc Burton had posed the question, "Can't a group of men be God?" only to be rebuffed by the practical Communists; in *The Grapes of Wrath*, when Casy says, "Maybe all men got one big soul ever'body's a part of," there is no spokesman for an opposing point of view. Set in a highly topical situation, *The Grapes of Wrath* shows a keen awareness of man as a political animal, existing somewhere between the tidepool and the stars, but, true to his personal and empirical attitude, Steinbeck refuses to be limited exclusively to that consciousness.

Steinbeck's interest in nonteleology as a way of approaching life and literature was first stimulated by his association with Ed Ricketts at the Pacific Biological Laboratories, and like the group-man theory, it rapidly moves in the fiction far beyond its scientific sources. Ricketts felt that people in a complex universe tended to search for its purpose before they had any comprehension of what it was—they asked the question, Why? before they tried to answer the question, How? Ricketts advocated instead what he called "is" thinking, which sought understanding without judgment and was therefore "capable of great tenderness, of an all-embracingness" that is rare otherwise. Steinbeck's fascination with this theory is indicated by the frequency with which he creates fictional characters who voice Rickett's opinions: Doc Burton in *In Dubious Battle*; Casy and, to some extent, Ma Joad in *The Grapes of Wrath*; and Doc in *Cannery Row*. But, especially in the novels written in the 1930s, Steinbeck consistently questions the social consequences and dangers of this rather passive view.

Doc Burton is one of the more appealing characters in *In Dubious Battle*; in a world of cruel and self-assured fanatics, he is gentle and tentative in his opinions; in a world of violence and destruction he aids and cures. He serves humanity without judging it; in a partisan setting, he has avoided taking sides. In his many debates with Mac, the Communist, he emphasizes his quest for pure knowledge, uncontaminated either by moral or historical labels: "I don't want to put on the blinders of 'good' and 'bad', and limit my vision. . . . I want to be able to look at the whole thing." Burton denies beginnings and ends, seeing only constant flux that prevents any practical, goal-oriented action. He is an enigma to Mac, who responds to his arguments with a mixture of revulsion and admiration, "In one way it seems cold-blooded, standing aside and looking down on men like that, and never getting yourself mixed up with them; but another way, Doc, it seems fine as the devil, and clean." Doc's mysterious disappearance from the novel indicates that in this particular dubious battle, when the ranks are drawn, there is simply no place for the man who tries to remain unsullied by partial commitment. To be "fine as the devil, and clean" is also to be intolerably isolated from human endeavor, as his departing remarks in the novel assert: "I'm awfully alone. I'm working all alone, towards nothing."

The Grapes of Wrath traces in more detail the wholesale transformation of two of its heroes, Casy and Tom, and the imminent conversion of the third, Ma Joad, away from "is" thinking to the search for both causes and ends. At the beginning of the novel, the former preacher, Jim Casy, is very much in the nonteleological mold of Doc Burton; he has given up his ministry to study his fellow mortals, of whom he says, nonjudgmentally, "There ain't no sin and there ain't no virtue. There's just stuff people do. . . . And some of the things folks do is nice, and some ain't nice, but that's as far as any man got a right to say." Casy, too, has a sense of living in a directionless flux, but unlike Doc Burton he gradually comes through his experiences to see a meaning and purpose in it—on the road west he observes of the migrants, "They's gonna come somepin outa all these folks goin' wes'—outa all their farms lef' lonely. They's gonna come a thing that's gonna change the whole country." Despite his initial rejection of sin, Casy is soon brought to the assertion that "they's somepin worse'n the devil got hold a the country, an' it ain't gonna let go till it's chopped loose." By the time of his death, Casy appears to have identified what is worse than the devil as California's rampant capitalism, and he gives his life to the ideal of defeating it.

Tom Joad is at first stolidly unimpressed by Casy's vaguely apocalyptic vision of the future; to Casy's admission that he mentally climbs barriers that have not yet been built, Tom replies, "I'm still layin' my dogs down one at a time." However, he is gradually led to realize, much as Steinbeck himself appeared to be doing, the dangers of such aimlessness. When his conversion to social activism comes, it is the result of personal experience rather than the preacher's rhetoric. This is a crucial difference between the radicalism of *In Dubious Battle* and that of *The Grapes of Wrath*: in the earlier novel, a rigid ideology is furthered by the emotional manipulation of the group; in the latter, the people themselves are educated empirically into their new activism. Tom's first advice to Ma Joad when she worries about the future is to "jus' take ever' day," an attitude that is qualified for the reader by the knowledge that it is the product of Tom's prison experiences in a powerless and dependent role. When Ma attempts to live by this ideal, it becomes a struggle to preserve the family unit against its assimilation into any wider group. As the futility of that struggle gradually becomes apparent, Ma, too, finally comes to recognize the need for a new vision of the future. She never relinquishes altogether her concern for the immediate future to the extent that Tom and Casy do, but she knows by the end that if people are ever to exist in more peace and security, it will be because of those who dedicated themselves to a final purpose instead of just "taking every day." Steinbeck's original attraction to the nonteleological view of the scientist is reversed when the fictional symbols in which he embodies it are the peculiar disasters of the depression for people who have formerly dedicated themselves to "is" thinking.

The last of Steinbeck's biological interests that found fictional symbols in his work during the 1930s is his sense of the mystery of ecology and especially of the mutual and sacred dependence of people and land. Like other American writers in the thirties, notably Faulkner and Caldwell, Steinbeck was interested in the special nature of the agricultural bond, since agribusiness and natural disasters seemed about to end it forever. It is explored early in his fiction in the pagan religious context of *To a God Unknown* in 1933; only later in the decade does the topic come to have a political dimension. *To a God Unknown* deals with the mystical union between the farmer, Joseph Wayne, and the homestead he acquires in California. Joseph's cult begins in a simple lust for the land, symbolized in a ritualized mating with it. He glories in its fertility, identifies a tree as the spirit of his dead father, makes sacrificial offerings to the land, and ultimately comes to identify with it so completely that he kills himself in a dry season in the certainty that his blood will water and renew the earth. Although this novel was seen by most critics as a kind of anthropological curiosity, the same identification with the land, both physically and spiritually, is apparent in the more contemporary and realistic Okies in *The Grapes of Wrath*, who affirm that the "place where folks live is them folks."

In *The Grapes of Wrath*, Steinbeck depicts what happens to the land as well as the people when the agrarian bond is broken. The tractors that come on to the land, driven by machinelike men who eat machine-made food, rape the land that had formerly been loved and cause its symbolic death. Thus the banks that drive the people off the land are shown to be committing not only a crime against humanity but also a sacrilege against the religion of agriculture. This attitude is identified by critic Chester Eisinger with Jeffersonian agrarianism, and he argues that, appealing as this philosophy may be, it is certainly an outmoded way of dealing with the problems of the Okies in the 1930s. However, while Steinbeck clearly displays some nostalgia for such notions, he also identifies them as part of the past that is irretrievable; in addition to the banks that tractor the people off the land, there are the dust storms that would ruin their livelihood anyway; their legal or moral right to stay is undermined by nature itself turning against them. The pantheism of the novel is rooted in hunger for fertile, productive land; it is useless to continue to worship land that is already dead, as Muley Graves and Granpa Joad do. Steinbeck demands adaptability as well as resilience in his species of farmers so that even at the nadir of the Joads' suffering in California, when Pa wishes only to return to Oklahoma, Ma insists that California, which has treated them so badly, is nevertheless "better land."

The religious element in Steinbeck's agrarianism that made reviewers of *To a God Unknown* wish that he could find more stable and relevant principles on which to build future novels proves capable in *The Grapes of Wrath* of supporting a highly political and topical thesis: "when property accumulates in too few hands it is taken away. . . . when a majority of the people are hungry and cold they will take by force what they need. . . . repression works only to strengthen and knit the repressed." Land hunger in Steinbeck is from his earliest works both a physical instinct and a religious need; in *The Grapes of Wrath,* when the days of homesteading are past, it becomes also a political principle.

The fact that Steinbeck's biological interests took the direction they did in his fiction in the 1930s is, of course, a direct consequence of the times in which he lived. Although Steinbeck was largely estranged from the cliques of radical literary activists, he was throughout the depression coming into more and more intimate contact with the human suffering it spawned. In 1934 he had written sardonically to a friend in New York, "I am pegged as a pessimistic writer because I do not see the millennium coming." By 1936, after he had done a series of reports for the *Nation* on migrant labor in California, he was writing to the same friend, "There are riots in Salinas and killings in the streets of that dear little town where I was born. I shouldn't wonder if the thing had begun. I don't mean any general revolt but an active beginning aimed toward it, the smouldering." This is a considerable progress in millennialist rhetoric in the space of two years, and what was largely responsible for Steinbeck's rather late awakening was the peculiar experience of California. Since much of the suffering and exploitation there arose as a consequence of the Dust Bowl migration, the exposure and consciousness of it came much later in the decade than the circumstances that gave rise to the main flowering of proletarian literature. By 1938 Steinbeck's letters show a repeated anguished emphasis on the explosive situation in California, the starvation and disease among migrant families, and the sabotaging of all efforts to help them by what he calls the "fascist" utilities and banks. Steinbeck was torn between his desire to write his fury into a work of fiction and a more pressing need to take direct action, "to help knock these murderers on the heads." One of his letters ends, "funny how mean and little books become in the face of such tragedies"; a few days later, he arranged for the proceeds of his articles to buy serum and codliver oil for the migrant children and then concluded in despair, "Of course no individual effort will help." A week or two later, he apparently decided that reporting might be the best medium: "I want to put a tag of shame on the greedy bastards who are responsible for this but I can best do it through newspapers." *The Grapes of Wrath* is thus very firmly grounded in the immediate turmoil of the California scene although it is necessary to add that it was not an immediate product. The first book Steinbeck wrote out of his anger was a bitter satire called *L'Affaire Lettuceberg*; he later rejected it because it was "mean" and "nasty" and, by dealing in half-truths, more likely to cause hatred than understanding. When he began work on *The Grapes of Wrath*, the need to take immediate action had been satisfied by his journalism and personal generosity; the need to vent his rage had been poured into the abandoned propagandistic novel that he knew was bad. Thus into *The Grapes of Wrath* he could distill the more measured results of a whole decade of intellectual and literary apprenticeship with a topic that was almost exclusively apt to his worldly experience.

There is one final factor in Steinbeck's intellectual background that plays an important role in his political novels and indeed, according to his friend Toni Ricketts, was the "real clue to his writing": this was what she characterized as "his hatred of the middle class." This appears to be not so much a class-conscious attitude in a political sense as a preference in cultural and moral values for lower-class people who lived with excess and abjured moderation. The excess might take the form of sexuality, drunkenness, gross appetite, or religious enthusiasm; Steinbeck was not so much interested in the specific manifestation of a zest for life as in abhorring the prudence, prurience, rigidity, and conformity that robbed people of the capacity for heroic conduct or the pursuit of dreams. His earlier, largely unpolitical fiction—*Cup of Gold, The Pastures of Heaven,* and *Tortilla Flat*—had all examined the stultifying effects of respectability, mediocrity, and stability on the human tendency to wildness and eccentricity. Although the Joads in *The Grapes of Wrath* are never so extravagant as the people in these early novels in their appetite and indulgences, they are certainly immoderate and nonconformist. Every member of the family is introduced by a tale of excess, from Tom's murder to Granma's religious ecstasies to Al's tomcatting, Uncle John's binges, and Ma's attack on a peddler with a live chicken. The Joads, however, are also generous, compassionate, and able to restrain their impulses when it is necessary for the common good. They are hardworking, not for acquisition but for survival and the pleasure of performing well. Only in *The Grapes of Wrath* do these qualities become politically class-conscious, since they are deliberately opposed to the "shitheels"—the worried, insecure businessmen with their languid, discontented wives, rushing across the country to California to indulge in gossip and vicarious living because they no longer have any vitality in themselves. Steinbeck's comments on the decadence of these people, of their pursuit of the artificial and perversion of the natural, come very close to the standard conventions of proletarian fiction, but for him they are very far from being leftist clichés, or a sentimental indulgence in primitivism. They are rather the logical development, in the political atmosphere of the depression, of an early and instinctive prejudice.

When *The Grapes of Wrath* was published, it shocked, offended, and made enemies for Steinbeck, but it also brought him instant fame, offers from Hollywood, membership in the Press Club, and a Pulitzer prize; he was now an acknowledged member of the literary set. He was completely unprepared for such a response. While the novel was in the publication process, he wrote repeatedly warning Viking against a large first edition. His later letters express surprise but little elation at the reception of it; he seems to have been exhausted, both physically and mentally, skeptical of any political action, and wholly disillusioned with the genre in which he had been working: "I've worked the novel . . . as far as I can take it." He loathed the newfound intrusions on his privacy and feared for his future integrity the consequences of "this damnable popularity." He determined to change directions, to abandon fiction altogether for scientific studies, to write a good book that few people would want to read. He foresaw himself becoming what he had so detested—respectable, consistent, satisfactorily assimilated. As with his late and largely empirical conversion to radical politics, Steinbeck needed to feel the actual destructive force of success on himself before he doubted the validity of his particular approach to art. It was a position to which one other notable radical writer had come by the end of the 1930s, but for James Agee the revulsion from the public's appetite for aesthetic images of human suffering preceded the writing of his great depression effusion, *Let Us Now Praise Famous Men*. With a topic and a political philosophy remarkably close to Steinbeck's, Agee's work helps to dramatize, by its almost nihilistic originality as well as by its ideological torment, both the advantages and disadvantages of the enduring value of *The Grapes of Wrath*, of Steinbeck's estrangement in California during the 1930s.

Let Us Now Praise Famous Men grew, like *The Grapes of Wrath*, from a specific experience of human suffering and from Agee's background in the depression, which was markedly different from Steinbeck's—at the center of the New York literary and radical world. From that he had acquired a distaste for the chic, left-wing affectation he observed, as well as for the fashionable new relevance of the artist. It was a distaste that led him to reject all the successful literary conventions of the 1930s for a work that he determined would be as unpalatable to the aesthetes of suffering as he could possibly contrive. He succeeded in creating a book that had in its own day no popular appeal and limited critical enthusiasm but has risen steadily in critical estimation ever since, so that it is not unusual now to see it hailed as the greatest literary achievement of the depression. By contrast, the reputation of *The Grapes of Wrath* in America had declined so much that in 1962, when Steinbeck was awarded the Nobel Prize, the *New Republic* rather ungraciously editorialized that it could not in any sense acknowledge that he was a great artist, or even nationally esteemed. Steinbeck's novel had succeeded in the 1930s not merely because of its topicality but also because of the skill with which he had documented the voices and lives of the migrants, the carefully fostered dialectical debate between the chapters and interchapters, the compassion with which the novel demanded a moral response from its readers. In contriving a technique, as well as an ideology, Steinbeck had come to discover the use of conventions such as documentary journalism, folk idiom, multiple protagonists, and ideological irony and symbolism that had become common in the thirties in the fiction of other left-wing writers, but in the eyes of a writer like James Agee, hackneyed and discredited. Steinbeck's isolation from Agee's world permitted his education in the field rather than the radical drawing-room; it enabled him to explore his biological interests free of ideological harassment and to evolve new vehicles for them in accordance with his emotional sympathies. Nevertheless, this freedom cost Steinbeck something in the loss of the kind of intellectual stimulus and debate that helped direct Agee towards the creation of a new literature of the left, rather than, as *The Grapes of Wrath* finally seems to be, the climax and culmination of the old. Perhaps, in this sense, Michael Gold's enthusiasm is its most fitting epitaph.

Metaphor, Metonymy, and Voice in Zora Neale Hurston's *Their Eyes Were Watching God*

Barbara Johnson

Not so very long ago, metaphor and metonymy burst into prominence as the salt and pepper, the Laurel and Hardy, the Yin and Yang, and often the Scylla and Charybdis of literary theory. Then, just as quickly, this cosmic couple passed out of fashion again. How did it happen that such an arcane rhetorical opposition was able to acquire the brief but powerful privilege of dividing and naming the whole of human reality, from Mommy and Daddy or Symptom and Desire all the way to God and Country or Beautiful Lie and Sober Lucidity?

The contemporary sense of the opposition between metaphor and metonymy was first formulated by Roman Jakobson in an article entitled "Two Aspects of Language and Two Types of Aphasic Disturbances." That article, first published in English in 1956, derives much of its celebrity from the central place accorded by the French structuralists to the 1963 translation of a selection of Jakobson's work, entitled *Essais linguistiques*, which included the aphasia study. The words "metaphor" and "metonymy" are not, of course, of twentieth-century coinage: they are classical tropes traditionally defined as the substitution of a figurative expression for a literal or proper one. In metaphor, the substitution is based on resemblance or analogy; in metonymy, it is based on a relation or association other than that of similarity (cause and effect, container and contained, proper name and qualities or works associated with it, place and event or institution, instrument and user, etc.). The use of the name "Camelot" to refer to John Kennedy's Washington is thus an example of metaphor, since it implies and analogy between Kennedy's world and King Arthur's, while the use of the word "Watergate" to refer to the scandal that ended Richard Nixon's presidency is a metonymy, since it transfers the name of an arbitrary place of origin onto a whole sequence of subsequent events.

From *Black Literature and Literary Theory*. © 1984 by Methuen, Inc. Originally entitled "Metaphor, Metonymy, and Voice in *Their Eyes Were Watching God*.

Jakobson's use of the two terms is an extension and polarization of their classical definitions. In studying patterns of aphasia (speech dysfunction), Jakobson found that they fell into two main categories: similarity disorders and contiguity disorders. In the former, grammatical contexture and lateral associations remain while synonymity drops out; in the latter, heaps of word substitutes are kept while grammar and connectedness vanish. Jakobson concludes:

> The development of a discourse may take place along two different semantic lines: one topic may lead to another either through their similarity or through their contiguity. The metaphoric way would be the most appropriate term for the first case and the metonymic way for the second, since they find their most condensed expression in metaphor and metonymy respectively. In aphasia one or the other of these two processes is restricted or totally blocked—an effect which makes the study of aphasia particularly illuminating for the linguist. In normal verbal behavior both processes are continually operative, but careful observation will reveal that under the influence of a cultural pattern, personality, and verbal style, preference is given to one of the two processes over the other.
>
> In a well-known psychological test, children are confronted with some noun and told to utter the first verbal response that comes into their heads. In this experiment two opposite linguistic predilections are invariably exhibited: the response is intended either as a substitute for, or as a complement to the stimulus. In the latter case the stimulus and the response together form a proper syntactic construction, most usually a sentence. These two types of reaction have been labeled substitutive and predicative.
>
> To the stimulus *hut* one response was *burnt out;* another, *is a poor little house.* Both reactions are predicative; but the first creates a purely narrative context, while in the second there is a double connection with the subject *hut:* on the one hand, a positional (namely, syntactic) contiguity, and on the other a semantic similarity.
>
> The same stimulus produced the following substitutive reactions: the tautology *hut;* the synonyms *cabin* and *hovel;* the antonym *palace,* and the metaphors *den* and *burrow.* The capacity of two words to replace one another is an instance of positional similarity, and, in addition, all these responses are linked to the stimulus by semantic similarity (or contrast). Metonymical responses to the same stimulus, such as *thatch, litter,* or *poverty,* combine and contrast the positional similarity with semantic contiguity.
>
> In manipulating these two kinds of connection (similarity and contiguity) in both their aspects (positional and semantic)—selecting, combining, and ranking them—an individual exhibits his personal style, his verbal predilections and preferences.

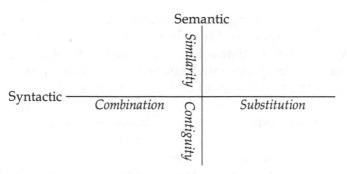

Figure 1

Two problems immediately arise that render the opposition between metaphor and metonymy at once more interesting and more problematic than at first appears. The first is that there are not two poles here but four: similarity, contiguity, semantic connection, and syntactic connection. A more adequate representation of these oppositions can be schematized as in Figure 1. Jakobson's contention that poetry is a syntactic extension of metaphor ("The poetic function projects the principle of equivalence from the axis of selection into the axis of combination"), while realist narrative is an extension of metonymy, can be added to the graph as in Figure 2.

The second problem that arises in any attempt to apply the metaphor/metonymy distinction is that it is often very hard to tell the two apart. In Ronsard's poem "Mignonne, allons voir si la rose . . .," the speaker invites the lady to go for a walk with him (the walk being an example of contiguity) to see a rose which, once beautiful (like the lady), is now withered (as the lady will eventually be): the day must therefore be seized. The metonymic proximity to the flower is designed solely to reveal the metaphoric point of the poem: enjoy life while you still bloom. The tendency of contiguity to become overlaid by similarity and vice versa may be summed up in the proverb, "Birds of a feather flock together"—"Qui se ressemble s'assemble." One has only to think of the applicability of this proverb to the composition of neighborhoods in America to realize that the question of the separability of similarity from contiguity may have considerable political implications. The controversy surrounding the expression "legionnaires' disease" provides a more comical example: while the name of the disease

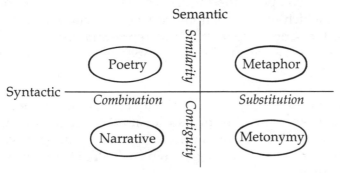

Figure 2

derives solely from the contingent fact that its first victims were at an American Legion Convention, and is thus a metonymy, the fear that it will take on a metaphoric color—that a belief in some natural connection or similarity may thereby be propagated between legionnaires and the disease—has led spokesmen for the legionnaires to attempt to have the malady renamed. And finally, in the sentence "The White House denied the charges," one might ask whether the place name is a purely contiguous metonymy for the presidency, or whether the whiteness of the house isn't somehow metaphorically connected to the whiteness of its inhabitant.

One final prefatory remark about the metaphor/metonymy distinction: far from being a neutral opposition between equals, these two tropes have always stood in hierarchical relation to each other. From Aristotle to George Lakoff, metaphor has always, in the Western tradition, had the privilege of revealing unexpected truth. As Aristotle puts it: "Midway between the unintelligible and the commonplace, it is a metaphor which most produces knowledge." Paul de Man summarizes the preference for metaphor over metonymy by aligning analogy with necessity and contiguity with chance: "The inference of identity and totality that is constitutive of metaphor is lacking in the purely relational metonymic contact: an element of truth is involved in taking Achilles for a lion but none in taking Mr Ford for a motor car." De Man then goes on to reveal this "element of truth" as the product of a purely rhetorical—and ultimately metonymical—sleight of hand, thus overturning the traditional hierarchy and deconstructing the very basis for the seductiveness and privilege of metaphor.

I should like now to turn to the work of an author acutely conscious of, and superbly skilled in, the seductiveness and complexity of metaphor as privileged trope and trope of privilege. Zora Neale Hurston, novelist, folklorist, essayist, anthropologist and Harlem Renaissance personality, cut her teeth on figurative language during the tale-telling or "lying" sessions that took place on a store porch in the all-black town of Eatonville, Florida, where she was born around 1901. She devoted her life to the task of recording, preserving, novelizing and analyzing the patterns of speech and thought of the rural black south and related cultures. At the same time, she deplored the appropriation, dilution and commodification of black culture (through spirituals, jazz, etc.) by the pre-Depression white world, and she constantly tried to explain the difference between a reified "art" and a living culture in which the distinctions between spectator and spectacle, rehearsal and performance, experience and representation, are not fixed. "Folklore," she wrote, "is the arts of the people before they find out that there is such a thing as art."

> Folklore does not belong to any special area, time, nor people. It is a world and an ageless thing, so let us look at it from that viewpoint. It is the boiled down juice of human living and when one phase of it passes another begins which shall in turn give way before a successor.

> Culture is a forced march on the near and the obvious. . . . The
> intelligent mind uses up a great part of its lifespan trying to awaken
> its consciousness sufficiently to comprehend that which is plainly
> there before it. Every generation or so some individual with extra
> keen perception grasps something of the obvious about us and
> hitches the human race forward slightly by a new "law." Millions
> of things had been falling on men for thousands of years before
> the falling apple hit Newton on the head and he saw the law of
> gravity.

Through this strategic description of the folkloric heart of scientific law,
Hurston dramatizes the predicament not only of the anthropologist but
also of the novelist: both are caught between the (metaphorical) urge to
universalize or totalize and the knowledge that it is precisely "the near and
the obvious" that will never be grasped once and for all but will only be
(metonymically) named and renamed, as different things successively strike
different heads. I shall return to this problem of universality at the end of
this essay, but first I should like to take a close look at some of the figurative
operations at work in Hurston's best-known novel, *Their Eyes Were Watching
God*.

The novel presents, in a combination of first- and third-person narration, the story of Janie Crawford and her three successive husbands. The
first, Logan Killicks, is chosen by Janie's grandmother for his sixty acres
and as a socially secure harbor for Janie's awakening sexuality. When Janie
realizes that love does not automatically follow upon marriage and that
Killicks completely lacks imagination, she decides to run off with ambitious,
smart-talking, stylishly dressed Joe Starks, who is headed for a new all-
black town where he hopes to become what he calls a "big voice." Later,
as mayor and store owner of the town, he proudly raises Janie to a pedestal
of property and propriety. Because this involves her submission to his idea
of what a mayor's wife should be, Janie soon finds her pedestal to be a
straitjacket, particularly when it involves her exclusion—both as speaker
and as listener—from the tale-telling sessions on the store porch and at the
mock funeral of a mule. Little by little, Janie begins to talk back to Joe,
finally insulting him so profoundly that, in a sense, he dies of it. Some
time later, into Janie's life walks Tea Cake Woods, whose first act is to teach
Janie how to play checkers. "Somebody wanted her to play," says the text
in free indirect discourse; "Somebody thought it natural for her to play."
Thus begins a joyous liberation from the rigidities of status, image and
property—one of the most beautiful and convincing love stories in any
literature. In a series of courtship dances, appearances and disappearances,
Tea Cake succeeds in fulfilling Janie's dream of "a bee for her blossom."
Tea Cake, unlike Joe and Logan, regards money and work as worth only
the amount of play and enjoyment they make possible. He gains and loses
money unpredictably until he and Janie begin working side by side picking
beans on "the muck" in the Florida everglades. This idyll of pleasure, work

and equality ends dramatically with a hurricane during which Tea Cake, while saving Janie's life, is bitten by a rabid dog. When Tea Cake's subsequent hydrophobia transforms him into a wild and violent animal, Janie is forced to shoot him in self-defense. Acquitted of murder by an all-white jury, Janie returns to Eatonville, where she tells her story to her friend Phoeby Watson.

The passage on which I should like to concentrate both describes and dramatizes, in its figurative structure, a crucial turning point in Janie's relation to Joe and to herself. The passage follows an argument over what Janie has done with a bill of lading, during which Janie shouts, "You sho loves to tell me whut to do, but Ah can't tell you nothin' Ah see!"

"Dat's 'cause you need tellin'," he rejoined hotly. "It would be pitiful if Ah didn't. Somebody got to think for women and chillun and chickens and cows. I god, they sho don't think none theirselves."

"Ah knows uh few things, and womenfolks thinks sometimes too!"

"Aw naw they don't. They just think they's thinkin'. When Ah see one thing Ah understands ten. You see ten things and don't understand one."

Times and scenes like that put Janie to thinking about the inside state of her marriage. Time came when she fought back with her tongue as best she could, but it didn't do her any good. It just made Joe do more. He wanted her submission and he'd keep on fighting until he felt he had it.

So gradually, she pressed her teeth together and learned how to hush. The spirit of the marriage left the bedroom and took to living in the parlor. It was there to shake hands whenever company came to visit, but it never went back inside the bedroom again. So she put something in there to represent the spirit like a Virgin Mary image in a church. The bed was no longer a daisy-field for her and Joe to play in. It was a place where she went and laid down when she was sleepy and tired.

She wasn't petal-open anymore with him. She was twenty-four and seven years married when she knew. She found that out one day when he slapped her face in the kitchen. It happened over one of those dinners that chasten all women sometimes. They plan and they fix and they do, and then some kitchen-dwelling fiend slips a scrochy, soggy, tasteless mess into their pots and pans. Janie was a good cook, and Joe had looked forward to his dinner as a refuge from other things. So when the bread didn't rise and the fish wasn't quite done at the bone, and the rice was scorched, he slapped Janie until she had a ringing sound in her ears and told her about her brains before he stalked on back to the store.

Janie stood where he left her for unmeasured time and thought.

She stood there until something fell off the shelf inside her. Then she went inside there to see what it was. It was her image of Jody tumbled down and shattered. But looking at it she saw that it never was the flesh and blood figure of her dreams. Just something she had grabbed up to drape her dreams over. In a way she turned her back upon the image where it lay and looked further. She had no more blossomy openings dusting pollen over her man, neither any glistening young fruit where the petals used to be. She found that she had a host of thoughts she had never expressed to him, and numerous emotions she had never let Jody know about. Things packed up and put away in parts of her heart where he could never find them. She was saving up feelings for some man she had never seen. She had an inside and an outside now and suddenly she knew how not to mix them.

This opposition between an inside and an outside is a standard way of describing the nature of a rhetorical figure. The vehicle, or surface meaning, is seen as enclosing an inner tenor, or figurative meaning. This relation can be pictured somewhat facetiously as a gilded carriage—the vehicle—containing Luciano Pavarotti, the tenor. Within the passage cited from *Their Eyes Were Watching God*, I should like to concentrate on the two paragraphs that begin respectively "So gradually . . . " and "Janie stood where he left her . . . " In these two paragraphs Hurston plays a number of interesting variations on the inside/outside opposition.

In both paragraphs, a relation is set up between an inner "image" and outward, domestic space. The parlor, bedroom and store full of shelves already exist in the narrative space of the novel: they are figures drawn metonymically from the familiar contiguous surroundings. Each of these paragraphs recounts a little narrative of, and within, its own figurative terms. In the first, the inner spirit of the marriage moves outward from the bedroom to the parlor, cutting itself off from its proper place, and replacing itself with an image of virginity, the antithesis of marriage. Although Joe is constantly exclaiming, "I god, Janie," he will not be as successful as his namesake in uniting with the Virgin Mary. Indeed, it is his godlike self-image that forces Janie to retreat to virginity. The entire paragraph is an externalization of Janie's feelings onto the outer surroundings in the form of a narrative of movement from private to public space. While the whole of the figure relates metaphorically, analogically, to the marital situation it is designed to express, it reveals the marriage space to be metonymical, a movement through a series of contiguous rooms. It is a narrative not of union but of separation centered on an image not of conjugality but of virginity.

In the second passage, just after the slap, Janie is standing, thinking, until something "fell off the shelf inside her." Janie's "inside" is here represented as a store that she then goes in to inspect. While the former paragraph was an externalization of the inner, here we find an internalization of the outer: Janie's inner self resembles a store. The material for this metaphor is drawn from the narrative world of contiguity: the store is the place where Joe has set himself up as lord, master and proprietor. But here Jody's image is broken, and reveals itself never to have been a metaphor but only a metonymy of Janie's dream: "looking at it she saw that it never was the flesh and blood figure of her dreams. Just something she had grabbed up to drape her dreams over."

What we find in juxtaposing these two figural mini-narratives is a kind of chiasmus, or cross-over, in which the first paragraph presents an externalization of the inner, a metaphorically grounded metonymy, while the second paragraph presents an internalization of the outer, or a metonymically grounded metaphor. In both cases, the quotient of the operation is the revelation of a false or discordant "image." Janie's image, as Virgin Mary, acquires a new intactness, while Joe's lies shattered on the floor. The reversals operated by the chiasmus map out a reversal of the power relations between Janie and Joe. Henceforth, Janie will grow in power and resistance, while Joe deteriorates both in his body and in his public image.

The moral of these two figural tales is rich with implications: "She had an inside and an outside now and suddenly she knew how not to mix them." On the one hand, this means that she knew how to keep the inside and the outside separate without trying to blend or merge them into one unified identity. On the other hand it means that she has stepped irrevocably into the necessity of figurative language, where inside and outside are never the same. It is from this point on in the novel that Janie, paradoxically, begins to speak. And it is by means of a devastating figure— "You look like the change of life"—that she wounds Jody to the quick. Janie's acquisition of the power of voice thus grows not out of her identity but out of her division into inside and outside. Knowing how not to mix them is knowing that articulate language requires the co-presence of two distinct poles, not their collapse into oneness.

This, of course, is what Jakobson concludes in his discussion of metaphor and metonymy. For it must be remembered that what is at stake in the maintenance of both sides—metaphor and metonymy, inside and outside—is the very possibility of speaking at all. The reduction of a discourse to oneness, identity—in Janie's case, the reduction of woman to mayor's wife—has as its necessary consequence aphasia, silence, the loss of the ability to speak: "she pressed her teeth together and learned how to hush."

What has gone unnoticed in theoretical discussions of Jakobson's article is that behind the metaphor/metonymy distinction lies the much more serious distinction between speech and aphasia, between silence and the capacity to articulate one's own voice. To privilege *either* metaphor *or* metonymy is thus to run the risk of producing an increasingly aphasic *critical* discourse. If both, or all four, poles must be operative in order for speech to function fully, then the very notion of an "authentic voice" must be redefined. Far from being an expression of Janie's new wholeness or identity as a character, Janie's increasing ability to speak grows out of her ability not to mix inside with outside, not to pretend that there is no difference, but to assume and articulate the incompatible forces involved in her own division. The sign of an authentic voice is thus not self-identity but self-difference.

The search for wholeness, oneness, universality and totalization can nevertheless never be put to rest. However rich, healthy or lucid fragmentation and division may be, narrative seems to have trouble resting content with it, as though a story could not recognize its own end as anything other than a moment of totalization—even when what is totalized is loss. The ending of *Their Eyes Were Watching God* is no exception: "Of course [Tea Cake] wasn't dead. He could never be dead until she herself had finished feeling and thinking. The kiss of his memory made pictures of love and light against the wall. Here was peace. She pulled in her horizon like a great fish-net. Pulled it from around the waist of the world and draped it over her shoulder. So much of life in its meshes! She called in her soul to come and see." The horizon, with all of life caught in its meshes, is here pulled into the self as a gesture of total recuperation and peace. It is as though self-division could be healed over at last, but only at the cost of radical loss of the other.

This hope for some ultimate unity and peace seems to structure the very sense of an ending as such, whether that of a novel or that of a work of literary criticism. At the opposite end of the "canonical" scale, one finds it, for example, in the last chapter of Erich Auerbach's *Mimesis*, perhaps the greatest of modern monuments to the European literary canon. That final chapter, entitled "The Brown Stocking" after the stocking that Virginia Woolf's Mrs Ramsay is knitting in *To the Lighthouse*, is a description of certain narrative tendencies in the modern novel: "multipersonal representation of consciousness, time strata, disintegration of the continuity of exterior events, shifting of narrative viewpoint," etc. "Let us begin with a tendency which is particularly striking in our text from Virginia Woolf. She holds to minor, unimpressive, random events: measuring the stocking, a fragment of a conversation with the maid, a telephone call. Great changes, exterior turning points, let alone catastrophes, do not occur." Auerbach concludes his discussion of the modernists's preoccupation with the minor, the trivial and the marginal by saying:

> It is precisely the random moment which is comparatively independent of the controversial and unstable orders over which men fight and despair. . . . The more numerous, varied, and simple the people are who appear as subjects of such random moments, the more effectively must what they have in common shine forth. . . . So the complicated process of dissolution which led to fragmentation of the exterior action, to reflection of consciousness, and to stratification of time seems to be tending toward a very simple solution. Perhaps it will be too simple to please those who, despite all its dangers and catastrophes, admire and love our epoch

for the sake of its abundance of life and the incomparable historical vantage point which it affords. But they are few in number, and probably they will not live to see much more than the first fore-warnings of the approaching unification and simplification.

Never has the desire to transform fragmentation into unity been expressed so succinctly and authoritatively—indeed, almost prophetically. One cannot help but wonder, though, whether the force of this desire has not been provoked by the fact that the primary test it wishes to unify and simplify was written by a woman. What Auerbach calls "minor, unimpressive, random events"—measuring a stocking, conversing with the maid, answering the phone — can all be identified as conventional *women's* activities. "Great changes," "exterior turning points" and "catastrophes" have been the stuff of heroic *male* literature. Even plot itself—up until *Madame Bovary*, at least—has been conceived as the doings of those who do *not* stay at home, i.e. men. Auerbach's urge to unify and simplify is an urge to re-subsume female difference under the category of the universal, which has always been unavowedly male. The random, the trivial and the marginal will simply be added to the list of things all *men* have in common.

If "unification and simplification" is the privilege and province of the male, it is also, in America, the privilege and province of the white. If the woman's voice, to be authentic, must incorporate and articulate division and self-difference, so, too, has Afro-American literature always had to assume its double-voicedness. As Henry Louis Gates, Jr, puts it in "Criticism in the Jungle": "In the instance of the writer of African descent, her or his texts occupy spaces in at least two traditions—the individual's European or American literary tradition, and one of the three related but distinct black traditions. The 'heritage' of each black text written in a Western language, then, is a double heritage, two-toned, as it were. . . . Each utterance, then, is double-voiced." This is a reformulation of W. E. B. DuBois's famous image of the "veil" that divides the black American in two:

> The Negro is a sort of seventh son, born with a veil, and gifted with second sight in this American world,—a world which yields him no true self-consciousness, but only lets him see himself through the revelation of the other world. It is a peculiar sensation, this double-consciousness, this sense of always looking at one's self through the eyes of others, of measuring one's soul by the tape of a world that looks on in amused contempt and pity. One ever feels his twoness—an American, a Negro; two souls, two thoughts, two unreconciled strivings; two warring ideals in one dark body, whose dogged strength alone keeps it from being torn asunder.
>
> The history of the American Negro is the history of this strife,—this longing to attain self-conscious manhood, to merge his double self into a better and truer self.

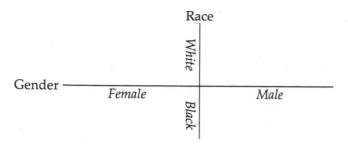

Figure 3

James Weldon Johnson, in his *Autobiography of an Ex-Colored Man*, puts it this way: "This is the dwarfing, warping, distorting influence which operates upon each and every colored man in the United States. He is forced to take his outlook on all things, not from the view-point of a citizen, or a man, or even a human being, but from the view-point of a *colored* man. . . . This gives to every colored man, in proportion to his intellectuality, a sort of dual personality." What is striking about the above two quotations is that they both assume without question that the black subject is male. The black woman is totally invisible in these descriptions of the black dilemma. Richard Wright, in his review of *Their Eyes Were Watching God*, makes it plain that for him, too, the black female experience is nonexistent. The novel, says Wright, lacks "a basic idea or theme that lends itself to significant interpretation. . . . [Hurston's] dialogue manages to catch the psychological movements of the Negro folk-mind in their pure simplicity, but that's as far as it goes. . . . The sensory sweep of her novel carries no theme, no message, no thought."

No message, no theme, no thought: the full range of questions and experiences of Janie's life are as invisible to a mind steeped in maleness as Ellison's Invisible Man is to minds steeped in whiteness. If the black *man's* soul is divided in two, what can be said of the black woman's? Here again, what is constantly seen exclusively in terms of a binary opposition—black versus white, man versus woman—must be redrawn at least as a tetrapolar structure (see Figure 3). What happens in the case of a black woman is that the four quadrants are constantly being collapsed into two. Hurston's work is often called non-political simply because readers of Afro-American literature tend to look for confrontational *racial* politics, not sexual politics. If the black woman voices opposition to male domination, she is often seen as a traitor to the cause of racial justice. But, if she sides with black men against white oppression, she often winds up having to accept her position within the Black Power movement as, in Stokely Carmichael's words, "prone." This impossible position between two oppositions is what I think Hurston intends when, at the end of the novel, she represents Janie as acquitted of the murder of Tea Cake by an all-white jury but condemned by her fellow blacks. This is not out of a "lack of bitterness toward whites," as one reader would have it, but rather out of a knowledge of the standards of male dominance that pervade both the black and the white worlds. The

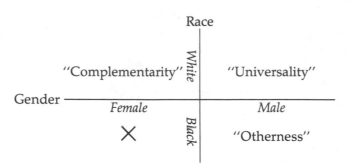

Figure 4

black crowd at the trial murmurs,"Tea Cake was a good boy. He had been good to that woman. No nigger woman ain't never been treated no better." As Janie's grandmother puts it early in the novel: "Honey, de white man is de ruler of everything as fur as Ah been able tuh find out. Maybe it's some place way off in de ocean where de black man is in power, but we don't know nothin' but what we see. So de white man throw down de load and tell de nigger man tuh pick it up. He pick it up because he have to, but he don't tote it. He hand it to his womenfolks. De nigger woman is de mule uh de world so fur as Ah can see."

In a very persuasive book on black women and feminism entitled *Ain't I a Woman*, Bell Hooks (Gloria Watkins) discusses the ways in which black women suffer from both sexism and racism within the very movements whose ostensible purpose is to set them free. Watkins argues that "black woman" has never been considered a separate, distinct category with a history and complexity of its own. When a president appoints a black woman to a cabinet post, for example, he does not feel he is appointing a person belonging to the category "black woman"; he is appointing a person who belongs *both* to the category "black" *and* to the category "woman," and is thus killing two birds with one stone. Watkins says of the analogy often drawn—particularly by white feminists—between blacks and women: "Since analogies derive their power, their appeal, and their very reason for being from the sense of two disparate phenomena having been brought closer together, for white women to acknowledge the overlap between the terms 'blacks' and 'women' (that is, the existence of black women) would render this analogy unnecessary. By continuously making this analogy, they unwittingly suggest that to them the term 'women' is synonymous with 'white women' and the term 'blacks' synonymous with 'black men'." The very existence of black women thus disappears from an analogical discourse designed to express the types of oppression from which black women have the most to suffer.

In the current hierarchical view of things, this tetrapolar graph can be filled in as in Figure 4. The black woman is both invisible and ubiquitous: never seen in her own right but forever appropriated by the others for their own ends.

Ultimately, though, this mapping of tetrapolar differences is itself a fantasy of universality. Are all the members of each quadrant the same? Where are the nations, the regions, the religions, the classes, the professions? Where are the other races, the interracial subdivisions? How can the human world be totalized, even as a field of divisions? In the following quotation from Zora Neale Hurston's autobiography, we see that even the *same* black woman can express self-division in two completely different ways:

> Work was to be all of me, so I said. . . . I had finished that phase of research and was considering writing my first book, when I met the man who was really to lay me by the heels. . . .
>
> He was tall, dark brown, magnificently built, with a beautifully modeled back head. His profile was strong and good. The nose and lips were especially good front and side. But his looks only drew my eyes in the beginning. I did not fall in love with him just for that. He had a fine mind and that intrigued me. When a man keeps beating me to the draw mentally, he begins to get glamorous. . . . His intellect got me first for I am the kind of woman that likes to move on mentally from point to point, and I like for my man to be there way ahead of me. . . .
>
> His great desire was to do for me. *Please* let him be a *man*! . . .
>
> That very manliness, sweet as it was, made us both suffer. My career balked the completeness of his ideal. I really wanted to conform, but it was impossible. To me there was no conflict. My work was one thing, and he was all the rest. But I could not make him see that. Nothing must be in my life but himself. . . . We could not leave each other alone, and we could not shield each other from hurt. . . . In the midst of this, I received my Guggenheim Fellowship. This was my chance to release him, and fight myself free from my obsession. He would get over me in a few months and go on to be a very big man. So I sailed off to Jamaica [and] pitched in to work hard on my research to smother my feelings. But the thing would not down. The plot was far from the circumstances, but I tried to embalm all the tenderness of my passion for him in *Their Eyes Were Watching God*.

The plot is indeed far from the circumstances, and, what is even more striking, it is lived by what seems to be a completely different woman. While Janie struggles to attain equal respect *within* a relation to a man, Zora readily submits to the pleasures of submission yet struggles to establish the legitimacy of a professional life *outside* the love relation. The female voice may be universally described as divided, but it must be recognized as divided in a multitude of ways.

There is no point of view from which the universal characteristics of the human, or of the woman, or of the black woman, or even of Zora Neale Hurston, can be selected and totalized. Unification and simplification are fantasies of domination, not understanding.

The task of the writer, then, would seem to be to narrate both the appeal and the injustice of universalization, in a voice that assumes and articulates its own, ever differing self-difference. In the opening pages of *Their Eyes Were Watching God* we find, indeed, a brilliant and subtle transition from the seduction of a universal language through a progressive de-universalization that ends in the exclusion of the very protagonist herself. The book begins:

> Ships at a distance have every man's wish on board. For some they come in with the tide. For others they sail forever on the horizon, never out of sight, never landing until the Watcher turns his eyes away in resignation, his dreams mocked to death by Time. That is the life of men.
>
> Now, women forget all those things they don't want to remember, and remember everything they don't want to forget. The dream is the truth. Then they act and do things accordingly.
>
> So the beginning of this was a woman, and she had come back from burying the dead. Not the dead of sick and ailing with friends at the pillow and the feet. She had come back from the sodden and the bloated; the sudden dead, their eyes flung wide open in judgment.
>
> The people all saw her come because it was sundown.

At this point Janie crosses center stage and goes out, while the people, the "bander log," pass judgment on her. The viewpoint has moved from "every man" to "men" to "women" to "a woman" to an absence commented on by "words without masters," the gossip of the front porch. When Janie begins to speak, even the universalizing category of "standard English" gives way to the careful representation of dialect. The narrative voice in this novel expresses its own self-division by shifts between first and third person, standard English and dialect. This self-division culminates in the frequent use of free indirect discourse, in which, as Henry Louis Gates, Jr, points out, the inside/outside boundaries between narrator and character, between standard and individual, are both transgressed and preserved, making it impossible to identify and totalize either the subject or the nature of discourse.

Narrative, it seems, is an endless fishing expedition with the horizon as both the net and the fish, the big one that always gets away. The meshes continually enclose and let escape, tear open and mend up again. Mrs Ramsay never finishes the brown stocking. A woman's work is never done. Penelope's weaving is nightly re-unraveled. The porch never stops passing the world through its mouth. The process of de-universalization can never, universally, be completed.

A Surfeit of Commodities:
The Novels of Nathanael West

Jonathan Raban

If Nathanael West did not exist, then Leslie Fiedler would probably have had to invent him. For West, after a couple of decades of critical *purdah*, has become a necessary figment of American literary mythology. Indeed, flicking over the pages of the PMLA bibliographies of the last ten years, one might reasonably assume that West's bones had long ago been picked clean by the assistant professors and their assiduous graduate students. The arrival, in the mid-fifties, of what is now confidently termed "the comic apocalyptic novel," occasioned an evangelical wave of ancestor baptism. In the search to legitimize recent writers like Joseph Heller, Terry Southern, Thomas Pynchon, Thomas Berger, and the young novelist Edward Stewart (whose *Heads* strikes me as a very clever pastiche of the Westian style), West has been posthumously credited with a wonderfully virile and promiscuous talent for parenthood. Like most mythical figures, his powers have been variously, and exaggeratedly labelled: First American Surrealist, Sick Comedian, Dreamdumper, Nightmarist, Social Critic (of all things), Laughing Mortician. And for the mythmakers, West had an almost embarrassing abundance of convenient attributes: he was a Jew who renounced his religion; he was briefly expatriated during the twenties; he went the right distance out to the political left in the thirties; he worked in, and wrote about, Hollywood; he died young in a violent accident at the

From *The American Novel and the Nineteen Twenties*. © 1971 by Edward Arnold Publishers Ltd.

first to open a West stall in the literary bazaar, puts the basic ingredients
of the myth beautifully in *Waiting for the End*:

> He is the inventor for America of a peculiarly modern kind of
> book, whose claims are perfectly ambiguous. Reading his fiction,
> we do not know whether we are being presented with a nightmare
> endowed with the lineaments of reality, or with reality blurred to
> the uncertainty of nightmare. In either case, he must be read as
> a comic novelist, and his anti-heroes understood as comic char-
> acters, still as much *shlemiels* as any imagined by Fuchs, though
> they are presented as sacrificial victims, the only Christs possible
> in our skeptical world. In West, however, humor is expressed
> almost entirely in terms of the grotesque, which is to say, on the
> borderline between jest and horror; for violence is to him technique
> as well as subject matter, tone as well as theme.

Reading Fiedler, like reading most recent critics of West who tend slavishly
to echo him, we hardly know whether we are being presented with a
novelist and his actual work, or with a plausible diagram of a certain kind
of writer, and a certain kind of literary technique, which arguably *ought* to
exist somewhere in the labyrinth of recent American fiction. In the literary
histories and the books on the modern novel, West most frequently exists
as a cipher for a style which is far more readily identifiable with, say,
Thomas Pynchon's *V.* than with his own *Miss Lonelyhearts*. And in the
earnest exegetical articles, symbolist explication of West's novels has gone
into a wonderland of its own, full of failed Christs, illusions masquerading
as realities, phallic guns and hatches, ritual deaths and *shlemiels* galore. But
all that is a long way away from the spikey, spoiled surface of the novels,
themselves, with their short sentences facetiously pursuing their own metaphors into absurdity; their desperate patter of gags working their way
through the prose like a nervous tic; characters like cartoons in livid crayon;
everywhere an atmosphere of the kind of surrealism which might have
been rigged up by an enterprising handyman in his back garden. Nowhere
can the jitterbugging craze have worked itself into the texture of literature
so successfully as in the frantic phrasing of West's style.

It's a profoundly maimed style; as unambiguous as a shriek. West's
work is pathetically incomplete: re-reading his novels one watches again
and again as the shrill personality of the author extrudes from behind the
papery mask of his assumed style. With most novelists of a comparable
public stature, the work is larger, more rounded, than the biography which
produced it; with West, one needs biography in order to understand the
peculiar hiatuses, the grammatical breaks, the awkwardnesses and the often
uncontrolled hysteria of a fictional *oeuvre* that has been fractured, even
ruined, by its own history.

West seemed destined to miss every available boat. He was six years
younger than Hemingway, eight years younger than Fitzgerald; and by the
time he graduated from college and joined the colony of expatriates in

Paris, his near-contemporaries were already established writers. He was an awkward, gangling figure with an acned face, who aspired to Brooks Brothers suits and the latest dance steps. He had neither the glamour of Hemingway's war service and apprenticeship as a newspaperman, nor the polish of Fitzgerald's Ivy Leaguery. Brown University in the early twenties sounds like a dull coltishly provincial establishment, where the sons of the small-professional and commercial middle class acted out a hammed pastiche of the Harvard-and-Princeton style. Worst, West was a Jew; he was born Nathan Wallenstein Weinstein, and grew up in a period when to be Jewish was to be stigmatized as a Robert Cohn, or one of Pound's Usurers, or Eliot's "The jew squats on the windowsill, the owner,/Spawned in some estaminet of Antwerp . . . " No Weinstein could join any of the fraternity clubs at Brown, or participate easily in the confident protestantism of the literary tone of the twenties. And West had an agonising sense of social propriety. He seems to have spent his time at Brown developing an edgy, imitative style that would hide his Jewishness under his Coca-Cola nickname of "Pep." John Sanford, who knew West in New York, wrote of him: "More than anyone I ever knew Pep writhed under the accidental curse of his religion. . . . He changed his name, he changed his clothes, he changed his manners (we all did), in short he did everything possible to create the impression in his own mind—remember that, in his own mind—that he was just like Al Vanderbilt. It never quite came off." Part of the Al Vanderbilt act consisted of West playing the country squire, surrounded by gun-dogs and toting a twelve-bore with which he was a spectacularly careless and inaccurate shot. He was an urban Jew who tried to storm WASP America with endless frantic mimicry; it's hard to miss the obsessive, yearning inadequacy which characterized his life style—a desperation channelled into the relentless acquisition of social masks. Dance floor lizard, hometown Raskolnikov, Paris bohemian (on a parental allowance), hotel clerk, hunter, movie writer . . . Whatever West did seemed to take on the characteristics of a theatrical role; a part to be learned and played out with slightly over-large gestures. Deeply embedded in his novels is the notion of life as a kind of vulgar, snobbish vaudeville show. Certainly West himself was adept at the painful clowning in which the touring performer gets up in rouge and worn white slicker suit, to go through a travesty of the high-life style.

He was, prototypically, a marginal man, perched uneasily on the edge of his society. His acute sense of social conformity led him into an infatuation with the values of the twenties which was so overdone that it turned insidiously into conscious parody. At the same time he inflected his own contortions with shrill, self-destructive irony; he was simultaneously inside and out, passionately involved in his own activity, yet able to mock it with a ribald series of Bronx cheers. In West's early work, the social style that one recognizes from the anecdotes of his classmates at Brown is readily turned into a literary trick—indeed becomes, at first, his sole piece of literary equipment.

In an unpublished, semi-autobiographical story called "L'Affaire Beano," he treated the experience of expatriation in a tone of such bland condescension that the writing itself becomes merely a crude mode of exorcism:

> "In order to be an artist one has to live like one." We know now that this is nonsense, but in Paris in '25 and '26 we didn't know it. "Artists are crazy" is another statement from the same credo. Of course all these ideas were foisted on us by the non-artists, but we didn't realize it then. We came to the business of being an artist with the definitions of the non-artists and took libels for the truth. In order to be recognized as artists, we were everything our enemies said we were.
>
> By the time I got to Paris, the business of being an artist had grown quite difficult. . . . When I got to Montparnasse, all the obvious roles had either been dropped or were being played by experts. But I made a lucky hit. Instead of trying for strangeness, I formalized and exaggerated the costume of a bond salesman. I wore carefully pressed Brooks Brothers clothing, sober but rich ties, and carried gloves and a tightly rolled umbrella. My manners were elaborate and I professed great horror at the slightest breach of the conventional. It was a success. I was asked to all the parties.

The confident air is too exaggerated; the inclusive use of "we" too strident. West adopts a strategy of unearned absurdity: by reducing everything to short, slangy sentences, phrased in glib generalities, he achieves a thin horse-laugh at the expense of the narrator, of Paris, of the whole generation embodied in that sweeping "we." The passage exhibits a barely veiled hysteria; it is *about* authorial distance; one feels West frantically disengaging himself from his subject, reaching for a language that is cool, urbane, above all, knowing. But West doesn't know when to stop, and the effect is blatantly unconvincing.

When West stepped off the boat from France, he had the manuscript of *The Dream Life of Balso Snell* in his valise. Talking to A. J. Liebling, he said that he had written his first novel as "a protest against writing books." Both the remark and the book itself are of a piece with West's nervously brash social style. *The Dream Life of Balso Snell* filters the figureheads of modernism—Dostoevsky, Huysmans, Dada, Joyce—through the vulgarity of undergraduate revue. It is an impertinent satire, remarkably devoid of cunning, and maintains a consistent, irritating air of cocking a snook at the teachers, as West flails inaccurately around his pond of fashionable names. The core material of the novel was apparently in existence by 1924, when West lent an *ur-Balso* manuscript to Quentin Reynolds, to use as a crib for a Spring Day speech. The surprise is that West could continue living with his skittish ephemerid until 1931, when the book was finally published.

Its optimistic target was to demolish western culture with a snigger; its effect is to set in motion the lineaments of a style of contrived bogusness—a style which, in *Miss Lonelyhearts* and *The Day of the Locust*, was to be sharpened into a literary weapon of considerable force and subtlety. For the intestines of the wooden horse, where *Balso Snell* takes place, contain the remains of a stew of partially digested rhetorics. The characters—John Raskolnikov Gilson, Miss McGeeney, Maloney the Areopagite—are ciphers enclosed by the platitudes of their own languages. Together they compose a kind of Bartholomew Fair of social and cultural clichés.

It is quite clear that West had little intention of satirizing his modern humours in any detail. The parodies of *Balso Snell* are parodies of parodies; they work on schoolboy notions of "literary English," "avant garde writing," "religious rhetoric" and so on. When West turns on specific authors, he assimilates them into a childish convention; as in the garbled pastiche of Molly Bloom's soliloquy at the book's end:

> Hard-bitten. Casual. Smart. Been there before. I've had policemen. No trace of a feminine whimper. Decidedly revisiting well-known, well-ploughed ground. No new trees, wells, or even fences.
>
> Desperate for life. Live! Experience! Live one's own. Your body is an instrument, an organ or a drum. Harmony. Order. Breasts. The apple of my eye, the pear of my abdomen. What is life without love? I burn! I ache! Hurrah!
>
> Moooompitcher yaaaah. Oh I never hoped to know the passion, the sensuality hidden within you—yes, yes. Drag me down into the mire, drag. Yes! And with your hair the lust from my eyes brush. Yes . . . Yes . . . Ooh! Ah!

Its badness is at least partially deliberate. For West's writing, by its very lack of satiric specificity, forces us to attend, not to the thing parodied (in this case *Ulysses*), but to the chaotic detritus of a consciousness brutally assaulted by this mess of styles, names, lists of objects. The random breaks, the structurelessness, the noisy nonsense, the constant posing of *Balso Snell* go to make up the actual subject of the book. And West is very good at recreating the stimuli of physical nausea as he lets his language cascade into a trough of absurdities. Again and again we are deluged by a style of gratuitous enumeration, as sentences reduplicate themselves in a runaway rhetoric, as repetitive as the flow of identical articles off an assembly line:

> "And Death?—bah! What, then, is there still detaining you in this vale of tears?" Can it be that the only thing that bothers me in a statement of this sort is the wording? Or is it because there is something arty about Suicide? Suicide: Werther, the Cosmic Urge, the Soul, the Quest, and Otto Greenbaum, Phi Beta Kappa, Age Seventeen—Life is unworthy of him; and Haldington Knape, Oxford, author, man-about-town, big game hunter—Life is too tiresome; and Terry Kornflower, poet, no hat, shirt open to the navel—Life is too crude; and Janey Davenport, pregnant, unmarried, jumps from a studio window in Paris—Life is too difficult.

Here is a style of writing which sets out to prove its own sogginess, its own inadequacy under the pressure of the objects which it is forced to catalogue platitudinously. The failed surface of *Balso Snell* represents West's attempt to exhibit language and a sensibility which have been raped to a point of retching exhaustion.

As a satire, *Balso Snell* is a pretentious flop. But as the inauguration of a style, it is an auspicious technical essay, marred by grandiose overreaching and by the intrusive uncertainty of the author. For West himself shows up anxiously every few pages, nudging the reader in the ribs, all too ready to explain just what he's trying to do. The book is full of passages with the ring of deadly earnestness about them: "An intelligent man finds it easy to laugh at himself, but his laughter is not sincere if it is not thorough. If I could be Hamlet, or even a clown with a breaking heart 'neath his jester's motley, the role would be tolerable. But I always find it necessary to burlesque the mystery of feeling at its source; I must laugh at myself, and if the laugh is 'bitter,' I must laugh at the laugh. The ritual of feeling demands burlesque and, whether the burlesque is successful or not, a laugh." This poses real problems. On the one hand, West cursorily tries to incorporate the passage itself with the other exhausted rhetorics of the book, by quoting "bitter" and slipping in the phrase about the broken hearted clown (then overdoing it with the archaism " 'neath"); on the other, he allows it to stand as a *propria persona* statement. For a book as bland in its general approach as *Balso Snell*, such lapses act as remarkable confessions of insecurity. They work like distress signals, shouts for help from the centre of a muddle he clearly doesn't fully understand. He becomes the victim of his own lucidity; his language runs away with him, as if the mask had commandeered the face behind.

For West's novels, though they aspire to burlesque and laughter, rarely manage to climb out of that state of anxious self-scrutiny. His second book, *Miss Lonelyhearts* (1933), is frequently credited with being West's most assured and controlled piece of fiction; if that is true, it is only because he had learned to incorporate his uncertainty into the design and texture of his writing. Originally he was going to subtitle *Miss Lonelyhearts: A Novel in the Form of a Comic Strip*—and the tautness of that initial idea has stayed with the book, in its use of short illustrative chapters, stylized language, and primary-coloured locations. The comic strip gives the novel its extraordinarily rapid tempo; working on West like a harness, so that his tendencies towards diversive extravaganza are kept firmly in check. But the apparent single-mindedness of *Miss Lonelyhearts* is deceptive: an uneasy tension throbs away in the novel, just under its carefully polished surface. (It is indicative of West's painstaking care with the book that he rewrote it more than six times: and, when working on it full-time, produced only 700-1,000 words a week.)

Like *Balso Snell*, *Miss Lonelyhearts* presents us with a menagerie of rhetorics; between them they make up a splintered portrait of a society that has become consumed by its own clichés. At the same time it is a novel which explores the possibility that the conventions of the Novel—its machinery of "plot" and "character" and psychological tensions and development—have been made unworkable by the urban industrial world of pulp media and cheapjack commodities. West does not merely create "two-dimensional" characters; he attempts to obliterate the notion of character altogether. For the people in *Miss Lonelyhearts*—Desperate, Broken-hearted, Sick-of-it-all, Mr. and Mrs. Doyle, Shrike, Betty and the rest—act simply as labels on which to stick a jaded, received language of sickening platitudes. The book basically belongs to them; it is their confusing and contradictory *noise* which assaults both the reader and Miss Lonelyhearts.

What then of Miss Lonelyhearts himself? The first phrase of the novel is "The Miss Lonelyhearts of the New York *Post-Dispatch* . . . " and West never fully allows him to disambiguate himself from that definite, but inanimate, article. He is a function; a vibrating diaphragm set in the centre of the communications business, as stereotyped in his available roles as the voices which beset him. He is described once in the book, and the description is made in such generic terms that it almost becomes a parodic satire on the convention of bodying-out the central "character" in all his particularities: "Although his cheap clothes had too much style, he still looked like the son of a Baptist minister. A beard would become him, would accent his Old-Testament look. But even without a beard no one could fail to recognize the New England puritan. His forehead was high and narrow. His nose was long and fleshless. His bony chin was shaped and cleft like a hoof." Compare this with the other descriptions in the book: of Shrike, "Under the shining white globe of his brow, his features huddled together in a dead, gray triangle"; of Mr. Doyle, "He looked like one of those composite photographs used by screen magazines in guessing contests"; of Mrs. Doyle, "Legs like Indian clubs, breasts like balloons and a brow like a pigeon." In all cases, the similes are there, not to illuminate, but to deaden the character. West robs each of them of any recognizably human attributes, and turns them into things. The language they speak is the mass-produced grammar and vocabulary of the newspaper, the magazine, the movie. Not only are they likened to objects, but on occasions become confused with objects. Thus in the chapter, "Miss Lonelyhearts and the Party Dress," Miss Lonelyhearts begins by encountering Betty (a splendid talking doll out of a woman's weekly) person-to-person, then slides rapidly, through a dialogue of resounding banality, into an object-to-object relationship: "He begged the party dress to marry him, saying all the things it expected to hear, all the things that went with strawberry sodas and farms in Connecticut. He was just what the party dress expected him to be: simple and sweet, whimsical and poetic, a trifle collegiate yet very masculine." This technique of synecdoche turns Shrike into a talking newspaperman's eyeshade, with his glibly cynical spiels; Doyle becomes merely an extension of his enormous cripple's shoe; and Miss Lonelyhearts himself grows into a walking evangelist's soapbox. By reducing his characters to these formulae West deadens our expectations of human sympathy or change: deeply rooted in the novel is the suggestion that the only way in which we can be surprised or moved is by the introduction of things so shocking or grotesque that they transcend all normal social categories. And this is the function of the letters—"*I sit and look at myself all day and cry. I have a big hole in the middle of my face that scares people even myself so I cant blame the boys for not wanting to take me out. My mother loves me, but she crys terrible when she looks at me.*" The only alternative to cliché is illiteracy; the only alternative to the conditioned social responses of the Shrikes and the Mrs. Doyles is gross deformity. But we should, I think, be honest enough to admit that the letters rise to such a level of crude extremity that they are merely funny. The predicaments to which they refer are so unimaginably awful that one takes refuge in the comic-proletarian humour of bad spelling and impossible grammar. If we are shocked by, say, the first or second letter in the book, they soon become a convention as predictable as Betty's homely flutings. The girl with the hole in the middle of her face turns, along with all the other characters in the book, into just another cliché. What is truly shocking is our own incapacity to respond to, or to make sense of, the human confusion which the novel appears to enact.

I say "appears to" because *Miss Lonelyhearts* works like a baited trap; it assaults the reader with extremities, then leaves him wondering, embarrassedly, about his own emotional inadequacy in the face of this battering. But West effectively prevents us from responding by deliberately deadening his characters and by turning even the most bizarre rhetorics in the book into cliché. What is real in the novel is the procession of images which focus, not on any fictional predicament inhabited by the characters, but on the dilemma of West the writer, the unwilling creator of this perverse menagerie.

For the central tone of the narrative is one of jokey circumspection; it pries, investigates, works in beautifully sharp visual flashes, constantly counterpointing the violent hysteria of the novel's social world. In the second chapter, for instance, Miss Lonelyhearts crosses a park on his way to the speakeasy: "He entered the park at the North Gate and swallowed mouthfuls of the heavy shade that curtained its arch. He walked into the shadow of a lamp-post that lay on the path like a spear. It pierced him like a spear." One is brought up sharp by that last sentence; it looks like a facetious indulgence, a piece of verbal by-play for which there shouldn't be room in a passage supposedly centring on Miss Lonelyhearts's agony over the desperation of his correspondents' lives. But in *Miss Lonelyhearts* there always is room; the narrative continually steps back and films in sardonic slow motion. In the middle of a violent row with Betty—"He began to shout at her, accompanying his shouts with gestures that were too appropriate, like those of an old-fashioned actor." The narrative is positively garrulous in its readiness to stop by the way and chat, throwing in eloquent, but static, similes. Its effect is to make the social situation both trivial and unreal; it offers an alternative world of objects and exact descriptions—a world of concretes: bottles ranged above a bar, the colour of tobacco smoke, a flapping newspaper, flagstones, clothes, domestic implements. Throughout the novel, West constantly shifts from his object-like people to objects themselves, which he treats with relish. His imagery is invariably more alive than the characters who occasion it, as if the ordering process of writing were of far greater importance than the people and events out of which novels are usually, if unfortunately, made.

The reader of *Miss Lonelyhearts* becomes its proto-author; his central problem is to shape the hectic and confused voices of the book into the stylized patterns offered him by West. The subject of the novel becomes the desperate play of sensibility as it attempts to reconcile the noisy, heterogeneous fragments of a mass-media world. The images become more contorted, to the point of growing surreal; the noises get louder; the paper characters dance frenziedly on the spot. But our attention remains fixed on the jugglery of West, the most psychologically convincing character in the novel, as he tries to keep all those multiple, crude voices and objects in balance. The trouble is that West seems to be in love with his own failure. The grotesquerie of the letters, of Miss Lonelyhearts's eventual death at the hands of Doyle, of the snatched sex and casual speakeasy brutality in the book, is carried out with a kind of sadistic delight. West's tone, as he transforms his people into mechanical devices or exhibits their pathetically stereotyped rhetorics, is never less than gay. He, not Miss Lonelyhearts, is the failed hero of the novel; he subsides under its pressures like an old-style tragedian, waving his arms and bellowing with obvious enjoyment.

As a novelist, West establishes himself by destroying his own creations with the easily-won indifference of a god. He grossly indulged himself in *A Cool Million* (1934), accurately subtitled, "The Dismantling of Lemuel Pitkin"; an extended act of writer's vengeance on the notions of "character" and "society." By reducing his hero to an innocent who is even flatter and more simple-minded than Alger's Ragged Dick, and by turning American fascism into a society more lurid than that of most horror comics, West gives himself the opportunity to write in a vein of extraordinary nastiness: "He also made an unsuccessful attempt to find Mr. Whipple. At the Salvation Army post they told him that they had observed Mr. Whipple lying quietly in the gutter after the meeting of the 'Leather Shirts,' but that when they looked the next day to see if he were still there they found only a large blood stain. Lem looked himself but failed even to find this stain, there being many cats in the neighbourhood." One would surely have to be very insensitive indeed to find this humorous; it goes considerably further than the letters in *Miss Lonelyhearts* in its direct exploitation of a literary trick, enabled only by the complete unreality of the fictional characters and situations involved. There is a totalitarian streak in West's writing; a tendency to turn his novels into Charentons, where he can victimize his witless characters at his pleasure. For a novelist, it seems an odd revenge.

And West appears to have realized this in the five years that followed before the publication of *The Day of the Locust* (1939). In Tod Hackett, the Tiresias-like artist through whose eyes we see the waste land of Hollywood,

West partially embodied his own predicament as a writer. When he first encounters Homer Simpson, the retired hotel clerk from Iowa, on the landing of the San Bernadino Arms, he behaves remarkably like West's authorial persona: "Tod examined him eagerly. He didn't mean to be rude but at first glance this man seemed an exact model for the kind of person who comes to California to die, perfect in every detail down to fever eyes and unruly hands." Through Tod, West is able to inflect his own aesthetic sadism with a degree of irony. But West and Tod jockey for position in the novel, and it's often difficult to determine who is in control where. So, after the marvellous description of Hollywood as a landscape of pure artifice and simulation, the last paragraph of chapter one reads: "It is hard to laugh at the need for beauty and romance, no matter how tasteless, even horrible, the results of that need are. But it is easy to sigh. Few things are sadder than the truly monstrous." Its tone is both apologetic and sententious. Does it belong to Tod or West? It reads like most professions of sentiment in West's fiction, as if it ought to go into quotation marks, yet its positioning in the chapter suggests that it is an authentic narrative voice which we must accept if we are to continue to collaborate with the novel. In combination with the passage describing Tod's specimen-hunting approach to Homer Simpson, it is a strong indicator of West's unease. In *The Day of the Locust*, he covers himself both ways by creating a promiscuous irony with which to ambiguate almost everything in the book.

The structure of *The Day of the Locust* is that of an exactly timed series of improvizations. It is built round its set-pieces: two celluloid battles, a Hollywood party, a cheap rooming house inhabited by the dreamers, a funeral, a cockfight and a gala première. Each of these major scenes are "long shots"; they display the characters at a distance and treat them through a filter of imagery that rubs out their individual details and emphasizes their generic characteristics. They are balanced by interlinking flashback-biographies and close-ups which continually test the individual characters against the large thematic patterns proposed by Tod as he assembles the material for his painting, *The Burning of Los Angeles*, and tacitly underwritten by West. This dialectical structure works smoothly and eloquently; for the first time, West is able to use the Novel as mode of exploration rather than flat statement.

More powerfully than ever before, the destruction of character grows organically out of the texture of the fiction. The magnificently realized location of Hollywood—the luric illusions of the studio lot and the Cape Cod colonial house in paper and plaster, the antiseptic smelling corridors of the San Bernadino Arms, the sickly, pervasive heat in which Harry Greener peddles his cans of home-made polish, the mawkish kitsch of the Californian way of love and death—provides a backdrop of epic dimensions, against which the characters scuttle pitifully, reduced to twitching puppets by the overpowering articulacy of their environment. And West manages his structural devices with a new cunning. In the fourth chapter, for instance, he alternates between brief, cruel portraits of the guests at

Claude Estee's party and their tinny dialogues; then, just when the rhythm of the section demands a new portrait of a partygoer, West introduces the black mass at the bottom of the darkened swimming pool: "A row of submerged floodlights illuminated the green water. The thing was a dead horse, or, rather, a life-size, realistic reproduction of one. Its legs stuck up stiff and straight and it had an enormous, distended belly. Its hammerhead lay twisted to one side and from its mouth, which was set in an agonized grin, hung a heavy, black tongue." It is perfectly timed, and the party never recovers from the insidious suggestion of that passage: the twisted penis and the hanging tongue carry, like sustained bass notes, into the next chapter, where the party migrates to a brothel to watch blue movies.

In *The Day of the Locust*, the shifts of tone are rapid and unexpected; West darts in and out of his characters like a skilled saboteur. Describing Homer Simpson's move into his cottage, he spends four paragraphs of neutral narrative, in which the reader is allowed temporarily to inhabit Homer as a character, before shifting, through an intermediary paragraph, into a passage of brilliantly managed detachment: "He got out of bed in sections, like a poorly made automaton, and carried his hands into the bathroom. He turned on the cold water. When the basin was full, he plunged his hands in up to the wrists. They lay quietly on the bottom like a pair of strange aquatic animals. When they were thoroughly chilled and began to crawl about, he lifted them out and hid them in a towel." This is far more fully developed, and less flashy, than the comparable images of *Miss Lonelyhearts*. Almost every character in the novel—Abe Kusich, the dwarf who is initially mistaken for a pile of soiled laundry; the cowboy, Earle Shoop, who has "a two-dimensional face that a talented child might have drawn with a ruler and compass"; Harry Greener who behaves like an overwound mechanical toy when he had his first heart attack—is transmuted into the kind of object that can be found on the garbage dumps of an industrial society. But West does not simply leave it at that; he gathers the threads of his images together to project them into a large and complete metaphor of estrangement. In Hollywood, the dreams are faked in the studios; the houses are faked on the hillsides; emotions are faked (consciously and with style) in Harry Greener's music hall routines; religion, and even death, are faked by the funeral industry (where Harry's shaved and rouged corpse is made to look "like the interlocutor in a minstrel show"); and people are faked in a relentless process of image-making. The novel itself works like a production line; it takes the scattered ingredients of a recognizably real Hollywood and turns them into the hard, bright patterns of cheap industrial design.

For West never allows us to lose sight of the artifice of his own novel; his carefully managed structure is often deliberately obtrusive. One watches the novelist keep Harry Greener alive until the time is ripe for the funeral; then West, without warning, snuffs him out. And Tod's insistent interior monologues, as he collects characters and bits and pieces for his painting, are a way of reminding us that it is the process of the novel that is at stake;

the characters and their situations are merely the bundles of hair and leaves and mud out of which the glittering structure may be composed. The final effect is of a lunatic baroque edifice which stuns the onlooker with its sheer brazenness, its air of suffocating overpopulation. *The Day of the Locust* obsessively accumulates its details; characters are switched into objects and added to the pile; objects themselves take on a bizarrely vivid life of their own; the landscape of Los Angeles is broken down into a heap of brightly painted junk. The apocalyptic finale, when the rioting mob lynch Homer Simpson, is both a description and an encapsulation of the process of the novel: the heat, stench, frustration and noise of a packed crowd is expanded to breaking point. Then one is left only with a quietened shuffle of people round an ambulance, while the artist goes into an hysterical imitation of the sound of its klaxon.

West never got beyond that point. His unease is taken to the edge of hysteria and left there. On the one hand there is the shrill confidence of his imagery, the harshly didactic rhythm of his sentences. He strains all the time for a literary voice that will carry the ring of the stern authoritarian, and rules his novels like a dictator. On the other, there is a strain of excruciatingly evident insecurity. His irony teeters between the gross (as in *A Cool Million*) and the nervously diffuse. His style of masquerade slips frequently into lapses of embarrassing earnestness. He is, pre-eminently, the novelist as victim.

West's fictional world is essentially one of objects, of commodities. When people enter it they become transfixed and assimilated into the dime-store jumble of parti-coloured rubbish. On this account, West is often called a surrealist (a title which he himself vehemently rejected). And, clearly, there are deliberate echoes of Huysmans's *A Rebours* in all of West's novels; the glutted consciousness, fed to the point of nausea with sensations, images, people, things, which forms the centre of each narrative often seems exactly like a coarsened and vulgarized version of Des Esseintes. It is almost as if Huysmans's hero had lived into the post-war boom of industrial manufacturing, and found his dreams on sale at every Woolworths.' But this is why West's work is a far cry from European surrealism; his wildly juxtaposed objects always belong to an explicitly commercial context. The passage most frequently quoted as evidence for his "surrealism" is that section from *Miss Lonelyhearts* in which Betty and Shrike compete for the fevered columnist's soul. Lying ill in bed—

> He found himself in the window of a pawnshop full of fur coats, diamond rings, watches, shotguns, fishing tackle, mandolins. All these things were the paraphernalia of suffering. A tortured high light twisted on the blade of a gift knife, a battered horn grunted with pain . . .
> A trumpet, marked to sell for $2.49, gave the call to battle and Miss Lonelyhearts plunged into the fray. First he formed a phallus of old watches and rubber boots, then a heart of umbrellas and

trout flies, then a diamond of musical instruments and derby hats, after these a circle, triangle, square, swastika. But nothing proved definitive and he began to make a gigantic cross. When the cross became too large for the pawnshop, he moved it to the shore of the ocean. There every wave added to his stock faster than he could lengthen its arms. His labours were enormous. He staggered from the last wave line to his work, loaded down with marine refuse—bottles, shells, chunks of cork, fish heads, pieces of net.

It is too easy merely to see that here are the lineaments of a painting by Ernst or Dali. We shouldn't miss the fact that the vision starts in a pawnshop; that the objects over which Miss Lonelyhearts exercises his sickened imagination are either pieces of rubbish or things in hock. West turns his hero into a crazed consumer, haphazardly patterning the goods on display; his revulsion is focussed on a peculiarly American style of mass commercial wastage. If it is surrealism, it is the home-town surrealism of the neighbourhood supermarket. One can echo this with passages from any of West's books; for instance, when Homer Simpson goes shopping in *The Day of the Locust*; "The SunGold Market into which he turned was a large, brilliantly lit place. All the fixtures were chromium and the floors and walls were lined with white tile. Coloured spotlights played on the showcases and counters, heightening the natural hues of the different foods. The oranges were bathed in red, the lemons in yellow, the fish in pale green, the steaks in rose and the eggs in ivory." Behind West's chilling, cartoonlike treatment of people and objects (and people-as-objects) there always lies the chink of money and the grinding of the industrial machine. He is a surfeited realist. The surface strangeness and "violence" of his novels never rises far above the simple level of being sickened by the excess of an overstocked refrigerator or a sweaty crowd on a Christmas-shopping spree.

It seems helpful to remember Fitzgerald's thorny transition from the twenties to the thirties. In *The Great Gatsby* he was able to allow Daisy to weep over the beauty of Gatsby's opulent shirts; to catalogue with open-eyed wonder the magnificence of that machine for gutting oranges and the brilliant yellow of Gatsby's car. But in *Tender Is the Night*, his tone hardens. Nicole, the child of American success, is discovered in a psychiatric clinic which is explicitly described by Fitzgerald as a kind of spunging-house for a society that is going sour on its own affluence. Nicole, the consumer heroine—for whose sake

trains began their run at Chicago and traversed the round belly of the continent to California; chicle factories fumed and link belts grew link by link in factories; men mixed toothpaste in vats and drew mouthwash out of copper hogsheads; girls canned tomatoes quickly in August or worked rudely at the Five-and Tens on Christmas Eve; half-breed Indians toiled on Brazilian coffee plantations and dreamers were muscled out of patent rights on new tractors— these were some of the people who gave a tithe to Nicole and, as the whole system swayed and thundered onward, it lent a feverish bloom to such processes of hers as wholesale buying, like the flush of a fireman's face holding his post before a spreading blaze. She illustrated very simple principles, containing in herself her own doom, but illustrated them so accurately that there was grace in the procedure, and presently Rosemary would try to imitate it.

—shakes hysterically in the bathroom, immersed in some obscure schizo-phrenic fit. Surrounded by the *embarras de richesse* which he acquires with Nicole (and which prominently includes another pneumatic rubber horse), Dick subsides into broken alcoholism. The wealth of possibilities which seemed once to extend, like the green light over Daisy's dock, has narrowed down to the rank aftertaste of used commodities. Fitzgerald accommodates these opposites in his fiction with a wonderful doubleness of vision; West works obsessively around only the seamy underside of that flowed dream.

For West had a more parochial, mean and hysterical talent than the best of his contemporaries. Like Nicole, he vividly expressed the ruin that came in the wake of the spree; but unlike her, and unlike Fitzgerald too, he never participated in the style which the spree temporarily enabled. Perhaps his novels have been overvalued because American literary history has needed a scapegoat—a novelist so violated that he stands as a symbol for the violent estrangement with which the thirties looked back on the hopes and excesses of the previous decade. He created a voice of shrill, high-pitched nausea; and his mutilated novels are as much symptoms as they are diagnoses of the disease.

I Thought I Knew These People: Richard Wright and the Afro-American Literary Tradition

Robert B. Stepto

One of the curious things about Richard Wright is that while there is no question that his best works occupy a prominent place in the Afro-American canon, or that a survey of Afro-American literature would be incomplete without him, many, including myself, find it difficult to describe his place in the Afro-American literary tradition. Part of this feeling may be attributed to a growing concern over how often "canon," "survey," and "tradition" have been casually treated as synonymous terms and unthinkingly interchanged. We all have distinctive, "working" definitions for these terms, but frequently in our teaching, if not so much in our writing, they are blurred and offered, perhaps in the same discussion or lecture, as three verbal lunges at a single vague but tacitly understood idea. When we try to clarify them and teach accordingly, teaching becomes infinitely more difficult, especially when one assumes the task of illuminating a tradition as opposed to following blindly dates of publication or of biography, or proceeding along the slightly more arduous path of identifying what are commonly held to be the "best" texts. An author's place in a tradition depends on how he reveals that tradition. It is not simply a matter of when his works were published but also of how they illuminate—and in some cases honor—what has come before and anticipate what will follow. In Afro-American literature particularly, the idea of a tradition involves certain questions about the author's posture not only among his fellow writers but also within a larger artistic continuum which, in its exquisite commingling of materials spoken, played, and written, is not the exclusive property or domain of the writer alone. Richard Wright is a fine writer, perhaps a great one; he has influenced, in one way or another, almost every important black writer who has followed him. But Wright forces us to face a consid-

From *Chant of Saints: A Gathering of Afro-American Literature, Art, and Scholarship*. © 1979 by The Board of Trustees of the University of Illinois. University of Illinois Press, 1979.

erable problem: to what extent may we qualify his place in the artistic tradition and still submit that he is unquestionably a participant in it? I don't pretend to be able to solve this problem, but I can explore three of the questions involved: What was Wright's posture as an author, and how did it correspond with models provided by the tradition? How do his works illuminate or complement those Afro-American texts preceding them? And, what has been his effect on our contemporary literature and culture? In answering these we will be a little closer to understanding Wright's place— or lack of one—in the tradition.

I

Many passages in Wright's works illustrate the issues concerning his authorial posture, but the following one from "I Tried to Be a Communist" seems particularly appropriate, partly because it is autobiographical and partly because it raises all the familiar arguments regarding Wright's posture toward his audience. In the passage, Wright describes what happened when he spoke before a unit meeting of black communists in Chicago:

> The meeting started. About twenty Negroes were gathered. The time came for me to make my report and I took out my notes and told them how I had come to join the Party, what few stray items I had published, what my duties were in the John Reed Club. I finished and waited for comment. There was silence. I looked about. Most of the comrades sat with bowed heads. Then I was surprised to catch a twitching smile on the lips of a Negro woman. Minutes passed. The Negro woman lifted her head and looked at the organizer. The organizer smothered a smile.

When the organizer finally breaks the silence, Wright recoils from his comments, significantly remarking, "His tone was more patronizing than that of a Southern white man. . . . I thought I knew these people, but evidently I did not." Then Wright informs us: "During the following days I learned . . . that I . . . had been classified as an *intellectual* . . . that the black Communists in my unit had commented upon my shined shoes, my clean shirt, and the tie I had worn. Above all, my manner of speech had seemed an alien thing to them. . . . 'He talks like a book,' one of the Negro comrades had said. And that was enough to condemn me forever as bourgeois." Wright's ambivalent attitude toward his race and its rituals is amply revealed here, and, while it is not a matter which should enter into our evaluations of his art, it does haunt and becloud our feelings concerning his place in the tradition. Aware of the vivid scenes in *Black Boy*, wherein racial bonds are shown to be either hypocritical or forms of submission, and recalling as well how he argues in "Blueprint for Negro Literature" for Negro writers to transcend "the nationalist implications of their lives," we are able to comprehend his behavior at the unit meeting but not necessarily approve of it. What brands him an intellectual in this instance is not, strictly speaking, his clean clothes or his articulateness. If this were the case, then most of the black preachers in America—whom Wright termed "sainted devils"—would bear the same mark and be cast from church and pulpit. That Wright "talks like a book" is closer to the heart of the matter, for it is Wright's *mode* of articulation, and the related matter of how he did not (or could not) acknowledge kinship with his black brethren while articulating the Party line, which most troubled his black audience and, in turn, bothers us.

Wright's refusal to partake of the essential intra-racial rituals which the situation demanded suggests that he was either unaware of, or simply refused to participate in, those viable modes of speech represented in history by the preacher and orator and in letters by the articulate hero. The question of articulation does not rest exclusively with matters of verbal facility, but, on a higher plane, with the expression of a moral consciousness which is racially-based. And of course this involves a celebration of those honorable codes of conduct among one's kin.

Wright's dilemma reminds one of Du Bois's short story in *The Souls of Black Folk* entitled "Of the Coming of John," in which the "black" John, John Jones, comes home from college to teach school and "rescue" his black townspeople from their "backwardness." His chance to address neighbors and kin occurs at the black Baptist church, and despite his college-honed elocution he fails miserably in his purpose, partly, one imagines, because he attempts to assault those rituals of behavior which the humble building in which he speaks both represents and reinforces. Divorced from the community, condemning blindly all intra-racial codes as formulae for submission, speaking an oddly-cadenced tongue, John Jones fails because of his inarticulateness; and as the story unfolds, he becomes the prototype for Bigger Thomas when he finally expresses himself by bludgeoning the "white" John, John Henderson, kissing his momma, and running away. Jones would have done well to take Wright's advice in "Blueprint" that one only transcends what is "national" in their lives by first embracing it. But he did not, and it is questionable whether Wright did either.

In both the story of John Jones and Wright's "I Tried to Be a Communist," the failure to articulate is at once a matter of the voice assumed and of how that voice relates to the audience at hand. While Jones did not speak to or of his audience, Wright compounded Jones's error by speaking beyond his immediate audience to another, which in this case was Big Brother. We might see our way to calling a truce and sounding a grace note if, when Wright states that the blacks condemned him as "bourgeois," we could be certain that he is employing both the Party-line and "black culture-based" senses of the term. This might have suggested his awareness, in retrospect, of the violation of intra-racial codes. But the evidence is, if not exactly to the contrary, at least unconvincing.

The "unit meeting" passage hints at many complaints laid at Wright's door, but none loom larger than Ellison's lament (*Shadow and Act*) that Wright "could not for ideological reasons depict a Negro as intelligent, as creative or as dedicated as himself." The charge pertains particularly to Bigger Thomas, but as we see in *Black Boy* and in "I Tried to Be a Communist," Wright's limited depiction of the Negro extends occasionally to self-portraits as well. It is hard to believe that the bumbling black writer alienating black folk and performing a poor job of propagandizing for the Party is supposed to be Wright himself, but for reasons neither wholly self-effacing nor wholly aesthetic it is, alas, poor Richard.

The issue is really Wright's idea of the hero, although I believe none of his critics put the matter quite this way. If we assume, as I do, that the primary voice in the tradition, whether in prose or verse or music, is a personal heroic voice delineating the dimensions of heroism by either aspiring to a heroic posture, as do the voices of Douglass and Du Bois, or expressing an awareness of that which they *ought* to be, as we see Johnson's Ex-Colored Man and Ellison's Invisible Man doing, then the mystery of what is unsettling about Wright's voice (and protagonists) begins to unfold. Bigger Thomas is hardly the only maimed or stunted or confused figure in Afro-American literature; this is not what makes him different. What *does* is his unawareness of what he *ought* to be, especially as it is defined not by the vague dictates of the American Dream but by the rather specific mandates of a racial heritage. When Ellison complains (*Shadow and Act*): "Wright could imagine Bigger, but Bigger could not possibly imagine Richard Wright. Wright saw to that." his lament is really that Wright did not place Bigger in the tradition. Interestingly enough, placing *Wright* in the tradition was exactly what Ellison tried to do in 1945 (but later renounced in "The World and the Jug" in 1963) when he argued that *Black Boy* was a blues in prose (*Shadow and Act*).

All in all, Wright's authorial posture is much like that of Booker T. Washington. Both men are, to use George Kent's phrase, "exaggerated Westerners," especially with regard to the voice and posture each perfected in order to reach those whom they perceived to be their audience. Responding to what might be termed the literary offences of Washington, Du Bois argued in *The Souls* that part of what was wrong with the Tuskegee Spirit was the degree to which "the speech and thought of triumphant commercialism" was indeed *becoming* that spirit, or at least the *expression* of it. Ellison makes a similar point about Wright when he says, " . . . Wright found the facile answers of Marxism before he learned to use literature as a means for discovering the forms of American Negro humanity" (*Shadow and Act*). In the case of both men, the speech and thought they espoused led to a necessary denial, at least in print, of certain Afro-American traditions. Hence, they were, in their authorial posture, exaggerated individuals alienated from their race and, to some degree, themselves. Even when they are about the task of creating themselves in autobiographies, their vision is shaped and possibly warped by this state of "exaggeratedness." Thus, in *Up from Slavery*, Washington models himself as the ideal fundraiser and public speaker and defers to the facile portraits of himself by journalists, while Wright, in *Black Boy*, suppresses his own extraordinary human spirit by rendering himself a black "biological fact."

But as with most comparisons there are distinctions to be made. Beyond all questions of era and place rests the simple fact that Washington was in control of the implications of his authorial posture while Wright was not. When, for example, Washington rebukes the models and motifs of the slave narratives by casting *Up from Slavery* in the vein of the Franklinesque source book and, to some degree, the Horatio Alger tale, we sense that this was the price he willingly paid to exchange his full life story for funds for Tuskegee and other, sometimes clandestine, projects. He knew what he was about and the dollars most certainly came rolling in. When Wright, on the other hand, even in the writing of *Black Boy*, embraces the example of Dreiser, Lewis, and Mencken far more than that of Toomer, Johnson, Hughes, or Hurston, we want to know what was the trade-off, what the exchange or sacrifice comparable to Washington's? In sum, Wright was more the victim of his posture than the master of it, and in this he is not alone in Afro-American letters. If he indeed occupies a prominent place in the tradition because of his views on author and audience, it is because the founders set aside a large space for confused men.

II

Turning to the question of how his books may confirm Wright's place in the tradition, we find ourselves on what seems to be surer ground but in the end is not. Despite Wright's apparent ignorance of Afro-American literature during his youth and rise to literary prominence, there are distinct links between certain preceding narrative types, the slave narrative and plantation tale in particular, and his own writings. But the question remains as to whether these links are mere repeated patterns or of the resilient stuff that establish author and text in an artistic continuum.

Native Son, for example, may be viewed as a plantation tale, not only because there are ties between it and the "revisionist" plantation tales of Charles W. Chesnutt, but also because certain features of setting, action, and character are recognizably those of a nineteenth-century American plantation society. The setting is roughly that of a plantation, with the slave quarters west of Cottage Grove Avenue, a respectful long block from the Big House of the Dalton's on Drexel Boulevard. Dalton may not be a slave-holding captain of early agri-business, but his immense profits do come from the land and from the hard toil of blacks in that, as president of the South Side Real Estate Company, he landlords over hundreds of over-priced rat-infested tenements, including that in which Bigger and his family lead their sorry lives. This provides the essential irony of the famous cell-block scene where Mrs. Thomas kneels before Mrs. Dalton and begs for her intervention, saying (*Native Son*): "Please, don't let 'em kill my boy! You know how a mother feels! Please, mam. . . . We live in your house.

394   Robert B. Stepto

... They done asked us to move. . . . We ain't got nothing . . . I'll work
for you for the rest of my life! . . . " Mrs. Thomas's plea is in part one for
Mrs. Dalton to honor a sense of commitment initially established by the
covenant between master and slave. He offer to work for the Daltons the
rest of her life is, under the circumstances, a gift she has already given and
will continue to give as long as she is trapped in one or another tenement
of Dalton's ghetto.

Besides the Daltons and Mrs. Thomas, there are other minor characters
such as Britten, who in his functions as a private eye turns out to be more
and more like an overseer. And of course there are the major characters,
Bigger, Mary Dalton, and, I would argue, Attorney Max. When George
Kent writes that "A major source of the power of *Native Son* derived from
Wright's ability to articulate the relevant rituals of black and white cultures—and Bigger's response to them," he refers to those rituals emphasizing the presence or absence of "rational drive, curiosity, revolutionary
will, individualism [and] self-consciousness." But he should have also mentioned those ritualized postures of the black male and white female which,
one imagines, have prevailed in the mainstream of the culture since the
races first came into contact. Despite her flirtation with communism, Mary
Dalton is still the young, white, and (as her Christian name implies) virginal
belle on the pedestal. She might at first sit alongside Bigger in the front
seat of her father's car, but in the end, she removes to the rear with her
boyfriend, Jan, only to reinforce the distance by reminding Bigger to cart
her trunk to the station in the morning. And so the shuttle is set in motion,
orders one moment, her drunken head on Bigger's shoulder the next. If
Bigger is confused, the police and newspapers are not: Mary is the white
beauty, Bigger the black brute.

These postures are, unfortunately in our world, timeless, and we
would be wrong to suggest that they are in some way the exclusive property
of the antebellum South. And because Mary and Bigger are in this sense
conventional types, we must wonder whether the third major character,
Attorney Max, is as well. Like Mary's boyfriend, Jan, Max resembles the
sympathetic white found in the slave narratives who is somewhat removed
from the system. But while Jan remains within the type—and is therefore
as one-dimensional as are most of the novel's characters—Max's status is
more problematic. While he never gains the intimacy with Bigger he so
desperately seeks, Max does nevertheless, more than any other, spark
Bigger's fleeting glimpse of the possibilities of life and of human communion. Moreover, as his courtroom speech implies, he sees, more than the
rest, how America has made Bigger far more than Bigger has fashioned
himself. Max's use of language is what allows him to break out of the
plantation tale type. It contrasts not only with Bigger's verbal deficiencies
and with the corruption of language by the State's Attorney and the press,
but also, on a subtler scale, with Mary and Jan's insensitive verbal gropings
across the racial chasm (" 'Isn't there a song like that, a song your people
sing?' ") which only fill Bigger with "a dumb, cold, and inarticulate hate."

Indeed, what most distinguishes *Native Son* from its antecedent plantation tale texts is not its bleak urban landscape but the fact that the traditional heroic modes of transcending travail in this world, such as the gift of uncommon insight and speech, have been given not to Bigger but apparently to Max instead. Thus, the issue of Bigger's sub-heroic posture is further confused by the question of whether Wright intends Max to be the novel's heroic voice and, by extension, Wright's voice as well.

All this brings us to Max's celebrated courtroom speech. If Max speaks for Wright, we must assume that he specifically does so in the courtroom episode where he is not only eloquent but forthright and compassionate. Yet this poses a considerable problem, for in implicitly espousing the classic liberal notion that truth will invariably foster justice, Max blunts the raw revolutionary fervor which Bigger generated and which first seduced the communists to come to his aid. In doing so, Max exchanges his credentials as a radical for a heroic posture which is very much in the American grain. Thus, while transcending the character type in the slave narratives which he first resembles, Max soon takes on the features of a familiar turn-of-the-century type, the "white moral voice," of whom Charles W. Chesnutt, in Afro-American letters, provides us with at least four examples. Max is, then, a revolutionary manqué; a reformer possessing a grand but ineffectual idealism which leaves him horror-struck before the fact of Bigger's pending execution.

If Max is *not* Wright's voice, or at least not the heroic voice in the novel, then we would expect him to be sketched ironically, with the stress falling on what may be less than heroic in his words and character. But this is not the case. What we have instead is a confusion of political language and purpose, compounded by the troublesome fact that Wright seems to have bestowed the gift of eloquence on Max with no clearly discernible end in mind.

The problem with Max seems to be a fictive equivalent of Wright's own dilemma in "I Tried to Be a Communist." In each case, the speaker's articulateness does not meet the needs of the occasion and in that sense is a kind of illiteracy, especially of the sort that is enforced by America's rituals along the color line. If, in *Native Son*, Max is indeed Wright's voice, it is not because of the content of his speeches but rather because he shares with his author a misperception of audience, grounded in what we may term an extraordinary and almost myopic innocence. Thus, despite the novel's many and varied images of American slave society, the absence of an articulate hero whose posture and language tends to modulate the forces of a hostile environment renders *Native Son* a most problematic novel in Afro-American letters.

Black Boy, on the other hand, is more clearly conceived and is hence the better of Wright's two greatest published works. The dominant voice of the book seems to be finally that of its author precisely because it has a fair measure of human proportion. To be sure, we are almost overwhelmed by those relentless passages in *Black Boy* in which Wright fashions himself a black "biological fact." But countering these are the moments of marvelous self-assertion, the Whitmanesque catalogs of sensual remembrances, and overall, the presence of a questing human being seeking freedom and a voice. Here, a hostile environment *is* modulated by an emerging, extraordinary figure, and the resulting narrative establishes a place for itself in the continuum founded by the slave narrative.

One may list a number of motifs *Black Boy* shares with the slave narratives—the violence and gnawing hunger, the skeptical view of Christianity, the portrait of a black family valiantly attempting to maintain a degree of unity, the impregnable isolation, the longing and scheming to follow the North Star resolved by boarding the "freedom train"—but the most enduring link is the motif (and, one might argue, the narrative form) of the narrator's quest for literacy. Frederick Douglass provides the most compelling statement (*Narrative of the Life of Frederick Douglass, An American Slave*) of how literacy and freedom are entwined goals when he relates:

> Very soon after I went to live with Mr. and Mrs. Auld, she very kindly commenced to teach me the A, B, C. After I had learned this, she assisted me in learning to spell words of three or four letters. Just at this point of my progress, Mr. Auld found out what was going on, and at once forbade Mrs. Auld to instruct me further, telling her, among other things, that it was unlawful, as well as unsafe, to teach a slave to read. To use his own words, further, he said,"If you give a nigger an inch, he will take an ell. A nigger should know nothing but to obey his master—to do as he is told to do. Learning would *spoil* the best nigger in the world. Now," said he, "if you teach that nigger (speaking of myself) how to read, there would be no keeping of him. It would forever unfit him to be a slave. He would at once become unmanageable, and of no value to his master. As to himself, it would do him no good, but a great deal of harm. It would make him discontented and unhappy." These words sank deep into my heart, stirred up sentiments within that lay slumbering, and called into existence an entirely new train of thought. It was a new and special revelation, explaining dark and mysterious things, with which my youthful understanding had struggled in vain. I now understood what had been to me a most perplexing difficulty—to wit, the white man's power to enslave the black man. It was a grand achievement, and I prized it highly. From that moment, I understood the pathway from slavery to freedom.

While Wright's quest for literacy was hardly this arduous, it was nevertheless difficult and, especially by the time he was nineteen and in Memphis, fraught with danger. As he intimates in *Black Boy*, there were white men who might have killed him had they known he was reading Mencken and Sinclair Lewis and absorbing their indictments of America. Unlike Douglass, Wright did not have to dupe white boys in the streets in order to learn how to cipher, but he did have to discover a sympathetic Irishman who secretly lent him his library card before he could break the isolation and read "books that opened up new avenues of feeling and seeing." And it was this reading, as well as the writing of stories and even commencement addresses, which prompted young Richard to follow the North Star and, in a supreme act of self-assertion, free himself.

All in all, our comparison of *Black Boy* and *Native Son* provides us with a number of strong, revealing contrasts, but none presses with greater urgency and portent than that of the self-assertive, self-aware narrator of *Black Boy* seeking literacy and a voice appositioned against the image of Bigger and his inert cohorts assaulted by the mindlessness of B-grade Hollywood films and the rhetoric of propaganda emanating not only from the communists but also from the Daltons, the government, and the press. Clearly, Wright could match his model of the writer described in "Blueprint" who is "something of a guide in [our] daily living," but it is remarkable that he did so only in the writing of his autobiography.

III

Despite what we've previously said about Wright's distance from the race and his problems concerning voice and audience, there is considerable evidence of his influence on and enshrinement by the contemporary black writer and critic. In 1964, while participating in a symposium on Wright, Saunders Redding declared: "Certainly, if we are in a renaissance, as it were, more or less similar, though very, very different from the renaissance of the Twenties, it is because of Richard Wright." Given the year in which Redding made this statement, one may assume that he was referring to the ascending careers of several writers, of whom Baldwin and Ellison might very well have topped the list. Their protests to the contrary, Baldwin and Ellison *were* influenced by Wright; one might even argue that a significant part of their drive to write derived from a desire to "humanize" Bigger. A great deal of ink has been spilled on this subject, and I won't contribute mine. Rather, I would like to explore briefly Wright's influence on the critics and authors of Afro-American literature of the last decade.

Perhaps the most obvious evidence of Wright's influence is provided by the titles of several widely disseminated studies of Afro-American literature published in the 1950s and 1960s. In addition to Baldwin's *Notes of a Native Son* (1955) and Cleaver's "Notes on a Native Son" in *Soul on Ice (1968)*, we have Edward Margolies's *Native Sons: A Critical Study of Twentieth-Century Negro American Authors* (1968). Yet another quasi-sociological survey of Afro-American writing, and one which systematically excludes black women writers (the title is no reasonable rationale for this), Margolies's book is hardly a ground-breaking performance. One imagines that it was rushed to print, as were many other titles, to meet the needs of the new market created by the rise of Afro-American Studies. But it is worth our attention because Margolies attempts, in a very modest way, to forge a critical approach to Afro-American literature based on the example and impact of *Native Son*. He writes in his introductory chapter:

> The example of *Native Son* enabled others to deal with a body of subject matter they had hitherto warily skirted. Wright opened up for Negro writers not only the bitterness of their lives, but other taboo matters as well—miscegenation, homosexuality, the white-Negro power structure, and even the singular freedom a Negro feels in a society that denies him any recognition of his humanity. The courage to "tell it the way it is" is the prime requisite of artistic integrity. Human revelation is the business of the artist; he must write about what he *knows* to be true—imaginatively or other-wise—and the first truths he must know are about himself. *Native Son* provided many Negro authors with these precedents. In its way it liberated them as no other book has done since.

We are not entirely happy with this statement; one hopes, for example, that Margolies's list of "taboo matters" beginning with miscegenation and ending with the "singular freedom" of the Negro is not supposed to reflect the order of their importance. But the idea of treating *Native Son* as some sort of watershed in Afro-American literature is not altogether amiss, especially if one wishes to investigate the course of Afro-American literary *art*. However, Margolies is centrally concerned with "the Negro's evaluation of his historical and cultural experience in this century"; for him, *Native Son* is a point of departure more for social scientific evidence than for the discovery of an artistic tradition.

As the Black Aesthetic critics and writers surfaced in the late sixties, partly in response to the critical inadequacies of approaches like Margolies's, they embraced Richard Wright as a novelist and also as an aesthetician. In some instances, however, it was not so much Wright but Bigger Thomas who, strangely enough, was promoted as the black artist's model. For example, Sarah Webster Fabio writes in her contribution to Addison Gayle's *The Black Aesthetic:* "No turning back, though. This is the day of Biggers and the ghosts of Biggers. Black writers—most of them poets plus—have always been barometers, even when America kept the bell jars on them. Have always been/still are/will be. Always traveling with ears to the ground; attuned to the drumbeats of the age." One assumes that Fabio, who usually makes better sense, is being rhetorical. Buried in here somewhere is the notion that black writers, armed with poems and novels for weapons, must "kill" as Bigger did in order to feel the pulse of time and, for the first time in their lives, feel free. As rhetoric this may be powerful and, for some, inspiring, but it hardly suggests a viable aesthetic ideal, nor does it pay proper credit to Richard Wright. Addison Gayle, however, offers a more fruitful line of inquiry when he correctly turns to the example of Wright, not Bigger, and argues:

> The task of pointing out northern duplicity was left to the black artist, and no writer was more effective in this undertaking than

Richard Wright. When Wright placed Bigger Thomas and Mr. Dalton in a northern setting and pointed up the fact that Bigger's condition resulted from Dalton's hypocrisy, he opened up a Pandora's box of problems for white liberals and Negro leaders, neither of whom could bring themselves to share his vision. . . . The liberal ideology—both social and literary— of the northern Daltons has become the primary target of the Afro-American writer and critic.

Above and beyond the issue of how Gayle views contemporary black writers and critics pursuing their muse, this statement is questionable as a "political" reading of *Native Son*. The total picture of liberal thought in the novel includes, as we've indicated before, the words and deeds of Attorney Max, even though it is through him that the most explicit and vitriolic condemnation of the Daltons is expressed. If a critic values such features in literature and actually intends to build an aesthetic upon such foundations, as Gayle apparently does, then Wright's inability to portray Max as a "pure" radical should conceivably becloud his view of *Native Son* as a seminal book. But apparently this is not a problem for Mr. Gayle. Our point is, however, that here is another attempt to trace a pattern in Afro-American literature which has *Native Son* as its source. As Margolies emphasizes the socio-cultural, Gayle, albeit with greater attention to the Afro-American artist's posture in society, stresses the political, the literary war against an ideology. Since each of these patterns has a considerable history beginning well before the publication of *Native Son* in 1940, one might say that both Margolies and Gayle are trying, from what often seems like opposite corners of the earth, to move toward an articulation of a tradition. But patterns aren't traditions, and even a combination of the Margolies and Gayle approaches does not illuminate all we want to know about books like *Native Son* and *Black Boy*. If indeed, as some are saying, the black art-as-sociology and Black Aesthetic theories of the 1960s are outmoded, it may be because the latter is but an extension and political radicalization of the former, and neither approach is fully in tune with the heartbeat of the artist and his art.

By and large, the chief limitation to most of the criticism of *Native Son* is that the critics have dwelled on what we may loosely call the novel's content. Whether *Native Son* actually shocked the proverbial banker's daughter (who might identify, one supposes, with Mary Dalton) as Wright hoped it would remains unclear. What *is* clear, however, is that Wright's critics have been preoccupied by those very features to the novel which are presumably distressing to proper young ladies. Generally, most of the criticism of *Native Son* falls into one of two categories: predictable, journeyman-like studies of imagery (light and dark; animal references) and symbolism (the soaring airplane, various timepieces, the Christian crosses); or, responses to those features which, as Baldwin has written, "whet the notorious national taste for the sensational." The problem, we discover, is that these approaches unduly isolate the text from the corpus of American and Afro-American literature and direct discussion of *Native Son* toward yet another ritualized, pseudo-scientific rehash of the Black Man's Plight.

As I have tried to indicate earlier in these pages, Wright's influence on the contemporary critic may lead to the pursuit of other types of questions. Our sense of an Afro-American literary tradition can be sharpened and enhanced, for example, by assaying Wright's departures from it. We need to develop what has already been ventured about Bigger and Wright's entanglement in the web of double-consciousness so that we may come to know them and the place of *Native Son* in the artistic continuum. We need to assess why, from the standpoint of artistic and even aesthetic considerations, Wright earnestly desired to become a jazz critic in the twilight of his career. Above all, we must not hesitate to discover the Americanness of Richard Wright. Such an activity is actually part of the legacy handed down by such pioneering Afro-American critics as William Stanley Braithwaite and Sterling A. Brown. Wright's departures from Afro-American traditions generally serve to confirm his place in the mainstream of American letters, and, for the moment, it seems like the knowledgeable Afro-American critic is best suited to articulate Wright's stature in both literary worlds.

Turning to Wright's influence on the contemporary black writer, especially those writers first published during the last decade, we find a predictable array of responses ranging from celebrations of Bigger to what we can only deem more thoughtful considerations of Wright's work which frequently re-examine those rituals of black and white cultures of which we've already spoken. The celebrations of Bigger more often than not represent the exploitation of these cultural rituals, and seem to be generated by psychological needs surfacing as strategies for political power, or by unadulterated greed. Writers are often found in the former camp (Eldridge Cleaver, for example), while the would-be artists behind the spate of "blaxploitation" films may be designated to the latter. If indeed, as Kichung Kim writes, "For many Black Americans . . . Bigger is probably the one character they find most authentic in all of American literature," we need not wonder why these writers and filmmakers have a considerable audience. None of this is Wright's doing or intention. The man who split the atom did not drop the bomb. However, like the scientist who foresaw the holocaust of Hiroshima, Wright, in his portraits of Bigger fantasizing at the movies and dreamily reading detective stories, seems to have prophesied what is a lamentable feature to our present cultural state. What he understandably could not foresee is that today not only is Bigger still in the audience, but his fantasized self is on the screen.

A far more honorable and direct response to Wright may be discovered in the recent fiction of black women authors. We have alluded to the effort to "humanize" Bigger but the attempts to revise and redeem Mrs. Thomas and both Bessies (the one in *Native Son* and the one in *Black Boy*), launched mostly by black women writers, must be mentioned as well. There is little written discussion of this; but looking at the literature itself, we can find types of Mrs. Thomas and both Bessies leading richer lives and having more going for them than a false church, a whiskey bottle, and, as Wright says of the Bessie in *Black Boy*, a peasant mentality.

Ann Petry's *The Street* (1946) and Toni Morrison's *The Bluest Eye* (1970) are two novels from what may be termed the antipodes of the contemporary period which support our point. Although Lutie Johnson in *The Street* is ultimately defeated by the dimensions of racism and sexism at work and at home in Harlem, she, unlike the Bessie in *Native Son*, possesses a fair measure of pride, will, and grace. The fact that near the end of the novel she kills her black lover, not to silence him, but because of the continual sexual and psychological assault he has made on her life, would suggest that Petry was about the task not only of redeeming Bessie but of revising Bigger as well.

In *The Bluest Eye*, virtually all of the black women, whether they be prostitutes or keepers of the hearth, are far more compelling, complex, and differentiated than Wright's. Mrs. Pauline Breedlove and her daughter, Pecola, may be likened to Mrs. Thomas and her daughter, Vera. Both sets of women are entrapped by the burdens of being poor, black, and female. But for all their woes, or perhaps because of them, Mrs. Breedlove and Pecola are the dreamers in Morrison's novel. Their dreams may be false and irredeemably warped—Mrs. Breedlove covets Jean Harlow's hair, Pecola desperately searches for blue eyes—but they dream just the same; they have an inner life. Most importantly, in terms of the tradition of the articulate hero, the arresting story of all the Breedloves (Pauline, Pecola, Sammy, and the father, Cholly) is told by a young woman, Claudia MacTeer, whose accumulation of the facts and rendering of the tale softens our horror while yielding her a special knowledge with which she can face and endure adulthood.

All in all, the black women novelists of our age seem to be agreeing with Alice Walker that "black women are the most fascinating creations in the world." Thus, out of necessity, they are turning to Toomer, Hurston, Brooks, and Petry, and not to the majority of black male writers for their models and encouragement. In this light, the rise of a feminine and sometimes feminist voice in contemporary Afro-American fiction may be directly related to the narrow and confining portraits of black women in earlier modern fiction, including that of Wright.

Besides the revision of characters, we also find evidence of the contemporary writer treating the aforementioned cultural rituals as lore handed down; as essential metaphors to be combined with others such as the heroic black athlete and the veil. For example, in "Heartblow," Michael Harper's series of poems for Wright in *Debridement* (1973), we find this poem entitled "Afterward: A Film":

Erect in the movies
with a new job,
Trader Horn
and *The Gay Woman*
unfold in a twinbill:
drums, wild dancing,
naked men, the silver
veils on the South Side.
He imagines nothing:
it is all before him,
born in a dream:
a gorilla broke loose
from his zoo
in a tuxedo: baboon.
You pick your red bottom.
The Daltons are the movies.

On my wall are pictures:
Jack Johnson, Joe Louis,
Harlow and Rogers:
"see the white god and die."

Underground I live in veils,
brick and cement,
the confession beaten out,
slung with hung carcasses,
a bloody cleaver grunting,
a dead baby in the sewer:
"all the people I saw were guilty."

Marked black I was shot,
double-conscious brother in the veil—
without an image of act or thought
double-conscious brother in the veil—

The rape: "Mrs. Dalton, it's me,
Bigger, I've brought Miss Dalton
home and she's drunk":
to be the idea in these minds,
double-conscious brother in the veil—
father and leader where is my king,
veils of kingship will lead these folks
double-conscious brother in the veil—
"see the white gods and die"
double-conscious brother in the veil—

The opening stanzas take two of Wright's most effective images of Bigger the empty vessel being inundated and filled by the celluloid flotsam of popular culture, and integrate them into one flowing portrait of assault, first at the theatre and finally in his quarters at the Dalton home. All this is done with careful and loyal attention to the text. The gorilla reference is, for example, almost a quotation of Jack's playful response to Bigger's musings over what it would be like to attend a party like that in *The Gay Woman*, only now the self-debasing racial comment at the heart of Jack's joking is fully exposed and relentlessly pursued. Furthermore, in the second stanza, mention of the photos on Bigger's walls at the Dalton's serves to remind us of how, according to Wright's vision, Bigger and Mary will encounter each other in a dance designed by warped yet powerful cultural and historical forces; a dance of psycho-sexual and racial ritual along the color line. In short, stanzas one and two present those cultural forces affecting Bigger in Book I of the novel as much as stanza three captures Bigger's mood in Book II.

In the third stanza, the series of images transports us back to the scene of Mary's dismemberment and forward to Bigger's confession while immersing us in Bigger's flight underground in Dalton's ghetto. The primary image is that of a hellish landscape, peopled by the victimized and oppressed, which the poet places in a historical continuum, not so much as Wright did by means of economic and political reference, but rather by ancient metaphor, the veil. Through this metaphor, Harper can now expand upon his image of Bigger until it approximates the fullest dimensions of the artistic continuum. Thus, in the remaining stanzas, the line *"double-conscious brother in the veil"* becomes at once a musical refrain and, like a repeated color in African woven cloth, the agent and source for a compelling visual rhythm.

In poems such as these, Wright, I feel, is restored to his proper stature as a participant in Afro-American letters. Harper's mining of Wright's primary images and placement of them in the continuum, as well as his implied suggestion that Wright deserves a place in the pantheon where we find Du Bois, yields the kind of evidence which balances all we know of Wright's shortcomings. And it is this balanced view of Wright, as an author who could argue "Tradition is no longer a guide. . . . The world has grown huge and cold" while providing us with archetypes which generations of writers would in turn place *in* the tradition he rejected, that begins to define his stature in the Afro-American tradition.

The Vision of Eudora Welty

Ruth M. Vande Kieft

Considering Eudora Welty's happy possession of a "good ear," her use, throughout her fiction, of her ears "as magnets," and the long challenge, most amazingly met in *Losing Battles,* of objectifying and projecting character almost solely through dialogue, it is extraordinary that she has visual gifts to match those of her hearing. Yet she has revealed a steady interest in painting and photography, says she "see[s] things in pictures," finds her talent for writing to be "quite visual," sees always, in her imagination, both what she reads and writes.

One Time, One Place (1971) is a testimony to her youthful gifts as a photographer—gifts human and visual rather than technical, though she did more than many an amateur might have done with her primitive photographic equipment. She subtitles the collection "A Mississippi Album," with all the intimacy, familial memory and affection which the term connotes. And the whole of her work might be so titled were it less impressive, public, universal. Her introduction to that album is a loving tribute to her place and its people during the Depression and a fitting prelude to her art, not only because many of her stories sprang from the same time and place, but because of what it tells us about her own visual gifts.

"Seeing" or "vision" is never a simple matter in literature. There is first of all the thing actually seen, the literal, and this primary level of vision raises several complex questions. Are things seen from near, or far, or the "middle distance"; from a fixed or moving point of view; sharply or vaguely? With what nuances of light, color, atmosphere? Is the seeing eye that of the author, a partially or wholly fictionalized narrator, one or more of the characters, or some inextricable combination of any two or three of these possibilities? Are the visual elements in the fiction chiefly the products of direct description, or metaphor and simile? Progressing to less literal

From *The Mississippi Quarterly* 26, no. 4 (Fall 1973). © 1973 by Mississippi State University.

implications of the term, further questions arise. Is the process one of seeing *to* some point at which vision, however arduous and strained, is stopped short? Or, alternatively, is it one of seeing *through* surfaces? And is it, finally, whatever has been achieved through imaginative wisdom, universal as well as individual truths captured and conveyed?

Obviously all of these elements and many more are involved in the consideration of any writer's vision, and I should be at a loss to discuss all of them in any detail here. I wish to focus, however, on two generalizations about vision in Miss Welty's fiction. First is the meeting of the literal vision—the way things are created, seen, "painted" by words—and the final vision of insight, imaginative wisdom, the meaning of persons, feelings, situations, events. Second is the paradoxical quality of that vision: the creative tension between, for example, objectivity and subjectivity, "hard-edge" observations executed with realistic clarity, and the impressionistic blur; the serious "rage for order" and the cheerful abandonment to the random and haphazard, chance-ridden, even chaotic; the patience and care with detail (the near vision) and the withdrawal to deep distances; frivolity and gravity; action and stasis; hiddenness and revelation; tragedy and comedy.

In short, singleness of vision is rarely to be found in this writer; rather ambiguity, paradox, above all, mystery. I find myself in partial agreement, therefore, with John F. Fleischauer, who has titled his discerning and carefully illustrated essay on Miss Welty's style "The Focus of Mystery." Fleischauer finds her style "dreamy, mysterious, remote." It seems unjust to present some of his conclusions without including samples of his supporting evidence, but here they are:

> It may be said that her prose moves in gradual surges from indefiniteness to increasingly focused details charged with intensity: that the progress itself is associative, uncertain (because of imprecise connectives), and ultimately neither firmly resolved nor defined. Culminations contain feelings and impressions, not facts. And throughout, Miss Welty's exclusive use of similes both exposes poetic relationships to the reader and keeps him from entering into them.

He finds, in Miss Welty's emphasis on clarity of vision and the necessity of focus, that "the apparently trivial becomes meaningful as part of the mystery of imaginative awareness; it does not become simply more clear." The small details Miss Welty selects from the random flow of life have the effect of "leaving what was obvious and irrelevant now poetic and mysterious"—transmuted from the meaningless to the alluring and portentous. Unless I misread him, Fleischauer seems troubled by all the vagueness in this focus on mystery: Miss Welty, he says, "wants [the reader's] acquiescence and appreciation rather than his trust in her assumed ability to solve his puzzles or to articulate his feelings"; she wins "not credibility and empathy but curiosity and delight." The method of *Losing Battles* (which he considers her greatest work), despite its use of a more "hidden" narrator, "has not changed the most central patterns of her style. The focus which changes to mystery has become the way of seeing that precludes total understanding, an awareness that Truth is truths, that significance is a vagary grasped privately by the individual and is never finally translatable."

With much of this I can agree, though not with Fleischauer's seeming identification of mystery with vagueness or confusion, his assumption that mystery hasn't its component of piercing clarity as well as its necessary mystification. I wonder too at his not seeming fully aware of the breadth of implication in those related ends of focusing: meditation and poetry. Above all, I cannot agree that Miss Welty lacks the ability or inclination to articulate clearly any character's, her own, or the reader's feelings, to be credible and to evoke empathy. Her tolerance and refusal to make strong judgments aids rather than hinders empathy. Furthermore, she does articulate both feelings and "truths," often obliquely, through imagery or symbolism, and on occasion explicitly, through direct statement; one could, were he so inclined, make a list of such "truths" to be gleaned from her work. She would wince at the idea, having indicated on several occasions that didacticism and philosophy are congenial neither to the functions of art nor her own temperament and artistic practice. Such a collection could, however, be made, as it could from the writings of certain authors whom she greatly admires: Jane Austen, Chekhov, E. M. Forster. It would add up to one writer's Truth. That she has made and won.

A writer's fund of life experience constitutes the raw material of his vision. She describes it in an essay called "Words into Fiction" as involving "how he sees life and death, how much he thinks people matter to each other and to themselves, how much he would like you to know what he finds beautiful or strange or awful or absurd, what he can do without, . . . how he imposes order and structure on his fictional world; and it is terribly clear, in the end, whether, when he calls for understanding in whatever way, he gets any." She wants communication, and it appears to me that she gets a great deal of it.

Fleischauer spends little time discussing *The Optimist's Daughter:* I think he would find it a further illustration of "the focus of mystery." Reynolds Price, in his wonderfully illuminating essay on what was at the time still a long story published in the *New Yorker*, sets out a position which seems almost totally opposed to that of Fleischauer. Once again, I find myself in partial disagreement with his conclusions. I take a similarly high view of what has since become the Pulitzer Prize-winning novel; whether it will prove to be Miss Welty's "strongest, richest work" among so many might be debated, but I am sympathetic to his statement that such an assertion "is tantamount to saying that no one alive in America now has yet shown stronger, richer, more useful fiction"; and I agree that a response to Miss Welty's fiction is "always a response to vision, literal eye-sight; she has the keenest eyesight in American letters— . . . as strange as it is unique." Price locates the uniqueness of Miss Welty's vision in the "stance and line-of-sight" of the "onlooker": what makes this stance unique is that her on-

lookers, unlike others in modern fiction, with few or momentary exceptions, do not particularly want to become "members"; they are without the
need or impulse to "join"; they are largely content with the benefits of
insight their apartness grants them, or are resigned to their status as on-
lookers. Price says further that in the early stories (he mentions specifically
the salesman in "The Hitch-Hikers," Audubon in "A Still Moment," Virgie
Rainey in *The Golden Apples*) "the last note is almost invariably rising, a
question; the final look in the onlooker's eyes is of puzzlement." (Here,
perhaps, he is sharing some of Fleischauer's reactions.) *The Optimist's
Daughter* veers from that pattern, he finds, because Laurel, "the woman at
the center," comes to a point where "mystery dissolves before patient
waiting"—before her "unbroken stare," which is "finally merciless—to her
dead parents, friends, enemies, herself; worst, to us."

Having been subjected to that merciless stare in the process of reading
and rereading the novel, I feel no inclination to dispute Reynolds Price's
conclusion. I wonder only whether that stare hasn't been present in her
fiction all along, and whether it is finally merciless at the close of *The
Optimist's Daughter*. Miss Welty has always had a clear view of the excesses
to which family love is prone, and its outside limits, together with love's
absolute primacy and enormous staying power over the long haul, except
for recuperative spaces, the completion of emotional cycles following or-
deals such as the death of a loved one, the devastation brought on by
unblinking tragic insight, or, contrastingly, the resurgence of primal joy.
And the long haul is no less than the duration of a life and its memory.

Obviously the short stories, especially the early ones, are more likely
to appear as "single mood" pieces than longer or later works, lacking a
clear resolution in the onlooker's mind. But I should like to illustrate some
of the characteristics of Miss Welty's vision with a story from each of the
first two collections of her stories, as well as the most important of her
subsequent works.

"A Memory" is illustrative of "puzzlement," yet it displays most of
the paradoxical qualities of vision which I have mentioned, as well as the
matching of external with internal vision. The pictures, actions, feelings
are conveyed through the memory of the narrator at some mature stage in
her later life. We see initially through the small frame of a rectangle the
young lady of the story makes with her fingertips to "look out at everything." The technique is self-consciously visual because the girl has been
taking painting lessons. Her attempt is to be objective—missing no detail
in that brilliant picture of "sun, sand, water, a little pavilion, a few solitary
people in fixed attitudes, and around it all a border of dark rounded oak
trees, like the engraved thunderclouds surrounding illustrations in the Bible"—but we see at once how subjective is her objectivity. The brightly lit
rectangle is described as "actually glaring" at her, as though noonday sunlight on sand and water might attack the exposed eye and the person behind
it. Furthermore, we notice that the order the young girl makes by the
framing device is a superimposed order which nature everywhere over-

spills. The girl is also governed by an obsessive need to categorize; make judgments on persons and events, predict, and by implication, control, through her grim and vigilant watching. Each "observation," she believes, may yield a "secret of life"; she is "obsessed with notions about conceal-ment," and feels that she must "wrest . . . a communication or a presen-timent" from any passing detail such as "the smallest gesture of a stranger."

This aspect of her vision is, then, not so much objective as an attempt at objectifying (a process she has not yet mastered), with the final purpose not of reflecting or capturing, still less of enjoying surfaces, but of disclosing hidden meaning. A rather fearful and unpleasantly driven state of mind, one might think—where is the joy in such seeing? Contradictorily, how-ever, it is called a "state of exaltation," either "heightened" or caused by her being in love. About this young girl's first love there is *nothing* objective, except the fact that she had recognized and categorized the state (she had "identified love at once" and subjects the small blond boy who is her innocent love object to her customary, though now even more fearful and wondering, observation—fear *for* him, and her inability to order, control, or even to know about his "frame" (environment), which she fills with unknown threats, like the thunderclouds around the biblical illustrations. Her love has no relation to reality, has never been communicated, endures its torments and raptures in the heady silence and inwardness of dreams. Specifically, *a* dream: of a moment when she touched the boy's wrist in passing, a "minute and brief encounter" which she dwells on "endlessly," until "it would swell with a sudden and overwhelming beauty, like a rose forced into premature bloom for a great occasion." The "dual life" of the child, as the narrator calls it, that of "observer and dreamer," expresses the dichotomy of her vision. The slow-rapid action of the hot-house rose would be typical of the dreamer's similes and feelings; "the water shone like steel" of the observer's.

Both observer and dreamer get a terrible jolt from the vulgar group of bathers who attack the beach, each other, the dignity and privacy of their own bodies. The observer records each nuance of their ugly, formless bod-ies, each violation of the principles of order and control involved in their attitudes, the senseless sounds they make, their chaotic activity, their heed-less energy unleashed like a storm on the beach. The images of the observer are as vivid as they are repellent: the man is smiling like a panting dog, and all the bathers appear "large and almost metallic, with painted smiles"; the woman has "bulbous descending breasts" which eventually seem to turn into the "mashed and folded sand" she empties out of her bathing suit; two little boys run in "wobbly ellipses"— one has straight white hair like "thistles in red sunlight" and cheeks "ballooned outward"; a girl is like a genie who may at any moment "burst in a rage of churning smoke" as from the "bottle" of her bright green bathing suit. The dreamer tries to escape, closes her eyes against the horror and glare of reality. Her internal images are soft and vague, hazily romantic: she feels the "shudder" of her wish "shaking the darkness like leaves," she senses the "heavy weight of sweetness"; but she cannot any longer recover the memory, the "long narrative" of the touch on the stair. When she finally opens her eyes to find "the blur of an empty beach," it is with a feeling of victimization—for the ravaged beach, the pavilion, above all for herself. She will now have to watch the boy "with this hour on the beach accompanying [her] re-covered dream and added to [her] love." The dreamer's love has been modified, though not lost.

Curious here is the paradox between the child's expectation—that meaning must be wrested from the *smallest* gestures and details, making her the active, even aggressive one—and what actually happens, which is that she is battered by large and violent gestures and recoils like a wounded snail into its shell, under which protective cover she has some mental and emotional adjusting to do. Love (and however "grotesquely altered in the outward world" this first love seems to the mature narrator, she never denies her youthful identification of it) involves self-exposure, laying one-self open to the risk of being seriously hurt. One who loves abandons his self-containment, security, inviolability, protection.

In her fascinating introduction to *One Time, One Place,* Miss Welty has a great deal to say about seeing—about the difference and relationship between a camera's eye and a human one. The camera's eye is a "shy person's protection, . . . not quite mine [though not because Miss Welty isn't shy], but a quicker and an unblinking one—and it couldn't see pain where it looked, or give any, though neither could it catch effervesence, color, transience, kindness, or what was not there. It was what I used, at any rate, and like any tool, it used me." After printing and drying her snapshots she looked at them long and hard. "I began to see objectively what I had there." She mentions first (and places first in her album) the courageously uplifted, weathered head of a black woman—"heroic," she calls it, accurately, "a face . . . full of meaning more truthful and more terrible and, I think, more noble than any generalization about people could have prepared me for or could describe for me now. I learned from my own pictures, one by one, and had to; for I think we are the breakers of our own hearts." Her reflection here is as vague as it is eloquent—and the picture *is* indescribable and heartbreaking. After noting the potentials and limitations of the camera—what it catches as well as misses—she celebrates the life it captures *if* there is a quick intelligence to click the shutter at the right—that is the fleetingly revelatory—moment (an art she "learned quickly enough"); and even more importantly, *if* there is a large capacity for imaginative self-extension, understanding, patience, a willingness to study and wait in order to receive the unspeakable meanings of a face, a gesture, a feeling, an event. If you wish to see, then, you must be quick as a camera's shutter and slow as a painter's or lover's attentive eye. "A snapshot is a moment's glimpse (as a story may be a long look, a growing contemplation) into what never stops moving, never ceases to express for itself something of our common feeling." You must be objective to learn and interpret, and you must be subjective, inward, *willing* to love. If you are not, you will never see anything of significance, never learn to put the true value on persons, events, relationships, never have to suffer any more than life happens to inflict on your own flesh. Which is why she adds cautiously, "I think we are the breakers of our own hearts." No one is forcing us to look or feel; only we ourselves determine the kind and degree of our seeing or caring.

The child in "A Memory" is already aware of these potentials and hazards of vision. Love has "heightened"hers; she is quick to record, slow and patient to divine and interpret. She waits for the revealing gesture. "Then when it does come, how unpredictable it turns out to be, after all." Her revulsion from vulgarity is her recognition of a value system ignorant of human dignity and privacy. As an adult, she does not forget her first love, immature as it was; her "memory" has retained it all, even, "unadulteratedly," the incident of the richly blooming touch. Because of the small boy's nosebleed she will always "be unable to bear the sight of blood." If that seems a foolish youthful squeamishness, we have only to remember that bloodshed, protracted, results in death.

" 'Lord, give me strength to see the angels when I am in Paradise,' he said. 'Do not let my eyes remain in this failing proportion to my loving heart always.' "

Who is this man with his strange problem of vision? It is Lorenzo Dow, the evangelist ("A Still Moment"), driving his horse along the Natchez Trace when it was still wilderness. There is nothing wrong with his sight; his senses are, in fact, unusually acute, enabling him to pass safely through danger. Nor is he insensitive to the beauty of nature —the fireflies bright and tireless, the birds singing of "divine love which was the one ceaseless protection. 'Peace, in peace.' " His problem is that he cannot always see with the steady penetration of serene faith through and beyond these distractingly lovely surfaces to the God who created them. He cannot make souls light up as the fireflies do. His hungry heart wants always fo see the flesh made Word, as his faith has convinced him the Word was made flesh. "God created the world, . . . and it exists to give testimony." But who, excepting the believer, is there to see and hear this testimony of creation? Lorenzo at his rare best, but he isn't enough, and he knows it. His vision must be shared; if there were a way to coerce it, he might. His is another instance of superimposing human sight on what exists in the outside world. The compulsion this time is not for making order but saving souls, transmuting men into angels. To Audubon Lorenzo says, "Life is the tongue: speak"; but Audubon has stopped using words except to record in his journal details which might otherwise be lost.

When the still moment comes as the snowy heron settles to feed in the soft sunset light, Lorenzo gives it "a triumphant look, such as a man may bestow upon his own vision." He thinks, "Praise God, His love has come visible." Thus, when Audubon kills the bird, the shock comes chiefly to Lorenzo's inward or spiritual sight. God has given the Love, and it seems to Lorenzo that "God Himself, just now, thought of the Idea of Separateness." How *can* God see as a man sees, in sequential time, and so, in a "scattering moment" destroy His own nearness and love? And yet, even as Lorenzo suffers from the tormenting question, the scene of the bird feeding recomposes itself in his memory: it is "as if nothing could really take away what had happened to him, the beautiful little vision of the feeding bird. Its beauty had been greater than he could account for. The sweat of rapture poured down from his forehead, and then he shouted into the marshes. 'Tempter!' "

Rapture? So soon after the "horror in its purity and clarity" Audubon had seen in Lorenzo's blue eyes? So soon after the near, imminent God who had made His Love visible seems to have withdrawn so far from human beings as to need a Lorenzo Dow to explain how and why they suffer? But there it is—*joy* springs up hard upon tragic vision; and Lorenzo, who tends to personify and allegorize every feeling, shouts "Tempter!" at that joy.

James Murrell, the outlaw, sees nothing of the outside world. He looks at it through dark eyes which appear to Audubon as "chinks," seeing "neither closeness nor distance, light nor shade, wonder nor familiarity." The eyes are "narrowed to contract the heart"; Audubon perceives an even physical connection, produced by tendons, between eyes, hands, and heart, which may be, respectively, either enlarged, active, receptive, or narrowed, arrested, closed off. Murrell's internal vision is filled with a fantastic plan of the diabolical Mystical Rebellion he hopes to lead; of the murders he has committed and plans to commit—imaginatively, ceremoniously, in the belief that at the moment of death his victims might "lighten their hold on the secret" of life's mystery, "let it fly free at death." When the still moment comes Murrell blinks into a haze, sees only "whiteness ensconced in darkness, as if it were a little luminous shell that drew in and held the eyesight." The brand of "H. T." on his thumb intrudes on the foreground of his sight; the plan of the Mystic Rebellion "dart[s] from him as if in rays of the bright reflected light." Incapable of looking outward, he yearns for someone to look straight into *him,* disclosing his conspiracy and crimes, his evil nature; accusing, then pitying him. The other two men will not look at him, so he turns back to the bird, thinking that "if it would look at him a dread penetration would fill and gratify his heart." Murrell's blind self-preoccupation, his satanic, egotistical dreams of glory, are a dead end. He persists in darkness, showing that where there is no outsight, genuine insight is precluded.

Audubon, the naturalist and painter, seems to have the finest vision possible. His capacity for looking outward, for observing with care, remembering and recording the details of nature, seems unlimited. In order to increase his knowledge he has placed himself as much as possible in the continuum of nature. Only his human self-consciousness appears to set him off from the total life of the wilderness into which he has plunged himself. Audubon seems, also, to have the artist's prerequisite for sight—

the attitude of wonder and love at the mystery and beauty of natural life, an eager openness of the inward self to the outside world. Yet for all his dedication to nature in its glorious "radiance," he too has a problem of vision. He cannot penetrate the "two darks" of his origin and his end which surround the "interval" of that radiance. He cannot see through or beyond nature, despite his ceaseless gazing. "When a man at last brought himself to face some mirror-surface he still saw the world looking back at him, and if he continued to look, to look closer and closer, what then? The gaze that looks outward must be trained without rest, to be indomitable."

Audubon's sight of the snowy heron is full and informed; his eyes "embrace" it in the distance, identify the bird's feeding habits, sex (female), instinctive behavior when human beings are in the vicinity. He shares with the other two troubled men the still moment when the three of them become like "three whirlwinds . . . drawn together at some center" where peace falls, the snowy bird's benediction at the far end of the vision. But immediately Audubon realizes that he cannot trust his memory to paint accurately, nor can he relax in his vigilant efforts to look *through* the mirror surface of nature. He raises his gun, closes his eyes, sees the heron perfectly there, in his memory, in "all its solitude, its total beauty," and shoots. He must kill the bird (gun before camera lens) in order to make the vision in his head one with the drawing to come from it, in order to *communicate* that vision, later, to all who might see. But the effort, he knows, cannot be fully successful. The object of a vision, and therefore the vision itself, cannot *belong* to a single person, not even the one best qualified for seeing. The essence of life cannot be recorded; its living beauty will "never be one with the beauty in any other man's head in the world." To be sure, Audubon had seen the bird "most purely at its moment of death"—was that perhaps because the enormity of his act had pressured and intensified his vision? Yet in that same moment of death, "in some fatal way, in his care for looking outward, he saw his long labor most revealingly at the point where it met its limit." How futile to kill in order to preserve. Death stops vision; beyond and through it there is no seeing. Nature is a "curtain of green" which cannot be penetrated or parted by the living. Memory, whether or not it is transposed into art, is the only means we have of preserving life in all its beauty, joy and pain, its infinite value.

The narrator of "A Still Moment" has visualized everything fully, in patterns, with almost balletic sequences of three dancers in solo, pas de deux, pas de trois, and a final sequence of solos. She has alternated swift and violent action with slow moments of reflection; frustration with rapture; the beautiful, still moment of revelation and freedom with moments of binding dilemmas. She shows both the powers and limitations of human sight, of spiritual and artistic love, the futility of trying to press where they cannot go. Her "unblinking stare" yields a double truth, of success in failure, or the reverse.

Delta Wedding provides images of how to *be* which are directly related with those of how to *see*. Though the point of view is parcelled out among several characters, and never given to its hero, George Fairchild, he is the person in the novel who has best mastered the related arts of seeing and loving. The women who hover around him—his sisters, nieces, wife—all know this. One of them, Dabney, the bride, watches him looking one day, and recognizes the authenticity of his vision:

> She saw Uncle George lying on his arm on a picnic, smiling to hear what someone was telling, with a butterfly going across his gaze, a way to make her imagine all at once that in that moment he erected an entire, complicated house for the butterfly inside his sleepy body. It was very strange, but she had felt it. She had then known something he knew all along, it seemed then—that when you felt, touched, heard, looked at things in the world, and found their fragrances, they themselves made a sort of house within you, which filled with life to hold them, filled with knowledge all by itself, and all else, the other ways to know, seemed calculation and tyranny.

This is very difficult from the aggressive, obsessed vision of the child in "A Memory," or even Audubon's, given his drive to record each small detail and his acceptance of the necessity of killing the birds he must paint. Perhaps such drives are essential to the artist's devouring eye, and George is not that— only a lover. But he is not merely passive, for he meets the butterfly with his "entire, complicated house" ready for it, and even more complicated houses for every human being he encounters: he takes them "one by one," as Shelley, one of his nieces, records in her diary. The meeting in George Fairchild of the inward and outward vision is unmistakable, and reveals itself markedly in a gesture, or rather an action: he risks being run over by a local train when he tries to release the foot of one of the cousins, simple-minded Maureen, whose foot is caught in a trestle. The action shows his abandon, the universality as well as particularity of his love.

Ellen Fairchild, mother, wife, sister, though an "outsider" or "onlooker," and not by nature a plantation mistress, is another benign eye in *Delta Wedding*. At the center of the busy household at Shellmound, she watches unobtrusively, intuitively, tenderly, all the developing persons and relationships about her, misses nothing, meets every quarrel and difficulty honestly and squarely, but tactfully. And she has the instinctive sense to withdraw for a half hour when the going gets rough: she simply faints. Both she and George exhibit a fine balance between inward and outward vision, and both are capable of sorting out the trivial from the important; of refusing protracted anguish about anything, or submitting to petty worries; of responding to joy wherever it upthrusts, regardless of strict morality or propriety.

The short-story cycle, *The Golden Apples*, exhibits sheer virtuosity in its use of point of view, most of all in "June Recital," which seems to me also the greatest story in that collection. Loch Morrison, a young boy supposedly confined to bed with malaria, enjoys a full view of the old abandoned MacLain house and its temporary occupants. Loch's head is stuffed with fantasies about wild men, giants, his big fig tree like "a magic tree with golden fruit . . . a tree twinkling all over." On this particular day, however, he watches closely the activities of Virgie Rainey and her sailor boyfriend, chasing each other in an upstairs bedroom, eating pickles and making love on a bare mattress; Miss Eckhart, the music teacher, setting fire to the parlor where the piano is; Booney Holifield, night watchman at the gin, sleeping in another bedroom through most of the excitement. Loch looks out, "all eyes like Argus, on guard everywhere," with and without his father's telescope, but his youth and ignorance of the histories and relationships of the persons involved prevent him from understanding what he sees: he takes Miss Eckhart for the sailor's mother, King MacLain for Mr. Voight, the ticking metronome for a time-bomb. Shortly before a peak moment when several of the "wanderers" in the cycle converge, Loch hangs on a tree branch upside down. He sees Old Man Moody and Mr. Fatty Bowles —the town marshal and his friend, cronies of Mr. Holifield come to wake him—and it seems in Loch's "special vision . . . that they could easily be lying on their backs in the blue sky and waving their legs pleasantly around, having nothing to do with law and order." They haven't, particularly; Loch's generally "upside down" view of things, his delight in freedom and lawlessness, forms a comic parallel and contrast to the "right side up" vision of his more conservative sister Cassie.

She has been dyeing scarfs in her room, preparing for a hayride, daydreaming. Her literal position prevents her from seeing what goes on in the MacLain house; yet her knowledge of and relationships to Virgie and Miss Eckhart give her the perspective through which the reader may interpret the events in the house. "Für Elise," the theme Miss Eckhart begins on the piano, sets off in Cassie's mind the chain of associations and memories unfolding the tragic history of the German-speaking music teacher so improbably placed in Morgana, Mississippi. Miss Eckhart's story is one of continual frustration, of passions and dedications apparently wasted and thwarted, the love and hope she has for Virgie, as her sole musically gifted student, rejected by the girl along with Miss Eckhart's hated metronome. At the climax of the story, when the fire is discovered and everybody in the house is routed, Virgie and Miss Eckhart come together on the sidewalk. This particular moment exactly coincides with the most hilarious sequence of comical if not farcical action leading to the convergence of Virgie with the "wall" of ladies spilling out from a Rook party, her half-naked sailor boyfriend, Old Man Moody's party, King MacLain, Loch in his nightie, and Cassie in her petticoat. It is one of the most striking juxtapositions of the comic and tragic in all of Miss Welty's fiction. Strangely, however, because of the time perspective of both narrator and characters, the moment or period of tragedy has passed. Late that night in her "moonlit bed" Cassie thinks about the "meeting" of Virgie and Miss Eckhart on the sidewalk, after Virgie had "clicked" nonchalantly through the Rook party:

> What she was certain of was the distance those two had gone, as if all along they had been making a trip . . . It had changed them. They were deliberately terrible. They looked at each other and neither wished to speak. They did not even horrify each other. No one could touch them now, either.
>
> *Danke schoen.* . . . That much was out in the open. Gratitude— like rescue—was simply no more. It was not only past; it was outworn and cast away. Both Miss Eckhart and Virgie Rainey were human beings terribly at large, roaming on the face of the earth. And there were others of them—human beings, roaming, like lost beasts.

That strikes me as clear-eyed, "unblinking" vision. It recognizes both the love and cruelty of which human beings are capable, and what time may do to both— deadening them by distance. It sees the anguished search for fulfillment of human beings as part of a vast natural panorama in which lost beasts also roam. But the vision isn't left on that broad, nonhuman plane, for the thoughts which push Cassie over into the literal dreamworld are of the Wandering Aengus in the Yeats poem which has been weaving in and out of her consciousness. "She slept, but sat up in bed once and said aloud, *'Because a fire was in my head.'* Then she fell back unresisting. She did not see except in dreams that a face looked in; that it was the grave, unappeased, and radiant face, once more and always, the face that was in the poem." Always, in Eudora Welty's fiction, the appetite, the quest for life reasserts itself, the radiant face of that expectant wanderer.

Nor is Cassie's vision about the distance between Virgie and Miss Eckhart at the stage of their last meeting the final one in the story cycle. The time comes, in the last story (titled "The Wanderers"), when Virgie, past forty, has learned the lessons of dedication and discipline—not as Miss Eckhart had planned them for her, by developing her musical gifts, but by staying on with her old mother, setting her supple fingers and strong hands to typing and such farm chores as milking cows. Kate Rainey, her mother, has just died; Virgie has endured all the rituals of the last rites, festive and sometimes funny as well as lugubrious in smalltown Mississippi. Virgie goes through stages of feeling numbed, dissociated, cleansed and liberated after a solitary swim in the Big Black River. Returning from the cemetery she remembers another return when she had come back home after running away at seventeen, and the fields had seemed to her bathed "in a kind of glory," all of nature meeting in herself a rebirth of joy and hope. "Virgie never saw it differently, never doubted that all the opposites on earth were close together, love close to hate, living to dying; but of them all, hope and despair were the closest blood—unrecognizable one from the other sometimes, making moments double upon themselves, and in the doubling double again, amending but never taking back."

Out of her mature view of life, Virgie conceives, perhaps for the first time, a full appreciation of Miss Eckhart, long since dead. Virgie remembers a picture Miss Eckhart had on her wall of Perseus holding up the head of Medusa—the uplifted arm of the hero, vaunting; she thinks of the roles of heroes and their victims, of the sequence of time in its moments, creating separateness. And beyond that, "only the secret, unhurting because not caring in itself—beyond the beauty and the sword's stroke and the terror lay their existence in time—far out and endless, a constellation which the heart could read over many a night." She sees how Miss Eckhart had given her own love and hate, absorbed and transmitted through her Beethoven. "She offered, offered, offered—and when Virgie was young, in the strange wisdom of youth that is accepting of more than is given, she had accepted *the* Beethoven, as with the dragon's blood."

And so, belatedly, Miss Eckhart's gift has been recognized and gratefully received; a cycle has passed, and Virgie, from her now deeply distanced perspective, understands more than she can articulate, only what she can share with an old black woman who sits with her in the rain under a big tree, "listening to the magical percussion, the world beating in their ears. . . . the running of the horse and bear, the stroke of the leopard, the dragon's crusty slither, and the glimmer and trumpet of the swan." The world has become as it was when the wanderers on the face of the earth were beasts: so have the human wanderers slipped back into nature, actual and mythical.

The story of Virgie Rainey and Miss Eckhart is only one of many which illustrate several of the paradoxes of Miss Welty's vision—the use of concrete detail and impressionism (the latter coming together most effectively in "Moon Lake"), the convergence of tragedy and comedy, despair and "primal joy," nearness and distance of perspective. She makes free use of myth as well as the symbolism of nature, and even these are used visually. One onlooker, Cassie, sees the wanderers "to be by their own nature rising—and so alike—and crossing the sky and setting, the way the planets did. Or they were more like whole constellations, turning at their very centers maybe, like Perseus and Orion and Cassiopeia in her Chair and the Big Bear and Little Bear, maybe often upside down, but terribly recognizable. It was not just the sun and moon that traveled." So do all those who search, like the wandering Aengus, for the golden apples of the sun. Extraordinary events turn them "upside down" (as Loch's inverted vision also upends them) in some slow propulsion of their own deepest motives and the mysterious workings of fate (in contrast with furious and frenzied terrestrial drives). But they are always "terribly recognizable," nothing but themselves, each revelatory gesture a personal mark or talisman, as much as a Panama hat or a swivel chair where the road goes by; yet ancient as the heroes and heroines of Greek mythology. For virtuosity as well as power of vision, I believe *The Golden Apples* to be one of Miss Welty's strongest works, and am pleased to note that in a recent interview she named it as being "in a way closest to my heart of all my books."

Losing Battles is a joyful noise made to life itself, a celebration: an extended psalm of praise, though interspersed with laments, and sung between silences. But even the silences are filled: they are those of the briefest and brightest heralding of dawn, a longer night of a boy's inward journey and a thunderstorm, a few moments of people closed in to all but themselves or one other, the silences of the eloquent dead and the unborn, and above all, of the narrator, who everywhere binds together with her own lyric voice. She keeps it stilled as author and interpreter of thoughts and feelings, but her inward vision goes out to meet and embrace this family with delight, amusement, and a large tribute to their courage in the teeth of several losing battles.

Despite the preponderance of dialogue, scenes and action are all clearly visualized. The day opens hotly on a bright new tin roof, there is a great domestic flurry, and the family begins to arrive in a clatter of burgeoning old cars, trucks and wagons, raising clouds of red dust that never get a chance to settle until nightfall. Judge Oscar Moody's Buick must be twice rescued, the second time when it is poised toward destruction on the brink of Lover's Leap. There is horseplay with an old schoolbus, a rickety and overused bridge about to collapse, endless activity to match the tales told, the family history spread out in a rambling and contrapuntal manner by various members of the clan. Endurance and zest, staying power to match that of the narrator and her characters, openness to common people, their amusements, concerns, pains, are required for this long auditory and visual feast of folk-talk and activity; and a wicked little thought may invade the mind of somebody who feels he's had enough of baby Lady May Renfro or yet another wave of barking dogs—W. C. Fields's notion that anybody who hates children and animals can't be *all* bad.

The novel, though comic in every important sense, is more than a series of hilarious sequences, providing further evidence of the paradoxical quality of its author's vision. Miss Julia Mortimer, a teacher whose history and purposes are tied in with the history of the Vaughn-Beecham-Renfro clan as well as the whole Banner community, seems to have fought a losing battle with ignorance; her rare victories, in the persons of receptive and successful students, have all scattered to other parts of the country, except for Judge Moody, who stays, at her urging but unwillingly, to work with his own people. She had chosen Gloria Short to be her successor. But Gloria betrayed her calling, in Miss Julia's eyes, by loving and marrying Jack Renfro. Gloria resists all claims and ties except those binding her to the intimate family group of her husband and child, and asks Jack wistfully during one of the few moments when she is alone with him in that crowded day of the reunion, "When will we move to ourselves?" That too seems a losing battle, for the family are "piled all over" Jack, and threaten to inundate her completely by putting together a fairly credible story of her origins which would make of her as much a Beecham as Jack. The war on dedication to aspirations and ideals alien to the community, the persistent battering down of personal doors marked "Private Keep Out," are serious matters in the novel, bordering on the tragic. And yet without compromise to any streak of cruelty or intolerance in these people, how the author sees love thriving, even the give and take of individuality! "Forgiving seems the besetting sin of this house," remarks Judge Moody in his melancholy voice; he might as well have called it loving.

The following passage is unusually spare with simile, which flows throughout the novel, but it shows how much can be done with the "outside" point of view Miss Welty uses in the novel. It is night; all of Granny's large family but the Renfros have left, though her cracked voice has been calling them not to leave. ("Parcel of thieves! They'd take your last row of pins. They'd steal your life, if they knew how.") She is very tired and confused, about to be put to bed, and then Jack comes to her and quietly kneels at the foot of her rocker. From deep out of her ninety-year-old memory-riddled mind and dimmed senses she must discover him again, this great-grandson who has become a man, and returned home:

> Granny lifted both her little trembling hands out of her lap and took something out of her bosom. She held it before her, cupped in her hands, then carried it toward him. Her face was filled with intent that puckered it like grief, but her moving hands denied grief. Then, in the act of bending toward him, she forgot it all. Her hands broke apart to struggle toward his face, to take and hold his face there in front of her. It was the little silver snuffbox that Captain Jordan in his lifetime had come by, that had been Granny's to keep for as long as anybody could remember, that rolled across the floor and down into the folds of the cannas.
>
> Jack let her trembling fingers make sure they'd found him, move over his forehead, down his nose, across his lips, up his cheek, along the ridge of his brow, let them trace every hill and valley, let them wander. He still had not blinked once when her fingers seemed to forget the round boundaries belonging to flesh and stretched over empty air.

All human vulnerability and tenderness are in those blind gestures and patient repose, brought to serene and steady focus by a writer who is shamed by neither.

Once part of experience and memory, the joyful noise of this novel recedes to some quiet, bright region of the mind and heart: it becomes, oddly enough, a book remembered visually. And if it seems more like a big brown country bucket than a Grecian urn, unsuited to visual display as a "period piece" of Southern literature, one senses that this novel of children of the Depression may some day also become a foster child of silence and slow time, though ready to resume its bumping clatter the minute anybody picks it up.

Near the close of her introduction to *One Time, One Place*, Miss Welty says, "We come to terms as well as we can with our lifelong exposure to the world, and we use whatever devices we may need to survive. But eventually, of course, our knowledge depends upon the living relationship between what we see going on and ourselves. If exposure is essential, still more so is the reflection. Insight doesn't happen often on the click of the moment, like a lucky snapshot, but comes in its own time and more slowly and from nowhere but within." *The Optimist's Daughter* shows every sign of a "lifelong exposure to the world," careful reflection, the wisdom of survival. To one young bereaved widow, the curtain of green had seemed too dense to be penetrated; nature only confused her with its disorderly fecundity, its rapid and pointless alternation of life and death. But another curtain had already been parted in that title story of Miss Welty's first collection, as a result of what had been for her a "continuing passion" ever since the days, some forty years ago, when she shifted from photography to story writing: "not to point the finger in judgment but to part a curtain, that invisible shadow that falls between people, the veil of indifference to each other's presence, each other's wonder, each other's human plight" (*One Time, One Place*). What makes *The Optimist's Daughter* so revelatory is that through the character of Laurel McKelva she is standing squarely inside, looking out from involvement in the most intimate of human love relationships—those between husbands and wives, parents and children—when they suffer under the heaviest attacks. Vision comes in this novel almost as it does to Judge McKelva when he gets his first warning that something is wrong with his eyes—in explosive flashes before and behind, flashes coming from the inside but registered as though they occurred outside.

Deprived of his vision after eye surgery, the Judge waits patiently for time to pass, to move forward to the event, his optimism had earlier assured him, when his impaired vision would be restored to normal. But his time does not move forward, or even stop, as does the big clock back in Mount Salus; it starts ticking backward, and there is reason to believe, from our observation of him through his daughter Laurel's eyes, that his memory too has become something of a "somnambulist." Laurel's has been that ever since the death of her husband in World War II, her mother's five-year struggle with blindness and the Judge's incapacity for following her along the tortuous ways of protracted suffering. His lack of the tragic sense, optimism, innocence deceived by misplaced pity, had led to his late marriage to a pretty, vulgar woman several years his junior, Fay Chisom. Fay's childish fixation on her own pleasure and brutal disregard of the doctor's orders concerning her husband's care or his feelings, form a kind of grotesque parody of the Judge's failure of his first wife in her final illness.

To Laurel, Fay is guilty not only of the senseless and selfish killing of her father in his weakened state, but of something far worse: the violation of the perfect marriage her parents had enjoyed until her mother's blindness began, of her mother's memory, position, home. Visual details enforce her sense of the violation: Fay's vermilion nail polish on her father's great-grandfather's desk; her mother's breadboard, handsomely crafted by Laurel's husband, Philip, now dirt-encrusted, hacked up from Fay's having used it to crack nuts. Laurel's inward journey begins after her father's funeral. She moves deeper and deeper into the house, starting with her father's library. On the last night she spends in the parental home she is forced into rooms which form the most congenial, and painful, contexts for her probing. The night is stormy; an additional, alarming presence in the house—that of a chimney swift "making free" of it—brings her to her parents' bedroom, now Fay's. There she suffers the first lightning flash of self-revelation she is to endure during the night when she realizes that for the sake of relief she would have been willing to tell her mother of Fay's crimes, produce the "damnable evidence," in order to be herself consoled.

The drumming of the bird on the door and Laurel's growing fear drive her finally into a little adjoining sewing room which contains her mother's secretary and her own study table, an old slipper chair, a trunk. She had slept in this small room as a child, securely close to her parents. The room is a retreat: "Firelight and warmth—that was what her memory gave her." Here, when her mother or sewing woman had worked, Laurel had made scraps of cloth fallen on the floor "into patterns, families, on the sweet-smelling matting, with the shine of firelight, or the summer light, moving over mother and child and what they both were making." Memory moves back now, first tenderly and nostalgically, then with increasing tough-mindedness, putting together the patterns of families: her mother's, "up home" in Virginia, especially impressions received on their annual visits there; her parents', beginning and continuing in joy until the time of affliction, ending in her mother's half-crazed sense of betrayal; her own brief and perfect marriage to Philip Hand. Insight comes to Laurel by way of remembered "outsight": images, incidents, scenes with resonance, many of them involving birds—horrible and frightening up close or out of place, beautiful at a distance.

Grandma's pigeons had come under her close scrutiny as a child. She had expected to feed them and enjoy it; they frightened her badly, she hated them, and never told anybody. "Laurel . . . had already seen a pair of them sticking their beaks down each other's throats, gagging each other, eating out of each other's craws, swallowing down all over again what had been swallowed before: they were taking turns. . . . the other pigeons copied them. They convinced her that they could not escape each other and could not themselves be escaped from." Her grandmother had reassured her, " 'They're just hungry, like we are.' " Though at some level Laurel had accepted that analogy as a child, she had not resigned herself to it, her sense of human privacy, dignity, inviolability being as strong as that of the child in "A Memory." To Laurel as adult, the aggressive behavior, the crude forms of family solidarity and individual selfishness revealed by the Chisoms, and to a lesser extent the more amusing Dalzells (Grandpa Dalzell had shared Judge McKelva's hospital room), are fresh evidence not so much of the "humanity" of pigeon behavior as its obverse.

But she cannot fence off her abhorrence of suffocating family "closeness" by limiting it to the offensive behavior of those who have no sense of pattern, of the meaning of their own experience or the life and death of loved ones. Even as a child, she knows how all "parents and children take turns back and forth, changing places, protecting and protesting each other," and as an adult she knows how husbands and wives repeat the process. She knows further what damaging forms both the protecting and protesting may take when love goes very deep, when sensibilities are fine, and will is strong. Laurel "did not any longer believe that anyone could be saved, anyone at all. Not from others." So, she believes, she could not have protected her dead father from Fay, her mother from her father, nor could either of her parents have been saved, before that, from each other.

Nor can Laurel be safe, even from her dead husband. At the end of her long vigil on that stormy night he calls back to her across the distance of years and death to demand his life, which, like an exceptionally complacent pigeon, she has been chewing and swallowing for so long, content to leave him in his secure, supposedly static place far from her home and family (Chicago) and time (the distant past)—part of a brief wedded life, ideal and idealized, polished to perfection by memory, never subjected to the hazards of a living, continuing human relationship, which, however beautiful in its beginnings, might have ended like her parents' in tragic misunderstanding and an alienation terminated only by death. While she listens, through the wind, to Philip's voice crying for life, "wanting it," demanding it of her now, she weeps "for what happened to life."

Exhausted from so much seeing ("Human kind cannot bear very much reality"), Laurel falls asleep in the chair, and is restored. She dreams of an actual incident when, riding on a train with Phil to be married in Mount Salus, they had at dawn seen from a high point, far below them, the beautiful confluence of the Ohio and Mississippi waters; and far above, "the long, ragged, pencil-faint line of birds within the crystal of the zenith, flying in a V of their own, following the same course down. All they could see was sky, water, birds, light, and confluence. It was the whole morning world." Pattern and harmony become visible—but they are not static. The rivers flow, the birds fly, she and Phil move forward in time and space. The prospect of joining her life with Phil's, the exhilaration of riding ahead together, "in front," makes her feel at that moment that they are "going to live forever." Phil is killed soon afterward, though not too soon for them to discover their complementary polarities, to give to each other something important and permanent in this brief marriage without blunders. And Phil is always remembered, can "still tell her of her life. For her life, any life, she had to believe, was nothing but the continuity of its love." The revelations of the preceding night have not brought cynicism in their wake, for Laurel, though obviously more inward and reflective than her father, is the optimist's daughter.

A few last trials await her: getting rid of the intruders—the chimney swift (" 'all birds got to fly, even them no-count dirty ones,' " says Missouri, reminding one of Grandma's comment on the offensive pigeons); the crass, snooping Mr. Cheek; finally Fay, the desecrator of the house, whom Laurel's mother had "predicted." In a brief but violent struggle with this bold woman who knows neither feeling nor love nor respect for the dead, she perceives that while Fay cannot hurt the past and what it holds, neither can she herself protect or affect it in any way. Yet memory, "the somnambulist," keeps it alive; memory, always vulnerable, is yet merciful; "it lives for us, and while it lives, and while we are able, we can give it up its due."

Laurel, having disposed of all her mother's letters and keepsakes, refuses now to take even the cherished breadboard. "Memory lived not in initial possession but in the free hands, pardoned and freed, and in the heart that can empty but fill again, in the patterns restored by dreams." Emptied of feeling the preceding night by her awareness of her parents' and her own complicity in the kind of selfishness and cruelty more comfortably assigned to vulgar and insensitive people or rapacious pigeons, Laurel's night dream of an actual event, a time of hope and expectation, refills her heart with love. Emptied once again by her confrontation with Fay, destroyer of the past and harbinger of a fearful future peopled with such types, Laurel's heart fills once again as she thinks of the durability of memory and the power of dreams to restore the internal harmony of patterns—the lives of loved ones and her own in relation to them, seen, interpreted, understood, absorbed with a changed, enlarged, enriched perspective.

Miss Welty's focusing in this novel has again led to meditation and poetry. Laurel McKelva's experience, turned into actual verse, might read something like the following lines from Eliot's *Four Quartets:*

> This is the use of memory:
> For liberation—not less of love but expanding
> Of love beyond desire, and so liberation
> From the future as well as the past. . . .
>   See, now they vanish,
> The faces and places, with the self which, as it could, loved
>   them,
> To become renewed, transfigured, in another pattern.

This far Miss Welty's vision, the internal meeting the external world, has carried her. It has been both consistent and varying, but always faithful to the reality of life's contradictions and complexities, and reflecting, in the constant resurgence of joy and hope in even this darkest of her recent works, the overriding joy she takes in the performance of her art. That too is clearly visible; we may walk into that joy open-eyed and surrender to its blessed contagion.

Biographical Notes

Edith Wharton (1862–1937). Born Edith Newbold Jones into a wealthy New York family, she was educated by her own reading, governesses, and frequent trips to Europe. She came out into New York society at a young age, and soon afterwards married Edward Wharton, a Harvard graduate. In 1899 she published a book of short stories, *The Greater Inclination*, and in 1900 *The Touchstone* appeared. Her first full-length novel was a historical romance, *The Valley of Decision* (1902). With the publication of *The House of Mirth* (1905), Wharton found what was to be her essential subject: the relationship between the individual and society, especially in the conventional Old New York of her childhood.

After 1907, Wharton moved permanently to France, developing friendships with, among others, Henry James and Bernard Berenson. She had become a very popular writer in America, with such successes as *The Fruit of the Tree* (1907), *Ethan Frome* (1911), *The Reef* (1912), and *The Custom of the Country* (1913). In 1920 she received the Pulitzer Prize for *The Age of Innocence*. *Old New York* (1924), *The Writing of Fiction* (1925), and her autobiography, *A Backward Glance* (1934), ensured her continued popularity. She wrote steadily until her death, and in all published 46 books, including travelogues, and numerous short stories.

Theodore Dreiser (1871–1945) was born in Terre Haute, Indiana, the ninth child of German-speaking parents. After attending Indiana University, Dreiser became a reporter on the Chicago *Globe*, working also in St. Louis and Pittsburgh before arriving in New York in 1894. His first book, *Sister Carrie* (1894), was suppressed soon after publication because of the publisher's wife's reaction to its harsh realism. Dreiser worked as an editor for *Butterick's*, a women's magazine, and eventually became head of the company. *Jennie Gerhardt* (1911) was followed by a trilogy based partially on the career of the Chicago magnate Charles T. Yerkes: *The Financier* (1912),

The Titan (1914), and *The Stoic* (published posthumously in 1947). With *An American Tragedy* (1925), Dreiser achieved success (and received criticism) for his description of an actual murder case of 1906.

Dreiser's other works include *The Hand of the Potter* (1918), *Twelve Men* (1919), and a series of autobiographical volumes: *The "Genius"* (1915), *Dreiser Looks at Russia* (1928), *A Traveler at Forty* (1913), *A Hoosier Holiday* (1916), and *Dawn* (1931). *The Bulwark* was published posthumously in 1946.

Willa Cather (1873–1947) was born in Virginia but moved at age nine to Nebraska. She was educated at the University of Nebraska, became a teacher, later a journalist, and finally a free-lance writer. Her first published work was a book of poems, *April Twilights* (1903, rev. 1933); a book of short stories, *The Troll Garden* appeared in 1905. She worked for six years in New York for *McClure's Magazine* but gave up journalism in 1912, after publishing *Alexander's Bridge*. Following the advice of Sarah Orne Jewett, Cather began to use her own background as the subject of her novels. *O, Pioneers!* was published in 1913, followed by *The Song of the Lark* (1915), *My Ántonia* (1918), and *One of Ours* (1922), for which she won the Pulitzer Prize.

Death Comes for the Archbishop (1927) and *Shadows on the Rock* (1931) indicate Cather's growing interest in Catholicism. *Lucy Gayheart* (1935) and *Sapphira and the Slave Girl* (1940) were her last novels. In *Not under Forty* (1936) Cather presents her ideas about fiction and acknowledges the influence of Flaubert, Henry James, and Sarah Orne Jewett on her work.

Gertrude Stein (1874–1946) was born in Allegheny, Pennsylvania, the youngest of five children. During her childhood both of her parents died, and Gertrude and her brother Leo were placed under the guardianship of their older brother, Michael, who continued to manage their father's estate and to provide for them throughout their lives.

Gertrude and Leo were very close; when he went to study at Harvard, she followed and began taking courses at Radcliffe, becoming especially interested in psychology. At the suggestion of William James, she undertook a series of experiments on automatic writing. In the autumn of 1903, after completing three years of medical school at Johns Hopkins, she joined Leo in Paris at 27 rue de Fleurus, the studio that became famous in the next several years for their extensive and daring collection of modern art.

Gertrude Stein began to write seriously in Paris, completing *Quod Erat Demonstrandum* (*Q.E.D.* or *Things As They Are*), *Fernhurst*, and *Three Lives*, as well as translations of Flaubert's *Trois Contes*, before 1907. She met Alice B. Toklas, her lifelong companion, in 1907. As her writing became more prolific and more experimental, Stein's circle of friends widened to include Matisse, Picasso, Hemingway, F. Scott Fitzgerald, Apollinaire, Gris, Marie Laurencin, Sherwood Anderson, and many other artists and writers. Stein's early and middle works include *Tender Buttons* (1915), *The Making of Americans* (1925), *Composition As Explanation* (published posthumously), *Lucy Church Amiably* (1930), and *How to Write* (1931). Following the great success of *The Autobiography of Alice B. Toklas*, published in 1933, Stein returned to the United States on a speaking tour. Her lectures are collected in *Lectures in America* and *Narration*. Returning to Paris, she continued to write throughout World War II and until her death of cancer in 1946. Much of her work was published posthumously by Yale University Press in the 1950s.

Sherwood Anderson (1876–1941) was born in Camden, Ohio, and left school at fourteen, eventually serving in the Spanish-American War in 1898. After marrying and settling down to manage a paint factory in Ohio, Anderson left his family and moved to Chicago to become an advertising copywriter and pursue his literary career. *Windy McPherson's Son* was published in 1916, followed by *Marching Man* in 1917. In 1919, Anderson published *Winesburg, Ohio*, a collection of stories of small-town life told in highly idiomatic prose. *Poor White* (1920) describes the effect of technology on a small town.

Anderson was part of the expatriate life in Paris in the 1920s, introducing Ernest Hemingway to Gertrude Stein and encouraging the career of William Faulkner. During this time he published collections of short stories, including *The Triumph of the Egg* (1921) and *Horses and Men* (1923), and the novels *Many Marriages* (1923), *Dark Laughter* (1925), and *Tar, A Midwest Childhood* (1926). At fifty-one, Anderson moved to Winesburg, Virginia, where he wrote personal editorial essays for two country weeklies he had bought. These essays appear in *Return to Winesburg* (1967). In his autobiography, *A Story Teller's Story* (1924), Anderson relates the story of his decision to leave his family for a career as a writer.

(Harry) Sinclair Lewis (1885–1951) was born at Sauk Center, Minnesota. Graduating from Yale in 1907, Lewis worked as a journalist and copy editor before publishing *Our Mister Wrenn* in 1914. With *Main Street* (1920) and *Babbitt* (1922), Lewis established an international reputation for his satires on American life. *Arrowsmith* (1925), *Elmer Gantry* (1927), and *Dodsworth* (1929) continued his literary success, and in 1930 Lewis became the first American to win the Nobel Prize for literature.

From *Ann Vickers* (1933) to *World So Wide* (published posthumously in 1951), Lewis wrote ten novels that failed to live up to the success of his earlier works. After spending his last years traveling in Europe, he died in Rome, and his ashes were returned to Sauk Center.

Katherine Anne Porter (1890–1980) was born in Indian Creek, Texas. Although she liked to claim a rather aristocratic Catholic background, it appears that she was raised, after her mother's death in 1902, by her Methodist grandmother, her father, and other relatives. At sixteen, she eloped, married a Catholic (divorced eight years later), and converted to Catholicism, at least for a time. She held jobs on newspapers in various cities and performed songs and poems on the Lyceum Circuit. In 1920, and intermittently thereafter, she lived in New York.

Henry Miller (1891–1980) was born in Brooklyn, New York, of German ancestry. After attending the City College of New York for two months, he worked at various jobs before becoming employment manager of the messenger department of Western Union in New York. In 1924, Miller decided to become a writer, and in 1930 he went to live in Paris. *Tropic of Cancer* was published in Europe in 1934, although its sexual frankness caused the book (along with Miller's later work) to be banned in the United States until well after World War II. *Black Spring* (1936) and *Tropic of Capricorn* (1939) continue in Miller's highly autobiographical style.

Miller went to Greece in 1939 and published his impressions of the country in *The Colossus of Maroussi* (1941). In 1940, he returned to the United States; *The Air-conditioned Nightmare* (1945) and *Remember to Remember* (1947) record his uneasy impressions of modern American life. Miller spent the rest of his life at Big Sur, on the California coast. His later work includes *The Books in My Life* (1952), *The Time of the Assassins: A Study of Rimbaud* (1956) and the sequence entitled *The Rosy Crucifixion: Sexus* (1945), *Plexus* (1949), and *Nexus* (1960).

Djuna Barnes (1892–1982) was born in Cornwall-on-Hudson, New York. Self-educated, she moved to New York City to write free-lance journalism. A short book called *The Book of Repulsive Women* appeared in 1915, with almost no critical notice. In 1919 she went to Paris and in 1923 published *A Book*. *Ryder* (1928) and *Ladies Almanack* (1929) were brief successes; with *Nightwood* (1936), Barnes achieved a critical success and the enthusiastic support of T. S. Eliot, who called the book "so good a novel that only sensibilities trained on poetry can wholly appreciate it."

After living briefly in England, Barnes returned to America in 1940. She settled in New York and published only *The Antiphon* (1958), and a collection of previously written short stories, *Spillway* (1962), before her death.

Jean Toomer (1894–1967) was born Nathan Pinchback Toomer in Washington, D.C., of mixed black (or Indian) blood. He attended the University of Wisconsin and the City College of New York. In 1922, Toomer met Waldo Frank, who encouraged him to write, and began to submit his work to *Broom*, *The Little Review*, and *Dial*. *Cane* (1923), for which Frank wrote the introduction, was inspired by a trip to Georgia in which Toomer sought out his Southern roots. Soon afterward, Toomer moved to New York, broke with Frank, and met and became a follower of the spiritualist George Gurdjieff. In 1924, Toomer renounced fiction "as he had practiced it" to commit himself to Gurdjieff and his teaching.

The rest of Toomer's life was chiefly devoted to his spiritualism, and his writing was solely concerned with promulgating Gurdjieff's philosophy.

John Dos Passos (1896–1970) was born in Chicago and educated at Choate

School and Harvard. After graduating in 1916, Dos Passos was in Spain studying architecture when America entered World War I. In *One Man's Initiation: 1917* (1920; reissued in an unbowdlerized form in 1969) and *Three Soldiers* (1921) Dos Passos related the disillusionment he experienced as an ambulance driver during the war. His next few years were spent as a newspaper correspondent. *Manhattan Transfer* (1925) represents Dos Passos's first effort to compose a novel by the interconnection of hundreds of disparate elements and differing points of view. In his trilogy, *U.S.A.*, Dos Passos uses this style to describe the first thirty years of the twentieth century in the United States, beginning with *The 42nd Parallel* (1930), through *1919* (1932), and concluding with *Money* (1936). His second trilogy, *District of Columbia*, describes American social history in the thirties and forties: *The Adventures of a Young Man* (1939), *Number One* (1943), and *The Grand Design* (1949).

By the end of the 1930s, Dos Passos came to see the political left as providing a limited solution to social or economic problems; instead he began to ally himself with a Jeffersonian view of democracy. This perspective is expressed in his *The Head and Heart of Thomas Jefferson* (1954) and a series of nostalgic works, among them *The Ground We Stand On* (1941), *Chosen Country* (1951), *The Theme Is Freedom* (1956), and *Prospects of a Golden Age* (1959).

F(rancis) Scott (Key) Fitzgerald (1896–1940), born in St. Paul, Minnesota, attended Newman School in New Jersey and Princeton University. During the first World War, he was stationed in the United States, where he spent his time in camp writing *The Romantic Egoist* (rewritten as *This Side of Paradise*) and courting Zelda Zayre, whom he married in 1920. When *This Side of Paradise* was published (1920), Fitzgerald became an immediate success. *Flappers and Philosophers* (1920), *The Beautiful and the Damned* (1922), and *Tales of the Jazz Age* (1922) confirmed Fitzgerald's place as a spokesman for a decadent generation of pleasure-seeking young Americans. *The Great Gatsby* (1920) and *All the Sad Young Men* (1926), written while Fitzgerald was in Europe, represent a more tragic view of this generation.

In 1927 Fitzgerald returned to America to write for Hollywood, but by 1928 he was back in Europe. During the next few years Zelda's mental instability grew, and Fitzgerald himself became increasingly alcoholic. *Tender Is the Night* (1934) offers Fitzgerald's perspective on the tragic and pathetic lives of Americans living hopelessly restless lives in Europe. Articles written in *Esquire* in 1936 (collected in *The Crack-Up*, 1945) detail Fitzgerald's physical and mental breakdown after he had returned to America to write for Hollywood again in 1937. In the last three years of his life, Fitzgerald worked on *The Last Tycoon* (unfinished, published posthumously in 1940) and wrote seventeen short stories. He died in 1940, in Hollywood.

William Faulkner (1897–1962) was born in New Albany, Mississippi, and brought up in Oxford County. He left school early, joined the Royal Flying

Air Corps in Canada in World War I (which ended before he was commissioned), and studied briefly at the University of Mississippi at Oxford. *The Marble Faun*, a collection of verse, was published in 1924 without much critical attention. Faulkner went to work for a newspaper in New Orleans, where he met and was encouraged by Sherwood Anderson; in 1926 *A Soldier's Pay* was published. Faulkner traveled briefly to Europe in 1926 but returned to Oxford, where he spent most of the rest of his life. *Mosquitoes* (1927) was followed by the first of his Yoknapatawpha novels, *Sartoris* (1929), but *The Sound and the Fury* (1929) was the first of his works to draw critical attention. *As I Lay Dying* (1930), *Light in August* (1932), and *Absalom, Absalom!* (1936) all continued Faulkner's literary success; only *Sanctuary* (1931) was poorly received by the critics, who thought it was too sadistic.

In *Go Down Moses* (1942), *These Thirteen* (1931), *Doctor Marino and Other Stories* (1934), and *Knight's Gambit* (1949) Faulkner's first-rate stories appear. *The Hamlet* (1940), *The Town* (1957), and *The Mansion* (1959) concern the rise to power of the Snopes clan. In 1950, Faulkner won the Nobel Prize. His later works include *Requiem for a Nun* (1951), *A Fable* (1954), and *The Reivers* (1962).

Ernest (Miller) Hemingway (1898–1961) was born in Oak Park, Illinois, and raised both in Oak Park and the Great Lakes region in Michigan, where his family had a vacation house. After school he worked as a reporter for a Kansas City newspaper, volunteered for service in World War I, and served as an ambulance driver near the Austro-Italian border, where he was wounded in 1918. Hemingway's war experience and his father's suicide caused him, in his words, to cease to be "hardboiled." After the War, Hemingway was a journalist in Toronto and Chicago. In 1921 he married Hadley Richardson, and the couple moved to Paris, where Hemingway wrote articles for Hearst newspapers. A memoir of his Paris years appears in *A Moveable Feast* (published posthumously in 1964).

With the influence of Gertrude Stein, Ezra Pound, and F. Scott Fitzgerald, Hemingway began to write fiction, and *In Our Time* appeared in 1925. *The Torrents of Spring* (1926) is a parody of Sherwood Anderson's style; with *The Sun Also Rises* (1926), Hemingway became both critically and popularly successful. *Men without Women* (1927) and *Winner Take Nothing* (1933) offer the classic, sparse Hemingway short-story style. *A Farewell to Arms (1929)* and *For Whom the Bell Tolls* (1940) have become his most popular novels. In between, Hemingway developed both his idiosyncratic style and his macho image with *Death in the Afternoon* (1932), *The Green Hills of Africa* (1935), and *To Have and Have Not* (1937). *Across the River and into the Trees* (1950) and *The Old Man and the Sea* (1952) ended a period of writer's block for Hemingway, and in 1954 he was awarded the Nobel Prize. In the last years of his life, Hemingway found it increasingly difficult to write, and on July 2, 1961, he shot himself at his home in Ketchum, Idaho. *Islands in the Stream* appeared in 1970 and *Garden of Eden* in 1986, both substantially edited.

Thomas Wolfe (1900–38) was born in Ashville, North Carolina, where his father was a stone-cutter and his mother ran a boarding house. He graduated from the University of North Carolina in 1920 and received an M.A. from Harvard in Theater in 1922. From 1924 to 1930 he taught English at New York University, and in 1929 *Look Homeward, Angel* was published. Wolfe's autobiographical work received mixed critical responses. Maxwell Perkins, his editor at Scribner's, apparently worked very closely with Wolfe on both his first novel and *Of Time and the River* (1935).

From *Death to Morning* (1935), *The Hills Beyond* (1941), *The Web and the Rock* (1939), and *You Can't Go Home Again* (1940) roughly parallel Wolfe's own life in his consistently autobiographical style. Wolfe died in 1938 after two operations for a brain infection following pneumonia. Several posthumous works, including two novels and a volume of short stories, were edited by George Aswell.

John Steinbeck (1902–68) was born in California and attended Stanford University, studying marine biology. He left school without taking a degree, became a laborer, and then decided to become a writer. *Cup of Gold* (1929) was a romantic novel about the buccaneer Sir Henry Morgan. With *Pastures of Heaven* (1932), *To A God Unknown* (1933), and *Tortilla Flat* (1935), Steinbeck developed his principal subject—laborers and migrant workers in the West—and began to write about it from the perspective of biological observation. *In Dubious Battle* (1936), *Of Mice and Men* (1937), and *The Grapes of Wrath* (1939) demonstrate his gradual identification with the "rural proletariat."

From *Cannery Row* (1945) to *Travels with Charley* (1962), Steinbeck wrote several novels, stories, and non-fiction works, including *East of Eden* (1952) and *The Winter of Our Discontent* (1961). He won the Nobel Prize in 1968.

Zora Neale Hurston (1903–60) was born in Eatonville, an all-black town in Florida. She left home at twelve to become a maid for a member of a traveling Gilbert and Sullivan troupe. After attending Howard University, she graduated from Barnard College in 1928. *Jonah's Gourd Vine* was published in 1934, and *Mules and Men* in 1935. After the publication of *Their Eyes Were Watching God* (1937), she traveled on a Guggenheim Fellowship to Jamaica, Haiti, and Bermuda to collect folklore, and in 1938–39 she worked for the W.P.A. collecting folklore in Florida.

Moses, Man of the Mountain (1939), *Dust Tracks on the Road* (1942), and *Seraph on the Sewanee* (1948) were her later publications. Before her death in a welfare home in 1960, she had worked as a maid, librarian, and reporter in Florida.

Nathanael West (1903–40) was born Nathan Wallenstein Weinstein in New York City. He studied at Brown University and lived in Paris for a time before returning to New York to be a hotel manager. *The Dream Life of Balso Snell* appeared in 1931, and with the publication of *Miss Lonelyhearts* (1933)

West developed an enthusiastic, if limited, following. After writing *A Cool Million* (1934)—another limited success—West went to Hollywood to write screenplays. *The Day of the Locust* (1939) is told in West's apocalyptic style, aiming his cynical satire at the classic example of the American dream: Hollywood. West and his wife were killed in a car crash while returning from a hunting trip in Mexico.

Richard Wright (1908–60) was born in Natchez, Mississippi. He was self-educated and worked at odd jobs in Memphis before moving to Chicago in 1934. He joined the Communist Party in 1936, and *Uncle Tom's Children*, a collection of short stories, was published in 1938. *Native Son* (1940) describes the career of Bigger Thomas, a black raised in Chicago slums, whose violent crime and subsequent execution are depicted by Wright as an existential dilemma.

After living in Mexico briefly in the early 1940s, Wright moved to Paris, where he lived until his death. *Black Boy* (1945), *The Outsider* (1953), *Black Power* (1954), *The Long Dream* (1958), and *Land Today* (published posthumously in 1963) were among his later publications.

Eudora Welty (1909–   ), born in Jackson, Mississippi, received her B.A. from the University of Wisconsin at Madison. After studying advertising at Columbia Business School in New York, she returned to Jackson. She began to write while working as a photographer in the mid-thirties for the W.P.A., and a collection of short stories, *A Curtain of Green*, was published in 1941. *The Robber Bridegroom*, a fairy-tale novel, appeared in 1942, followed by *The Wide Net and Other Stories* in 1943. During the War she wrote reviews of battle reports under the pseudonym Michael Ravenna.

Delta Wedding (1946), *The Golden Apples* (1949), *The Ponder Heart* (1954), and *The Bride of Innisfallen* (1954) all take place in the Mississippi delta community that has been her home for most of her life and the primary subject in most of her work. *Losing Battles* (1970), *The Optimist's Daughter* (1972), and the non-fiction works *The Eye of the Story* (1978) and *One Writer's Beginnings* (1983) have been her most recent works.

Contributors

Harold Bloom, Sterling Professor of the Humanities at Yale University, is the author of *The Anxiety of Influence, Poetry and Repression,* and many other volumes of literary criticism. His forthcoming study, *Freud: Transference and Authority,* attempts a full-scale reading of all of Freud's major writings. A MacArthur Prize Fellow, he is general editor of five series of literary criticism published by Chelsea House.

Mary Suzanne Schriber is Associate Professor of English at Northern Illinois University. Her works on Sherwood Anderson, Edith Wharton, and Henry James have appeared in *Studies in Short Fiction, American Literary Realism,* and *Studies in the Novel.*

John J. Conder teaches at Vanderbilt University and is the author of *Naturalism in American Fiction.*

Phyllis Rose is Professor of English at Wesleyan University. Her publications include *Woman of Letters: A Life of Virginia Woolf* and articles on Huxley and Woolf in *Victorian Newsletter* and *Women's Studies.*

Clive Bush is Lecturer in English and American Literature at the University of Warwick, England, and the author of *The Dream of Reason: American Consciousness and Cultural Achievement from Independence to the Civil War.* He is at work on a book dealing with Henry Adams, Gertrude Stein, and William James.

Benjamin T. Spencer is Professor Emeritus of English, Ohio Wesleyan University, and the author of *Patterns of Nationality* and several books and articles on American literary nationalism.

James Lea is the author of *Katzanzakis: The Politics of Salvation.*

433

Joseph Wiesenfarth is Professor of English at the University of Wisconsin at Madison. His publications include *Henry James and the Dramatic Analogy*, *The Errand of Form*, and numerous essays on Henry James and George Eliot.

Alan Warren Friedman has taught British and American Literature at the University of Texas since 1964. He has published books on Lawrence Durrell and essays on Philip Roth, Bernard Malamud, Joyce Cary, and Joseph Conrad.

Carolyn Allen teaches in the English department at the University of Washington at Seattle.

Barbara E. Bowen, Assistant Professor of English at Wellesley College, has published a study of the poetry of Gwendolyn Brooks and is completing a dissertation on the problem of representation in Shakespeare's plays.

Charles Marz has written on Dos Passos for *Studies in the Novel*.

Bruce Michelson is Assistant Professor of English at the University of Illinois at Urbana. His essays on Mark Twain and Richard Wilbur have appeared in *American Literature, The Southern Review*, and *The Massachusetts Review*.

Maria DiBattista is Assistant Professor of English at Princeton University and specializes in nineteenth- and twentieth-century fiction. She is the author of *Virginia Woolf's Major Novels: The Fables of Anon*.

Donald Monk is Lecturer in American Literature in the Department of American Studies of the University of Manchester.

Cleanth Brooks is Gray Professor of Rhetoric Emeritus, Yale University. He is the author of *The Hidden God: Studies in Hemingway, Faulkner, Yeats, Eliot, and Warren, William Faulkner: Toward Yoknapatawpha and Beyond*, and *William Faulkner: First Encounters*, as well as many other books of literary criticism.

James G. Watson is Associate Professor of English at the University of Tulsa, and the author of *The Snopes Dilemma: Faulkner's Trilogy* and essays in *Fifty Years of Yoknapatawpha* and *Faulkner Studies*.

Patrick O'Donnell is Assistant Professor of English at the University of Arizona. His publications include *John Hawkes* and *Journeying to the Center: Time, Pattern, and Transcendence in William Golding's Free Fall*.

Ihab Hassan, Vilas Research Professor of English and Comparative Literature at the University of Wisconsin at Milwaukee, is the author of *The Dismemberment of Orpheus: Toward a Postmodern Literature, Paracriticism: Seven Speculations of the Times*, and *The Right Promethean Fire: Imagination, Science, and Cultural Change*.

John Graham is Associate Professor of Speech at the University of Virginia and the author of, among other works, *The Writer's Voice* (1973) and *Lavater's Essays on Physiognomy: A Study in the History of Ideas* (1979).

Wesley A. Kort is Professor of Religion at Duke University. Among his publications are *Shriven Selves: Religious Problems in Recent American Fiction* and *Narrative Elements and Religious Meaning.*

Morris Beja is Professor of English at Ohio State University and has published *The Wooden Sword: Threatener and Threatened in the Fiction of James Joyce's "Dubliners"* and *"A Portrait of the Artist"* as a Young Man, as well as articles on Aidan Higgins and Herman Melville.

Sylvia Jenkins Cook, who teaches in the department of English at the University of Missouri, has written *From Tobacco Road to Route Sixty-Six* and numerous articles dealing with politics, feminism, and literature in the 1930s.

Barbara Johnson is Professor of Romance Languages and Literatures at Harvard University. Her publications include *Défigurations du langage poétique, The Critical Difference,* a translation of Jacques Derrida's *Dissemination,* and an edition of *The Pedagogical Imperative: Teaching as a Literary Genre.*

Jonathan Raban is the author of *Mark Twain: Huckleberry Finn* and *Old Glory: An American Voyage.*

Robert B. Stepto is an Associate Professor of English, Afro-American Studies, and American Studies at Yale University. He is the author of *From Behind the Veil: A Study of the Afro-American Narrative* and a coeditor (with Dexter Fisher) of *American Literature: The Reconstruction of Instruction.*

Ruth M. Vande Kieft is a Professor at Queens College, New York, and the author of *Eudora Welty, Patterns of Communication,* and other works on southern fiction.

Bibliography

EDITH WHARTON

Ammons, Elizabeth. *Edith Wharton's Argument with America*. Athens: University of Georgia Press, 1980.

Gimbel, Wendy. *Edith Wharton: Orphancy and Survival*. New York: Praeger, 1984.

Howe, Irving, ed. *Edith Wharton: A Collection of Critical Essays*. Englewood Cliffs, N.J.: Prentice-Hall, 1962.

Lawson, Richard H. *Edith Wharton*. New York: Frederick Ungar, 1977.

Lindberg, Gary H. *Edith Wharton and the Novel of Manners*. Charlottesville: University of Virginia Press, 1975.

McDowell, Margaret B. *Edith Wharton*. Boston: Twayne Publishers, 1976.

Walton, Geoffrey. *Edith Wharton: A Critical Interpretation*. Rutherford, N.J.: Fairleigh Dickinson University Press, 1970.

Wershoven, Carol. *The Female Intruder in the Novels of Edith Wharton*. Rutherford, N.J.: Fairleigh Dickinson University Press, 1982.

Wolff, Cynthia Griffin. *A Feast of Words: The Triumph of Edith Wharton*. New York: Oxford University Press, 1977.

THEODORE DREISER

Dowell, Richard, ed. *An Amateur Laborer: Theodore Dreiser*. Philadelphia: University of Pennsylvania Press, 1983.

Elias, Robert. *Theodore Dreiser: Apostle of Nature*. Ithaca: Cornell University Press, 1970.

Gerber, Phillip L. *Theodore Dreiser*. New York: Twayne Publishers, 1964.

Hussman, Lawrence E. *Dreiser and His Fiction: A Twentieth-Century Quest*. Philadelphia: University of Pennsylvania Press, 1983.

437

Kazin, Alfred, and Charles Shapiro, eds. *The Stature of Theodore Dreiser: A Critical Survey of the Man and His Work*. Bloomington: Indiana University Press, 1955.

Lehan, Richard. *Theodore Dreiser: His World and His Novels*. Carbondale: Southern Illinois University Press, 1969.

Lundquist, James. *Theodore Dreiser*. New York: Frederick Ungar, 1974.

Lydenberg, John, ed. *Dreiser: A Collection of Critical Essays*. Englewood Cliffs, N.J.: Prentice-Hall, 1971.

McAleer, John J. *Theodore Dreiser: An Introduction and Interpretation*. New York: Holt, Rinehart, and Winston, 1968.

Moers, Ellen. *Two Dreisers*. New York: Viking Press, 1969.

Pizer, Donald. *The Novels of Theodore Dreiser: A Critical Study*. Minneapolis: University of Minnesota Press, 1976.

Salzman, Jack, ed. *Theodore Dreiser: The Critical Reception*. New York: David Lewis, 1972.

WILLA CATHER

Arnold, Marilyn. *Willa Cather's Short Fiction*. Athens: Ohio University Press, 1984.

Bailey, Jennifer. "The Dangers of Femininity in Willa Cather's Fiction." *Journal of American Studies* 16, no. 3 (December 1982): 391–406.

Daiches, David. *Willa Cather: A Critical Introduction*. Ithaca: Cornell University Press, 1951.

Gerber, Phillip L. *Willa Cather*. Boston: Twayne Publishers, 1975.

McFarland, Dorothy Tuck. *Willa Cather*. New York: Frederick Ungar, 1972.

Murphy, John J., ed. *Five Essays on Willa Cather: The Merrimack Symposium*. North Andover, Mass.: Merrimack College, 1974.

Randall, John Herman. *The Landscape and the Looking Glass: Willa Cather's Search for Value*. Boston: Houghton Mifflin, 1960.

Schroeter, James Mervin, ed. *Willa Cather and Her Critics*. Ithaca: Cornell University Press, 1967.

Slote, Bernice, and Virginia Faulkner, eds. *The Art of Willa Cather*. Lincoln: Department of English, University of Nebraska—Lincoln, 1974.

Stouck, David. *Willa Cather's Imagination*. Lincoln: University of Nebraska Press, 1975.

Van Ghent, Dorothy. *Willa Cather*. Minneapolis: University of Minnesota Press, 1964.

Woodress, James. *Willa Cather: Her Life and Art*. New York: Pegasus, 1970.

GERTRUDE STEIN

Bridgman, Richard. *Gertrude Stein in Pieces*. New York: Oxford University Press, 1970.

Copeland, Carolyn. *Language and Time and Gertrude Stein*. Iowa City: University of Iowa Press, 1975.

DeKoven, Marianne. *A Different Language: Gertrude Stein's Experimental Writing*. Madison: University of Wisconsin Press, 1983.

Hoffman, Frederick. *Gertrude Stein*. Minneapolis: University of Minnesota Press, 1961.

Hoffman, Michael. *The Development of Abstractionism in the Writings of Gertrude Stein*. Philadelphia: University of Pennsylvania Press, 1965.

————. *Gertrude Stein*. Boston: Twayne Publishers, 1976.

Neuman, Shirley. *Gertrude Stein: Autobiography and the Problem of Narration*. Victoria, B.C.: English Literary Studies, Department of English, University of Victoria, 1979.

Simon, Linda, ed. *Gertrude Stein: A Composite Portrait*. New York: Avon, 1974.

Steiner, Wendy. *Exact Resemblance to Exact Resemblance: The Literary Portraiture of Gertrude Stein*. New Haven: Yale University Press, 1978.

Sutherland, Donald. *Gertrude Stein: A Biography of Her Work*. New Haven: Yale University Press, 1951.

Walker, Jayne. *The Making of a Modernist: Gertrude Stein from* Three Lives *to* Tender Buttons. Amherst: University of Massachusetts Press, 1984.

SHERWOOD ANDERSON

Anderson, David D. *Sherwood Anderson: Dimensions of His Literary Art—A Collection of Critical Essays*. East Lansing: Michigan State University Press, 1976.

Howe, Irving. *Sherwood Anderson*. New York: Sloane, 1951.

Rideout, Walter, ed. *Sherwood Anderson: A Collection of Critical Essays*. Englewood Cliffs, N.J.: Prentice-Hall, 1974.

Sutton, William A. *The Road to Winesburg: A Mosaic of the Imaginative Life of Sherwood Anderson*. Metuchen, N.J.: Scarecrow Press, 1972.

Tanner, Tony. *The Reign of Wonder: Naivety and Reality in American Literature*. Cambridge: Cambridge University Press, 1965.

Walcutt, Charles. *American Literary Naturalism, A Divided Stream*. Minneapolis: University of Minnesota Press, 1956.

Weber, Brom. *Sherwood Anderson*. Minneapolis: University of Minnesota Press, 1964.

White, Ray Lewis, ed. *The Achievement of Sherwood Anderson*. Chapel Hill: University of North Carolina Press, 1966.

SINCLAIR LEWIS

Bradbury, Malcolm, and David Palmer, eds. *The American Novel and the Nineteen Twenties*. Stratford-upon-Avon Studies, 13. London: Edward Arnold, 1971.

Brown, Daniel R. "Lewis' Satire—A Negative Emphasis." *Renascence* 18 (Winter 1966): 63–72.

Dooley, David. *The Art of Sinclair Lewis*. Lincoln: University of Nebraska Press, 1967.

Grebstein, Sheldon. *Sinclair Lewis*. New York: Twayne Publishers, 1962.

Griffin, Robert J., ed. *Twentieth-Century Interpretations of "Arrowsmith".* Englewood Cliffs, N.J.: Prentice-Hall, 1968.

Light, Martin. *The Quixotic Vision of Sinclair Lewis*. West Lafayette, Ind.: Perdue University Press, 1975.

————, ed. *Studies in "Babbitt."* Columbus, Ohio: Charles E. Merrill, 1971.

Lundquist, James. *Guide to Sinclair Lewis*. Columbus, Ohio: Charles E. Merrill, 1970.

————. *Sinclair Lewis*. New York: Frederick Ungar, 1973.

Schorer, Mark, ed. *Sinclair Lewis: A Collection of Critical Essays*. Englewood Cliffs, N.J.: Prentice-Hall, 1962.

————. *Society and Self in the Novel*. New York: Columbia University Press, 1955.

Yoshida, Hiroshige. *A Sinclair Lewis Lexicon with a Critical Study of His Style and Method*. Tokyo: Hoyu Press, 1976.

KATHERINE ANNE PORTER

DeMouy, Jane. *Katherine Anne Porter's Women: The Eye of Her Fiction*. Austin: University of Texas Press, 1983.

Givner, Joan. *Katherine Anne Porter: A Life*. New York: Simon and Schuster, 1982.

Hardy, John. *Katherine Anne Porter*. New York: Frederick Ungar, 1973.

Hartley, Lodwick, and George Core, eds. *Katherine Anne Porter: A Critical Symposium*. Athens: University of Georgia Press, 1969.

Hendrick, George. *Katherine Anne Porter*. New York: Twayne Publishers, 1965.

Liberman, Myron. *Katherine Anne Porter's Fiction*. Detroit: Wayne State University Press, 1971.

Mooney, Harry John, Jr. *The Fiction and Criticism of Katherine Anne Porter*. Pittsburgh: University of Pittsburgh Press, 1957; rev. ed. 1962.

Nance, William L., S. M. *Katherine Anne Porter and the Art of Rejection*. Chapel Hill: University of North Carolina Press, 1964.

Unrue, Darlene Harbour. *Truth and Vision in Katherine Anne Porter's Fiction*. Athens: University of Georgia Press, 1985.

Warren, Robert Penn, ed. *Katherine Anne Porter: A Collection of Critical Essays*. Englewood Cliffs, N.J.: Prentice-Hall, 1979.

————. "Katherine Anne Porter (Irony with a Center)." *Kenyon Review* 4 (1942): 29–42.

West, Ray B., Jr. *Katherine Anne Porter*. Minneapolis: University of Minnesota Press, 1963.

HENRY MILLER

Gordon, William A. *The Mind and Art of Henry Miller*. Baton Rouge: Louisiana State University Press, 1967.

Hassan, Ihab. *The Literature of Silence: Henry Miller and Samuel Beckett.* New York: Knopf, 1968.

Mailer, Norman, ed. *Genius and Lust*: *A Journey through the Major Writings of Henry Miller.* New York: Grove Press, 1976.

Manning, Hugo. *The It and the Odyssey of Henry Miller.* London: Enitharmon Press, 1972.

Mathieu, Bertrand. *Orpheus in Brooklyn: Orphism, Rimbaud, and Henry Miller.* The Hague: Mouton, 1976.

Mitchell, Edward B., ed. *Henry Miller: Three Decades of Criticism.* New York: New York University Press, 1971.

Nelson, Jane. *Form and Image in the Fiction of Henry Miller.* Detroit: Wayne State University Press, 1970.

White, Emil, ed. *Henry Miller: Between Heaven and Hell.* Big Sur, Calif., 1961.

Wickes, George. *Henry Miller.* Minneapolis: University of Minnesota Press, 1966.

————, ed. *Henry Miller and the Critics.* Carbondale: Southern Illinois University Press, 1963.

Widmer, Kingsley. *Henry Miller.* New York: Twayne Publishers, 1963.

DJUNA BARNES

Baldwin, K., and David K. Kirby, eds. *Individual and Community: Variations on a Theme in American Fiction.* Durham, N.C.: Duke University Press, 1978.

Baxter, Charles M. "A Self-Consuming Light: *Nightwood* and the Crisis of Modernism." *Journal of Modern Languages* 3, vol. 5 (July 1974): 1175–87.

Burke, Kenneth. *Language as Symbolic Action: Essays on Life, Literature, and Method.* Berkeley: University of California Press, 1968.

Greiner, Donald J. "Djuna Barnes' *Nightwood* and the American Origins of Black Humor." *Critique* 17, vol. 1 (1975): 41–54.

Gunn, Edward. "Myth and Style in Djuna Barnes' *Nightwood.*" *Modern Fiction Studies* 19 (Winter 1973–74): 545–55.

Kannenstine, Louis. *The Art of Djuna Barnes: Duality and Damnation.* New York: New York University Press, 1972.

Pochoda, Elizabeth. "Style's Hoax: A Reading of Djuna Barnes' *Nightwood.*" *Twentieth Century Literature* 22 (May 1976): 179–91.

Scott, James B. *Djuna Barnes.* Boston: Twayne Publishers, 1976.

Sutton, Walter. "The Literary Image and the Reader: A Consideration of Spatial Form." *Journal of Aesthetics and Art Criticism* 16, vol. 1 (September 1957): 112–23.

Williamson, Alan. "The Divided Image: The Quest for Identity in the Works of Djuna Barnes." *Critique* 7 (Spring 1964): 58–74.

JEAN TOOMER

Antonides, Chris. *Jean Toomer: The Burden of Impotent Pain.* Photocopy of typescript. Ann Arbor: University Microfilms International, 1975.

Benson, Brian Joseph. *Jean Toomer*. Boston: Twayne Publishers, 1980.

Davis, Charles T. "Jean Toomer and the South: Region and Race as Elements within a Literary Imagination." In *Black Is the Color of the Cosmos*. New York: Garland Publishing, Inc., 1982.

Golding, Alan. "Jean Toomer's *Cane:* The Search for Identity through Form." *Arizona Quarterly* 39, vol. 3 (Autumn 1983): 197–213.

Gysin, Fritz. *The Grotesque in American Negro Fiction: Jean Toomer, Richard Wright, and Ralph Ellison*. Bern: Francke, 1975.

Krasny, Michael Jay. *Jean Toomer and the Quest for Consciousness*. Photocopy of typescript. Ann Arbor: University Microfilms International, 1982.

MacKethan, Lucinda Hardwick. "Jean Toomer's *Cane:* The Pastoral Return." In *The Dream of Arcady: Place and Time in Southern Literature*. Baton Rouge: Louisiana State University Press, 1980.

Turner, Darwin T. *In a Minor Chord: Three Afro-American Writers and Their Search for Identity*. Carbondale: Southern Illinois University Press, 1971.

JOHN DOS PASSOS

Becker, George. *John Dos Passos*. New York: Frederick Ungar, 1974.

Belkind, Allen J., ed. *Dos Passos, the Critics, and the Writer's Intention*. Carbondale: Southern Illinois University Press, 1971.

Brantley, John D. *The Fiction of John Dos Passos*. The Hague: Mouton, 1968.

Colley, Iain. *Dos Passos and the Fiction of Despair*. Totowa, N.J.: Rowman and Littlefield, 1978.

Davis, Robert Gorham. *John Dos Passos*. Minneapolis: University of Minnesota Press, 1962.

Hook, Andrew Dunnett, ed. *Dos Passos: A Collection of Critical Essays*. Englewood Cliffs, N.J.: Prentice-Hall, 1974.

Morse, Jonathan. "Dos Passos' *U.S.A.* and the Illusions of Memory." *Modern Fiction Studies* 24, no. 4 (Winter 1977–78): 543–56.

Rosen, Robert C. *John Dos Passos: Politics and the Writer*. Lincoln: University of Nebraska Press, 1981.

Sartre, Jean-Paul. *Literary and Philosophical Essays*. London: Rider and Co., 1955.

Wagner, Linda Welshimer. *Dos Passos: Artist as American*. Austin: University of Texas Press, 1979.

Wrenn, John H. *John Dos Passos*. New York: Twayne Publishers, 1961.

F. SCOTT FITZGERALD

Allen, Joan M. *Candles and Carnival Lights: The Catholic Sensibility of F. Scott Fitzgerald*. New York: New York University Press, 1978.

Bruccoli, Matthew, ed. *F. Scott Fitzgerald in His Own Time: A Miscellany*. Kent, Ohio: Kent State University Press, 1971.

Bryer, Jackson, ed. *The Short Stories of F. Scott Fitzgerald: New Approaches in Criticism*. Madison: University of Wisconsin Press, 1982.

Callahan, John F. *The Illusions of a Nation: Myth and History in the Novels of F. Scott Fitzgerald*. Urbana: University of Illinois Press, 1972.

Cowley, Malcolm, ed. *Fitzgerald and the Jazz Age*. New York: Scribner's, 1966.

Eble, Kenneth, ed. *F. Scott Fitzgerald: A Collection of Criticism*. New York: McGraw-Hill, 1973.

Fahey, William A. *F. Scott Fitzgerald and the American Dream*. New York: Crowell, 1973.

Lehan, Richard D. *F. Scott Fitzgerald and the Craft of Fiction*. Carbondale: Southern Illinois University Press, 1966.

Miller, James E. *F. Scott Fitzgerald: His Art and His Technique*. New York: New York University Press, 1964.

Mizener, Arthur, ed. *F. Scott Fitzgerald: A Collection of Critical Essays*. Englewood Cliffs, N.J.: Prentice-Hall, 1963.

Sklar, Robert. *F. Scott Fitzgerald: The Last Laocoon*. New York: Oxford University Press, 1967.

Stern, Milton. *The Golden Moment*. Urbana: University of Illinois Press, 1970.

Way, Brian. *F. Scott Fitzgerald and the Art of Social Fiction*. London: Edward Arnold, 1980.

WILLIAM FAULKNER

Brodhead, Richard, ed. *Faulkner: New Perspectives*. Englewood Cliffs, N.J.: Prentice-Hall, 1983.

Brooks, Cleanth. *William Faulkner: First Encounters*. New Haven: Yale University Press, 1983.

Davis, Thadious M. *Faulkner's "Negro": Art and the Southern Context*. Baton Rouge: Louisiana State University Press, 1983.

Fowler, Doreen. *Faulkner's Changing Vision: From Outrage to Affirmation*. Ann Arbor: University Microfilms International Research Press, 1983.

Gresset, Michel, and Patrick Samway, eds. *Faulkner and Idealism: Perspectives from Paris*. Jackson: University Press of Mississippi, 1983.

Irwin, John T. *Doubling and Incest/Repetition and Revenge: A Speculative Reading of Faulkner*. Baltimore: Johns Hopkins University Press, 1973.

Kartiganer, Donald. *The Fragile Thread: The Meaning of Form in Faulkner's Novels*. Amherst: University of Massachusetts Press, 1979.

Matthews, John T. *The Play of Faulkner's Language*. Ithaca: Cornell University Press, 1982.

Mortimer, Gail L. *Faulkner's Rhetoric of Loss: A Study in Perception and Meaning*. Austin: University of Texas Press, 1983.

Sensibar, Judith L. *The Origins of Faulkner's Art*. Austin: University of Texas Press, 1984.

Sundquist, Eric J. *Faulkner: The House Divided*. Baltimore: Johns Hopkins University Press, 1983.

ERNEST HEMINGWAY

Brenner, Gerry. *Concealments in Hemingway's Works*. Columbus: Ohio State University Press, 1983.

Giger, Romeo. *The Creative Imagination: Hemingway's Iceberg Theory*. Bern: Francke, 1977.

Grebstein, Sheldon Norman. *Hemingway's Craft*. Carbondale: Southern Illinois University Press, 1973.

Lee, A. Robert. *Ernest Hemingway: New Critical Essays*. London: Vision; Totowa, N.J.: Barnes and Noble, 1983.

Meyers, Jeffrey, ed. *Hemingway: The Critical Heritage*. Boston: Routledge and Kegan Paul, 1982.

Noble, Donald R., ed. *Hemingway: A Reevaluation*. Troy, N.Y.: Whitson Publishing Company, 1983.

Suobada, Frederic J. *Hemingway and* The Sun Also Rises: *The Crafting of a Style*. Lawrence: University Press of Kansas, 1983.

Wagner, Linda Welshimer, ed. *Ernest Hemingway: Five Decades of Criticism*. East Lansing: Michigan State University Press, 1974.

Weeks, Robert Percy, ed. *Hemingway: A Collection of Critical Essays*. Englewood Cliffs, N.J.: Prentice-Hall, 1962.

Williams, Wirt. *The Tragic Art of Ernest Hemingway*. Baton Rouge: Louisiana State University Press, 1981.

THOMAS WOLFE

Field, Leslie A., ed. *Thomas Wolfe: Three Decades of Criticism*. New York: New York University Press, 1968.

Gurko, Leo. *Thomas Wolfe: Beyond the Romantic Ego*. New York: Crowell, 1975.

Holman, Clarence Hugh, ed. *The Loneliness at the Core: Studies in Thomas Wolfe*. Baton Rouge: Louisiana State University Press, 1975.

McElderry, Bruce R. *Thomas Wolfe*. New York: Twayne Publishers, 1964.

Reeves, Paschal, ed. *Thomas Wolfe and the Glass of Time*. Athens: University of Georgia Press, 1971.

Rubin, Louis D., Jr., ed. *Thomas Wolfe: A Collection of Critical Essays*. Englewood Cliffs, N.J.: Prentice-Hall, 1973.

Ryssel, Fritz. *Thomas Wolfe*. New York: Frederick Ungar, 1972.

Steele, Richard. *Thomas Wolfe: A Psychoanalytic Literary Criticism*. Philadelphia: Dorrance, 1976.

Turnbull, Andrew. *Thomas Wolfe*. New York: Scribner's, 1967.

JOHN STEINBECK

Davis, Robert M., ed. *Steinbeck: A Collection of Critical Essays*. Englewood Cliffs, N.J.: Prentice-Hall, 1972.

Garcia, Reloy. *Steinbeck and D. H. Lawrence: Fictive Voices and the Ethical Imperative.* Muncie, Ind.: John Steinbeck Society of America, Ball State University, 1972.

Hayashi, Tetsumaro, ed. *Steinbeck's Literary Dimension: A Guide to Comparative Studies.* Metuchen, N.J.: Scarecrow Press, 1972.

——. *Steinbeck's Women.* Muncie, Ind.: John Steinbeck Society of America, Ball State University, 1979.

Levant, Howard. *The Novels of John Steinbeck: A Critical Study.* Columbia: University of Missouri Press, 1974.

Marks, Lester Jay. *Thematic Design in the Novels of John Steinbeck.* Paris: Mouton, 1969.

O'Connor, Richard. *John Steinbeck.* New York: McGraw-Hill, 1970.

Owens, Louis. *John Steinbeck's Re-Vision of America.* Athens: University of Georgia Press, 1985.

Simmonds, Roy S. *Steinbeck's Literary Achievement.* Muncie, Ind.: John Steinbeck Society of America, Ball State University, 1976.

ZORA NEALE HURSTON

Bone, Robert. *Down Home.* New York: G. P. Putnam's Sons, 1975.

Holloway, Karla F. C. *A Critical Investigation of Literary and Linguistic Structures on the Fiction of Zora Neale Hurston.* Photocopy of typescript. Ann Arbor: University Microfilms International, 1979.

Howard, Lillie P. *Zora Neale Hurston: A Non-Revolutionary Black Artist.* Photocopy of typescript. Ann Arbor: University Microfilms International, 1980.

——. *Zora Neale Hurston.* Boston: Twayne Publishers, 1980.

Jenkins, Joyce. *To Make a Woman Black: A Critical Analysis of the Women Characters in the Fiction and Folklore of Zora Neale Hurston.* Photocopy of typescript. Ann Arbor: University Microfilms International, 1978.

Johnson, Gloria. *Hurston's Folk: The Critical Significance of Afro-American Folk Tradition in Three Novels and the Autobiography.* Photocopy of typescript. Ann Arbor: University Microfilms International, 1980.

Turner, Darwin T. *In a Minor Chord: Three Afro-American Writers and Their Search for Identity.* Carbondale: Southern Illinois University Press, 1971.

Walker, S. Jay. "Zora Neale Hurston's *Their Eyes Were Watching God: Black Novel of Sexism.*" *Modern Fiction Studies* 20 (Winter 1974–75): 519–27.

NATHANAEL WEST

Brown, Daniel R. "The War within Nathanael West: Naturalism and Existentialism." *Modern Fiction Studies* 20 (Summer 1974): 181–202.

Comerchero, Victor. *Nathanael West: The Tuning Fork.* Microfilm of typescript. Ann Arbor: University Microfilms International, 1962.

Cramer, Carter M. *The World of Nathanael West: A Critical Interpretation.* Emporia: Kansas State Teachers College, 1971.

Hyman, Stanley Edgar. *Nathanael West*. Minneapolis: University of Minnesota Press, 1962.

Light, James F. *Nathanael West: An Interpretative Study*. 2nd ed. Evanston, Ill.: Northwestern University Press, 1972.

Madden, David, ed. *Nathanael West: The Cheaters and the Cheated: A Collection of Critical Essays*. Deland, Fla.: Everett/Edwards, 1973.

Martin, Jay, ed. *Nathanael West: A Collection of Critical Essays*. Englewood Cliffs, N.J.: Prentice-Hall, 1971.

Reid, Randall. *The Fiction of Nathanael West: No Redeemer, No Promised Land*. Chicago: University of Chicago Press, 1967.

Widmer, Kingsley. *Nathanael West*. Boston: Twayne Publishers, 1982.

RICHARD WRIGHT

Avery, Evelyn. *Rebels and Victims: The Fiction of Richard Wright and Bernard Malamud*. Port Washington, N.Y.: Kennikat Press, 1979.

Bakish, David. *Richard Wright*. New York: Frederick Ungar, 1973.

Fabre, Michel. "Richard Wright: Beyond Naturalism." In *American Literary Naturalism: A Reassessment*, edited by Yoshinobu Hakutani and Lewis Fried. Heidelberg: Carl Winter, 1975.

———. *The Unfinished Quest of Richard Wright*. Trans. Isabel Barzun. New York: William Morrow, 1973.

Felgar, Robert. *Richard Wright*. Boston: Twayne Publishers, 1980.

Gysin, Fritz. *The Grotesque in American Negro Fiction: Jean Toomer, Richard Wright, and Ralph Ellison*. Bern: Francke, 1975.

Hakutani, Yoshinobu, ed. *Critical Essays on Richard Wright*. Boston: G. K. Hall, 1982.

Kinnamon, Kenneth. *The Emergence of Richard Wright: A Study in Literature and Society*. Urbana: University of Illinois Press, 1972.

Ray, David, and Robert M. Farnsworth, eds. *Richard Wright: Impressions and Perspectives*. Ann Arbor: University of Michigan Press, 1973.

EUDORA WELTY

Desmond, John F., ed. *A Still Moment*: Essays on the Art of Eudora Welty. Metuchen, N.J.: Scarecrow Press, 1978.

Devlin, Albert. *Eudora Welty's Chronicle*: A Story of Mississippi Life. Jackson: University Press of Mississippi, 1983.

Dollarhide, Louis D., and Ann J. Abadie, eds. *Eudora Welty: A Form of Thanks*. Jackson: University Press of Mississippi, 1979.

Evans, Elizabeth. *Eudora Welty*. New York: Frederick Ungar, 1981.

Howard, Zelma Turner. *The Rhetoric of Eudora Welty's Short Stories*. Jackson: University and College Press of Mississippi, 1973.

Kreyling, Michael. *Eudora Welty's Achievement of Order*. Baton Rouge: Louisiana State University Press, 1980.

MacKethan, Lucinda. *The Dream of Arcady: Place and Time in Southern Literature*. Baton Rouge: Louisiana State University Press, 1980.

Manz-Kunz, Marie Antoinette. *Eudora Welty: Aspects of Reality in Her Short Fiction*. Bern: Francke, 1971.

Prenshaw, Peggy Whitman, ed. *Eudora Welty: Critical Essays*. Jackson: University Press of Mississippi, 1979.

Vande Kieft, Ruth. *Eudora Welty*. New York: Twayne Publishers, 1962.

Acknowledgments

"Convention in the Fiction of Edith Wharton" by Mary Suzanne Schriber from *Studies in American Fiction* 11, no. 2 (Autumn 1983), © 1983 by Northeastern University Press. Reprinted by permission.

"Dreiser's Trilogy and the Dilemma of Determinism" by John J. Conder from *Naturalism in American Fiction: The Classic Phase* by John J. Conder, © 1984 by The University Press of Kentucky. Reprinted by permission of the publisher.

"Modernism: The Case of Willa Cather" by Phyllis Rose from *Modernism Reconsidered* (Harvard English Studies, no. 11) edited by Robert Kiely, © 1983 by the President and Fellows of Harvard College. Reprinted by permission of Harvard University Press.

"Toward the Outside: The Quest for Discontinuity in Gertrude Stein's *The Making of Americans*" (originally entitled "Toward the Outside: The Quest for Discontinuity in Gertrude Stein's *The Making of Americans; Being a History of a Family's Progress*") by Clive Bush from *Twentieth Century Literature* 24, no. 1 (Spring 1978), © 1978 by Hofstra University Press. Reprinted by permission of the editor.

"Sherwood Anderson: American Mythopoeist" by Benjamin T. Spencer from *American Literature* 41, no. 1 (March 1969), © 1969 by Duke University Press. Reprinted by permission.

"Sinclair Lewis and the Implied America" by James Lea from *Clio* 3, no. 1 (October 1973), © 1973 by Robert H. Canary and Henry Kozicki. Reprinted by permission.

"Negatives of Hope: A Reading of Katherine Anne Porter" by Joseph Wiesenfarth from *Renascence* 25, no. 2 (Winter 1973), © 1973 by the Catholic Renascence Society, Marquette University. Reprinted by permission of the editor.

"Personal Narrators Playing God and Man: Henry Miller's Henry Miller" by Alan Warren Friedman from *Multivalence: The Moral Quality of Form in the Modern Novel* by Allen Warren Friedman, © 1978 by Louisiana State University. Reprinted by permission of the publisher.

" 'Dressing the Unknowable in the Garments of the Known': The Style of Djuna Barnes's *Nightwood*" by Carolyn Allen from *Women's Language and Style* (Studies in Contemporary Language, no. 1) edited by Douglas Buttorff and Edmund L. Epstein, © 1978 by E. L. Epstein. Reprinted by permission of the publisher.

"Untroubled Voice: Call and Response in Jean Toomer's *Cane*" (originally entitled "Untroubled Voice: Call and Response in *Cane*") by Barbara E. Bowen from *Black Literature and Literary Theory* edited by Henry Louis Gates, Jr., © 1984 by Methuen, Inc., Barbara E. Bowen, Brandt and Brandt, and Indiana State University. Reprinted by permission. This essay originally appeared in *Black American Literature Forum* 16, no. 1 (1982).

"Dos Passos's *U.S.A.*: Chronicle and Performance" (originally entitled "*U.S.A.*: Chronicle and Performance") by Charles Marz from *Modern Fiction Studies* 26, no. 3 (1980), © 1980 by the Purdue Research Foundation. Reprinted by permission.

"F. Scott Fitzgerald: The Myth of Gatsby" (originally entitled "The Myth of Gatsby") by Bruce Michelson from *Modern Fiction Studies* 26, no. 4 (Winter 1980–81), © 1980 by the Purdue Research Foundation. Reprinted by permission.

"The Aesthetic of Forbearance: Fitzgerald's *Tender Is the Night*" by Maria DiBattista from *Novel: A Forum on Fiction* 16, no. 1 (Fall 1977), © 1977 by Novel Corp. Reprinted by permission.

"Fitzgerald: The Tissue of Style" by Donald Monk from *Journal of American Studies* 17, no. 1 (April 1983), © 1983 by Cambridge University Press. Reprinted by permission.

"Faulkner on Time and History" by Cleanth Brooks from *William Faulkner: Toward Yoknapatawpha and Beyond* by Cleanth Brooks, © 1978 by Yale University. Reprinted by permission of Yale University Press and the author.

"Literary Self-Criticism: Faulkner in Fiction on Fiction" by James G. Watson from *The Southern Quarterly* 20, no. 1 (Fall 1981), © 1981 by The Southern Quarterly. Reprinted by permission.

"The Spectral Road: Metaphors of Transference in Faulkner's *As I Lay Dying*" by Patrick O'Donnell from *Papers on Language and Literature* 20, no. 1 (Winter 1984), © 1984 by the Board of Trustees of Southern Illinois University. Reprinted by permission.

"Hemingway: Valor against the Void" by Ihab Hassan from *The Dismemberment of Orpheus* by Ihab Hassan, © 1971, 1982 by Ihab Hassan. Reprinted by permission of the author and the University of Wisconsin Press.

"Ernest Hemingway: The Meaning of Style" by John Graham from *Ernest Hemingway* edited by Arthur Waldhorn, © 1973 by McGraw-Hill, Inc. Reprinted by permission. This essay originally appeared in *Modern Fiction Studies*, © 1961 by the Purdue Research Foundation, West Lafayette, Indiana 47907.

"Human Time in Hemingway's Fiction" by Wesley A. Kort from *Modern Fiction Studies* 26, no. 4 (Winter 1980–81), © 1980 by the Purdue Research Foundation, West Lafayette, Indiana 47907. Reprinted by permission.

"Why You Can't Go Home Again: Thomas Wolfe and 'The Escapes of Time and Memory'" by Morris Beja from *Modern Fiction Studies* 11, no. 3 (Autumn 1965), © 1965 by the Purdue Research Foundation, West Lafayette, Indiana 47907. Reprinted by permission.

"Steinbeck, the People, and the Party" by Sylvia Jenkins Cook from *Literature at the Barricades: The American Writer in the 1930s* edited by Ralph F. Bogardus and Fred Hobson, © 1982 by The University of Alabama Press. Reprinted by permission of the publisher.

"Metaphor, Metonymy and Voice in Zora Neale Hurston's *Their Eyes Were Watching God*" (originally entitled "Metaphor, Metonymy, and Voice in *Their Eyes Were Watching God*") by Barbara Johnson from *Black Literature and Literary Theory* edited by Henry Louis Gates, Jr., © 1984 by Methuen, Inc. Reprinted by permission of the publisher and the author.

"A Surfeit of Commodities: The Novels of Nathanael West" by Jonathan Raban from *The American Novel and the Nineteen Twenties* (Stratford upon Avon Series) edited by Malcolm Bradbury and David Palmer, © 1971 by Edward Arnold Publishers Ltd. Reprinted by permission of the publisher.

"I Thought I Knew These People: Richard Wright and the Afro-American Literary Tradition" by Robert B. Stepto from *Chant of Saints: A Gathering of Afro-American Literature, Art, and Scholarship* edited by Michael S. Harper and Robert B. Stepto, © 1979 by The Board of Trustees of the University of Illinois. Reprinted by permission of the University of Illinois Press and the author.

"The Vision of Eudora Welty" by Ruth M. Vande Kieft from *The Mississippi Quarterly* 26, no. 4 (Fall 1973) (Special Eudora Welty issue), © 1973 by Mississippi State University. Reprinted by permission.

Index

Abel, Darrel, 246–47

Absalom, Absalom! (Faulkner), 9, 10, 13, 16, 244, 247, 248, 256, 261, 430

"Absolution" (Fitzgerald), 224

Across the River and into the Trees (Hemingway), 297, 320, 327–29, 430

Adams, Henry, 42, 77–78, 104, 111, 112, 137, 138

Adventures of a Young Man, The (Dos Passos), 429

Adventures of Huckleberry Finn, The (Twain), 12, 179, 349

"Afternoon of a Cow" (Faulkner), 266, 267, 268

"Afterward: A Film" (Harper), 401–3

Agee, James, 348, 358, 359

Age of Innocence, The (Wharton), 30–32, 34, 425

Ain't I a Woman (Watkins), 372

Air-Conditioned Nightmare, The (Miller), 428

Alexander's Bridge (Cather), 65, 426

Alger, Horatio, 207, 383, 393

Algren, Nelson, 15

All the King's Men (Warren), 253

All the Sad Young Men (Fitzgerald), 429

American Scene, The (Henry James), 2

American Slave, An (Douglass), 396

American Tragedy, An (Dreiser), 2, 426

Ammons, Elizabeth, 27

Anderson, Sherwood, 2, 9, 101–13, 264, 426, 427, 430

Ann Vickers (Lewis), 427

Antiphon, The (Barnes), 428

Apollinaire, Guillaume, 426

"Apology for Crudity, An" (Anderson), 113

April Twilights (Cather), 426

A Rebours (Huysmans), 386

Arendt, Hannah, 80

Aristotle, 80, 86–87, 94, 253, 364

Armies of the Night (Mailer), 137

Arnold, Matthew, 84, 256

Arp, Jean, 62

Arrowsmith (Lewis), 5, 116, 120–21, 125, 427

Artist Looks at Nature, The (Sheeler), 64

"As Adam Early in the Morning" (Whitman), 170

As I Lay Dying (Faulkner), 9, 10–12, 13, 16, 269–83, 430

Aswell, Edward C., 343

Aswell, George, 431

Auerbach, Erich, 369–70

Augustine, Saint, 137, 138, 139, 241, 250, 259

Auroras of Autumn, The (Stevens), 8

Austen, Jane, 407

Autobiography (Franklin), 207, 211

453

Autobiography of Alice B. Toklas, The (Stein), 427
Autobiography of an Ex-Colored Man (Johnson), 370–71

Babbitt (Lewis), 116, 119–20, 125, 427
"Babylon Revisited" (Fitzgerald), 5, 6, 7, 224
Backward Glance, A (Wharton), 425
Baird, Helen, 263, 264–65, 267
Baker, Carlos, 293, 315, 316
Bakhtin, Mikhail, 214
Baldwin, James, 397, 399
Balzac, Honoré de, 67, 103, 241, 304
Barnes, Djuna, 147–62, 428
"Battle Hymn of the Republic, The" (Julia Ward Howe), 259
"Battler, The" (Hemingway), 289–90, 318
"Bear, The" (Faulkner), 249
Beautiful and the Damned, The (Fitzgerald), 429
Beckett, Samuel, 293
Bellamy, Edward, 105
Bellow, Saul, 16
Bennett, Arnold, 67
Benton, Thomas Hart, 75
Berenson, Bernard, 425
Berger, Thomas, 375
Bergson, Henri-Louis, 94, 239–48
Between the Acts (Woolf), 68
Bewley, Marius, 202
Beyond Desire (Anderson), 106, 111
Bhagavad-Gita, 58
Big Money, The (Dos Passos), 186, 187, 429
"Big Two-Hearted River" (Hemingway), 290, 317, 318
Birth of the Clinic, The (Foucault), 84
Birth of Tragedy, The (Nietzsche), 247
Bishop, Elizabeth, 13
Bishop, John Peale, 209–10, 225
Black Aesthetic, The (Gayle), 398
Black Boy (Wright), 390, 392, 393, 395–97, 399, 400, 432
"Black Music" (Faulkner), 266
Black Power (Wright), 432
Black Spring (Miller), 144, 428
Blake, William, 8, 11, 88, 233
Bleikasten, Andre, 265
"Blueprint for Negro Literature" (Wright), 390, 391, 397

Bluest Eye, The (Morrison), 401
Book, A (Barnes), 428
Book of Repulsive Women, The (Barnes), 428
Books in My Life, The (Miller), 428
Booth, Wayne C., 141
Bourne, Randolph, 187
Bouvard, Loïc, 239–40
Braithwaite, William Stanley, 400
Brancusi, Constantin, 62, 74
Bride of the Innisfallen, The (Welty), 432
Brodkey, Harold, 17
Brooks, Cleanth, 9, 10
Brooks, Gwendolyn, 401
Brooks, Van Wyck, 102, 108
Broom, 428
Brown, Norman O., 78, 95
Brown, Sterling A., 400
Bryer, Jackson R., 195
Bullough, Edward, 340
Bulwark, The (Dreiser), 38, 426
Buñuel, Luis, 94
Burden of Southern History, The (Woodward), 259–60
Burke, Edmund, 256
Burke, Kenneth, 160–61
Butterick's, 425
Byron, George Gordon, Lord, 15, 16

Cabell, James Branch, 263
Camus, Albert, 286
Cane (Toomer), 163–77, 428
Cannery Row (Steinbeck), 353, 431
Cantos, The (Pound), 74
Carmichael, Stokely, 371
Carnegie, Andrew, 187, 188
Carringer, Robert, 189
Cather, Willa, 1–5, 61–75, 426
"Cat in the Rain" (Hemingway), 289
Cellini, Benvenuto, 137, 138, 139
Cervantes, Miguel de, 14, 69, 103
Cézanne, Paul, 75, 86, 263, 268, 286
Chekhov, Anton, 407
Chesnutt, Charles W., 393, 395
Chicago Globe, 425
Chopin, Frédéric, 97
Chosen Country (Dos Passos), 429
"Clean Well-Lighted Place, A" (Hemingway), 288, 294
Cleaver, Eldridge, 397, 400
Coindreau, Maurice, 266

Colossus of Maroussi, The (Miller), 428

"Comedian as the Letter C, The" (Stevens), 1

Composition As Explanation (Stein), 426

Comte, Auguste, 256

Confessions (Saint Augustine), 241

Conrad, Joseph, 5, 6–7, 9, 10, 12, 107, 197, 221, 225, 226, 232, 246, 248, 339

Cool Million, A (West), 16, 22, 383, 386, 431–32

"Cornhuskers" (Sandburg), 108

Cowley, Malcolm, 9, 102, 218, 290

"Cracked Looking-Glass, The" (Porter), 134

Crack-Up, The (Fitzgerald), 234, 235, 236, 429

Crane, Hart, 5, 13, 16, 259

Creative Evolution (Bergson), 94

Creative Mind, The (Bergson), 245, 246

Creel, George, 187, 189

"Criticism in the Jungle" (Gates), 370

"Cross Country Snow" (Hemingway), 318

"Crossing Brooklyn Ferry" (Whitman), 138

Crying of Lot 49, The (Pynchon), 13, 16

Culler, Jonathan, 166

Cup of Gold (Steinbeck), 348, 357, 431

Curtain of Green, A (Welty), 432

Custom of the Country, The (Wharton), 27, 30, 33, 425

Daiches, David, 61

Dali, Salvador, 73, 387

Dance of Life, The (Matisse), 75

Dante, 138–39, 245, 325, 326, 327, 328

Dark Laughter (Anderson), 103, 105, 106, 108, 109, 110, 111, 427

Davis, Lambert, 252–53

Dawn (Dreiser), 426

Day of the Locust, The (West), 5, 16, 22, 379, 383–86, 387, 432

"Day's Work, A" (Porter), 131–32, 133

Dear Scott/Dear Max (Kuehl and Bryer), 195

Death Comes for the Archbishop (Cather), 1, 2, 62, 65, 68, 70–71, 75, 426

Death in the Afternoon (Hemingway), 301, 430

"Death in the Woods" (Anderson), 103

Debridement (Harper), 401

Debs, Eugene, 187, 190

Delta Wedding (Welty), 413–14, 432

de Man, Paul, 281, 364

Democracy in America (Tocqueville), 255

Desmoiselles d'Avignon, Les (Picasso), 74, 86

DeMott, Benjamin, 140

Derain, André, 74

Dial, 428

"Diamond as Big as the Ritz, The" (Fitzgerald), 224

Dickens, Charles, 12, 69, 191

Dickinson, Emily, 14

"Dilemma of Determinism, The" (William James), 37, 51

Discreet Charm of the Bourgeoisie (Buñuel), 94

District of Columbia (Dos Passos), 429

Divine Comedy (Dante), 138, 325, 327, 328

Doctor Martino and Other Stories (Faulkner), 266, 430

Dodsworth (Lewis), 116, 123–24, 125, 427

Donaldson, Scott, 315, 320

Donne, John, 169, 295

Donovan, Josephine, 148, 149

Dos Passos, John, 5, 59, 179–93, 214, 428–29

Dostoyevsky, Fyodor, 14, 140, 191

Douglass, Frederick, 392, 396

Down and Out in Paris and London (Orwell), 145

"Downward Path to Wisdom, The" (Porter), 128–29, 133

Doyle, Peter, 17

Dream Life of Balso Snell, The (West), 16, 21, 378, 379–80, 431

Dreiser, Theodore, 2, 9, 37–59, 74, 102, 103, 104, 393, 425–26

Dreiser Looks at Russia (Dreiser), 426

Dubliners (Joyce), 14

Du Bois, William, 174, 370, 391, 392, 403
Duncan, Isadora, 190
Dunciad, The (Pope), 96
Dust Tracks on the Road (Hurston), 431

East of Eden (Steinbeck), 431
Edel, Leon, 70, 71
Education of Henry Adams, The (Adams), 42, 137, 138
Edwards, Paul, 54
"Egg, The" (Anderson), 110
Einstein, Albert, 49
Eisinger, Chester, 355
Elective Affinities (Goethe), 85
Elias, Robert, 49, 56
Eliot, T. S., 5, 6, 7, 9, 11, 13, 14, 16, 73, 74, 167–68, 224, 226, 246, 248, 257, 261, 268, 377, 423, 428
Ellison, Ralph, 171, 172, 371, 391–92, 397
Ellmann, Mary, 148, 149
"Elmer" (Faulkner), 265, 267
Elmer Gantry (Lewis), 116, 121–22, 125, 427
Emerson, Ralph Waldo, 3, 46–47, 56, 59, 103, 104, 108, 253, 259
Endymion (Keats), 5
"Equation Inevitable, The" (Dreiser), 50–51
Ernst, Max, 387
Esquire, 429
Essais Linguistiques (Jakobson), 361
"Essential Tragedy of Life, The" (Dreiser), 49
Ethan Fromme (Wharton), 425
Euphues (Lyly), 83
Everest, Wesley, 187, 190
"Experience" (Emerson), 108
Eye of the Story, The (Welty), 432

Fabio, Sarah Webster, 398
Fable, A (Faulkner), 8, 10, 242, 430
"Factor Called Chance, The" (Dreiser), 37
Fall of Hyperion, The (Keats), 5, 7
Fanny Hill (Cleland), 137
Farewell to Arms, A (Hemingway), 15, 290, 292–93, 307, 311–12, 317, 318–20, 430
Faulkner, William, 1, 8–12, 13, 14, 16, 102, 152, 219, 239–60,

261–68, 269–83, 355, 427, 429–30
"Feminist Style Criticism" (Donovan), 148
Fernhurst (Stein), 426
Fiedler, Leslie, 375–76
Fields, W. C., 418
Fifth Column, The (Hemingway), 295
Financier, The (Dreiser), 37–59, 425
"Financing Finnegan" (Fitzgerald), 224
Firbank, Ronald, 20
First Forty-Nine Stories, The (Hemingway), 13
Fisher, Philip, 185
Fitzgerald, F. Scott, 1, 2, 5–8, 9, 10, 13, 14, 20, 104, 195–207, 209–22, 223–37, 337, 376–77, 387–88, 426, 429, 430
Fitzgerald, Zelda, 195, 429
Flags in the Dust (Faulkner), 256, 268
Flappers and Philosophers (Fitzgerald), 429
Flaubert, Gustave, 1, 73, 74, 210, 241, 426
Fleischauer, John F., 406–7, 408
"Focus of Mystery, The" (Fleischauer), 406
Ford, Henry, 188, 190, 257
Ford, John, 12
Forster, E. M., 6, 115, 407
42nd Parallel, The (Dos Passos), 183, 184, 429
For Whom the Bell Tolls (Hemingway), 15, 295–97, 302, 303–4, 305–6, 307, 309, 310–11, 312, 320, 321–23, 327, 430
Foucault, Michel, 79, 84, 95
Four Quartets, The (Eliot), 423
Frank, Jacob, 17, 21, 22
Frank, Manfred, 270–71
Frank, Waldo, 171, 428
Frankenthaler, Helen, 75
Franklin, Benjamin, 137, 138, 139, 145, 207, 211, 212
Freud, Sigmund, 2, 7, 9, 17, 18–19, 67, 288
From Death to Morning (Wolfe), 431
Frost, Robert, 13, 16, 145
Fruit of the Tree, The (Wharton), 425
"Fullness of Life, The" (Wharton), 26, 34
Fussell, Paul, 186

Galsworthy, John, 67
Gates, Henry Louis, Jr., 370, 374
Gauguin, Paul, 19, 74, 75, 103
Gayle, Addison, 398–99
Gay Woman, The, 401, 403
Geismar, Maxwell, 122–23
"Genius," The (Dreiser), 426
Gide, André, 12
Go Down, Moses (Faulkner), 9, 252, 253, 256, 258, 430
"God Rest You Merry Gentlemen" (Hemingway), 14, 294
God-Seeker, The (Lewis), 116–17, 118, 121, 125
Goethe, Johann Wolfgang von, 83, 85
Gold, Herbert, 103
Gold, Michael, 347–48, 359
Golden Apples, The (Welty), 408, 414, 417, 432
Golden Bough, The (Frazer), 75, 198
Gone with the Wind (Mitchell), 235, 257
"Gradual Making of *The Making of Americans*, The" (Stein), 82, 84
Grand Design, The (Dos Passos), 429
Grant, Ulysses S., 212–13, 222
Grapes of Wrath, The (Steinbeck), 348, 350, 351, 352–53, 354–59, 431
Gravity's Rainbow (Pynchon), 16
Great Days, The (Dos Passos), 186
Greater Inclination, The (Wharton), 425
Great Expectations (Dickens), 137, 138
Great Gatsby, The (Fitzgerald), 2, 5–6, 13, 16, 195–207, 210–11, 226, 227–31, 387, 429
Grebstein, Sheldon, 115, 316
Green Hills of Africa, The (Hemingway), 430
Griffin, Robert J., 118
Gris, Juan, 426
Ground We Stand On, The (Dos Passos), 429
Guernica (Picasso), 75
Gurdjieff, George, 428

Hambourg, Jan, 2, 70
Hamlet, The (Faulkner), 9, 430
"Hands" (Anderson), 102
Hanna, Thomas, 242

Hardie, W. F. R., 94
Hardy, Thomas, 2–3, 62, 127, 132
Harper, Michael, 175, 401–3
Harris, Frank, 138, 139
Hartman, Geoffrey, 164
Hawthorne, Nathaniel, 9, 107, 210, 224
Haywood, William D., 187, 188, 190
"He" (Porter), 131–32, 133
Head and Heart of Thomas Jefferson, The (Dos Passos), 429
Heads (Stewart), 375
Hearst, William Randolph, 187
"Heartblow" (Harper), 401
Heart of Darkness (Conrad), 5, 6–7
Hegel, Georg Wilhelm Friedrich, 84–85, 99
Heller, Joseph, 375
Hemingway, Ernest, 1, 2, 9, 10, 12–16, 20, 72–73, 75, 86, 137, 145, 214, 225, 236, 285–99, 301–13, 315–29, 376–77, 426, 427, 430
Herodotus, 347
Hill, Joe, 187, 190
Hills Beyond, The (Wolfe), 431
"Hills Like White Elephants" (Hemingway), 293
"Hitch-Hikers, The" (Welty), 408
Hoffman, Frederick J., 287
Hollander, John, 4
"Hollow Men, The" (Eliot), 5, 6–7
"Homage to Switzerland" (Hemingway), 294
Homer, 211–12, 213, 215, 217, 245
Home Town (Anderson), 108
Hoosier Holiday, A (Dreiser), 426
Hopalong Cassidy (Mulford), 207
Horses and Men (Anderson), 110, 427
House of Mirth, The (Wharton), 26–27, 29–30, 33, 425
Housman, A. E., 263
Howe, Irving, 102, 103
Howe, Julia Ward, 259
Howells, William Dean, 107
How to Write (Stein), 426
Hughes, Langston, 176–77, 393
"Human Universe" (Olson), 91
"Humor" (Freud), 18–19
Hurston, Zora Neale, 361–74, 393, 401, 431
Huxley, Aldous, 20
Huysmans, Joris-Karl, 378, 386
Hyman, Stanley Edgar, 17

Iliad (Homer), 256
"In Another Country"
    (Hemingway), 293
"In a Strange Town" (Anderson),
    107
"Indian Camp" (Hemingway), 289,
    318
In Dubious Battle (Steinbeck),
    349–51, 352, 353–54, 431
Ingersoll, Robert Green, 105
In Our Time (Hemingway), 286,
    288–90, 317–18, 430
Intruder in the Dust (Faulkner), 242,
    253
Invisible Man (Ellison), 171
Irving, Washington, 123
Irwin, John T., 8
Islands in the Stream (Hemingway),
    430
"I Tried to Be a Communist"
    (Wright), 390, 391, 392, 395

Jackson, Andrew, 212, 236, 263
Jackson, Stonewall, 329
Jakobson, Roman, 361–63, 368
James, Henry, 1, 2, 3, 8, 9, 14, 65,
    71, 190, 191, 210, 213, 226, 233,
    425, 426
James, William, 37, 38, 51, 52, 59,
    80–81, 83, 84, 92, 99, 426
Jarret, Mrs. Edwin, 217
Jefferson, Thomas, 104, 253
Jennie Gerhardt (Dreiser), 425
Jewett, Sarah Orne, 1, 2, 72, 73, 426
"Jilting of Granny Weatherall, The"
    (Porter), 133
Job, The (Lewis), 118
Johnson, James Weldon, 370–71,
    392, 393
Jonah's Gourd Vine (Hurston), 431
Jonson, Ben, 145
Joyce, James, 11, 14, 68, 73, 74, 75,
    77–78, 152, 186, 190, 197, 209,
    211–12, 213, 217, 220, 222, 246,
    248, 261, 331–32, 335, 339, 343,
    378
"Joy in the House" (Wharton), 34
"June Recital" (Welty), 414–16
Jung, Carl Gustav, 67
Jurgen (Cabell), 263

Kafka, Franz, 299
Katz, Leon, 78, 83, 85

Keats, John, 5, 6, 7, 8, 10, 43–44,
    47, 218, 225, 246
Kennedy, John F., 361
Kenner, Hugh, 261
Kent, George, 392, 394
"Killers, The" (Hemingway), 293
Kim, Kichung, 400
Kim (Kipling), 12
King, Richard H., 8
Kingsblood Royal (Lewis), 116,
    124–25
Kipling, Rudyard, 12
Kit Brandon (Anderson), 102, 110
Klee, Paul, 75
Knight's Gambit (Faulker), 430
Kolodny, Annette, 148, 149
Kronborg, Thea, 73–74
Kuehl, John, 195

Ladies Almanack (Barnes), 428
"L'Affaire Beano" (West), 378
L'Affaire Lettuceberg (Steinbeck), 357
LaFollett, Robert, 187
Lakoff, George, 364
Landseer, Edwin Henry, 70
Land Today (Wright), 432
"L'Après-Midi d'un Faune"
    (Faulkner), 265, 266
Lardner, Ring, 228
Last Tycoon, The (Fitzgerald), 5,
    235–37, 429
Laurencin, Marie, 426
Lawrence, D. H., 5, 19, 67, 68, 74,
    140, 190, 294
"Leader of the People, The"
    (Steinbeck), 351
Lectures in America (Stein), 427
Lettters to His Mother (Wolfe), 331
Let Us Now Praise Famous Men
    (Agee), 358
Levin, Harry, 286
Lewis, Edith, 69
Lewis, R. W. B., 170
Lewis, Sinclair, 5, 103, 115–25, 393,
    396, 427
Liebling, A. J., 378
Life, 254, 255
Life Studies (Lowell), 235
Light in August (Faulkner), 9, 10, 13,
    16, 244, 246, 256–57, 430
"Light of the World, The"
    (Hemingway), 294
Lincoln, Abraham, 104, 109

Lindbergh, Charles, 111
Lippman, Walter, 120
Liszt, Franz, 97
Little Review, the, 106–7, 108, 428
Locke, John, 83
Long Dream, The (Wright), 432
Long Gay Book, A (Stein), 82
Look Homeward, Angel (Wolfe), 332, 334–35, 336, 341, 342, 345, 431
"Loom Dance" (Anderson), 111
Losing Battles (Welty), 405, 406–7, 417–19, 432
Lost Lady, A (Cather), 1–2, 3, 66
"Love Song of J. Alfred Prufrock, The" (Eliot), 167–68
Lowell, Robert, 235
Lucy Church Amiably (Stein), 426
Lucy Gayheart (Cather), 426
Lyde, Marilyn, 32
Lyly, John, 83
Lynn, Kenneth, 179

McAleer, John J., 38
McClung, Isabelle, 2, 70
McClure, Michael, 94
McClure's Magazine, 426
"Machine Song" (Anderson), 111
Madame Bovary (Flaubert), 370
"Magic" (Porter), 131, 133
Magritte, René, 64, 73
Mailer, Norman, 14, 16, 137, 145
Maine, Henry James Sumner, 256
Main Street (Lewis), 115, 117–19, 121, 123, 125, 427
Making of Americans, The (Stein), 77–100, 426
Malamud, Bernard, 16
Malcolm X, 139
Mallarmé, Stéphane, 266
Malory, Thomas, 347
Manhattan Transfer (Dos Passos), 5, 179, 184, 191, 429
Mansion, The (Faulkner), 430
"Man Who Became a Woman, The" (Anderson), 110
Man Who Died, The (Lawrence), 19
Many Marriages (Anderson), 427
Marble Faun, The (Faulkner), 265, 266, 430
Marching Man (Anderson), 427
Margolies, Edward, 397–98, 399
Marionettes (Faulkner), 264

Marius the Epicurean (William Horatio Pater), 223
Marsh, Reginald, 188
Marx, Karl, 84–85, 90, 294
Masters, Edgar Lee, 108
Matisse, Henri, 74, 75, 79, 426
Maud (Tennyson), 6
Maugham, Somerset, 19
Maupassant, Guy de, 14
Mayday (Faulkner), 263–65, 266–67, 268
"May Day" (Fitzgerald), 196–97
Meade, Julian, 343
Melanctha (Stein), 79
Melville, Herman, 9, 14, 19, 100, 210
Memoirs (Anderson), 106, 107, 108
"Memory, A" (Welty), 408–10, 411, 414, 421
Mencken, Henry L., 393, 396
"Mental Traveller, The" (Blake), 8, 233
Men without Women (Hemingway), 293, 430
Messianic Idea in Judaism, The (Scholem), 16
Metamorphoses (Ovid), 197, 198–99
"Michael" (Wordsworth), 10
Mid-American Chants (Anderson), 105, 108, 109
"Mid-American Prayer" (Anderson), 108
Miller, Henry, 137–46, 428
Mimesis (Auerbach), 369–70
Minter, David, 8, 12
Miss Lonelyhearts (West), 13, 14, 16, 17–21, 22, 376, 379, 380–83, 385, 386–87, 431
"Miss Zilphia Gant" (Faulkner), 244
"Mr. Bennett and Mrs. Brown" (Woolf), 67
Mitchell, Margaret, 235
"Modern Fiction" (Woolf), 67
Modigliani, Amedeo, 74
Moll Flanders, The Fortunes and Misfortunes of the Famous (Defoe), 137
Moon and Sixpence, The (Maugham), 19
"Moon Lake" (Welty), 417
Moore, George, 20
Moore, Henry, 62
Moore, Marianne, 86
Morgan, Henry, 431

Morgan, J. P., 187, 188, 190
Morris, Wright, 215
Morrison, Toni, 401
Mortal No, The (Hoffman), 287
Moses, Man of the Mountain
    (Hurston), 431
Mosquitoes (Faulkner), 263–64, 267,
    430
Moveable Feast, A (Hemingway), 137,
    430
Mules and Men (Hurston), 431
Murphy, Sara, 13
My Ántonia (Cather), 1, 2, 3–4,
    62–63, 65, 68, 69–70, 426
My Life and Loves (Harris), 138
"My Old Man" (Hemingway), 290

Narration (Stein), 427
Narrative of the Life of Frederick
    Douglass (Douglass), 396
Nation, the, 356
Native Son (Wright), 393–95, 397–98,
    399, 400, 401, 432
Native Sons: A Critical Study of
    Twentieth-Century Negro
    American Authors (Margolies),
    397–98
"Natural History of the Dead, A"
    (Hemingway), 14
Nature (Emerson), 46–47
Nausea (Sartre), 286
"Necessity for Contrast, The"
    (Dreiser), 52
Newman, Barnett, 75
New Masses, the, 347
New Republic, 347, 358
"New Testament, A" (Anderson),
    107
New Yorker, 407
New York Times, 188
Nexus (Miller), 428
Nichomachean Ethics (Aristotle),
    86–87, 94
Nietzsche, Friedrich Wilhelm, 2,
    8–9, 81, 246–47, 257
Nigger of the Narcissus, The (Conrad),
    225
Nightwood (Barnes), 147–62, 428
Nin, Anaïs, 145
1919 (Dos Passos), 183, 187, 189,
    429
Nisbet, Robert, 255–56
Nixon, Richard, 361

"Noon Wine" (Porter), 129–31, 133
Norris, Frank, 38, 313
Nostromo (Conrad), 6, 9
"Notebooks, The" (Stein), 82
Notes of a Native Son (Baldwin), 397
"Notes on a Native Son" (Cleaver),
    397
Notes on Life (Dreiser), 37, 40, 43,
    45, 49, 50, 51, 52
Not under Forty (Cather), 61, 426
"Novel Démeublé, The" (Cather),
    67
"Now I Lay Me" (Hemingway), 293
Number One (Dos Passos), 429
"Nun, the Gambler, and the Radio,
    The" (Hemingway), 294

"Ode on a Grecian Urn" (Keats), 7,
    245
"Ode to a Nightingale" (Keats), 218
"Ode to Indolence" (Keats), 10
Odyssey (Homer), 75
Of Mice and Men (Steinbeck), 431
"Of the Coming of John" (Du Bois),
    391
Of Time and the River (Wolfe), 332,
    333, 335–37, 338, 340, 431
O'Hara, John, 15
O'Keeffe, Georgia, 70, 73
"Old Cumberland Beggar, The"
    (Wordsworth), 10
Old Man and the Sea, The
    (Hemingway), 297–98, 301, 304,
    316, 321, 323–24, 430
"Old Man at the Bridge"
    (Hemingway), 15
Old New York (Wharton), 425
Olson, Charles, 91
Omoo (Melville), 19
One Man's Initiation: 1917 (Dos
    Passos), 429
One of Ours (Cather), 426
One Time, One Place (Welty), 405,
    410–11, 419, 420
One Writer's Beginnings (Welty), 432
"On Privacy" (Faulkner), 254
"On the Art of Fiction" (Cather), 2
O Pioneers (Cather), 1, 62, 63,
    65–66, 68, 426
Optimist's Daughter, The (Welty),
    407, 419–23, 432
Orozsco, José Clemente, 75
Orwell, George, 145, 226

Our Mister Wrenn (Lewis), 427
"Out of Nazareth" (Faulkner), 263
Outsider, The (Wright), 432
Ovid, 197–99, 207
Ozick, Cynthia, 16

Parr, Susan Resneck, 244–45
"Part of Earth, A" (Anderson), 102
"Passage to India" (Whitman), 104
Pastures of Heaven, The (Steinbeck), 348, 357, 431
Pater, Walter, 9
Pater, William Horatio, 3, 4–5, 20, 223
Perhaps Women (Anderson), 111–12
Perkins, Maxwell, 195, 431
Perosa, Sergio, 234
Petry, Ann, 401
Picasso, Pablo, 74, 75, 86, 426
Picture of Dorian Gray, The (Wilde), 223
Piper, Henry Dan, 224
Plato, 80
Plexus (Miller), 428
Plimpton, George, 286
Plumed Serpent, The (Lawrence), 19
Plutarch, 347
Poetics (Aristotle), 253
Pollock, Jackson, 75
Ponder Heart, The (Welty), 432
Poor White (Anderson), 102, 105, 106, 108, 110, 427
Porter, Katherine Anne, 127–36, 427
"Portrait of Elmer, A" (Faulkner), 267–68
Portrait of the Artist as a Young Man, A (Joyce), 335
"Potash and Perlmutter" (Cather), 2
Pound, Ezra, 2, 13, 62, 74, 104, 223, 257, 377, 430
Price, Reynolds, 407–8
Principles of Psychology, The (William James), 81
"Problem, The" (Emerson), 59
"Problem of Progress and Purpose, The" (Dreiser), 52–53
Professor's House, The (Cather), 1, 2, 3, 64, 65, 70
Prospects of a Golden Age (Dos Passos), 429
Proust, Marcel, 137, 138–39, 186, 191, 241, 332, 333, 339
Pusey, Edvard Bouverie, 241

Putnam, Samuel, 288
Puvis de Chavannes, Pierre-Cécile, 71, 74–75
Pylon (Faulkner), 261
Pynchon, Thomas, 14, 16, 375, 376

Quest for Community (Nisbet), 255–56
Quod Erat Demonstrandum (Q.E.D. or Things As They Are) (Stein), 426

Rabelais, François, 287
Racing Form, the, 286
Redding, Saunders, 397
"Redemption through Sin" (Scholem), 16
Reed, John, 187
Reef, The (Wharton), 425
Reivers, The (Faulkner), 430
Remember to Remember (Miller), 428
Remembrance of Things Past (Proust), 137
Requiem for a Nun (Faulkner), 430
Return to Winesburg (Anderson), 427
Reynolds, Quentin, 378
Rhetoric of Fiction, The (Booth), 141
Richardson, Dorothy, 147, 148
Richardson, Hadley, 430
Ricketts, Ed, 349, 353
Ricketts, Toni, 357
Ricoeur, Paul, 270
Rimbaud, Arthur, 234
Robber Bridegroom, The (Welty), 432
Robbins, Susan, 149
Rockefeller, John D., 230
Romantic Egoist, The (Fitzgerald), 429
Romeo and Juliet (Shakespeare), 67
Ronsard, Pierre de, 363
Rosen, Charles, 97
Ross, Alan, 375
Rosy Crucifixion, The (Miller), 428
Roth, Philip, 16
Rothko, Mark, 75
Rousseau, Jean Jacques, 137, 138, 139
Rovit, Earl, 316
Rubin, Louis D., Jr., 345
Ruskin, John, 256
Ryder (Barnes), 428

Sacco, Nicola, 187
Sacred Fount, The (Henry James), 8, 233

"St. Augustine and the Bullfight"
    (Porter), 134–35
Salinger, J. D., 112
Sanctuary (Faulkner), 9, 13, 16, 244,
    430
Sandburg, Carl, 108
Sanford, John, 377
Santayana, George, 96
Sapphira and the Slave Girl (Cather),
    426
Sartoris (Faulkner), 430
Sartre, Jean-Paul, 96, 286
Satyricon (Petronius), 198
Scholem, Gershom, 16, 17, 21
Schönberg, Arnold, 97
Schorer, Mark, 119
Scott, Sir Walter, 116, 257, 304
Scribner, Charles, 14
Secret Agent, The (Conrad), 10, 226
Secret Sharer, The (Conrad), 5
Self-Reliance (Emerson), 56
Sensibar, Judith L., 9
Seraph on the Sewanee (Hurston), 431
Sewell, Elizabeth, 287
Sex and Character (Weininger), 85
Sexus (Miller), 428
Shadow and Act (Ellison), 172, 391–92
Shadows on the Rock (Cather), 1, 426
Shakespeare, William, 12, 245, 246
Sheeler, Charles, 64, 73
Sheffield, Carlton, 348
Shelley, Percy Bysshe, 5, 139
*Sherwood Anderson and Other Famous
    Creoles* (Faulkner), "Foreword"
    to, 263
Ship of Fools (Porter), 132–33
"Short, Happy Life of Francis
    Macomber, The" (Hemingway),
    294
Sister Carrie (Dreiser), 74, 425
"Soldier's Home" (Hemingway),
    290, 317, 318
Soldier's Pay, A (Faulkner), 430
"Some Notes on Defining a
    'Feminist Literary Criticism' "
    (Kolodny), 148
"Song for Lonely Roads"
    (Anderson), 109
Song of Myself (Whitman), 88
Song of the Lark, The (Cather), 64, 65,
    68, 426
"Song to New Song" (Anderson),
    109
Sontag, Susan, 101, 184

Sophocles, 245
Soul on Ice (Cleaver), 397
Souls of Black Folk, The (Du Bois),
    391, 392
Sound and the Fury, The (Faulkner),
    8, 9, 10, 13, 16, 241, 242, 250,
    261–62, 263, 268, 430
Southern, Terry, 375
Spillway (Barnes), 428
Spoon River Anthology (Masters), 108
Sportsman's Sketchbook, A
    (Turgenev), 4
Stanley, Julia, 149
Steadman, William, 188
Stein, Gertrude, 75, 77–100, 104,
    112–13, 197, 426–27, 430
Stein, Jean, 244
Stein, Leo, 86, 426
Stein, Michael, 426
Steinbeck, John, 347–59, 431
Stendhal, 210
Stern, Milton, 203
Stevens, Wallace, 4, 8, 13, 14, 16
Stevick, Philip, 141
Stewart, Edward, 375
Stieglitz, Alfred, 109, 110
"Still Moment, A" (Welty), 408,
    411–13
Stoic, The (Dreiser), 37–59, 426
Story of a Novel, The (Wolfe), 331,
    333, 335, 336, 337–38
Story Teller's Story, A (Anderson),
    104, 108–9, 110, 112, 427
Stranger, The (Camus), 286
Street, The (Petry), 401
Sun Also Rises, The (Hemingway), 2,
    13, 14, 16, 214, 290–92, 304–5,
    306, 308, 309, 310, 311, 313,
    320, 324–27, 328, 430
Swanburg, W. A., 39, 49
Swift, Jonathan, 79
Swinburne, Algernon Charles, 265

Taine, Hippolyte-Adolphe, 256
"Tale of Margaret, The"
    (Wordsworth), 10
Tales of the Jazz Age (Fitzgerald), 429
Tanner, Tony, 101, 112
Tar, A Midwest Childhood
    (Anderson), 427
Tate, Allen, 257
Tender Buttons (Stein), 426

Tender Is the Night (Fitzgerald), 5, 7–8, 209–22, 230–34, 236, 387–88, 429
Tennyson, Alfred, 6
Thackeray, William Makepeace, 6, 211
"Theft" (Porter), 131, 133
Their Eyes Were Watching God (Hurston), 365–69, 371, 373, 374, 431
Theme Is Freedom, The (Dos Passos), 429
Theory of the Leisure Class, The (Veblen), 216
"Theory That Life Is a Game, The" (Dreiser), 40
"There Was a Child Went Forth" (Whitman), 170
These Thirteen (Faulkner), 430
Things As They Are (Stein), 426
This Side of Paradise (Fitzgerald), 223, 226, 429
Thoreau, Henry David, 14, 103
"Three Day Blow, The" (Hemingway), 318
Three Lives (Stein), 426
Three Soldiers (Dos Passos), 179, 429
Time of the Assassins: A Study of Rimbaud, The (Miller), 428
Titan, The (Dreiser), 37–59, 426
To a God Unknown (Steinbeck), 347, 355, 356, 431
"To Autumn" (Keats), 10
Tocqueville, Alexis de, 89, 255, 256
To Have and Have Not (Hemingway), 15, 294–95, 430
Toklas, Alice B., 426
Tolstoy, Leo, 14
Toomer, Jean, 163–77, 393, 401, 428
Torrents of Spring, The (Hemingway), 430
Tortilla Flat (Steinbeck), 357, 431
"Totems in Steel" (Sheeler), 73
"To the Garden the World" (Whitman), 170
To the Lighthouse (Woolf), 68, 369
Touchstone, The (Wharton), 28–29, 425
Tourneur, Cyril, 12
"Toward a Feminist Aesthetic" (Stanley and Robbins), 149
Town, The (Faulkner), 430
Trader Horn, 401
Traveler at Forty, A (Dreiser), 426

Travels with Charley (Steinbeck), 431
Trilling, Lionel, 2, 6, 101, 103, 112
Triumph of the Egg, The (Anderson), 427
Trois Contes (Flaubert), 426
Troll Garden, The (Cather), 426
Tropic of Cancer (Miller), 141–42, 143, 144, 145–46, 428
Tropic of Capricorn (Miller), 143, 144–45, 428
Turgenev, Ivan Sergeyevich, 4, 14, 103, 140
Twain, Mark, 9, 12, 14, 103, 104–5, 107, 112, 138, 139, 179, 210, 349
Twelve Men (Dreiser), 426
Twilight Sleep (Wharton), 27–28
Typee (Melville), 19

Ulysses (Joyce), 14, 74, 75, 196, 268, 332, 335, 343, 379
Uncle Tom's Children (Wright), 432
"Undefeated, The" (Hemingway), 293
Unvanquished, The (Faulkner), 256
Up from Slavery (Washington), 392–93
U.S.A. (Dos Passos), 179–93, 214, 429

V. (Pynchon), 376
Valentino, Rudolph, 188, 190
Valley of Decision, The (Wharton), 425
Van Ghent, Dorothy, 70, 71
Van Gogh, Vincent, 140
Vanity Fair (Thackeray), 211
Vanzetti, Bartolomeo, 187
Veblen, Thorstein, 187, 216
Virgil, 70, 325, 326
Vlaminck, Maurice de, 74

Wagner, Richard, 97
Waiting for the End (Fiedler), 376
Walker, Alice, 401
"Wanderers, The" (Welty), 416–17
Warren, Robert Penn, 13, 15, 253, 257
Washington, Booker T., 392–93
Waste Land, The (Eliot), 1, 6, 9, 74, 75, 196, 198
Watkins, Gloria, 3?2

Waves, The (Woolf), 68
Wayne, Anthony, 212
"Way You'll Never Be, A"
    (Hemingway), 294
Web and the Rock, The (Wolfe), 332,
    333, 338–39, 340–41, 342–43,
    431
Webster, John, 12
Weininger, Otto, 85–86
Wellington, first duke of, 81
Wells, H. G. 2, 67
Welty, Eudora, 405–23, 432
West, Nathanael, 5, 14, 16–23,
    375–88, 431–32
Wetherill, Richard, 64
Wharton, Edith, 1, 6, 25–35, 65, 425
Wharton, Edward, 425
Whistler, James Abbott McNeill, 103
Whitman, Walt, 13, 14, 16, 17, 88,
    94, 102, 103, 104, 111, 112, 113,
    138, 139, 145, 170, 176, 259
Wide Net and Other Stories, The
    (Welty), 432
Widmer, Kingsley, 142, 144
Wilde, Oscar, 16, 20, 74, 223
Wilder, Thornton, 347–48
Wild Palms, The (Faulkner), 9, 240,
    243, 255, 265
Williams, Sherley, 172
Williams, William Carlos, 13, 103
Wilson, Edmund, 5, 141, 237,
    293–94, 347
Wilson, Woodrow, 187, 188, 189,
    190
Wimsatt, William K., 3
Windy McPherson's Son (Anderson),
    105, 106, 109, 427

"Wine of Wyoming" (Hemingway),
    294
Winesburg, Ohio (Anderson), 101,
    102, 106, 108, 427
Winner Take Nothing (Hemingway),
    294, 430
Winter of Our Discontent, The
    (Steinbeck), 431
Wolfe, Thomas, 2, 9, 140, 259,
    331–46, 430–31
Women and Angels (Brodkey), 17
Woodlanders, The (Hardy), 3
Woodward, C. Vann, 259–60
Woolf, Virginia, 61, 67, 68, 71, 73,
    147, 148, 186, 190, 369
"Words into Fiction" (Welty), 407
Wordsworth, William, 3, 10, 13, 83
World of Sex, The (Miller), 140–41
World So Wide (Lewis), 427
Wright, Richard, 371, 389–403, 432
Writing of Fiction, The (Wharton),
    425
Wyatt, David M., 8

Xenophon, 347

Yeats, William Butler, 7, 14, 20, 247,
    257, 416
Yerkes, Charles T., 425
You Can't Go Home Again (Wolfe),
    338, 341–42, 344, 431
Young, Philip, 299, 315

Zola, Émile, 313